W9-BSC-242

THE
CAMBRIDGE EDITION OF
THE LETTERS AND WORKS OF
D. H. LAWRENCE

THE LETTERS OF D. H. LAWRENCE

GENERAL EDITOR
James T. Boulton
Professor of English Studies, University of Birmingham

EDITORIAL BOARD
David Farmer, *University of Tulsa, Oklahoma*
Gerald Lacy, *Angelo State University, Texas*
Warren Roberts, *University of Texas at Austin*
Andrew Robertson, *University of Birmingham*
Keith Sagar, *University of Manchester*
George Zytaruk, *Nipissing University College, Ontario*

PR
6023
.A93
Z53
1979

THE LETTERS OF D. H. LAWRENCE

VOLUME I

September 1901 – May 1913

EDITED BY

JAMES T. BOULTON

$29.50

58096

CAMBRIDGE UNIVERSITY PRESS

CAMBRIDGE

LONDON NEW YORK MELBOURNE

10-2-80

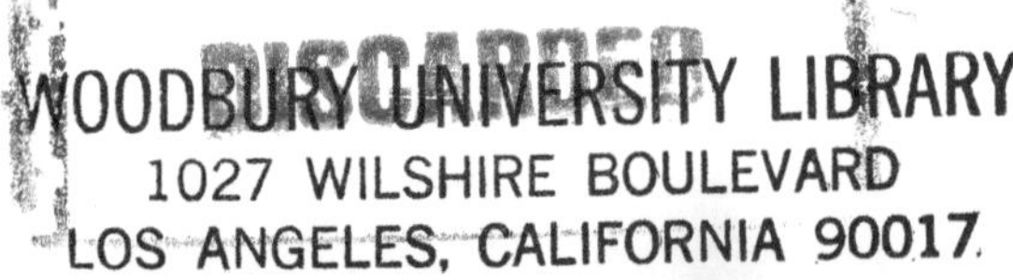

Published by the Syndics of the Cambridge University Press
The Pitt Building, Trumpington Street, Cambridge CB2 1RP
Bentley House, 200 Euston Road, London NW1 2DB
32 East 57th Street, New York, NY 10022, USA
296 Beaconsfield Parade, Middle Park, Melbourne 3206, Australia

Introductory material and editorial apparatus © Cambridge University Press 1979. Letters of D. H. Lawrence: copyright 1932 by the estate of D. H. Lawrence; copyright 1934 by Frieda Lawrence; Copyright 1933, 1948, 1953, 1954, © 1956, 1957, 1958, 1959, 1960, 1961, 1962, 1967, 1969 by Angelo Ravagli and C. Montague Weekley, executors of the estate of Frieda Lawrence Ravagli; © the estate of Frieda Lawrence Ravagli 1979.

First published 1979
Reprinted 1979

Printed in the United States of America
Typeset at the University Press, Cambridge, England
Printed and bound by Vail-Ballou Press Inc., Binghamton, New York

Library of Congress Cataloguing in Publication Data

Lawrence, David Herbert, 1885–1930.

The Letters of D. H. Lawrence.

Includes index.

CONTENTS: v. 1. September 1901–May 1913.
1. Lawrence, David Herbert, 1885–1930 – Correspondence.
2. Authors, English – 20th century – Correspondence.
I. Boulton, James T.
PR6023.A93Z53 1979 823'.9'12 [B] 78-7531
ISBN 0 521 22147 1

CONTENTS

ILLUSTRATIONS

PREFACE

In his letters 'Lawrence has written his life and painted his own portrait. Few men have given more of themselves in their letters. Lawrence is there almost in his entirety' (Aldous Huxley). This in itself is justification enough for the present edition. The letters are biographical documents of the highest importance in that they inform us about his discernible life; but, in addition, they contain unique evidence for the 'biography of an emotional and inner life' to which Lawrence referred in the Preface to his *Collected Poems*. Through them we come close to the creative mind and whole personality of the private individual, Lawrence. We also acquire an intimacy with the man and the spirit which played a public rôle and exerted a formative influence on the modern consciousness. This influence, impossible briefly to formulate or precisely to estimate, is permanent. It has been variously welcomed and lamented; it is rarely denied.

Lawrence was involved in the life of his time to an unusual extent: the range and number of his correspondents, people of diverse interests and activities, make this plain. To mention a few – Edward Garnett, E. M. Forster and Bertrand Russell, Mark Gertler, Edward Dahlberg and Giuseppe Orioli, David Eder, Max Mohr and Lady Cynthia Asquith – at once brings into focus international spheres of creative literature and criticism, philosophy, psychology and politics, art and publishing. This is merely a handful of names; it is enough to suggest that Lawrence's letters both illuminate and evaluate innumerable facets of the early twentieth century.

Furthermore – their wider significance aside – his letters are a delight to read. The expressive vividness, explosive energy and imaginative resourcefulness which are characteristic of Lawrence in other *genres*, are abundantly present in what the eighteenth century called 'the familiar letter'. Pope believed the letter should convey 'thoughts just warm from the brain without any polishing or dress, the very *déshabille* of the understanding': Lawrence achieved this to a degree that Pope could not have begun to imagine or desire.

For the first time all Lawrence's available letters – those to which he contributed as well as those originating with him – will be published in their entirety. ('Letters' here includes postcards, of which he wrote hundreds.) The editors have not felt it legitimate to exclude any. Nor have any been excised or bowdlerised. It is unfortunately not possible to reproduce in printed form the flippant, angry or sometimes obscene remarks scrawled across Frieda Lawrence's letters or his own; but, though inevitably muted in force and visual impact, none is excluded.

By adhering to the principle of inclusiveness this edition differs in one fundamental respect among many from its main predecessors. In his *Letters of D. H. Lawrence* (1932) Aldous Huxley selected from the texts available to him; he excised passages (often without due notice) as well as omitting names to avoid giving offence. Harry T. Moore in his *Collected Letters of D. H. Lawrence* (1962) adopted Huxley's principles though including a far greater array of letters. Neither editor provided detailed annotation nor revealed his sources. Yet they were the pioneers; they saved many texts from extinction; and they stimulated the taste of a large reading public for Lawrence as a letter-writer. Since 1962 the letters to certain particular individuals – such as Louie Burrows, S. S. Koteliansky, Martin Secker, E. D. McDonald, Thomas and Adele Seltzer – have appeared in book-form. Other letters, before and after that date, were pressed into service in the autobiographies of the recipients (like those by Catherine Carswell and Grace Lovat Fraser) and in biographies of Lawrence himself. Still others have been published, singly and in groups, in an astonishing variety of periodicals. Many are inaccurately printed, few are adequately annotated. And, lastly, a large and ever-increasing number remain unpublished. The grand total published and unpublished is over 5,500.

Whenever manuscripts were available – and the exceptions are relatively small in number – they have provided the basis for the texts printed in this edition. Published sources have been used where there are no others. (Volume I, for example, contains many letters written to Jessie Chambers; she destroyed all Lawrence's letters to her but incorporated extracts – several of them mere fragments – in her *Personal Record*; consequently reliance on her book is necessarily extensive.) Both in this and later volumes editors also face the familiar problem of the letter which is known to have existed but has now vanished. Sometimes its contents are at least partly accessible, quoted perhaps in correspondence between Lawrence's friends or in a secondary source. On these occasions the letter is entered in the chronological sequence and its contents reported or summarised as the case may be (within square brackets). If no reliable information exists about its contents, then a letter is ignored, though a footnote may enable the editor to draw attention to its having been written.

Even from his early years the survival-rate of Lawrence's letters is gratifying. Some correspondents from that early period nevertheless remain unrepresented. With the exception of a single postcard to Lawrence's mother, no letters to his parents exist. None has survived to his intimate college friend, Thomas A. Smith; nor (beyond a note recently discovered) to Agnes Holt whom, briefly, he thought of marrying; nor – except for Arthur McLeod and Philip Smith – to his colleagues at Davidson Road School. Letters are known to have been addressed to all these; it is also certain, in the case of Tom Smith, Agnes Holt and one teaching colleague, that disenchantment with the later Lawrence led them to destroy letters from him. Manuscripts belonging to other recipients doubtless met the same fate: one such person is reputed to have held a public burning of all Lawrence manuscripts in his possession. But – with a single known exception – no correspondent has been moved to destroy any Lawrence letter during the lifetime of the present project. On the contrary, manuscript owners have been exceedingly generous and co-operative: without their kindness the edition would not have been possible.

Manuscripts of letters have been discovered in over 110 locations throughout the world. The size of holdings varies enormously: the collections of private owners and of public institutions vary from as few as one manuscript to over 1,000 at the University of Texas at Austin.

If there is a matter for regret, it is that letters *to* Lawrence are relatively rare. Yet this is not surprising: he travelled extensively, he travelled light and he loathed 'possessing things'. Even his own manuscripts were of little account: '...I should be glad if you could drop the MS itself into a spare drawer. It is such a nuisance carting the lumber about.' It was therefore inconceivable that he would hoard letters written to him. Some have survived, nevertheless, mainly in the form of carbon-copies retained by the senders: whenever appropriate they will be quoted in footnotes so as to make his own letters more intelligible as well as to show how he responded *ad hominem* to every correspondent.

The edition has been planned as a whole, but the eight volumes will appear singly. Though they will be published in succession and as rapidly as possible, each volume must be in a measure self-sufficient. Each will therefore contain a detailed chronology, illustrations and maps appropriate to the particular span of years; a skeleton-index of persons, publications and places (the comprehensive critical index being reserved for the final volume); and a substantial introduction. The introduction will not provide a full, sequential biography of Lawrence – the chronology gives that in outline – nor a literary assessment of his letters or published works. The purpose of the introduction is – while making use of biographical and historical knowledge – rather to offer a critical assessment of the person Lawrence was during the years covered by a volume, the principal events or experiences that helped to shape him, and the people he chiefly encountered (whether or not they were important correspondents). It is hoped, therefore, to equip the general reader with the requisite understanding and information and the well-informed reader with some new insights. A full statement of editorial practices and a genealogical table of Lawrence's family will be found only in this volume.

J. T. B.

ACKNOWLEDGEMENTS

The Editorial Board is grateful for the enthusiastic agreement of the copyright holders, Laurence Pollinger & Co., executors of the Estate of Frieda Lawrence Ravagli, and of Lawrence's publishers, Messrs William Heinemann Ltd in Britain and Viking Press in the USA, that this edition should be produced.

Profound gratitude is due to the owners of manuscripts for their willingness to make Lawrence's letters available. The identity of those whose property is used in this volume is evident in the list of cue-titles given below.

Particular thanks are appropriate to the Leverhulme Trust for a research grant to the General Editor, 1973–7, and to the Universities of Nottingham, Birmingham, and Texas at Austin for official support and administrative facilities. The General Editor has benefited from the unfailing co-operation of the University Librarians and their staffs at Nottingham and at Birmingham.

Some individuals deserve special mention. The Editorial Board is indebted to Mr Michael Black, the Publisher, Cambridge University Press, whose personal commitment to the project and critical interest at every stage have been the source of great encouragement. The General Editor for his part must acknowledge the continuing support of his editorial colleagues and in particular of Dr Warren Roberts – together with his assistant Lin Vasey – for the efficiency and generosity of the editorial centre at the Humanities Research Center, Austin. Mr Andrew Robertson, formerly research assistant to the General Editor, has made a major contribution to the progress of the edition, and whatever success it achieves. His appointment to the Editorial Board is proof of the confidence he enjoys. Dr Carl Baron of Downing College, Cambridge, has given liberally of his time and freely of his expert knowledge of Lawrence to the great benefit of the edition. And Dr David Garnett, whose family was intimately associated with Lawrence's early career as a writer and who was himself a close friend of Lawrence, has put both his manuscripts and his remarkable memory at the service of the edition.

In an undertaking of this nature innumerable people, with complete disinterestedness, give of their professional skills and readily answer enquiries both about clearly important matters as well as about those which seem – though in the end seldom prove – either trivial or irrelevant. The General Editor hopes that each such individual receives due mention; if any is omitted, it is through oversight and not intention; and he begs the indulgence of anyone thus apparently slighted. Among those whose assistance with the production of this volume should be publicly acknowledged are: Professor Miriam Allott; Miss Louise A. Annand; Mr Colin Bailey; Mrs Barbara Barr; Mr Michael Bennett; Mr A. Birtles; Mrs Emily G. Brooks; Professor C. A. Burns; Dr M. Butler; Mr F. W. Cammack; Mr W. H. Clarke; Mr W. Cracknell; Mr Guy Collings; the late Professor T. W. Copeland; the late Miss Helen Corke; Miss Grace Cranston; the Chief Librarian and his staff, Central Library, Croydon; the Director of Education and his staff, Croydon; the Editor, *Croydon Advertiser*; Mr J. Davies; Mr T. R. Davis; Dr E. Cunningham Dax; Professor Emile Delavenay; Mr J. W. Dettmer; Professor R. L. Draper; Mrs E. Duncan-Jones; Dr V. Edden; Professor I. Ehrenpreis; Mr A. D. Elmslie; Mrs G. Falla; Dr Brian Finney; Miss A. Foster; Mr P. P. Francis; the late Mrs Grace Lovat Fraser; Mr Roland Gant; Mrs E. Goodband; Dr A. R. Griffin; Mrs N. Haselden; Mr John Hathaway; Mr Sidney Herbert; Mr and Mrs C. Hine; Mrs E. L. Hollingshead; Dr Enid Houghton; Mrs Ann Howard; the late Mr E. G. Inwood; Professor Ivor Keys; Mr G. F. King; Professor Mark Kinkead-Weekes; Professor J. Kinsley; Mr George Lazarus; Professor Philip McNair; Professor Harry T. Moore; Mrs Margaret Needham; the Librarian and staff of the Berg Collection, New York Public Library; the Librarian, *Nottingham Guardian Journal*; Nottinghamshire County Librarian and his staff; Mr H. G. Pearson; Mr D. J. Peters; Mr David Phillips; the late Mr Laurence Pollinger; Professor Frederick R. Pottle; Dr Margaret Radford; Mr Anthony Rota; Mr P. Sarll; Mr I. A. Shapiro; Dr I. Small; Professor Horton Smith; Dr A. Leigh Smith; Mrs H. M. Snowswell; the late Professor T. J. B. Spencer; Professor A. Subiotto; Mr R. C. Swift; Mrs G. Tring; Mr F. Webster; Miss L. E. Williamson; Mr Paul Wilson; Mrs W. Wilson; Mr Oliver Wood; Dr John Worthen. Special thanks have been earned by Dr Frank K. Robinson, University of Tennessee, who is responsible for translating Lawrence's letters in German throughout the edition; by Margaret Boulton for her invaluable help with proof-correcting; and by Miss Jennifer Wootton and Mrs Anne Buckley for their excellent secretarial assistance.

For permission to use copyright material in the introduction and for the purpose of annotation, gratitude is expressed to: Ernest Benn Ltd; the Berg Collection, New York Public Library, Astor, Lenox and Tilden Foundations; the late Miss Helen Corke; Mrs N. Haselden; Messrs W. Heinemann; Humanities Research Center, University of Texas at Austin; Hutchinson Publishing Group Ltd; the Society of Authors and Estate of Katherine Mansfield; University of Nottingham; Lord Stow Hill; and the late Mr Martin Secker.

Illustrations in this volume have been made available through the generosity of: Miss L. Annand; Dr W. J. D. Annand; Mr W. H. Clarke; Mr G. Collings; Messrs Constable & Co.; Mr W. Cracknell; Dr. E. C. Dax; Editor of *Der Islam*; Mr J. W. Dettmer; Mr A. D. Elmslie; Messrs Faber & Faber Ltd; Mrs D. Falla; the late Mrs G. Lovat Fraser; Dr D. Garnett; Mr R. Garnett; Messrs W. Heinemann; Mrs E. Hilton; Dr E. Houghton; Mrs A. Howard; Humanities Research Center, Austin, Texas; Miss E. Jennings; Mrs N. Littler; Mr J. Lord; Mrs M. Needham; University of Nottingham; Nottinghamshire County Library; Dr K. Sagar; the late Mr M. Secker; Dr A. L. Smith; Mrs H. M. Snoswell; Miss L. E. Williamson; Mr O. Wood.

Lawrence's chosen phoenix device has been engraved afresh for this edition by Reynolds Stone.

RULES OF TRANSCRIPTION

The editors provide not a diplomatic transcription of Lawrence's manuscripts but an edited text which is accurate and reliable. Editorial intrusion on readers' interest in what Lawrence himself wrote has been kept to a minimum, though relevant scholarship has been used in notes to clarify his meaning and elucidate his references. The rules which have directed editorial practice are as follows:

1. Spelling. Inadvertent misspellings which might puzzle the reader are corrected but reported in the notes. No attempt has been made to standardise eccentricities (e.g. 'aimiable').

2. Capitalisation and punctuation. Lawrence's manuscripts are strictly followed in these respects, with the following exceptions:

(a) Incomplete quotation marks are completed and where the end of a sentence lacks all pointing a full stop is supplied. Both emendations are silent.

(b) Since Lawrence's use of single and double inverted commas is inconsistent and might occasionally affect a reader's understanding of his meaning, the current British usage (single inverted commas surrounding a quotation and double for a quotation within a quotation) has been adopted throughout.

3. Torn or mutilated Manuscripts. A reconstructed text is supplied where possible, within square brackets. Where it proves impossible, five spaces are shown within square brackets and 'MS torn' or 'MS mutilated' is reported at the first occurrence in a particular letter.

4. Deletions or alternative readings. Where Lawrence deletes or replaces a complete word, his first thought is recorded in a note (e.g. family] father). If the deletion is illegible, in the text three points are shown within square brackets. This device is also used when postmarks are partly illegible.

5. Interlineations and marginalia. These are silently transferred into the text.

6. Abbreviations. Contractions or abbreviations which may perplex some readers are expanded in square brackets. A proper name is expanded (e.g. J[essie]) on its first occurrence in any letter; if it recurs in the same letter, Lawrence's abbreviation is retained. 'And' replaces the ampersand.

7. Italics. Words underlined by Lawrence are italicised. In addition – whether he underlined them or not – titles of independent publications or works of art (paintings, sculptures, pieces of music) are italicised. Titles of essays, short stories or poems are shown in single inverted commas.

8. Foreign languages. Where a complete letter or postcard is in a foreign language, the original text is immediately followed by a translation in square brackets. Where a sentence or more within a letter is in a foreign language, a translation is given in a footnote. Certain foreign words or phrases are also translated in the notes.

9. Place of writing and date. The address as given by Lawrence appears on a single line, commas being supplied where necessary to separate the elements. Where Lawrence omits an address, it will be supplied (when known) in square brackets.

The date as given on the manuscript appears below the address-line. When Lawrence omits all date-information, a conjectural date is provided in square brackets. If the reasons for a conjectural date are obvious (e.g. from the postmark in the headnote) no explanation will be provided; if, in the editor's view, justification of a date is required, it will be placed in a footnote.

10. Signature. Lawrence's normal manner was to sign himself by his initials alone or by initials and surname. These forms will be shown as either 'DHL' or 'D. H. Lawrence'.

11. Postscript. Wherever this is positioned on the manuscript (in the margin, at the top or at the end of a letter), it will be placed after the signature as if it were a new paragraph.

12. Joint letters. Letters written jointly by Lawrence and another person (usually Frieda) are presented in their entirety. The point at which one writer takes over from the other is announced: [Lawrence begins] or [Frieda Lawrence begins]. Where one writer inserts a single remark into the text of the other, this will be shown: e.g. [Lawrence interjects: No wonder I have the hump].

EDITORIAL APPARATUS

13. Numbering of letters. Since Lawrence often wrote more than one letter on the same day, sometimes two to the same recipient, scholars may find it inconvenient to refer to letters by date and recipient. Therefore all letters are numbered in sequence throughout the edition.

14. Heading. Following the number, each letter is introduced by the name of the recipient and the date (suitably bracketed where it is conjectural).

15. Headnote. This contains information on the source of the text of each letter and, if it has been previously published, its *first* appearance. The order followed is:

(a) Location of the manuscript used (e.g. MS Corke). (Where the editor is dependent on a printed source, this will obviously be omitted.) The following abbreviations are used: TMS = typed manuscript; TMSC = typed manuscript copy; AMSC = autograph manuscript copy; TSCC = typescript carbon copy.

(b) If the text is from a picture postcard, a brief description of the verso (e.g. PC v. Norman Tower, Christchurch), usually taken from the printed caption. If the description is editorial, it is shown in square brackets.

(c) Postmark information.

(d) If already published, the first printing (e.g. Huxley 304).

If the manuscript has not been previously published, the final element reads: 'Unpublished'.

Lawrence's letters already published have been variously printed in their entirety or partially, by excerpts as long as a paragraph, as short as a phrase. In order to show the extent to which a text was first printed (in (d) above), the following convention is used: where at least half the letter appeared, the reference is simply by cue-title and page (e.g. Huxley 304); where less than half was published, the reference begins, 'cited in' (e.g. cited in Violet Hunt, *The Flurried Years*, p. 151).

16. Footnotes

(a) In notes Lawrence himself is referred to as DHL.

(b) Acronyms are not used for any other person, but editors will not hesitate to employ the short name which Lawrence would have used (e.g. Kot for S. S. Koteliansky, or Brett for Hon. Dorothy Brett).

(c) Individuals named by Lawrence are identified at their first significant mention. Since cross-references are not normally provided later in the same volume to these biographical sketches, the index will – by the use of bold type – inform the reader where to find the main descriptive note. Nicknames and shortened forms of proper names are also indexed.

CUE-TITLES

Cue-titles are employed both for manuscript locations and for printed works. Each volume will contain lists of those cue-titles which are used in it. The following appear in this volume:

A. Manuscript locations

BL	British Library
Clarke	Mr W. H. Clarke
CEduc	Croydon Education Department
Corke	the late Miss Helen Corke

Garnett, D.	Dr David Garnett
Hale	Mrs Phyllis M. Hale
Harrison	Mr R. Austin Harrison
Heinemann	Messrs W. Heinemann
Jeffrey	Mr Frederick Jeffrey
Martin	Mr John Martin
NCL	Nottinghamshire County Libraries
NWU	Northwestern University
NYPL	New York Public Library
Pollinger	Laurence Pollinger Ltd.
Ridgway	Mrs Margaret Ridgway
Roberts, F. W.	Dr Warren Roberts
Sharpe	Mr Michael C. Sharpe
SIU	Southern Illinois University
Temple	Mr Frederic-Jacques Temple
UCB	University of California at Berkeley
UCLA	University of California at Los Angeles
UInd	University of Indiana
ULiv	University of Liverpool
UN	University of Nottingham
UT	University of Texas at Austin
Whiteson	Mrs Mary Whiteson

B. Printed works

(The place of publication is London unless otherwise stated.)

Allott	Kenneth Allott and Miriam Allott, 'D. H. Lawrence and Blanche Jennings', *Review of English Literature*, I (July 1960), 57–76
Boulton	James T. Boulton, ed. *Lawrence in Love: Letters to Louie Burrows.* Nottingham: University of Nottingham, 1968
Corke, *Neutral Ground*	Helen Corke. *Neutral Ground.* Barker, 1933
Corke, *Croydon Years*	Helen Corke. *D. H. Lawrence: The Croydon Years.* Austin: University of Texas, 1965
Delavenay	Emile Delavenay. *D. H. Lawrence: L'Homme et la Genèse de son Œuvre.* 2 volumes. Paris: Librairie C. Klincksieck, 1969

DHL Review	James C. Cowan, ed. *The D. H. Lawrence Review*. Fayetteville: University of Arkansas, 1968–
Draper	R. P. Draper, ed. *D. H. Lawrence: The Critical Heritage*. Routledge & Kegan Paul, 1970
E.T.	E.T. [Jessie Wood]. *D. H. Lawrence: A Personal Record*. Jonathan Cape, 1935
Ewing	Majl Ewing, ed. *Eight Letters by D. H. Lawrence to Rachel Annand Taylor*. Pasadena, California: Castle Press, 1956
Fraser	Grace Lovat Fraser. *In the Days of my Youth*. Cassell, 1970
Frieda Lawrence	Frieda Lawrence. *Not I, But the Wind...* Santa Fe: Rydal Press, 1934
Heilbrun	Carolyn G. Heilbrun. *The Garnett Family: The History of a Literary Family*. New York: Macmillan, 1961
Huxley	Aldous Huxley, ed. *The Letters of D. H. Lawrence*. Heinemann, 1932
Lawrence–Gelder	Ada Lawrence and G. Stuart Gelder. *Young Lorenzo: Early Life of D. H. Lawrence*. Florence: G. Orioli [1931]
Moore, *Intelligent Heart*	Harry T. Moore. *The Intelligent Heart*. New York: Farrar, Straus, and Young, 1954
Moore	Harry T. Moore, ed. *The Collected Letters of D. H. Lawrence*. 2 volumes. Heinemann, 1962
Nehls	Edward Nehls, ed. *D. H. Lawrence: A Composite Biography*. 3 volumes. Madison: University of Wisconsin Press, 1957–9
Pollak	Paulina S. Pollak, 'The Letters of D. H. Lawrence to Sallie and Willie Hopkin', *Journal of Modern Literature*, III (February 1973), 24–34
Roberts	Warren Roberts, *A Bibliography of D. H. Lawrence*. Rupert Hart-Davis, 1963

Secker	Martin Secker, ed. *Letters from D. H. Lawrence to Martin Secker 1911–1930.* [Bridgefoot, Iver] 1970
Tedlock, *Lawrence MSS*	E. W. Tedlock. *The Frieda Lawrence Collection of D. H. Lawrence Manuscripts: A Descriptive Bibliography.* Albuquerque: University of New Mexico, 1948
Tedlock	E. W. Tedlock, ed. *Frieda Lawrence: The Memoirs and Correspondence.* Heinemann, 1961
TLS	*The Times Literary Supplement*

MONETARY TERMS

tanner = sixpence (6d) = 2½p.
bob = one shilling (1/-) = 5p.
half-a-crown = 2/6 = 12½p.
quid = £1.
guinea = £1/1/- = £1.05.

LAWRENCE: A GENEALOGY

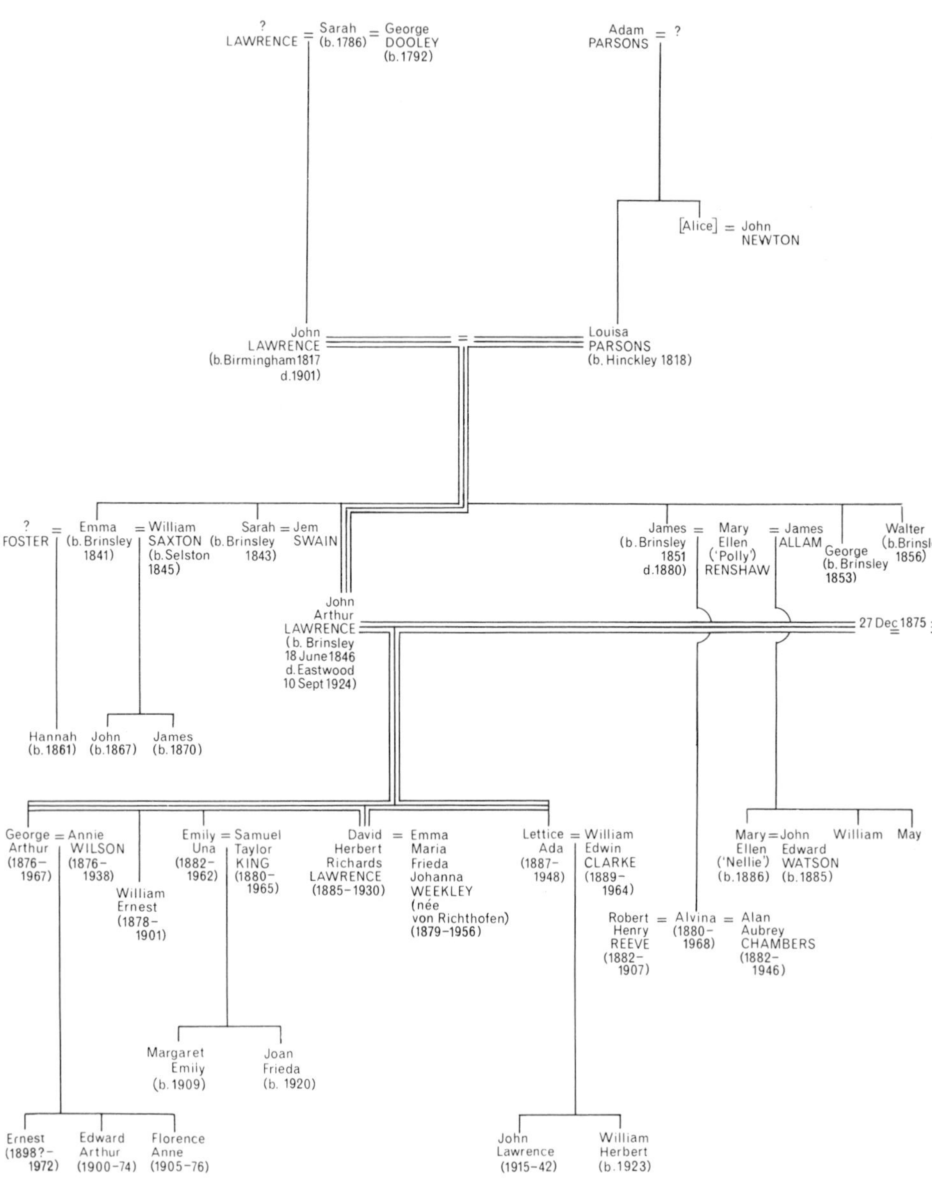

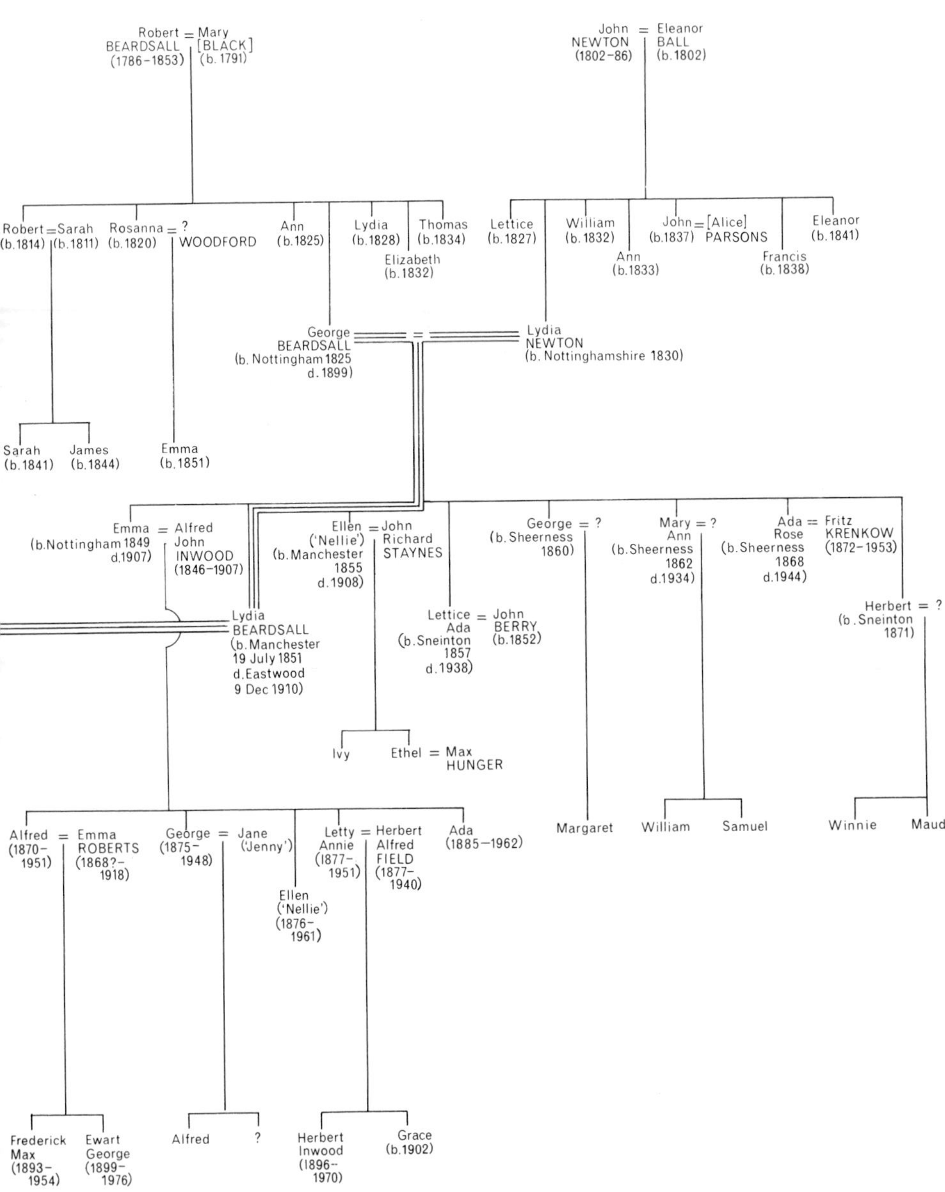

Robert BEARDSALL (1786–1853) = Mary [BLACK] (b. 1791)
John NEWTON (1802–86) = Eleanor BALL (b. 1802)
Robert (b. 1814) = Sarah (b. 1811)
Rosanna (b. 1820) = ? WOODFORD
Ann (b. 1825)
Lydia (b. 1828)
Thomas (b. 1834)
Elizabeth (b. 1832)
Lettice (b. 1827)
William (b. 1832)
Ann (b. 1833)
John (b. 1837) = [Alice] PARSONS
Francis (b. 1838)
Eleanor (b. 1841)
George BEARDSALL (b. Nottingham 1825 d. 1899) = Lydia NEWTON (b. Nottinghamshire 1830)
Sarah (b. 1841)
James (b. 1844)
Emma (b. 1851)
Emma (b. Nottingham 1849 d. 1907) = Alfred John INWOOD (1846–1907)
Ellen ('Nellie') (b. Manchester 1855 d. 1908) = John Richard STAYNES
George (b. Sheerness 1860) = ?
Mary Ann (b. Sheerness 1862 d. 1934) = ?
Ada Rose (b. Sheerness 1868 d. 1944) = Fritz KRENKOW (1872–1953)
Herbert (b. Sneinton 1871) = ?
Lydia BEARDSALL (b. Manchester 19 July 1851 d. Eastwood 9 Dec 1910)
Lettice Ada (b. Sneinton 1857 d. 1938) = John BERRY (b. 1852)
Ivy
Ethel = Max HUNGER
Margaret
William
Samuel
Winnie
Maud
Alfred (1870–1951) = Emma ROBERTS (1868?–1918)
George (1875–1948) = Jane ('Jenny')
Ellen ('Nellie') (1876–1961)
Letty Annie (1877–1951) = Herbert Alfred FIELD (1877–1940)
Ada (1885–1962)
Frederick Max (1893–1954)
Ewart George (1899–1976)
Alfred
?
Herbert Inwood (1896–1970)
Grace (b. 1902)

LAWRENCE: A CHRONOLOGY, 1885–1913

11 September 1885	Lawrence born at Eastwood, Nottinghamshire
1891? – 1898	Beauvale Board School, Eastwood
14 September 1898 – July 1901	Pupil at Nottingham High School
Late 1901	Clerk with J. H. Haywood Ltd, Nottingham
c. 4 April 1902	A month at Skegness convalescing after pneumonia
October 1902 – July 1905	Pupil-Teacher at British School, Eastwood; from March 1904 attended part-time at Pupil-Teacher Centre, Ilkeston
1904	King's Scholarship
June 1905	Great Yarmouth, Hunstanton, etc.
July 1905	University of London Matriculation
August 1905 – September 1906	Uncertificated assistant teacher, British School, Eastwood
August 1906	Family holiday at Mablethorpe, Lincolnshire
September 1906 – June 1908	Student at University College, Nottingham
10?–24? August 1907	Family holiday at Robin Hood's Bay, Yorkshire
7 December 1907	'A Prelude' published in *Nottinghamshire Guardian*
8–22? August 1908	Family holiday at Flamborough, Yorkshire
16 September 1908	Leicester 'for a week or two'
25 September 1908	Unsuccessful interview for a teaching post in Stockport
26? September – 3? October 1908	'A week in London' including interview at Croydon
11 October 1908	To Croydon: teacher at Davidson Road School
23 December 1908 – 10 January 1909	Eastwood for Christmas
10 January – 8 April 1909	Croydon
8–18 April 1909	Eastwood for Easter
18 April – 29 July 1909	Croydon (Whitsuntide holiday 28 May – 6 June)
29–31 July 1909	At Harrow-on-the-Hill staying with his aunt, Mrs Berry

31 July – 14 August 1909	Family holiday at Shanklin, Isle of Wight
14–29 August 1909	Eastwood
29 August – 23 December 1909	Croydon
c. 11 September 1909	In London to meet Ford Madox Hueffer
November 1909	Sequence of poems, 'A Still Afternoon', in *English Review*
23 December 1909 – 9 January 1910	Eastwood for Christmas
9 January – 24 March 1910	Croydon
February 1910	'Goose Fair' in *English Review*
24 March – 3 April 1910	Eastwood for Easter
3 April – 13 May 1910	Croydon
April 1910	Sequence of poems, 'Night Songs', in *English Review*
13–22 May 1910	Eastwood for Whitsuntide holiday
22 May – 28 July 1910	Croydon
28 July – c. 8 August 1910	Eastwood
c.8–15 August 1910	Holiday in Blackpool, Fleetwood and Barrow-in-Furness; returns to Eastwood
22–28 August 1910	At Leicester: Mrs Lawrence seriously ill
28 August 1910	Returns to Croydon for Autumn term
4 September 1910	Leicester
6–9 October 1910	Eastwood; visits Nottingham's Goose Fair
22–23 October 1910	Eastwood
October 1910	'Three Poems', in *English Review*
5–7 November 1910	Eastwood
c.15 November 1910	Breaks 'betrothal of six years standing' to Jessie Chambers
24 November – 13 December 1910	Eastwood
3 December 1910	At Leicester: becomes engaged to Louie Burrows
9 December 1910	Mrs Lawrence dies
13–24 December 1910	Croydon
24–31 December 1910	Holiday in Brighton with Ada Lawrence and Frances Cooper
31 December 1910 – 8 January 1911	Quorn (home of Louie Burrows)
8 January – 14 April 1911	Croydon
19 January 1911	*The White Peacock* published in New York (20 January in London)
14–23 April 1911	Eastwood. Matlock with Louie Burrows on Easter Monday
23 April – 5 June 1911	Croydon

5–11 June 1911	Quorn, Eastwood and Leicester for Whitsuntide holiday
12–16 June 1911	Croydon
16–25 June 1911	Eastwood (holiday for George V's coronation)
June 1911	'Odour of Chrysanthemums', in *English Review*
25 June – 27 July 1911	Croydon
27 July 1911	Quorn
29 July – 12 August 1911	Holiday in North Wales with Louie Burrows and Ada Lawrence
12–27 August 1911	Eastwood, Eakring, Shirebrook, Lincoln, Quorn
27 August 1911 – 4 January 1912	Croydon
September 1911	'A Fragment of Stained Glass', in *English Review*
13–15 October 1911	First visit to Edward Garnett at The Cearne, near Edenbridge, Kent
27–29 October 1911	Quorn and Eastwood
November 1911	Review of *Contemporary German Poetry*, in *English Review*
4 November 1911	Two poems in *Nation*
18–19 November 1911	The Cearne
19 November 1911 – 4 January 1912	Ill with pneumonia at Croydon
January 1912	Reviews of *The Minnesingers* and *The Oxford Book of German verse*, in *English Review*
4 January–3 February 1912	Leaves Croydon; two days at Redhill; then at Bournemouth for convalescence
3–9 February 1912	The Cearne
4 February 1912	Breaks engagement to Louie Burrows
9 February–25 March 1912	Eastwood (with visits to Nottingham, Shirebrook, Worksop, Eakring)
February 1912	'Second Best' in *English Review*
5 March 1912	Resignation from teaching post confirmed by Croydon Education Department
16 March 1912	'The Miner at Home' in *Nation*
17? March 1912	Meets Frieda Weekley
25–31 March 1912	Bradnop, Staffordshire; returns to Eastwood
25–29 April 1912	London (and at The Cearne with Frieda, 27–28 April)
29 April 1912	Via Leicester to Eastwood
3 May 1912	London; leaves England with Frieda

4–8 May 1912	Metz
8–11 May 1912	Trier
11 May 1912	To Waldbröl (via Coblenz, Nieder Lahnstein, Troisdorf, Hennef)
11 May 1912	First three of eight 'Schoolmaster' poems in *Saturday Westminster Gazette*, 11 May – 1 June
19 May 1912	In Bonn
23 May 1912	*The Trespasser*
24 May 1912	To Munich and Wolfratshausen
25 May – 1 June 1912	Beuerberg (the 'honeymoon')
1 June – 5 August 1912	Icking
June 1912	A poem, 'Snap-Dragon', in *English Review*
3 August 1912	'German Impressions: I. French Sons of Germany', in *Saturday Westminster Gazette*
5 August 1912	Leaves Icking for Tyrol and Italy
7 or 8 August 1912	Glashütte
10–27 August 1912	Mayrhofen
10 August 1912	'German Impressions: II. Hail in the Rhineland', in *Saturday Westminster Gazette*
28 August 1912	Dominicushütte
29 August – 2 September 1912	Sterzing
2–5 September 1912	To Riva (via Meran, Bozen, Trient)
5–17? September 1912	At Riva
18 September 1912 – 30 March 1913	Gargnano, Lago di Garda
December 1912	'Snap-Dragon', in *Georgian Poetry 1911–1912*
February 1913	*Love Poems and Others*
22 March 1913	'Christs in the Tirol', in *Saturday Westminster Gazette*
March 1913	'The Soiled Rose', in *Forum*
March 1913	'The Georgian Renaissance', a review of *Georgian Poetry 1911–1912*, in *Rhythm*
30 March – 11 April 1913	San Gaudenzio
11 April 1913	To Verona
14 April 1913	To Munich (via Innsbruck)
19 April – 17 June 1913	Irschenhausen; thence to England
29 May 1913	*Sons and Lovers*

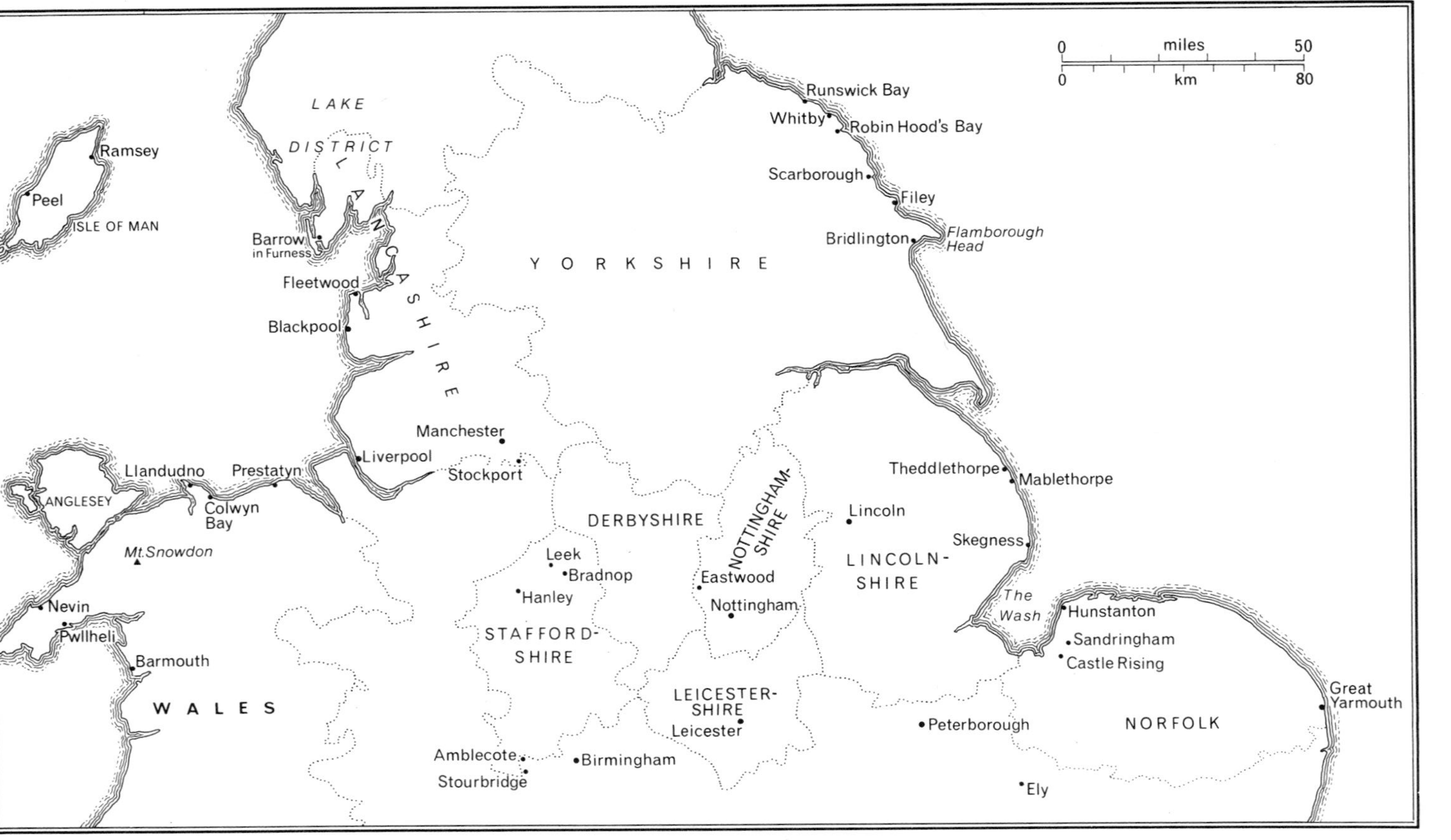

Map 1. Northern England and Wales with county boundaries (c. 1910)

Map 2. South-east England with county boundaries (c. 1910)

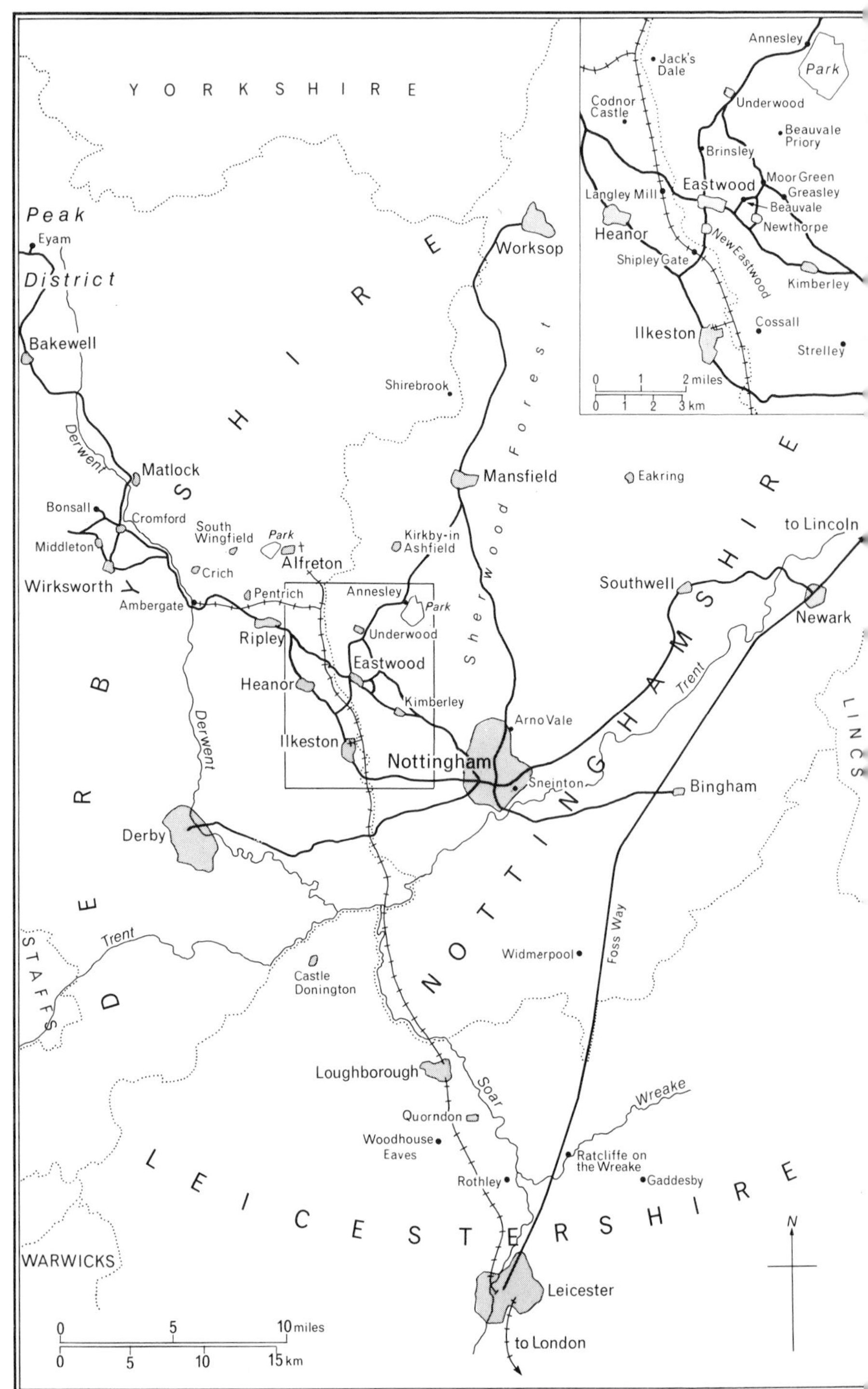

Map 3. Eastwood and Nottingham (c. 1910)

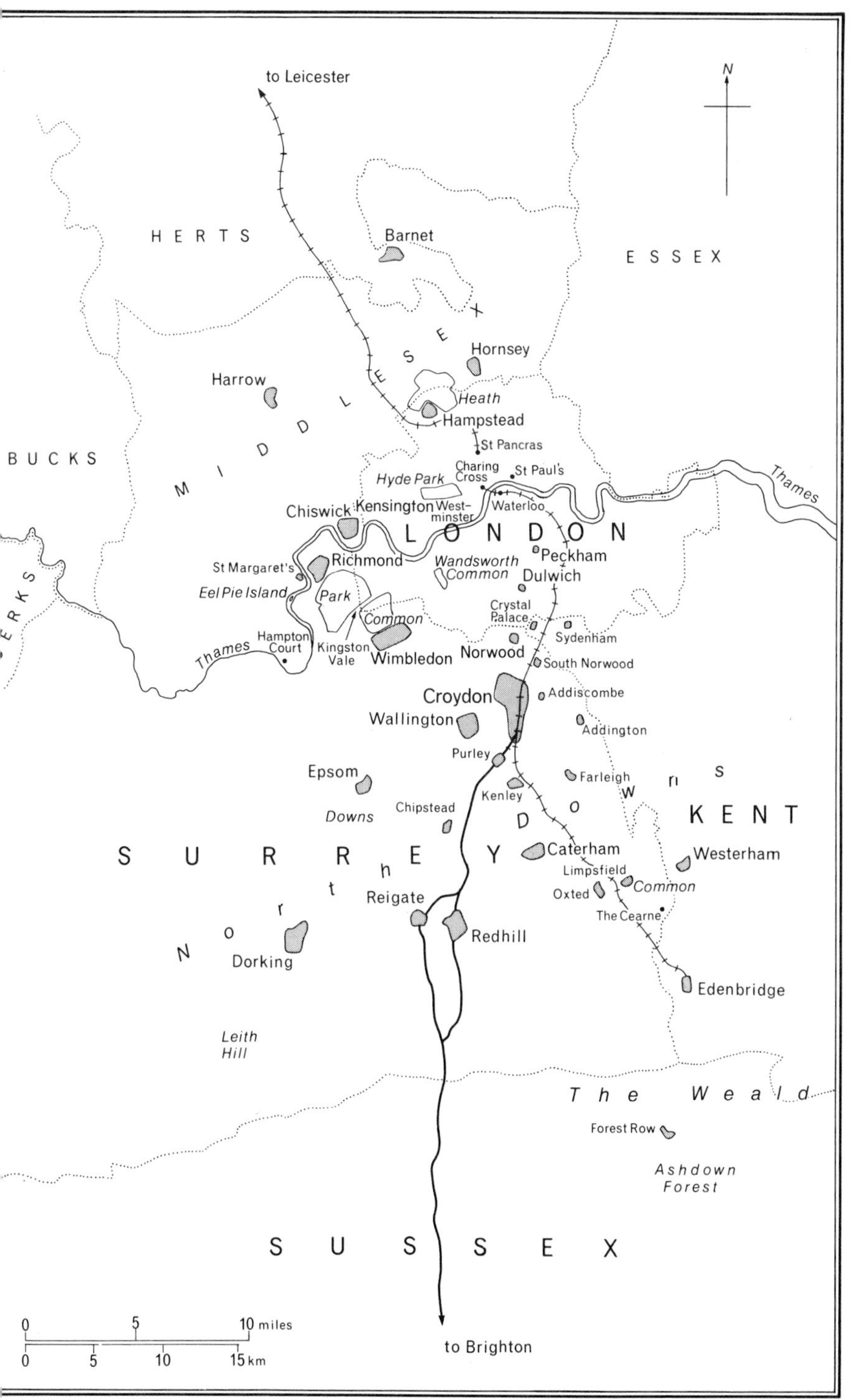

Map 4. Croydon and London (c. 1911)

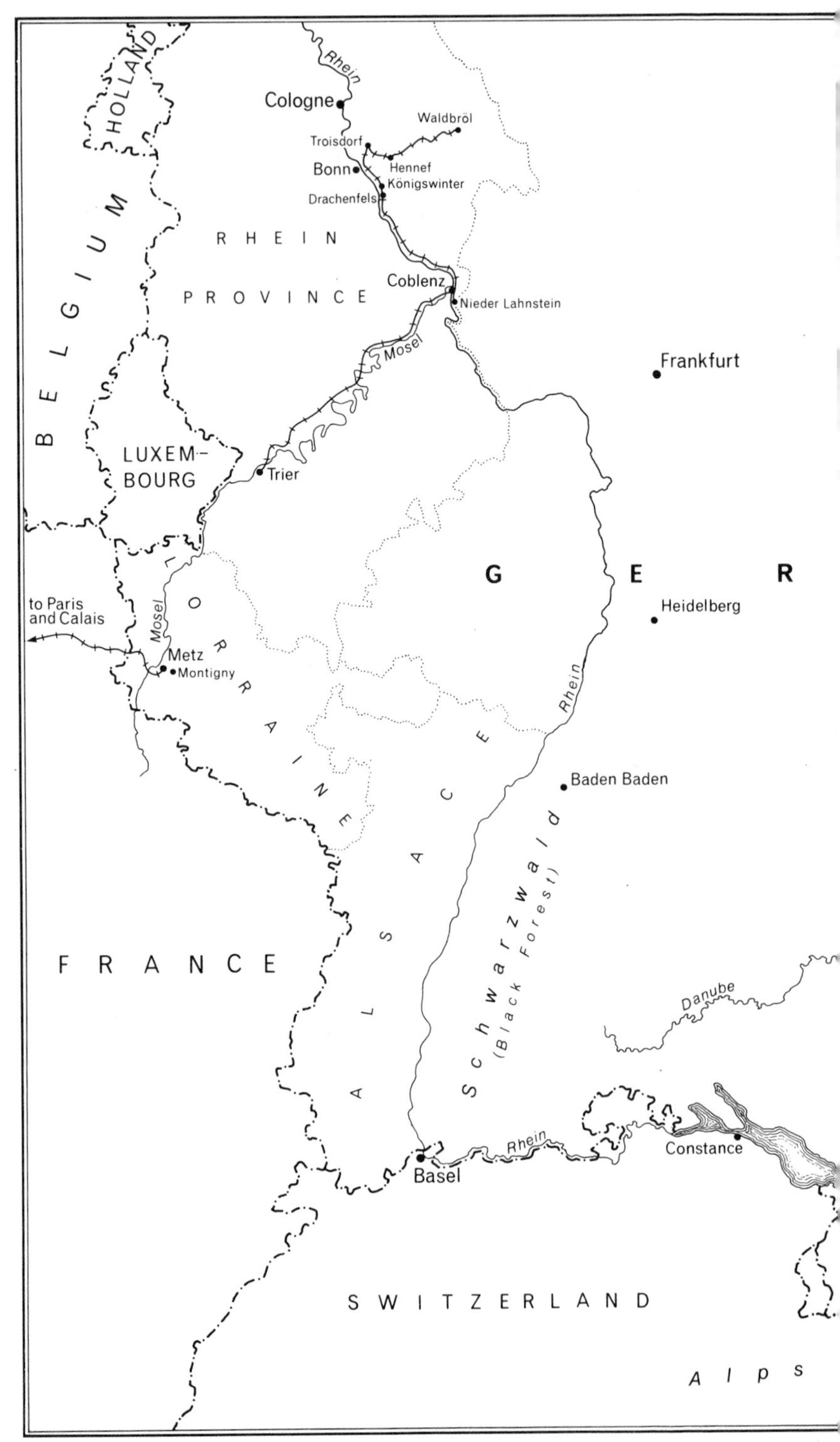

Map 5. Germany 191

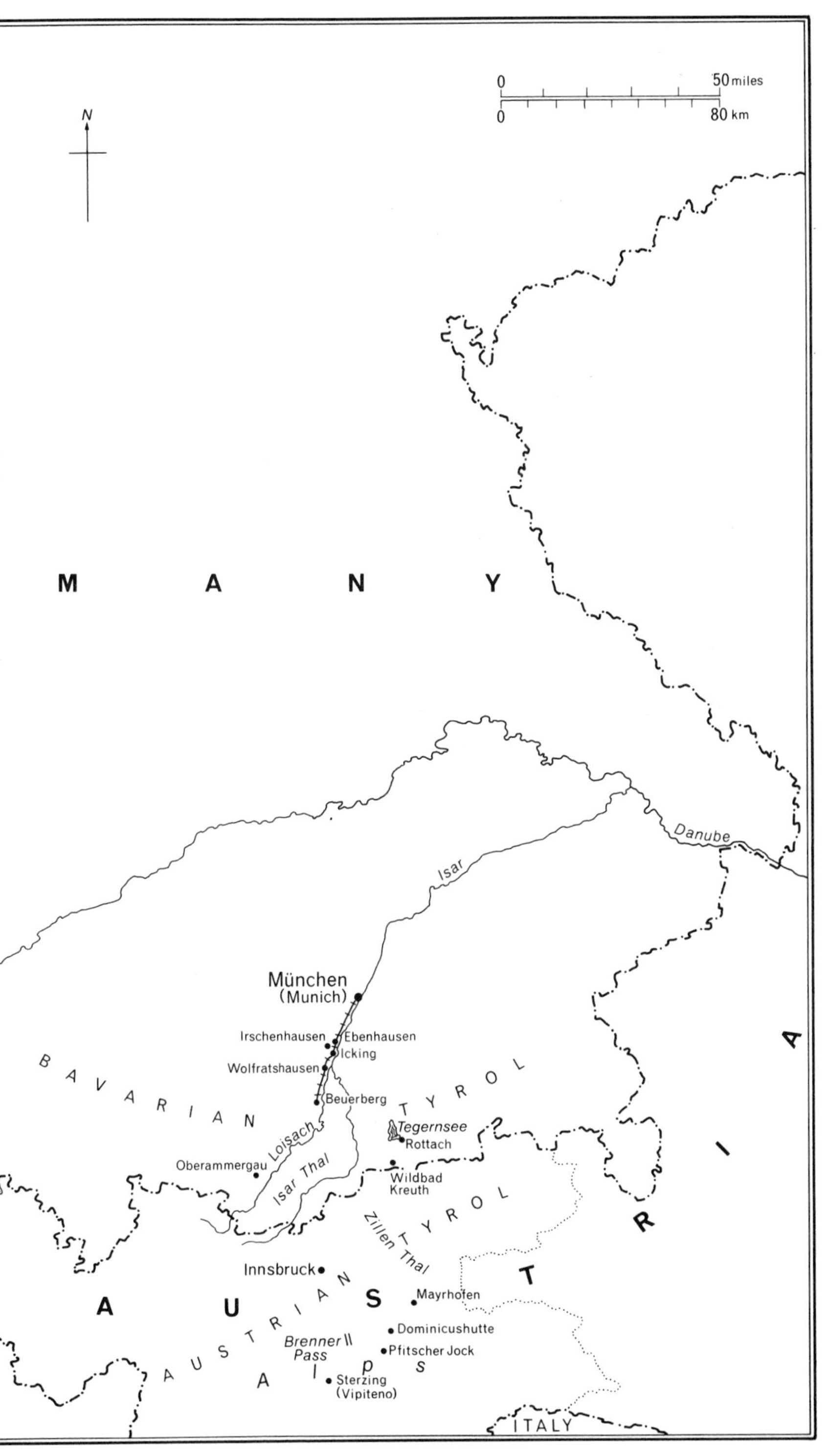

0
50 miles
0
80 km
N
M A N Y
Danube
Isar
München
(Munich)
Irschenhausen
Ebenhausen
Icking
Wolfratshausen
Beuerberg
B A V A R I A N T Y R O L
Loisach
Tegernsee
Rottach
Oberammergau
Isar Thal
Wildbad
Kreuth
Zillen Thal
T Y R O L
A U S T R I A
Innsbruck
Mayrhofen
A U S T R I A N A l p s
Dominicushutte
Brenner Pass
Pfitscher Jock
Sterzing
(Vipiteno)
ITALY

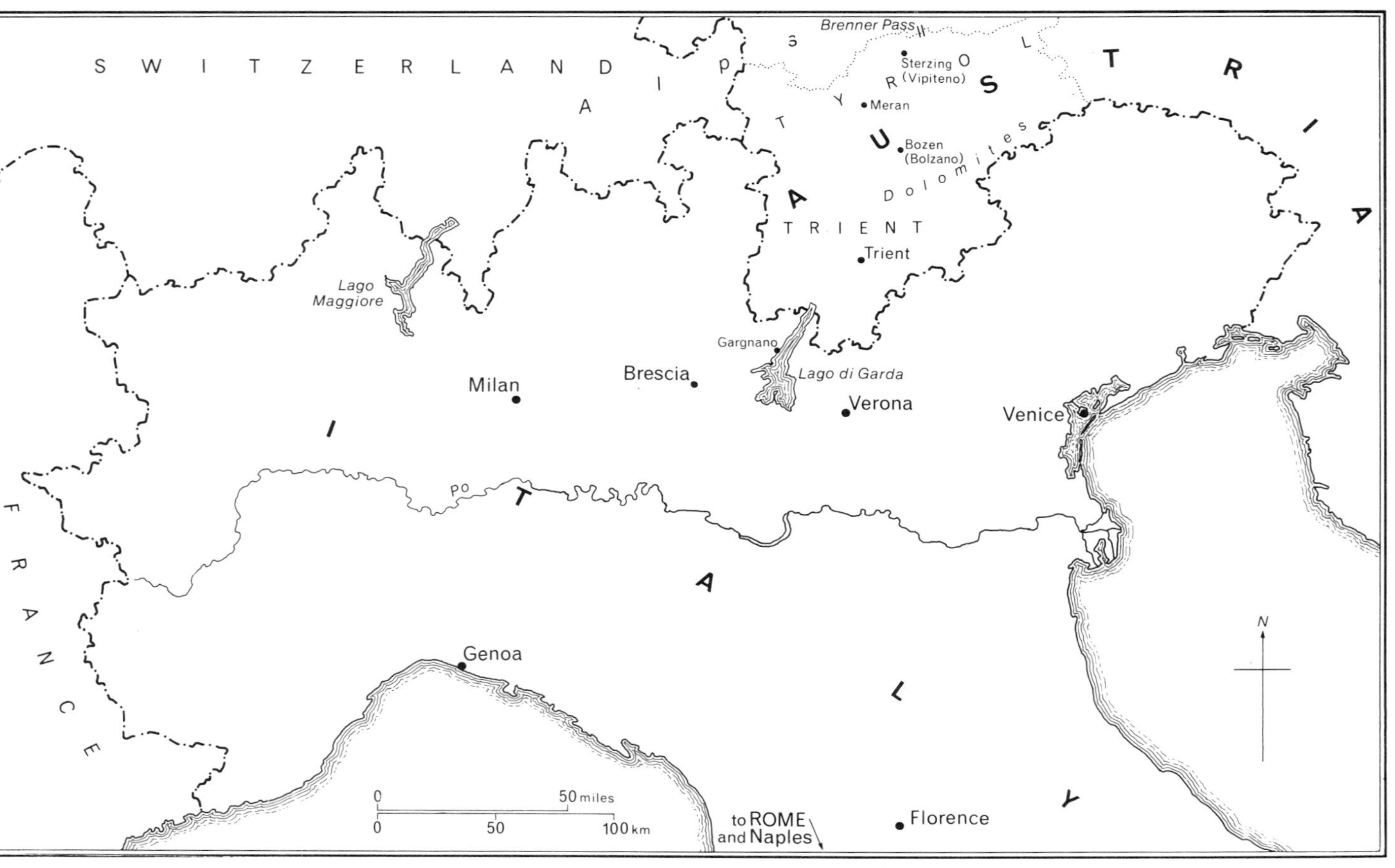

Map 6. Northern Italy (c. 1913)

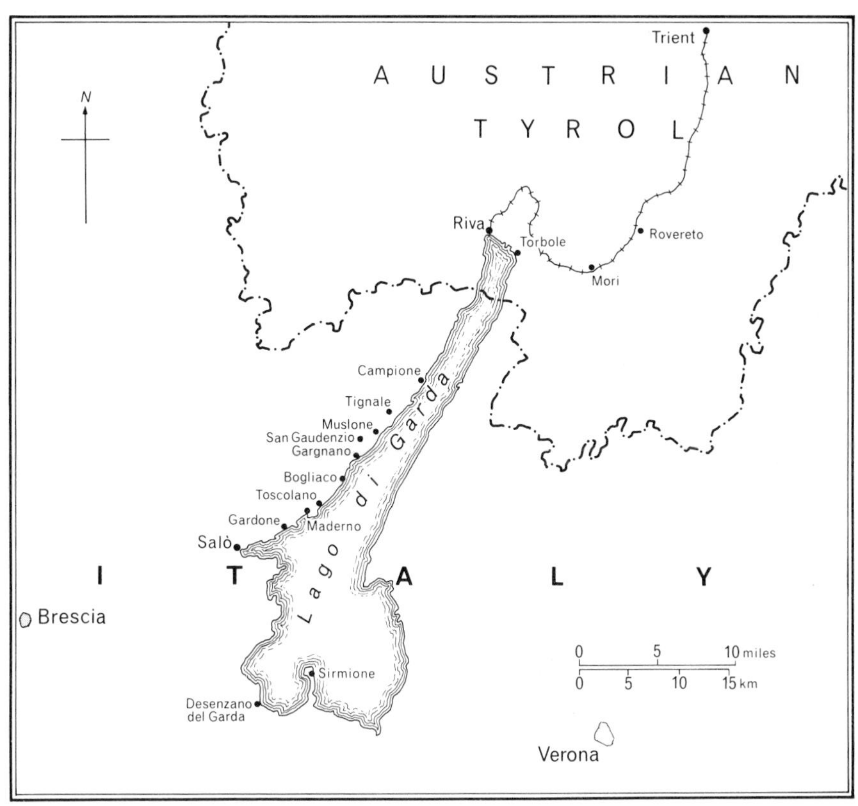

Map 7. Lago di Garda, Northern Italy (c. 1912)

INTRODUCTION

The volume opens with a formal letter dictated for the sixteen-year-old David Herbert Lawrence by his brother Ernest in stiff, commercial English; the last letter coincides with the publication of *Sons and Lovers* and marks 'the end of [his] youthful period'.[1] The period between – almost twelve years – in absolute terms is short: its significance can scarcely be exaggerated. In these years Lawrence grew from a provincial schoolboy into a mature man; from a working-class adolescent under the tutelage of a possessive mother he became a published writer who had eloped with a woman of aristocratic family, the wife of one of his college professors; from the mining village, Eastwood, he had moved to the metropolitan centre of literary sophistication and thence to Italy. Multiplicity of experience, emotional and physical adventure, intellectual growth, 'culture-shock' and creative achievement: these engage our attention in the letters which follow.

In an attempt to describe and account for Lawrence's remarkable development, the private and personal nature of his letters compels our attention to the writer himself, but also to the people and events that helped to create the setting to which he responded and in which he grew. The people are those with whom Lawrence chiefly came into contact either in personal relationships or by letter, or both; people who exerted influence on him and who, in turn, felt his influence. The events are diverse, including literary and cultural experiences as well as happenings either calculated or fortuitous.

Without question, his mother was the dominant figure in his early life: the portrait of Mrs Morel in *Sons and Lovers* makes that abundantly clear. (He wrote to her every week for nearly two years from Croydon:[2] every letter has disappeared.) Mrs Lawrence has frequently been described by her son's biographers or memorialists; all insist on the toughness of her personality, her emotional vitality and intellectual sharpness. She read voraciously, loved discussion of philosophical or religious subjects, had submitted verses to local journals (though none has been discovered in print) and generally was a person 'of considerable refinement and culture'.[3] Of nearly comparable importance was the girl to whom Lawrence was unofficially engaged for six years until November 1910: Jessie Chambers. Her *D. H. Lawrence: A Personal Record* by 'E.T.' – the most valuable first-hand account of Lawrence's early years – reveals her own emotional vulnerability; but there is also evidence of shrewd judgement, integrity and literary sensitivity. She was

[1] Letter 577. [2] Letter 252. [3] Nehls, i. 9, 22.

profoundly in his debt; he was indebted to her for the shape of his entire career. 'The girl...launched me...on my literary career, like a princess cutting a thread, launching a ship.'[1]

In his early manhood he relied mainly on women for both intellectual stimulus and emotional satisfaction: 'I am always opening my heart to some girl or woman', he wrote in May 1908.[2] In varying degrees they were women of independent mind, resolute and decisive. Mrs Lawrence was manifestly such; so was Jessie Chambers (despite certain features in the portrait of Miriam in *Sons and Lovers*); and so was Louie Burrows to whom Lawrence became officially engaged on 3 December 1910. His emotional commitment to Louie, though intense in the early stages, proved short-lived; it was probably never as complete and certainly not so enduring as hers. Academically she was his equal at University College, Nottingham, and her modest creative ability earned his praise. He expected she would write short stories 'very likely as good as W. W. Jacobs'; he regarded her as co-author of his story 'Goose Fair' and shared with her the fee received for it.[3] Louie was devoted to the cause of women's rights and was in close touch with members of one of the leading suffragist societies, the Women's Social and Political Union (one member wrote to her, in November 1911, from custody at Bow Street Police Station). Frequent attempts were doubtless made to enlist Lawrence's support for the women's cause both by Louie and also by two others among his female friends: Alice Dax and Blanche Jennings. Alice Dax was the more militant: her suffragist activities brought about her transfer as a Post Office clerk from Liverpool (where she worked with Blanche Jennings) to the Isle of Man. Later, after her marriage, she was prominent in the Eastwood socialist group, on the local council in the village of Shirebrook and in the affairs of the Workers' Educational Association. It was at her home (in late 1907 or early 1908) that Lawrence met Blanche Jennings whose visit may well have been linked with a suffragist rally in Nottingham. Politically radical like her friend, she too was one of the 'new women', free of the conventional mores inherited in different degrees by Jessie Chambers and Louie Burrows. Lawrence welcomed the opportunity to write to her. She was slightly older than he; she was detached from the local scene but acquainted with it; and he could be flirtatious, indulge his theatricality and boisterous fun, and experiment with literary tone and style.

Lawrence's female companions were of great consequence. They were all highly articulate and delighted in the exchange of ideas. They composed his first audience as readers and critics of his short stories and of the early

[1] 'Autobiographical Sketch', *Phoenix II*, p. 593. [2] Letter 47.
[3] Letters 144 and 149.

versions of *The White Peacock*. And either individually or collectively they were responsible, into his early manhood, for the education of his feelings. Intellectually and emotionally he developed under their influence.

The maturing process did not, however, depend solely on Lawrence's female friends. His father's contribution must be taken into account though, during the period covered by this volume, Lawrence himself was unable to recognise – much less, acknowledge – it. Later – in the essay, 'Enslaved by Civilisation', 1929 – he gloried in his father's lack of formal education, seeing him then as admirably untamed and free. A man of unsophisticated but powerful feelings, John Arthur Lawrence was one in whom a bullying stubbornness co-existed with a capacity for tenderness. He revelled in the close and boisterous male companionship that stemmed from his work down the pit; he delighted equally if not more so in the beauty and vitality of the natural world. From him Lawrence probably inherited his own astonishing familiarity and sympathy with that world, particularly with animals, that is so frequently remarked. For influence on young Lawrence's intellectual growth, however, we have to look to two other men. William Hopkin was one. Considerably older than Lawrence, he was an established local politician; he had his own weekly column in the Eastwood newspaper, the *Eastwood and Kimberley Advertiser*; and Lawrence had the opportunity to meet national politicians at Hopkin's house – Philip Snowden, Ramsay MacDonald and Keir Hardie among them.[1] Hopkin was, also, a leading member of and contributor to the Congregational Literary Society founded in Eastwood in 1899 by the Rev. Robert Reid, himself a principal figure in the affairs of the Lawrence family. Reid was obviously central in that Congregational upbringing for which Lawrence expressed gratitude in his late essay (1928), 'Hymns in a Man's Life'. Reid had a keen mind, enjoyed a broad range of intellectual enquiry and loved debate: Lawrence's recently discovered letters to him take these qualities for granted. They also assume in him compassion and understanding.

Lawrence was himself a member of the Literary Society; Jessie Chambers gives the impression that they were both keen participants, but we cannot know how regularly he attended. Nevertheless, available to him through Society meetings were papers on subjects ranging from literature, politics and music (both sacred and secular) to geography, history and travel.[2] At an annual cost of one shilling, the 3–400 members could have heard, in the first year, papers on Burns, Thomas Hood, Browning, early English drama,

[1] Cf. Nehls, i. 134–5.

[2] For this information I am indebted to D. M. Newmarch, 'D. H. Lawrence's Chapel', unpublished M.Phil. thesis, University of York, 1976.

Goldsmith, Tennyson and Longfellow. Alice Dax's husband, Henry, spoke several times on biological topics; the Rev. A. R. Henderson (whom Lawrence heard from the pulpit) talked on Morley's *Life of Gladstone*; a paper on Tennyson's *Idylls* was followed by a vote of thanks from Lawrence's Eastwood headmaster, W. Whitehead; and Alice Dax's frequent contributions to discussions were noted in the local newspaper. Indeed, either in its intellectual concerns or through its members, or both, the Literary Society probably stimulated Lawrence's development very significantly.

Contemporary with the early years of the Literary Society was the period (1898–1901) Lawrence spent at Nottingham High School, an independent day school of ancient foundation. The influence it exerted on his intellectual growth has been curiously underestimated. He may well have felt an outsider at the school; the distance he travelled daily from Eastwood made it inevitable that he would be debarred from many extra-curricular activities; but the quality of the education he received cannot be disregarded.[1] He was taught by some able graduate-teachers under Dr James Gow (who became headmaster of Westminster School in London at the same time as Lawrence left the High School); he studied a broad curriculum (though strangely excluding Latin), including Natural Sciences as well as English language and literature, History, French and German. Interestingly, the emphasis in English and History was predominantly on the seventeenth century; this was also to be his chosen area of specialisation in those subjects at University College, Nottingham. The three years Lawrence spent at the High School exposed him for the first time to academic rigour of a formal kind; this school year by year sent boys with Open Scholarships to Oxford and Cambridge; and to ignore its impact on him would be foolish.

Also largely ignored has been the lasting importance to Lawrence of a set of books he found at home: *The International Library of Famous Literature*, edited by Richard Garnett (1899) in twenty volumes. Potentially they offered him a wider literary education than either the High School or – the next stage of his formal education – the Pupil-Teacher Centre at Ilkeston. (The curriculum at the Centre is summarised in Lawrence's letter to *The Teacher*.)[2] As Jessie Chambers remarked, the Garnett *Library* was 'regarded with a reverence amounting to awe';[3] originally the set belonged to Lawrence's dead brother Ernest whose passion for cultivation doubtless intensified Lawrence's own. Justifiably Jessie added: 'Lawrence must have

[1] See D. J. Peters, 'Young Bert Lawrence as pupil at city High School', *Nottingham Guardian Journal*, 22 March 1972.

[2] Letter 14.

[3] E.T. 92.

made many literary acquaintances through the medium of these volumes.' The letters which follow here frequently confirm the accuracy of her supposition.

Garnett's anthology – surely one of the most remarkable even in a period of Smilesian self-help – printed substantial extracts (over thirty pages in many instances) from works originating as far afield as Russia and China, Europe and America. Horace, Euripides, Seneca, Spenser, Bacon, Shakespeare, Pope, Swift, Goethe, Renan, Tolstoy, George Eliot, Schopenhauer, Emerson and Verlaine: all are represented, among many others. Through this brilliantly selected *Library* Lawrence probably made his first acquaintance with such major writers or, say, with Mrs Humphry Ward, Björnson, Bliss Carman, Béranger, H. R. Haweis or Harrison Ainsworth. Many of the works quoted or alluded to in his early letters appear in Garnett's volumes. Browning's 'Hervé Riel', Burns's 'To a Mouse', W. S. Gilbert's 'Yarn of the Nancy Bell', Hood's 'Bridge of Sighs', Jerrold's 'Mrs Caudle's Curtain Lectures', Edwin Arnold's 'The Light of Asia' and Whitman's 'O Captain, my Captain' provide some examples. In his paper, 'Art and the Individual' (delivered at Easter or Whitsuntide 1908, in Eastwood), Lawrence refers to the Laocoön;[1] in August 1909 he sent postcard reproductions of it to two friends: his interest may have derived from Garnett's 4,000-word extract from Lessing's *Laocoön* illustrated by a picture of the sculpture. Helen Corke recalls lending Olive Schreiner's *Story of an African Farm* to Lawrence;[2] Garnett may have introduced him to the book many years before. When he rejoiced at the purchase of Baudelaire's *Fleurs du Mal* for ninepence in Charing Cross Road,[3] part of his delight may have been to possess complete and in French the poems of which Garnett had printed two in translation. Or, as a final example, Lawrence's knowledge of *Manon Lescaut* and his belief that Dumas in *La Dame aux Camélias* was indebted to Prévost may have originated in a reading of Garnett's 13,000-word extract from the novel and a shorter one from the play. In any case when, on 15 June 1908, he was eagerly anticipating the experience of watching Sarah Bernhardt in the play, Lawrence's expectations had probably been shaped by Garnett's striking illustration of Bernhardt as Dumas' famous courtesan. The caption to the illustration reads: 'Sarah Bernhardt as Camille'. In Dumas' novel and play the character's name is Marguérite Gautier; but in Matilda Heron's translation (1856), both the play and the leading rôle are called 'Camille'. It was Heron's version that Garnett reprinted in the *Library*; it is therefore

[1] 'Art and the Individual', *Phoenix II*, p. 224.

[2] Helen Corke, *In Our Infancy* (Cambridge, 1975), p. 184.

[3] Letter 179.

tempting to link that fact directly to Lawrence's remark to Blanche Jennings: 'As Camille I think [Bernhardt] will be thrilling.'[1]

Much here is necessarily conjectural: one cannot know precisely the extent to which Lawrence explored Garnett's *Library*. Yet, though single examples of 'influence' can be regarded as coincidental, in the mass they become weighty evidence; they lead to the confident assertion that Lawrence was and perhaps remained greatly indebted to this astonishing anthology. One of Garnett's intentions was to introduce English readers to American literature[2] (Bret Harte contributed one of the introductory essays to be found in each volume): this may prove significant to a discussion of the background of Lawrence's later work, *Studies in Classic American Literature*. In any event, together with the Eastwood Mechanics' Institute library (which Lawrence and Jessie Chambers plundered every Thursday evening),[3] Garnett's twenty green-backed volumes provided the basis for a generous liberal education. They offered 'infinite riches in little room'.[4]

The letters and Lawrence's biographers afford glimpses into the formal education he received at University College, Nottingham, during his teacher-training course (1906–8); the famous passages in *The Rainbow* record, through the character of Ursula, his disenchantment with it. What has so far remained unexplored is the intellectual and moral calibre of the people with whom he was in close contact at this period. Jessie Chambers, Louie Burrows, Alice Dax and Blanche Jennings have been considered; three more (hitherto unknown or underestimated) may now be added.

First a college contemporary previously unidentified but clearly important: Thomas Alfred Smith. Like Lawrence he came from a working-class home; his father was an engine-driver, his mother a farmer's daughter. The two undergraduates struck up a warm friendship: Smith was the only male friend not from Eastwood whose home (in Lincoln) Lawrence visited, and his admiration for Lawrence was intense. Smith read Chemistry; he obtained a First Class Honours B.Sc. (London) in 1910; he was awarded a postgraduate scholarship – an '1851 Exhibition' – and went to Göttingen to study for his doctorate under the distinguished Professor Wallach. (His parents encouraged this move partly to sever his relationship with Lawrence.) Smith's subsequent career is summarised later: it is enough here to observe that, in 1945, as Director with the British Control Commission in Germany, he was responsible for the dismantling of the German chemical industry. He was,

[1] Letter 49.
[2] Richard Garnett, *International Library of Famous Literature* (1899), i. xvf.
[3] E.T. 92–3.
[4] Richard Garnett, *International Library of Famous Literature*, i. xiv.

then, a man of considerable distinction; Lawrence derived pleasure from his company; and Smith's achievements should dispel any lingering doubts about the quality of mind Lawrence met with during his college years.

The second person to be noted is one of Lawrence's teachers, possibly one of the only two for whom he admitted any respect whatever:[1] Ernest Alfred Smith, popularly known as 'Botany' Smith. Though he was doubtless partly responsible for Lawrence's achieving a Distinction in Botany in his Teacher's Certificate, he made a major contribution in other ways. At a time when Lawrence was undergoing a painful struggle to reach a religious and philosophical equilibrium, Smith was important. He had some academic competence in philosophy, sociology and ethics (he was a particularly successful extra-mural teacher in these subjects); his interest in theology later led him to become a Unitarian minister. Lawrence had cause to be grateful to him: 'You were my first live teacher of philosophy.'[2] Smith was not, like Robert Reid, speaking from an achieved dogmatic position; rather was he, like his young pupil, philosophically adventurous and religiously undogmatic. He helped Lawrence to grow. 'You showed me the way out of a torturing crude Monism, past Pragmatism, into a sort of crude but appeasing Pluralism.' It would be foolish to inflate Smith's importance on the basis of this rather opaque sloganising; equally perverse would be to suggest that it contributed nothing to the Lawrence of 1927 who believed that 'Monism is the religion of the cut-off...There is a *principle* in the universe, towards which man turns religiously.'[3]

Lawrence's uncle by marriage, Fritz Krenkow, is the third person worth particular attention. His largely intellectual influence was reinforced by his wife's interest in Lawrence as a painter. Lawrence sent his aunt Ada three 'sketches' in November 1908; in April 1911 he started a painting for her – 'she needs another' (possibly suggesting that she occasionally sold paintings for him); and he was prepared to lend her money in October 1911 from his own scarce resources.[4] Ada may, then, have had some importance; her husband certainly had. It must be admitted that, in April 1912, Lawrence wrote from the Krenkows' house in Leicester: 'I hate this house – full of old books, gloomy as hell, and silent with books';[5] but what these remarks chiefly reflect is his excitement at having just stayed overnight with Frieda Weekley and his eagerness for their elopement four days later. A truer picture comes earlier. On a postcard from Leicester, 21 September 1908, he wrote: 'My friends here are books – nothing but books...Uncle is always working

[1] Letter 60.
[2] Letter 135.
[3] Letter 3 August 1927.
[4] Letters 85, 260 and 316.
[5] Letter 424.

away at his Arabic, and I sit reading French, wishing I could tackle Spanish and Italian, of which there are such a lot of delightful books here.'[1] What we see here is a young man's excited reaction to perhaps the only private library he had yet intimately explored; his reaction, too, to a private scholar (later to have an international reputation) who made the inadequacy of most of his college teachers even more obvious. Fritz Krenkow, a German national (until his naturalisation in 1911) worked as a cashier in a Leicester hosiery firm; in his spare time he was a scholar-editor and translator of Arabic texts, and lexicographer. From 1907 he published frequently in the *Journal of the Royal Asiatic Society* and other learned journals, mainly German; his edition of the *Poems of Tufail Ibn Auf al-Ghanawi and At Tirimmah Ibn Hakim At-Ta'yi* was ready in 1906, though it did not appear until 1927; and he continued to produce editions and other important work until shortly before his death in 1953. He was Professor of Islamic Studies at the Muslim University of Aligarh 1929–30; the University of Leipzig awarded him an honorary Ph.D. in 1929; and at Bonn he held an honorary professorship in Arabic Language and Literature in the early 1930s. Krenkow's dedication to scholarship and his intellectual energy could not fail to have their impact on the young Lawrence. Krenkow, we know, prompted Lawrence to translate into English verse some Arabic Fellah songs which he had himself translated into German. It is inconceivable that his influence ceased there.

Krenkow was significant for another reason: as well as acquiring an increasing reputation in the world of scholarship, he represented contact with Europe, its literature and culture. By contrast, when Lawrence moved to his teaching post in Croydon in 1908, he was provincial. He had indeed lost his 'mental and moral boyhood' and gained in 'scepticism';[2] he was no longer 'the sweet, innocent, mystical lad' of earlier years;[3] but he remained severely limited in experience. Except for family holidays at Mablethorpe and Robin Hood's Bay, and a couple of other visits to the Lincolnshire coast, his world was bounded by Eastwood and Nottingham. That is, his physical world. In reading and in his imaginative life, he was richly equipped. He had already eagerly begun and was to continue to exercise his painterly skills by copying the works of others – Brangwyn, Girtin, Peter de Wint among them – and in consequence to develop his 'visionary awareness'.[4] In terms of education he had been thoroughly taught at a grammar school for three years, been placed in the first eleven candidates in England for the King's Scholarship (which would pay the fees for his college training) and in the First Class in the Teacher's Certificate. And he had the advantages of the nonconformist

[1] Letter 63.
[2] Letter 47.
[3] Letter 53.
[4] 'Making Pictures', *Phoenix II*, p. 605.

culture into which he was born. Ford Madox (Hueffer) Ford's record of a visit to Eastwood provides insights into the living quality of this culture: 'All the while the young people were talking about Nietzsche and Wagner and Leopardi and Flaubert and Karl Marx and Darwin...the French Impressionists and the primitive Italians and [they would] play Chopin or Debussy on the piano.'[1] Ford's vivid description may be fanciful to some extent, but it was an exaggeration in degree, not an invention of kind. Yet, despite Lawrence's cultural sophistication he remained closely identified with particular people and specific places. His profound attachment was to his mother and Eastwood, the Chambers family and Haggs Farm. In October 1908 when he had to move to Croydon, outside the familiar group, he shocked Jessie Chambers with a letter 'like a howl of terror...everything was strange, and how could he live away from us all? He dreaded morning and school with the anguish of a sick girl...cut off from us all he would grow into something black and ugly...'[2]

This reaction is not surprising; more so was the speed with which he accommodated himself to his new circumstances. He maintained contact with his familiars by letter; he proposed visiting George Hill whom he had known as a clerk in the Eastwood office of the mine-owners Barber, Walker & Co. but who was now head of the firm's sales office in London; and he was quickly on intimate terms with the London branch of his mother's family, particularly with his cousin Ellen ('Nellie') Inwood. (She developed a passion for him; when he fell in love elsewhere she suffered a total nervous collapse.) Manifestly, then, Lawrence's first instinct was to strengthen the bonds which held him to his past: he was 'a stranger in a strange land'.[3] Yet within a fortnight he was overcoming his 'loneliness and despair'.[4] As Jessie Chambers was shocked by the intensity of his homesickness, so she probably was by the speed of his recovery from it. Helen Corke presented her fictionally in *Neutral Ground* as Theresa and attributed to her the comment: 'London *has* isolated him...He, of all men, needs his own folk near him – their sympathy is essential to his life and work.'[5] This dependence on 'his own folk' proved not to be so complete as expected. The explanation is necessarily complex, but its principal elements must again be presented in terms of culture and personalities.

Lawrence certainly needed and quickly developed intimate relationships. Many of his teaching responsibilities in Croydon were irksome, but his

[1] Ford Madox Ford, *Return to Yesterday* (1931), p. 392.
[2] Letter 68.
[3] Letter 69.
[4] Letter 71.
[5] Corke, *Neutral Ground* 301–2.

sympathies were at once engaged by his pupils. Some of them endured poverty such as he had seen in Nottingham but had not directly encountered before. Davidson Road School Log records on 13 December 1907 (before Lawrence's arrival, but his letters confirm that the situation continued): 'Free breakfast given to the number of 102 during the week...28 children were discovered to be in want of boots. Many of these scholars were in a deplorable condition.' They aroused his compassion; his headmaster testified that Lawrence for his part enjoyed his pupils' 'entire regard, respect and confidence'.[1] As for his peers, although the headmaster and some colleagues were unexciting, Lawrence discovered one who shared his own interests and others from neighbouring schools who were congenial. Outstanding on his own staff was Arthur William McLeod; over sixty letters were written to him over the years. He was more academically inclined than Lawrence; he read for a degree (London B.A. in Greek) – which Lawrence explicitly refused to do – and so was qualified to transfer to grammar-school teaching; but devotion to books cemented their friendship. McLeod's library, particularly of classical literature, modern poetry and fiction, supplied Lawrence and Frieda when they were later in northern Italy and almost totally deprived of books. Conventional and conservative though McLeod was, his literary sensitivity and scholarship together with his personal integrity (he was the only colleague in whom Lawrence confided about Frieda), made his friendship of considerable and continuing importance.

Two other Croydon teachers were significant for Lawrence: one fleetingly, the other much more profoundly. The first was a vivacious and attractive girl, Agnes Holt; for a short time he contemplated marriage with her. She had other plans and a mind of her own. Lawrence was introduced to the second, Helen Corke, by the senior mistress in his own school, Agnes Mason. Helen Corke was undoubtedly his most important woman friend in Croydon. She shared many of his interests – literature, German, art and music; she supervised and assisted in the copying of the final manuscript from which *The White Peacock* was set up in proof; her own private tragedy was transmuted by Lawrence into subject-matter for *The Trespasser*; and concurrent with these shared activities there developed an intense emotional attachment. Helen Corke was at times a focus for Lawrence's extremes of feeling – passionate physical desire or bitter irony verging on hatred. While writing *The Trespasser* Lawrence imaginatively 'became' Siegmund and in consequence suffered an agonising conflict between his impersonal, artistic self and his personal feelings; but it became clear that no permanent,

[1] Nehls, i. 150.

harmonious relationship was possible. 'Repulsed', 'Coldness in Love', 'Release' and 'Passing visit to Helen': such poems written at this time vividly convey Lawrence's passion and frustration, tension and pitiless scorn.

His teaching responsibilities, his colleagues like Agnes Mason and McLeod who at once took a personal interest in him, his deep affection for the children of his landlord and the vicarious intimacy with Eastwood sustained through Hill and Ellen Inwood: all such factors enabled Lawrence quickly to adjust to his new surroundings. So also did his fascination with London; he soon came to feel 'remarkably at home in London, remarkably cheerful and delighted'.[1] The beauty of the countryside close to the city surprised and excited him; it helped to compensate for the loss of that beloved rural scenery near Eastwood celebrated in *The White Peacock*. His letters frequently refer to a new range of cultural opportunities which dwarfed those available to him in Nottingham: concerts and theatres in Croydon and London; exhibitions at the Royal Academy or the Dulwich Art Gallery; or the architecture of the 'capital of commercialdom...magnificent temples built by the swelling intelligence of Men'.[2] Yet Lawrence's world remained book-centred: plays, concerts, lectures may have been momentarily enthralling but 'the true heart of the world is a book...The essence of things is stored in books.'[3] 'I don't seem to need, at least I don't feel the need, of much food of new ideas, or of too new sensations. My books are enough.'[4]

In this respect one of the crucial events during Lawrence's stay in Croydon – coinciding almost exactly with his arrival there – was the appearance of the first issue of the *English Review* in December 1908. He obviously bought each number as it came out; he persuaded the Chambers family to do so;[5] he hectored Blanche Jennings – 'Do you take the *Review* – if not, then you ought';[6] and more courteously encouraged Louie Burrows to subscribe to this 'very fine and very "new"' journal. 'It is the best possible way to get into touch with the new young school of realism.'[7] His own reading, both of the contents of the *Review* and also of what it reviewed and recommended, came at once under its influence. And in terms of his personal life, directly and indirectly the *English Review* was to have a more formative and ultimately transforming effect on Lawrence than any other experience before his meeting with Frieda Weekley.

The leading spirit in founding the *English Review* was Ford Madox Hueffer

[1] Letter 67.
[2] Ibid.
[3] Letter 88.
[4] Letter 95.
[5] E.T. 156.
[6] Letter 102.
[7] Letter 127.

as he then was. The periodical, he announced in his first Editorial, was 'devoted to the arts, to letters and ideas'.[1] The first issue amply justified him (and sold about 2,000 copies). It opened with Hardy's 'Sunday Morning Tragedy'; then followed Henry James's 'The Jolly Corner', Joseph Conrad's 'Some Reminiscences', John Galsworthy's 'A Fisher of Men', W. H. Hudson's 'Stonehenge', Tolstoy's 'The Raid' and H. G. Wells's *Tono-Bungay*, Volume 1. And socio-political 'ideas' were not neglected. The journal's political colouring is suggested by the explicit commendation given to Stephen Reynolds' *A Poor Man's House*, the inclusion of W. H. Davies's observations on 'How it Feels to be Out of Work', together with proposals for a contributory old age pension scheme devised by Arthur Marwood for 'John Doe, a member of the proletariat'.[2] (It becomes perhaps easier to understand why a miner's son from the Midlands, when he was a 'genuis' – as Hueffer invariably described him – should be so warmly and immediately fêted by the *Review's* inner coterie.) Contributors to the second number included Anatole France (writing in French), R. B. Cunninghame Graham, Vernon Lee and Theodore Watts-Dunton (who printed and discussed a previously unpublished poem by D. G. Rossetti). This level of distinction among the contributors was sustained to such a degree that when, in June 1911, Hueffer's successor as editor, Austin Harrison, felt obliged to rebut the *Spectator's* charge that the *English Review* dumped 'garbage...on the nation's doorstep',[3] he could adduce the signatures of over ninety writers of the first and 'top second' rank: all had written for the *Review*. In addition to those already named, the list included Shaw, Bridges, Yeats, Bennett, Gorky, Chekhov, De la Mare, Lowes Dickinson, Edward Thomas, and Ramsay MacDonald as well as Lawrence himself. No other English literary periodical of this century could assemble a comparable array of contributors.

Its concern with 'ideas', the general political and sociological issues of the day, must be underlined: the *Review* was not merely belletristic. Hueffer announced that there would be 'no party bias';[4] in fact there was a bias and it was left-wing. Nor was it accidental that the affairs of Russia and eastern Europe were fairly prominent. For several years Hueffer had been acquainted with leading Russian revolutionaries such as Prince Kropotkin, Stepniak (Kravchinsky) and Volkhofsky; Hueffer's brother-in-law, David Soskice, had only recently escaped from Siberia. Indeed Soskice's attempts to save the *Review*, when Hueffer's funds could not sustain it beyond the first twelve issues, offer a valuable insight into the journal's readership both actual and hoped-for. Part of his endeavours were directed towards engaging the

[1] *English Review*, i (December 1908), 158.
[2] Ibid. i. 163, 168–75.
[3] See Letter 276 and n. 8, p. 277.
[4] *English Review*, i. 159.

support of Cambridge dons and an interesting correspondence developed with Edward Granville Browne, Professor of Arabic, who had himself written for the *Review*. This distinguished scholar believed it essential to keep the journal alive if only 'for the sake of having open for us a channel whereby to put forward sound views on Foreign Policy... it has become *vital*, I think, to encourage an independent Review like the *English Review*'.[1] Browne regarded the *Review* as a medium for 'advanced', intellectually searching as well as politically challenging opinions. His letters to Soskice make clear that the journal was keenly read by some academics but, having canvassed financial support for it among other Cambridge Fellows, Browne was confirmed in his first suspicions – that 'the "intellectuals" are generally not rich, while the rich are not intellectual'.[2] There was irony in the sequel. Hueffer decided that Soskice and his friends were 'revolutionary' extremists and he persuaded the wealthy industrialist and anti-socialist Sir Alfred Mond (later Lord Melchett) to buy the *Review*. He did – and at once replaced Hueffer as editor by Austin Harrison. Harrison was by no means an incompetent editor, but it proved impossible to sustain the *Review's* high achievements. By February 1913 Lawrence could be sarcastic: 'the *English Review*, – a shilling monthly, supposed to be advanced and clever'; four months later, sadly, he thought it 'piffling'.[3]

However when, in June 1909, Jessie Chambers sent some of Lawrence's poems to Hueffer, she could not have acted more decisively. At a stroke, albeit unwittingly, she 'launched' him on his literary career. She introduced him to a discriminating editor, to a highly intelligent public and to the world of professional authorship.

'Hueffer is splendid', Lawrence assured Louie Burrows in November 1909.[4] Not only did he publish in the *English Review* the first writing to appear under Lawrence's own name; he established a link between Lawrence and the *Review* which was to persist until 1923 (thirty-five issues included his works). Hueffer also acted as a constructive critic of *The White Peacock* (he was to be more destructive of *The Trespasser*), and gave Lawrence entry to the literary circles of the capital. 'I *do* so much', Lawrence had said in December 1908, 'want to know, now, the comrades who are shuffling the days in the same game with me':[5] he was referring to the writings of his contemporaries; Hueffer made it possible for him to meet the writers themselves. In mid-November 1909 he was introduced by Hueffer to the

[1] Letter, Browne to Soskice, 9 July 1909 (Soskice MSS).
[2] Letter, Browne to Soskice, 2 June 1909 (Soskice MSS).
[3] Letter 547; letter to Edward Garnett, 10 June 1913.
[4] Letter 132.
[5] Letter 92.

fashionable and formidable Violet Hunt; she was Hueffer's mistress but she was, besides, generally recognised as one of the leading women novelists of the time. On the same day, through Hueffer again, Lawrence met Ernest and Grace Rhys, and H. G. Wells; two days later, this time through Violet Hunt, he met Ezra Pound and the actress Ellaline Terriss, as well as Elsie Martindale (Hueffer's wife) and Mary Cholmondeley, both of them novelists and essayists. He was indebted to Rhys and Hueffer for a second meeting with Pound and also with Yeats, Ernest Radford and Rachel Annand Taylor. Through Pound he became acquainted with the American singer Grace Crawford, and the Australian singer Florence Schmidt (married to the sculptor, Francis Derwent Wood); and through Rachel Annand Taylor he briefly encountered a brilliant young architect, Adrian Berrington. So was Lawrence's circle enlarged. Hueffer did more. He gave Lawrence a letter of introduction and commended his first novel to the leading publisher of the day, William Heinemann; he may also have introduced him or spoken of him to Heinemann's partner Sydney Pawling, whom Hueffer had known for years. Later he certainly invited Harley Granville-Barker, the well-known dramatist and critic, to read and comment on Lawrence's plays. It seems clear, too, that Lawrence had the freedom of the *English Review* office at 84 Holland Park Avenue, where literary manuscripts were 'stuffed into the splendid but shabby Spanish cabinet that had, [Hueffer] liked to say, once belonged to the Duke of Medina-Sidonia'.[1] At any rate, in November 1909 Lawrence incorporated into a letter to Grace Crawford a hitherto unpublished poem by Francis Thompson: Hueffer published it in the *Review* two months later.[2]

Whatever Hueffer's personal defects – and they were many – Lawrence's debt to him was inestimable. Lawrence acknowledged it: 'he is a really fine man, in that he is so generous, so understanding, and in that he keeps the doors of his soul open, and you may walk in'; he 'was the first man I ever met who had a real and a true feeling for literature'.[3] By 1912 Lawrence was complaining to De la Mare – 'I suffered badly from Hueffer re Flaubert and perfection'[4] – but, inscribing for Hueffer a copy of *Love Poems and Others* in 1913, he acknowledged his profound indebtedness: 'Remembering that he discovered me.'[5]

Perhaps Hueffer's most significant contribution to Lawrence's career and development as a professional writer was the introduction he provided to the

[1] Arthur Mizener, *The Saddest Story: A Biography of Ford Madox Ford* (1971), p. 167.
[2] Letter 133, p. 145 and n. 5.
[3] Letter 128; 'Preface to *Collected Poems*', *Phoenix*, p. 253.
[4] Letter 461.
[5] Douglas Goldring, *South Lodge* (1943), p. 63.

man he dubbed 'London's literary – if Nonconformist – Pope',[1] Edward Garnett (son of Richard Garnett). Hueffer and Garnett had been acquainted since boyhood; it was through Garnett that Hueffer had met Conrad and the trio had taken the lead in the discussions which led to the founding of the *English Review*; and Garnett's brother Robert was Hueffer's (much used) legal adviser. It was virtually inevitable that Garnett and Lawrence would meet. And, as is plain with hindsight, it was quasi-symbolic that Lawrence's first letter to him was written from Quorn, Louie Burrows' home.[2] Here was the point of intersection between Lawrence's old and new lives: the fading attraction of teaching – an orthodox and secure profession, associated in his mind with a traditional home and family life – opposed to the increasing fascination of the adventure and self-fulfilment possible to the full-time writer. Many years later Louie recalled how Lawrence became 'avid for new experiences' during the Croydon period.[3] She was inescapably the loser.

Soon after letters were first exchanged with Garnett, in August 1911, Lawrence almost *sotto voce* began to warn Louie that he might leave the teaching profession. So much had already changed. He had broken his unofficial engagement with Jessie Chambers in November 1910. The loss of his mother on 9 December 1910 wrenched him apart, left him permanently scarred and snapped the strongest link with his birthplace. He continued to write to and be generous towards his Eastwood friends (and particularly his sister Ada), but he recognised that 'the old clique is broken: it will never be restored'.[4] 'I *don't* want to come to Eastwood', he wrote to Ada in February 1911.[5] The literary world had become all-absorbing. Martin Secker in June 1911 offered to publish a volume of his short stories; in August Austin Harrison was requesting contributions to the *English Review*; and Edward Garnett offered assistance in placing his stories, critical advice on his manuscripts and, as reader for Duckworth, influence with yet another publisher. Lawrence himself knew that he was writing quickly, prolifically and well. The end of the old life with its conventional aims was foreshadowed in a letter to Louie Burrows, 15 September 1911:

> Should you be cross if I were to – and I don't say I shall – try to get hold of enough literary work, journalism or what not, to keep me going without school. Of course, it's a bit risky, but for myself I don't mind risk – like it.... I am really rather, – very – sick of teaching when I want to do something else.[6]

Within two weeks of his first meeting Garnett on 5 October 1911, Lawrence

[1] Mizener, *The Saddest Story*, p. 107.
[2] Letter 302.
[3] Private family letter, 26 February 1962.
[4] Letter 168.
[5] Letter 228.
[6] Letter 309.

visited him at the Cearne, his home in Kent. This now replaced Eastwood and Quorn as the pivot of Lawrence's existence.

The Cearne represented for Louie Burrows, Jessie Chambers and, as it proved, Helen Corke, 'advanced', unconventional attitudes to love and marriage. '[Garnett] and his wife consent to live together or apart as it pleases them... they are content to be a good deal apart.'[1] Louie associated the house with suspicions of sexual impropriety; she believed Garnett had suggested 'that "Sex" was necessary for the development of [Lawrence's] authorship'.[2] For Lawrence the Cearne represented intellectual energy, books and debate about literary issues: 'we discussed books most furiously'; 'beer, apples, a big fire, and a jaw till midnight'.[3] Much of the writing discussed was his own. From 'Intimacy' and 'Two Marriages' (later entitled 'The Witch à la Mode' and 'Daughters of the Vicar') to *Sons and Lovers* and 'The Sisters', together with his plays and poems (though he suspected Garnett of not caring much for verse), virtually everything Lawrence wrote from August 1911 to the end of the period covered by this volume was submitted for Garnett's critical appraisal. Lawrence relied on him to 'trim and garnish', 'to barber up' his manuscripts for the publisher.[4] Indeed the assumption which the two men increasingly shared was that Lawrence would abandon teaching and devote himself to authorship. Thus as well as encouraging Lawrence in his resolve and engaging with him in literary-critical debate, Garnett acted in an entrepreneurial capacity on his behalf. 'Garnett is going to introduce me to quite a lot of people. I am not keen on it, but he says my business is to get known.'[5] Hence the meeting with R. A. Scott-James at the Cearne. He was the literary editor for the *Daily News* and, like Garnett, closely acquainted with writers such as Bennett, Galsworthy and Wells; he could be encouraged to take an interest in Lawrence's writings, ensure that the press took due note of his publications, or perhaps open up opportunities in journalism. Frank Harris had a comparable significance. As Lawrence subsequently acknowledged, 'Garnett...introduced me to the world.'[6]

In one sense Lawrence had already been introduced to the world. The reviewer Henry Savage believed that 'with *The White Peacock* Lawrence may be said to have arrived at once'.[7] The novel was widely and generally favourably reviewed when it appeared in January 1911; it provoked some local hostility in the Eastwood area; but – as the letter from Mrs Villiers-Stuart demonstrates[8] and Savage's remark confirms – professional writers

[1] Letter 321.
[2] Private family letter, 14 January 1962.
[3] Letters 321 and 523.
[4] Letters 537 and 549.
[5] Letter 321.
[6] 'Preface to *Collected Poems*', *Phoenix*, p. 253.
[7] Nehls, i. 210.
[8] Letter 319.

had begun to recognise the seeds of greatness. Before these could flourish, Lawrence had finally to break with the stifling regimen of teaching.

The circumstances which prompted the break were adventitious; again they were associated with the Cearne. On 19 November 1911 Lawrence caught a chill while working in the garden there with Garnett; pneumonia followed; and Lawrence barely survived. From 20 November he never taught again; his determination not to return to Davidson Road School was reinforced by medical advice; and he eventually resigned his post on 28 February 1912. A month's convalescence at Bournemouth in January gave him the opportunity to revise *The Trespasser*, but the illness, as he told Helen Corke, had changed him 'a good deal'.[1] He used the same phrase to Louie Burrows: 'My illness has changed me a good deal.'[2] One might suspect that the illness, however serious, was a convenient pretext or that Lawrence was rationalising in order to terminate two relationships which had become irksome – were it not for an outspoken letter from his sister Ada to his fiancée. 'It's surprising how very much changed Bert is since his illness, and changed for the worse too, I think...his flippant and really artificial manner gets on my nerves dreadfully...I wouldn't marry a man like him, no, not if he were the only one on the earth.'[3] Of course the purpose of this letter was to console Louie Burrows when Lawrence (writing from the Cearne) broke their engagement on 4 February 1912. Yet Ada was – he had declared – his 'one, *real* relative in the world';[4] she was unlikely so wildly to exaggerate as to tell a complete falsehood. Whatever the exact truth, Lawrence was now determined to act decisively; to go abroad; and specifically to visit relatives of Fritz Krenkow at Waldbröl in Germany.

In March 1912 he met Frieda Weekley, the German wife of Ernest Weekley, the Professor of French who had taught Lawrence at University College, Nottingham: their meeting seems providentially timed in this chronological sequence. At least Lawrence was psychologically prepared for it. His earlier warning to Louie Burrows had been prophetic: 'I go straight, like a bullet, towards my aim. I cannot loiter by the way...I cut straight through like a knife to what I want. I cannot, cannot slowly enjoy watching the rose open...I love my rose, and no other: and when I can have her I shall want no other.'[5] Approximately six weeks after their first meeting, Lawrence and Frieda eloped to Germany (travelling to Metz, the home of Frieda's parents).

They had spent one night at the Cearne shortly before leaving. This – as

[1] Letter 379.
[2] Letter 383.
[3] Ibid. p. 361, n. 2.
[4] Letter 230.
[5] Letter 236.

well as his importance to Lawrence the professional author – gave Garnett a central place in their joint affection. 'Frieda sort of clings to the idea of you', Lawrence assured him, 'as the only man in England who would be a refuge'; 'I feel as if you were father and brother and all my relations to me – except wife.'[1] When they first met Edward's son, David Garnett, at Icking near Munich on 24 July 1912, though they immediately came to relish his distinctive charm and vitality, he was welcome because of their debt to his father. (Similarly, in early 1913, when Antonia Almgren – the estranged wife of a Swedish artist – and her child desperately needed a refuge, Lawrence offered assistance because she was a close friend of the Garnett family.) McLeod, too, was an object of continuing affection and trust; together with Garnett he could be relied upon to send books, to have a sympathetic regard for Lawrence's well-being, and to respond to his need for friendly intercourse. Friendship Lawrence urgently wanted; he was well aware that 'folk' would readily 'wipe their dirty mouths' on him because of Frieda.[2] The only people whose friendship was not rooted in literary interests but to whom – almost as surrogate parents – he could soon write openly and trustingly about her were Sallie and Willie Hopkin: 'I want you and [Frieda] to be friends always. Some time perhaps she – perhaps we – shall need you.'[3] It was to them that he wrote in the same letter after a week's 'honeymoon' at Beuerberg in the Bavarian Tyrol, in late May 1912: 'I love Frieda so much I don't like to talk about it. I never knew what love was before.' Gradually, during the six months by Lake Garda in northern Italy (September 1912 – March 1913), his sister Ada and other old friends were told about Frieda, or Lawrence assumed that rumour had informed them of the 'scandal'. But his attachment to the past was now dependent on very few individuals. 'The Cearne is after all the nearest place to home that I've got.'[4] The 'new enterprise of living' was with Frieda; it was with her that he would 'start living';[5] the emphasis was therefore on a new life which owed nothing to the past. Thus the agonies caused by Frieda's indecision about her children or by her husband's indecision about a divorce had to be endured for the sake of the future: 'I want to rough it and scramble through, free, free.'[6]

Concurrent with this discovery of selfhood, emotional security and satisfaction through his passionate commitment to Frieda was a striking development in his maturity and self-confidence and therefore in his creative achievement. Certain individuals and some external circumstances provided

[1] Letters 452 and 495.
[2] Letter 536.
[3] Letter 457.
[4] Letter 560.
[5] Letter 445.
[6] Letter 472.

stimulus and encouragement. Walter de la Mare, for example, was a source of both. It was as Heinemann's 'reader' that he became acquainted with Lawrence, but Lawrence's recently discovered letters to him suggest that De la Mare's interest went beyond his professional duties. Though dissatisfied with *Sons and Lovers* when the manuscript was offered to Heinemann, he advised Lawrence on a possible selection of the poems which were subsequently published as *Love Poems and Others* and, according to his lights, was an encouraging critic. Then, despite Lawrence's own reservations, *The Trespasser* (May 1912) had a generally favourable press. Basil de Selincourt thought the book 'full of exquisite perceptions'; its style was 'not only poetical but clear and incisive also'; and 'the psychology is penetrative and convincing'.[1] The *New York Times Book Review* considered it 'not only the frankest of serious contemporary novels; it comes near to being the best'.[2] Mitchell Kennerley, who published the American edition of *The Trespasser*, was so satisfied with his countrymen's reception of the book that he sought and obtained Duckworth's agreement to handle the American edition of *Sons and Lovers*.[3] And even if one reader adjured Lawrence 'to repent before it was too late, before [he] and [his] books were consumed in the fire of wrath',[4] another stranger wrote to congratulate him. This was the talented artist and illustrator Ernest Collings with whom he was to maintain an often important correspondence until 1917. Moreover in September 1912 two other major English publishers – Hutchinson and Fisher Unwin (the latter prompted by Austin Harrison) – expressed a strong desire to publish his future works.[5] In the same month Edward Marsh, compiling the first of his volumes of *Georgian Poetry*, sought Lawrence's agreement that his poem 'Snap-Dragon' should be included.[6] The link between the two men was Edward Garnett; once again he had helped to introduce Lawrence 'to the world'; and, as is clear, the world was increasingly willing to listen.

The completion and then the publication of *Love Poems and Others* in February and *Sons and Lovers* in May 1913 powerfully fortified Lawrence's self-confidence. Edward Thomas thought 'the book of the moment in verse is Mr D. H. Lawrence's'; Ezra Pound was (in September 1913) to consider it 'the most important book of poems of the season'.[7] With the exception of 'Bei Hennef' which celebrated Lawrence's love for Frieda, *Love Poems* incorporated poems about his Nottingham and Croydon years, about Jessie Chambers, Louie Burrows and Helen Corke. In short, it recorded his emotional and imaginative response to a life that had ended. Also therapeutic

[1] Draper 47.
[2] Draper 50.
[3] Letter 553, p. 522, n. 5.
[4] Letter 511.
[5] Letter 503, p. 458, n. 4.
[6] Ibid. p. 459.
[7] Draper 51, 53.

was the writing and lengthy revision of *Sons and Lovers*. Here for the first time he committed his resources on a large scale to getting into imaginative perspective the two central relationships of his early years: with his mother, particularly, and also with Jessie. Though complete success did not come at once in the case of Mrs Lawrence, the battle for Lawrence's independence from her had been consciously joined. But the achievement was greater than merely personal. And, importantly, he knew it. Technically it represented greater maturity: it had 'form'. Lawrence had endured sustained criticism on this score about his earlier writings, particularly from Hueffer. Now he could assure Walter de la Mare and Garnett that the form was organic: 'the development...is slow like growth.'[1] Thematically, too, the novel had a large contemporary relevance: 'It's the tragedy of thousands of young men in England.'[2] More than anything else it was this conviction of having written a great novel which would be read by the perceptive young – by people like David Garnett and Harold Hobson (who had shared with Lawrence and Frieda the walk over the Alps in August 1912) – that imbued Lawrence with a vigorous, creative confidence. 'I think...I have inside me a sort of answer to the *want* of today: to the real, deep want of the English people, not to just what they fancy they want. And gradually, I shall get my hold on them.'[3] Similarly he was convinced that he could, as a playwright, pioneer a reaction against 'the rather bony, bloodless drama' of Shaw, Galsworthy and Granville-Barker, 'the rule and measure mathematical folk'.[4] In fact Lawrence was certain that he could write 'bigger stuff than any man in England'.[5] The confidence was not misplaced: before *Sons and Lovers* was published, the first draft of 'The Sisters' (subsequently transformed into *The Rainbow* and *Women in Love*) was completed.

Sons and Lovers signalled 'the end of [Lawrence's] youthful period'. The final letter to Helen Corke – the last in the volume – written on the day of the novel's publication, 23 May 1912, confirms it. In that letter he precludes the possibility of any further correspondence with her; he accepts that he will never hear again from Jessie Chambers; and he acknowledges himself a 'different person' from the man they had formerly known. The letter is, indeed, a solemn gesture of rejection and affirmation. Lawrence rejects the 'several lives' in his past; he rejects his country; and he places his confidence in his creative ability together with the love he shared with Frieda. 'We two are alone.' His belief that life would not 'unsaddle' him, 'not much, any more', was to prove false. More prophetic was a remark of two years before: 'I shall never rest in this life – not long.'[6]

[1] Letter 516.
[2] Ibid.
[3] Letter 544.
[4] Ibid.
[5] Letter 574.
[6] Letter 273.

THE LETTERS

1. To J. H. Haywood Ltd., [September? 1901]

Text: Lawrence–Gelder 70–1.

[3 Walker Street, Eastwood]
[September? 1901]

Gentlemen,[1]

In reply to your ad. in today's *G[uardian]* for a junior clerk, I beg to place my services at your disposal. I am sixteen years of age, and have just completed three years' course at the Nottingham High School.[2] Although I have not had any business experience in accounts yet, I studied book-keeping and obtained two prizes for Mathematics, as well as one for French and German.[3]

If desired, I shall be pleased to furnish you with the highest references as to character and ability, both from my late masters and the Minister in this town.[4]

Should you favour me with the appointment I would always endeavour to merit the confidence you place in me.[5]

Trusting to receive your favourable reply, I beg to remain, Gentlemen,

Yours obediently, D. H. Lawrence

[1] John Harrington Haywood (1829?–1912) owned a firm (founded in 1830 by his father John Shrewsbury Haywood) which manufactured 'Surgical, Athletic, Veterinary and Magnetic Appliances' at 9 Castle Gate, Nottingham. He was the prototype of Mr Jordan in *Sons and Lovers* (Duckworth, 1913). Ada Lawrence and Stuart Gelder (Lawrence–Gelder 70) claimed that DHL's eldest brother, William Ernest (1878 – 11 October 1901), 'wrote this application'. This seems confirmed in *Sons and Lovers*, chap. 5: 'William had written out a letter of application couched in admirable business language, which Paul copied with variations.' DHL must have written at his brother's dictation not later than 3–5 October 1901 when Ernest visited Goose Fair in Nottingham (Nehls, i. 39).

[2] DHL, sixteen on 11 September 1901, was a scholarship holder at the school September 1898 – July 1901.

[3] School records confirm prizes for Mathematics at Easter 1899 and July 1900, and a Form Prize at Easter 1900. Prizes in French and German are not recorded.

[4] Rev. Robert Reid: see p. 31 n. 1.

[5] DHL's application was successful. In 'Myself Revealed' (later entitled 'Autobiographical Sketch') he wrote: 'After leaving school I was a clerk for three months' (*Sunday Dispatch*, 17 February 1929).

2. To Edmund and Sarah Chambers, [April? 1902]

Text: E.T. 28.

['Sandsea', South Parade, Skegness, Lincolnshire]
[April? 1902]

[In one 'long descriptive' letter to the Chambers 'family in general' Lawrence 'said that he could stand in his aunt's drawing-room and watch the tide rolling in through the window'.][1]

3. To Jessie Chambers, [3? October 1903]

Text: E.T. 40; PC.

[3? October 1903]

[Lawrence 'sent [Jessie][2] a postcard from the café where they[3] had tea at a table in a window overlooking the whole panorama of the Fair,[4] and he managed to convey the full flavour of his palpitating excitement'.]

4. To Jessie Chambers, [3? October 1903]

Text: E.T. 40.

[97 Lynn Croft, Eastwood]
[3? October 1903]

[When Lawrence got home after his visit to Goose Fair 'he wrote a long account of what they had done, and headed the letter "The Diary of a Butterfly to a Moth"'.]

[1] One of several letters written to the Chambers family (at the Haggs Farm, Underwood, near Eastwood) when DHL was convalescing after an attack of pneumonia. He spent a month in Skegness at a '"select" boarding-house' (E.T. 28). This establishment was managed by his maternal aunt Ellen ('Nellie') Staynes (1855–1908) from 1901 to c. 1908. In the headnote the Chambers family 'in general' are represented by the parents, Edmund (1863–1946) and Sarah Ann (1859–1937). (See also May Chambers' account of the letters from Skegness; Nehls, iii. 577.)

[2] Jessie Chambers (1887–1944) – known also as 'Muriel' and 'the Princess' – was the prototype for Miriam in *Sons and Lovers*. A childhood friend of DHL, later a pupil-teacher and then (1910) an assistant mistress in a Nottingham school, she was responsible for sending some of DHL's MSS to Ford Madox Hueffer in 1908 and thus for his first significant publications. m. John R. Wood 1915. Her centrally important memoir of DHL – *D. H. Lawrence: A Personal Record*, 1935 – was published as 'by E.T.'. These initials recall the principal character in her novel 'Eunice Temple' (earlier entitled 'The Rathe Primrose') which was a fictionalised account of her relationship with DHL. She destroyed the MS of the novel together with the letters exchanged between them. (For a fuller portrait see Helen Corke, 'D. H. Lawrence's "Princess": A Memory of Jessie Chambers', *The Croydon Years*, Austin, Texas, 1965, pp. 17–45.)

[3] A party of unnamed friends who had gone 'for a jaunt round the Fair' (E.T. 40).

[4] Goose Fair, Nottingham's annual three-day fair, beginning on the first Thursday in October (1–3 October 1903).

5. To Gertrude Cooper, [23 October 1903]

Text: MS Clarke; PC v. The University, Nottingham; Postmark, Eastwood OC 23 03; Moore 1.

[97 Lynn Croft, Eastwood]
[23 October 1903]

Do you[1] like this, it's not cats.[2] I passed this place every day going to school, and I've sat for one exam in it.[3] What about 'Two in a hammock'.[4] We're going to Beauvale on Sunday to hear Ferguson are you?[5] DHL

6. To Ethel Cooper, [23 October 1903]

Text: MS Clarke; PC v. Castle Entrance, Nottingham; Postmark, Eastwood OC 23 03; Moore 1.

[97 Lynn Croft, Eastwood]
[23 October 1903]

Thanks very much for your ppc.[6] I guess you know this place. Remember me from Kirkby.[7] DHL

7. To Gertrude Cooper, [31 October 1903]

Text: MS Clarke; PC v. Peterborough, – Town Hall; Postmark, Peterborough OC 31 03; Moore 1.

[31 October 1903]

Here we are, safe and sound. Been to Cathedral. DHL

8. To Gertrude Cooper, [10 November 1903]

Text: MS Clarke; PC v. Lincoln Cathedral; Postmark, Eastwood NO 10 03; Unpublished.

[97 Lynn Croft, Eastwood]
[10 November 1903]

This makes the 9th so call it 'nonem'. DHL

1 The addressee Gertrude ('Grit') Cooper (1885–1942), was a childhood friend of DHL at Lynn Croft, Eastwood. She suffered from tuberculosis; by 1919, possibly after her father's death in 1918, made her home with Ada, DHL's sister; and was buried in the same grave as DHL's parents and brother, Ernest.

2 The reference is obscure.

3 The University College building (where DHL probably sat the exam by which he won his scholarship to the school) is approximately half a mile from Nottingham High School.

4 Presumably a reference to the rhyme often contributed to autograph albums and accompanied by a drawing of an amatory couple falling out of a hammock: 'Two in a hammock intended to kiss/All of a sudden they ended like – sıɥʇ'.

5 DHL was proposing to listen to a famous Methodist preacher, Rev. Dr Joseph Ferguson (1838–1904), President of the Primitive Methodist Conference in 1891 and at this time Minister at Brierley Hill, Staffordshire.

6 The addressee, Gertrude Cooper's sister Ethel (1887–1905) was a clerk with Langley Mill Co-operative Society.

7 Kirkby-in-Ashfield, approximately nine miles from Eastwood.

9. To Gertrude Cooper, [21 January 1904]

Text: MS Clarke; PC v. New-Eastwood. Canal Side; Postmark, Eastwood JA 21 04; Moore 2.

[97 Lynn Croft, Eastwood]
[21 January 1904]

Thanks for ppc. I have wondered when it was coming. Send me the Chapel if you have any of our own views, I should like it. Good Luck for the coming year.
Yours DHL

10. To Gertrude Cooper, [27 February 1904]

Text: MS Clarke; PC v. Swans Black and White;[1] Postmark, Eastwood FE 27 04; Moore 2.

[97 Lynn Croft, Eastwood]
[27 February 1904]

This is *not* a coloured one, but I think it's lovely. Really one of the nicest I've seen, I consider. Is it going to be hide and seek again? DHL

11. To Edith Holderness, [30 June 1904]

Text: MS UT; PC v. The Old Village, Shanklin, I[sle of] W[ight]; Postmark, Eastwood JU 30 04; Unpublished.

[97 Lynn Croft, Eastwood]
[30 June 1904]

At last – my long-made promise is at last fulfilled. This is absolutely the prettiest card I could get, do you like it?[2] We're having a quarterly exam at Centre so I have to work jolly hard.[3] How does the weather go down, I love it, but it makes me feel so awfully tired – or lazy, I dont know which.
DHL

12. To Gertrude Cooper, [18 August 1904]

Text: MS Clarke; PC v. Cromford, Via Gellia; Postmarks, Bonsall and Matlock-Bath AU 18 04; Moore 2.

[18 August 1904]

Have ridden thro here about an hour ago. Am now in Bonsal post-office. Going to Bakewell this afternoon. A lovely time. DHL

1 DHL initialled the verso of the postcard.

2 DHL initialled the verso of the postcard. The addressee Edith ('Kitty') Holderness, was the daughter of George Holderness, headmaster of the British School, Albert Street, Eastwood (where DHL was a pupil-teacher, October 1902 – July 1905, and an uncertificated teacher August 1905 – September 1906). She became a teacher herself and was infants' mistress at Eakring, Nottinghamshire, when her father moved there as headmaster.

3 DHL attended part-time at the Pupil-Teacher Centre at Ilkeston, Derbyshire, March 1904 – July 1905.

13. To Edith Holderness, [ante 25 March 1905]
Text: MS UT; Unpublished.

[97 Lynn Croft, Eastwood]
[ante 25 March 1905]

Dear Kitty,

Why didn't you bring me your book yourself – I was expecting you all evening. Now I am consumed with impatience to open the parcel and cannot till I get home. Naughty girl to cause me to be teased thus.

Quant au livre de ton père, il est plus beau que je pouvais rever.[1] I am almost ashamed to accept such a magnificent book. Tell him I am very grateful – I cannot myself, je perd les mots.

Come down tonight – you and Nellie[2] – I shall have seen your books then. Oh, my photo proofs have come, so you may criticise them.[3]

Au revoir – yours – the 'man' almost overwhelmed – DHL

14. To The Editor, *The Teacher*, [ante 25 March 1905]
Text: The Teacher, 25 March 1905.

[97 Lynn Croft, Eastwood]
[ante 25 March 1905]

My schoolmaster showed me the first issue of your paper, and I at once recognised its merits, and ordered one for myself. Needless to say, I have continued to take it ever since.[4] I consider it of the greatest help to any student in our profession. I have always found that the courses of study contained in *The Teacher* have an originality which is very pleasing and instructive. The lessons on geography and history bring the important points clearly into view, and the mathematics are splendid practice to anyone who

[1] 'As for your father's book, it is finer than I could have dreamed... I am speechless.' Edith's father, George Holderness, was headmaster of the British School, Eastwood, from at least 1902 to 1908; he had gone to Eakring by 1912 and stayed until at least 1916 as headmaster of the Public Elementary School. On this occasion, as DHL's headmaster, Holderness was presumably rewarding DHL's success in being placed among the top eleven candidates in the entire country for the King's Scholarship (which he had taken in December 1904). The Scholarship results were publicly declared on 25 March 1905 but – as the next letter makes clear – at least the outstanding candidates had been informed beforehand. Hence the dating of this letter.

[2] Edith's sister, Ellen Mary Holderness.

[3] DHL had been asked to submit a photograph for publication along with his letter in *The Teacher* (see letter following).

[4] The results of the King's Scholarship examination were published in *The Teacher* (founded 7 November 1903) on 25 March 1905. The outstanding candidates had been invited to estimate the contribution of the journal's 'Scholarship Course' to their success: DHL's tone and manner are thus not surprising. (When printed in *The Teacher*, his letter was accompanied by a photograph.)

would have every rule in its different forms at his command. Especially valuable are the Science and English, the former being particularly adapted for those who cannot enjoy the benefits of a laboratory. I consider the *Teacher* a first class magazine for teachers; it is eminently practical and yet has an intellectual chatty tone which is very charming.

During my study I used:— *English:* Evan Daniel, and Meiklejohn; *History:* Ransome and Gardiner; *Arithmetic:* Christian and Collar; *Geography:* Gill and Meiklejohn.[1] I have been teaching for two years and a half, and until March of last year received my instruction from Mr. G. Holderness, headmaster of the Eastwood British School. In that month, however, I obtained permission to attend the Ilkeston Centre, and there I received the greatest assistance from the Principal, Mr. T. A. Beacroft.[2]

15. To Ernest Woodford, [c. March 1905]

Text: MS Sharpe; Unpublished.

[97 Lynn Croft, Eastwood]
[c. March 1905]

[Woodford wrote to congratulate Lawrence on his success in the King's Scholarship examination and asked if he were still in touch with Thomas Marsden, a mutual friend at Nottingham High School.[3] Lawrence replied that 'they had lost touch because their dispositions were not compatible'.]

16. To Jessie Chambers, [c. 25 April 1905]

Text: E.T. 70.

[97 Lynn Croft, Eastwood]
[c. 25 April 1905][4]

1 DHL probably referred to some or all of the following: English: Evan Daniel, *The Grammar, History and Derivation of the English Language* (1881); John M. D. Meiklejohn, *The English Language* (1886; 12th edn 1895), or *English Literature: a new history and survey* (1904). History: Cyril Ransome, *An Advanced History of England* (1895; 5th edn 1901), or *A Short History of England* (1887; 12th edn 1901); Samuel R. Gardiner, *Outline of English History* (1881), or *A Student's History of England* (1890). Arithmetic: Gilbert A. Christian and George Collar, *A New Arithmetic* (1897; 3rd edn 1899). Geography: George Gill, *Gill's Imperial Geography* (1886), or *The Oxford and Cambridge Geography* (1886); John M. D. Meiklejohn, *A Short Geography* (1889), or *A New Geography* (1889; 22nd edn 1899).

2 Thomas Alfred Beacroft (1871–1925), Head of Ilkeston Pupil-Teacher Centre, 1899–1913; then became organising Inspector of elementary education in Ilkeston.

3 Ernest John Woodford (b. 1884) and Thomas Haynes Marsden (1886–1964) were DHL's two closest associates at the High School. (This information, together with the summary of DHL's letter given above, was contained in a letter from Woodford to Mr Michael Sharpe, 4 November 1957.)

4 On Easter Monday, 24 April 1905, DHL had made a half-hearted suggestion which Jessie could not accept that they should be formally engaged. The 'note' arrived 'a couple of days later' (E.T. 70).

['. . .a note came from Lawrence saying he hoped [Jessie] was not grieving.']

A man can do so many things. He reads, he paints, he can get across his bicycle and go for a ride, but a woman sits at home and thinks. ['He added that he would come up on the Friday and read some French with [Jessie].']

17. To Jessie Chambers, [June 1905]

Text: E.T. 75.

[97 Lynn Croft, Eastwood]
[June 1905]

[Lawrence wrote to Jessie 'of the misery of'] pen-driving in the city heat.[1]

18. To Lydia Lawrence,[2] [12 June 1905]

Text: MS Clarke; PC v. [Fishing boat] Returning Home, Gorleston; Postmark, Great Yarmouth JU 12 05; Moore 2.

[12 June 1905]

We have come down here by boat – it is such a jolly little place.

Ada[3] is dispensing tea while we are writing. It has been such a ripping day and the sea is so lovely.

DHL

19. To Jessie Chambers, [14 June 1905]

Text: MS UN; PC v. Below Potter Heigham; Postmark, Hunstanton JU 14 05; Nehls, iii. 599.

[14 June 1905]

We've done Castle Rising and Sandringham on our way here.

We passed this place on Monday. We are having a fine time – been paddling all afternoon – now we're at tea on the sea front.

DHL

[1] DHL sat the London Matriculation examination in June 1905 (information from his application-form for a post with Croydon Education Committee, 16 September 1908).

[2] Lydia Lawrence née Beardsall (1851–1910), DHL's mother. b. Manchester, daughter of a dockyard engineer; the family lived at Sheerness c. 1860–8, before returning to Nottingham. Qualified as a teacher. M. John Arthur Lawrence (1846–1924), a miner, on 27 December 1875. (For a description see Lawrence–Gelder 20–5.)

[3] Lettice Ada Lawrence (1887–1948), DHL's younger sister. She attended the Pupil-Teacher Centre, Ilkeston, qualified as a teacher and first taught at Somercotes near Alfreton. Subsequently taught at Eastwood Elementary School until her marriage to William Edwin Clarke, 4 August 1913.

20. To Constance Burrows, 6 July 1905
Text: MS UN; Boulton 173.

Lynn Croft, Eastwood, Notts.
6th July 1905.

Dear Miss Burrows,[1]

I return to you your album,[2] little improved I fear. Yet I have found much pleasure in trying to embellish it, hoping that I might give you a moment's gratification.

This is an opportune time for the expression of my gratitude for the help you gave me at Centre; I trust I was not too troublesome a pupil, I can avouch for the patience of the mistress. Centre days are happy days, I wish they could be repeated.

If at any time it were possible for me to be of assistance to you, I shall be most delighted to do what is in my power;

I am Yours Sincerely D. H. Lawrence

21. To Jessie Chambers, [January? 1906]
Text: E.T. 62.

[97 Lynn Croft, Eastwood]
[January? 1906][3]

[Lawrence 'painted a study of fruits for [Jessie], figs and dark green leaves, and sent it with a note saying it was a gift of a day of his life'.]

22. To Jessie Chambers, [February 1906]
Text: E.T. 62.

[97 Lynn Croft, Eastwood]
[February 1906]

['One day in February' Lawrence sent a note by Mr Chambers asking Jessie 'to meet him at the entrance to High Park wood.']

[1] Constance Burrows, older cousin of Louie and daughter of Campbell Burrows; assistant mistress at the Pupil-Teacher Centre, Ilkeston, until June 1904; she was then appointed jointly to the Centre and to a local school.

[2] i.e. autograph album.

[3] The chronology of Jessie Chambers's account (E.T. 62) suggests that this note was written between Christmas and April 1906, and probably earlier than February.

23. To Jessie Chambers, [February? 1906]

Text: E.T. 107.

[97 Lynn Croft, Eastwood]
[February? 1906][1]

What am I doing to you? You used to be so vigorous, so full of interest in all sorts of things. Don't take too much notice of me. You mustn't allow yourself to be hurt by Maupassant or by me.

24. To Louie Burrows, [September 1906]

Text: MS UN; Boulton 1–2.

[97 Lynn Croft, Eastwood]
[September 1906][2]

Dear Louie,[3]

I am going to quizz your essay, not in the approven school-mistress style, but according to my own whimsical idea, which you may or may not accept. First of all I will find fault.

I do not like the introductory paragraph, it is like an extract from a Catalogue of Pictures for sale at some auctioneers. Nor am I quite sure that you are justified in saying that other artists have failed in depicting eastern colours as well as the painter of *Homer.*[4] In fact the painting is not, I think, remarkable for its colour scheme, but for its striking personal characters and grace and harmony of form. Those are particulars of this essay. Then as to your style as a whole.

Like most girl writers you are wordy. I have read nearly all your letters to J[essie], so I do not judge only from this composition. Again and again you put in interesting adjectives and little phrases which make the whole piece loose, and sap its vigour. Do be careful of your adjectives – do try and be terse, there is so much more force in a rapid style that will not be hampered

1 Jessie Chambers states that she was 'only 19' when DHL 'bought Maupassant's *Tales* for [her] to read' (E.T. 107). (She was nineteen on 29 January 1906.) 'Then a few days later' he sent this note.

2 Dated by Louie Burrows.

3 Louisa ('Louie') Burrows (1888–1962), DHL's financée from December 1910 to February 1912. Knew DHL from c. 1900; 1902–6 attended the Pupil-Teacher Centre, Ilkeston, and, with DHL, became a student at the Day Training College of University College, Nottingham. Awarded a First Class Teacher's Certificate, 1908. Continued a teacher until a year after her marriage to Frederick Heath, April 1941. DHL referred to her in his Preface to *Collected Poems*, 1928, as 'the woman of "Kisses in the Train" and "Hands of the Betrothed"'. (For further information see Boulton ix-xxviii.)

4 Louie may have been describing *Homer Singing his Iliad at the Gates of Athens*, painted 1811, by Guillaume Le Thière (1760–1832), owned by Nottingham Castle Art Gallery.

by superfluous details. Just look at your piece and see how many three lined sentences could be comfortably expressed in one line.

I know my essay was squeezed down almost to incoherence because I did not want it to be too long. I am very glad you saw how I had compressed it; if I had filled in and merged off my thoughts Miss B[ecket][1] would not have accused me so strongly of confusion.

Again, don't use hackneyed adjectives. 'Shapely heads – fallen heroes – white beard on aged breast' you know these are in everybody's mouth. If you would write, try to be terse and in some measure original – the world abounds with new similes and metaphors.

I wish you had studied the characters of the picture more than the City – the Greek Art – the magnificent carvings. Things which are obvious are worth no more than a mention. If you cannot tell people of something they have not seen, or have not thought, it is hardly worthwhile to write at all. Try and study people, and the living soul which is the essence of mankind. If you have externals, they must represent something. I write to you as a would-be aspirant after literature, for I know you are such.

I like above all things your enthusiasm, and your delightful fresh, youthful feeling. Don't be didactic; try and make things reveal their mysteries to you, then tell them over simply and swiftly, without exaggerating as I do. I think you will do well. You are brighter than Jessie, more readable, but you are not so powerful. You will doubtless succeed far better than I who am so wilful. Be your own bright ingenuous self, and you are sure to make a delightful impression.

I am going to make my next try now. Let me see what you do – I am all interest.

Yrs DHL

25. To Jessie Chambers, [8? September 1906]

Text: E.T. 135.

[97 Lynn Croft, Eastwood]
[8? September 1906][2]

[Lawrence had his photograph taken and sent a copy to the Chamberses with a note for Jessie saying that] the troublesome original would probably come up and bother [her] the next day.

[1] Edith Mary Becket (d. 1952), lecturer in the Department of Education, University College, Nottingham.

[2] Jessie Chambers relates the writing of this to DHL's twenty-first birthday (E.T. 134–5).

26. To Reverend Robert Reid, 24 October 1906

Text: MS UN; Unpublished.

Lynn Croft, Eastwood.
24 Oct. 1906

Dear Mr Reid,[1]

I am very disappointed that I am not able to take an Arts course in college, and this is because I have no Latin.[2] Would it be possible for you to give me some assistance in acquiring a knowledge of the language, so that I might take up a course next year.

I am aware that I am trespassing considerably on your time and goodness, but I see no other way than to ask you.

Pardon me if I am too bold,

I am Yours Sincerely D. H. Lawrence

27. To Louie Burrows, [c. 29 October 1906]

Text: MS UN; Boulton 2–3.

[97 Lynn Croft, Eastwood]
[c. 29 October 1906]

Dear L.,

You see how splendidly Madame[3] has crushed me. She has asked me now to write the essay she wanted – viz the Description of a Picture. I'm not quite sure whether I shall comply – if so[4] I shall merely do it as a written exercise.

She told me some of my phrases are fine, but other ludicrous; that I was not entirely incapable of writing, but mixed up some sense with a great amount of absurdity. Therefore I must restrain myself to writing just what other people think, and are therefore willing to accept.

Bien – I consent – I am merely a pupil, therefore I must work by rule. I only wish Madame were not so ready to laugh at us as silly infants. Are you still thinking of contributing to the *Gong*? I saw a number in the Library, and thought it a very mediocre publication. I do not think I shall try to be admitted as a contributor.[5]

[1] Rev. Robert Reid (1868–1955), Congregational Minister at Eastwood, 1897–1911; founder and first President of the influential Congregational Literary Society (see D. M. Newmarch, 'D. H. Lawrence's Chapel', unpublished M.Phil. thesis, University of York, 1976, pp. 50–64); and a close friend of DHL's mother. (For obituary see *Congregational Church Year Book* (1956), p. 522.)

[2] Professor Amos Henderson had persuaded DHL 'to take up an Arts degree course' (E.T. 75); for this a competence in Latin would be required. DHL took the Intermediate Arts course in this subject (information from his application to Croydon Education Committee, 16 September 1908).

[3] Possibly Miss Becket (see p. 30 n. 1).

[4] so] I do.

[5] In his 'Preface' to *Collected Poems* DHL confessed: 'I had offered the little poem "Study" to the Nottingham University Magazine [*Gong*], but they returned it' (*Complete Poems*, ed. V. de S. Pinto and Warren Roberts, 1964, ii. 851).

Write me your opinions and criticisms – your advice if you like – I shall like it.

J[essie] is not very well – has a very bad cold her brother[1] told me. May is married on Thursday[2] – I shall go if it is fine, and will tell you thereof. Shall I let J. see the essay? I shall look for a note from you this afternoon. I like people to criticise me – even Madame. Also I forgot to say that my thoughts expressed in the essay are in hopeless muddle – most likely it's true, but it is hardly encouraging to be told so many unpleasant things. That essay took me about 4 hrs – the next I do shall not occupy me more than 45 minutes, and it will then be better.

I want to see your attempt – do not be afraid, I am not exacting, nor carping; give me your book this afternoon, with the various papers in it, if you have time please. DHL

28. To Louie Burrows, [November? 1906]

Text: MS UN; Boulton 3–4.

[97 Lynn Croft, Eastwood]
[November? 1906]

Dear Louie,

I have hardly seen you this week to know how you are progressing – or retrogressing. Things are not very rosy, are they? I feel a bit flat. Miss Beckett surprised me with those marks – both yesterdays and Mondays. How did you go on? I am sick of work, there is no end to it.

Have you developed any new ideas or plans? Let me know if you do. When I saw J[essie] on Sunday she seemed much better – she had written you she said. When she has anything interesting to tell you that is not private show me the letter will you? She and I do not know much of each other nowadays. It is my fault – my temper is so variable – yet I do not like to lose her intimate acquainta[nce][3] and she never writes me letters.

Did I tell you Birdie[4] gave me 9/10 for my essay, and did not vouchsafe a single remark or correction, but let me severely alone. I was surprised – I should have liked her opinion – generously expressed – better than her silence. Do you know any more about the *Gong* – have you sat down yet to adorn it. For goodness sake send me some news either of yourself or someone

[1] Probably Alan Chambers (see p. 34 n. 4).

[2] Muriel May Chambers (1883–1955), Jessie's sister, m. William Holbrook on 1 November 1906. (DHL was clearly writing a few days before this date: hence the conjectural date given to his letter.)

[3] MS torn.

[4] Annie Florence Bird (1859–1921), lecturer in Education, University College, Nottingham.

else, for everything is as dull as the day. I am slogging Latin – how I suffer. Would I had a little leisure to employ myself congenially. How many had you for yesterdays history – I was surprised not to see your name on the board. But don't worry, satisfactory[1] work here only means gratification of a sum of individual fads – most teasing.

DHL

29. To Louie Burrows, 24 December 1906

Text: MS UN; Boulton 4.

Lynn Croft, Eastwood, Notts.
24th Dec. 1906.

My dear Louie,

I saw Jessie's card from you before I saw my own. Is not that remarkable? You see I had just run up to get some holly, when their post came. I want to know if you will come over on Wednesday to take tea with us. Ada and mother would be so glad to see you, and Jessie is coming down.

Come in the morning, about half past ten if possible, so that we may have a long and jolly time. Now don't refuse. Let us know what train you will come by and we will meet you at Shipley Gate. I think 10.30 or 11.0 would be a nice time. At any rate, suit yourself on the score of time.

Wishing you all a very [?happy] Christmas –

I am, Yours D. H. Lawrence

30. To Louie Burrows, [29 December 1906]

Text: MS UN; PC v. Flowers and Fruits;[2] Postmark, Eastwood DE 29 06; Boulton 5.

[97 Lynn Croft, Eastwood]
[29 December 1906]

I shall be pleased to come on Monday by the train arriving in the Junction[3] at 2.36 or thereabouts. Ada cannot come, as you will remember she was already claimed for that time, but I expect Jessie will gladly acquiesce, tho. I have not yet seen her.

DHL

[1] satisfactory] it is only the

[2] DHL initialled the verso of the postcard.

[3] i.e. Ilkeston Junction station.

31. To Reverend Robert Reid, 20 February 1907

Text: MS UN; Unpublished.

Lynn Croft, Eastwood.
20 Feby. 1907

Dear Mr. Reid,

I shall not have to trouble you any further on Thursday, since Professor Henderson[1] has proffered his assistance during college hours in my study of Latin. I was exceedingly surprised when he suggested it, as I did not even know he was aware of my intentions. However, I willingly accepted, seeing that thus I should no longer continue to inconvenience you, to whom I am so deeply indebted already, and that it will be a slight saving of my time.

Accept my heartfelt gratitude for your past kindness, and for the assurance I have that I may always appeal to you in difficulty.

I am, Yours very Sincerely D. H. Lawrence

32. To Louie Burrows [29 March 1907]

Text: MS UN; Postmark, Eastwood MR 29 07; Boulton 5–6.

Lynn Croft, Eastwood, Notts.
Good Friday 1907

Dear Louie,

If this wonderful weather holds we shall have a delightful day on Monday. The train we have decided on leaves the Junction at 10.33 – the Town[2] at 10.42 – arrives in Langley Mill at 10.52, and in *Alfreton* 11.8. So if you take the train at the Junction we shall join you at Langley Mill and we will skip off for Alfreton. Thence we go across the Park and about four miles on to Wingfield.[3] There I suppose we shall eat dinner, and after a time proceed on to Crich. We shall arrive there – D.V. – about teatime, and if you would care to we could buy tea, though before we carried all the tuck we had – a good quantity – except sixpennyworth of bread and butter. Jessie and Alan are going – Gertie, Frances Ada[4] and I. We shall be delighted to have Ethel[5]

[1] Amos Henderson (1864–1922) was Normal Master (i.e. Head of the Day Training College), University College, Nottingham, 1890–1905; Professor of Education, 1905–22. (According to Jessie Chambers (E.T. 75) Henderson's assistance was short-lived: 'the professor at College was unable to give him the extra help he had promised'.)

[2] Ilkeston Town station.

[3] The route was through Alfreton Park to South Wingfield.

[4] Respectively: Jessie Chambers and her older brother Alan Aubrey (1882–1946) who later married Alvina Reeve (née Lawrence) and subsequently emigrated to Canada; Gertrude Cooper; Frances ('Frankie') Amelia Cooper (1884–1918), a teacher at Beauvale School who later died of tuberculosis; and Ada Lawrence.

[5] Etheldreda Helen Burrows (1890–), Louie's sixteen-year-old sister.

if she would care to go with us. Let us hope for a nice time. I should think we shall leave Ambergate by the 7.45 which arrives in the Junction at 8.52. So Ethel would be home quite early. You will come home with us for the night, and after dinner on Tuesday it is proposed we all proceed to the Haggs for a united gathering. That night you will spend with Jessie, and Wednesday afternoon is set aside for a picnic up at the New House farm, near Annesley.[1] If we should be late from the picnic you will stay with us again till Thursday.

How elaborate it all sounds – but if it may come to pass how jolly it will be! I trust everything will meet with your approval. Remember me to your mother and father,[2] and the little ones.

I am Yrs Sincerely D. H. Lawrence

33. To Ellen Holderness, [August 1907]

Text: MS UT; PC v. 'A Bit' in Robin Hood's Town; Postmark, Robin Hoods Bay [. . .]; Unpublished.

[August 1907]

Hope you are still having a good time. It is splendid here[3] – wish you could see the bay, the steep hills with straggling streets of stone houses – like Derbyshire – the moors with ling and heather – everything. Our weather keeps splendidly fine. DHL

34. To Mabel Limb, [15 August 1907]

Text: MS Clarke; PC v. Street View, Robin Hood's Bay; Postmark, Robin Hoods Bay Station AU 15 07; Moore 3.

[15 August 1907]

It has rained all this afternoon so I have time to write you.[4]

This place is charming – a wide bay with two bold headlands and a sea of changing color. Behind are the moors, with the heather just coming out. I will bring you a bit. Hope you are well. Love – DHL

[1] New House Farm, Annesley was usually occupied by the farm bailiff to Annesley Colliery Co.; in 1907 the bailiff was John Herbert.

[2] Louisa Ann (1865–1954) and Alfred Burrows (1864–1948). Alfred Burrows, formerly a draughtsman in a Nottingham lace factory, had just become a peripatetic handicrafts teacher in Leicestershire. The family lived in Cossall, near Eastwood; by April 1908 they had moved to Quorn, Leicestershire. (For further information see Boulton ix–xi.)

[3] This holiday most likely provided the setting for DHL's story, 'The Shadow in the Rose Garden' (first called 'The Vicar's Garden' and probably written in 1908). Jessie Chambers remarked: 'The actual garden he describes I believe is one we visited at Robin Hood's Bay on one of our annual holidays' (Delavenay 694).

[4] Mabel Limb (1886–1909), a childhood friend who lived at 6 Percy Street, Eastwood.

35. To Gertrude Cooper, [20 August 1907]

Text: MS Clarke; PC v. Rigg Mill, Whitby; Postmark, Thorpe AU 20 07; Unpublished.

[20 August 1907]

Another beautiful day here. We have been to Rigg Mill across the moors about 5 miles picnicing – all of us. It was delightful, and the mill is a bonny little spot in such a secluded dell. You would love the heather, and the clouds of harebells, and the many different ferns.

Ada's eyes are quite better and her foot almost so – she has walked about seven miles today. Mab[el] and Frances are exceedingly well, I think. We are dreading returning to you. Love. DHL

Hope you are better than Emily[1] says you were.

36. To Edmund and Sarah Chambers [ante 24 August 1907]

Text: Nehls, iii. 601.

[ante 24 August 1907]

[When Lawrence was away at the seaside 'letters describing Robin Hood's Bay made [Mrs Chambers] remark: "I think he must be writing a book." She looked grave. "I'm afraid for him," she added. "With his ideas, he could set the world on fire."']

37. To Reverend Robert Reid, 15 October 1907

Text: MS UN; Unpublished.

Lynn Croft, Eastwood, Notts.
15 Oct. 1907.

Dear Mr Reid,

I should be very glad to hear your treatment of some of the great religious topics of the day,[2] and regret that I cannot attend an evening class. As it is my nights are all too short for the amount of work I ought to put into them.

Reading of Darwin, Herbert Spencer, Renan, J. M. Robertson, Blatchford and Vivian in his *Churches and Modern Thought* has seriously modified my

[1] Emily Una ('Pamela') King (1882–1962), DHL's eldest sister. m. Samual Taylor King (1880–1965), 5 November 1904.

[2] DHL together with Jessie and Alan Chambers proposed to ask Reid to 'define his position' with regard to the agnostic authors whom DHL had read. A joint letter to Reid was projected. Jessie Chambers recalled: 'Probably the thought of his mother held him back, for the letter was never sent to the minister' (E.T. 85). Though the joint letter did not materialise, DHL appears to have acted independently.

religious beliefs.[1] A glance through J. R. Campbell's *New Theology* suggested to me that his position was untenable, indeed almost incomprehensible to an ordinary mind that cannot sustain a rationalist attitude in a nebulous atmosphere of religious yearning.[2] I do not think Campbell solves any problems; I do think he is practically an agnostic, – and a mystic.

But I should like to know whether the Churches are with him on the subjects of the Miracles, Virgin Birth, The Atonement, and finally, the Divinity of Jesus. And I would like to know, because I am absolutely in ignorance, what is precisely the orthodox attitude – or say the attitude of the nonconformist Churches to such questions as Evolution, with that the Origin of Sin, and as Heaven and Hell.

I know these are tremendous issues, and somehow we hear of them almost exclusively from writers against Christianity.

Reading the *Rise of the Dutch Republic* I am staggered by the astounding difference between the accepted doctrines of various ages.[3] It seems remarkable too, that change has always originated in a people antagonistic to the Church. It is essential that we should understand the precise position of the Church of today.

Pardon me if I sound presumptuous and write with the assurance and inflatus of youth. I do not know how to take my stand

and am Yours Sincerely D. H. Lawrence

[1] Jessie Chambers (E.T. 112–13) confirms that DHL's reading in his second year at University College, Nottingham (1907–8), included: Charles Darwin, *On the Origin of Species* (1859); Herbert Spencer (probably *First Principles of a New System of Philosophy*, 1860); and Ernest Renan, *The Life of Jesus* (1863; English translation 1864). It is not possible precisely to identify his knowledge of John Mackinnon Robertson, author of *A Short History of Christianity* (1902), *Essays in Ethics* (1903), *Pagan Christs* (1903), etc., though he does mention Robertson's *Letters on Reasoning* (1902) in Letter 107. On Robert Blatchford's *God and my Neighbour* (1903), see Letter 39. The work by Philip Vivian (Harry Vivian M. Phelips) is *The Churches and Modern Thought: an inquiry into the grounds of unbelief and an appeal for candour* (1906).

[2] Jessie Chambers (E.T. 83–4) lays particular stress on the challenge represented by Reginald John Campbell's *New Theology* (1907). Resulting from a discussion of this work, 'such things as the Virgin Birth, the Atonement, and the Miracles we talked out and discarded as irrelevant to the real matter of religion'.

[3] John Lothrop Motley's *Rise of the Dutch Republic* (1855) was given to DHL by the Chambers family as a birthday present (E.T. 82).

38. To Louie Burrows, 20 October 1907

Text: MS UN; Boulton 6–7.

Lynn Croft, Eastwood, Notts.
20 Oct. 07

Dear Louie,

I have a request to make. Perhaps you know that the *Nottm. Guardian* asks for three Christmas stories, and offers a prize of £3 for each.[1] I have written two just for fun, and because Alan and J[essie] asked me why I didn't, and so put me upon doing it to show I could. I may write a third.

They ask for an Amusing Adventure, a Legend, and an Enjoyable Christmas. But one person may not send in more than one story. So will you send in the Amusing in your name?[2] They say 'In sending a story each person undertakes it is his or her original work and property which has never been published.' That is rather a sneezer, but I don't see that it matters, for I make the story your property, and you will write it out again according to your taste – will you?

It is the Amusing I want you to send, because it is the only one that is cast in its final form. I want you to write it out again in your style, because mine would be recognised. Indeed you may treat it just as you like. I am sorry to take up your time – but would you mind? If not I will bring you the story and give full instructions. The legend you shall read when you come and see us, which will be next Saturday if you please, or the foll. Sat if you prefer.

If you have scruples do not hesitate to say so. The story, if published, [...] bears a nom-de-plume, and I am pretty nearly certain that the Amusing will *not* be accepted, though the Legend may. So you would be fairly safe in sending it, and I see no wrong. However, that you must decide.

I have not seen J this week end owing to the atrocity of the weather. But I will post your note to her.

I await your reply. and am Yrs. DHL

[1] Details of the competition appeared in the *Nottinghamshire Guardian*, 8 October 1907. Prizes were offered for 'the best story of the Most Enjoyable Christmas the writer remembers or has ever heard of'; 'the most amusing Christmas story which the competitor can narrate'; and 'the best Legend of Some Historic Building within the four counties' (of Nottinghamshire, Derbyshire, Leicestershire, Lincolnshire). The scenes and actions of all stories had to occur in these four counties; competitors were restricted to residents in that area and were required to use a nom-de-plume. MSS were required by 9 November.

[2] Louie Burrows submitted 'The White Stocking' on DHL's behalf (the MS is described by Brian Finney, *Studies in Bibliography*, 28 (Charlottesville, Virginia, 1975), 322); it was later re-written and included in *The Prussian Officer and Other Stories* (Duckworth, 1914). DHL himself submitted the 'Legend' (using Beauvale Abbey as the 'Historic Building') which later became 'A Fragment of Stained Glass'. The 'Enjoyable Christmas' story, apparently written last, was 'A Prelude'; sent in by Jessie Chambers under the nom-de-plume 'Rosalind', it won a prize and was printed with Jessie Chambers as the author in the *Nottinghamshire Guardian*, 7 December 1907 (see Roberts Plate vii).

39. To Reverend Robert Reid, 3 December 1907

Text: MS UN; Unpublished.

Lynn Croft, Eastwood, Notts.
3rd Dec 1907.

Dear Mr Reid,

I send you my heartfelt thanks for the books – the 'Antidotes' as Ada, punning, calls them. During the Christmas holiday I will read them scrupulously.

As you say, violent, blatant writers against Christianity do not affect me – I could not read *God and My Neighbour* with patience. It is this way. By nature I am emotional, perhaps mystical; also I am naturally introspective, a somewhat keen and critical student of myself. I have been brought up to believe in the absolute necessity for a sudden spiritual conversion; I believed for many years that the Holy Ghost descended and took conscious possession of the 'elect' – the converted one; I thought all conversions were, to a greater or less degree, like that of Paul's.[1] Naturally I yearned for the same, something the same. That desire was most keen a year ago, and during the year before that, when I had to fight bitterly for my authority in school. Through all that time I was constantly making the appeals we are urged to make, constantly bewildering myself as to what I should surrender – 'Give yourself' you say. I was constantly endeavouring to give myself, but Sir, to this day I do not understand what this 'giving' consists in, embodies, and includes. I have been moved by Mr. Lane,[2] by Ritchie's[3] dramatic fascination, by your earnest and less intoxicating appeal. Yet in the moments of deepest emotion myself has watched myself and seen that all the tumult has risen like a little storm, to die away again without great result. And I have watched for the coming of something from without; – it has never come. You will not say 'Because you watched'; you will not talk about the 'Lord's good time' – then was the need, *now* it is much less, and grows smaller. Now I do not believe in conversion, such conversion. I believe that a man is converted when first he hears the low, vast murmur of life, of human life, troubling his hitherto unconscious self. I believe a man is born first unto himself – for the happy developing of himself, while the world is a nursery, and the pretty things are to be snatched for, and pleasant things tasted; some people seem to exist thus right to the end. But most are born again on

[1] Acts ix. 3–19.

[2] Probably James Lane, a pharmacist in Radford, Nottingham, and a member of Radford Congregational Mission, who underwent a spectacular conversion in 1903 and became an unofficial lay preacher testifying to his experience.

[3] Rev. David Lakie Ritchie (1864–1951), Principal of Nottingham Theological Institute (later called Paton College), 1904–19, and of Montreal Congregational College, 1919–28.

entering manhood; then they are born to humanity, to a consciousness of all the laughing, and the never-ceasing murmur of pain and sorrow that comes from the terrible multitudes of brothers. Then, it appears to me, a man gradually formulates his religion, be it what it may. A man has no religion who[1] has not slowly and painfully gathered one together, adding to it, shaping it; and one's religion is never complete and final, it seems, but must always be undergoing modification. So I contend that true Socialism is religion; that honest, fervent politics are religion; that whatever a man will labour for earnestly and in some measure unselfishly is religion.

I have now only to state my position with regard to Christianity. At the present moment I do not, cannot believe in the divinity of Jesus. There are only the old doubts in the way, the old questions. I went through the lowest parts of Sneinton to Emily's to dinner when she lived in Nottingham – it had a profound influence on me. 'It cannot be' – I said to myself 'that a pitiful, *omnipotent* Christ died *nineteen hundred* years ago to save these people from this and yet they are here.' Women, with child – so many are in that condition in the slums – bruised, drunk, with breasts half bare.[2] It is not compatible with the idea of an *Omnipotent*, pitying Divine. And how, too, shall I reconcile it to a belief in a *personal* God. I cannot be a materialist – but Oh, how is it possible that a God who speaks to all hearts can let Belgravia go laughing to a vicious luxury, and Whitechapel cursing to a filthy debauchery – such suffering, such dreadful suffering – and shall the short years of Christ's mission atone for it all? I do not want them to be punished after death – what good then, when it is all irremediably done? 'God can touch their hearts,' you say, giving me examples, as Mr Henderson[3] did, 'of the terrible, wild and blasphemous man who was saved at last.' Then why not touch these people at once, and save this enormity, this horror? 'His ways are inscrutable' – you say – what comfort can I draw from an unknowable. 'Faith' – you say. 'And faith is,' you might continue,[4] 'belief in a hypothesis

[1] who] that

[2] Cf. John Foster Fraser, *Life's Contrasts* (1908), pp. 211, 213: '...a warren of hovels within an area of half a mile in the poorest part of the town – that of Sneinton'. 'I am not a squeamish man, and have seen some of the industrial sores in various parts of the world; the brutal exploitation of labour in Chicago, the Hebrew sweatshops in the East End of London. But I do not recall ever having been so sick as when...I went round the Nottingham slums. Nowhere in this world have I seen such vile conditions, such decrepit, foul, insanitary houses as I found in an alley in Nottingham.'

[3] Rev. Alexander Roy Henderson (1862–1950), Minister of Castle Gate Congregational Church, Nottingham, 1902–19; 1921–39 Principal of Paton (Congregational) College, Nottingham. He preached frequently at Castle Gate Congregational Church, February – December 1907, particularly on conversion (paying special attention to St Paul, St Augustine, Luther and Bunyan).

[4] continue] say

that cannot be proved.' – But sir, there must at least be harmony of facts before a hypothesis can be framed. Cosmic harmony there is – a Cosmic God I can therefore believe in. But where is the human harmony, where the balance, the order, the 'indestructibility of matter' in humanity? And where is the *personal, human* God? Men – some – seem to be born and ruthlessly destroyed; the bacteria are created and nurtured on Man, to his horrible suffering. Oh, for a God-idea I must have harmony – unity of design. Such design there may be for the race – but for the individual, the often wretched individual?

I care not for Blatchford or anybody. I do not wage any war against Christianity – I do not hate it – but these questions will not be answered, and for the present my religion is the lessening, in some pitiful moiety, the great human discrepancies.

I have tried to write to you honestly – this is the first time I have ever revealed myself. Of course I know there is much of the wilfulness of youth in it all – some little arrogance perhaps that you will pardon me. I thought it fair that you should have some explanation of myself from me – but it is a subject I can never discuss. I wish to thank you for your late sermon – and sermons. There seems some hope in a religion which will not answer one with fiats and decrees.

Again, I ask your pardon for all this incoherent display

and am Yours very Sincerely D. H. Lawrence

40. To May Holbrook, [11 ? December 1907]

Text: MS UN; Nehls, iii. 608–9.

Lynn Croft, Eastwood, Notts.
Wed. night.

Dear May,

The tale is Jessie's; do not accept any such reports.[1] Whoever can have promulgated it? The miserable cacklers in Eastwood are always so ready to jump to conclusions and bandy names.

Do not say anything to those at the Haggs, it would make them feel so uncomfortable, perhaps vexed – I am Yours D. H. Lawrence

[1] The reference is to 'A Prelude' published under Jessie Chambers's name on 7 December 1907 (see p. 38 n. 2). For the background to the controversy see Nehls, iii, 608–9.

41. To Louie Burrows, 23 December 1907

Text: MS UN; Boulton 7–8.

Lynn Croft, Eastwood, Notts.
23 Dec 1907

My dear Louie,

You will not mind accepting these few words of Tolstoï in memory of 'The White Stocking'? You, who love to romance, look at the blue binding and think of it, years hence, catching your eye in your study as you sit writing your newest novel. Then give a sigh for our abortive effort – or better, give a smile. I am sure Tolstoï will be interesting to you – and see how good I am to choose thus for you.

If you accept Jessie's invitation for Christmas day I expect you will stay a few days and come down to us for one of them. But I expect you will stay at home until the 30th. In that case I shall wait to hear from you concerning our visit to you. Thursday will be an excellent day for us all except Ada – she is then engaged. Friday also is good – then everybody is at liberty. If you prefer that we should come Thursday Ada bids you say so – she would be very loth to put you to any inconvenience.

While you are over here we propose having a discussion among ourselves on the ultimate questions of philosophy raised in the education class – a discussion of a 'Universal Consciousness' for instance – the matter with which we left off last Wednesday.

You do not mind accepting Tolstoï, do you? Be good, sweet maid, and acquiescent.[1] That is the only way a maid may be good from a man's point of view. 'Take from my mouth the wish of – increasing fulness of life and thought'. I am—Yrs D. H. Lawrence

42. To Jessie Chambers, [28 January 1908]

Text: E.T. 139.

[97 Lynn Croft, Eastwood]
[28 January 1908][2]

When I look at you, what I see is not the kissable and embraceable part of you, although it is so fine to look at, with the silken toss of hair curling over your ears. What I see is the deep spirit within. That I love and can go on

[1] Charles Kingsley, 'A Farewell. To C.E.G.', l. 9 ['...maid, and let who can be clever'].

[2] Jessie Chambers prefaces this letter with the remark: 'On my twenty-first birthday [29 January 1908] Lawrence sent me a long letter...' (E.T. 138). DHL is assumed to have written it the previous day. (Cf. *Sons and Lovers*, chap. 10. In the original, unrevised MS of the novel the letter written to Miriam 'when she was twenty-one' contained more striking similarities of phrase to the text printed here.)

loving all my life....Look, you are a nun, I give you what I would give a holy nun. So you must let me marry a woman I can kiss and embrace and make the mother of my children....The anguish that impinges so cruelly upon you now comes only from your association with me. Once you have passed out of my orbit life holds nothing but sunshine for you, of that I am convinced.

43. To G. K. Chesterton, [March? 1908]

Text: E.T. 155.

[97 Lynn Croft, Eastwood]
[March? 1908][1]

[Lawrence 'had sent some of his work to an author, whose weekly article in the *Daily News* we often read and discussed, asking him if he would give his opinion as to its merit'.]

44. To Blanche Jennings, 15 April 1908

Text: MS ULiv; cited in Allott 58.

Lynn Croft, Eastwood, Notts.
15 April 1908

Dear Miss Jennings,[2]

Since you belong to a class which I conceive of as scorning conventional politeness – don't ask me 'what class?' – I am going to be just natural, which is to be rude. I wish you – I feel like one on the brink of a cold bath – to read and criticise some writing of mine that purports to be a novel.[3] There, I am in!

I feel you laughing – and you know what a Sensitive Plant is a young, sentimental man of some slight ability and much vanity! So pray cease to giggle – I won't beg your pardon for the word – and listen while I tell you

[1] Jessie Chambers dates the letter as 'some weeks or even months' before 'the end of his last term in College'. Chesterton (1874–1936) had a regular Saturday column in the *Daily News*, 1901–13 (see Dudley Barker, *G. K. Chesterton*, 1973, pp. 218–19). The letter has not survived.

[2] Blanche May Rust Jennings (1881–1944). b. Liverpool. On leaving elementary school became a Post Office counter-clerk. Keen socialist and suffragist. Eventually appointed to Head Post Office, Liverpool; retired 1941 as superintendent of Leece Street Office. She met DHL only once, probably late 1907 or early 1908 at Alice Dax's house following a Nottingham rally for women's rights.

[3] The two earliest versions (completed June 1907 and April 1908) were entitled 'Laetitia'; 'Nethermere' became the title of the third version (written at Croydon); and *The White Peacock* was finally selected in June 1910.

with earnestness, pathos, and some glory what a fool I am: In the first place it is a novel of sentiment – may the devil fly away with it – what the critics would call, I believe, an 'erotic novel' – the devil damn the whole race black[1] –, all about love – and rhapsodies on spring scattered here and there – heroines galore – no plot – nine-tenths adjectives – every colour in the spectrum descanted upon – a poem or two – scraps of Latin and French – altogether a sloppy, spicy mess. Now madam – I offer you the dish. You will do me honour if you will taste.

If you would be so good, you would make a really good judge of it on the emotional side, I believe. I would not ask you to criticise it so much as a work of art – by that, I mean applying to it the tests of artistic principles, and such-like jargon – don't smile too soon, my head is not very swelled, I assure you;– but I would like you to tell me frankly whether it is bright, entertaining, convincing – or the reverse. Don't base your conception of its lucidity on the style of this letter – I hold that the parentheses are by far the most important parts of a non-business letter – and don't be afraid of my feelings. If you say something violently nasty I shall say 'Dear me, the woman's[2] taste and judgment are not yet well cultivated' – and I shall become quite fond of you, seeing in myself the person meet to cultivate in you the requisite amount of good taste and discrimination.

I have not showed the stuff to Mrs Dax.[3] It is remarkable how sensitive I am on her score. You know, or you will know – or perhaps you will never discover it – my fondness for playing with the 'Fine Shades', for suggesting rather than telling, for juggling with small feelings rather than dashing in large ones – this Mrs. Dax would at one time entirely have scorned, and even now I am not sure of her. Do you not notice a change in her? – a softness, an increasing aesthetic appreciation of things instead of mere approval on utilitarian grounds, or because of appeal to a strong, crude emotion? – do you remark an increasing personal, individual, particular interest which takes the place of her one-time sweeping general interests – in Woman, for instance, instead of in a woman and some women; in humanity rather than in men; in Aked's[4] capacity to move crowds rather than his ability to lighten

[1] Cf. *Macbeth* v. iii. 11.

[2] woman's] lady's

[3] Alice Mary Dax (1878–1959). b. Liverpool; attended Central School; joined the Post Office and became a colleague and friend of Blanche Jennings. Shared her enthusiasm for socialism and suffragism. m. Henry Richard Dax on 2 November 1905 and moved to Notts. Active in local affairs at Shirebrook; inaugurated local Nursing Association; prominent member of Congregational Literary Society, Eastwood. Keen social reformer. Emigrated to Australia 1951.

[4] Rev. Charles Frederic Aked (1864–1941), a 'progressive' Baptist Minister whom Alice and Henry Dax admired and Blanche Jennings probably heard. Educated at Midland Baptist College and University College, Nottingham. First pastorate at Syston, Leics. (1886–8); later

up a little corner in the big obscurity and cosmos of Alice Mary. She is a much gentler, broader woman; she is broader because she is not so broad, not so general, not so sweeping. Come now and find defiance in her eyes if you can, defiance, scorn which is proud because it is weak after suffering, and scathing for the same reason, such as it used to be. I attribute it to maternity – she attributes it to me. Are you interested?

You will allow me to be polite? You will allow me to say I hope you will not be bored or offended. I know I am trespassing – it is a word invented in Hell – or before socialism, eh? – on your time, your patience, and your goodness. There – that's sloppy, isn't it? Oh dear, I am not accustomed to writing to women[1] of your class – I wish you'd let me be really shamefully polite, or the opposite.

Oh, by the way, did Mrs Dax ever answer the question you asked me as to what is true humour. If she did not, I am anxious to reply, as you non-sentimental, practical, battling people are the most arrant sentimentalists alive. I am prepared to prove my words. It is not I, but *you*, who suffer from rude emotions. You have put aside many popular sentimentalities, and you call that ridding yourself of sentiment. As a matter of fact, it is just on the ground of sentiment you – pardon the pronoun, I mean those practical, warlike, socialistic people of whom I have met a few – are weakest; your likings and hates are unruled, unchastened, while your approvals are well balanced. It is aesthetic culture you need, not intellectual. To scorn emotions is to be a tottering emotionalist. Sentiment should be examined, analysed, known just as judgments – facts, if you like – are analysed. I am defending myself. But ask Mrs Dax.

You are bored again, I feel. But I warn you, beware when you call me a sentimentalist.

I wonder if I really offend you. If I do, just say so. When you write, pray continue to call me David – since it suits me so well – and since it puts you in the position of safe, wise elder who will smile with an experienced woman's lenity at my absurdities; it is a position you have taken; and to be sure, I am very young – though twenty two; I have never left my mother, you see.

I apologise for my prolixity – but I'm forgetting again. Hope you've enjoyed this long letter as you ought to have done; – that's the style, eh? I shall look for a letter from you.

and am Yours D. H. Lawrence

at Pembroke Chapel, Liverpool, 1890–1907. Emigrated to USA 1907. Author of *The Courage of the Coward* (1905), etc.

[1] women] ladies,

45. To Louie Burrows, 21 April 1908

Text: MS UN; Postmark, Eastwood AP 21 08; Boulton 8–9.

Lynn Croft, Eastwood, Notts.
21st April 1908.

My dear Louie,

It is dull and gloomy; the paper says 'rain or snow later'; the way is long and lonely; I am rather tired; I have the inevitable cold. Shall I pile up and continue to pile up? At seven I got up – give me one morsel of credit for that, pray – and cleaned my boots – the sum of your disfavour is decreasing like wrath in the eyes of a girl melting into pity – and I shaved. But as I shaved and looked at myself, and asked my reflection how myself fared, I fell out with myself, and saw that that same estimable person would not make good company today. Therefore, out of magnanimous consideration, I sat down after shaving and poked the fire, and as the dust and ashes drizzled over the bar, I made up my mind to spare you. By this time you are on your knees in gratitude to me for staying away. I am an expert, am I not, at making excuses? I have had many friends.

I am truly sorry not to come today – but it is better not. Why have you gone so far – why couldn't you stay within unwearying distance?[1] You will not be vexed, will you?

Last week I did not go to Leicester. My aunt is very ill – this morning we hear that she can hardly last another day.[2] How *can* I go and see her – how can I? It is enough to suffer my mother's sighs, and to feel the current of her thoughts like an uneasy quivering note of sad music. Oh for some blessed Nirvána!

'Om, Mani Padme, Om! the Dewdrop slips
  Into the shining sea.'
'Unto Nirvána – he is one with Life yet lives not.'
'– Nirvána – where the Silence lives'[3]

Still, it would be frightfully slow after a bit, would it not? I have done with my crude philosophising, my thin-air metaphysical rant. I don't care a rap for the beginning of things – it is too far away, and I'm short-sighted – I don't care a button for the end of things – I cannot be sure of Certif[icate] result.[4] Amen! I have sung the Requiem of my Soulfulness – aren't you glad? I'm taking Horace's advice

[1] The Burrows family had recently moved to Quorn, Leicestershire.

[2] Ada Rose Krenkow, née Beardsall (1868–1944), DHL's maternal aunt; she had lived in Leicester since 1906.

[3] Edwin Arnold, *The Light of Asia* (1879), viii. 289–92.

[4] Teacher's Certificate; the results were declared in October.

'Dona praesentis cape laetus horae et
Linque severa.'[1]

which is quite trite, merely:

'Take with a glad heart what the day gives, and stop bothering.'

Au revoir, – jusqu'à jeudi. I trust you and J[essie] are having a good time – have you yet fallen on each other's necks and poured out your hearts in girlish sympathy?

'Est et fideli tuta silentio
Merces.'[2]

which is

'There is a safe reward awaits faithful silence.'

I shall go empty away[3] – shall I not? Et vous?

Goodbye Yrs DHL

46. To Jessie Chambers, [May? 1908]
Text: E.T. 148.

[97 Lynn Croft, Eastwood]
[May? 1908][4]

[Jessie sent Lawrence half a crown to pay for the repair of his bicycle brake. 'He sent a letter of incoherent protest, but he promised to get it done.']

47. To Blanche Jennings, 4 May 1908
Text: MS ULiv; cited in Allott 59, 62, 63.

Lynn Croft, Eastwood, Notts.
4 May 1908.

Dear Miss Jennings,

With hot, boyish impatience I looked for a letter from you. 'Well! well!' I soothed myself at last 'my epistle is like parsley seed, it has gone to pay a few visits to the devil, but it will germinate and put out leaves at last.'[5] It did – I was right (I am always) – it produced some ten or eleven crisp little leaves from you, promising little leaves, unclosed as yet, their chief quality being a healthy greenness. You know that people say parsley seed goes seven

[1] Horace, *Odes* III. viii. 27–8 ['...horae Linque...']
[2] Horace, *Odes* III. ii. 25–6.
[3] Cf. Luke i. 53.
[4] The date of this letter appears to fall between the College Concert on 25 April 1908 (see E.T. 146 and Boulton 174) and the end of the College year (E.T. 148), 4 July 1908.
[5] English proverb: see M. P. Tilley, *Dictionary of Proverbs in England in 16th and 17th Centuries* (Ann Arbor, 1950) P62; the *Oxford Dictionary of Proverbs* (1970), p. 610, cites this usage by DHL.

times (some are moderate, discarding the holy number as unfit, and say five) to the Old Lad, it is so long a-germinating. However, since you have been enjoying yourself so richly –. By the way, what did you wear as a bridesmaid? – did you 'wear a wreath of roses'?[1] Oh Lord! Did you blush? Did you weep a tear or two? Lord! Lord!!

But I had promised to make my bow to you quite 'comme il faut', this time, even as if I were in a frock coat and a pink carnation (think of it!), discarding my cap and bells; (but which, think you, is the motlier motley? – frock, carnation, and white waistcoat or my jingle cock's comb?); but I meant to show you plainly I *could* cease to be absurd. It[2] must be the thought of you, though, makes me absurd. (read that as you will).

Let's make a bargain – I'll call you a girl if you will style me a man – Oh luxury! Do you jest when you say 'it is usual in persons of your *sex* to wish to be styled girl'? – is there some hidden sarcasm in that? – did you think I, one of the meaner sex, aspired to the glorious title of 'girl' – nay – 'write me down a *Man*'.[3] (the quotation is hardly changed at all, is it?)

No, no, I will stop fooling. Do you know, I have wandered dangerously near the indigo land, the region of blues that we all can see in the distance (if we have any art in our souls). Don't be surprised if I vanish in blue mist, and talk to you, like a sad God, from the cloud.

Mrs Dax, having become somewhat fond of me, so that I am elder brother of my sweet little Phyllis ? or that sturdy little Eric Cunninghame, one or the other of whom is so long in coming, though I have decided it is my dear little Phyllis? (I want her Phyllis Maud, or Phyllis Corinna – Mrs Dax suggests the hideous Phyllis Irene) who is on the way,[4] let me repeat, Mrs Dax having become somewhat fond of me, and perhaps not wishing my pretty sister Phyllis? to take up all her affection (when she comes, naughty, tardy Phyllis?), she has suggested that she might enjoy reading my chatter, my own chattering 'Laetitia', in bed. I have given it to her – but it will make rummy sick food. Therefore (I am going to write now with logical severity) I shall not be able to send you the work immediately, especially as Mrs Dax, having read the first four chapters (little ones), says that though the first two are good enough, the other pair is very bad, which I can quite believe, and which

[1] Thomas H. Bayly's poem, 'She wore a wreath of roses'.

[2] It] But

[3] Cf. 'write me down an ass', *Much Ado About Nothing*, IV. ii. 78.

[4] Alice Dax was expecting a child and had been discussing possible names. In fact Eric Cunningham Dax was born on 18 May 1908. (Educated at Cambridge and the University of London, he qualified as a doctor in 1934; various appointments in psychiatry in England and Australia. Since 1969 Co-ordinator in Community Health Services, Tasmania.) Mrs Dax had a second child Phyllis Maude, b. 6 October 1912. (Educated at Letchworth and London; she qualified as a nurse; emigrated to Australia.)

makes it plain that I must read the damned stuff, and once more write out afresh great pieces of it. As I do not expect Mrs Dax to give me back my tiresome girl 'Laetitia' until my sweet pink sister Phyllis? has had a fortnight in which to oust me, and as even then I have the re-writing to do, it may be July, or August before I can burden you. You do not mind, do you? Say, aren't you glad?

Because you are nearly a stranger, and one may always scatter the seeds of ones secret soul out to a stranger, hoping to find there fertile soil to replace the exhausted home earth, to which we will not, even cannot, confide what is precious to us; so, because you are a cold stranger, and not my mother or my bosom friend, I will come to you for sympathy with that sore, that sickness of mine which is called 'Laetitia', 'Laetitia', of whom my mother will say nothing except 'I wish you had written on another line' – of whom Mrs Dax says scarcely anything, not being very interested. But you are not a cold stranger – you are a good deal like me in temperament, I think.

You know when I first went to Coll., I was in the Normal Classes, taught by a woman and one man[1] whom I could teach myself with excellent advantage (the woman is a mother to me, treating me as a wilful, spoilt boy – lots of women do that, dear creatures – and the man defers to me) – three parts of my time I was bored till college boredom became a disease. Moreover I was suffering acutely from Carlyliophobia,[2] which you will understand if that rabid philosopher has ever bitten you; and lastly, I was sore, frightfully raw and sore because I couldn't get the religious conversion, the Holy Ghost business, that I longed for. It was imperative that I should do something, so I began to write a novel – or rather, I resumed a work I had begun some months before – two years last Easter. College gave me nothing, even nothing to do – I had a damnable time there, bitten so deep with disappointment that I have lost forever my sincere boyish reverence for men in position. Professors and the rest of great men I found were quite small men – they quibbled forever over the woman and the friend in Shak's Sonnets, reading lectures written twenty years before (that is true), droning out nonsense about Langland for long, dreary hours – they were evidently small men, all wind and quibbles, flinging out their chaffy grain to us with far less interest than a farm-wife feels as she scatters corn to her fowls. So I lost my reverence, and my reverence was a big part of me – and having lost my reverence for men, my religion rapidly vanished. Now I respect some men, I deeply respect some of our Professors, but I revere none, no one, not one

[1] Either Miss A. F. Bird or Miss E. M. Becket and Professor Amos Henderson, all on the staff of the Department of Education, University College, Nottingham.

[2] Jessie Chambers recalled DHL's keen reading of Carlyle in Spring 1906 (E.T. 101–2).

in the length and breadth of the world. Likewise I respect religion; but dear me, it isn't often respectable.

Well, when my boyhood – and I was[1] a born boy, cut out for eternal boyishness – began to drop from me as the grains drop one by one from a head of oats, or ten at a time when rudely shaken, then I began to write. Consequently I wrote with crude sentimentality, being sick, having lost the health of my laddishness, all the humour that was the body of my mind's health dead. I finished the first writing last June – since then I have written the whole thing again. But I have been busy at Coll. this year – and I have been irritated between duty to swot Latin and trigonometry and my impulse to write. So, much of Laetitia is poor stuff, I fear, and I shall have it all to do over again.

I shrink from the thought of anyone's reading that work – if I were not vain and poor I should like to put it in the fire. Mrs Dax has had it a fortnight, and says 'I have not had time to read your papers – I'll read them in bed' – meantime I have taken her a vol. of Ibsen – she has read it – she has read another book – and I took her yesterday another big green book.[2] Of course she thinks I don't care many damns about Laetitia (I don't know sometimes myself whether I do) – but as a matter of fact my mind is sore, and it waits for the ointment of somebody's sincere criticism. I cannot cure myself of that most woful of youth's follies – thinking that those who care about us will care for the things that mean much to us. Only one girl, who is in love with me,[3] and whom I do not love (I am the sad god in blue mist now), cares deeply for my writing; but she is valueless because she approves too much: – valueless as a critic, I mean. There – look how serious I am. I have been writing a long time, and I have all my work to do for the exam in June – every bit of work to begin and finish for the Certif[icate] in June. And I am poor – and my mother looks to me – and I shall either have to wear motley all my days and be an elementary school teacher, or be an elementary school-teacher without motley – a lamentable figure I should cut – unless I can do something with that damned damnation of a Laetitia, which is almost the sole result of my coll. career – except, of course, loss of my mental and moral boyhood, and gain in scepticism.

[1] was] am

[2] 'One of the most treasured possessions of the Lawrence household was a set of large volumes bound in green cloth containing long extracts from famous authors. The books had belonged to [DHL's deceased brother] Ernest, and were regarded with a reverence amounting to awe' (E.T. 92). The set (also described in the opening stage directions to DHL's play, *A Collier's Friday Night*, Secker, 1934) was the *International Library of Famous Literature* ed. Richard Garnett, 20 volumes (1899).

[3] Jessie Chambers.

Have I bored you this time – Lord, what a fool I am? I am always opening my heart to some girl or woman, and they wax sympathetic, but they are fools with no alloy of wisdom. I have my grain of sense somewhere – it prevents my falling in love – it prevented my becoming 'converted' to religion.

But where is my motley – my motley! Think of a naked fool – with patches even on his skin – here and there – patches of blushing soreness – a naked fool – oh Lord! Give me my motley, my motley – and burn this letter, this portrait of my patched, naked folly. Yrs DHL

48. To Blanche Jennings, 13 May 1908

Text: MS ULiv; cited in Allott 63.

Lynn Croft, Eastwood, Notts.
13 May 1908.

Hail, Blessed Damosel,[1] you are a genius: you have invented the letter which does not begin with a kiss, a letter altogether un-Judas-like.[2] I have an aversion to kissing people straight off – I have somewhat of a distaste for being caressed (except on occasions). So you have had the blissful courage to shed that formality – that 'Dear —,' – that 'My dear —' greeting which is like being kissed by one's Auntie in the street. You are delicious. To rip straight off with 'Really David, if I went in for dignity –' is nearly as good as if a parson should arise in his pulpit and say right out,[3] with no prayings and slobber 'Sit up – put your hearts in your pockets out of the way, and prepare your wits. You're going to think tonight about a few little things.' You won't endear me any more – nor I you. Bonum!

Now I've been sweet to you, have I not? Prepare then. You are shamefully unappreciative – I treat you to beautiful eulogies, and you fling them back at me with scorn. Any person of the slightest wit is flattered at being called a 'Devil'. Dear me – if only half the world were devils, what a brilliant and happy time we should have! Again, think of the subtle compliment when I 'infer that you are green'. It is a metaphor borrowed from the vegetable kingdom signifying youthfulness, virility, beauty, health, and capacity for delicate and extremely valuable work. All these I attributed to you, and you

[1] DHL's fascination with D. G. Rosetti's poem or painting, 'The Blessed Damozel', is confirmed in a remark made about him by one of his University teachers, Professor Ernest Weekley, and recorded by Frieda Weekley: 'I am sure he is a poet I could see it in his face, when I referred to the "blessed Damozel"' (MS UT F88 Misc; see *Library Chronicle, University of Texas at Austin*, n.s. 6, December 1973, p. 98). Frieda attributes the remark to 1910; it is more likely to have been 1908.

[2] Cf. Matthew xxvi. 48–9.

[3] right out] straight off

scorn them. Would you rather I had called you etiolate, flaccid and the like? Oh, the feminine mind! We poor males are forever strewing pearls. Don't say I have 'patches of boy' – I resent being called piebald.

Laetitia is *not* romantic – she is not Meredithian. I'm not going to touch her– she'll come to you in all her gawky rude condition, for Mrs Dax will never read her, and will never cease to pretend that she *will*, so the only way out will be to request that Laetitia should be packed among the baby clothes and brought to you when the Mother flees into Egypt with the supreme creature.[1]

Babies are all right when they are not spotted and mottled like souse – brawn – collared head,[2] whatever you call it; they're all right when their mother's nowhere about, and when they're asleep – so there! I *do* like babies! You needn't groan when a girl is born – she may in time be the mother of a man! Phyllis Maud is *not* atrocious. It is a madrigal, it is a lyric in Trochaic[3] dimeter. Look at it Phȳlliš Māūd. There are the light, tripping syllables of 'Phyllis' suggesting the bright, sweet, merry creature, and there is the sonorous dignity of Maud which tells the girl will have a soul – she will not be a frippet – I could read Shelley to her, and she would look at me with grand understanding eyes. If only she might be a Phyllis Maud! One name is *not* sufficient for anyone – there is unity and perfection in a Trinity. Do you think the idea of the mystic oneness of three is empty and barren? It is not. I don't like your miserable lonely single 'front name'. It is so limited, so meagre; it has no versatility; it is weighed down with the sense of responsibility; it is worn threadbare with much use; it is as bad as having only one jacket and one hat; it is like having only one relation, one blood relation, in the world. Never set a child afloat on the flat sea of life with only one sail to catch the wind. I am called Bertie, Bert, David, Herbert, Billy, William and Dick; I am a full rigged schooner; I have a wardrobe as complete as the man's-about-town.

I shan't tell you another thing about that girl. As for my forte, nothing and everything is my forte. I could write a good novel, if I thought about it enough. I could do anything in that line. I could write crits. – but who wants me to – who would have 'em? How shall I squeeze my jostled, winded way into journalism,[4] who kick everybody that cramps me and confines me

[1] Cf. Matthew ii. 13–14.

[2] i.e. the meat of a pig's head preserved and prepared for eating.

[3] Trochaic] Iambic

[4] This was not merely an idle thought. On 26 September 1908 when DHL went to Croydon for an interview for a teaching post, he stayed with his cousin Alfred Inwood (1870–1951) – then London Editor of the *Sheffield Telegraph* – and made a point of enquiring from him 'how to start in journalism' (see 'The Day D. H. Lawrence came for Advice', *The Times*, 22 March 1963).

and is a vulgar selfish lout. I *don't* boast about my sense – I have to make it my boast that I am smart enough to be a fool.

Do you know what I shall do when I am out of college? I shall write drivelling short-stories and the like for money. I am learning quite diligently to play the fool consistently, so that at last I may hire myself out as a jester, a motley to tap folks on the head fairly smartly with a grotesque stick – like Shaw does.[1] In Laetitia there is, I would declare it in the teeth of all the jabbering critics in the world, some beautiful writing – there are some exquisite passages, such as I shall not write again, because – well, because most folks out of motley are such fools. You say I have a sane critic in Mrs Dax – a sane critic in a woman who is fond of me! – and you know human nature! She is careful of me. She says 'here the boy has written cleverly – the words are well strung' – then with a frown she reads on, commenting 'the lad hasn't done his lesson so well here – that is flawed English even to my untutored eyes.' So she carefully criticises, like a mother who reads her son's school essay. She does not know that I must flaw my English if I am to be anything but a stilted, starched parson. How can I be wilful and whimsical in good English? But wilful and whimsical I ought not to be, according to Mrs Dax, – in a novel. How can a woman whose feelings flow in such straight canals follow me in my threadings, my meanderings, my spurts and my sleepings!

You may certainly read that paper on 'Art and the Individual'[2] – better 'Art and Individual Development' – when I have written it out again. In its present scrappy condition you would not enjoy it; most likely you never would, for that matter.

I have been trying, for some time back, to learn to cork up that irritable geyser which I call my soul. A bit of mud, or stick or any irritant and up it bubbled and spurted, much to the amusement of the bystanders. But soon my soul will be a manageable thing; it will only play for pennies; I shall cork it up when the crowd won't pay; in time it will cool down, and become, not a geyser, but a little cold pond with mud banks. Eh, my soul is my great asset and my great misfortune. But I am choking it with mud and stones; I am cooling it, or people are cooling it for me, by making it work, when it doesn't want, and for dirt. As true as I am born, I have the capacity for doing something delicately and well. As sure as I am poor, I am being

[1] George Bernard Shaw (1856–1950).

[2] This paper (first printed in Lawrence–Gelder 245–68) was given to an Eastwood discussion group either at Easter or Whitsuntide 1908 (Delavenay 682 and n.). The group met on Thursday evenings to discuss social problems in order to advance 'a more perfect social state'; on this occasion it consisted of Jessie and Alan Chambers, Henry and Alice Dax, William and Sallie Hopkin, an unnamed couple and DHL himself.

roughened down to a blunt blade; I am already rusting; I will not take the trouble to polish myself. My greatest happiness, I am sure, lies in being coarse, strong, not easily vulnerable; in a word common-place, like the rest of the dull blades and flat muddy pools. Pah, I don't care a damn whether you fancy me conceited or not! I am voluntarily wearing off the fine edge of my character. Had I been rich, I should have been something Ruskinian (– blessed poverty!). Now I shall be nothing – and am content.

I don't know where I shall get a place. The Notts Council will not; or have not kept situations for us. There is a glut of certificated teachers. We are cheap – we are a drug in the market. We are twenty two, and have earned nothing. We have prepared, and are not wanted. We are the nations servants, and we must live on our mothers, and eat of our father's sweat. *Never* advise anyone to be a teacher.

I have written myself into a bad temper. My geyser *will* persist in bubbling; but it is a mild bubble, is it not? Oh, it is losing life! Hurrah for a sluggish, dormant soul –

'Bubble, bubble
(Brings) Toil and trouble'[1]

Thank Heaven, I've no more paper. Yrs DHL

49. To Blanche Jennings, 15 June 1908

Text: MS ULiv; cited in Allott 63–4.

Lynn Croft, Eastwood, Notts.
15 June 1908

Vale! Vale!

I was very sorry to hear from Mrs. Dax yesterday that you had been sick; have a few days in bonny Wales quite set you up again? – pray be quite plump by the time I see you next. How can one be thin and a Hedonist; who has heard of a skeleton with a soul of fat self-sufficiency and zest in mere being? Pray, pray, chase a healthy layer of flesh – it is such a perfect armour for a poor, shivering, tortured soul.

I was afraid from your long silence, that I had at last succeeded in boring you to extremity. Indeed I know my last letter was a 'bavardage' – but who can defend oneself against one's own liver? You may humiliate the spirit and subjugate the flesh – but what can be done against the liver? Nevertheless, I contend that the things one sees and says via the liver are as true, in proportion, and are as real, as are the things which come along with perfect

[1] *Macbeth* IV. i. 10 ['Double, double...'].

health. If 'things are not what they seem'[1] it is because we can't see with liver and with unjaundiced vision at once.

Assez de bavardages. Tonight I am going to see Sarah Bernhardt in *La Dame aux Camélias.*[2] As Camille I think she will be thrilling. You know she always sticks to French. *La Dame aux Camélias* is largely founded, I believe, on *Manon Lescaut*, a very early novel of passion, which perhaps you have read.[3] I got a 4½d translation for Mrs Dax, and to my eternal triumph, she read it without a smile, a scoff, or an upheaval of the nose; in fact, she was somewhat deeply impressed. If you do not know *Manon Lescaut* I will send it you – this 4½d copy; and if you are good I will tell you about la divine Sarah in my next letter.

I regret that I have not yet been able to remit you that vapouring of mine on 'Art'; I have very little time to write it out – do you mind waiting a little longer?

Almost I am forgetting what it is my chief intention to say. You know that Mrs Dax is coming to Liverpool shortly with her son. It was my idea that she should bring you that M.S.S. of mine,[4] but since she has read it, and expressed her opinion in some half-dozen laughing lines of amused scoffing, I am inclined to repent having asked you to inflict yourself with the mass. I doubt whether Mrs Dax will ever say much more to me about the stuff – she is not impressed, or ill impressed; see then how execrable it must be. I am inclined to blush for myself – I know there is such a lot of crude sentimentality in it, and youthful gusty sighing, bungling insupportable. Nevertheless, there is some real good stuff – a good deal that Mrs Dax never sees, for she only cares about whether such people could really exist, and live like other folk in the midst of neighbours, chapels and mothers-in-law; whereas I don't care a damn whether they live or whether they don't – there are some rather fine scenes and effects. If you will allow me, however, I will retract my request, and keep the stuff at home, put it away in some dark obscurity of a desk for a year or two, whence I can take it when I am a wiser and less sad man tha[n][5] when I wrote it,[6] and, with much amusement, I can sort it out and have a bonfire. I must not be a laughingstock – I must hide the stuff –

1 Longfellow, 'A Psalm of Life', l. 4.

2 Bernhardt played the part of Marguérite Gautier in Alexander Dumas *fils* dramatic adaptation of his own novel (1852), at the Theatre Royal, Nottingham, 15 June 1908.

3 DHL's supposition is not strictly accurate. L'Abbé Prévost's *Manon Lescaut* appeared in 1731; Marguérite Gautier was modelled on Marie Duplessis, a Paris courtesan in the 1840s.

4 i.e. 'Laetitia'.

5 MS reads 'that'.

6 Cf. Coleridge, 'The Rime of the Ancient Mariner', l. 624 ['A sadder and a wiser man'].

'Nisi ventis debes ludibrium'.[1]

That is a young man's motto – it means 'lest thou owe the winds a laughingstock' – I ought to substitute 'filiis' or 'virginibus' for 'ventis', but it wouldn't scan. I remember I warn my hero with those words

'Nisi ventis debes ludibrium'.

If, however, you would be disappointed (Oh Heaven!) at my retaining the stuff, tell me, and Mrs Dax shall bring it. Better, ask her advice – you will then no doubt be cured of wanting.

I am going to see Sarah Bernhardt – I don't care a damn about that stuff – I have not yet got a job – I do so hope you are well. –

I am Yours D. H. Lawrence

50. To Jessie Chambers, [16 June 1908]

Text: E.T. 109.

[97 Lynn Croft, Eastwood]
[16 June 1908][2]

[The day after seeing Sarah Bernhardt in *La Dame aux Camélias* Lawrence 'wrote to [Jessie] that the play had so upset him that at the end he rushed from his place and found himself battering at the doors until an attendant came and let him out. He ran to the station to find the last train gone, and had to walk home. He added,'] I feel frightened. I realize that I, too, might become enslaved to a woman.

51. To Blanche Jennings, 25 June 1908

Text: MS ULiv; cited in Allott 69.

Eastwood
25 June 1908

As a disciple of the 'Love-thyself' school, you will forgive me that I write you in pencil. I am so lazy; having just gathered some gooseberries for a pudding, and picked them out here on our little mat of grass, sitting in the united shade of an elder and a lilac bush, I am disinclined to go indoors to the table, I am unwilling to leave this deck-chair; I refuse to swot; let me write to you then, me lounging here on the grass, where the still warm air

[1] Horace, *Odes* I. xiv. 15–16. As DHL goes on to observe, the quotation occurred also in the MS of 'Laetitia', but was deleted from fol. 534 when DHL was writing 'Nethermere'.

[2] Dated with reference to p. 55 n. 2.

is full of the scent of pinks, spicy and sweet, and a stack of big red lilies a few yards away impresses me with a sense of hot, bright sunshine. Now the vivid potentillas just move in a little breeze that brings hot breath of hay across the permanent spice of pinks. From the field at the bottom of the garden I hear the 'chack' and jingle of a[1] horse-rake; the horse is neighing; there, they come into sight between the high larkspur and the currant bushes!; the man sits like a charioteer; his bare arm glistens in the sun as he stretches forward to pull up the tines; they have gone again. It is a true mid-summer day. There is a languorous grey mist over the distance; Shipley woods, and Heanor with its solid church are hidden today; no, I can just see a dense mark in the mist, which is Heanor; but Crich is gone entirely. The haze just falls on Eastwood; the church is blue, and seems fast asleep, the very chimes are languid. Only the bees are busy, nuzzling into some wide white flowers;– and I am busy too, of course.

This all sounds very idyllic; does it not? Well, we will leave it so, eh? Pity to hunt out the ugly side of the picture when nature has given you an eye for the pretty, and a soul for flowers, and for lounging in the lozenge lighted shade of a lilac tree.

I am very sorry you have been dipped so deeply into the blues. Let me drowse you out a little sermon, will you? I will labour it out like the church clock slowly lets fall the long hour. It has just struck twelve. I wonder if I can keep awake. I think, you know, Hedonism won't wear. I think life is only a joke when you are sure it's most serious and right; when you know the great procession is marching, on the whole, in the right direction, then, to be sure, the creatures in the menagerie are comical, and their capers are too funny. But before you can see the fun you must be earnestly certain of the wonder of this eternal progression – The little lozenge lights are sliding round my pencil quaintly; but the sun they come from is keeping on in its grand course. (If I write a bit canting, it is because I am almost dreaming.) My poor little philosophy is like that. I think there is a great purpose which keeps the menagerie moving onward to better places, while the animals snap and rattle by the way. So I laugh when I see their grimaces, if these do not hinder the march. I am sure I can help the march if I like. It is a valuable assurance.

But the folks who see the funny side of things suffer horribly at times from loneliness. It is a sad thing to be the only spectator at a farce. So religion is a most comforting companion; it is absolutely necessary to many who would drop and never recover without it; then love is next precious, love

[1] a] the

of man for a woman; one should feel in it the force that keeps the menagerie on the move (you may read that as narrowly as you like, since you're not a poetess); lastly, a passionate attachment to some work which will help the procession somehow is a safety against the loneliness of not wanting to laugh at the farce, and of having no one with whom to weep.

You will see from what it pleases me to call my 'philosophy', that I have still some religion left; I would give a great deal to fall in love; it would be a magnificent thing for me to fall in love; meanwhile, I keep up my confidence, writing this, that, and the other, cultivating my soul, sure that it can give good help sometime to the march of the procession. How do you manage? When you turn your face to the wall, is everything quite blank? That is very triste. When I turn my face to the wall I laugh, seeing my own grimaces. I am never utterly navré, desolate.

A lady-bird has settled on my hand, black, with six scarlet spots. She is so gay in her little trotting that she wakes me from my preaching dream. Now she has gone – for a moment I saw her spread wings glitter. My preaching dream has gone too. Aren't you glad?

A girl has just come to our neighbour, asking him to go and take a swarm of bees 'off the corran bushes, again' the gate'. Listening to her has quite roused me. Am I answering your letter?

Laetitia, damn her, you shall have her. I wish I might never hear of her again. But you will not dare to laugh too much – I shall threaten you with Victorine Cow.[1] Mrs Dax read that tale to me, and I promised faithfully never to tell you. I laughed, of course – who could help it? – but the thing was tragic, never-the-less. Mrs Dax didn't see it – and I didn't want to preach. But that a girl should be so sapped by civilisation and society as to act as did that Cow of a girl – why, it is terrible. For it is possible, is it not, to find a girl such a beast? I don't think I know one such, for[2] there is something different in Eastwood air.

My exams are on – they continue till July 4th.[3] Today and tomorrow, however, are holidays. I ought to be swotting, but I don't want, therefore I will not. I am scandalously unprepared; I cannot rouse myself to study things I am not interested in; consequently, I cannot have anything but a poor result. It does not trouble me – exams are among the grimaces that I will laugh at. I have not got a job – I will not write for any more – I cannot bear to advertise myself. They will give me a place at Nottm. when there is one.

[1] Perhaps Blanche Jennings had written a story under this title. It has not been traced in published form.

[2] for] but

[3] The final examinations for the Teacher's Certificate.

Sarah Bernhardt was wonderful and terrible.[1] She opened up the covered tragedy that works the grimaces of this wonderful dime show. Oh, to see her, and to hear her, a wild creature, a gazelle with a beautiful panther's fascination and fury, laughing in musical French, screaming with true panther cry, sobbing and sighing like a deer sobs, wounded to death, and all the time with the sheen of silk, the glitter of diamonds, the moving of men's handsomely groomed figures about her! She is not pretty – her voice is not sweet – but there she is, the incarnation of wild emotion which we share with all live things, but which is gathered in us in all complexity and inscrutable fury. She represents the primeval passions of woman, and she is fascinating to an extraordinary degree. I could love such a woman myself, love her to madness; all for the pure, wild passion of it. Intellect is shed as flowers shed their petals. Take care about going to see Bernhardt. Unless you are very sound, do not go. When I think of her now I can still feel the weight hanging in my chest as it hung there for days after I saw her. Her winsome, sweet, playful ways; her sad, plaintive little murmurs; her terrible panther cries; and then the awful, inarticulate sounds, the little sobs that fairly sear one, and the despair and death; it is too much in one evening. She played Manon Lescaut exactly – and it was dreadful.

Don't let that little fool shove a lot of mental rubbish on you. Systematic reading be damned! You might as well say 'proteids one week, carbohydrates next, then hydrocarbons.' I find that by reading what I feel I want to read, I get the most benefit. Then my soul keeps bonny and healthy. So if you feel like going for something wildly emotional, like *Jane Eyre*, or Balzac, or *Manon Lescaut*, you *have* it, and don't let that pragmatical ass shove shredded wheat down you when you want the red apples of feeling. Above all things, women should refuse to be dominated, or even domineered, by the insolent 'intellectuals'.

I wish I were in Liverpool. I wish I could get hold of some rope that is fastened to some van of the menagerie. I don't want to drowse along in the edge of the dust all my life. Ah well! I am lazy – I will *not* run in the heat. But, from a distance, I will try and give some help to lotus-eaters like myself.

Concerning holidays. We generally go somewhere for a fortnight – all of us; with friends, some ten people. Last year we went to Robin Hood's Bay, near Whitby – it was delightful. I have written to Runswick Bay, Barmouth, and the Lincs. coast for digs, and in none of these places can we be accommodated. We almost thought of Peel. But nearly all houses with 2

[1] The effect of Bernhardt's performance is also reflected in *The White Peacock*, I.3. (For a portrait of her as Marguérite Gautier, see *The Library Chronicle of the University of Texas at Austin*, December 1973, p. 75.)

sitting rooms and 5 bedrooms – or one sitting and 5 beds. – are let for the time we want them – the first two weeks in August. – The holidays go from 24th July to 23rd Aug. – we could take any fortnight out of that date, I think – Can you give me any advice? If so, tell me quickly.

You are sick of me for once, I know. Vale! D. H. Lawrence

52. To Louie Burrows, 10 July 1908

Text: MS UN; Postmark, Eastwood JY 10 08; Boulton 9–10.

Lynn Croft, Eastwood, Notts
10th July 1908

My dear Louie,

I have been conjuring up pictures of you dictating in most sweetly pronounced college terms to your flock of admiring and revering youngsters.[1] How has it been? Have you yet lost that precious jewel, that Holy Grail of teachers, your precious perfect good temper? Have you yet summoned a trembling little mortal in thunder tones to the terrors of the strap? Have you yet flung yourself down in the railway carriage reciting in soul-sick tones:

'Tomorrow, and tomorrow, and tomorrow
Creeps in this petty pace from day to day;
And all our yesterdays have lighted fools
The way to dusty death.'[2] – 'And I wish one of 'em had lighted me.'? Have you? – then you have my heart-felt sympathy. Have you not? – Then accept my hearty congrats – but wait till next week before you crow.

Hasn't this been a — week? I have several times been black in the face. 'The hay is cut, the clover's shut' – but I cannot go wielding the fork – I have stewed indoors till I am sick in – Little Mary.[3] – – –.

Next week, if it is fine, I hope to be in the hay. Should the Sat. be a blazer, I must remain in the hay, since, as usual, I am an indispensable factor in the well-being of things. 'He that putteth his hand to the hay-fork' – you know the rest;[4] – I suppose one farming implement is as good as another. So I don't know quite when I can come to Quorn. How would it be to leave it till the holiday? You know we don't go away till the 8th – and I guess you will not depart earlier. Command me, however, I am as submissive as Puck.

[1] Since finishing her exams on 4 July (like DHL), Louie had begun teaching at St Mary's School, Castle Street, Leicester; she remained there till the end of the year.

[2] *Macbeth* V. v. 19–20, 22–3.

[3] i.e. the stomach (colloquial, from J. M. Barrie's *Little Mary*, first performed 1903).

[4] Luke ix. 62 ('No man, having put his hand to the plough, and looking back, is fit for the kingdom of God').

I have no word of a holiday – I mean, fool that I am, of a job.

I want to read some Verlaine[1] to you – fun! – I shall see your eyes swing round.

I remember Saturday – it is as good as *Alice in Wonderland.*

I expect to hear from you – give me your school address.

Yours. DHL

53. To Blanche Jennings, 17 July 1908

Text: MS ULiv; Moore 18–21.

Lynn Croft, Eastwood, Notts.
17 July 1908.

I will try to obey your behest, and write you in a sweet mood, though my mouth is sore with eating white currants, and my inside is sore with a little sad news. However, as you can neither taste my currants nor my sorrow, I will spare you the effects of both as far as possible.

Why do you write me when you have only five minutes to spare? Perhaps you are very much occupied. Quant à Laetitia, I shall receive your pronunciations with pleasure; say something nice about her if you can, please, for my heart of hearts is very sore also on that young lady's score; I shall be content and amused with your animadversions. Would you have liked Cyril analysed as a personnage? – it would never do; he is a young fool at the best of times, and a frightful bore at the worst. Moreover, the first person allows of whimsicality in treatment. You will find plenty of Cyril; Mrs. Dax found too much; 'it is too full of moods', she said; the moods were such as she does not see in her own real actual Cyril;[2] – and a woman can always read a man through and through – through and through. So the moods disquieted Mrs. Dax; they were unfamiliar pages to her; they were therefore affected, not genuine; at any rate something was the matter. 'Too suggestive of moods.' Your friend may read Laetitia, as she, the former, is not acquainted with me. It seems to me my little girl's circle of feminine acquaintances is soon to be quite large; she has not a single male friend, poor child. Tell me something about this interested lady – I'm sure I'm covered with confusion because of her goodness – and tell me what she will condescend to say.

I am astonished that you liked that last letter of mine – I always read 'boredom' in your long silences. As for being a clod, there are indeed lots of things I should miss if I were such (I accept your gracious assumption

[1] Paul Verlaine (1844–96).

[2] DHL himself.

that I am not) – things that I would gladly spare myself. To be poor and sensitive is to be twice cursed. But I forget, I promised to be sweet.

Let me repeat, a bout of desolation, or a bout of the liver, helps to *establish* a sense of proportion. As for love – if it is unhappiness, then a great sorrow is better than a host of petty vexations and mean cares and pleasures. The great thing is to love – therein lies the excitement, the fundamental vibration of the life force. As to being loved, it is not so essential. As somebody or other says 'In every love affair, one party loves the other "se laisse aimer"' – 'let's himself love' – often 'lets himself be loved',[1] – no more. Yet the lover is, or should be if he has any nobility of character, infinitely better for his passion.

The secret of religion is, I think, that one can remain a child without losing any of one's importance. As a matter of fact, most folks are afraid to grow up; that's why they defer it so long. Real independence and self-responsibility are terrifying to the majority; to *all* girls, I think. As a child crying with toothache gets a small comfort by knowing that his mother is awake listening and grieving for him, and gets great comfort, even real cure, if only his mother will leave her bed and come and hold him in her arms till he goes to sleep, so the grown-ups, sick with an ailment for which there is no dentist, weep themselves better in the arms of the Christ. Think of the phrases 'The everlasting arms' – 'safe on Jesu's breast'.[2] They are the words of grown up children. For myself, if there were any woman to whom I could abandon myself, I should find infinite comfort if she would nurse me, console me, soothe me, and tell me I should soon be better. I miss religion for this only; that I have now no season when I can really 'become again as a little child'[3] – and make my querulous little complaint into the ear of a deep sympathy. This is a confession for a man to make, is it not? It is surprising, too, how women – one woman – yearns to nurse me and soothe me. But I will not have it. When you come to think that we are such transitory little dots, it is no wonder we are sometimes lonely. Religion, work, love all link us on to an eternity – the one of singing, the other of influencing, the last of being. You think the middle one best – I like both the last two.

Many thanks for the trouble you took enquiring for digs on our behalf. I think we shall like Flamboro. I can make a kindred spirit of almost any body; my spirit is one of the versatile hob-nobbing sort. As for a complete

1 A commonplace of uncertain origin. (Thackeray introduces it in translation in *Vanity Fair*, (1848), chap. 13; Galsworthy quotes it in French in *The Dark Flower* (1913), III.V.)

2 Deuteronomy xxxiii. 27; perhaps 'Safe in the arms of Jesus, safe on his gentle breast', from the popular hymn by Frances Jane Van Alstyne (1868).

3 Matthew xviii. 3 ['become as little children'].

kindred spirit – I know none – I am learning, and the lesson is almost complete, to do without a familiar spirit in my hours of real deep feeling; I am never in deadly, ludicrous earnest with anyone now as I used to be. Do I hear your say 'What ho!'? Madam – my sentiments entirely.

I have not yet got a situation. Just glance at the Liverpool educational advts. for me, will you? I should like to come to your cosmopolitan city – and I dont care a damn where I go – my dear demoiselle, you would be a 'kind kin' to my frivolous spirit, would you not? Don't say nasty things about yourself when you write – leave that to other folks.

I will send you that paper on Art when I have heard from you your judgments on Laetitia.

It goes without saying, of course, that a fool with my variety of follies should have turned his capering wits to the trapeze of verse. I am willing to afford you more amusement when Laetitia and my dithyrambs on aesthetics are exhausted. I will send you a 'morceau' for your delectation. Fie, fie – don't smile. I declare – I am forced to wave my own banner as vehemently as any suffragette, being in such a tiny minority of one – that my verses are tolerable – rather pretty, but not suave; there is some blood in them. Poetry now a days seems to be a sort of plaster-cast craze, scraps sweetly moulded in easy Plaster of Paris sentiment. Nobody chips verses earnestly out of the living rock of his own feeling: You know Verlaine's famous verse.

'De la musique avant toute chose
Et pour cela préfère l'impair
Plus vague et plus soluble dans l'air
Sans rien en lui qui pèse ou qui pose'[1]

Literally, it runs 'Let us have music before everything, and, to obtain it, we will choose a subtle irregularity with nothing which balances and makes weight.' Something undecided, vague, suggestive. I like it, but will not practise it. Before everything I like sincerity, and a quickening spontaneous emotion. I do not worship music or the 'half said thing.' Do you like poetry?

I am sick of the rain. I want to get into the hay. I want summer and action. Much feeling and fancying are wearying in the extreme. I want action, heat, boisterousness.

The red lilies are dead, and the white Madonna lilies hold their place. The rich scent in the evening, and the waxen religious look of the flowers does not please me. They recall inevitably the sweet, innocent, mystical lad who was me ten years ago.

[1] Verlaine, 'Art Poétique', ll. 1–4 (in *Jadis et Naguère*, 1885).

Pah – you will be sick of me.

Auf wiedersehen (I wonder when I shall see you again).

Yrs D. H. Lawrence

54. To Louie Burrows, 29 July 1908

Text: MS UN; Postmark, Giltbrook JY 31 08; Boulton 11–12.

Lynn Croft, Eastwood, Notts.
29 July 1908

My dear Châtieuse,

On my stream of consciousness has often sailed a cockle boat carrying your tawny image, but the fragile idea of a letter to you which your boat had in tow got wrecked before it came to harbour and set up motor responses. Cependant – now I write, you are not cross, hein?

This I hear from J[essie] of your coming to the Haggs is very jolly. 'Swiftly walk over the Western Wave, Daughter of Night.'[1] You will come? – you must come. Surely nothing will happen to prevent you – if it does I shall jerk my thumbs off – à la mode italienne. Come for Bank Holiday[2] – we are arranging some simple little jaunt; stay till the week end – I want to read to you Verlaine – I want to laugh like a fiend with you at some behaviours of our friends over here.

All last week, and all this, I have been in the hay. Hardly do I know myself; I have cast my tender skin-of-college culture (don't dare to say it never grew) – my hands are pachydermatous (Hurray!) – and still jolly sore; my manners are – dear me, dear me, Mrs Grundy![3] – my exquisite accent, beloved of Billy,[4] is gone; as the corns rose on my hands so grew gruffness in my speech. You will like me, you hussy. Alas, I forget, I have been to the dentist; I have two teeth out in front; steel yourself against the sight of me. On Sunday we worked in the fields till nearly three o'clock; the righteous went by to church; the bells did ring; we worked and sweated. Monday night we camped out – under the haystack; a tramp came to join us; he mistook us for fellow tramps;[5] it took all Neville's[6] (he was there – with Alan and I) virtuous and

[1] Shelley 'To Night', l. 1 ['...Spirit of Night'].

[2] i.e. August Bank Holiday, Monday, 3 August 1908.

[3] i.e. the figure of conventional prudery from Thomas Morton, *Speed the Plough* (1798).

[4] Possibly a reference to William ('Billy') H. Newton, a Lecturer in Education at Nottingham University College.

[5] DHL used this incident (more fully described in the letter following) in *The White Peacock* I. 3 and in his story 'Love among the Haystacks'.

[6] George Henry Neville (1886–1959). b. Eastwood; early and very close friend of DHL; fellow pupil at Nottingham High School. Became a teacher at Gilt Hill School and at Amblecote, Stourbridge; Headmaster at Bradnop, Staffs, in 1912; and in July 1912 master at Armitage Elementary School, near Rugeley, Staffs.

indignant 'side' to convince the poor devil of our immeasurable superiority. I have one or two tales to tell you – they will not go onto paper, for I want tones of voice. Do come.

I have no news of a job yet – don't care many – jerks of the thumb.

Au revoir – ma chère bohémienne Yrs DHL

55. To Blanche Jennings, 30 July [–3 August] 1908

Text: MS ULiv; cited in Allott 64, 71–3.

Lynn Croft, Eastwood, Notts.
30 July 1908

I give you my hand; see, if I were in Liverpool, and you are not really conventional, I would kiss you. You have written me charmingly, for which I thank you, and, as I am in a mood which should please you, I will begin a reply at once.

About half an hour ago I came in from the hay field, where I have been working for the last fortnight. I[1] have had a bath, a delicious cold bath, and have eaten half a fruit pie. Now I am as complacent as a god.

My hands are brown, hard, and coarse; my face is gradually tanning. Aren't you glad? I have really worked hard; I can pick alongside a big experienced man; indeed I am fairly strong; I am pretty well developed; I have done a good deal of dumb-bell practice. Indeed, as I was rubbing myself down in the late twilight a few minutes ago, and as I passed my hands over my sides where the muscles lie suave and secret, I did love myself. I am thin, but well skimmed over with muscle; my skin is very white and unblemished; soft, and dull with a fine pubescent bloom, not shiny like my friend's. I am very fond of myself. I like you because I can talk like this to you.

You tell me I have no male friends. The man I have been working with in the hay is the original of my George,[2] – lacking, alas, the other's subtlety of sympathetic discrimination which lent him his nobility. But I am very fond of my friend, and he of me. Sometimes, often, he is as gentle as a woman towards me. It seems my men friends are all alike; they make themselves, on the whole, soft-mannered towards me; they defer to me also. You are right, I value the friendship of men more than that of women. Do not suppose I have no men friends. I could show you two men who claim me as their heart's best brother; there is another, home for the vacation, who has been with me every available moment[3] – till I am tired, I confess. But of David

[1] I] Since then I

[2] Alan Chambers, the original of George Saxton in 'Laetitia'.

[3] The three friends were, respectively: Alan Chambers, George Neville and probably Richard Pogmore.

and Jonathan[1] – it is as impossible as magnificent love between a woman and me. It is like this (I am going to hold forth). You measure a friend by the breadth of his understanding; by understanding I mean that delicate response from the chords of feeling which is involuntary. Various folk vibrate to various frequencies, tones, whatever you like. Now a woman's soul of emotion is not so organised, so distinctly divided and active in part as a man's. Set a woman's soul vibrating in response to your own, and it is her whole soul which trembles with a strong, soft note of uncertain quality.[2] But a man will respond, if he be a friend, to the very chord you strike, with clear and satisfying timbre, responding with a part, not the whole, of his soul. It makes a man much more satisfactory. But then the soul of a man is a stubborn and unwieldy instrument. Ever so many chords are slack, and won't sound; most of the subtle semi-notes are missing; you may call from him the notes of the scale of C, but hardly more; the deep bottom tones, and the shrill, sharp notes at the top which verge on madness, they are all missing, and one must turn to a woman. Set up her response, and the whole range of her chords of feeling vibrates with incoherent frenzy. But better a woman vibrating with incoherent hum than a man altogether dumb, eh? So to make a Jonathan for me, it would take the natures of ten men such as I know to complete the key board. Any man might say exactly the same. To make a real wife for me would need a woman with a great range of swift and subtle feeling; a woman whose melody of soul is not numbed by the murmur of her whole soul answering at once, when there is no call for such an answer; a vague, wearing sound; like bees in a great lime tree, hidden altogether, so that the tree seems to be speaking and saying nothing. Women can feel, but often, very often, they do not understand, understand in their souls, I mean.

Most people marry with their souls vibrating to the note of sexual love – and the sex notes may run into beautiful aesthetics, poetry and pictures, and romance. But love is much finer, I think, when not only the sex group of chords is attuned, but the great harmonies, and the little harmonies, of what we will call religious feeling (read it widely) and ordinary sympathetic feeling. After marriage, most folks begin to slacken off the chords of their nature, and confine themselves to a little range. It is a great shame. Laetitia, you see, responded, and that very weakly, to Leslie, only in the sex melody. It needed that the other chords of her nature, the finer, should be jangled in an agony of discord before she realised how much she was sacrificing. Most women realise it too late, don't they? Of course I give Lettie credit for a far

[1] Cf. 2 Samuel i. 26. (DHL considered 'the story of David and Jonathan one of the finest in the world': see 'Art and the Individual', in Lawrence–Gelder 267.)

[2] quality] tone

finer soul than the majority of women; and George, for his part, than men. I am not sure whether the chords of sex, and the fine chords of noble feeling do not inevitably produce a discord; in other words, whether one could possibly marry and hold as a wife a woman before whom one's soul sounded its deepest notes. I am half inclined to think that a man must marry on the strength of sex sympathy, with as much accompanying beauty of harmony as possible, like Handel's, Schubert's, or Verdi's music, but *not* with Mozarts organ tones. It is a cruel, stultifying shame when married folk give up their friends. But you are sick of this, and so am I.

I have worked a long fortnight in the hay, with my friends, men, three men, whom I really love, in varying degrees. There are two great fields at Greasley,[1] running to the top of a sharp, irregular hillside, with the Baron's[2] – the Vicar's garden on one side, and low, wild rushy fields on the other; with the immense grey church tower sleeping quietly, with no sound of bells, behind silver poplars; with big lime trees, murmuring, and full of the scent of nectar, stretching along; with the hillside, scattered with trees, and a thick wood at the top, rising in front, and the white road climbing up it, with little carts creeping along to Nottingham, or a motor occasionally flashing down in a cloud of dust; and, far away, from the brow of the top field you can see the viaduct spanning the blue valley, and beyond that, the purple gloom of Ilkeston. From morning till night I have worked in the fields, when the willows have glittered like hammered steel in the morning, till evening when the yellow atmosphere seemed thick and palpable with dense sunshine at evening. You might have found me crawling from side to side on the horse rake, bending, then a jingle as the tines fell behind the winrow;[3] you might have heard the whirr of the file as I sharpened the bristling machine-knife under the hornbeam; you could have seen me high on the load, or higher on the stack, like a long mushroom in my felt hat, sweating, with my shirt neck open. In the evening, as we moved, we four men, turning the silvered swaths, we sang the songs we learned at school, and then my beloved Schumann, and Giordani.[4] One evening we slept out under the stack. As we were dropping asleep one of us jumped up with an exclamation – and I heard the whining answer of a tramp 'It's all right, young 'un, I'm only luikin' fer a rough 'un, like yer sen.' It took all my friend's excellent English and refined accent to convince him that we were not of the great fraternity.

1 They were rented by Edmund Chambers (Lawrence–Gelder 51).
2 Baron Rev. Rodolph von Hube (1834?–1910), Vicar of Greasley, 1866–1907 (whom DHL portrays as Baron Rudolf von Ruge in 'The Merry-go-Round'). At the time of this letter, the Vicar was Rev. Claude Cyprian Thornton.
3 i.e. as the prongs of the rake fell to the rear of the line in which the hay was raked for drying.
4 Robert Schumann (1810–56) and Giuseppe Giordani (c. 1744–98).

Then he whined 'Well, can 'e lay me dern somewheer, I shanna dö no harm?' 'Tell the poor devil to lie down, and shut up' said I across my sleepiness. It rained in the night. In the morning we found the old fellow on the other side the stack, burrowed underneath it like a rat. His bald, grey lined head made me shiver. There he lay, while we wandered round in the drizzle, hugging our rugs under our chins, looking for dry chips. We lit a fire in a little shed, smelling strongly of horses, and made coffee in a milk tin, piling hay on the fire, and blowing it into a glowing mass, while one held the can on the end of a hayfork.

The hay is finished now. Three stacks we have got in. This week is for rest. On Saturday we go to Flamboro for a fortnight. Today – Bank Holiday,[1] we are having a picnic at Beauvale Abbey – not far away. Mother and the weary will drive. Alice Gall is going – Emily – George – a fellow something like Leslie – Louie[2] – a girl I am very fond of – a big, dark, laughing girl – do you remember her? Tomorrow we shall be in the fields again, pulling and finishing the stacks; Louie, Emily, and George will be there (these are not their proper names, and the people are not like the fictions) – we shall have some fun; Wednesday we shall walk to Codnor Castle – we shall be out all day, returning to the Haggs (a farm, the home of my friends) – where, in the low parlour, I shall read Verlaine to the girls (in French – the nut-brown eyes of Louie will laugh and scold me; the soft dark eyes of Emily will look at me, pensive, doubtful – not quite sure what I mean) – and perhaps I'll read Whitman; we shall walk arm in arm through the woods home in the moonlight. Thursday we have a party at home, when we sing; we learn then our songs, our Schumann, Giordani, Schubert and the song classics; we shall play bridge and be jolly. Friday is left for packing, and for escorting Louie to the station; Saturday we go to Flamboro. A good week, eh?

I have lots of tales to tell you, if I had time. I have just made a ripping match between George and my cousin, a young widow.[3] I'll tell you the history of my cousin Tim sometimes – she is a queer girl – her life has been full of strangeness. I have a tale to tell you about Alice Gall – but that must wait also. Alice is reproduced *faithfully* from life.

Now I'll answer your letter. Your remarks on Laetitia are exceedingly just.

[1] The remainder of the letter was written on 3 August 1908.

[2] With the exception of Louie Burrows each person is here referred to by the appropriate name in 'Laetitia': Alice Gall = Alice Hall (see p. 232 n. 1); Emily = Jessie Chambers; George = Alan Chambers; 'a fellow something like Leslie' = George Neville.

[3] Alvina ('Tim') Reeve (1880–1968), daughter of DHL's paternal uncle James Lawrence and aunt Mary Ellen. m. (1) Robert Henry Reeve (1882–1907), carpenter; (2) Alan Chambers, 15 October 1910.

If you think it worth the trouble, I will write the thing again, and stop up the mouth of Cyril – I will kick him out – I hate the fellow. I will give Lettie a few rough shakings; I will keep Alice all the way through – by the way, she called me a devil yesterday, damned me on Saturday – she is a tartar – and a treat. The sheep[1] worrying incident is real – actual – dogs get a sheep-worrying habit – they have the instinct to begin with.

Thanks very much for the notes. They will be valuable. I wish there had been more of them. You will be sick of it if you have to read it again; but tell me, please, everything you can think of. Have you anything to say on the Annable part? Is it really coarse (Mrs Dax says it is)? Shall I introduce more characters? Shall I leave out lots of incidents? I *will* leave out Cyril, the fool.

You do not like poetry – I will not bother you. When you go to your friend's, tell me about it, about her. I am interested.

I have written to Egypt for a job. It doesn't bother me very much whether I get one immediately or not.

We are *not* conventional. Our set is a bit astonishing. Mr Dax[2] is quite shocked when he goes out with us – Mrs Dax also. You are all rather badly town-stamped – city bred.

As you have prophesied, my nose is out of joint at Mrs Dax's – the nose of my interest is knocked off. Mrs Dax asks me to go, and then she is quite hopeless. She has no mind left; she has no interest in anything but 'Son'. Hélas.

The sun is gay on the nasturtiums and marigolds. A gypsy woman has come. She wants a few marigolds. 'I dew so love 'em in broth.' The church clock strikes eleven. I am going to meet Louie. In the intervals of writing I have been talking to my friend, who is sitting with me on the grass, and showing him how the deaf and dumb are taught[3] to speak; so pardon me my scrappiness.

Once more, I kiss my hand to you. D. H. Lawrence

I have such heaps more things to tell you.

[1] sheep] rabbit

[2] Henry Richard Dax (1873–1962). b. Liverpool; educated at Council School and Liverpool Institute. Qualified as pharmacist (MPS, 1902) and Fellow of the British Optical Association. m. 2 November 1905. Worked in Tonbridge Wells; chemist in Eastwood and (from 1911) in Shirebrook; emigrated to Australia, 1952.

[3] taught] led

56. To Louie Burrows, [10 August 1908]

Text: MS UN; PC v. Thornwick Bay, Flamborough; Postmark, Bridlington AU 1 [...] 08; Boulton 12.

[10 August 1908]

Thanks for your note – I think Thursday will suit us nicely. I cannot yet make arrangments – will write you tomorrow. We are having a ripping time – do you think you could get down here[1] – it is so delightful? Till tomorrow then –

Love from all DHL

57. To Louie Burrows, [11 August 1908]

Text: MS UN; PC v. In the Four-Arched Cave, Flamborough Head; Postmark, Flamborough AU 11 08; Boulton 12.

[11 August 1908]

Dear Louie,

We will come on Thurs.[2] if it is quite fine. We propose to walk – start about 8.0 or 8.30 and arrive at Filey[3] about 12.0, or thereabouts. Meet us at the Station – we will try to get there by 12.0. You will come in by the 10.25 perhaps, and have a look round. You might come out to meet us a very little way on the Flam[borough] (Brid[lington]) Rd. DHL

(our train returns at 8.50 p.m. hope this will suit you) – we may get a later.)

58. To Louie Burrows, [15 August 1908]

Text: MS UN; PC v. Rocks at Flamborough; Postmark, Flamborough AU 15 08; Boulton 13.

[15 August 1908]

Good old Filey! – did it improve your cold? Make haste to be well and come to Flamboro. Will you come Tuesday, Wednesday or Thursday? Any day will suit us. We have Alan to despatch on Monday, after that we are prepared to enjoy a day with you and Ethel. Write and say times etc. Shall we have another day at Filey?

Yrs DHL

59. To Louie Burrows, [18 August 1908]

Text: MS UN; PC v. The North Landing, Flamborough; Postmark, Bridlington AU 18 08; Boulton 13.

[18 August 1908]

Ma chère Louise,

Your card comes too late for me to reply as you ask. Our posts go out at 6.0 a.m and 5.0 p.m – is it not ridiculous. I have just received your card;

[1] While DHL was on holiday at Flamborough (with his mother and other friends), the Burrows family were holidaying at Scarborough.

[2] Thurs.] Sat.

[3] Filey] Brid

it is seven o'clock and drizzling with rain. I am afraid tomorrow may be wet. If it is, come Wednesday; if Wed. is wet, come Thursday. Is the earlier train too early? Tide is high now about 9.0, you know, so we want you to come quite early. Mother is anxious for you to come – and why do you not mention Ethel – is she not coming? – if so, why not? We wanted you both. Alan is gone – Tim desolate. You *must* be well – I hope for a jolly day.

DHL

60. To Blanche Jennings, 1 September 1908

Text: MS ULiv; cited in Allott 62–3.

Lynn Croft, Eastwood, Notts
1 Sept. 1908

I have forgotten all the interesting things I had to tell you, so now I am free to write. You make me laugh when you say I sound superior and am a trifle conceited and lofty. I am very conceited, but not lofty; Oh ma foi, non! I am like a bit of hummocky ground, with many little amusing eminences – but Alpine – Oh dear No! I have a pretty good time of it, although I am a poor unemployed wretch still. My chief fortune is that I can amuse myself readily and well; I am rarely bored, and I can enjoy myself heaps on very little. As for swimming – I do a little disport myself in the water, but at the moment I was out of breath, and a man looks so lovely struggling in sea-water as clear and green as a late evening light. I am a real jolly animal – thorough as you like; I could continue so for ever, if folks would let me; and be rid of the disease of soulfulness.

It is as undesirable to be city bred as it is to be bred in corsets and trained in a school for young ladies, dear heart. That remainds me of my loftiness; Alice Gall was with us at Flamboro; she and I always talk in the broadest slang; she sits on my knee and makes mocking love to me; she is a delightful little devil. As for kissing – I never kiss but out of devilry – I hate slobber of all sorts. 'Little ways' – I have scores, scores; my worst fault is that I would always give folks their own ways if it didn't seriously inconvenience me; I am too cowardly to refuse.

Give a man that damned rot 'Laetitia'? I'm not such a fool. I told you most men had only about four strings to their souls; my friends are such. I talk to them about intellectual things, sex matters, and frivolities, never about anything I care deeply for. I also fish their souls out of them – they are so much more easy to analyse than a woman. I have a tale to tell – no, I have not.

I simply roll at the opinions of your friend. You have made me acquainted with her in them, and I love her. I like women like that, if they're old enough. Tell her to forgive me – I'm very sorry for my naughty escapade.

I did Laetitia about a year ago. The Father incident is not unnecessary – there is a point; there are heaps of points; I told you there would be, but you have not bothered to find them; quite rightly, too. I will re-write some time, and your suggestions will be valuable. Do you feel me bowing to you? One little thing I will say seriously. Laetitia was written during[1] the year that I changed from boyhood to manhood, my first year in college. It is a frightful experience to grow up, I think, it hurts horribly; but when you have got over it, it is delightful. College disappointed me painfully; there are only four or five respectworthy people in the place, and only one or two whom I knew and felt superior to myself – I am speaking of professors. Now though I am conceited, one of the cruellest shocks I ever had was to find that half the pro's in college were not superior to me in intellect or character. I am timid before people whom I respect as my superiors, but I feel confident even to insolence before my inferiors. One can feel after a very short time whether a man is superior or inferior. Then the prof's in coll. went on in such a miserable, jog-trot, earn-your-money manner that I was startled; then I came to feel that I might as well be taught by gramophones as by those men, for all the interest or sincerity they felt. I doubted them, I began to despise and distrust things; I lost my rather deep religious faith; I lost my idealism and my wistfulness, and I wrote Laetitia in that year. Now I have weaned myself from folks and God and my young dreams; I don't care very much for things, anything; I believe in life, and am determined not to waste myself battling against the worlds inertia and contrariness. Hurray!

I don't want to tell you any more psychology, I am such a gassy fool. Let us shut up now forever about Laetitia; don't send her to me until I go away, unless she lumbers you up too much.

Mrs. Dax is getting better; she looks young and pretty and winsome with the little one; he is better too, now, doesn't cry so much, and is getting rather fatter.

I am sorry you don't like men, they are interesting, more solid than women. I am sorry, but I fear you are rather lonely, and don't feel rich in the possession of your own soul. Could you not make it so that your soul is a delicious companion of delight to you?

I send you the long promised paper on Art. Don't let the tone offend you; I confess I am a school teacher. Would your friend like it, think you? Give me your opinion of it please – nice and freely, so.

[1] written during] written at during

Yesterday I was in the corn; it was a horrid cynicism on harvesting, with that wretched rain. The oats are thin and poor – so different from last year. There were some bonny harvest days then.

If I do not get a job I shall go visiting some of my genteel relatives – at Hampstead Heath or Leicester.[1] Then I will write you a sweet mincing letter. This is very rough and stale. – I cry your pardon.

D. H. Lawrence

61. To Louie Burrows, 2 September 1908

Text: MS UN; Postmark, Eastwood SP 2 08; Boulton 14–16.

Lynn Croft, Eastwood, Notts.
2nd Sept 08.

Ma chère Louise,

So you command me to write you something lively! Divessa, (fem. of Dives, not some young person out of the *Faery Queene*), flourishing on seventy-five quid a year commands poor Lazarus whose soul is covered with sores to whistle her a comic song.[2] My days are spent in uttering that mournful lament 'Meine Ruh is hin, mein Herz ist schwer' – 'My peace is gone, my heart is sore' (Do you know 'Gretchen at the Spinning Wheel'?).[3] Truly I am in a sad state, although I am getting fatter. I have used pounds of paper in applications; when I am not singing 'Meine Ruh' I am repeating to myself the verses of my testimonials 'Mr D H Lawrence has just completed a two years' course of training at this College. We have never had a student –' I can recite two long testimonials by heart[4] – Post time is a period of painful suspense – about 8.30 a.m. and 7.0 p.m. – when the postman should come. He brings me a letter – the house holds its breath – 'We beg to inform you that your application was not successful' – the devils! And you ask *me* to write something lively. The most amusing thing I can do is to console myself that I am not in your shoes. Ah, would it were holidays for ever! I don't want to begin work in school, oh dear no; I only want the filthy lucre. I hate school, I love an eternal holiday – Hurray!

Another lugubrious tale! We began to cut the corn on Monday. The crop is thin and wretched; the knife cottered and clogged vilely; it rained; I am sure Hell is a cold wet place; they invented the fiery business somewhere in Arabia, by the bright Saharas sunny strand; my hell has a N.E. wind and

[1] DHL's cousin Ethel and her husband Max Hunger lived in Ardwick Road, Hampstead; his aunt and uncle-in-law, Ada and Fritz Krenkow lived at 20 Dulverton Road, Leicester.

[2] Cf. Luke xvi. 20.

[3] Schubert set to music the words ('Gretchen am Spinnrade') by Goethe.

[4] For the text of one testimonial, see Moore, *Intelligent Heart* 71.

rain varying from drizzle to pelting sleet. On Monday I expiated all the sins I ever committed, and all that I ever inherited. Two of us raked out after the damned machine; plodded over the sticky field with its thin dragged stubble, to the corner where we must wait for the machine; there we squatted by a little hedge, and got wetter and more like 'Canterbury' lamb. Such is harvesting, harvesting the oats.

'The little god works wonders in Alan'! Lord, Lord, the poor lad's tipsy with a foolish gibbering intoxication. He has not enough of the choleric element to give his passion colour, so he trots off like a fussy spaniel to pay his court. Lord, Lord! When the oats will be gathered I do not know. The rain, oh the rain!

Me, with sores on my soul (most of 'em painted on); me, on my doorstep; me, the unemployed, I lift up my hands to heaven and thank a beneficent deity that I am not as that opulent girl reaping another harvest in Leicester. Mais félicitez Ethel de ma part.[1] (I won't trust myself in English.)

Keep up your courage, I implore you; think what an expense a funeral would be, and how like a wretched Sansjoy[2] I should look in a black tie and a crape band round my arm. When J[essie] told me of your expectations for the end of last week I said 'I should think she won't be such a brute. Think how it would knock some poor body about "laying her out".' Be of good cheer, and get those chapters ship-shape; I know it will be harder work for you to make them tidy than it was to originate them, but screw your courage to the sticking point[3] – in other words 'Hold on tight, Eliza'.[4] I shall look soon for that bit of dainty literature from you, don't be lazy.

I am highly interested in your cricket score; I am contemplating writing a Lay in its honor – after the manner of Horatius.[5]

'But the Captains brow was sad
And the Captain cursèd low
And darkly looked she at score
And darkly at the beaux'

———
———
———
———

[1] 'But congratulate Ethel from me.'

[2] See Spenser, *The Faerie Queene* I. ii. 25ff.

[3] *Macbeth* I. vii. 60 ['...sticking-place'].

[4] Perhaps an allusion to the Eliza about whom Barry Pain (1864–1928) wrote a number of tales: *Eliza* (1900), *Eliza's Husband* (1903), etc. 'Hold on' was one of her favourite phrases.

[5] Cf. Macaulay, 'Horatius', *Lays of Ancient Rome* (1842), xxviff.

Then forth strode bold Louisa
The mistress of the field
Her chin was high, her arm was strong
The trusty bat to wield

———

———

———

———

Louisa struck out wildly
And high the dust did rise
Then as she bolted down the pitch
Caught the fieldsman in her eyes.
! ! !

The Kaleïdoscope[1] I find a bit too kaleïdoscopic; it is too confused for my poor English sense; I can't make out the pattern, and the suggestion is only such as makes me feel puzzled. Let's translate it.

'In a street in the heart of a dream city comes a moment that seems a fragment repeated from a life before this, an instant at once vague and clear – – – Ah, that sun through the rising mist!

Oh, that cry away on the sea, that voice in the forest! – like when one knew nothing about the causes of things –. A slow awakening after the soul has inhabited many bodies – things will be more the same than they were before (what the last line means I don't know).

In this street in the heart of a magic town where street organs grind out jigs in the evenings, where there are cats on the side-boards of the cafés, and where bands go playing down the streets – It will be so fatal for one to believe there is any death for it.'

It recalls moments such as one has felt – but it is all so intangible – I dont know what death has to do with it.[2] Give your Français[3] an English translation of the thing and ask him where you are wrong, and to kindly explain; he had better explain in French.

I cannot say when I shall come to Leicester; think of the weather. I like to play; I like to feel childish and irresponsible, it is possible to be so much more gay. This morning when the postman had brought me that kind 'not successful' I bethought myself of my old dodge for peeping into the future, one I borrowed from *La Jeune Sibérienne*, that is, sticking a pin in the bible

[1] Verlaine's poem 'Kaléidoscope', ll. 1–13, in *Jadis et Naguère*.

[2] DHL's perplexity was caused by a misunderstanding of Verlaine's line: 'Ce sera si fatal qu'on en croira mourir.'

[3] Probably Leroy, Louie's French pen-friend; they regularly exchanged letters till 1914.

on a certain verse (at hazard), and reading one's fate.[1] I stuck Zachariah – I did not know that old boy had a book to himself – and it said 'And on the 4th day of the 9th month news came unto Somebody or other.'[2] I have therefore high expectations from Friday's post.

Hope I'll see you soon. I'm glad you can write to me as a last (and, I'm afraid, rather unsuccessful) escape from boredom.

Vous me flattez. Au revoir DHL

62. To Louie Burrows, 12 September 1908

Text: MS UN; Postmark, Eastwood SP 12 08; Boulton 17.

Lynn Croft, Eastwood, Notts.
12 Sept. 08.

Louisa Carissima,

Your good memory surprises and flatters me; I offer you a thousand thanks for your congrats.[3] You, also, why do not you write me cheerfully, me, a poor hungry unemployed, still employed busily transcribing my testimonials. I shall soon mark myself as 'unsaleable goods', and withdraw from the market.

How wicked you are to rebuke me for the tone of my last letter; not only am I called upon to make you smile, but to make you smile on the right side when everything wears a wrong face because school is a bit purgatorial. I am much interested in the matrimonial adventures of your Sandowian[4] assistant – I have never heard of him before, by the way; tell me when the new meek assistant embarks on similar adventures. Mr Mott[5] must have derived his name from the fool's attire in which his ancestors were clad; he himself seems eligible for the motley. The only thing to do with a fool is to treat him as such – an object to laugh at.

After much nibbling of bad cake you come to the almond paste at last: I'm coming to Leicester on Wednesday, to stay for a week or two. Damn it, no, the corn isn't in, but I'm sick of it! One Sat. I'll come to Quorn, shall I? What is the name of your school – and where is it? I'll come to look for you on Thursday – at 4.30 eh? My aunt's address is 20 Dulverton Rd – somewhere near the Foss.[6] Is it a hundred miles from you? We'll have a few trips round town – hurray! I am biking in on Wednesday. On the way I hope

[1] The reference is to the novel (Paris, 1825) by François Xavier de Maistre (1763–1852), in *Œuvres Complètes* (Paris, 1939), pp. 326–7.

[2] Zechariah vii. 1.

[3] On his twenty-third birthday, 11 September 1908.

[4] i.e. muscular, after 'strong-man' Eugen Sandow (1867–1925).

[5] Herbert H. Mott (b. 1864) had been on the staff of St Mary's School for sixteen years.

[6] The Foss Way, originally one of the great Roman military roads.

to be able to have the model for my teeth taken. Alas, the poor hiatus in my upper jaw!

Do you want me to bring you any book or anything? I shall expect at least a card from you before Wed.

A jeudi, donc DHL

63. To Mabel Limb, [21 September 1908]

Text: MS Clarke; PC v. Municipal Buildings, Leicester; Postmark, Leicester SP 21 08; Unpublished.

[20 Dulverton Road, Leicester]
[21 September 1908]

Here am I in Leciester. You in old Eastwood, are you still getting fatter. I hope so.

My friends here are books – nothing but books, except I go out with my Aunt. Uncle[1] is always working away at his Arabic, and I sit reading French, wishing I could tackle Spanish and Italian, of which there are such a lot of delightful books here.

This is a pretty house – so still, so deeply carpeted. It is too quiet for me – I wish I could hear you speak across the miles to me. DHL

64. To Louie Burrows, [25 September 1908]

Text: MS UN; PC v. Stockport, Vernon Park; Postmark, Manchester SEP 25 08; Boulton 18.

[25 September 1908]

Unsuccessful here – tomorrow must go to Croydon after another.

I am writing on a Manchester car. Stockport is a dirty ugly place – I'm rather glad I've not got it. Hope I get Croydon.[2] DHL

[1] Fritz Johann Heinrich Krenkow (1872–1953). b. Schönberg, Mecklenburg. Came to England 1894; naturalised 1911. Associated with hosiery firm in Leicester from 1899, and later in Beckenham. For many years a part-time scholar, from 1921 Krenkow fully devoted himself to the study of Arabic poetry and to lexicographical scholarship. 1929 honorary doctorate from University of Leipzig. 1929–30 Professor of Islamic studies, Muslim University, Aligarh; 1931–5 Professor of Arabic Language and Literature, University of Bonn. Retired to Cambridge. m. (1) Ada Rose Beardsall (2) Ann Savidge. (For obituary see *Der Islam*, 31 (1954), 228–36.)

[2] DHL was probably interviewed for the post at Croydon on 28 September 1908, having stayed with Alfred Inwood (see p. 52 n. 4). (His application, 16 September 1908, names his referees as Professor Amos Henderson, George Holderness and Rev. Robert Reid.)

65. To Louie Burrows, [6 October 1908]

Text: MS UN; PC v. Sunflowers; Postmark, Eastwood OC 6 08; Boulton 18.

[97 Lynn Croft, Eastwood]
[6 October 1908]

Dear Louie,

You see I am now at home. I had a pleasant ride on Sat. evening, and another yesterday. My bike behaved like a gentleman, and the paints did not rattle off, and the flowers did not die. I spent all Sunday painting those nasturtiums;[1] they look rather pretty; ask Auntie to show you the thing when you call for the paints. I don't suppose it matters when you go, but I would just drop my aunt a card if I were you. She will be glad to see you again, I know, for she was quite taken. I have not yet heard from Croydon, but expect a letter tomorrow. Bristowe[2] has just written to say he can find me employment very shortly, but I have written and refused, with thanks. No more Notts. C[ounty] C[ouncil] for me. I wish Saturday were coming over again. Regards to all. Adieu. DHL

Je vous enverrai une lettre et votre conte en deux ou trois jours.[3]

DHL

66. To Louie Burrows, 7 October 1908

Text: MS UN; Postmark, Eastwood OC 7 08; Boulton 19–20.

Lynn Croft, Eastwood, Notts.
7 Oct. 1908

Liebeste Ludwigin,[4]

I have read your tale; it is very jolly; I'm sure it will take if you write it out again once or twice.[5] The great thing to do in a short story is to select the salient details – a few striking details to make a sudden swift impression. Try to use words vivid and emotion-quickening; give as little explanation as possible (e.g. – the facts about the keepers being in certain parts of the wood at certain times); make some parts swifter, (e.g. – the girl's adventure in the night – that is not a rush enough); avoid bits of romantic sentimentality like Crewsaders and too much Wishing Well; select some young fellow of

[1] Most likely a reference to the oil-painting, 'Nasturtiums' (*Paintings of D. H. Lawrence*, ed. M. Levy, 1964, monochrome reproductions plate 1). *Paintings* dates it c. 1903; that it should be dated 1908 is strongly supported by this reference and by its having been painted on the verso of a photograph of Ada Krenkow who is mentioned in the letter (see *Young Bert: an exhibition of the early years of D. H. Lawrence*, Castle Museum, Nottingham, 1972, pp. 63–4).

[2] Charles John Bristowe (1862–1911), the first Director of Education for Nottinghamshire.

[3] 'I will send you a letter and your story in two or three days.'

[4] 'Dearest Louie' ['Liebste'].

[5] Louie Burrows' story has not survived.

your acquaintance as a type for your lover, and think what he probably would do – Bonnie and the girl are good, but the young keeper is not well defined; be *very careful* of slang; a little is as much as most folks can stand. Send it me again when you have re-written it; I am interested.

I have to begin work at Croydon on Monday;[1] I go down on Sunday. My school is the Davidson Rd; my salary £95. That's all I know.

In certif[icate] – I called in Coll. and Pa[2] seized me and took me upstairs – I have distinction in French, Botany, Maths. and Hist. and Geog:[3] Never anything in English – is it not a joke? I could not see anything but Education against your name, but only had a slight glance at the list. I don't know any results besides mine – Miss Domleo has French and English[4] – I did not see anyone with four – but my glance at the list as Pa turned it over was most cursory.

Soon I shall be far away in Croydon; alas, unhappy fate which sends me from the few people with whom my heart would wish to stay. But Christmas! – that is the magic word I conjure with.

I am immensely busy rushing round to see everybody. Oh the lamentations heard abroad!

I've bought one of those round cloth hats, and look so comical therein. I would like to see you laugh at me. Oh, I must close.

Adieu; adieu – one kiss? DHL

Am coming into Nottm on Saturday – must be at the Dentist at 4.0. Shall I see you – where? I shall bike – if fine. DHL

67. To Blanche Jennings, 9 October 1908

Text: MS ULiv; Moore 28–30.

Lynn Croft, Eastwood, Notts.
9th Oct. 1908.

I am having a dreadful time bidding folk good-bye. My heart is 'serré' – I shall soon have nothing inside my chest but the spent fragments of my organ of affection. Seven girls are coming to tea today to weep a farewell tear into our best saucers with fragile fleeting poppies on them; seven other

[1] The School Log at Davidson Road confirms that DHL took up his post on 12 October 1908.

[2] Professor Amos Henderson.

[3] Despite Jessie Chambers' claim (E.T 82) that DHL achieved a distinction in Education, he correctly recorded his distinctions in four papers (History and Geography jointly forming one examination). See *List of Training College Students who completed their period of training on 31st July 1908* (HMSO 1909), p. 41.

[4] DHL reported Louie Burrows' and Mary Domleo's results accurately. Mary B. Domleo, a prize-winner at the end of her first training year, obtained a First Class Teacher's Certificate (with DHL and Louie Burrows) in 1908 (see *List of Training College Students*, p. 113).

girls will be left weeping at home, into their everyday saucers of white stone. Mon Dieu, this atmosphere of tears and separation is painful – 'God send Sunday', as the world says. I have a job at Croydon; I must begin work on Monday; I leave home on Sunday morning.

Since writing you I have been to Stockport and Manchester, vile, hateful, immense, tangled, filthy places both, seething with strangers; I have also spent a week in London, pompous, magnificent capital of commercialdom, a place of stately individualistic ideas, with nothing Gothic or aspiring or spiritual. The arches there are round and complete; the domes high for the magnification of the voices below; the pillared temples are banks and business houses. I felt remarkably at home in London, remarkably cheerful and delighted; it is so frankly mundane, that one is never tortured. Verily, London is restful, as quiescent as a dinner with J.P.'s. It is Lincoln and Ely that are still, and set the soul a-quivering. Silence is strange and mystical and wearying; a row is a calm to the soul; it is the noble, the divine, the Gothic that agitates and worries one – round-arched magnificent temples built by the swelling intelligence of Men are gratifying and comforting. Also the people in London do not feel so strange; they are folk who have come down the four winds of Heaven to this center of convergence of the Universe; people in Manchester and Stockport and the awful undignified provincial towns are like races of insects running over some food body; one naturally gravitates to London; one naturally flees from the cotton centres.

I am appointed assistant master in the Davidson Rd schools, Croydon – or South Norwood, I hardly know which. My standard – IV; my salary £95. Croydon is a clean, decent, and I think healthy place. It is enough.

Pray do not trouble about that paper on Art; I did not want *it*, I wanted your acknowledgment. I'm glad you like it – I had much rather you found it to your taste than that your friend 'J' should. She is a Ruskinite; well, *all* Ruskinites are not fools. Does she herself 'make haste to see that none are in need of employment, food, or raiment', or does she spend the bulk of her time – her leisure – in reading appreciated novels and serious if not profound discourses on all manner of irrelevant subjects; in listening to lectures on Pre-Raphaelitism and the Ideal Home; in attending concerts and Shaw-plays? I wrote the paper for her, not for the Bottom Dog; but because I would ask her to make up her mind to turn her nose from the slum-stink, she is offended on behalf of poor, hungry, stinking humanity; as a matter of fact the sniffs she takes are few and cautious; then, with the memory of a bad odor in her nostrils, or the report of a bad odor in her ears, she holds her head high and waxes indignant; feels virtuous on the strength of that same 'righteous indignation'. What devil was it that decreed that above all things men (and women supremely) must to themselves seem superbly virtuous? The deep damnation of self-righteousness sticks tight to every creed, to every 'ism' and every 'ite'; but it lies thick all over the Ruskinite, like painted feathers on a skinny peacock.

As for the paper, keep it as long as you like, give it to whom you like, and do you think I could do anything with it? Where could I send short stories such as I write? not to any magazine I know of – can you advise me. I will take to writing frivolously and whimsically if I can – if I could but write as I behave! There, I've had twenty years experience in dishing up my strong flavoured feelings in a nice smooth milk sauce with a sprinkle of nutmeg or cinnamon; but I've only had a few months of experience in making melted butter to be served with my writing.

I'm glad you're living in 'opulent idleness'. I've had three weeks of it[1] (no, mine was bourgeois idleness, that only keeps two maids) and I find it exceedingly suitable to me.

Concerning Daisy Lord, I am entirely in accord with you.[2] If I had my way, I would build a lethal chamber as big as the Crystal Palace, with a military band playing softly, and a Cinematograph working brightly; then I'd go out in the back streets and main streets and bring them in, all the sick, the halt, and the maimed;[3] I would lead them gently,[4] and they would smile me a weary thanks; and the band would softly bubble out the 'Hallelujah Chorus'.

I have no more time. I will send you my new address. Write to me from Hunst[anto]n, if you have time. At least I need not bid you goodbye. What damnable fate puts the length of England forever between us? Do not talk about the 'sere and yellow';[5] you sound nervous. There are the roses of sixteen blooming in your vivid phraseology. Besides, who cares about growing old! Moonlight is as beautiful as sunlight, and night-flowers have more sweetness if less hot colour than poppies and marigolds.

So no more 'old maid' business; you're quite as young as I am. In some things I'm grey old.

À l'Eternité, donc DHL

What are your names 'B.M.R.'?

Whats the M.R.? Mary Rose? It sounds Rossettian.

[1] With the Krenkow family at Leicester.

[2] Daisy Lord was sentenced to death in July 1908 for the murder of her illegitimate child; on 15 August the death-sentence was commuted to life imprisonment; on 14 September a protest meeting – largely organised by women suffragists – tried (unsuccessfully) to obtain her release.

[3] Luke xiv. 21 [A.V.: 'the poor and the maimed, and the halt'].

[4] Isaiah xl. 11 ['shall gently lead...'].

[5] A cliché deriving from *Macbeth* v. iii. 26.

68. To Jessie Chambers, [12? October 1908]

Text: E.T. 151.

[12 Colworth Road, Addiscombe, Croydon]
[12? October 1908]

['On his second day in Croydon Lawrence sent me [Jessie] a letter that gave me a shock. It was like a howl of terror. People were kind, he said, but everything was strange, and how could he live away from us all? He dreaded morning and school with the anguish of a sick girl. Finally he said he felt afraid for himself; cut off from us all he would grow into something black and ugly, like some loathsome bird...In a postscript he told me not to say anything of this to his mother, he had written to her that everything was all right and he was getting on well.']

69. To Mabel Limb, [15 October 1908]

Text: MS Clarke; PC; Postmark, Croydon OC 15 08; Moore 31.

12 Colworth Rd, Addiscombe, Croydon.
Thursday evening

My dear Mabel,

Here am I a stranger in a strange land.[1] Croydon is a big rambling place, not very interesting, but clean and open. I have the best of digs with exceedingly nice people[2] in a smart, quiet quarter. The schools are big, new, and finely appointed, but teaching is wearisome here, there is so much red tape, and so little discipline. I shall like it better with use, though. I have not yet got over the strangeness. Already I am introduced to some very nice people – but times goes slowly, slowly towards Christmas and home again.

I find I can go to London by motor-bus for fourpence. I am not so far from the Crystal Palace – I can see it from the school playground. So I could get up to see Mr. Hill at Hornsey fairly cheaply, I guess.[3] Will you send me his address, for I've forgotten it? This place suits me, but it makes me so heavy and sleepy. Be well – I want to see you plump at Christmas.

Regards to all and love from DHL

[1] Exodus ii. 22 (A.V.).

[2] John William Jones (1868–1956), Superintendent School Attendance Officer in Croydon; formerly with the Manchester (1891–1903) and Cumberland (1903–7) School Boards. He served in Croydon, 1 February 1907 – March 1936. His wife, Marie Jones née Blaylock (1869–1950), was formerly a teacher.

[3] George W. Hill, a clerk in the Barber, Walker & Co. Head Office at Nethergreen, Eastwood, until c. 1903; then became head of the firm's London sales office. Later he joined the coal factors, Brentnall & Cleland, Brentford. (For a photograph of Hill see G. C. H. Whitelock, *250 Years in Coal* (n.d.), p. 48.)

70. To Gertrude Cooper, [17 October 1908]

Text: MS Clarke; PC v. Cheapside; Postmark, London OCT 17 08; Unpublished.

12 Colworth Rd, Addiscombe, Croydon.
[17 October 1908]

Dear Gert,

Here I stand with all London rumbling round me, thinking of you. I wish you could see the shops and the folks here – do, my dear, come down for a day with Fran[ces], you would enjoy it. Is the world very still without me? do your Brussels grow well? DHL

71. To Louie Burrows, 23 October 1908

Text: MS UN; Boulton 20–1.

12 Colworth Rd, Addiscombe, Croydon
23 Oct. 1908

Dear Louisa,

I cry peccavi to your unuttered reproach. The fact of the matter is I'm sick to death of telling the same thing to different folk. I've spent 4/- in stamps since I've been here, and written an unholy host of letters. It is so amusing – they all sound breathless – my letters, I mean.

Here goes. I have excellent digs. Mrs Jones was a schoolmistress in Manchester – Jones is superintendent of school attendance officers here. They are both delightful people – he has rather a lot of his own sayings which he considers savoury, and which he must repeat to me – otherwise –. But I like his missis best. Then there is Winnie, a jolly quaint little maiden of five – she is 'infatuated with me', Mr Jones says, manipulating the syllables of the big word cautiously; then there is a baby which is sometimes good.[1] But I'm ever so much at home here – I am really lucky. I have a room to myself – when Win. or her Dad are not in – and good and copious (save the word) food for 18/- per wk. Digs are not half bad.

School – a great big new red-brick imposing handsome place, with a fair amount of open space – looking across in front over great stacks of timber, over two railways to Norwood where the musichall folk live in big houses among the trees, and to Sydenham, where the round blue curves of the Crystal Palace swell out into view on fairly clear days. Inside all is up to date, solid and good. Class rooms open off a big hall – like Gladstone Street[2] –

[1] The two children were Winifred (1903–) and Hilda Mary (1908–).

[2] An Ilkeston school very close to the Pupil-Teacher Centre; probably used for teaching practice.

but classrooms here on one side only. There is plenty of accommodation – floors are block wood – thirty dual desks for forty five boys – all very nice. But the head is a weak kneed windy fool[1] – he shifts every grain of responsibility off his own shoulders – he will not punish anybody; yourself, when you punish, you must send for the regulation cane and enter the minutest details of the punishment in the Pun. book – if you do. Discipline is consequently very slack and teaching is a struggle; but it's not so bad – we shall soon be comfy. At any rate one is not killed by work. I have St[andar]d IV – 45 lads – there is much pretence of high flown work – not much done.

I am rapidly getting over my loneliness and despair; soon I'll settle down and be quite happy here. But there don't seem to be many nice folk here. They are all glib, but not frank; polite, but not warm. Lord, Lord, – I went to a literary society conversazione and nearly discovered the North Pole – such poor fools.[2]

I am making a vain attempt to study – I never get anything done. Somehow I cannot bring my nose down to a good swot. I feel the lack of somebody to be lively with – somebody to swear at and fall out with and enjoy. Pray translate yourself here. Your letter was 'killing'. I shall preserve it.

Au revoir – soyez sage. DHL

72. To Mabel Limb, [24 October 1908]

Text: MS Clarke; PC v. The Pond Garden, Hampton Court Palace; Postmark, London 24 OC 08; Unpublished.

12 Colworth Rd, Addiscombe, Croydon.
[24 October 1908]

Dear Mab,

I have sent you one card – have I not. I do not want you to forget me. Will you send me George Hill's address, please?

I have been to Hampton Court today – it is a most lovely place. I should just like to take you there. Now I am in London, writing in cousin Nellie's[3] room. Do you remember her – she stayed with us you know in Walker St.?

[1] Philip Frank Turner-Smith (1866–1961), formerly headmaster of Dering Place School, South Croydon (see Helen Corke, *In Our Infancy*, Cambridge 1975, p. 133), had become head of Davidson Road School in November 1907. In April 1913 he transferred as head to Norbury Manor School and remained till retirement in 1927. (In March 1927 DHL sent a message for the reception given in Smith's honour.)

[2] Possibly a meeting of the English Association (Nehls, i. 88).

[3] Ellen Inwood (1876–1961), daughter of Alfred John Inwood (1846–1907) and DHL's maternal aunt, Emma née Beardsall (1849–1907). She made men's silk ties and cravats.

Do write me a little letter, there's a dear. I am very well, and am getting quite jolly. DHL

Love to Mama and Emmie[1] – one kiss. x.

73. To Blanche Jennings, 26 October 1908

Text: MS ULiv; cited in Allott 64–5.

12 Colworth Rd., Addiscombe, Croydon.
26 Oct. 1908.

Dear Miss Jennings,

You will not be cross with me if I write you childishly. I am very tired, and have a little head ache. School is a conflict – mean and miserable – and I hate conflicts. I was never born to command; I do not want to command. So the lads and I have a fight, and I have a fight with my nature, and I am always vanquished. I have been setting my foot down – nothing in the world is so hard for[2] me as to be firm, hard, stern. I can be cruel, but not stern. So I struggle with my nature and with my class, till I feel all frayed into rags. Think of a quivering grey hound set to mind a herd of pigs and you see me teaching; forgive the flattering comparison. I suppose it will put grit into me, but it is painful. There, I won't lament any more. I think I ought to be an elegiac poet: for ever singing my own elegy. I wonder that my specs. are not moist with tears (Mr. Dax has saddled my nose, willy-nilly).

I am wondering whether you will encourage me. I ought to continue to study for a degree, but I do not want to study – I shall have to make quite a shattering effort to do it. So I have pretty well decided to give up study; and to comfort my poor soap-bubble of a soul with writing. Everybody says study; I say I won't. Do aid and abet me! I dread your giving me more maternal advice – in this vein: 'get on – take your degree – then you can hope to leave the elementary teaching that you hate. Writing is only putting more wind into your soap-bubble of a soul – to burst it.' I want to have another whack at Laetitia, to take the sentimentality out of her. I long to be a dear little God, and evolve her soul, or metempsychose it. I want to have my own way somewhere; I want some little space where I may enjoy the iridescence of the soap-bubble. Now do you play the noble heroine of romance, and send me forth into the mythical fields of literature wearing your badge. Be a sweet Una to me, and I will be Ye Redcrosse Knight, sallying forth to slay the foul brood of Errour, and to overcome Sans Joy.[3]

[1] Emmeline and Mabel (the addressee) were daughters of William T. Limb (1858–1928). Emmeline was a close friend of Ada Lawrence and bridesmaid at her wedding in 1913.

[2] hard for] hard as

[3] Cf. p. 74 n. 2.

All this is a prelude to my request that you will send me here part of Laetitia. Send me a bit of the dear girl, and after a while the other bit. She is a lump to send all at once, bless her! We will count up the stamps when she has come home to me, when I can put her sweet limbs together again, and mend her as Isis mended the scattered fragments of the beautiful Truth, whom the bull-god had trampled and torn in the open wastes of the desert world. Hooray, there's a bit of wild Egyptology![1] Soon I shall have pulled out my ears as long as a donkeys, with mad metaphors; like the ears of the Inca weighted with ornament.

Give me some sound advice concerning Laetitia, the joyful one. Shall she spread her soul over the same sort of paper – would you get another kind? Shall I make her longer or shorter, fatter or frailer, a Burne-Jonesian or a Moore?[2] I will certainly squash the sticky juice of sentimentality out of her. But advise me again there's a dear soul.

You will be home by now – and in harness. I would rather drudge than fight, any day. In drudgery, one's own self is quiet, resting, preparing to come to fruition; but a struggle is a storm, a wild east wind. Most fighting is ignoble – drudgery need not be; it is no more than a sort of workhouse dress, not necessarily degrading.

Here I have found no-one with whom I shall grow intimate. I do not care. My landlady is a splendid woman – my landlord is affable and plays chess worse than I do – What more can I want? Do you know, I regret rather keenly that I cannot see you and hear you. The loss is mine. I go easily onto paper – there is quite a lot of *me* in a letter; in return I get – no, not from you, oh no – a bundle of news. I hate letters that one might entitle 'News of the Month – the Slowcombe Advertiser'. I should like you for a companion – you would suit me. Damn my Fate!

I will dry up. I will mark forty five pieces of execrable composition on the Battle of Crècy. My cry is 'Eloi, Eloi, lama Sabachthani?'[3]

You were a good soul to write me so promptly before. You were a good soul to play the noble Roman matron, or the Spartan mother. I regret that I cannot respond, and be the spartan boy; I *will* cry when the fox gnaws my bowels; and I will choose you, my Spartan mother, to weep to. I have to smile when I write to Eastwood – to you I'll only grin occasionally through my grimaces.

[1] Annotations in DHL's copy of Palgrave's *Golden Treasury* (1896 reprint, p. 62), to Milton's 'Ode on Christ's Nativity' confirm his interest in 'Animal gods of Egypt'.

[2] Sir Edward Burne-Jones (1833–98), and Albert Moore (1841–93), Pre-Raphaelite painters. (The 'longer' and 'frailer' features belong to women in Burne-Jones's paintings.)

[3] Mark xv. 34 quoting Psalms xxii. 1 ('My God, my God, why hast thou forsaken me?').

Hurray – one thing I can do – I can juggle with words: get a white rabbit out of a silk hat, or a turtle dove out of a black saucepan – into which I had only rattled peas. Hurray – I like having a bit of fun with words.

Write to me soon if you are not busy. Don't be a Spartan mother, or I shall laugh – which will be worse than my tears.

Farewell – I should love to talk to you. I daren't say 'Au revoir'.

Farewell DHL

74. To Jessie Chambers, [November ? 1908]

Text: E.T. 88.

[12 Colworth Road, Addiscombe, Croydon]
[November ? 1908][1]

You are so just. I guess you never punish the wrong kid. As for me, I put up with them until I can stand them no longer, then I land the nearest, and as likely as not, he's innocent.

75. To Jessie Chambers, [November ? 1908]

Text: E.T. 151.

[12 Colworth Road, Addiscombe, Croydon]
[November ? 1908][2]

[Lawrence 'began to explore London, and to write about the lights that flowered when darkness came'.]

76. To Blanche Jennings, 4 November 1908

Text: MS ULiv; Moore 33–5.

12 Colworth Rd., Addiscombe, Croydon
4th Nov 1908

My dear Bee,

I'll call you Bee, as Mrs Dax does – not a busy bee – not quite a burly bumble bee – one of those smaller, lighter little summer bees that hum about so much and roll in the sunshine – and make no store. May I? Thanks!

I have received 'Laetitia'. I feel a frightful fool when I look at the great parcel. I regret very much the trouble I have given you; I have been a poor beardless fool – I would not deny being so still. I began to read – it is poor

1 Presumably from Croydon after DHL had some experience of full-time teaching.

2 Jessie Chambers places this letter after the early 'phase of acute homesickness' and before Christmas 1908 (E.T. 151).

stuff, with just a taste here and there of palatable matter. Mrs Dax told me her opinion – she is wrong – she is no judge of style – she likes style as she likes *not* people – well-bred, accurate, carefully attired – she dresses herself in grey costumes – she is like the whole world, she likes things 'superior'.

I do not know James Lane Allen[1] – am dying to make his acquaintance. Surely, surely you are Brontë bitten in your taste in heroes; you cannot have got over the 'Rochester–Moore' stage[2] (I presume you are well acquainted with *Shirley* and *Jane Eyre*, two of my favourite English books). Strong stern men bore and irritate me; their strength lies in their insusceptibility to half the influences that deflect mortality. I never admire the *strength* of mountains and fixed rocks; but the strength of the sea that leaps and foams frantically and slips back in a tame underwash; strength that laughs and winks, that mocks, and mocks; and broods awhile, and is sullen – I am fascinated by that sort. Adam Bede was strong enough – with a bull's strength. The little cripple in *Mill on the Floss* was strong[3] – but a woman despised his frailty. Pah – I hate women's heroes. At the bottom women love the brute in man best, like a great shire stallion makes one's heart beat.

I am sorry you have an 'irritable temper'; it means you have a nervous temperament of fine susceptibility with no felt pad of health and humour and contempt to keep the chords from vibrating – health for a pad, and humour or contempt to apply it – by turns. I have an irritable temper, but it's generally cushioned down – except when I'm not well, or when I'm screwed up to a new pitch – as I am here. I am becoming now accustomed to my new pitch.

I have decided to crucify my body – and with it my hopes for financial success. I believe if I cared to talk education from behind the fence of an Arts degree I could soon get a soft job – well paid; but I can't do what I don't want to do. I shall try writing again; I don't believe I shall ever do much at it. My nature is versatile and volatile. At present I am painting for dear life, and enjoying myself immensely. I have just finished my third landscape[4] – I began the first ten days ago. At this moment my fingers are

[1] James Lane Allen (1849–1925), American author. (For bibliography see Grant C. Knight, *James Lane Allen and the Genteel Tradition*, 1935.)

[2] Rochester in Charlotte Brontë's *Jane Eyre* (1847) and Robert Gérard Moore in her *Shirley* (1849). (On DHL's 'fascination' with *Jane Eyre*, see E.T. 98.)

[3] Philip Wakem in George Eliot's novel (1860). Cf. E.T. 97–8: 'Lawrence adored *The Mill on the Floss*, but always declared that George Eliot had "gone and spoilt it half way through". He could not forgive the marriage of the vital Maggie Tulliver to the cripple Philip.'

[4] DHL gave three landscapes to the Jones family: they may be those referred to here. One is a copy of *A Harvest Scene – an Outdoor Sketch* by Peter de Wint (1784–1849) which DHL probably saw in *English Water-Colour*, ed. Charles Holme, Pt. 3 (cf. p. 196 n. 5). The second seems to be indebted to the work of the Norwich School, perhaps Henry Bright (1814–73);

greasy with oil paint (my sketches are water), for I have rushed round to the other side of the table and snatched the brush from my landlord's hand to prevent his further corrupting an old daub of his, his only child of his creative mind. He is an inflated frog, but a very decent chap.

Don't regret that you cannot 'lay bare bits of your soul'. I sometimes feel as if I'd stood like a naked slave in the market, under the glances of a crowd of fools safely swathed in stupidity. Ho! Ho! – I beg your pardon – I don't mean it.

School is better. I can teach better when I know my lads individually. It is one of my weaknesses that I cannot work on averages and 'in totos'. I can't teach the average lad, because I cannot find him, so I gradually slog away at fifty creatures varying from youthful seraphim through all the tribes of things winged and footed, to the condemned, hated, useless housefly. But I should love to laugh with my boys, to play with them, and be a bit naturally riotous with them. They recognise this; when I am giving them a history lesson they are enforcing it by pretending to shoot arrows at me, drawing back the bow with vigour, and looking at me with brown bright eyes. I rebuke them sternly, but my heart is laughing. Oh my discipline! – My old boys liked me nearly as much as I loved them.

I have ordered *Eugénie Grandet* – of Balzac, – for you, in memory of Laetitia. It is one of the finest novels out of the heart of a man. You will forgive the poor 'Everyman' edition;[1] I know no other. The poor wretches here did not stock it – I shall not get it till Saturday. Tell me if you don't want it, and I'll get another.

I feel that frequent interruptions are making me stupid. Winnie insists on my going upstairs to see Guy Fawkes martyred in the next garden[2] – robed in an ancient 'best blouse'. Just drop me a card if you don't want *Eugénie* – she's paid for, but we can swop. Forgive me if I'm a crude ass.

I wish you were here. Again the eternal farewell. Yrs DHL

the third may owe something to John Linnell (1792–1882). (DHL's interest in 'English water-colour artists, from Paul Sandby and Peter de Wint and Girtin' is made clear in his essay 'Making Pictures', 1929, *Phoenix II*, p. 605.)

1 Trans. Ellen Marriage, preface by George Saintsbury (1907).

2 If this occurred on 'Guy Fawkes Day', 5 November, the letter was presumably written over two days.

77. To Frances Cooper, [7 November 1908]

Text: MS Clarke; PC v. Horton Lane, Epsom; Postmark, Epsom NO 7 08; Unpublished.

[7 November 1908]

Dear Fran,

Here is a charming little place for you, and a lovely county. It is ideal for biking. Thanks very much for your letter – you'll forgive me for not replying. I have heard nothing from G[ertie] and Mabel.

Best love DHL

78. To Louie Burrows, [7 November 1908]

Text: MS UN; PC v. Mickleham Church; Postmark, Dorking NO 7 08; Boulton 21–2.

[7 November 1908]

Dear Lou,

Now I've seen sweeter country than Quorn and Woodhouse. Down here it is wonderful. The masses of gorgeous foliage, the sharp hills whose scarps are blazing with Autumn, the round valleys where the vivid dregs of Summer have collected – they have almost intoxicated me. Your letter was exceedingly interesting. I'm sure Mr Smith is quite a ravishing person.[1] Come, come, Louise! DHL

I've come thro Epsom to Dorking – am going on to Reigate.

79. To Gertrude Cooper, [7 November 1908]

Text: MS Clarke; PC v. Dorking – Tillingbourne Waterfall; Postmark, Dorking NO 7 08; Unpublished.

[7 November 1908]

Ah, this is a lovely place – and you should see the rich folk riding horseback through the lanes, and the young girls trotting on their cobs. It is very beautiful all through the county – clean and glorious. Dont forget me.

DHL

80. To May Holbrook, [7 November 1908]

Text: MS UN; PC v. Dorking, Glory Woods; Postmark, Dorking NO 7 08; Nehls, iii. 611–12.

[7 November 1908]

Forgive me for not sending you sooner – I thought you would have the Haggs news. I should love you to be here to ride with me through Surrey – it is

[1] Not identified.

a most sweet and lovely county. The roads are perfect – and the masses of gorgeous foliage almost dazzle one. It is exceedingly beautiful. Let me have a line from you some time, will you. My address 12 Colworth Rd, Addiscombe, Croydon. I think of you often – and Will.[1] Yrs DHL

81. To Mabel Limb, [7 November 1908]

Text: MS Clarke; PC v. Suspension Bridge. Reigate; Postmark, Reigate 7 NO 08; Unpublished.

[7 November 1908]

Dearest Mab,

Have I ever thanked you for your letter – if not I do so now – heartily. Mr Hill has asked me to go and see him. I shall go soon.

Today I've ridden through Epsom and Dorking to this place. It is very beautiful – something like Derbyshire but Surrey is a softer, sweeter county.

Love to all. DHL

82. To Blanche Jennings, 11 November 1908

Text: MS ULiv; cited in Allott 65, 74.

12 Colworth Rd, Addiscombe, Croydon
11 Nov. 1908.

My dear Bee

Those people down in Croydon have at last delivered poor *Eugénie* to me. Since you have not stated your disinclination to receive her, I conclude you are as yet unacquainted with her. She is exceedingly beautiful. I consider the book as perfect a novel as I have ever read. It is wonderfully concentrated; there is nothing superfluous, nothing out of place. The book has that wonderful feeling of inevitableness which is characteristic of the best French novels. It is rather astonishing that we, the cold English, should have to go to the flashy French for level-headed, fair, unrelenting realism. Can you find a grain of sentimentality in *Eugénie*? Can you find a touch of melodrama, or caricature, or flippancy? It is all in tremendous earnestness, more serious than all the profundities of German thinkers, more affecting than all English bathos. It makes me drop my head and sit silent. Balzac can lay bare the living body of the great Life better than anybody in the world. He doesn't hesitate at the last covering; he doesn't point out the absurdities of the intricate innumerable wrappings and accessories of the body of Life; he goes straight to the flesh; and, unlike De Maupassant or Zola, he doesn't

[1] May's husband, William Holbrook (b. 1884), a general stoneworker. m. 1 November 1906; he emigrated to Canada, March 1914; May joined him the following year.

inevitably light on a wound, or a festering sore. Balzac is magnificent and supreme; he is not mysterious nor picturesque, so one never sees his portrait.

I have nearly read Laetitia. It bores me mightily in parts. You can none of you find one essence of its failure: it is that I have dragged in conversations to explain matters that two lines of ordinary prose would have accomplished far better; I must cut out many pages of talk, and replace them with a few paragraphs of plain description or narrative; secondly, one is cloyed with metaphoric fancy; thirdly, folk talk about themes too much; – slight incidents – such as the sugar in *Eugénie*[1] – should display character, not fine speeches; fourthly, I don't believe Lettie ever did break her engagement with Leslie – she married him. The construction – changeable and erratic as it is – is defensible; there are some fine, swift bits, e.g. the latter half of the party; there are some strong scenes, e.g. – the churchyard scene with Annable, the motor accident, and, for a moment, Leslie's appeal to Lettie when he comes to her sick; and also the death of the father; there is some rare suggestiveness – the burial of the keeper, the idiot girl 'Christmas'.[2] The 'father' scene is *not* ugly and superfluous. I will defend my construction throughout.

The characters are often weak – the men – George and Leslie especially. Lettie herself is not bad. The rest are undeveloped. What the whole thing needs is that the essential should be differentiated from the non-essential. I will have another go at it this winter. The theme is abominable – I blush for myself.

You will not mind my referring to it again. With a true womanly wit, you fell out with details that didn't matter. Tell me where you differ from me in the above opinions, please – if you are not bored.

Things are going fairly comfortably. School is quite decent; Hell would become palatable with use.

I do not think I have anything to tell you. This is one of my stupid nights. If you have not read *Eugénie Grandet*, I shall consider I have been kind to you even in making you read Laetitia (dont be offended at my language) – (I shall change the name of the thing); who would not travel through such a sloppy valley of afflictions to come so near to the well of Life in *Eugenie*.

I kiss your hand. DHL

P.S. I am a silly little ass.

P.P.S. I'm no worse than most folk.

[1] Balzac, *Eugénie Grandet*, chap. 3.

[2] There is no mention of this character in the MS from which *The White Peacock* was eventually printed. Presumably she disappeared from the story when DHL rewrote the novel soon after arriving in Croydon.

83. To Frances Cooper, [14 November 1908]

Text: MS Clarke; PC v. Hadley High Stone, (site of the Battle of Barnet 1471) near Barnet; Postmark, Barnet NO 14 08; Unpublished.

[14 November 1908]

I thought this might be a little interesting historically. Barnet is a sleepy, small place – one can hardly believe oneself so near to London.

I heartily sympathise with you and Mabel. How do you like green bedsteads. Tell Gert to do it mildly. Love. DHL

84. To Louie Burrows, 16 November 1908

Text: MS UN; Postmark, Croydon NO 16 08; Boulton 22–3.

12 Colworth Rd. Addiscombe, Croydon
16 Nov 1908

My dear Louie,

Your letter – rather your p.c. – somewhat alarms me. Is school so bad that you think of chucking up before you get another job? From my heart, I am sorry. I thought you had got over the most devilish time; I thought you were comparatively comfortable; I thought Mr Smith was a great consolation. Are you knocked up? Why don't you write me a letter? What has put a coldness in your heart 'envers moi'? Can I guess?

I am so sorry the fight of school is too long, too painful for you. My God, it is bitter enough at the best; it is the cruellest and most humiliating sport, this of teaching and trying to tame some fifty or sixty malicious young human animals. I have some days of despair myself – this has been one. We are not allowed to punish, you know, unless we send to the boss' desk for the regulation cane, and enter up full particulars of the punishment in the cane-book. The boss is nice, but very flabby; the kids are rough and insolent as the devil. I had rather endure anything than this continual, petty, debasing struggle. Shortly I shall be good for very little myself. But this is one of my black days: it is not really so bad: not so bad. I shall get on a level some time. Now I am off balance; my life will not go; the machinery of my soul is all deranged by these shocks of conflict. It is not broken – I shall recover soon – I may even be happy.

Write and tell me how you are. Why will you be funny half out of spite – why will you be trivial? Well, well, we must make belief we are whole, but most of us are being ground down under one millstone or another.

Forgive me if I am a wet blanket. You make me feel a bit downy, with your news. Tell me how all the world is – tell me you are better.

DHL

Dont you think my seriousness rather comical – I do?

85. To Louie Burrows, 24 November 1908

Text: MS UN; Postmark, Croydon NO 24 08; Boulton 23–4.

12 Colworth Rd, Addiscombe, Croydon
24 Nov 1908.

My dear Louise,

What desolating little letters for my Louise to write – Louise with her arch insouciance, and sportful frivolity. Never mind, my dear; there is a bladder of indigo hanging over every poor young devil's head, and it must squash sooner or later and paint things a black purple. It'll all wash off again – won't it – this damned indigo? – when you have altered your circumstances. It is a cruel position to put you in, in full fight with all that is barbarous and devilish in youthful mankind on the one hand, and with all that is supercilious, and snobbish, and mean, and fault pecking – inspectors, know yourselves – on the other. I'm glad you're chucking up. I would do it straight away, before I got another school, if I were you. Why should you sell – not yourself, because you keep your suffering – but all the sunshine out of yourself for £75 dirty quid. I feel myself swelling with bad language.

As for me – it only needs that I gird up my loins, and take to arm me for the fight the panoply[1] of a good stinging cane – and me voilà! I am making things hum this week: you can guess what things.

Don't be naughty and reserved with me. You know the wells of my sympathy are really profound – the surface just winks a little bit wickedly. I understand your position now too perfectly to treat your confessions with levity. I swear I am a sweet Father Confessor. But seriously, my dear girl, my blood runs hot when I think of the suffering and indignity you are exposed to for the sake of a dirty pittance. If – if –.

What about your writing? Are you too used up to do any now? It is a shame. As for me I have not much time, and not enough tranquillity of soul. My amusements are painting; (go to Aunties and see the three sketches I have sent her) and playing chess with Mr Jones, and larking with Hilda Mary, our eight month, jolly baby. It comforts me inexpressibly if I am a bit downy (that is not often) – to see her bright hazel eyes laughing into mine, and to feel her fat little hands spreading over my face and trying to grasp it. She is such a jolly little beggar – you should hear her laugh when I dance her round the room, or play hide and seek with her.[2]

I hope you will soon be settled – but don't be desperate – it doesn't really

[1] Charles Wesley's hymn, 'Soldiers of Christ arise', ll. 11–12 ['. . .arm you for. . .'].

[2] Cf. E.T. 157: 'He was very fond of [Hilda Mary] and often spoke about her in letters.' DHL's two 'Baby-Movements' poems, 'Running Barefoot' and 'Trailing Clouds', *English Review*, iii (November 1909), 565, were prompted by this affection.

matter – and don't take anything (I don't mean arsenic – but any job that offers). Your soul is developing its bitter rind of maturity – it must do so, sooner or later, unless you remain forever immature, as most folks do. When you have a good rind you are safe.

Au revoir – soyez encore gai. Yrs DHL

86. To Mabel Limb, [28 November 1908]

Text: MS Clarke; PC v. Picturesque Devon, Bickleigh Vale, Nr Plymouth; Postmark, Croydon NO 28 08; Moore 37.

[12 Colworth Road, Addiscombe, Croydon]
[28 November 1908]

Dearest Mab,

Doesn't this picture remind you of our old days? Ah, my dear, those days were the gems of our lives, were they not.

I hear how much better you are getting, and I rejoice. Myself I am ever so well – this is a fat place. Christmas is almost here. The shops are dressed. Next week I am going up to London to see them there. I am also going up to London tomorrow, to see Cousin Nellie again. Do I not jaunt about now? I shall have such a lot to tell you when I come home, it will be so jolly. Give my love to your Mother and father – I hope your mother is better. Try and keep Emmie good, [I][1] know she's a handful.

With Love DHL xxx.

87. To Jessie Chambers, [December? 1908]

Text: E.T. 119

[12 Colworth Road, Addiscombe, Croydon]
[December? 1908][2]

['Sometimes when he had particularly enjoyed a book he would send it to me [Jessie] with urgent instructions to leave off whatever I might happen to be doing and read it immediately. In this manner he sent me Charles Doughty's *Adam Cast Forth*, and I was especially to note where Eve, after long separation, finds Adam, and he tells her to bind herself to him with the vine strands,[3] lest they be separated again by the Wind of God.'[4]]

[1] MS reads '&'.

[2] Jessie Chambers places this letter after DHL's departure for Croydon and before Spring 1909 (E.T. 119–20).

[3] Doughty, *Adam Cast Forth* (1908), p. 15. It is Adama (Eve) who suggests they bind themselves together.

[4] Jessie Chambers adds: 'Another time, in swift enthusiasm, he sent me Francis Thompson's essay on Shelley; and again there came [Swinburne's] *Atalanta in Calydon*, and my attention was directed to the lyrics of the choruses.'

88. To May Holbrook, 2 December 1908

Text: MS UN; Nehls, iii. 612–13.

12 Colworth Rd, Addiscombe, Croydon.
2 Dec. 1908.

My dear May,

I was surprised and pleased to see your handwriting, once so familiar, now so rarely received. What a quaint, serious girl you are! Do you feel like a chrysalis opening too late, when the Spring and the Summer have passed? Bless me – it is only June with you.

One does seem buried in Eastwood – but the grave is no deeper there than elsewhere. There is a cousin of mine who lives in the heart of London – not far from Picadilly.[1] She is thirty two, and has worked in a sort of warehouse all her life (in a really nice job). She is more unlearned, and less developed than anyone I have ever met, of her years. Towns oftener swamp one than carry one out onto the big ocean of life. Townspeople are indeed glib and noisy, but there is not much at the bottom of them. They are less individual, less self-opinionated and conceited than country people, but less, far less serious. It is with them work, and after work, conscious striving after relaxation. In Eastwood, people work, and then drift into their small pleasures; here they pursue a shallow pleasure, and it leaves no room for a prolific idleness, a fruitful leisure. Do not lament a town so much. Truly, there are meetings, and, better, theatres and concerts. But meetings are places where one develops an abnormal tone, which it takes some time to soften down again, and theatres and concerts have not much staying power. The true heart of the world is a book; there are sufficient among your acquaintances to make a complete world, but you must learn from books how to know them. A book is better than a meeting. The essence of things is stored in books; in meetings and speeches the essence is diluted with hot water and sugar, and may be a dash of fire spirits. Read, my dear, read Balzac and Ibsen and Tolstoi and think about them; don't take offence at them; they were great men, all, and who are we that we should curl our lips. One thing that a townsman does *less* frequently than the countryman – that is to lift his head in the scorn that has never understood. Pardon me for my preaching; you provoke it; you make me feel serious.

Shall I tell you something about school? Oh Davidson Rd is a fine red place – new and splendid! There is a great hall, with wood block floor; dumb-bells and Indian clubs hang round the walls. The class rooms open off one side; large, lofty rooms, with dual desks; everything smooth and bright and neat. I have St[andar]d IV – about 50 boys now. They are queerly mixed.

[1] Ellen Inwood (see p. 84 n. 3).

Six are the orphans of actors and acresses, who live in the Actors home near us.[1] They are delightful boys, refined, manly, and aimiable. The other week we had Beerbohm Tree and Cyril Maude and other big actresses and actors round to see them in school.[2] Then I have eight lads from the Gordon Home; waifs and strays living by charity.[3] They are of insolent, resentful disposition; that is only superficial, owing to training, I think. When they are forced to respect you (by the cane) – they linger round you to do little things for you. Poor devils – they make me jolly mad, but I am sorry for them. I have boys who will leave me at Christmas to go to a fairly expensive Grammar School;[4] and I have lads whose five bare toes peep at me through their remnants of boots as they sit in the desks, boys who cannot drill, because their boots and clothing will not allow of it. We have free meals and free breakfasts now the winter is on. It is rather pitiful to see them gathered in the canteen for dinner – some sixty or seventy boys and girls. The canteen is a mission room, with pictures of the feeding of the ten thousand and Peter smiting the rock.[5] Hélas – not much water runs from the smitten rock of charity. Some of my boys have the thin lips, and the dreadful upwrinkling of nervous brows characteristic of the underfed. Ours is a strange, incoherent school. The boss is a delightful man (a bit of a fathead sometimes, but kind as an angel!) – but he is a weak disciplinarian. The tone of the school is lax, and to establish oneself and to keep ones equilibrium is not easy.

As for my digs – they are fine. We have the jolliest fat baby, eight months old. You cannot tell how fond I am of her; her fine hazel eyes laugh at me so brightly, and her soft fingers wandering over my face and grasping at my cheeks speak to me so cunningly. Then Freddy[6] is a quaint, jolly maiden. I took her up town on Saturday to see the shops; we went into a great draper's where there is a Father Christmas Cave, and bears, and – and paradise all in one nook. The bairnie pays threepence, and the Real Father Christmas gives her a bundle of toys. We did enjoy ourselves, Freddy and I.

1 1908–14 the Actors' Orphanage Fund (now the Actors' Charitable Trust) rented 32–4 Morland Road, Croydon, to accommodate orphans and illegitimate children of actors and actresses. The children attended local schools.

2 The visit occurred on 23 October 1908 (Davidson Road School Log Book). (Sir) Beerbohm Tree (1853–1917), actor-manager; Cyril Maude (1862–1951), actor-manager and, in 1908, President of the Orphanage Fund.

3 From 1903 the Church of England Society for Providing Homes for Waifs and Strays ran a home at 24 Morland Road, Croydon, for 30 boys (cf. Helen Corke, *In Our Infancy*, p. 153). (They figure prominently in DHL's early story, 'A Lesson on a Tortoise'.)

4 Most likely Selhurst Grammar School.

5 Perhaps the feeding of the 5,000 (Matthew xiv. 21) – mentioned at the opening of 'Lessford's Rabbits' (*Phoenix II*, p. 18) – and Moses smiting the rock (Numbers xx. 11).

6 i.e. Winifred Jones.

On Saturday I am going to London to see the great shops. I wish you might come to[o].

My regards to Will and Love to you. DHL

89. To Louie Burrows, [12? December 1908]

Text: MS UN; Boulton 24.

[12? December 1908][1]

Are you going to have your photograph taken this term? I[2] am dubitous[3] whether I shall confer a benefit on mankind by having mine taken and thus transmitting my charms through the ages.

90. To Blanche Jennings, 15 December 1908

Text: MS ULiv; cited in Allott 74–5.

12 Colworth Rd, Addiscombe, Croydon
15 Dec. 1908

My dear Bee,

You will be thinking that your insinuation 'if ever you write to me again' was a prophecy. But surely you did not expect that I should remain forever silent towards you! Don't make foolish, feminine insinuations. I am as constant as the wind – which, as it is sure to blow again, is very trustworthy.

Referring to Balzac. Do sometime, get a few more vols of him from Everyman. Begin with *Old Goriot* – then try the *Asses Skin* – then *Atheists Mass*.[4] But I remember that the Walter Scott people publish a fine collection of Balzac's short stories for 1/-.[5] You must not fall out with the homilies of so old a writer as Balzac. Think of what one is treated to in Scott and Thackeray – and George Eliot by way of padding and moral and reflection, and you'll see that Balzac lets you off cheap. Besides, you are so thoroughly out of sympathy with anything that savours of christianity that a little tenderness towards it alarms you to disgust. Balzac was pretty atheistic – but he was vastly sympathetic – and to be sympathetic is to be rarely antipathetic. You women, when you turn, you are like Lot's wife, pillars of salt, immutable;[6] you can never turn again and look with calm generous eyes

[1] This note was placed at this point among her MSS by Louie Burrows herself. DHL refers in the letter following to his having been photographed.

[2] term? I] term? Why? I

[3] i.e. dubious (dialect).

[4] *Old Goriot* (1907) and *Wild Ass's Skin* (1906), trans. Ellen Marriage; *The Atheist's Mass*, trans. Clara Bell (1907); each volume was introduced by George Saintsbury.

[5] *Balzac: Shorter Stories*, trans. W. Wilson (Walter Scott, 1890).

[6] Genesis xix. 26.

on a thing that has disappointed and disillusioned you. Pray why so much curl of the lip in pronouncing the words 'rather Christian'. I do not believe in a Godhead even – not a Personal God – but the sound of Christianity does not rile me. As for the 'gush' about the kiss[1] – it *was* a crisis in Eugénies life – a most productive crisis. Think – if you kissed a man on the mouth – what it would mean to you. I have kissed dozens of girls – on the cheek – never on the mouth – I could not. Such a touch is the connection between the vigorous flow of two lives. Like a positive electricity, a current of creative life runs through two persons, and they are instinct with the same life force – the same vitality – the same I know not what – when they kiss on the mouth – when they kiss as lovers do. Come to think of it and it is exceedingly rare that two people participate in entirely the same sensation and emotion; but they do when they kiss as lovers, I am sure. Then a certain life-current passes through them which changes them forever; another such effect is produced in a mother by the continual soft touchings of her baby. Somehow, I think we come into knowledge (unconscious) of the most vital parts of the cosmos through touching things. You do not know how I feel my soul enlarged through contact with the soft arms and face and body of my Hilda Mary – who is 9 months old today. I know my phraseology is vague and impossible. But there must be some great purposeful impulses impelling through everything to move it and work it to an end. The world says you feel the press of these impulses, you recognise them, in knowledge – science; but I, joining hands with the artists, declare that also and supremely the sympathy with and submission to the great impulses comes through *feeling* – indescribable – and, I think unknowable. There is something of this idea behind Balzac's homily on the kiss, I think.

As for a book on music – the way to learn about music is to listen to it, and think about it afterwards. The only book I know is Haweis's *Music and Morals* – it is not new – it is not startling – but it is good, I think.[2] Look through a catalogue in one of your big free libraries – in the music section – you'll find something newer there. I love music. I have been to two or three fine orchestral concerts here. At one I heard Grieg's *Peer Gynt* – it is very fascinating, if not profound. Surely you know Wagner's operas – *Tannhäuser* and *Lohengrin*.[3] They will run a knowledge of music into your blood better than any criticisms. We are withering nowadays under the barren warmth

[1] Balzac, *Eugénie Grandet*, chap. 9.

[2] Hugh R. Haweis, *Music and Morals* (1871). An extract from it occurs in the *International Library of Famous Literature*, xviii. 8319–34 (see p. 50 n. 2).

[3] Helen Corke asserts that, in 1909, DHL's 'only experience of Wagner's music had been a performance, in Nottingham theatre, of *Tannhäuser*, when he reacted against the stridency of the Venusberg music' (*DHL Review*, vii (1974), 231–2).

of other people's opinions, and second hand knowledge. It doesn't matter much how little you *know*, so long as you are capable of feeling much, and giving discriminate sympathy. That's why I like you so much – that's why I like women – they are so suggestible – on the whole – and they respond so heartily.

Thank the Lord we break up on the 23rd at noon. I am ready for a holiday. School however, is not bad. I have smitten the Philistines with the rod, and they are subdued.[1]

I have had my photo taken; if you would like one I'll send you one. But if you are like Mrs Dax, and think photos a sentimental folly – I shall be glad to spare you. For heaven's sake don't be polite. Would you rather have a photo or Titterton's poems[2] – you *must* choose.

Goodnight, dear Blanche Mary. DHL

91. To Blanche Jennings, 22 December 1908

Text: MS ULiv; Moore 41–3.

12 Colworth Rd., Addiscombe, Croydon
22 December 08

My dear Blanche,

I am astonished that you have the folly to choose a portrait of me instead of Tittertons unlovely *Love Poems.* Indeed they are not worth lamenting, even if the photo is fit for nothing but the album-cemetery; I do not relish the idea of being a tombstone there.

Anyone would think I were an Erewhonian,[3] or that the photographers were, they make me look so sweet on paper. Indeed I know I am not near so fair as I am pictured – but I am not in my Sunday clothes – and I am not glassy. I strolled into the shop one Saturday morning while waiting for a bus to take me to London – I did not smile, for, somehow, I felt ridiculous. Surprising, is it not?

I am sorry you fell across Haweiss; he does not ill suit me. I have snatched at Ernest Newman;[4] had I thought of him I should have felt happy and content, for then my prestige had been safe. As it is, you are quite sweet in your disquisition on the Composers. Absolute music is not intended to have any relation to ideas, I think. It has no more meaning[5] than the wind

[1] 2 Samuel viii. 1.

[2] William R. Titterton, *Love Poems* (1908).

[3] Alluding to the emphasis given to physical well-being in the imaginary country of Samuel Butler's *Erewhon* (1872).

[4] Ernest Newman (formerly William Roberts) (1868–1959), music critic; wrote *Elgar* (1904), *Richard Strauss* (1904), *Wagner* (1904), *Musical Studies* (1905), etc.

[5] meaning] music

round the house, or the cries of sea gulls over the low surf. Who knows what thought, or meaning, or ideas are behind a larkie's singing – there ain't any; and composers are mostly birds who sing up in the air – unless they're Angeluses, so much to order – by the yard; – and there isn't thought behind music, but the music is behind the thought, music behind the idea, music the first wild natural thing, and thought is the words writ to the music, the narrow rows of words with little meanings. There *is* no *meaning* no verbal, ideational meaning to the *Pastoral Symphony* – or any other. If it's a pastoral symphony, and its a man-bird who writes it, we don't begin 'Here Thyrsis sits a-piping – tra-la-la-' 'Baa-Baa-tra-la-la.' 'The sheep cease to nibble and wag their tails – diddle-dee – For the flowers are unfolding under Phyllis' foot as she comes – diddle diddle dum – die-doooo.' There ain't no meaning, and if there is, there oughtn't to be. All that is sayable, let it be said, and what isn't, you may sing it, or paint it, or act it, or even put it in poetry. I don't care a damn about the technique and technicalities (I mean the second) – of music. Thackeray is very fine, I love him; Scott is a trifle flat nowadays, but it's largely my fault. You don't know how to read 'em. Folks *will* want things intellectually done, so they take refuge in George Eliot. I am very fond of her, but I wish she'd take her specs off, and come down off the public platform. 'I wouldn't mind if they spoke the truth, but they don't.' I take it 'they' refers to christians – and that the reference ends there. My dearest, most veracious, lily white Blanche, who does more 'twisting for the glory of their own pet cults' than the modern theorists. G[eorge] B[ernard] S[haw] is always grinning suavely or satanically through his legs after performing some contortion in honor of his own pet cult. So with the rest of 'em. Believe none of 'em, and all of 'em. There's a vein of truth in 'em all – else they wouldn't be alive – it's a question of more or less. The ghosts of falsity that wait on Christianity are forever surging before your eyes, but those little shades of untruth that attend on GBS and Socialism are hid by red whiskers and exorcised by a trick of giddy words.

I *do* know a fair amount about Life. Life has four dimensions, not two. Probably I know more about the middle and the bottom sea than does many a many-leagued sailor. If I cross the seas in a little boat I never touch the waters; I can but judge them generally. But bathing and paddling in the pools by the shore – see, I know how salt it is, how buoyant, and how it moves. I don't pretend to know how to behave at a big dinner, at a big ball; I am in total ignorance of aristocratic life – save from books; and I cannot tell a 'femme perdue' by the look of her, as most men seem to be able to do. No, I don't know much of *life* – but of Life. – I *do not* poke into peoples souls; peoples souls come flowing round me and

WOODBURY UNIVERSITY LIBRARY
1027 WILSHIRE BOULEVARD
LOS ANGELES, CALIFORNIA 90017

touching me, and I feel them. I *never* consciously poke; – yes, I have done once – only once.

Hilda Mary Jones is a giddy damsel of nine months. She is fat, bonny; she can laugh like a blackbird in a bush; her eyes are the brightest, gayest things I know. She is very fond of me.

As for Eugénies kiss – an unconscious artist often puts the wrong words to the right feeling. So long as the feeling's right, it doesn't matter so much.

I do not see the *Sunday Chron*[*icle*] – I like Hubert.[1] I like you.

Why is not my simile sound? Must I say I am like a particular wind – or that my feeling is sure to set again in a certain direction like the wind – what the devil do you want.

I am sorry your Christmas is spent among the derelict joys of other folk. It's sure not to be nice. I wish it were nicer. See, see, my wishes won't go down my pen; see, I can't sing them; see, I am dumb. DHL

P.S. I did not know I was guilty of a flowery style. And that and 'dash and abandon' are rather antithetical, are they not?

I do not feel particularly dashing – but I don't care many damns about anything. I don't decorate myself much though.

92. To Blanche Jennings, 31 December 1908

Text: MS ULiv; cited in Allott 70.

Lynn Croft, Eastwood
31 Dec. 1908.
(How easily I write the old address!)

Sweet Bee,

Is it my turn to write? It strikes me it is your's. But I like you so much I will give you two pennies for one.

The little red book you sent me delighted me like a glass of wine poured out for me. But the wine was home-made; it was elderberry, turbid, inky, flat, with a rough medicinal flavor suggestive of colds on the chest. 'The Shropshire Lad' is, I presume, a lad.[2] He gives himself out a ploughman; I could conceive him a little independent farmer; but that he really has broad shoulders I will not believe. He is thin, gloomy, I swear; he sits by the fire after a raw day's singling the turnips, and does not doze, and does not talk,

[1] The pseudonym of the journalist responsible for the first two columns on the front page of the *Sunday Chronicle*. He often wrote on topical political issues; Blanche Jennings may have been alluding to his subject-matter on the previous Sunday, 20 December 1908: 'Love and Illusion: The Question whether a man or woman "can truly love twice".'

[2] A. E. Housman, *A Shropshire Lad* (1896).

but reads occasionally Blatchford, or perhaps *Night Thoughts*;[1] he is glum; Death has filched the pride out of his blood, and there is the conceit of death instead in his voice. Do you know anything of A. E. Housman? He is no poet; he can only sing the stale tale of the bankruptcy of life, – in death. I believe he comes of a consumptive family; I believe he himself is consumptive. Bah! To a man, and supremely to a man who works in the wholesome happiness on a[2] farm, Life is the fact, the everything: Death is only the ''To be concluded' at the end of the volume. *A Shropshire Lad* ought not to be bound in red: black and white, or grey, are his colours. Nevertheless, I thank you heartily for the volume. I have now a passion for modern utterances, particularly modern verse; I enjoy minor poetry, no matter how minor; I enjoy feeling that I can do better; I have a wicked delight in smashing things which I think I can make better; besides, I *do* so much want to know, now, the comrades who are shuffling the days in the same game with me. I put out my hands passionately for modern verses, and drama – and, in less degree, novels. Do not think because I rave at Bernard Shaw I don't like him. He is one of those delightful people who give one the exquisite pleasure of falling out with him wholesomely. Same with lots of 'em.

As for Greiffenhagen's *Idyll*,[3] it moves me almost as much as if I were fallen in love myself. Under it's intoxication, I have flirted madly this christmas; I have flirted myself half in love; I have flirted somebody else further, till two solicitous persons have begun to take me to task; it is largely the effect of your *Idyll* that has made me kiss a certain girl till she hid her head in my shoulder; but what a beautiful soft throat, and a round smooth chin, she has; and what bright eyes, looking up! Mon Dieu, I am really half in love! But not with the splendid uninterrupted passion of the *Idyll*. I am too conscious, and vaguely troubled. I think it is a good thing I must go back to Croydon. Where there is no 'abandon' in a love, it is dangerous, I conclude; mother declares the reverse. By the way, in love, or at least in love-making, do you think the woman is always passive, like the girl in the *Idyll* – enjoying the man's demonstration, a wee bit frit[4] – not active? I prefer a little devil – a Carmen – I like not things passive. The girls I have known are mostly so; men always declare them so, and like them so; I do not.

[1] Edward Young, *The Complaint, or Night Thoughts on Life, Death and Immortality* (1742–4).

[2] MS reads 'on of a'.

[3] The first of many references (one as late as 9 July 1916) to the pictorial representation of a passionate embrace, *The Idyll*, by Maurice Greiffenhagen (1862–1931). Blanche Jennings owned a coloured reproduction of the painting; she might have sent DHL her own copy or, more likely, one of many reproductions to be found on Christmas cards, postcards etc. The original, first exhibited in the Royal Academy (1891), might have been seen by Blanche Jennings in the Walker Art Gallery, Liverpool.

[4] i.e. alarmed.

We have had some bubbling fun this Christmas. I wish sincerely you *were* here. But we have had some devilish fun, too. I found a fellow a girl in the midsummer.[1] He is a friend of mine, but he takes his love, as he has taken his life, with such stolid, complacent comfort that I was sick. On Saturday and Sunday we flirted with his girl; she kissed me at the stiles; she ran sliding down the slides with me, and had scarce a look for him. Poor devil, he was as mum as a sulky crow. Oh Lord! But on Monday morning he was at her house before many cocks had crowed, and they kissed and made it up, they kissed, and made it up, not with tears, but with cocoa and bacon – Cocoa and bacon! – And she told me – Mon Dieu!

Did you like my photo? It is not bad. It represents me in gross; it has no subtlety; there is no insight in it; I like it exceedingly; I like myself bluff, rather ordinary, fat, a bit 'manly'.

I love the snow, and the cold, and the slides, and ice, and the dull orange skies. But today, the day has gone no further than the garden wall; the trees have dripped yellowly, and the slush has melted and trickled; the cat, as she walked across the grass, lifted and shook her paws, pettishly shook her feet; the birds are like black rags; the starlings swing on the wire line, and cannot keep balance, and scutter off; they dispute the yard with a blackbird, whose bright orange bill is the gayest thing I've seen today, for even the chaffinches and the bull-finch which have darted out of the mist all day seemed dulled by the weather; blue-tits are absolutely dingily chilly to look at today. I'm glad the gas is lighted.

I am writing in my true Eastwood vein. Here I am a bigger fool than in Croydon. When you see Mrs Dax give her my – my – regards. I am going to see H[enry] R[ichard][2] tonight.

This letter – see, I take it under the mistletoe and there is a kiss for you.

DHL

93. To Jessie Chambers, [1909?]

Text: E.T. 121.

[12 Colworth Road, Addiscombe, Croydon]

[1909?]

I read nothing serious now, only Pushkin, very polished and elegant, and the delicate irony of Anatole France's *Isle des Pinguins.*[3]

[1] Alan Chambers and Alvina Reeve.

[2] Henry Richard Dax.

[3] The French text of *L'Ile des Pingouins* was published in England, November 1908. (It was reviewed by Joseph Conrad in *English Review*, i (December 1908), 188–90; perhaps significantly, Conrad also remarked on France's 'delicate irony'.)

94. To Louie Burrows, 12 January 1909

Text: MS UN; Boulton 25–6.

12 Colworth Rd, Addiscombe, Croydon
12 Jan 1909[1]

My dear Louise,

How is the mistress of the thirty? – how are the thirty? – how is the Kingdom? – who killed the mouse? – was it killed, or merely frightened to death by the shrieks? – or did you get a little boy to do the deed? – do your subjects tremble at the sway of your sceptre? – are you a grand personage in Ratcliffe[2] (it should be Mousecliffe)? – do you prepare your biceps in preparation for the irate mothers? – do you sneak down the byways, avoiding the highways? – does your landlady[3] think you will stand more fattening, or has she decided to reduce your flesh by regulated diet? – do you love the parson? – or is he a curate? – is there anything or anyone to relieve the deadly monotony? – except the thirty? – and the mouse? – and the occasional inspector? do you want any instructions regarding your work in school? – such as how to model mice in clay and cardboard? – or make petticoats – if so, you know where to apply. I do not know the Mistress of Mousehole cum Squeake – how shall I address this majesty? Princesses and Persons of Authority must be rather lonely; but power will jam much stale bread. Besides, one is lonelier in a crowd than in a 'cum Squeake' with thirty. Here, where one can only herd a few of the shaking multitudes, the herdsman is mucky and insignificant and heavy with indignity. But when the whole flock baa's after one's petticoats, it must be different; it must gladden the heart. Is it not so?

What do you propose to do with your nights, Louise? Read the *Life of Charlotte Brontë*[4] and weep? – Let it bide a bit, don't let bitterness for poor Carlotta blind your eyes to the young merits of your flock. Will you write – don't begin too soon? Will you draw? – do, it will soothe you, and make yourself a companion to yourself.

We had a devilish jolly time at Christmas: Lord, we were imps; I know three or four folk who would love to shake me. Do you?

I wish I were your assistant in your Kingdom – prime minister, so to speak. Lord, what larks we'd have. I do detest the hundred miles which push you so far off. I should love to visit you in Cum Squeake.

It is you who must write and tell me things. You are a new person to me.

Don't get puffed up. DHL

[1] 1909] 1908
[2] Ratcliffe-on-the-Wreake, a Leicestershire village where Louie Burrows took up the post of headmistress of the Church of England school on 1 January 1909.
[3] Mrs Pearl Root, The Hall Lodge, Ratcliffe-on-the-Wreake.
[4] By Elizabeth Gaskell (1857).

95. To Blanche Jennings, 20 January 1909

Text: MS ULiv; cited in Allott 66, 76.

12 Colworth Rd, Addiscombe, Croydon.
20 Jan. 1909.

My dear Bee,

Your letter makes me laugh at myself. I am 'a heart-bruising friend', am I?; better that than a heart-breaker, though to be sure I never thought my light words dealt such deep blows. While the smile lasts, I'll just write to show you I am smiling – no no, I should grin.

It is not exactly home-sickness. You see there are so many lees, so much mud at the bottom of the wine of me (wine, I say!) – that after any little shaking of change I am turbid. Every time I have been poured from the bowl of circumstance and environment into a fresh vessel, then have the clouds come up from the bottom of me, and for some time the sunshine can find no road in me. I think it is my liver which is upset by nervous excitement. I get much better of this absurdity, but still it comes, and I expect it. Very rarely have I been able to enjoy the first weeks of anything, even a holiday, because I am always a bit sick as the result of my change. So I've had a little bout now; peculiar time, when I can write for myself, but not letters. The baby poem[1] I'll send you is a bit of Friday's work. I'm coming round now – it makes me mad that I am such an ass. Moreover I never tell folks – and hardly anybody knows – only mother. Why, if I only go to the baths I am all deranged (not mentally – I won't allow it!) for a few days, and it is not the result of the water, but of psychic disturbance. The pictures on Saturday made me worse – quite sad to see – on Sunday. Lots of folk are like it – to a more or less degree. I always remember poor Charlotte Brontë, who was much worse than I. That's enough of my homesickness. I have only this to add; that I should have been far happier and better as a farm-labourer than as anything out on the choppy seas of social life.

Since coming back I have set down to write in earnest – now verses – now Laetitia: I am astonished to find how maudlin is the latter. It needed to come out here to toughen me off a bit; I am a fearful, sickly sentimentalist.

I envy you your lectures and your music. But I do not care very much; somehow I don't seem to need, at least I don't feel the need, of much food of new ideas, or of too new sensations. My books are enough. What I do love are little volumes of poetry, quite fresh acquaintances. I do thank you for the *Shropshire Lad*, though I stick to it his poetry is rotten. I have got W H Davies' *Nature Poems*,[2] and those poems which *are* nature poems –

[1] 'Ten Months Old': see below.

[2] W. H. Davies (1871–1940), *Nature Poems and Others* (1908).

like those about rain – and leaves – and robins – are delightful – about cities, purblind and nonsensical. I have had a lot of Yeats – he is vapourish, too thin. Now I have *City of the Soul*: Alfred Douglas has some lovely verses; he is affected so deeply by the new French poets, and has caught their beautiful touch. But, being a Lord, the fat-head writes 'A Prayer' – 'Images of Death' 'Ennui', 'Garden of Death', just because he feels himself heavy with nothing and thinks it's death when its only the burden of his own unused self.[1] Bah! Do you remember Gissing's *Henry Ryecroft* – a tour de force, the *Times* calls it[2] – I agree – but Henry Ryecroft says that the essence of art is to express the zest of Life, whatever that may be.[3] Nevertheless, he means something to me, and I accord. Machen – a writer to the *Academy* I believe – says that the touchstone of art is ecstasy – whatever that may be.[4] I think he means crying about the mysteries and possibilities. But 'ecstasy' leads to so much vapour of words, till we are blind with coloured wordiness. But I say, all mysteries and possibilities lie in things and happenings, so give us the things and happenings, and try just to show the flush of mystery in them, but don't begin with a mystery and end with a foolish concrete thing, like taking Death and making a figure with 'yellow topaz eyes – each a jewel',[5] or a vulgar bestial *Mammon*, with long teeth, as Watts does. Some of Watts pictures are commonplace, and a trifle vulgar. But look at his *Love and Death*[6] – its beauty lies in the aesthetic unknowable effect of line, poise, shadow, and then in the blurred idea that Death is shrouded, but a dark, embracing mother, who stoops over us, and frightens us because we are children. It is no good trying to model a definite figure out of a mystery; it only cheapens the great thing. Watts' mystical pictures are half failures,

[1] Poems entitled 'Prayer', 'The Image of Death', 'Ennui', 'The Garden of Death' were included by Lord Alfred Douglas (1870–1945) in *The City of the Soul* (1899).

[2] George Gissing (1857–1903) in *The Private Papers of Henry Ryecroft* (1903) was reviewed in the *Times Literary Supplement*, 6 February 1903, pp. 38–9. The reviewer commented: a '*tour de force* of authenticity never of revelation'.

[3] 'One might define Art as: an expression, satisfying and abiding, of the zest of life', *Henry Ryecroft* I. xx.

[4] Arthur L. J. Machen (1863–1947) contributed regularly to the *Academy*, 8 June 1907–29 August 1908. DHL's reference is to Machen's enunciation of the doctrine of ecstasy, first made (and often repeated) in *Hieroglyphics* (1902): 'If ecstasy be present, then I say there is fine literature...Substitute, if you like, rapture, beauty, adoration, wonder, awe, mystery, sense of the unknown, desire for the unknown. All and each will convey what I mean...in every case there will be that withdrawal from the common life and the common consciousness which justifies my choice of "ecstasy" as the best symbol of my meaning. I claim, then, that here we have the touchstone which will infallibly separate the higher from the lower in literature' (edn 1912, p. 24).

[5] Alfred Douglas, 'The Image of Death', ll. 6–7 ['...(Each eye a jewel)'].

[6] *Mammon* (in the Tate Gallery), 1885; *Love and Death* (in the Bristol Art Gallery), 1875. (For other comments on Watts see DHL, 'Art and the Individual', Lawrence–Gelder 259, 264.)

and you cannot *say* what the successes mean or teach: you can *say* what the failures were meant to mean and teach.

I feel I am arguing for my own sake, for my own soul; because I have been reading Machen.

But you will perhaps appreciate the few verses I send you in the light of what I say. I want to write live things, if crude and half formed, rather than beautiful dying decadent things with sad odors.

Forgive me now if I bore you. Do not mind to write me a newsy letter. I felt cross this morning when you ended – I was interested.

My landlord sits at the piano growing ecstatic over some chords which prelude a music-hall song. Now he reads me the words. Oh, Mon Dieu, Mon Dieu, I have lost my laugh! – for the little present.

I wish you could come to London. I am poor – I am always poor – nice people always remain poor, unless the High Gods intervene.

Farewell DHL

Ten Months Old.[1]

See how she snuggles against my neck –
My wee mouse –
And her fingers move in the ruts of my ears
And my throat is wet with her tears.

———

I can just see the nape of her white little neck
My pale, wet butterfly –
The rest is a cloud of thistle down
Soft, tickling brown.

———

I cannot call her 'Sweet Joy' now –[x]
My wee squirrel –
She is no longer two days old –
'Twas a tale soon told.

———

And dark now is the sky that she came through[x]
– My white bird –
Heavy with drops of the first keen rain
– Tears for her pain.

———

There, press your hot red cheek against mine
– My own baby –

[1] The child in question was Hilda Mary Jones. (See *Complete Poems*, p. 864, for revised text.)

There, for the heat of it causes a smart,
Stinging down to my heart.[1]

This is perhaps the first teething song; perhaps you know Meredith's 'Where did you come from baby dear?'[2] – and Blake's

'I have no name
I am but two days old – Sweet Joy I'll call thee'[3]

– those are the references[x]

Cherry Robbers.[4]

Under the long dark boughs, like
jewels aflame
In the hair of an eastern girl,
Hang strings of crimson cherries, like
gifts of shame
Half hid by a wanton curl

Under the glistening cherries, with
folded wings
Three dead birds lie:
Pale breasted throstles, and a black-
bird, poor robberlings
Branded with red dye.

Up the garden, laughing, a girl
comes to me,
Cherries hung round her ears,
Offers me her scarlet fruit – I will see
If she has any tears. –

A Winter's Tale[5]

Yesterday the fields were only grey with
scattered snow,

[1] l. 9 now –] any more
[2] From the novel by George MacDonald (1824–1905), *At the Back of the North Wind* (1870), p. 226; the poem is included in *Poetical Works* (1893), ii. 158.
[3] William Blake, 'Infant Joy', *Songs of Innocence*, ll. 1–2, 9 ['. . . I call thee'].
[4] Published in *Love Poems and Others* (Duckworth, 1913). (The same incident, involving Miriam and Paul, occurs in *Sons and Lovers*, chap. 11.)
[5] Published in *The Egoist*, 1 April 1914.

And now the longest brown grass-leaves
hardly emerge;
Yet her deep footprints scar the snow, and
go
On towards the pines on the hill's white
verge

I cannot see her, since the mist's white
scarf
Obscures the purple wood, and the dull
orange sky;
But she's waiting, I know, impatient
and cold, half
Sobs struggling into her frosty sigh

Why does she come so promptly, when
she must know
That she's only the nearer to the
inevitable farewell?

The hill is steep, and in the snow
my steps are slow –
Why does she come – she knows
what I have to tell

Renaissance.[1]

We have bit no forbidden apple –
Eve and me –
Yet the splashes of day and night
Falling round us no longer dapple
The same Eden with purple and white.

This is our own still valley,
My Eden, my home.
But the day shows it vivid with feeling
And the pallor of night does not tally
With the dark sleep that once covered the ceiling

---

[1] For another early draft of this poem see *Complete Poems*, pp. 908–9. A version entitled 'Renascence' was published in *Love Poems*.

My little red heifer – go and look at her eyes –
She will calve tomorrow.
Take the lantern, and watch the sow, for fear she grab
 her new litter
With red snarling jaws; let yourself listen to the cries
Of the new-born, and the unborn, and the old owl, and
 the bats as they flitter.

And wake to the sound of the wood-pigeons, and lie and listen
Till you can borrow,
A few quick beats from a wood pigeon's heart: then rise
See the morning sun on the shaken iris glisten
And say that this home, this valley, is wider than Paradise

I have learned it all from my Eve,
This warm, dumb wisdom.
She's a finer instructress than years
She has shown me the strands that weave
Us all one in laughter and tears

I didn't learn from her speech –
Staggering words.
I can't tell how it comes
But I think her kisses reach
Down where the live web hums.[1]

This is supposed to be a song on the education of love. The first two verses a statement – the next two telling how the world is become pale of meaning – the last a reflection.

96. To Jessie Chambers, [February? 1909]

Text: Delavenay 690.

[12 Colworth Road, Addiscombe, Croydon]
[February? 1909]

You have done what I couldn't, you have got distinction in English.[2]

[1] l. 10 sleep] night

[2] Jessie Chambers had taken the examination for the Acting Teacher's Certificate (a qualification for teachers not educated at a Training College) in December 1908 (Delavenay 686). The *List of Successful Candidates* (1909), p. 17 confirms her Distinction in English and Pass in French.

97. To Jessie Chambers, [February ? 1909]

Text: E.T. 152.

[12 Colworth Road, Addiscombe, Croydon]
[February ? 1909][1]

You – the anvil on which I have hammered myself out.

98. To Louie Burrows, 9 February 1909

Text: MS UN; Boulton 26–7.

12 Colworth Rd, Addiscombe, Croydon.
9.2.09.

My dear Louise,

You do not want me to come so urgently, do you, ma mie? For you know; – out of a host of difficulties, I will give you two:

I am short of money and worse than that: do you think J[essie], you, and I make a happy triangle? I have a large spicing of devilry and perversity in me; it is more flagrant since I left home; somebody has a bad time when we three meet. Do you not feel it? It gets between my teeth. You understand, do you not? I am sorry I have said it – but – but – – –.

I am glad you are so heavenly. No – I do not know you when there is a murmur of content in your throat like the cooing of doves. Who ever did know you destitute of a grumble and an animosity; not that they were predominant; oh no, they only gave a flavor to the whole, like my devilry does me. But when the days get warmer; when the wild flowers are out, then I will come to you. I promise you. I am impatient for the day.

It is nice to attain one's majority.[2] It is nice to walk, to learn to toddle; there is a great satisfaction in it; there are also, generally, many nasty bumps and much trepidation and anguish of spirit. I am glad you are going to be major. One has always felt behind you the threatening (!!) shadows of Mr and Mrs Burrows. I am glad you are going to walk abroad with no shadow but your own. Damn the hundred miles that push between us; I damn them through my clinched teeth.

I send you a volume of Ibsen;[3] I send it before your birthday; there is generally a blank before a long awaited day. I have a second volume that I will send you on Saturday. Read, in these plays, the 'Pretenders' first, the 'Vikings' second, and 'Lady Inger' last, so that the first may be best. 'The

[1] A conjectural date on the basis of the chronological sequence in E.T.

[2] Louie Burrows was twenty-one on 13 February 1909.

[3] Probably *Ibsen's Prose Dramas*, ed. William Archer (1890–1906), vol. 3, containing 'Lady Inger', 'The Vikings' and 'The Pretenders'.

Pretenders' is by far the best of the three – I will say no more, that you may form your own judgments.

I went up to the Academy on Saturday. The winter collection is magnificent.[1] They have some sad, wonderful pictures of the French peasant Bastien Lepage; how sad they are too; grey, with not one gleam of light; that is literal. Then there is our Sargent, a man of startling vigor and brilliance – and cold heart. Leighton has a magnificent piece – the *Garden of Hesperides*; Millais is only so-so; Waterlow is exquisite; so is Adrian Stokes. There is a Norwegian – Fritz Thaulow – original – striking – very much like Ibsen.

There – I'll send you the other vol soon. Write and tell me if you are not satisfied with me. With all good wishes, I am Yrs DHL

99. To Louie Burrows, 12 February 1909
Text: MS UN; Boulton 27–9.

12 Colworth Rd, Addiscombe, Croydon
12 Feb. 1909.

My dear Louise,

This is the eve of your majority, and I guess you are wildly excited. People send you presents; I wonder why; to comfort you for the loss of your youthful insouciance? to congratulate you that you have come into your inheritance? Well, you at any rate are to be congratulated on the last score. You have a good fortune of vigour, and lusty Atalantan strength; there is a treasure of good blood and good health come down to you from countless generations; when your wild ancestors frisked about in meagre wolf-skins, Lord, what wild eyed, shaggy, massive blunderbusses they were; you have plenty of fresh savage blood – Hurray! Can't you just frisk! You have inherited no old sorrow, no dim uneasy culture; you lucky young Amazon. Why do I send you 'Rosmersholm' and 'Hedda Gabler'?[2] But really, my dear, you must

[1] It was devoted to the private collection of the late George McCulloch (1848–1907) and was a source of much contention. The artists named by DHL (together with their pictures exhibited in the Winter collection) are as follows: Jules Bastien-Lepage (1848–84), *The Potato-Gatherers, Pauvre Fauvette, Pas Mèche*; John S. Sargent (1856–1925), *On his Holiday: Salmon-fishing in Norway, Salmon*, two portraits of George McCulloch and one of Master Alec McCulloch; Lord Leighton (1830–96), *The Garden of the Hesperides, The Daphnephoria*; Sir John Millais (1829–96), *Sir Isumbras at the Ford, In Perfect Bliss, Lingering Autumn*; Sir Ernest Waterlow (1850–1919), *The Orphan, Autumn Glory*; Adrian Stokes (1854–1935), *The Setting Sun, The Edge of the River*; Fritz Thaulow (1846–1906), *A River in an Autumn Sunset, A River in Winter with Trees, A Factory in Norway* and *An Old Factory in Norway*. (Thaulow's snow scenes impressed DHL: see the poem 'A Snowy Day at School', *Complete Poems*, ii. 865.)

[2] Probably *Ibsen's Prose Dramas* ed. Archer, vol. 5, containing 'Rosmersholm', 'The Lady from the Sea' and 'Hedda Gabler'.

be on bowing acquaintance with these people. You, in happy thoughtless – in your comparative jolly savagery of leopard skins and ox-hide buskins – well, I sent you 'The Vikings'; – you will only stare in young, tawny wonder at the pale spectre of 'Rosmersholm', and the new-fangled madness of 'Hedda Gabler'.

You will like 'The Lady from the Sea' – all English people do; you will say it is the best. 'Hedda Gabler' is subtlest, profoundest – and, I think, truest; least imaginary. Never mind, what have you to do with truths, you, you Atalanta; you would make a good Bacchante, but for your training. You are all right bossing a little show and flinging your big arms about. You would be better on horseback, riding like the devil. Well, well, the world won't let us be young, if it can help it – damn it. I salute you, you breezy Atalanta. You are a woman, remember, so you may run with Hippomenes, or you may enter for contest in Corydon; you might, but for your training. Be jolly, and tell Ibsen's people they are fools; you'll be right.

Why do you ask me about great men, naughty. You know it is a question of the books you have to get 'em from, rather than the choice you may make for yourself. What books have you? I would select a few typical people: Julius Caesar, Hannibal, Attila, Julian the Apostate, Constantine; one or two of the great saints: Jerome, Anthony, St Francis of Assisi, Catherine of Siena, Thomas à Becket; then Charlemagne, Bayard, Roland, Cœur de Lion, Christopher Columbus; then H[enr]y VIII, William the Silent, Peter[1] the Great; Oliver Cromwell, Chas IX of Sweden,[2] Kosciusko, Garibaldi; Napoleon; you might have stuck in Robespierre or Danton after Cromwell; you please yourself about Nelson, and Washington, and Abraham Lincoln and so on. Will this do.

Mr Jones is waiting for the letter. Give my regards to all; to J[essie] – is she with you. Tell her I'll write her soon; and I'll write Hilda.[3]

Be jolly – be a woman Yrs DHL

[1] Silent, Peter] Silent, Peter Martin Luther, Peter.

[2] MS reads 'Sweeden'.

[3] Hilda Shaw (1885?–1913?), a contemporary of DHL and Louie Burrows at University College, Nottingham, where she too gained a First Class Teacher's Certificate. She corresponded with Louie until at least 1912.

100. To May Holbrook, 16 February 1909

Text: MS UN; Postmark, Croydon FE 16 09; Nehls, iii. 614–15.

12 Colworth Rd., Addiscombe, Croydon.
16 Feb. 1909.

My dear May,

I guess you have moved, and I am not sure of your postal address, but I venture a little letter to you.

It seems such a short time since I came back, although it is nearly six weeks. The weeks spin round noiselessly like a balanced wheel; suddenly one realises it is Friday night, and that one has two days in which to please one's self. It is very comfortable, but not stimulating. I find my soul slowing down into comfort; it is tiresome to have even to write a letter. But I have gathered myself for a moment.

We have flitted; not from the house, but we have come to dwell in the drawing room, making it now the dining[1] room. It is a small place, but bright; at the back, away from the little, still street. You know we are on the very edge of the town; there are great trees on the Addiscombe Rd, at the end of Colworth. Here, in this room, there is a glass door, opening onto our little garden. Beyond the grey board fence at the bottom rises the embankment, a quiet, grassy embankment of a light railway that runs from the great lines – S.E and the London, Brighton. In the dark, as if suspended in the air, little trains pass bright and yellow across the uncurtained door. The little trains have only one carriage, something like a tram car, and often there are no passengers; sometimes two, taking the space of one, fancying themselves secure in the privacy of a corner. It is quaint, like looking out on the world from a star, to watch them jog slowly past. Indoors, Hilda Mary is hanging onto my legs, laughing up at me. She has brilliant hazel eyes, so round and daring. Soon I shall take her and get her to sleep. She does not like to go to bed, but I am a good 'dustman'.[2] I hold her tight and sing – roar away at the noisiest songs. This subdues her, she tucks her face in my neck and toddles off to 'bo',[3] while her hair tickles my nose to a frenzy. It is very still outside; you can just hear the trams hum as they start from the terminus beyond the embankment.

I went to London a week last Saturday, to the winter exhibition at the Academy. It is very strange out West, down Piccadilly, on Saturday morning. There are women such as I have never seen before, beautiful, flowing women, with a pride and grace you never meet in the provinces. The proud, ruling

[1] dining] drawing

[2] i.e. one who encouraged a child to sleep.

[3] i.e. bed.

air of these women of the stately West is astounding; I stand still and stare at them. In the square in front of Burlington House, carriages are trotting sumptuously round and round waiting while the ladies are walking through the gallery. There are some glorious pictures. The most notable painter is a French Peasant, Bastien Lepage. Ah, you should see a beautiful woman in dark velvet costume with great orange feathers flowing onto her shoulders stand looking at *Pauvre Fauvette*. She looks, she pouts, her mouth relaxes. 'Too sad' she says to the gentleman. 'But the country does desolate one like that; I have felt like it myself.' She moves on to a romance picture of Abbey, and talks brightly about Maurice Hewlett.[1] *Pauvre Fauvette* is a terrible picture of a peasant girl wrapped in a lump of sacking; you feel her face paint itself in your heart, and you turn away; the sorrow is too keen and real. The academy is full of magnificent works.

I went in the afternoon to Hornsey, to see George Hill. On the Sunday he took me to the Alexandra Palace. It is a ghastly place, all sham, sham chalk statues, sham stone, wood and paint, sham trees, sham everything, and everything dirty, broken, the sham exposed. My heart feels sick to think of it. And there, on Sunday afternoon, in the great hall, there was an organ recital. The organ is big and good; but the gathering! There were some three or four hundred people, all that respectable class of poor city people such as one never sees in Croydon. All unhealthy, weedy, impoverished specimens. The worst of it was, there was hardly one face to look at; I shouldn't mind their figures, if their faces were interesting. There was no character, no anything; they were very much like John Willie Oldershaw[2] – Mon Dieu!

You will be happy now out at Moorgreen. I cannot quite understand where you are. Is it this side George's?[3] Tell me – is it on the Moorgreen main road? I do not know Price's. I know Renshaws, Mrs Rollings, Cunningham's, – no more. I hope you are well. Have you heard of Emily's baby girl.[4] Give my regards to Will and to everyone. Yrs DHL

P.S. Nelson's series of 7d modern writers is very good – get H. G. Wells' *Kipps*, – only sevenpence. Then get something of G. Gissing, and the others.[5] DHL

[1] Edwin Austin Abbey (1852–1911), R.A., painter and decorative artist. In the Winter collection 1909, he exhibited two paintings: *Richard Duke of Gloucester, and the Lady Anne* (1896) and *Lear and Cordelia* (1898). Maurice Henry Hewlett (1861–1923), novelist, poet and essayist.

[2] Oldershaw was employed in an Eastwood grocery store; later, c. 1930, he had his own business in Basford, Nottingham.

[3] Not identified.

[4] Margaret King (b. 9 February 1909), DHL's niece.

[5] Wells's *Kipps* (1905) had appeared in the famous library of red cloth-covered volumes the previous month. The only Gissing novel in print in 'Nelson's 7d' was *The Odd Women* (1893).

101. To Louie Burrows, 28 February 1909
Text: MS UN; Postmark, Croydon MR 1 09; Boulton 29–31.

12 Colworth Rd., Addiscombe, Croydon.
28 Feb. 1909.

Ma chère Louise,

I have been reviling myself these last ten days for my ingratitude in not replying and thanking you for the snowdrops. They were so beautiful – alas, they are dead. At first I could not reply to you, because the flowers made me long so much for the country, for Ratcliffe on Wreake, and the mill bank covered with snowdrops. Flowers are scarce here. Mrs Jones buys a bunch of box-leaves and laurel – funereal evergreen, enough for one vase – it is two pence. In the town the flower sellers are gay and brilliant; but in the daytime the flowers are dear, and one is not there to buy late at night. Besides, the mimosa, the vivid scarlet anemones, and the flaccid narcissi from the flower-trays in the street are not snowdrops gathered in the mill garden, on the banks of the Wreake. The snowdrops one buys in bunches, with their poor little noses packed tight together, turned upwards to the winter sky, like white beans stuck in a green cup – these are not snowdrops gathered in the mill garden on the banks of the Wreake – these are not snowdrops from under the hazel brake in the steep dell in the woods of Strelley.[1] Louisa, oh Louisa, my heart aches for the country, and those splendid hours we have had. The town too is good; it has books, and people; it is not so desolating; one cannot there be lonely enough to feel the wistful misery of the country; above all, the town is valuable for the discipline it gives one's nature; but, in the end, for congenial sympathy, for poetry, for work, for original feeling and expression, for perfect companionship with one's friends – give me the country. In the end – after a while – a year or two – I shall come back into the country. If I can, I too shall take a headship in the country – not quite so small as yours, oh Louisa, school-mistress Louisa – but I too shall not be very exacting.

School is really very pleasant here. I have tamed my wild beasts – I have conquered my turbulent subjects, and can teach in ease and comfort. But still I long for the country and for my own folks. I think one never forms friendships like those one forms at home, before twenty. I have no need, I have no desire, to fold these new people into my heart. But the old folks –!

To cure me of my madness for the country I took a trip last week to Wimbledon, through Kingston Vale, over to Richmond Park, and back over Wimbledon Common. Kingston Vale is lovely – beautiful groves of silver

[1] About half-a-mile east of Cossall, Louie's childhood home.

birch more silvery than any I have seen. Richmond Park is glorious; it is history, it is romance, it is allegory, it is myth. The oaks are great and twisted like Norwegian tales, like the Vikings; the beeches are tremendous, black like steel – Robin Hood, and Sir Galahad have travelled through the bracken up the steep little hills, the nymphs and satyrs have sported round the ponds, where surely there are naiads. You would love Richmond, Louisa; together, we should spend a perfect day there. Some time in the summer, do come here for a week end. Have you any relatives in London? But do come down here some time. Wimbledon Common, too, is fascinating: ladies, gentlemen, grooms, girls, galloping on horseback over the heath and down hill through the birch-woods; Territorials playing at war all over the great common; scarlet coated golfers moving like vivid flowers; the old windmill – the great view of Surrey – come with me to Wimbledon too sometime.

What do I write. I continue that old work of mine.[1] Sometime, I hope, it will be finished. I have to do it over and over again, to make it decent. Some time, surely, it will be of some value – and then you shall read it too.

We are only six weeks from Easter. What are your plans, if any? The time will soon be upon us. What are your plans?

I wrote Hilda a long letter – and she has replied with a longer. I must write her again. I do not love writing letters, though.

What books do you read now. I have read much modern work since I came here, Joseph Conrad, and Björnsterne Björnsterne,[2] Wells, Tolstoi. I love modern work. You have more time than I to write – write long letters.

Au revoir DHL

102. To Blanche Jennings, 6 March 1909

Text: MS ULiv; Moore 50–2.

12 Colworth Rd, Addiscombe, Croydon
6[3] March 1909.

My dear B,

Now, have you been attributing to me a fit of the blues, or an influenza, or a love affair? – well then, you're quite mistaken. I am merely well and busy – why I am busy, I don't know, for I get nothing done – which should mean that I do nothing; but time seems to have got an astonishing knack of dissipating, evaporating like spilled wine – quickly, unnoticed. What sort of wine-stains it leaves I can't tell. But since Christmas – oh – a rather long

[1] The novel still at this time called 'Laetitia'.

[2] Björnstjerne Björnson (1832–1910), Norwegian poet, novelist and dramatist.

[3] 6] 2

yesterday! – and it is two months that I have been back at school. I must be growing up – or grown up – since old Time walks with such big strides; but, my heart, I don't lament it; it is very fine. What fools they were who shook their heads over vanishing youth; my youth was the most acute and painful time I shall ever see, I'll bet. You see I don't care now – which makes all the difference. I don't care a damn about my future prospects, therefore I am free from school worry and a host of things; I do not need the friendship of the folks here – so I don't care what I do. There is nothing so delightful – an open handed carelessness; such freedom.

You are a pale person – must be, since you swallow huge pink pills![1] Now, don't be a pale person – I do like you to be – what? – Hedonistic. – nice and red-corpusculary – sanguine. Do you really think life is hardly worth living? It is worth lots of living if you can only have your own jinks, kick your young heels to the tune of the pulse of the world.

My letters are always momentary – moody, if you like to be nasty. Now I have just finished Wells' *Tono-Bungay* – in the *English Review*.[2] Do you take the *Review* – if not, then you ought. At any rate, you *must*, *must* read *Tono-Bungay*. Now knock down my perky beak by calmly replying that you *have* read *Tono Bungay*. It is the best novel Wells has written – it is the best novel I have read for – oh, how long? But it makes me so sad. If you knew what a weight of sadness Wells pours into your heart as you read him – Oh, Mon Dieu! He is a terrible pessimist. But, Weh mir, he[3] is, on the whole, so true. One has a bitter little struggle with one's heart of faith – in the ultimate goodness of things. One thing Well's lacks – the subtle soul of sympathy of a true artist. He rigidly scorns all mysticism; he believes there is something in aestheticism – he doesn't know what; but he doesn't do his people justice. To be sure George Ponderevo's uncle is a little bladder, but Wells' need not scoff at the little fellows feelings when he is stirred to the full depth of his soul. Everybody is great at some time or other – and has dignity, I am sure, pure dignity. But only one or two of Wells' people have even a[4] touch of sincerity and dignity – the rest are bladders. 'By their works ye shall know them'.[5] – But – Mon Dieu – you shan't.

'What I aspired to be
And was not, comforts me'[6]

1 Allusion to a famous advertisement: Parkinson's – 'Pink pills for pale people'.
2 *Tono-Bungay* was serialised in the first four issues of the *English Review*, December 1908–March 1909.
3 he] his
4 a] at
5 Matthew vii. 20 ['...their fruits...'].
6 Browning, 'Rabbi Ben Ezra', ll. 40–1.

But Wells is there complete in George Ponderevo, and it is – oh it is just heart-breaking to me.

The snow – Hell is a slushy, cold, wet place, – I have said it a thousand times, – where one walks with ever-soddened boots. Oh, I am sick of this soppy cold mess of a world.

It is Spring – I always know it is Spring by feeling. I always have a restlessness, a suddenness, a hotness, in spring. Why! Why! – life is very still. Even here near London – life is a still pool – or a puddle. I want – I want – I want – – –! How do you feel? What do you want?

I was going to tell you something about the pictures in the Academy. Bastien Lepage, the French Peasant painter, had three terrible pictures – ah yes, haunting. Life must be dreadful for some people. Grey pictures of French peasant life – not one gleam, not one glimmer of sunshine – that is speaking literally – the paint is grey, grey-green, and brown. The peasant woman is magnificent – above all things, capable: to work, to suffer, to endure, to love – not, oh Bastien Lepage, oh Wells! Oh the God that there isn't! – to enjoy. The little girl – Pauvre Fauvette minding her gaunt cow beneath a gaunt bare tree, wrapped in a horrid sacking, she, too is navrante. That little pinched face looking out of the sack haunts me and terrifies me and reproaches me. Oh – that it should be true. It seems that the great sympathetic minds are all overwhelmed by the tragic waste, and pity, and suffering of it. Those great unsympathetic minds, like Sargent – are sardonic. Sargent is wonderful – he takes my breath away.

Two weeks ago I went through Kingston Vale to Richmond Park and back over Wimbledon Common. Kingston Vale is sweet and beautiful – a glade with groves of glistening silver birch trees, and a brook, and full of sunshine, with flashing birds – very sweet and dear and graceful. Richmond Park is one of the few remaining parts of the old world of romance. The hills rise up and look on the great oaks writhing and twisting – the beeches are tremendous steel shafts – there are broad spaces and great fierce groves, where the pale deer flee, where, I vow, there are dryads and fauns, where you might find a Viking asleep, where there are outlaws and knights in armour and ladies who exist solely to be succoured. The ponds – the ponds are marvels. Do you know Maurice Hewlett's *Forest Lovers*?[1] It is not nearly so good as Richmond Park. And do you want to see the romance and showy life of today? Go on Wimbledon Common. The horsemen and the horsewomen dash and canter down the hill among the birch groves; on the great common, with the windmill in one corner, with the hills of Surrey

[1] Published 1898.

running far south, the Territorials play a game of war, the golfers in their vivid scarlet coats play a game of golf, dotted conspicuously far and near over the great plateau, the ladies play a game of strolling negligently in full view – grooms canter with their charges – girls trot, and fathers gallop. It is very fascinating. I love it, and have[1] a day of almost perfect happiness. Surely, surely Bastien Lepage and Wells are not the Truth, the Whole Truth, and Nothing but the truth.

Do be bonny and well. *Do* not talk about your years. You should spend yourself with a full hand, generously.

I am having one or two delightful little flirtations – quite little, but piquant.

Adieu – I wish you were nearer. DHL

103. To Louie Burrows, 11 March 1909

Text: MS UN; Postmark, Croydon MR 11 09; Boulton 31–2.

12 Colworth Rd., Addiscombe, Croydon
11 March 1909

My dear Louise,

Now that the flowers are almost dead I write to thank you for them. They have looked lovely on the table. I have had them in a low dish. Now only a few snowdrops and primroses remain, so they are in a little vase. Snowdrops are exquisite little things; poor little mites! – long into the night – we don't go to bed with the sun – they have poised with spread wings over the piano, wide-spread wings that are pathetically lifted in a hopeless flight. It was better in the day when the canary sang – but after eleven o'clock – near midnight – when Dick sat secure in his false night – immune[2] in the dark blue wrapping of an old apron – poor little things – they were still wide spread. I enjoyed the winter aconites immensely – they are very delicate and pure in their colouring. They are found wild a few miles out from here; the boss brought some to school. Do these grow wild round Mousehole?

We have had some despicable weather – I can hardly say vile enough things about it. How have you found it? Of course, in town, it is not quite so bad as in the country. But I have to cross a piece of wild waste land on my way to school – land where the grass is wild and trodden into mud – where the brick-layer's hammer chinks, chinks the funeral bell of my piece of waste land – and there the mud is inexpressible.

I am just going down town to a lecture by some pot or other on Arithmetic

[1] have] had
[2] immune] secure

– I guess I shall be bored – We had a lecture on geography last week by Dr Herbertson[1] – a very great gun from Oxford – and he bored me excruciatingly. I liked Margaret von Wyss[2] on Nature Study – very much. I am sick of meetings and one thing and another.

In a month today I shall be home. Great Scott – Christmas is yesterday – Easter tomorrow. Tempus fugit. We are grown up.

What are you going to do at Easter? Are you coming over? I hope the weather will pick up before then – the brute! I must have a day with you somehow. Perhaps when we take our Easter Monday jaunt we may meet.

You have soon established a circle of friends – and they make much of you, do they? Oh lucky girl – the world has always a cosy corner for thee if thou turn thy face to look for it.

I am very sorry to hear of your father's accident. I hope he is better now. Remember yours was only such a little note.

Au revoir – Miss Country Mouse DHL

104. To Louie Burrows, 28 March 1909

Text: MS UN; Postmark, Croydon MR 28 09; Boulton 32–5.

12 Colworth Rd, Addiscombe, Croydon
28 March 09.

My dear Louise,

You shocking girl – fancy talking about 'Coals to Newcastle' as a figure for Snowdrops to me digging in the City! And I make verses to those same 'Coals'! Louisa – you are the same wild barbarian – do not ever pretend to be cultivated.

I am sorry you have been knocked up. The Roots[3] will cure you. At any rate your life is very comfy. Why do you tell me *about* the funniness of your world in general, and never give me the fun. It is not fair. I don't like '*abouts*' – I want some of the real stuff of the fun.

Here fun is fast and furious, as you will see if you take a London paper. It is election – voting day on Monday.[4] There are great crowds surging

[1] Andrew John Herbertson (1865–1915), Reader in Geography, Wadham College, Oxford, from 1905, Professor from 1910.

[2] Clotilde von Wyss, Lecturer in Nature Study in the London Day Training College and author of *Beasts and Birds: a Nature Book for Boys and Girls* (1910), *Gardens in their Seasons* (1912), etc. (In October 1909 she was appointed tutor for a course on Nature Study for teachers: Croydon Education Committee Report, 18 October 1909.)

[3] Cf. p. 105, n. 3.

[4] The by-election at Croydon, 29 March, was the scene of keen activity by the suffragettes. The National Union of Women's Suffrage Societies campaigned vigorously. At a meeting chaired by Miss Cameron on 17 March they attacked the Liberal candidate J. E. Raphael,

through the streets – there is a searchlight wandering overhead through the darkness – there are cinematographs at upper-storey windows, there are Suffragettes in thousands and tens of thousands processing and crying in the wilderness – the place is strident with voices and placards – rustling with leaflets and pamphlets.

I was in the fun the other night; I was in the mad grip of the crowd before the Suffragettes. If you had felt the surge, the vicious rush of one solid mass of men towards the car where the two women were alone, one standing crying scorn on the brutes, the other sitting with dark, sad eyes! 'If men cannot control themselves' said Miss Cameron 'it is time women had some power to control them.' We in front heard, and the fellows yelled. Then the whole mob howled and like one shoulder, the hundred men in the mob pressed onto the car, threatening to overturn it. The women gave way – inch by inch the car retreated – amid howls and yells of derision. The searchlight splashed down the street on the close pack white faces and dark mouths – Louisa, have you seen such, you barbarian? – it would have frightened your fresh, barbarian heart.

I went to the radical van. A handsome, sensitive man with a face of extraordinary pallor was trying to speak,[1] and the mob was enjoying itself. Chant to yourself, to the tune of the Bow chimes, which had just rung out from the Town Hall clock 'Sit down, Sit down – sit down, sit down' – and so on – varying it with 'Shut up, Shut up – Shut up Shut up.' Think of fifty fools chanting together, while the words of hot, painful conviction were crushed on your lips. Yap to yourself 'Hodge, Hodge, Hodge, Hodge' some thousand times, and imagine fifty throats yapping in unison whilst you uttered the cry of your heart. Speak your deep convictions to somebody, and let them insult you and heckle you and call you a liar. Louisa,[2] tell me about your farmers who fall out. I tell you about the town, where a sensitive, handsome man of culture is tortured for three long hours. When at last his voice breaks, and a word becomes a screech – the crowd jeers to shake the little red stars high up. There was a big, splendid woman in the wagon, a woman with full, oval face – great swinging ear-rings, and gold ornaments along her arms. See her put her hand on the arm of the speaker, and look up pleading that he should not let it hurt him – that he shall not answer in wrath; he looks down at her with his pale drawn face and does not see her.

through a speech by Christabel Pankhurst. They particularly harrassed the Conservative candidate Sir Robert Trotter Hermon-Hodge, later Baron Wyfold (1851–1937); he had declared his opposition to their cause; he also won the election. (See the *Times* account on 29 March 1909.)

[1] Probably the Labour candidate, F. Smith.

[2] Louisa] Louie

He goes on with his speech – he lifts his hat, and the dark hair falls on his forehead – he is overwhelmed in the din, and his eyes glitter from side to side. The woman stands behind knitting her brows, and opening her mouth pitifully with bewilderment and despair. She too is a barbarian, big and splendid – but smoothed and shapely through the grooming of great world. She mounts the side of the cart boldly – and aloft there, laughs out a splendid laugh to the mob, and lifts her arm to them for respite – in vain. Their souls are lusted with cruelty. Louisa, is the twang of the Roots quaint – and is there nothing more in life? Louisa, do any of your youngsters limp to school; through the snow or the fine weather, limp to school because they are crippled with broken boots. Have you seen wounds on the feet of your boys, from great mens boots they wear which are split across. My dear old button boots – they are barely recognisable under the front desk. Have you seen the children gathered to free breakfasts at your school – half a pint of milk and a lump of bread – eighty boys and girls sitting down the bare boards? Louisa, my dear, life is not gentle, and amusing, and pleasant, I am afraid.

I went to the Dulwich Art Gallery yesterday – took the car to the high level of the Crystal Palace, and looked out over the great glade, to Westminster far in the distance, and the mist of all London between. I felt a long way from home and the quaint, amusing country. I went down the long College hill to the gallery. It is a lovely and lovable little place, full of old, fascinating pictures – Colonel Lovelace looking with full, womanly glance; the saddening face of Chas II – pale Chas I[1] – all the old people in one dear nook. There is a fine collection of Dutch pictures – Cuyp, Teniers, Wouverman, Jordaens, Hobbema, Van der Helder,[2] and the rest. I love the human, sturdy, noble Dutchies. There are one or two charming Watteaus, some splendid Guido Renis, three or four great Murillos, and Velasquez, and Titian, and Reynolds and the rest. Many quaint interesting Poussins – such a splendid little gallery – so little, so rich. I should like to take you – and then to the Academy, to see the moderns. In the old pictures sorrow is beautiful; in the new it is awful – Bastien Lepage; the old is the divine sorrow of fruitfulness, the new is the cruel sorrow of destruction. Louisa, my dear, thou art a century or so behind – and I am at the tip of the years. So thou art very comfortable and charming, and I am uncomfortable and a nuisance.

[1] The three portraits mentioned by DHL are of Richard Lovelace (catalogue no. 363), artist unknown; (no. 424) Charles II, ascribed to John Greenhill; (no. 414) Charles I, 'a copy after Van Dyck'.

[2] A slip of the pen for 'Velde'. Dulwich possesses works by both Adriaen and Willem Van der Velde.

I should like to come to see you – I should like you to come and see me.

Addio DHL

105. To Jessie Chambers, [c. 1 April 1909]

Text: E.T. 89.

[12 Colworth Road, Addiscombe, Croydon]
[c. 1 April 1909][1]

['When spring came he wrote with delight about the flowering almonds, and sent me [Jessie] a box of the blossom because we had never seen the miracle of the flowering almond in our countryside.']

106. To Louie Burrows, 4 May 1909

Text: MS UN; PC; Postmark, Croydon MY 4 09; Boulton 35.

Croydon
4 Mai 09.

Ma chère Louise,

Mille mercis du livre – il est arrivé aujourd'hui, et je le trouve charmant. Je vais copier quelques-uns des tableaux – vous me permettrez de le retenir pendant quelque temps, n'est ce pas?

Ne m'avez vous pas écrit un billet pour accompagner le livre ou pour m'en prévenir? – je n'en ai pas reçu. Vous n'êtes pas fachée contre moi, assurément. J'attends avec impatience quelque chose de votre part, car il est étrange que le livre soit venu sans aucun mot. Une bonne poignée DHL

[My dear Louise,

A thousand thanks for the book – it came today, and I found it delightful. I am going to copy some of the pictures – you'll let me keep it for a little while, won't you?

Didn't you write me a note to go with the book or to let me know about it beforehand? – I haven't had one. You're not cross with me, surely. I am anxious for something from you, because it's odd that the book came without any word. Warm regards DHL]

[1] The year is suggested by Jessie Chambers's chronology, the month by the known climatic conditions in 1909: almond blossomed at Kew on 31 March (see *The Croydon Natural History and Scientific Society: Rainfall of Croydon District 1905–22* for March–April 1909).

107. To Blanche Jennings, 8 May 1909

Text: MS ULiv; cited in Allott 60–1, 75, 76.

High St, Rottingdean, Sussex.
8 May 09.

Ah, I have not spoken to you for ages – I am becoming less talkative, I believe. At any rate, I hate writing letters. But now I am alone at Rottingdean, and it is dark outside, and the sea is still, and there is only Grimm's *Fairy Tales* in the room, besides the Church Magazine, and although Grimm is a pal of mine, yet I do not want him tonight, so I'm going to write to you, not, indeed, because I've nothing else to do, but because I want to. My poor English! – my lamentable epistolary style! Never mind, I don't care a damn if you dont.

You sound saddish – sort of disillusiony – 'life's a bad joke' sort of tone. Believe me, you want a change. You want pitching out into a new lot of folks, who'd rouse all your latent activities – you sort of cultivate three flower-beds in your cottage-garden soul: mustard and cress – yes they *are* flowers if they run to seed – for family use; flat pansies-of-thought for the oldish woman in Wales who has the rotten taste not to like me, and some purple emotional violets for your own private use, that you keep well hid under leaves, but which give you a violent odour of sentiment, néanmoins. Bah, you have never mirrored a poppy on your retina – nor a tiger-lily, nor deuced nasturtiums – leastwise, if you ever have, you've forgot it. What a beastly habit of metaphor I have. Do you know, you ought to leave Liverpool, and make a new start in – say – London. Bah, you are merely declining for lack of stimulus. Look at Mrs Dax – she has lost all that dam-foolery of faddishness about this that and the other – chiefly the ethics of society and woman – and come to her senses as an ordinary woman, 'cause she's married and got a child, and 'll have more sometime!

You can't appreciate *Manon Lescaut*. What can you appreciate but something with a series of labels attached, bearing scientific names? You have cultivated a sort of[1] ethic-intellectualism – flat thought-pansies – to the exclusion of everything sweeping and throbbing. *Manon Lescaut* is fine – you're narrow. You've shut up your vitalities in a few tight boxes – like J. M. Robertson.[2] I have just finished Dostoièvskys *Crime and Punishment* – which he – J. M. Robertson – considers the finest book written – I believe you told me so – at any rate I read it somewhere. He is a poor fool. He has called *me* fool often enough in his damned *Letters on Reasoning* and such like, but now it's my turn – he's an arrant ass to declare *Crime and Punishment*

[1] of ethic] of aesthetic

[2] Cf. p. 37, n. 1.

the greatest book – it is a tract, a treatise, a pamphlet compared with Tolstoi's *Anna Karénina* or *War and Peace*. Read *Anna Karénina* – no matter, read it again, and if you dare to fall out with it, I'll – I'll swear aloud. Besides, you've just read what's not worth reading of Wells: *War of the Worlds* and such like arrant rot – because theyre theoryish. Read *Kipps*, *Love and Mr Lewisham*, and read, *read*, *Tono Bungay*; it is a great book.

I have come to Rottingdean, to the sea, because the weather was too much for me. I biked this morning down to Brighton – over the Downs, north and south – between the banks thick bossed with primroses, and hazel brake all deep in bluebells and primroses. I have drunk beer in a pub, where they talked in lovely Sussex that I couldn't understand. I have lain an hour on the sharp shelving shingle on Brighton beach, and the sun has soaked through my shut eyelids into my eyes, and I'm giddy still with it. Brighton is splendid – big, stately, magnificent, with a sea like pale green jewels – is lapis lazuli green? – and all wavering, shimmering, intermingling with purple – lovely – inexpressible. But Brighton is stately, and Im not, so I pushed my way through the wind, and here I am at Rottingdean – and I thought I was going to be a second Miss Charlesworth, and get blown over the cliff.[1] I have been up on the downs – I have pushed a poor sheep's head back through the bars of the fold where it had jammed it like Mrs Jelliby's boy[2] – if it was her boy – and the sheep bells tinkled abruptly – the sheep and lambs were folded on the sheltered side of the hill. The downs are all like a cloth when two people are shaking it unevenly – and full of shadows and lights – and on the sunny side there are cowslips out. I have watched the sun swim and go – I was terrified to see the swimming sun sink so quickly and deliberately behind the round hill where the windmill stands up stately but a bit ridiculous. Then Brighton in the red fusing light looked like a wonderful imagined place, and the lights on the sea just played about, and me, I played with them, and the wind ruffled the water back, and right up in the sky were two ruddy clouds flung together, and they were perfect, like two lovers at last met in a kiss, now they have met in the winds, and his head was hid in the tossed glitter and beauty of her hair that the wind shook, and his naked body flung towards her. It was fine. I imagined it all for myself. A fellow sat with his arm round a girl's waist on the cliffs – My God, these folks don't

[1] DHL is referring to the minor *cause célèbre* involving the supposed death of May ('Violet Gordon') Charlesworth. Her 'death' by falling from a cliff near Llandudno was reported on 4 January 1909. It was soon disbelieved and within about a fortnight disproved. The press kept the case before the public through the continuing investigation and subsequent prosecution. Charlesworth was finally sentenced (February 1910) to three years penal servitude for fraud and conspiracy.

[2] See Dickens, *Bleak House*, chap. 4.

know how to love – that's why they love so easily. I am superstitious – that is I dwell on things, and read my own promises of life in them, though I never believe or act upon them – and I saw a promise of the Annunciation of Love for me. Nevertheless, though you grin, it was wonderful.

I went down on the wide beach, where nobody was, because the stretches of sand are wet and chalky, and the rocks are rough and pooly – only three shrimpers waded along the wonderful outspreading ruffling water, pushing their great nets before them, stopping, picking out the little objects, and moving on again through the marvellous green light overflushed with ruddy gleams. The sand was wet, and aswim with yellow and red fires – then the lights of Brighton came out like night flowers opening, and I came home to write to you.

I am grown up – I am tremendously grown up – well, I don't care if you won't believe it, it's truth.

I'd tell you about school only you take me too seriously.

When I go home, I'll send you the first four *English Reviews*, if you like – they've got *Tono Bungay* complete in them. I wonder if Mrs Dax has done with them.

What are you delicate for – why aren't you strong. I knit my brows with vexation over you.

There are some great fat unwieldy Glory rosebuds on the table. But, they are a bit withered. They remind me of English folks with their bulgy sentimentalities and their formless emotionalism that never expands.

I've said enough. How shall I close – you are so far away – you grow farther off. Fare well DHL

Do be happy – why dont you get fat?

My hands are as red as fire-lit sands, with biking through the sunny day.

108. To Louie Burrows, [22 May 1909]

Text: MS UN; PC v. Coulsdon Church. Caterham; Postmark, Caterham Valley MY 22 09; Boulton 36.

[22 May 1909]

I have not written that letter – I am *so* lazy. Today I've had a ripping time out on the North Downs. You *would* have enjoyed it had you been with me. Your flowers lasted such a long time – you would hardly believe the great admiration they received.

I *will* cycle to Quorn for a day. I want to go to Leicester too. Perhaps I may stay there the night. It will be towards the week-end. I must see how I can arrange it. Auntie told me you had been to see her – you are a favourite of her's.

When will you come to London? Will you stay the night at Croydon, like J[essie][1] – or is it too improper?

When I see you at Whit – will you tell me the news that you are going to tell me sometime. I am looking forward to seeing you. The weather is glorious and I revel in it. We have a holiday next Wednesday – I think I may go to the Derby at Epsom. Au revoir DHL

109. To Helen Corke, [June? 1909]

Text: Huxley 2.

[12 Colworth Road, Addiscombe, Croydon]
[June? 1909][2]

...I admit your accusation of impressionism and dogmatism. Suddenly, in a world full of tones and tints and shadows I see a colour and it vibrates on my retina. I dip a brush in it and say, 'See, *that's* the colour!' So it is, so it isn't...

110. To Louie Burrows, 22 June 1909

Text: MS UN; PC; Postmark, Croydon JU 22 09; Boulton 36–7.

Addiscombe.
22 June 09.

Time is barren, and my wits are sterile in these grey days – so I am not productive enough for a letter. It *is* a fraud you can't come to Shanklin. Are you really going to wait till the 10th of July – a fortnight on Saturday? – it seems a long time. Things are going rather slowly here – how is the Mousehole? Has the Cat of Fate committed many depredations yet? – She was on the warpath when last you wrote, and the mice were scuttling about pit-a-pat with grief and woe. Those drawings, alas – I got them ready, and some malicious fiend made off with them; I must wait till I get some more. I'm very sorry. How are you? Addio. DHL

[1] Jessie Chambers had visited DHL for a weekend earlier in May 1909. She stayed at his lodgings (see Delavenay 701).

[2] Dated by Helen Corke.

Helen Corke (1882–1978) the subject of DHL's 'Helen' poems, taught at Dering Place Mixed School, Croydon (under Philip F. T. Smith as headmaster until he left for Davidson Road School in November 1907). Introduced to DHL by her friend and mentor Agnes Mason. She was taught the violin by Herbert Baldwin MacCartney, the 'Siegmund' of *The Trespasser* (Duckworth, 1912); the novel was based largely on her 'Freshwater Diary'. Through DHL she formed a close friendship with Jessie Chambers. Author of *Neutral Ground* (1933), *Lawrence and Apocalypse* (1933), several books on economic reform, etc. Her autobiography, *In Our Infancy* (Cambridge, 1975) describes her relationship with DHL.

111. To Louie Burrows, 30 June 1909

Text: MS UN; Boulton 37–8.

12 Colworth Rd, Addiscombe, Croydon.
30 June 09.

My dear Louie,

What am I to write to you about? There is only one thing to confess, and that is that I have been cross this last week or so; I think it must be the weather.

I wish you were coming on Saturday, instead of the following. I just feel like a fuddle.[1] I vote we don't go to The Tower – that we go straight down to St. Pauls – then down the Strand to Trafalgar Square. You can choose for yourself there. Either you can have a glance through the National Gallery, to look at the Corot and the Velasquezs and the Rembrandts, or you can go straight down to the Embankment, to Westminster and the Tate Gallery. You will do as J[essie] did, I presume, bring lunch, and eat it by the River, then we will get tea in Town. After tea we will go into Hyde Park for a little time, and then we can go east again to the theatre – we *will* go to the theatre – we'll go to Drury Lane, where there is an Italian Opera Company: no we won't, we'll go to Covent Garden Opera, and I hope Tetrazzini will be singing.[2] Since you are not going to have a holiday, I don't see why you shouldn't have a real downright fuddle on that memorable day. To be sure I am not very well off – I wish I were not so handicapped for cash – so that I cannot pay the heavy ex's, but I want a giddy time with you. I am always so disappointed that I am so poor and that I cannot stand the treat altogether.

Life is flowing very slowly just now. Why *aren't* you coming on Saturday – I think it will be fine. Why will it be more convenient to come on the 10th?

I have got your book of pictures yet; shall I send it, or let you take it? What time do you come – there is not the slightest fear of my missing you. By the way, you will come to Marylebone – G[reat] C[entral] – wont you? I want some particulars. If you come G.C. we shall be fairly well west to start with, and you could go to Marble Arch[3] straight off and walk down Oxford St to see the great shops, if it so likes you, and we could move East, finishing at St Pauls before the theatre.

I am glad you are writing stories. I can't do 'em myself. Send me them, please, and I'll see if I can put a bit of surface on them and publish them for you. We'll collaborate, shall we? – I'm sure we should do well. At any

[1] Colloquialism for a drinking bout; DHL means 'a good time'.

[2] Luisa Tetrazzini (1871–1940) was to sing in Donizetti's *Lucia di Lammermoor* at the Royal Opera House, Covent Garden, on Saturday 10 July 1909.

[3] Marble Arch] Hyde Park

rate send me the tales at once, and I'll send em to the publisher some time or other in your name.

Be good, now, and keep a good stock of energy and spirits for your coming to London.

Till I see you, farewell DHL

Neville wants your address – I am giving it him. He wishes – wistfully – you were going with us to Shanklin. I am sure he would be gone on you if you'd let him – and for all you say you dont, I know you rather like him.

112 To Jessie Chambers, [July? 1909]

Text: E.T. 119.

[12 Colworth Road, Addiscombe, Croydon]
[July? 1909][1]

Do you mind if, *in the novel*, I make Emily marry Tom?[2]

113. To Louie Burrows, [26 July 1909]

Text: MS UN; PC. Postmark, Croydon JY 26 09; Boulton 38–9.

[12 Colworth Road, Addiscombe, Croydon]
[26 July 1909]

Vous[3] devriez me penser longtemps à vous écrire. J'ai envoyé le cinq schellings – cela était la somme, n'est ce pas – 5/-? – Je l'ai mise à la poste aujourdhui.[4] Bientôt, avant la fin de la semaine, je vous enverrai l'autre histoire[5] – je ne l'ai pas encore préparée tout à fait. Je suis heureux à apprendre que vous allez à Barrow. Certainement, donnez beaucoup de choses de ma part à notre petite Nina.[6] Je vous y écrirai. Mon addresse à Shanklin, c'est

[1] The conjectural date takes account of several factors: this letter is later than the 'brief moment of harmony' (E.T. 119) probably experienced during Jessie Chambers's weekend in Croydon in May 1909; it precedes the Shanklin holiday (in August) and the completion of 'Nethermere' (later *The White Peacock*) in November (see Letter 128).

[2] Emily is a fictionalised portrait of Jessie Chambers; she has a close association throughout *The White Peacock* with Cyril (DHL); but finally she marries Tom Renshaw.

[3] Vous] Tu

[4] DHL had submitted his short story 'Goose Fair' to the London and Provincial Press Agency, to be placed with a publisher. The Agency wrote (20 July 1909) requesting a registration fee of 5s. DHL sent the Agency's letter to Louie Burrows; it is preserved among the Burrows MSS (UN MS LaB 186).

[5] Presumably the story sent with his next letter.

[6] Nina Stewart – a contemporary of Louie and DHL at College – lived at Barrow-in-Furness. She remained a correspondent of Louie until at least 1930 (see Boulton xxvii–xxviii).

c/o Mrs Holbrooks,[1] Fern Villa, Carters Rd, Shanklin, I.o.W.

Nous y allons le Samedi – et vous partez pour Barrow le même jour, n'est ce pas? J'espère que vous continuez d'être de bon coeur – les vacances commencent le jeudi, heuresement. Addio. DHL

[You must think me a long time writing to you. I have sent the five shillings – that was the amount, wasn't it – 5/-? – I have posted it today. Soon, before the end of the week, I will send you the other story – I haven't quite done it up yet. I am delighted to know that you are going to Barrow. You must certainly give my best wishes to our little Nina. I will write to you there. My address at Shanklin is c/o Mrs Holbrooks, Fern Villa, Carters Road, Shanklin, Isle of Wight. We shall go there on Saturday – that's the same day as you go to Barrow, isn't it? I hope you continue in good spirits – mercifully the holidays begin on Thursday. Goodbye. DHL]

114. To Louie Burrows, 27 July 1909

Text: MS UN; Boulton 39–40.

12 Colworth Rd, Addiscombe, Croydon.
27 July 09.

My dear Louise,

Here is your tale – you will not like it. But tell me what you think of it. After Thursday, till Saturday, my address is

c/o Mrs Berry,[2] Low Hill, Roxburgh Park, Harrow on the Hill.

– then, after Saturday, Shanklin. – Fern Villa, Carters Rd. I told you, did I not, that I had sent the five bob to the Press Agency. I had forgotten all they said in the letter, so don't know whether they wanted anything else. You may go whacks with me in that, if you like, and then we will go whacks in the profits[3] – when they come: 'Ah, woful when!'[4]

We are in a bit of a muddle. Did I tell you that father went and had an accident last week, and that they are not sure whether he and mother will be able to come down on Saturday? I shall be raving mad if they can't, but I'm hoping for the best. We are having about five hours in London before proceeding to Portsmouth – it is very giddy to contemplate. I am beginning to get excited, although the weather is so damnable that if the most milky saint in heaven had to endure it he'd curdle your blood with wicked language.

[1] Mrs Holbrooks has not been traced: Fern Villa was an apartment building and the apartments are not separately listed.

[2] Lettice Ada Berry née Beardsall (1857–1938), DHL's maternal aunt.

[3] i.e. share the 5s. fee and share the proceeds.

[4] Coleridge, 'Youth and Age', l. 6.

I assure you, by the way, that my stories are most freezingly polite. The nom de guerre, as you will see, is a happy mixture of you and me: you are the body, I the head. Qu'en dites vous? I believe you are utterly unrecognisable under my figurehead.

My cold is somewhat better – I have not done any more tales. I shall be glad to see your other buds – when we get back from the holiday – Shanklin and Barrow. I will send you a line there and I'll greet Nina by the way. Don't let my tone in 'Cupid and the Puppy'[1] influence you – you write in your best sentimental vein. I send it to school to occupy your dinner hour.

Au revoir, donc, DHL

115. To Louie Burrows, [2 August 1909]

Text: MS UN; PC v. Shanklin, I.O.W.; Postmark, Ventnor 2 AU 09; Boulton 40.

Fern Villa, Carter Rd, Shanklin.
[2 August 1909]

Here we are, in a most lovely place. We are sitting on the cliffs among the bracken looking down through the ash-trees at the sea. The sea is shimmering pale green and purple (do you remember the pictures in the Tate?). There are eight men-of-war in the offing, and the guns are muttering in salutes as the King's ship passes.[2] We are on the way to Ventnor – walking over the cliffs. Give my regards to Nina – I hope she is well. Why do you want to copy out the 'Cupid'? – what for? Addio DHL

116. To Mabel Limb, [3 August 1909]

Text: MS Clarke; PC v. Ventnor. I.W looking West; Postmark, Shanklin AU 3 09; Moore 55–6.

Fern Villa, Carter Road, Shanklin, I.o.W.
[3 August 1909]

Dear Mab,

Don't I wish you were here: it is the most charming place imaginable. We walked over to Ventnor yesterday – even mother managed it, and it is four and a half miles. It is sunny and warm, and so pretty. Mother has been wishing you might be with us, for certainly it would do you good. I was *so* sorry to hear all the bad news of you[3] and your father: it is very cruel

[1] Presumably the title of Louie's short story mentioned in the opening sentence, and re-written by DHL.

[2] On 31 July 1909 the Home Fleet was reviewed in the Solent by Edward VII and on 2 August by Czar Nicholas II of Russia who was visiting the King.

[3] Most likely the illness which led to Mabel Limb's death in December.

altogether. I begin to hate Eastwood, things happen so cruelly and so perversely there. Love DHL

We saw the fleet as we walked along – heard them saluting the Czar's vessel as he passed. DHL

117. To May Holbrook, [10 August 1909]

Text: MS UN; PC v. View from Chine Hill, Shanklin – Isle of Wight; Postmark, Shanklin AU 10 09; Nehls, iii. 615–16.

[Fern Villa, Carter Road, Shanklin]
[10 August 1909]

How is the world using you? Whenever I look over the cliffs far down at the sea I think of you: you have an affection for high white cliffs, have you not? We sailed round the Island yesterday, calling at Ventnor and Ryde – and Southsea on the mainland – and Sandown. It was delightful. We passed close to the Needles – they are not a scrap like needles: they are great, ragged lumps of white rock walking out into the sea, and a lighthouse at the end. You have no idea how pretty the Solent and Spithead are – such shimmering iridescent running water. I am coming to tea with you next week – invite me. DHL

118. To Louie Burrows, [10 August 1909]

Text: MS UN; PC v. Osborne-House (Isle of Wight). – Mosaic Corridor; Postmark, Shanklin AU 10 09; Boulton 40–1.

[Fern Villa, Carter Road, Shanklin]
[10 August 1909]

Thanks for your card: are not we having ripping weather? We spent the day at Cowes on Friday – at the regatta – and we went over Osborn House:[1] it was very nice, but Queens have poor taste – German and vulgar. Yesterday we sailed round the Island – it was ripping – steamed a long way between the iniquitous ironclads – the Dreadnought[2] was in the harbour. Give my regards to Nina – what day shall I ride over to Quorn? DHL

[1] The favourite home of Queen Victoria. A Royal Naval College was opened there in 1903.

[2] The famous battleship, launched in 1906. In 1909 it was the flagship for the Commander-in-Chief Home Fleet.

119. To Jessie Chambers, [ante 14 August 1909]

Text: E.T. 158.

[Fern Villa, Carter Road, Shanklin]
[ante 14 August 1909]

['Lawrence wrote to [Jessie] from Shanklin, a long descriptive letter about the island and the fun they all had bathing.']

120. To Louie Burrows, [18 August 1909]

Text: MS UN; PC; Postmark, Nottingham AUG 18 09; Boulton 41.

[43 Laurel Street, Nottingham]
[18 August 1909]

I am writing at my brother's,[1] in Nottingham. It is he who is the holy man[2] – not I. He is ill, and mother and I are come to see him. I am so sorry I could not come today: last night I went for Alan's bike, to be ready for the morning. When I was at the top of Underwood hill the rain came on and I was drenched. The bike was not ridable this morning, and I have a cold. Mater does not want me to come while the weather is unsettled, she was so upset about my state yesterday – poor ma, she takes trifles so seriously. I will write you a letter tomorrow or so – j'ai une petite nouvelle, mais elle n'est pas bonne. Envoyez moi, s'il vous plait, le conte de Cupide.[3] Je l'enverrai à un 'Mag'. Je me fâche beaucoup de n'avoir pu venir. J'écrirai une lettre demain.[4] Yrs DHL

121. To Louie Burrows, 19 August 1909

Text: MS UN; Postmark, Eastwood AU 19 09; Boulton 41–2.

Lynn Croft, Eastwood, Notts.
19 Aug 09.

My dear Louie,

I am very sorry if you have been disappointed again – don't expect me any more, the devil holds the whip hand of affairs. I had engaged myself out today, tomorrow, Saturday, and four or five times next week. When there is only left one day, odd, here and there, and there is the weather to contend

[1] DHL's eldest brother, George Arthur Lawrence (1876–1967). First apprenticed to the picture-framing trade; later a textile engineer; and finally manager of Standard Engineering Co., Nottingham. Well-known as a Baptist preacher; nationally prominent in the Liberal Party.

[2] A reference to the printed heading on the postcard: 'St. Ann's Well Road and Edwin Street Baptist Mission'.

[3] Cf. p. 133, n. 1.

[4] 'I have a bit of news but it isn't good. Please send me the Cupid tale. I'll send it to a "Mag". I'm very cross at not being able to come. I'll write a letter tomorrow.'

with, and somebody else's old bike, and ma's, and my own temper – Oh Lordy Lordy, it's enough to make you swear.

Then my little news – damn it! When I was at Shanklin the agency people wrote me to say that they had received my letter, but no p[ostal] o[rder] – that they would have written before, but that they awaited my word, thinking I had made a mistake. I believe it is a palpable lie – I will not send them any more money. I shall ask them for the 'Goose Fair' back, if they don't write me soon. There is a new Magazine coming out – should be out now – *The Tramp*.[1] I'm going to send my tales direct to the mags now: so let me have the Puppy, and I'll go through it and revise it and send it; send me any more of yours you want to see 'slaughtered' – and send me those you wish to preserve as they are, so that I may crit them. I am beastly disappointed about one thing and another, but it's no use letting on. When does your mother come back – where has she gone? – are the children with her? – how do you like housekeeping? For the Lord's sake, send me that draft of a novel, I bet it would amuse me. You know, your forte would be short stories – it will take you at least three years to write a novel – at school.

Are you cross? – well, so I am also. Devil take everything!

Valete DHL

122. To Arthur McLeod, [26 August 1909]

Text: MS UT; PC v. 'Laokoon' Rom. Vatikan; Postmark, Eastwood AU 26 09; Unpublished.

[Lynn Croft, Eastwood, Notts]

[26 August 1909]

Thanks for the bonny view of Devon. Rocky coast scenery is much alike in all parts. It is so still here that I am almost oppressed – shall not regret coming back to town. I hope the post won't spoil this *Laocoon* – I spotted it in Nottingham,[2] and at once I wanted to send it to you[3] – don't know why.

à lundi.[4] DHL

[1] In fact *The Tramp*, founded and edited by Douglas Goldring, did not begin publication until March 1910; it ran for one year (see Goldring, *South Lodge*, 1943, p. 57ff).

[2] Perhaps on the occasion just after DHL's return from Shanklin, described by Jessie Chambers (E.T. 160): '...Afterwards he strode along to one of the picturesque old shops near the Castle, where he bought some photographs of Greek statuary.'

[3] Arthur William McLeod (1885–1956), assistant master at Davidson Road School, Croydon, 1907–13; graduated B.A. in Greek, King's College, London, 1907; from 1913 taught (under Philip F. T. Smith as headmaster) at Norbury Manor School; then became, successively, headmaster of Ingram School (c. 1920), Winterbourne School (1922), Heath Clark (1929), and finally (1934) of the John Ruskin High School until retirement in 1946. DHL's closest friend at Davidson Road; their shared enthusiasm for literature is reflected in Helen Corke's *Neutral Ground* (1933) where McLeod appears as Howard Phillips, 'the one man among his colleagues with whom Derrick [DHL] found anything in common' (p. 288). McLeod is MacWhirter in *The Trespasser*; also described in Helen Corke's *In Our Infancy*, pp. 122, 188–9.

[4] The new term began on 30 August 1909 (School Log).

123. To Alice Dax, [c. 26 August 1909]

Text: MS Hale; PC v. 'Laokoon' Rom. Vatikan; Unpublished.

[c. 26 August 1909][1]

Had a decent journey last night – am now en route to Lincoln. Will write you later, from London.

Yrs DHL

Arrange these as I number them No. 1.[2]

124. To Louie Burrows, 11 September 1909

Text: MS UN; Postmark, Croydon SP 11 09; Boulton 42–3.

12 Colworth Rd, Addiscombe, Croydon
11 Sept. 09.

My dear Louise,

It is so nice of you to remember me – how did you know the date? I am very fond of Jefferies, and the pieces in the *Open Air* are so many of them down here.[3] There is always a tiny pain in receiving – I suppose it comes from a lurking sense that we get more kindness than we deserve.

I have been very busy this week, or I would have written to you. I have never even written for the story from those people. Is the address:

London and Provincial Press Agency, 26 Shaftesbury Avenue, W.

If not, write and correct me, then will I demand back your, my, story.

The truth is, I am very much occupied with some work of my own. It is supposed to be a secret, but I guess I shall have to tell you. The editor of the *English Review* has accepted some of my Verses, and wants to put them into the *English Review*, the November issue.[4] But you see they are all in the rough, and want revising, so this week and so on I am very hard at work, slogging verse into form. I shall be glad when I have finished: then I may

[1] It is assumed that DHL bought two copies of the *Laocoon* on the same occasion (see previous letter n. 2).

[2] Mrs Dax's daughter recalls that DHL sent her mother three postcards (which would be numbered 1–3) of a similar type; nos. 2 and 3 have been lost.

[3] Louie had sent a copy of Richard Jefferies (1848–87), *The Open Air* (1885) for DHL's birthday on 11 September.

[4] In June 1909 Jessie Chambers sent some of DHL's poems – possibly without his consent – to Ford Madox Hueffer, editor of the *English Review* (see Nehls, i. 102–6). Five poems ('Dreams Old and Nascent' I and II; 'Baby Movements' I and II; 'Discipline'), under the general title 'A Still Afternoon', appeared in the November issue.

get on with the prose work. The editor, Ford Madox Hueffer,[1] says he will be glad to read any of the work I like to send him – which is a great relief, is it not? No more thieving agencies for us. Before I do anything with the Puppy tale, I want to write it out again, and I don't know when I shall have time to do that. I never thought of myself blossoming out as a poet – I had planted my beliefs in my prose.

I am glad to hear you managed your inspectors so well – you are a dab. I wish I were in Nottingham at this moment – it is two o'clock – to be going with you to the theatre. I should very much like to see *Strife*.[2] Last week I went to the Lyceum, to see Justin McCarthy's *Proud Prince* – never saw such rot in my life.[3]

Mary is responsible for this shocking page – she is larking with me as I write on my knee – another onslaught!

What devilish weather we're having! Can you keep happy?

Addio DHL

125. To Jessie Chambers, [c. 11 September 1909]

Text: E.T. 163–4.

[12 Colworth Road, Addiscombe, Croydon]
[c. 11 September 1909][4]

[Hueffer] is fairish, fat, about forty, and the kindest man on earth. Last night I dined with celebrities, and to-night I am dining with two R.A.s, but I'd give it all up for one of our old evenings in the Haggs parlour.

[1] Ford Madox Hueffer (later Ford) (1873–1939), novelist and editor. Grandson of the painter Ford Madox Brown. Collaborated with Conrad on two novels, *The Inheritors* (1901) and *Romance* (1903). Founded the *English Review*, December 1908, and edited it for a year (see Goldring, *South Lodge*, pp. 14–56), publishing work by Wells, Conrad, James, Hardy, Tolstoy, Yeats, Bennett, E. M. Forster, Ezra Pound, Wyndham Lewis, Edward Thomas, etc. Several novels followed, including *The Good Soldier* (1915) and the tetralogy *Parade's End* (1924–8), and autobiographical volumes. (See *Mightier than the Sword*, 1938, for an account of his association with DHL.)

[2] *Strife* (1909), the latest play by John Galsworthy (1867–1933), was acted at the Theatre Royal, Nottingham, 6–11 September 1909, by William Mollison and his London company.

[3] Matheson Lang in the title-rôle of the play by McCarthy (1830–1912) opened at the Lyceum on 4 September 1909. The *Times* reviewer (on 6 September) was not much more impressed than DHL.

[4] Jessie Chambers records that DHL saw Hueffer in September 1909 (E.T. 163).

126. To Jessie Chambers, [post 11 September 1909]

Text: E.T. 164.

[12 Colworth Road, Addiscombe, Croydon]
[post 11 September 1909][1]

['Lawrence began begging me [Jessie] to go and see him in London. He had so much to tell me and to show me. He had written a play,[2] and there were poems it was] too much fag [to copy out. He also wanted me to meet the girl he had almost decided to marry.']][3]

127. To Louie Burrows, [16 October 1909]

Text: MS UN; Boulton 44.

12 Colworth Rd, Addiscombe, Croydon
17 Oct 09.

Dear Louisa,

Here I am at last, and I have got 'Goose Fair'.[4] See what you think of it. I am sorry I have kept the pictures so long.[5]

You ask me first of all what kind of a 'paper' is the *English Review*: It is a half-crown magazine, which has only been out some twelve months. It is very fine, and very 'new'. There you will meet the new spirit at it's best: and, if you belong to the N[ational] U[nion] [of] T[eachers], you can get the *Review* at much reduced rates. It is the best possible way to get into touch with the new young school of realism, to take the *English Review*. In this month's issue, there is a particularly fine story 'The Nest' – such a one as you would find nowhere but in the *English*, and a magnificent story.[6] My four pieces of verse come out next month: I am not taking a nom de plume: I feel rather daft when I think of appearing, if only in so trivial a way, before the public.

You ask me also how you will get your stories typed. You must send them to a professional typist: look in any newspaper among the Authors, Agencies list in the adverts, and you will see men wanting to type M.S.S. for about 8d per 1000 words. Since a short story is only about 3 or 4 thousand words,

1 Jessie Chambers dates this letter 'soon after the meeting with Hueffer' recorded in the previous letter (E.T. 164).

2 Jessie Chambers identifies this play as *A Collier's Friday Night* (E.T. 166).

3 Agnes Holt (1883–1971), a fellow-teacher in Croydon. m. Walter E. Blanchard (d. 1951), 5 August 1911, Headmaster of Ramsey Grammar School, Isle of Man, 1911–22; she herself taught English and French at the school from September 1911. (She later destroyed all the letters she had received from DHL.)

4 DHL had recovered his MS from the London and Provincial Press Agency.

5 Cf. Letter 106.

6 A story by Anne Douglas Sedgwick, *English Review*, iii (October 1909), 392–425.

it would not ruin you to have one done, when you got a really good one. I return you the 'Goose Fair' – you may as well keep it entirely. If I had it I should write it all out again, and vivify in places: but you will use your own discretion. When you have got your story from J[essie], let me see it. I am always interested. But pray, do not write *too* romantically: write as near to life as possible. You needn't be pessimistic or cynical, but it is always best to be true. The *English Review* is finely truthful, on the whole.

I went to Wagners *Tristan and Isolde* last night, and was very disappointed.[1] I would much rather have seen *Strife*. *Tristan* is long, feeble, a bit hysterical, without grip or force. I was frankly sick of it.

I am glad your school thrives so well. For myself, I am sick of things: I shall go to France as soon as I can. Forgive me for being so long writing.

Yours DHL

127a. To Agnes Holt, [November? 1909]

Text: MS NCL; Unpublished.

[12 Colworth Road, Addiscombe, Croydon]
[November? 1909][2]

I have only this minute come back – Hueffer kept me. Will you come round here? It is not very comfy, place in a muddle, kids rampant. How is it at Lyndhurst? If you're crowded, come here, as soon as possible, will you?

I'm sorry Im late. DHL

128. To Blanche Jennings, 1 November 1909

Text: MS Uliv; cited in Allott 61, 67, 75.

12 Colworth Rd, Addiscombe, Croydon
1st November 09

Dear Bee,

I was thinking of you only on Saturday morning and thinking how in the ordinary insignificant manner our chapter had dribbled to an end. What's this – an epilogue or a new chapter?

[1] The Royal Carl Rosa Opera Company performed at the Grand Theatre, Croydon, 11–16 October 1909. Since *Tristan and Isolde* was staged only on Friday 15 October, DHL's letter must have been written on 16, not 17, October.

[2] DHL was seeing Agnes Holt frequently during this period but, since his message cannot be linked with a particular visit to Hueffer, the date must remain uncertain.

The MS itself had subsequently been slipped into one of two books presented and inscribed by DHL to Agnes Holt: Thomas Sturge Moore's *The Rout of the Amazons* (inscribed 'Xmas 1909') or Francis Thompson's *The Hound of Heaven* ('22 March 1910'). (Both books are now in the Nottinghamshire County Library.)

Thanks very much for your card: it is generous of you. I will not return to the end of the last chapter – only to say that I have no idea wherein I insulted you. You see I say so many things, and put my head under your veil to say them: it is almost inevitable I should say quite the wrong thing some time. I am sorry.

I think no youth was ever more verbose than I: it is amusing to remember. But I am waxing vastly more reticent: I cannot write letters now: the only ones I accomplish are those to my mother. – But tell me what you think of the verses, will you?[1] – if it is worth while. Do you take the *Review*? – in October's, the verses of Rachel Annand Taylor were exceedingly good:[2] did they rile you? What do you think of Ford Madox Hueffer's 'A Call'?[3] I think it has more art than life. I have been up to see him twice – he is a really fine man, in that he is so generous, so understanding, and in that he keeps the doors of his soul open, and you may walk in: you know what I mean: I likewise have a habit of admitting whosoever will into my intimacy, a habit of which the south, and school, are curing me. I have just sent up to Mr Hueffer my novel, which I have re-written, and which is much altered. I have added a third part, have married Lettie and Leslie and George and Meg, and Emily to a stranger and myself[4] to nobody. Oh Lord – what a farce.

I have got a new girl down here:[5] you know my kind, a girl to whom I gas. She is very nice, and takes me seriously: which is unwisdom. I do *not* believe in love: mon Dieu, I don't, not for me: I never could believe in anything I cannot experience or, which is equivalent 'imagine'. I can't help it: the game begins, and I play it, and the girl plays it, and – what matter what the end is!

I have been out a good bit lately: to the theatre and so forth. I found *Don* at the Haymarket, very good, on Saturday.[6] Really, I am very busy: either I am writing stuff, or going out, alone or with Miss H[olt], or rarely, reading

[1] Presumably DHL's poems published in *English Review*, November 1909 (see p. 137, n. 4).

[2] Rachel Annand Taylor (1876–1960), Scottish poet and biographer, whose 'Three Poems' – 'The Epilogue of the Dreaming Women'; 'The First Time'; 'The Masque of Proteus' – appeared in *English Review*, iii (October 1909), 378–9. She published *Poems* (1904); *Rose and Vine* (1909); *The Hours of Fiammetta; a sonnet sequence* (1910); *Leonardo the Florentine* (1927), etc. Gilbert Murray described the second volume as 'poetry of intense imagination and exquisite craftsmanship...defiantly and mockingly anti-modern, and instinct with a rich and dreamlike beauty of phrase'. DHL first met her at the home of Ernest and Grace Rhys (see Letter 180).

[3] This was published in four parts, August–November 1909 (*English Review*, iii. 93–134, 282–314, 460–76, 629–52).

[4] Cyril Beardsall.

[5] Agnes Holt.

[6] The comedy by Rudolf Besier (1878–1942) opened on 12 October 1909.

or painting: then when I begin to write a letter to you, suddenly I wax sceptical of everything. I must stop.

Have you read Arnold Bennet's *Old Wives' Tale – Daily Mail* sixpenny?[1] – Have you read John Galsworthy's *Man of Property* – paper, 6d?[2] Get them if you have not. What did you think of 'The Nest' in the October *Review*: it was wonderfully fine? Have you got any new books? Have you got any of Synge's plays – the *Playboy of the Western World* – I should like to read them: but I know the little volume beginning or ending with *Riders to the Sea*.[3] Have you ever been able to get hold of one of George Moore's – *Evelyn Innes* or another? I want that. What did you think of *Tono Bungay*?

How is the world with you? I feel like a nihilist: I do not care much for anything, and am ready to rebel if there is cause.

I hope life is not a dull hunger to you. Addio DHL

129. To Louie Burrows, [3? November 1909]

Text: MS UN; Boulton 45.

[12 Colworth Road, Addiscombe, Croydon]
[3? November 1909]

Dear Lou,

Many thanks for your suggestion. If there is anything else, you alter it.

What I want you to do is to send in the story[4] for the Christmas prize competition: get a *Guardian* and see what it says.[5] The prize per story is £3, and they keep the copyright. They would print your name: are you satisfied? You will also have to swear that the story is yours – but what does it matter! If we win we go whacks, according to agreement. Do you recognise the people? – a glorified Lois Mee (is she glorified) and a glorified (?) Taylor?[6]

Tom Smith is just the same:[7] no worse, I think. We had a very good time

[1] The novel (1908) by Bennett (1867–1931) appeared in this format, October 1909.

[2] Published, Heinemann, July 1907.

[3] *Riders to the Sea* (1905) by John Millington Synge (1871–1909) was published (along with *In the Shadow of the Glen*, 1904) at 1/- in the 'Vigo Cabinet Series' (E. Mathews), December 1907.

[4] 'Goose Fair'.

[5] The *Nottinghamshire Guardian* did not carry the rules of a short story competition in 1909. DHL was (wrongly) assuming that there would be a competition as in 1907.

[6] Lois Mee was a fellow-student at University College, Nottingham, and presumably is the 'Lois' in the story. 'Taylor' was probably Lewis Taylor, another College contemporary, the original of Will Selby.

[7] Thomas Alfred Smith (1886–1966), a fellow-student at University College, Nottingham. Graduated B.Sc. (London), 1st Class Honours, 1910; in 1913 was awarded 1851 Exhibition for research at Göttingen University towards Ph.D; outbreak of war intervened. 1914 commissioned in 5th Bn. Lincs. Regiment; 1915–19 seconded to H.M. Explosives Factory,

– went to the Haymarket to see *Don* – jolly good! We enjoyed ourselves. I saw Machen: he is the same blithering cocky fool.[1]

You will have seen the *Review* by now: they sent me a complimentary copy. Yes, tell me what you think, I am really anxious to know. Have you done any more at the story of yours?

I have not been up to much just lately: forgive me if I do not write any more, I am tired tonight. School is all right, but the weather! Floods – and the fog has blown down thick from London today.[2] Addio DHL

130. To Jessie Chambers, [14? November 1909]

Text: E.T. 164.

[12 Colworth Road, Addiscombe, Croydon]
[14? November 1909][3]

It is snowing, and I ought to be out on Wimbledon Common with a girl, a teacher here...I have almost made up my mind to marry her as soon as I get some money. I think I shall. I am almost sure I shall.

131. To Jessie Chambers, [post 14 November 1909]

Text: E.T. 164.

[12 Colworth Road, Addiscombe, Croydon]
[post 14 November 1909][4]

[Lawrence wrote to Jessie 'that his sister complained that he went about too much and did not send money home.'] But then I am in digs. I can't hang about the house as if I were at home.

Oldbury, Worcestershire. 1921–9 worked as industrial chemist with Anglo-Persian Oil Co., in Wales, Iran, etc.; 1929–30 with British Controlled Oilfields Ltd. in Trinidad and Venezuela; 1931–45 with War Office (Explosives Directorate) and Ministry of Supply, finally as Deputy Director of Explosives. 1945–8, as Director with Control Commission in Germany responsible for the dismantling of Germany's chemical industry. m. Elsie Hardstaff, 24 May 1915.

1 Perhaps John S. Machin, a fellow-student at College.

2 *The Croydon Natural History and Scientific Society: Report of the Meteorological Committee for 1909* (1910), records 3 November as being 'especially foggy'. Thus, in conjunction with DHL's visit to the Haymarket on 30 October, 3 November is taken as the date for this letter.

3 *The Croydon Natural History and Scientific Society: Rainfall of Croydon District 1905–22* records snowfall on 14, 15, 16 and 23 November 1909; DHL's meeting with Agnes Holt was probably arranged for a weekend; and this suggests 14 November as the most likely date for his letter.

4 Jessie Chambers places this letter in sequence after the previous one and before the account of her visit to London at the end of November.

132. To Louie Burrows, 20 November 1909

Text: MS UN; Boulton 46–7.

12 Colworth Rd, Addiscombe, Croydon
20 Nov. 09.

My dear Louie,

If I don't write you, don't be cross. I am so busy.

Concerning 'Goose Fair'. You will have got the rules, and you will have found, I think, that I could not send in the tale for the competition. If you think I might, I am quite willing to have the thing under my own name: only you can legally claim that the tale is as much your child as mine.

Last Sunday I went up to lunch with Ford Madox Hueffer, and with Violet Hunt, who is rich, and a fairly well-known novelist.[1] They were both delightful. Hueffer took me to tea at Ernest Rhys': he edits heaps of classics – Dents Everyman's, for instance. He is very nice indeed, and so is his wife, Grace Rhys, who writes stories.[2] After tea we went on to call on H. G. Wells who also lives up at Hampstead.[3] He is a funny little chap: his conversation is a continual squirting of thin little jets of weak acid: amusing, but not expansive. There is no glow about him. His two boys, in pale blue dressing gowns, came in and kissed us goodnight.

Hueffer is reading my novel. He says it's good, and is going to get it published for me. He also says I ought to get out a volume of verse, so you see how busy I am.

I went on Tuesday to Violet Hunts 'at home' at the Reform Club in Adelphi Terrace, on the Embankment. It was very jolly. Elizabeth Martindale[4] and Ellaline Terriss[5] and Mary Cholmondeley[6] were there – and Ezra

[1] Isobel Violet Hunt (1866–1942), novelist and biographer. Daughter of pre-Raphaelite painter, Alfred W. Hunt, and grew up in Rossetti circle. Wrote for *Pall Mall Gazette*; active suffragist; published novels – *Unkist, Unkind!* (1897), *The Wife of Altamont* (1910), *The House of Many Mirrors* (1914) – short stories, and memoirs, *The Flurried Years* (1926). Though she was never legally married to Ford Madox Hueffer, from 1911 she was known for some years as 'Mrs Hueffer'.

[2] Ernest Rhys (1859–1946) had edited Dekker's plays (1888), and *The Lyric Poets* (1894–9), as well as Everyman's Library. Grace Rhys (1865–1929) had collaborated with her husband on some Everyman's volumes but also wrote novels (*Mary Dominic*, 1898; *The Wooing of Sheila*, 1901) and children's books.

[3] Herbert George Wells (1866–1946), leading novelist and controversialist. His most recent publications were *Kipps* (1905), *Tono-Bungay* (New York, 1908), and *Ann Veronica* (October 1909).

[4] Hueffer's wife, Elsie née Martindale (1876–1949), signed herself Elizabeth Martindale when she published essays (see *English Review*, iii (August–November 1909), 88–92, 426–36; iv (January 1910), 249–56) and her novel, *Margaret Hever* (1909). (See Douglas Goldring, *The Last Pre-Raphaelite* (1948), p. 150.)

[5] Mary Ellaline Terriss (1871–1971), a well-known variety actress; m. (Sir) Seymour Hicks, 1893. (See *Ellaline Terriss: By Herself and with Others*, 1928.)

[6] A minor novelist (1859–1925); her satirical novel *Red Pottage* created a stir in 1899.

Pound.[1] He is a well-known American poet – a good one. He is 24, like me, – but his god is beauty, mine, life. He is jolly nice: took me to supper at Pagnani's, and afterwards we went down to his room at Kensington. He lives in an attic, like a traditional poet – but the attic is a comfortable well furnished one. He is an American Master of Arts and a professor of the Provençal group of languages, and he lectures once a week on the minstrels [at][2] the London polytechnic. He is rather remarkable – a good bit of a genius, and with not the least self consciousness.

This afternoon I am going up to tea with him and we are going out after to some friends who will not demand evening dress of us. He knows W B Yeats[3] and all the Swells. Aren't the folks kind to me: it is really wonderful. Hueffer is splendid: I have met a gentleman indeed in him, and an artist.

There, I have no time. Write and tell me your news, I like to receive letters.

Forgive me this rude haste, will you Yours DHL

133. To Grace Crawford, 21 November 1909

Text: MS UT; Fraser 136.

12 Colworth Rd, Addiscombe, Croydon
21 Nov. 09.

Dear Miss Crawford,[4]

Here is the 'morceau' of Francis Thompson:[5] no 'Hound', but an exquisite little thing written as most of Thompson's are on a dim sad day when the dew stays grey on the grass. Poor Thompson! Poor me and my rhetorics!

I did love those jolly young washerwomen of Naples, and the tearful

1 Ezra Pound (1885–1972) had been dismissed from his post at Wabash College, Indiana, travelled in Europe and now settled in London. His *Personae* and *Exultations* appeared in 1909.

2 MS reads '&'.

3 William Butler Yeats (1865–1939), Irish poet, dramatist and critic, had established his reputation with *Poems* (1895) and more recently his 8-volume *Collected Works in Verse and Prose* (Stratford-on-Avon, 1908).

4 Grace Crawford (1889–1977), born in Paris of American parents; brought to England in 1896 and remained. Studied singing, piano and ballet. Friendly with Violet Hunt and particularly with Ezra Pound. m. artist and designer Claud Lovat Fraser, February 1917 (he died 1921). (See Grace Lovat Fraser, *In the Days of my Youth*, 1970.)

5 The poem, 'Absence', by Francis Thompson (1859–1907) – famous for 'The Hound of Heaven' (in *Poems* 1893) – was first published in *English Review*, iv (January 1910), 185–6, i.e. six weeks after DHL wrote it out and included it in this letter. (With one exception, the only variants between DHL's copy and the text in *English Review* are in accidentals; the exception is in l. 46 where DHL writes 'bliss its pain', and the *Review* prints 'bliss is of pain'.)

Tuscan maids.[1] It is fine of you to bring them back so jolly and so tearful. – And a gentle painter, like Fantin Latour,[2] could have made a beautiful harmony in pink, with ghosts of old Italian loves in the shadows, as you stood under the lamp against the wall.

– What are winter cherries –![3]

It is a shame to break the moment from its stalk, to wither[4] in the vase of memory, by thanking you. Addio D. H. Lawrence

What an ass I am!

134. To Agnes Holt, [27 November 1909]

Text: E.T. 165; PC.

[27 November 1909][5]

['Lawrence sent a postcard to his possible fiancée telling her that he would take [Jessie] to see her in the morning.']

135. To Ernest Smith, [5 December 1909]

Text: MS BL; Moore, *Intelligent Heart* (Grove Press edn 1962), p. 102.

[12 Colworth Road, Addiscombe, Croydon]

[5 December 1909][6]

[Lawrence wrote 'mainly about school and his work there: he was asking Mr. Smith's[7] advice about buying a microscope for school. Later he says:]

[1] The reference is to Neapolitan and other folk-songs which DHL loved to hear Grace Crawford sing.

[2] Ignace Henri J. T. Fantin-Latour (1836–1904).

[3] DHL and Grace Crawford had argued about the 'sprays in the drawing-room; he called them Cape gooseberries and [she] winter cherries' (Fraser 136).

[4] to wither] and put

[5] This card was written (probably in Selfridge's) during Jessie Chambers's visit to London 'at the end of November' (E.T. 164). On the same day she and DHL went to see Alfred Sutro's *Making a Gentleman* which ran at the Garrick Theatre 13 September – 4 December 1909.

[6] The text is taken from Jessie Chambers's letter to S. S. Koteliansky, 15 July 1937; in that she quotes from DHL's letter to Smith. Smith had recently sent the original (now lost) to her to read. She dates DHL's letter 'exactly a week' after she and he visited Hueffer and Violet Hunt (on 28 November 1909).

[7] Ernest Alfred Smith (1872–1942) was the 'lecturer popularly known as "Botany" Smith' whom Jessie Chambers describes as the only member of staff at University College, Nottingham, with whom DHL had anything approaching a personal relationship (E.T. 76). Smith (B.Sc. London 1895) was Assistant Lecturer, then Lecturer in Botany, 1894–1908; he became Normal Master, then Lecturer in Psychology and finally organiser of University extra-mural Tutorial Classes, before moving to Manchester College, Oxford, in 1916, to study for the Unitarian Ministry. From 1918 till his retirement in 1937 he served congregations in Manchester and Wandsworth, London. Published *Religion and its Social Expression* (1932).

Life seems to me barbarous, recklessly wasteful and destructive, often hideous and dreadful: but, on the whole, beautiful...I owe you a debt. You were my first live teacher of philosophy: you showed me the way out of a torturing crude Monism, past Pragmatism, into a sort of crude but appeasing Pluralism [and then almost apologises for writing!']

136. To Louie Burrows, 11 December 1909

Text: MS UN; Postmark, Croydon DE 11 09; Boulton 47–8.

[12 Col][1]worth Rd, Addiscombe, Croydon
11 Dec. 09.

My dear Louie,

What a wretch I am to neglect you so long! In truth, I am become a shocking correspondent. I have not any news to tell.

I sent the story, with another I have written, up to Ford Madox Hueffer on Thursday. He will tell me what to do with them.[2]

I am going up to dine with Ezra Pound tonight. We shall meet a crowd of other literary folk. I will tell you about it later. Next week I am going up to Grace Rhys to meet various poetry people. I am to take some of my unpublished verses to read. I do not look forward to these things much. I shall feel such a fool. I shall be able to tell you all about things at Christmas.

I hear Ada has asked you over for a few days. That is all right! And she is going to see you? I *must* squeeze in a day this time, at Quorn. I will see what mother says. I hope the weather will be fine, and we can have a giddy time. I am anxiously awaiting Christmas – are not you? I am sick of this term.

Have you heard the BSc. results – everybody failed except one second year man: T A Smith, Preston, Morrison,[3] everybody. Sad, is it not? I am very sorry for T.A.S.

Don't be cross with me for not writing. You write to me instead. There is only a fortnight. A Noël DHL

137. To Grace Crawford, 12 December 1909

Text: MS UT; Fraser 138–9.

12 Colworth Rd, Addiscombe, Croydon
12 Dec. 09.

Dear Miss Crawford,

What a jolly girl you are! Do you know, when Pound was asleep – I stayed with him last night – when he had hidden the glories of his head under the

[1] MS torn.

[2] i.e. 'Goose Fair' and 'Odour of Chrysanthemums'.

[3] Probably James H. Preston and James Morrison whose names appear among those of students in the Day Training Department, University College, Nottingham.

counterpane, and was asleep, sighing like a child, I was watching you dancing all the time, and it was so strange.[1] At one moment it was you; then it was a flock of wagtails at the waterside, dipping their little black heads and tossing them up again, running on the margin of the water, then flashing into a rustle of flight, their wings suddenly spread out white and black; and, it seemed blue, for that was the ruffle and upcatch of your skirts. You were gone again in a second, and it was the peewits wheeling and swinging over a wild patch of blue scabious, black as they stoop down, then suddenly lifting white and glistening, and it was you again, raising your face. I saw the seagulls low on a misty blue sea, spreading their long wings, flying round and round, and stooping to touch the water: then it was your arms and your hands picking at your skirts. Just as I *was* going to sleep, a great[2] wild swan came with black feet flying up against me, and startling me again: then I knew it was only you coming down on me in your dance.

'Oh glory, when is she going to stop dancing?' I said to myself, and I stared at the red embers withdrawing into the ashes like a winter sun into the mists. I heard dear old St. Mary Abbott chime four.[3] We had been in bed two hours. Then you danced [a]way, and did not come back. Pound was quite oblivious. I was near to nudging him in the back and asking him if he could see anything. But I refrained.

If you dance for me on Saturday, then perhaps the folks at Rhys' will seem only like so many penguins, and I can rave at them in bad verse brilliantly. Command your humour. A Samedi – cinq heures D. H. Lawrence

Forgive this rotten paper.

138. To William Heinemann, 15 December 1909

Text: Huxley 1.

12 Colworth Road, Addiscombe, Croydon
December 15th, 1909

Dear Sir,[4]

I have just received the accompanying letter from Mr. Ford Madox

[1] For the occasion alluded to see Fraser 138.

[2] a great] it was a great

[3] Pound lived 'in a lodging house in the little paved court behind St Mary Abbot's, Kensington' (Goldring, *South Lodge*, p. 47).

[4] William Heinemann (1863–1920), leading English publisher. Trained with Kegan Paul, Trench and Trübner; began independently in 1890 and was joined by Sydney Pawling in 1893. Established a brilliant fiction list including Stevenson, Kipling, Galsworthy, Conrad, Maugham and Wells. Commissioned Constance Garnett's Russian translations. Published DHL's *The White Peacock*, 1911, but refused *The Trespasser* and *Sons and Lovers*; Heinemann Ltd took over the publication of all DHL's titles on 30 January 1935.

Hueffer.[1] I hasten to forward it to you, and in doing so to offer you the novel of which he speaks.

It is my first. I have as yet published nothing but a scrap of verse.[2] At the moment I feel a trifle startled and somewhat elated by Mr. Hueffer's letter, but already a grain of doubt is germinating in me.

I hope you will allow me to send you the MSS. Of course I am willing to fulfil all Mr. Hueffer's injunctions. I know nothing of the publishing of books. Yours sincerely D. H. Lawrence

139. To Louie Burrows, [22 December 1909]

Text: MS UN; Boulton 48.

12 Colworth Rd.
23 Dec 09

Dear Lou,

I am so tired. It is nearly midnight. I have just finished packing – I go home tomorrow.[3] I hope you'll like Benson.[4]

When are you coming to us? Oh, I have been so busy – such a rush! I feel as if I had not had a rest for years. But we'll make everything straight in the holiday.

A jolly, jolly Christmas to you. I shall see you before the new year.

Vale DHL

140. To Grace Crawford, 23 December 1909

Text: MS UT; Fraser 139–40.

Lynn Croft, Eastwood, Notts.
23rd Dec. 09

Dear Miss Crawford,

I hope my verses wont offend you.[5] I know they are poor enough. But do you like my little card?[6]

In the old days, they used to shed their blood for their ladies. Nowadays,

1 Not extant.

2 In *English Review*, November 1909.

3 Term ended at noon on 23 December 1909 (School Log), on which day DHL travelled home (Letter 140 was written from Eastwood on 23 December); thus although DHL dated this letter 23 December he actually wrote it before midnight on 22nd.

4 Perhaps (Sir) Francis (Frank) R. Benson (1858–1939), actor-manager. His theatrical companies regularly toured provincial theatres.

5 The verses (printed below), written on DHL's Christmas card, are an early version of 'Song' in *The Egoist*, 1 April 1914 (later entitled 'Flapper', *Complete Poems*, i. 46).

6 A Christmas card of DHL's own design, with water-colour decorations: bluebells and bees (p. 1), and a daddy-long-legs (p. 4).

we take our 'ruddy drops'[1] and patiently transform them, and lay the essence on paper for you: – then, woe is me, what a nothing it looks! Would you rather have a dented shield and a broken lance and a dread name? They would never look ridiculous, as our things do – eh? You are American. But you do prefer this form of gore – the transformed – don't you, even if it looks foolish?

I hope you will be very gay for Christmas.

Then till the new year, farewell. D. H. Lawrence

Song

Love has crept out of her sealèd
    heart
As a field bee, black and amber
Breaks from the winter-cell, to clamber
Up the warm grass where the
    sunbeams start.

Love has crept into her summery
    eyes
With glints and coloured glimmerings
Such as lie along the folded wings
Of the bee before he flies

But I with a ruffling impatient
    breath
Have loosed the wings of the wild
    young sprite;
He has shook them out in a
    reeling flight,
And over her words he hasteneth

Love flies delighted in her voice:
  The hum of his glittering, drunken wings
  Sets quivering with melody the common things
That she says, and my soul's wild roses
    rejoice

To greet you this Christmas D. H. Lawrence

[1] Cliché deriving from *Julius Caesar* II. i. 289.

141. To Louie Burrows, 30 December 1909

Text: MS UN; PC; Postmark, Eastwood DE 30 09; Boulton 48.

Eastwood
30/12/09

Chère Louise,

Pourquoi ne nous avez vous pas écrit? Nous attendons de vos nouvelles. Vous allez venir le Samedi, n'est ce pas – le jour de l'An? Dites nous l'heure, et nous allons vous rencontrer au station. Empressez de me répondre.

DHL

[Dear Louise,

Why haven't you written to us? We are waiting for news of you. You are coming on Saturday, aren't you – New Year's Day? Let us know the time, and we shall meet you at the station. Let me hear soon. DHL]

142. To Jessie Chambers, [1910?]

Text: E.T. 122.

[12 Colworth Road, Addiscombe, Croydon]
[1910?][1]

[Lawrence 'picked up W. H. Hudson's *South American Sketches* for two-pence and passed it on as a wonderful find, and at various times he sent me [Jessie] a volume of *Don Quixote*, promising to try and find the companion volume, one of Burns' *Letters*, and Sterne's *Sentimental Journey*, drawing my attention to the beautiful type and the fine old leather bindings.']

143. To Jessie Chambers, [1910?]

Text: E.T. 122.

[12 Colworth Road, Addiscombe, Croydon]
[1910?]

[Lawrence 'would sometimes write,] I'm sending you a Whitmanesque poem,[2] [when he was enclosing one of his own.']

[1] The letters referred to here together with the one following were written after March 1909 (the publication date of Hudson's *South American Sketches*) and, according to Jessie Chambers's sequence, apparently in the year of Mrs Lawrence's death, 1910.

[2] 'Whitman's *Leaves of Grass* was one of [DHL's] great books', E.T. 122.

144. To Louie Burrows, 23 January 1910

Text: MS UN; Boulton 49.

12 Colworth Rd, Addiscombe, Croydon
23 Jan 10

My dear Louise,

Do not be cross with me if I do not write letters. I scribble so much, I can only set to a letter with greatest difficulty.

Thanks for the enclosures. I have re-written the 'White Stocking'. 'The Chimney Sweeper' is much improved, I think'[1] You need, I think, to elaborate a bit: do a bit of character drawing, and give your locality: you want to give more setting: the figures are all right, but examine the scene '*pictorially*' – it is not there. Gather the picture – get the essentials for *description* – present to the eye. The conversation is very amusing. I should offer it to the *Guardian*. You have a certain quaint little talent of your own, but it is superficial. Accept it as such – and make the best of it – then you'll do things very likely as good as W. W. Jacobs.[2]

My novel is practically accepted. I went up to Wm Heinemann on Friday: he read me his readers crits:[3] mostly good. I am to alter a bit in parts, then the thing will come out, and I shall have royalties.

Fordy has given up the *English*. Austin Harrison wrote me that he would be glad if I would continue to submit my work to him.[4] Is he the man that wrote the 'Puntilla'?[5] I think so.

You must study the presentation – be a little more accurate – for instance, would they see the white and blue of the eyes of a man lifted up against the sky, therefore in shadow? – would the creeper in the chimney see 'white flesh'? Why did the kid do it? Where is the place? Describe the seen 'particularly', and the butcher, and Siah – put a paragraph or two in front to show *why* the sweep should behave so – don't tell us, show him in the situation which leads up to it. Then send the tale to the *Strand*[6] – they would very probably have it.

Mrs Jones likes the tale very much. Get W W Jacobs out of the

[1] A short story by Louie Burrows.

[2] William Wymark Jacobs (1863–1943), author of over twenty volumes of short stories between 1896 and 1926.

[3] The reader was Frederick M. Atkinson (see p. 162 n. 5).

[4] Hueffer was responsible for the *Review* until December 1909. By then he had lost £2,800 on it. Sir Alfred Mond bought the journal at a nominal price, dismissed Hueffer and replaced him by Austin Harrison (see Goldring, *South Lodge*, pp. 52–5). Harrison (1873–1928), son of Frederic Harrison, remained editor until 1923.

[5] Harrison's story appeared in the *English Review*, iv (January 1910), 208–22.

[6] The *Strand Magazine*, founded in 1891.

sevenpenny Nelsons, and read his amusing tales, and study their development.[1] You should do as well. Farewell now – DHL

145. To Blanche Jennings, [28 January 1910]
Text: MS ULiv; cited in Allott 61, 67.

12 Colworth Rd, Addiscombe, Croydon
28 Jan. 09

My dear B.,

I have been writing like the devil lately – I suppose He is a literary gentleman – so have had no epistolary energy. Tonight I am taking a rest, having exhausted my immediate duties and my inclinations.

I have a few little newses to tell you. First – there is a story of mine coming in the Feby. *Review*.[2] Second – Heinemann is going to take my novel and publish it, giving me royalties. That's all for the moment.

How are you? What do you want me to tell you about – my latest love?[3] Well – she's off again – I don't like her. She's rather a striking girl with much auburn hair. At first, she seems a person of great capacity, being alert, prompt, smart with her tongue, and independent in her manner. She is very popular with men, and goes out a good bit. She's going for 27. I have been out with her a good bit. Now I'm tired of her. Why? – She's so utterly ignorant and old fashioned, really, though she has been to college and has taught in London some years. A man is – or was – a more or less interesting creature, with whom one could play about with smart and silly speech – no more – not an animal – mon dieu, no! – I have enlightened her, and now she has no courage. She still judges by mid-Victorian standards, and covers herself with a woolly fluff of romance that the years will wear sickly. She refuses to see that a man is a male, that kisses are the merest preludes and anticipations, that love is largely a physical sympathy that is soon satisfied and satiated. She believes men worship their mistresses; she is all sham and superficial in her outlook, and I can't change her. She's frightened. Now I'm sick of her. She pretends to be very fond of me; she isn't really; even if she were, what do I care! – but if she were, she wouldn't be the timid duffer she is, declaring things dreadful, painful, hateful; life not worth living, life a degradation etc etc.; she would be interested in life; she lapses into sickly sentimentality when it is a question of naked life.

[1] Only Jacobs's *The Lady of the Barge* had been published (in November 1907) in Nelson's famous series.

[2] 'Goose Fair', *English Review*, iv (February 1910), 399–408. This detail (among others) confirms the error in DHL's dating of this letter.

[3] Agnes Holt.

I have been sick of her some little time. At Christmas an old fire burned up afresh, like an alcohol flame, faint and invisible, that sets fire to a tar barrel. It is the old girl, who has been attached to me so long.[1] It is most rummy. She knows me through and through, and I know her – and – the devil of it is, she's a hundred and fifty miles away. We have fine, mad little scenes now and again, she and I – so strange, after ten years, and I had hardly kissed her all that time. She has black hair, and wonderful eyes, big and very dark, and very vulnerable; she lifts up her face to me and clings to me, and the time goes like a falling star, swallowed up immediately; it is wonderful, that time, long avenues of minutes – hours – should be swept up with one sweep of the hand, and the moment for parting has arrived when the first kiss seems hardly overkissed. She is coming to me for a week-end soon; we shall not stay here in Croydon, but in London. The world is for us, and we are for each other – even if only for one spring – so what does it matter! What would my people and hers say? – but what do I care – not a damn! – they will not know.

'*I* am the master of my fate
I am the captain of my soul'[2]

I wonder why I tell you all these things, that I would not breathe to another soul! Because you ask me, I suppose. But put my letter in the fire, will you please! And tell me – do *you* think I am wrong?

You can get *Evelyn Innes* and *Sister Teresa* for 4½d each – Fisher Unwin I believe. Send me *Esther Waters*, will you, as you promised.[3] I have only read *Ann Veronica*, of any note, lately.[4] It is not very good – not to be mentioned beside *Tono-Bungay*.

Do not be a long, long time in writing to me. I am always glad to receive your letters.

Why are you sad? – tell me. What is the matter, that you have so discordant a note? – Tell me. What do you want? But what we all want, madly, is human contact. That I find more and more – not ideas; – transference of feeling – human contact.

I will tell you about a new girl[5] – a girl who '*interests*' me – nothing else – next time I write – a girl here – call her Helène – she is very interesting.

Goodbye – Human Contact – remember! – that's what I want.

Goodbye DHL

[1] Jessie Chambers.
[2] W. E. Henley (1849–1903), 'Invictus', ll. 15–16.
[3] Fisher Unwin published George Moore's *Evelyn Innes* (1898) in a 6d edn, 1901, and his *Sister Teresa* (1901) at 6d in 1909. Moore's *Esther Waters* (1894) was published at 6d by Scott, 1899.
[4] H. G. Wells's novel (October 1909) created an immediate sensation.
[5] Helen Corke.

146. To Jessie Chambers, [February 1910]

Text: Delavenay 694.

[12 Colworth Road, Addiscombe, Croydon]
[February 1910][1]

I didn't show you 'Goose Fair'; you wouldn't care for it.

147. To Florence Wood, 28 February 1910

Text: MS UT; Moore, *Priest of Love* 114.

12 Colworth Rd, Addiscombe, Croydon
28 Feby 1910

Dear Mrs Wood,[2]

I regret very much that I must send back the tickets.[3] It was so jolly nice of you to send them to me: I feel a meagre sinner returning them to you. But I am just convalescent from a sickness.[4] I have been laid up in bed for some days, watching the tassel of the blind swinging endlessly and mournfully across the grey wet sky. It would have given me real pleasure to have been at the Bechstein tomorrow evening: but I may not be out at that time.

I am very sorry. But you will have a full glad audience, so I do not matter. I shall call and see you some Saturday evening[5] if I may, to thank you personally. Yours Sincerely D. H. Lawrence

148. To Jessie Chambers, [March? 1910]

Text: E.T. 181.

[12 Colworth Road, Addiscombe, Croydon]
[March? 1910][6]

I have always believed it was the woman who paid the price in life. But I've made a discovery. It's the man who pays, not the woman.

[1] Jessie Chambers dates this letter at the time of the publication of 'Goose Fair', February 1910.

[2] Florence Mary Wood (1873–1969), née Schmidt, Australian-born concert singer. Trained by Steffani; friend of Caruso and Busoni; she made a considerable reputation in London. m. 25 March 1903 Francis Derwent Wood (1871–1926), R.A., sculptor. 1908–13 lived in King's Road, Chelsea. DHL was introduced to them by Pound.

[3] Mrs Wood had sent tickets for the vocal and pianoforte recital she was to give with the pianist Elsie Hall (1877–1976), in the Bechstein Hall, 1 March 1910 (see *Times* announcement, 26 February 1910).

[4] DHL was absent from school 8–11 February (School Log).

[5] The Derwent Woods' musical parties on Saturday evenings from c. 1903–25 were a feature of London's artistic life.

[6] Jessie Chambers appears to date this letter shortly before Easter, (27 March) 1910.

149. To Louie Burrows, 9 March 1910

Text: MS UN; Boulton 50.

Davidson Rd Boys School, South Norwood, SE.
9 March 1910

My dear Louie,

I have got the cheque at last for 'Goose Fair', and I hasten to remit you. It is not a vast sum that I send you, but it is worth having, and being the first-fruits of your literary tree, you ought to make much of it. I think I told you I could not do anything with the other story.

Austin Harrison has just sent me the proofs of some verses which he is putting in next month, and as they are just the verses I don't want him to put in, I am rather mad.[1] However, we may not as yet have our own way over these things.

Are you really getting sick of your little school? I am tired myself of being here, but I cannot think of moving till the autumn. I must grin and abide till then. I have nearly finished the novel ready for the publisher. You will also see another story of mine in the May *Review*.[2]

Could you send me a box of hazel catkins. If you could, I should be very much obliged, but don't put yourself to any trouble over them. The spring is also very beautiful here – in Hampton Court and in Richmond it has arrived with a wonderful silken bravery of green and crocus flowers. I could write you prose poems, if I had time.

Tomorrow night I am going up to the Rhyses to meet some celebrities, and to read some of my own verses.[3] I am not very keen, and not very much interested. I am no Society man – it bores me. I like private people who will not talk current clippings. What do you want to do? What have you in mind? – anything? Pray tell me all the interesting things that are happening inside you – I know they are happening.

When you see Tom Smith give him a kiss from me and tell him I am much too bashful to tell him all about myself that he asks. You may tell him if you like.

I'm in a devilish hurry as usual, but I like to get your letters and hear your news.

Forgive me DHL

[1] A group of five poems under the general title 'Night Songs' appeared in the *English Review*, v (April 1910), 4–8.

[2] There was nothing by DHL in the May *Review*. 'Odour of Chrysanthemums', the next to appear, was published in June 1911.

[3] See the account by Ernest Rhys (Nehls, i. 129–32) of this or a similar occasion when Yeats and Pound were the 'celebrities'.

150. To Jessie Chambers, [c. 9 March 1910]

Text: Delavenay 703.

[12 Colworth Road, Addiscombe, Croydon]
[c. 9 March 1910][1]

You have done me great good, my dear. Only I want you here with me. It is as if I cannot rest without you near me, you goodly thing, good to be near, to touch and to hold.

151. To Helen Corke, [c. 17 March 1910]

Text: Corke, *Neutral Ground* 263.

[12 Colworth Road, Addiscombe, Croydon]
[c. 17 March 1910][2]

Are you greatly offended with me?[3] If so, I will wear a becoming humility in your presence – I will stand at an approved distance from the wall you have built about you. But, nevertheless, my tenet holds good...You have no authority for building the wall...

How long will you try to hide yourself? You need people. You are alive...You cannot cover yourself under 'the snows of yesteryear'.[4] Your warmth would melt them.

152. To Jessie Chambers, [c. 23 March 1910]

Text: Delavenay 703.

[12 Colworth Road, Addiscombe, Croydon]
[c. 23 March 1910][5]

I was very nearly unfaithful to you. I can never promise you to be faithful. In the morning she [Alice Dax] came into my room, you know my morning sadness. I told her I was engaged to you. But it is all finished now with her – there is no more sitting on the doorstep.

[1] Jessie Chambers dates this letter in the week following her weekend visit to Croydon, 5–6 March 1910.

[2] Helen Corke (privately) dates this letter before Easter 1910; it is thus conjecturally placed in mid-March.

[3] In Helen Corke's *Neutral Ground*, Derrick Hamilton (DHL) encloses this letter with a story he has asked Ellis (Helen Corke) to look over.

[4] From the poem by François Villon, trans. D. G. Rossetti as 'Ballad of Dead Ladies', ll. 8, 16, 24, 28.

[5] Jessie Chambers must have confused Whitsuntide with Easter in her account of this letter and the related visit of Alice Dax to London. This visit was not between Easter and Whitsuntide but before Easter: Strauss's *Elektra* which Mrs Dax and DHL saw together ceased performance on 19 March 1910. Thus the letter written 'a few days' (Delavenay 703) after Mrs Dax returned home could not have been later than the date conjectured. (On the popularity of the famous Beecham season of *Elektra*, see *English Review*, v (April 1910), 172–9.)

153. To Jessie Chambers, [c. 5 April 1910]

Text: E.T. 181.

[12 Colworth Road, Addiscombe, Croydon]
[c. 5 April 1910][1]

['Almost immediately on returning to Croydon he wrote, apparently very much disturbed, saying that he found he had to write the story of Siegmund...[2] It was in front of him and he had got to do it. He begged [Jessie] to go to Croydon and make the acquaintance of "Helen".'[3]]

154. To Sydney Pawling, 11 April 1910

Text: MS Heinemann; Unpublished.

12 Colworth Rd, Addiscombe, Croydon
11th April 1910

Dear Mr Pawling,[4]

I send you herewith the MS. of my novel 'Nethermere'. It has been a new labour of Hercules. A good deal of it, including the whole of the third part, I have re-written. To be sure, it needed it. I think I have removed all the offensive morsels, all the damns, the devils and the sweat. I hope nothing of the kind remains. My own skin is not super-sensitive, so I can hardly judge what will make delicate people dither. But to my fancy, it is now all quite suitable even for the proverbial jeune fille – a kind of exquisite scented soap, in fact.

I am sorry the manuscript is in such scandalous disarray, but I have done my best to keep it tidy. I am sorry, also, that I could not compress it any further. It is a pity, but I could not cut my man to fit your cloth. I have snipped him where I could, and have tried to make him solid. If there is anything further I can do, I shall be very glad. I am the most docile, the most amenable of pens. I sincerely hope you will like the novel now.

Yours faithfully D. H. Lawrence

[1] DHL's school re-opened on 4 April 1910 (School Log).

[2] '*The Saga of Siegmund* [later *The Trespasser*] was begun during the fortnight succeeding the Easter holidays', Helen Corke, *DHL Review*, vii (1974), 233. On 'Siegmund' himself, Herbert Baldwin MacCartney, see Helen Corke, *In Our Infancy*, facing p. 53, and p. 144ff.

[3] A letter from Jessie Chambers to Helen Corke, 30 June 1911, implies that they first met on 3 July 1910 (UN MS LaM 6).

[4] Sydney S. Pawling (1862?–1923), publisher. Nephew of the founder of Mudie's Library, Pawling joined Heinemann as his partner about 1893. A perspicacious reader and skilled negotiator, he was the essential foil to the ebullient Heinemann. In 1910 they were co-directors; Pawling continued after Heinemann's death in 1920.

155. To Sydney Pawling, 27 April 1910

Text: Huxley 1–2.

12 Colworth Road, Addiscombe, Croydon
27th April, 1910.

Dear Mr. Pawling,

With reference to your letter of the 25th.[1] I think the novel is complete and final in its form as I have sent it you; also I think you will not find it actually so lengthy as the weight of the manuscript might lead one to suppose. The book is, I believe, much shorter than *Tono-Bungay* and about the length of *Jane Eyre*, or rather less, I estimated it. I will delete as much as I can in phrases and perhaps here and there a paragraph from the proofs, but there are now no passages of any length that I could take out.

I have written about half of another novel.[2] I wonder what you would think of it.

Yours sincerely, D. H. Lawrence

156. To Helen Corke, [11 May 1910]

Text: MS UT; cited in Huxley 3, 4.

[12 Colworth Road, Addiscombe, Croydon]
[11 May 1910][3]

I had a letter from Muriel[4] yesterday morning. She knew she had won. She wrote very lovingly, and full of triumphant faith. Since when, I have just lain inert. It is extraordinary, how I seem to have lost all my volition. She will take me as she would pick up an apple that had fallen from the tree when a bird alighted on it. I seem to have no will: it is a peculiar dull, lethargic state I have never known before. And now Muriel writes and says she will come on Saturday, and bring me an excursion ticket, and go home with me by the 6.25. And I say 'Bien – venez', – no more. And she will come. But the time might be next year, or in the after-death, or never, so it seems to me unreal. I cannot feel it beforehand. Till Saturday I shall merely wait in lethargy:[5] I can do no other. Yet I have a second consciousness somewhere actively alive. I write 'Siegmund' – I keep on writing, almost mechanically: very slowly, and[6] mechanically. Yet I don't think I do Siegmund injustice. Somewhere I have got the ballad of 'Sister Helen' – Rossetti's – beating

[1] This is confirmed by Pawling's MS note, 'April 25', on the previous letter.

[2] *The Trespasser.*

[3] In her autobiography Helen Corke says that DHL wrote this letter 'two days before the schools close for the Whitsuntide holidays' (*In Our Infancy*, p. 182). The schools closed on 13 May (School Log).

[4] i.e. Jessie Chambers.

[5] in lethargy] in absolute lethargy

[6] and] but

time. I couldn't repeat it, but yet I beat and beat through the whole poem, with now and again a refrain cropping up:

'Nay of the dead what can you say
Little Brother?'

or again

'O Mary, Mother Mary
Three days today between Hell and Heaven'

and again

'What of the Dead between Hell and Heaven
Little Brother.'[1]

[You?][2] are part of his immortality. That is what would make me go wild, if I woke up. You see, I know Siegmund is there all the time. I know you would go back to him, after me, and disclaim me. I know it very deeply. I know I could not bear it. I feel often inclined, when I think of you, to put my thumbs on your throat.

Muriel will take me. She will do me great, infinite good – for a time. But what is awake in me shivers with terror at the issue. Whatever happens, in the near present, I can't help it – I cannot.

You will sleep with Siegmund in the holiday. A revulsion from me, and put out your arms with passion into the dark, to him. And he will come – more or less – as sleep and inactivity.

When I finished the *Bacchae*, on Tuesday night, the last words

'And the way shall be pointed out, strangely
It shall not go either this way, as ye expected, nor
that way, as ye thought:
But elsewhere, unthought, unknown.'

Bien – I leave it – I must rise up and teach. I [cannot][3] see you before the holiday. Yet Agnes wants me to go to tea tomorrow. I may not.

Vale D. H. Lawrence

[1] D. G. Rossetti, 'Sister Helen', ll. 25–6, 6–7, 27–8 ['Nay now of...']. The poem was included in Richard Garnett's *International Library of Famous Literature*, xii. 5693–700. See also E.T. 146 for DHL's interest in the poem.

[2] The MS is mutilated, probably eliminating one line (or more) of text. Helen Corke reproduced part of the letter in *Neutral Ground*, 263–4; at this point her text reads: 'Little Brother!" I know exactly how Domine clings to you... You are part...'

[3] Helen Corke supplies this word, *In Our Infancy*, p. 183.

157. To Louie Burrows, [19 May 1910]

Text: MS UN; PC; Postmark, Eastwood MY 19 10; Boulton 51.

Eastwood
Thursday

Ma chère Louise,

It is ↓↓ , this weather. Pouring all morning, and every morning. I am afraid we shall not get to Leicester at this rate. When are you coming to Cossall?[1] Is there any chance of our seeing you? Wish you could come over tomorrow – Friday – to tea. – Things do criss-cross disgustingly.

Vale D. H. Lawrence

158. To Jessie Chambers, [c. June 1910]

Text: Delavenay 685.

[12 Colworth Road, Addiscombe, Croydon]
[c. June 1910]

[Lawrence 'read *The Story of an African Farm* and wrote to [Jessie]'] It will wring your woman's heart when you come to read it.[2]

159. To Helen Corke, 1 June 1910

Text: MS UT; Huxley 2–3.

Davidson Rd Boys School, South Norwood, S.E.
1st June 1910

I am wearing a pink carnation. Poor Agnes,[3] she looks woe-begone. So far, I admire her. Now, I am urging her to begin to work – paint, write letters, play. I think she will regain her independent individuality. If not – well. But don't be too kind to her: it will weaken her.

Heinemann was very nice: doesn't want me to alter anything: will publish in Sept. or October, the best season: we have signed agreements concerning royalties, and I have agreed to give him the next novel.[4] Will he want it? This transacting of literary business makes me sick. I have no faith in myself at the end, and I simply loathe writing. You do not know how repugnant

[1] The village near Eastwood where Louie had lived before her family moved to Quorn.

[2] Helen Corke, *In Our Infancy*, p. 184, implies that DHL borrowed the book from her and read it c. June 1910. (This does not necessarily conflict with the evidence supplied by Jessie Chambers.)

[3] Agnes Holt.

[4] The contract, dated 2 June 1910, gives the title of the book as 'provisionally: – Nethermere'; agrees to 15% royalties on normal sales; and binds DHL to offer Heinemann his next novel on the same terms.

to me was the sight of that 'Nethermere' MSS.[1] By the way, I have got to find a new title. I wish, from the bottom of my heart, the fates had not stigmatised me 'writer'. It is a sickening business. Will you tell me whether the Saga is good? I am rapidly losing faith in it. – Oh, I am rather disappointed that Austin Harrison has again omitted to put my story in the *Review*: I expect he's forgotten – mislaid it.[2]

I assure you, I am not weeping into my register. It is only that the literary world seems a particularly hateful yet powerful one. The literary element, like a disagreeable substratum under a fair country, spreads under every inch of life, sticking to the roots of the growing things. Ugh, that is hateful. I wish I might be delivered.

I shall not see you till Saturday. Then, unless you deny, we will go into the downs. I will look for you at the Grey Hound[3] at 10.0 oclock. If it should be wet, I will come round later in the morning, – unless you deny, – and we'll go somewhere.

You don't know how inimical I feel against you. C'est moi qui perdrai le jeu.[4]

Vale D. H. Lawrence

What we cannot bear, is deliberately to allow those we care for to think ill of us. It is a high test of courage.

160. To Frederick Atkinson, 14 June 1910

Text: MS UT; Unpublished.

12 Colworth Rd, Addiscombe, Croydon
14 June 1910

Dear Mr Atkinson,[5]

I remember you did not wish me to send back to you the *Devious Ways* proofs at Bedford Street. I am sorry, but I have been so careless as to lose your private [addr][6]ess. Will you send it me, a[nd] then I will forward the proofs, which I have read.[7]

To tell you the truth, *Devious Ways* bored me. It is very gawky: it's like

[1] Cf. p. 43 n. 3.

[2] Cf. p. 156 n. 2.

[3] The Greyhound Hotel in central Croydon, a convenient meeting-place. (DHL occasionally drank there with his landlord, J. W. Jones. Nehls, i. 83.)

[4] 'I myself will be the loser.'

[5] Frederick MacCurdy Atkinson, resident reader and general editor for Heinemann at 21 Bedford Street, London, for several years up to 1911 (having been introduced to the post by George Moore). Responsible for many of Heinemann's important authors. A notable translator, e.g. Louis Thiers, *Memoirs of M. Thiers* (1915); O. Aubry, *Eugénie, Empress of the French* (1939).

[6] The MS is damaged.

[7] Heinemann had already published Gilbert Cannan's *Devious Ways* in March 1910.

a lad who's been to a fair and come home with a tin sword, a tin trumpet, and some gingerbread. I could do with the England parts, but the abroad stuff is ridiculous. It is amusing to see Cannan striding the world like a colossus:[1] so puny.

I have not yet thought of a title for that thing of mine: that is to say, I have thought of hundreds of titles, and rejected them all. They go in groups. I will tell you, then perhaps you will mark out which you think is the right tack.

Group I – which is designed to give a truly rural odour and at the same time a touching picture of the futility of agitated humanity:

'Lapwings' (sad, lamentable birds – recall my effusions) – 'Pee wits' (the same) – 'The Cry of the Peacock' (a discordant row of selfishness triumphant – please refer to the keeper-graveyard-Lady An[nabel[2] scene?]) – 'The White Peacock' (to wit [...]

Group II – take a parable to explain a parable – brilliant philosophical method. -:

'The Talent in the Napkin' (a lovely title – Lettie folds her talent in the napkin of Leslie) – 'The Talent, the Beggar, and the Box' (quite Oliver Hobbesy).[3] But I weary myself and you. –

Bid me to persevere – and send me the other address.

Yours Sincerely D. H. Lawrence

161. To Helen Corke, 21 June 1910

Text: MS UN; cited in Huxley 3.

12 Colworth Rd, Addiscombe, Croydon
21 June 1910

Once again, Helene, I must answer your word: 'you had better not see me again.'[4] Once more, I say 'Bien', and proceed to disobey.

You see, you are very hard. But if our alliance breaks down often in the beginning, like a new machine, it will be the stronger in the end: for we repair and strengthen the weaknesses when they are discovered to us. I will be patienter, and 'plus sage'. – 'In the evening we are very wise concerning the spent day, but we're never wise enough for the coming morrow.' Eh bien!

[1] *Julius Caesar* I. ii. 135–6 ['the narrow world...'].

[2] Lady Annabel is replaced by Lady Chrystabel in MS of *The White Peacock*, fol. 461 (II. iv).

[3] John Oliver Hobbes, pseudonym of Pearl Mary Teresa Craigie (1867–1906). DHL is alluding to her choice of such titles as *The Gods, Some Mortals and Lord Wickenham* (1895) or *The Dream and the Business* (1906).

[4] In her *Neutral Ground*, p. 267 Helen Corke gives a version of the letter which DHL was probably answering here.

You see, when I am out with you for a day, and you, practically, ignore my presence all the time:– perhaps it is my vanity: the second of your two conclusions: '– the giftie'.[1] – But you have a wonderful blindness. I am exceedingly sensitive to other people, to their wants and their wishes: you hardly at all. You have a cruel blindness. – It is not sexual: that is another mistake you make: it is very rarely sexual. With your spiritual eyes, you fix me with a 'stony Britisher'.[2]

I would yield to you if you could lead me deeper into the tanglewood of life, by any path. But you never lead: you hunt from behind: 'jagt man tiefer ins Leben'.[3]

Nay, how gladly will I bend and follow you if you will lead. But you will not. Nor will you walk with me, en camarade. You hang away somewhere to the left.

I am wrong to be impatient and ironical: but surely, for my impatience, we are wiser.

I was thinking today: how can I blame the boys for breaches of discipline. Yet I must not only blame, I must punish. Once I said to myself: 'How can I blame – why be angry?' Then there came a hideous state of affairs. Now I say: 'When anger comes with bright eyes, he may do his will. In me, he will hardly shake off the hand of God. He is one of the archangels, with a fiery sword: God sent him – it is beyond my knowing.'

I ask you for nothing unnatural or forced. But a little thunder may bring rain, and sweet days, out of a sultry torpor.

I will come and see you after a day or two. Gradually we shall exterminate the sexual part. Then there will be nothing, and we can part. Inevitably, you must go on weed-killing – grass in the gravel path.

Muriel is not coming also this week, she says. I should like to go to 'Louise' on Saturday. Addio D. H. Lawrence

162. To Grace Crawford, 24 June 1910

Text: MS UT; Fraser 142–3.

12 Colworth Rd, Addiscombe, Croydon
24 June 1910

Dear Miss Crawford,

I am ashamed to return *Elga*. Half a dozen times, when I have been in London, on Saturday evening, I have stood in Picaddilly Circus, and swung

[1] Robert Burns, 'To a Louse', l. 43 [i.e. the talent *To see oursels as others see us!*].

[2] Cf. Tennyson, *Maud* I. xiii. 22, 'a stony British stare'.

[3] Gerhart Hauptmann, *Elga* (Berlin, 1905), Scene 5 ['jagt einen immer tiefer...': 'drives one deeper and deeper into life']. The copy of *Elga* belonged to Grace Crawford (see letter following); DHL and Helen Corke had been reading it together (see *In Our Infancy*, p. 236).

from one foot to the other – 'Shall I go – shall I not go?' Then I have turned away to Charing Cross, kicking the bits of paper in the road. – I am sorry: I ought at least to have sent the book back. I am sorry, too, it is so much battered. I have read it out of doors a good deal: it has been much in my pocket: now I am the more ashamed at its condition.

Truly, I am a fool, very much flawed even in folly. It is partly shyness – confusion, but chiefly an unnecessary sort of pride. Perhaps you will understand, and not be offended. Indeed, why should you care.

I liked the poetry of *Elga*, but not the humanity. The conception is clumsy, and blustering, like most German things, in its melodramatic presentation. – (a sentence like that makes me feel inclined to[1] say 'Ooray!'). But I like Hauptmann's elder-bushes and moonshine better than his cracked-cardboard Starschenskis and Oginskis.[2] Elga herself is a bit better.

Pound was at Hueffer's when I called on Sunday week. He was just back from Sermione[3] – which he announces as the earthly paradise. Perhaps the tree of wisdom is there, always in blossom, like a gorse bush. At any rate Pound's David Copperfield curls[4] – perhaps you never saw them: like bunches of hop-leaves over his ears – they were cut. They used to make me quote to myself: 'Good wine needs no bush.'[5] His great grandfather's black satin stock, which would throw into relief the contour of his chin four months ago, had given place to a tie of peach-bloom tint and texture. He wore a dark blue cotton shirt, no vest, and a Panama hat. What is the guise? – sort of latest edition of jongleur?[6] Italy had improved his health; I was glad of that. It had not improved his temper: he was irascible. He discussed, with much pursing up of lips and removing of frown-shaken eyeglasses, his projection of writing an account of the mystic cult of love – the dionysian rites, and so on – from earliest days to the present. The great difficulty was that no damned publisher in London dare publish it. It would have to be published in Paris. Then how about the sales. I suggested its being written in French,

[1] to] of

[2] Hauptmann presents a flashback to Count Starschenski's former life (he is now a monk) when he was deceived by Elga who was having an affair with her cousin Oginski. 'Elder-bushes and moonshine' refer to the play's Gothic atmosphere.

[3] On the peninsula at the southern end of Lake Garda, Brescia, N. Italy.

[4] Cf. *The White Peacock* III. vii; '[Lettie] had under her wing a young literary fellow, who affected the "Doady" style – Dora Copperfield's "Doady". He had bunches of half-curly hair and a romantic black cravat...' (For DHL, *David Copperfield* was 'pre-eminent' among Dickens' novels: see E.T. 95.)

[5] Alludes to the bush (of ivy in deference to Bacchus) which was hung at a vintner's door.

[6] The reference to the mediaeval entertainer alludes to Pound's current interest in Provençal poetry and the Troubadours. (He had lectured on them at the Regent Street Polytechnic in January 1909.)

like *Vathek* or *Salomé*:[1] impertinence on my part. But how was this matter of publishers to be arranged – – –? – It was a knot. – At the crowing of a cock we saw[2] the ground illuminated with a golden race of chickens: the offspring of the crow.

Pound, as perhaps you know, was returning to America by last Saturday's boat. Having had all the experiences possible for a poor man, he will now proceed to conquer riches, and explore the other hemisphere. He will sell boots – there is nothing in that blown egg, literature. I ventured that he should run a Cinematograph: a dazzling picture palace; for which valuable suggestion he tendered me a frown.

I am afraid I am a bit of a pig. – My affairs, like those of my friend, go a bit criss-crossy. It is very probable I shall have to return in September to home, to a little mining village in the midlands. Bóhze moï.[3]

I have just fetched from off the doormat a letter from one of Heinemann's men[4] cursing me because I can't find a title for that novel. The youngster of the house is weeping – she is two and a half – because I suddenly departed when she was riding to Banbury Cross on my foot.[5]

I bid you hasty farewell. D. H. Lawrence

My respects to Mrs and Mr Crawford.[6]

163. To Frederick Atkinson, 24 June 1910

Text: MS UT; Unpublished.

12 Colworth Rd, Addiscombe, Croydon
24 June 1910

Dear Mr Atkinson,

Your letter finds me immersed in correspondence: it is a good time to reply to you[7] – I thought eleven days quite a normal interval. It seems more meet to apologise for this undue promptitude. (– O odious assonance!)

As for titles, I am no good at them. They come in hustling crowds, like Unemployed when a job is going. Like Unemployed, they are a sorry lot. They tire me. That 'White Peacock' must be shot: it is a bird from the pen of Wilkie Collins or of Ibsen.

[1] Both works originally appeared in French: William Beckford (1759–1844), *Vathek* (Lausanne, 1786) and Oscar Wilde (1854–1900), *Salome* (Paris, 1893).
[2] we saw] we all saw
[3] 'My God.'
[4] F. M. Atkinson (about *The White Peacock*).
[5] The nursery rhyme, 'Ride a cock-horse to Banbury Cross'.
[6] Theron Clark Crawford (1849–1925), American political journalist (with Joseph Pulitzer); settled in England 1897; financial manager of Buffalo Bill's (William Cody's) Wild West Show. Wrote *English Life* (New York, 1889), etc. m. Inez Randall (1854–1916).
[7] you] it

'Now droops the milk-white peacock
like a ghost.'[1]

Nay, I would not for worlds capture *that* poor creature and haul it round in a 'one-object show'. –

Out of a heap of things – my projected titles would stock a curio shop – let me venture timidly [to] offer you this (I feel like a small dealer creeping up to my scornful and only purchaser) – this idea of 'Tendrils'. 'Tendrils' is what 'George' is always putting forth. He's like white bryony, that flourishes tendrils hysterically for things that are out of reach.

'Tendril Outreach' – or 'Outreaching Tendrils' or 'Outreach of Tendrils'.

What damned folly! – I beg your pardon.

The other book goes pretty well. A month will see it cast. Then I shall leave it a month or two, after which I will chisel it and shape it as best I can. It is horribly poetic: Covent Garden market, floral hall. I shall never do anything decent till I can grow up and cut my beastly long curls of poetry. I look at the clouds[2] go past, and I say to myself, of this new book: 'Now, by the stamp of Heaven, that's rather fine.' – I read newspaper crits, I listen to the advice of my best friends, and I curse inwardly, saying, 'Under the seal of commonsense, my lad, you are a naked fool.'

And so from hour to hour, we ripe and ripe.[3] When I have *finished* a writing, I hate it. In it, I am vulnerable, naked in a thickly clothed crowd. Dont send me that M.S.S. to revise again. Let the proofs be the next thing, please.

If you approve the Tendrils, tell me please. Vale! D. H. Lawrence

164. To Grace Crawford, 1 July 1910

Text: MS UT; Unpublished.

12 Colworth Rd, Addiscombe, Croydon
1st July 1910

Dear Miss Crawford,

You are very jolly to write as you do. I shall be in London on Sunday, lunching, perhaps, with Mr Byles of the stern jaw.[4] It is much too wet for you to golf. May I call on you on Sunday, if your are at home?

1 Tennyson, 'The Princess', vii. 181.

2 clouds] crowds

3 *As you Like It* II. vii. 26.

4 Réné Boileau Byles, close friend of Hueffer who had invited him to be business manager of the *English Review*. (For Hueffer's tribute to him see *Return to Yesterday*, 1931, pp. 235–7, 242, 378.) Formerly managing editor for Alston Rivers, publisher; for a time subsequently business manager of *New Statesman*. (See Goldring, *South Lodge*, pp. 58–61.)

I shall be delighted with the *Versunkene Glocke*. I confess, I have read only a papery translation.[1] Yours Sincerely D. H. Lawrence

165. To Grace Crawford, 9 July 1910

Text: MS UT; Fraser 144–5.

12 Colworth Rd, Addiscombe, Croydon
9th July 1910

Dear Miss Crawford,

Herewith the *Lute of Jade*:[2] it is a ghastly little object, but then, this yellow is truly oriental. I have seen little Burmese gentlemen, very tiny, like sprigs of golden privet, skating like bits of yellow machinery round and round the Crystal Palace rink: and they did look unhappy. Poor Orientals: even the *Lute of Jade* is sick yellow with us. When it talks it is moving – but scarcely musical: full of the lofty Chinese spirit, abstract and noble, which I admire so much – it is the same in their paintings in the British Museum – but the lute itself chinks rather like brass pennies. 'On the Banks of Jo-Yeh' is one of the best: the third verse is very good.[3]

This little volume has wandered variously: for three months a soldier friend of mine had it in barracks down at Plymouth:[4] I believe he's responsible for the markings: I never, by any chance, line or annotate a book:[5] but he's a horribly sententious fellow. If you like the book – I am tired of receiving it through the post:– a book parcel – raised expectations – and then–!

I have just hanged my latest hero:[6] after which I feel queer. Winnie, who is seven, is tying Mary's head up in a vivid yellow piece of butter-muslin. Mary is two and three months: she rather likes the idea of a gipsy-snood of glaring yellow: she purses up her lips and stands quite still, as Winnie

[1] *Versunkene Glocke* (1897), a play by Gerhart Hauptmann. Heinemann published a verse translation, *Sunken Bell*, by Charles H. Meltzer (1900).

[2] *A Lute of Jade: Being Selections from the Classical Poets of China*, ed. L. Cranmer-Byng (1909).

[3] 'On the Banks of Jo-yeh' by Li Po; stanza 3 runs:

But who are these, the cavaliers
That gleam along the river-side?
By three, by five they dance with pride
Beyond the willow-line that sheers
Over the trellised tide.

[4] The 'friend' was Helen Corke's brother, Arthur Stanley Corke (1885–1953), whom DHL met at the Corkes' home in Croydon. In Autumn 1909 he returned from China after five years military service; he was stationed in Plymouth until discharged from the Army. (See Helen Corke, *In Our Infancy*, pp. 127–8, 205.)

[5] This is not wholly true: DHL's copy of Palgrave's *Golden Treasury* is annotated; see also E. Delavenay, *Revue Anglo-Américaine*, xiii (1936), 234–8.

[6] Siegmund MacNair in *The Trespasser*.

winds round and round her neck with a piece of string. She looks at me to see if I approve: being dressed up, she is coy, she is very serious: the butter-muslin hardly suits her hazel eyes and fine bronzy hair: she has snatched off the snood, and is dancing with rage because she can't get off the string which is round her neck, yards of it. Winnie is terribly flustered: Mrs Jones shouts from afar: I rescue her.

Between me and the *Lute* and the muslin, I shall call this a study in yellow: remember Oscar Wilde's verse?[1] – Be thankful you have never to hang your hero. It leaves you with an uncomfortable strangled feeling in your neck, and a desolation of death – below the diaphragm.

Finally: I am bidden to Hueffer's to tea on Sunday. If I call on you then, it must be in the afternoon about 3.0. But I remember that your brother and his little family will be with you –![2]

There is a lesson in Italian –! Vale! D. H. Lawrence

If *Ambergris* smells like 'Crowley', it is pretty bad.[3] Civet cats and sperm whales – ugh!

166. To Frederick Atkinson, 15 July 1910

Text: MS UT; Unpublished.

12 Colworth Rd, Addiscombe, Croydon
15 July 1910

Dear Mr Atkinson,

I despair of finding any title for that book. Now, if I say to myself 'I will think of a title', my gorge rises with nausea. Won't one of those do? 'Crab-apples' seems to me as good as any.

Do you think Mr Pawling will let me have the proofs before long? Our holiday commences on the 28th inst. After that date I shall be away, and my address had better be that of my home – 'Lynn Croft, Eastwood, Notts'. I shall be away from Croydon for five weeks. I should like to get the proofs done with by the end of August. Tonight I shall write my last half dozen pages of the new work. I am inclined to be rather proud of it; but those who belong to the accurate-impersonal school of Flaubert will flourish large shears over[4] my head and crop my comb very close: so I will not crow. During the next six or seven weeks I will lend the book to one or two of my people:

[1] Wilde's 'Symphony in Yellow', *The Centennial Magazine*, February 1889.

[2] Jack Crawford (1878–1968); his second wife Dorothy (1885–1976); and his daughter Clare (b. 1904).

[3] DHL had borrowed Grace Crawford's copy of *Ambergris: a Selection from the Poems of Aleister Crowley* (1910).

[4] over] of

then I will overhaul it rigorously: then I will send it to you. But in the interim I should like to get the proofs of the first book finished, so that I could be quite free to take up the second again. I like to have clear breathing room.

Intercede with Mr Pawling for me, will you? He is a large and weighty man of affairs: in his presence I feel like an extinguished glow-worm under a lamp-post: when I think of writing to him, the stopper dives into the neck of my bottle of words, and there sticks firm. I am an ass.

I am sorry if I'm a nuisance. Yours Sincerely D. H. Lawrence

167. To Grace Crawford, 24 July 1910

Text: MS UT; Fraser 145–6.

12 Colworth Rd, Addiscombe, Croydon
24 July 1910

Dear Miss Crawford,

I ought to have written an answer to your note before. Of course I quite understood. Did you have a good time? – do you enjoy the youngster?[1] – I guess you do.

I went to Hueffer's.[2] What was my dismay, on running up the stairs, to be received open-armed by a waiter. I was so astonished I could neither find him a card nor tell him my name. At last he bawled my announcement, and I found myself in what seemed like a bargain sale. The room was packed. Breathless, I shook hands with Hueffer and Violet Hunt. She was tremendous in a lace gown and a hat writhed[3] with blue feathers as if with some python. Indeed she looked very handsome. She had on her best society manners. She is very dexterous: flips a bright question, lifts her eyebrows in deep concern, glances from the man on her right to the lady on her left, smiles, bows, and suddenly, – quick curtain – she is gone, and is utterly somebody else's, she who was altogether ours a brief second before.

I knew not a soul. I talked a little while to a weird great-uncle of Hueffers, then to a pretty and more-intimidated-than-I-was new secretary of Ford Madox, and then to the large, fair round cheeked sister of our host, who was married to a Russian.[4] In the intervals I stared at the folk. Once, opposite

[1] Her niece, Clare Crawford.

[2] At 84 Holland Park Avenue.

[3] writhed] with

[4] The three guests were respectively: William Michael Rossetti (1829–1919), strictly not Hueffer's 'great-uncle' but invariably addressed as 'Uncle William'; Olive Thomas, known as 'Hermosa', 'beautiful and austere...an admirable secretary for a literary man to have' (Violet Hunt, *The Flurried Years*, p. 22); and Juliet Hueffer, married to David Soskice, head of a Russian Law Bureau in Lincoln's Inn Fields (see David Garnett, *The Golden Echo*, 1953, pp. 38–9).

me, seated by the black piano, was a scarlet lady, also ticketed: 'To be had an approval'. She looked at me, I looked at her: we waited. Then Hueffer carted me off to his sister, and I shall never know the scarlet lady. She had a red satin frock on, short and very skimpy. She reminded me of a Christmas cracker. She was piquant in appearance. I expect she would have been quaint, like Judy in a show, to talk to. But I shall never hear her. Alas!

I liked Hueffer's sister: she was straight, frank, jolly – I liked her. But I wish Hueffer wouldn't introduce me as a genius.[1] When a fellow hasn't enough money to buy a decent pair of boots, and not enough sense to borrow or steal a pair, he's ticketed 'genius' as a last resource: just as they call things 'very desirable' when nobody on earth wants them.

When I was coming away, Miss Hunt was talking. She wouldn't look at me: I dare not for my life interrupt her. I fled. Was that criminal? I think I am quite out of favour with Miss Hunt. I'm sorry: I wish she liked me.

On Thursday I am going home. I shall be away for five weeks. Perhaps I shall be in London again in six weeks. Then if I may, I will come and see you. I have not been up to town this fortnight.

I return Crowley: didn't like it. May I keep *Einsame Menschen* for a time?[2] I have begun it: it is horribly tiresome with dialect, and Ibsenishly dry: but I'll stick it.

Give my regards to Mrs and Mr Crawford.

Yours D. H. Lawrence

I've been trying to sing 'O Cessate'![3]

168. To Louie Burrows, 24 July 1910

Text: MS UN; Boulton 51–2.

12 Colworth Rd, Addiscombe, Croydon
24 July 1910

My dear Lou,

Thanks for your letter. I am shockingly remiss.

I'm sorry life is so dead-level with you. Coteshael I always thought a very craggy place – what has happened to it?[4]

So you're going to Scarboro for three weeks! I am swearing because the holiday this year is so muddled. But I am determined to go away. I am going

[1] Hueffer claimed that, from reading the first paragraph of DHL's 'Odour of Chrysanthemums', he at once recognised and announced him as a 'genius' (see *Mightier than the Sword*, pp. 98–9).

[2] A play by Gerhart Hauptmann (1891), translated as *Lonely Lives* by Mary Morison (1898).

[3] Scarlatti's 'O cessate di piagarmi' became 'the signature tune' of Grace Crawford's friendship with DHL (see Fraser 135). She first sang it for him on 20 November 1909 and frequently thereafter.

[4] The name of Louie Burrows's parents' home in Cheveney Lane, Quorn, from early 1908.

with Neville to Blackpool, I think, for the second week in the holiday. To tell the truth, I rather look forward to escaping the annual feminine party this year. The old clique is broken: it will never be restored I expect.

We break up on Thursday – I shall get home the same day I think. I think I shall go Midland:[1] have not quite decided. School is very decent just now: I've only about 20 kids, and they are very amenable.

I was thinking that, if I went to Blackpool I would like to run up to Barrow and see Nina. Do you think it would be proper for two young men to call there? But I think I'll write her a note. Her address is 44 Nelson St, is it not? I hope we may have a good time.

Fancy Tom Smith's stopping in Loughboro to swot. I had said I would spend a day or so with him, at Lincoln or somewhere. Tell me what his Loughboro address is, will you, and I'll write him. Perhaps he'd come to me for a day or two. I'll ask him.

I do not know what J[essie] is thinking of doing this holiday, not having heard from her to that effect. Do you know?

As for the literary affairs, they are tiresome. They are worrying me for another title for the first book – let them go to blazes. They have sent me back a rather nice story from the *English*[2] – asking me to cut it 5 pages: a devilish business. I have finished another book – nearly – but what the world will say to it I do not know. However, things will, I think, begin to develop now. How slow literature[3] is. As to 'Matilda'[4] – when I looked at her I found her rather foolish: I'll write her again when I've a bit of time.

Those *Red Mag.*[5] fatheads – are you doing them anything? Do you ever see the *Tramp*? Thats not a bad mag. I don't know what books to recommend. Go to Nelsons Sevenpenny, and get *Odd Women* – *White Fang* – *The Pit* – *The Octopus* – *The Farm of the Dagger* – *The House with the Green Shutters* – all good.[6]

Let me hear from you. Good luck for the holiday. D. H. Lawrence

1 i.e. London Midland and Scottish Railway.

2 Probably 'Odour of Chrysanthemums' which was already in proof from the *English Review*; the first proofs, dated 10 March 1910, are among Louie's papers. (See James T. Boulton, *Renaissance and Modern Studies*, xiii (1969), 5–48).

3 literature] life

4 Perhaps a short story which has not survived.

5 The first number of the *Red Magazine* appeared in 1908.

6 *Odd Women* (1893) was by George Gissing; *White Fang* (1906) by Jack London (1876–1916); *The Pit* (1903) and *The Octopus* (1901) by Frank Norris (1870–1902); *The Farm of the Dagger* (1904) by Eden Phillpotts (1862–1960); and *The House with the Green Shutters* (1901) by G. Douglas (pseudonym for George Douglas Brown, 1869–1902). All were available in Nelson's 7d edition.

169. To Helen Corke, [31 July 1910]

Text: MS Corke; Postmark, Eastwood AU 1 10; cited in Helen Corke, *D. H. Lawrence's Princess* (Thames Ditton, 1951), p. 13.

Lynn[1] Croft, Eastwood, Notts.
Sunday 31 July

Liebe Helene,

How are you? I began to write to you at sunset: Now it is starlight, big scintillating stars: it is nearly midnight. I am as miserable as the devil.

But how have you found the Island? How often have I thought of you. I wish with all my soul I were with you in Freshwater – but the incongruity![2] How sick it makes one!

Muriel met me. She is very pretty and very wistful. She came to see me yesterday. She kisses me. It makes my heart feel like ashes. But then she kisses me more and moves my sex fire. Mein Gott, it is hideous. I have promised to go there tomorrow, to stay till Thursday. If I have courage, I shall not stay.[3] It is my present intention not to stay. I must tell her. I must tell her also that we ought finally and definitely to part: if I have the heart to tell her. But you see, my cousin,[4] who loves her brother, has been telling me tonight that at home, at her home, none of them care for her, for Muriel, not much: that they did not want her to go back home: that she asked them, could she go? Then, when she looks at me so forlorn, I feel I must kiss her even to gladden her a bit. But I do not want to go tomorrow. I am a rather despicable object. But can I hurt her so much. I wish I had not come home. I wish fate wouldn't torture one with these conjunctions – and you in Freshwater.

Never mind – we shall pull everything through alright. Do not forget me, and do not smile too wearily as you read.

Auf wiedersehen D. H. Lawrence

The writing is so bad because Mater is waiting for me to go to bed – won't leave me up.

1 Lynn] 12 Lynn

2 Helen Corke was staying at the same house in Freshwater, Isle of Wight, where she and Herbert MacCartney had stayed in July–August 1909 (see *In Our Infancy*, p. 189).

3 DHL did not stay; he broke with Jessie Chambers on Monday, 1 August 1910 (cf. E.T. 182).

4 Alvina Reeve.

170. To Grace Crawford, 4 August 1910

Text: MS UT; Fraser 147–8.

Lynn Croft, Eastwood, Notts.
4 August 1910

Dear Miss Crawford,

Remember, you said 'let me have a line from you.' I have no other excuse for writing.

You are jolly lucky to go to Norway. I spend my time humming Grieg and thinking of 'Arne'.[1]

Here I am at home. You may as well know what it's like: even though you may not be interested. – My father is a coal miner: the house has eight rooms: I am writing in the kitchen, or the middle parlour as it would be called if my mother were magniloquent – but she's not, she's rather scornful. It is cosy enough. There's a big fire – miners keep fires in their living rooms though the world reels with sun-heat – a large oval mahogany table, three shelves of study-books, a book-case of reading-books, a dresser, a sofa, and four wooden chairs. Just like all other small homes in England.

My mother, who is short and grey haired, and shuts her mouth very tight, is reading a translation of Flaubert's *Sentimental Education*,[2] and wears a severe look of disapproval. My father is out – drinking a little beer with a little money he begged of me. My sister, who is tall and slender and twenty three years old, has cycled to the theatre in Nottingham with her sweetheart.[3] I have a married brother and a married sister[4] – they do not count.

The sun is just setting; The large window on my left looks west, so when I turn my head, I see over the large daisies and the lilies the many chimneys of the town – a town village – shining red, and behind them the assertive church tower, and then at the back, some four or five miles off, another misty village with a square church-tower blocked on the sky on the top of the hill. The hill runs level like a low bluish panelling right along the sky, some four miles off. The clouds are yellow and orange in horizontal stripes. We have a big horizon.

This morning I read, wrote a little, and cycled to Heanor. This afternoon I went to sleep in among the gorse-bushes on the dry grass. This evening I sulk a bit because life seems dreary: it generally does at home.

[1] Grieg in *Haugtussa*, op. 67, set to music the poems by Arne Garborg published 1 May 1895. Garborg (1851–1925) was a major Norwegian poet and source of inspiration for Grieg; he became leader of the Landsmäl movement.

[2] *L'Education sentimentale* (Paris, 1870) was translated by D. F. Hannigan (1898).

[3] William Edwin Clarke (1889–1964). b. Eastwood. Educated at Nottingham High School; trained as a tailor by his father; 1912, set up his own business in Ripley, Derbyshire. m. Ada Lawrence, 4 August 1913.

[4] George Arthur Lawrence and Emily Una King.

But don't set this effusion down to egotism.

I have just finished my second novel. If you were in England I'd give you the MSS to read. You'd like it.

I am waiting for the proofs of the first book. Heinemann promised them to me for this week.

Next week I am going to Blackpool for eight or ten days. It is a crowded, vulgar Lancashire seaside resort. I am going with a man friend:[1] I shall enjoy it: you would think it hideous.

Drop this letter in the fire – if you have one – will you; and if I am a bore, forgive me. I am waiting that Italian lesson. How do you pronounce 'Chianti'?

Addio D. H. Lawrence

171. To Jessie Chambers, [c. 6 August 1910]

Text: E.T. 182.

[97 Lynn Croft, Eastwood]
[c. 6 August 1910][2]

Do read Barrie's *Sentimental Tommy* and *Tommy and Grizel.*[3] I've just had them out of the library here. They'll help you to understand how it is with me. I'm in exactly the same predicament.

172. To Helen Corke, [15 August 1910]

Text: MS UT; PC v. Rustic Bridge in Chine, Shanklin, Isle of Wight; Postmark, Eastwood AU 15 10; Moore 63.

[97 Lynn Croft, Eastwood]
[15 August 1910]

The unexpected will never cease to happen. Why did you not go to Plymouth? What in the world are you doing?[4] I give it up. It is true, I don't know what to say – not even enough to fill a postcard – you take the wind out of my sails.

DHL

[1] George Neville.

[2] This 'importunate note' is assigned by Jessie Chambers to 'within a week' of the break with DHL on 1 August 1910.

[3] On DHL and James Barrie's *Sentimental Tommy* (1896) and *Tommy and Grizel* (1900), see H. A. Mason, *Cambridge Quarterly*, iv (Spring 1969), 197–8.

[4] Helen Corke and Jessie Chambers had intended to spend a holiday with Arthur Corke and his family in Plymouth; their arrival coincided with the threat of a general railway strike; and at Arthur Corke's suggestion they returned to Croydon the following day (see Helen Corke, *In Our Infancy*, pp. 205–6).

173. To Louie Burrows, [19 August 1910]

Text: MS UN; PC v. Ancient Wall Painting in Chaldon Church; Postmark, Eastwood AU 19 10; Boulton 53.

[97 Lynn Croft, Eastwood]
[19 August 1910]

Have you heard from Auntie. I am going into Leicester, with Page,[1] on Monday morning, and expect to see you there. I at least will come to Quorn as you suggest on Tuesday morning, and we'll have a full day.

Regards DHL

174. To William Hopkin, 24 August 1910

Text: MS NCL; Huxley 4.

20 Dulverton Rd, Leicester
24 Aug 1910

Dear Mr Hopkin,[2]

I am very sorry that I cannot be at home to tea and talk with you tomorrow. Mother is laid up here, and I must certainly stay with her until Saturday. She came for a holiday with my aunt, and whilst here a tumour or something has developed in her abdomen. The doctor looks grave and says it is serious:[3] I hope not. But you will understand, will you not, why I cannot keep my promise for tomorrow. I am disappointed. I seem to have lost touch altogether with the old 'progressive' clique:[4] in Croydon the socialists are so stupid, and the Fabians so flat. It would have been jolly to talk with you about things. I'll say my millionth damn!

Give my regards to Mrs Hopkin and to Enid.[5]

Yours very Sincerely D. H. Lawrence

[1] Possibly George H. Page, a fellow-student at Nottingham.

[2] William Edward Hopkin (1862–1951), prominent figure in Eastwood political and intellectual life. Originally colliery clerk, then Post Office clerk. Leading member of Congregational Literary Society; active supporter of Socialist Democratic Federation; and radical journalist with a weekly column (pseudonym 'Anglo-Saxon') in *Eastwood and Kimberley Advertiser*. Urban District councillor for forty-five years; J.P.; and Aldermanic member of Nottinghamshire County Council. Presented as Willie Houghton in *Touch and Go* (Daniel, 1920) and as Lewis Goddard in 'Mr Noon' (in *A Modern Lover*, Secker, 1934). m. (1) Sallie A. Potter (d. 1923), (2) Olive Lizzie Slack, 1925. (See memoir, *William Edward Hopkin*, by Noel M. Kader, [Eastwood, 1977].)

[3] Lydia Lawrence was taken ill at the home of her sister Ada Krenkow; Dr James Eddy (1869–1943), a close friend of the Krenkows, diagnosed a cancer.

[4] The Eastwood Socialists including William and Sallie Hopkin and Alice Dax (together with their visitors such as Ramsay MacDonald, Philip Snowden, Beatrice and Sidney Webb).

[5] Sallie A. Hopkin (d. 1923), ardent feminist. Presented as Pattie Goddard in 'Mr Noon'. Enid, her daughter (b. 1896).

175. To Jessie Chambers, [c. 24 August 1910]

Text: E.T. 182.

[20 Dulverton Road, Leicester]
[c. 24 August 1910][1]

['Before the holiday was over I [Jessie] had a pathetic message, telling me of his mother's illness, that was to prove fatal.']

176. To Louie Burrows, [2 September 1910]

Text: MS UN; PC; Postmark, Croydon SP 2 10; Boulton 53.

Croydon –
Friday

My dear Louie,

Many thanks for your letter: you are very good. I understand mother is worse. I am going to Leicester on Sunday by the half-day trip.

I sent mother some of the first batch of proofs of the novel. She will not be able to read them. Ask Auntie to let you have them when you go again, and you shall have the rest.

There is no need to worry about me – I'm all right.

Regards to everybody. D. H. Lawrence

177. To Sydney Pawling, 8 September 1910

Text: MS Heinemann; Unpublished.

12 Colworth Rd, Addiscombe, Croydon
8th Sept 1910

Dear Mr Pawling,

I received this evening your letter and cheque, for which I thank you sincerely.[2] I am very grateful to you for writing thus immediately upon your return.

The proofs are progressing as well as a neuralgia in my eyes will allow them.

Yours Sincerely D. H. Lawrence

[1] Dated with reference to the previous letter and the re-opening of Davidson Road School on 29 August 1910 (School Log).

[2] DHL was responding to Pawling's letter (TSCC Heinemann) also dated 8 September 1910:

Dear Mr. Lawrence,

I am sorry the proofs of your book are so delayed. I have much pleasure in enclosing our cheque for £15 on account of general royalties to be earned.

I shall be very glad to see you when you have time to come up to town and if there is anything I can do I shall be only too pleased. I am only back in business to-day, so there has been some delay in answering your letter. Yours very truly.

178. To Louie Burrows, 9 September 1910

Text: MS UN; Boulton 54.

12 Colworth Rd, Addiscombe, Croydon
9th Sept. 1910

My dear Lou,

Here are some more proofs. Mother may not read them, may she? If she wants them, take them her. They are duplicates, thanks, so I needn't bother really about the mistakes.[1] I go through the other set twice.

Hueffer wrote me this morning concerning the second novel. He says it's a rotten work of genius, one fourth of which is the stuff of masterpiece.[2] He belongs to the opposite school of novelists to me: he says prose *must* be impersonal, like Turguenev or Flaubert. I say no.

I'm glad mater is fairly. I am looking after myself this week, having a cold.

I'm so glad you like the proofs: it is comforting.

Now I'm sleepy – been so busy.

Goodnight Yours D. H. Lawrence

179. To Louie Burrows, 18 September 1910

Text: MS UN; Boulton 54–5.

12 Colworth Rd, Addiscombe, Croydon
18 Sept 1910

My dear Lou,

Here are the last of the proofs: I am devoutly thankful to be done with them. You will not, I am afraid, care for the third part: tell me whether you do, as I am rather anxious concerning it. It is hard to represent in so short a space a fifteen years' development. I'm glad you like the title.

I was very sorry to hear of your uncle Will's accident.[3] It makes me shiver to think of. I tore my hand a tiny bit on the fence on Friday. When I looked at that, and thought what your uncle's accident must be, it made me feel quite sick.

[1] This set of galley-proofs, lacking p. 59, has survived (at the University of California, Los Angeles).

[2] Hueffer later described 'half the MS' he saw (though what stage of composition DHL had reached is not clear): 'It was a *Trespassers* much – oh, but much! – more phallic than is the book as it stands and much more moral in the inverted-puritanic sense...the whole effect was the rather dreary one of a schoolboy larking among placket-holes, dialoguing with a Wesleyan minister who has been converted to Ibsen.

...As it was it had the making of a thoroughly bad hybrid book and I told him so' (*Mightier than the Sword*, p. 121).

[3] William Burrows, art-teacher and water-colourist; he taught first at Chaucer Street, Ilkeston, later at Loughborough and Leicester.

I am glad your father is getting on. Yesterday I had a little note from mother herself, and she says she is better again this week end than she was on Monday and Tuesday. But she would never let me know how bad she was.

I propose to go home for the week-end at the Fair: I should come on Thursday night and stay till Sunday night. I hope mother will keep pretty well.

There will be three poems in the October *English*,[1] but Austin Harrison is still full up of prose, so the story must wait. However, it can wait. The novel may be out in a month.

I did not know sheet 59 was missing. I cannot find it anywhere, so I must have sent it off with the original proofs. However, I'll look again.

It is very warm now, and I'm sleepy, I'll spend this Sunday afternoon as I did last: in bed, dozing. I go out all Saturday – walk 15 or 20 miles. I work all Sunday morning – then I don't feel ashamed to sleep all Sunday afternoon. You will laugh, I know.

It would be jolly to go blackberrying with you at Quorn just now.

Regards to everybody. Addio DHL

I've got Baudelaire's *Fleurs du Mal* – got them for 9d in Charing Cross Rd on Friday: it was a fine capture. I'll read some to you when there is an opportunity. They are better than Verlaine. DHL

180. To Rachel Annand Taylor, 30 September 1910

Text: MS UCLA; Ewing [5].

12 Colworth Rd, Addiscombe, Croydon
30th Sept 1910

Dear Mrs Taylor,

Our 'English Association' vague,[2] middle-class Croydonians mostly ladies, lingering remnants of the Pre-Raphaelites – asked me to give a paper on 'A Living Poet'.[3]

'I will give you,' I said, 'Rachel Annand Taylor.'

'Excuse me,' they said, 'but how do you spell it.'

I have got the *Fiammetta* (*I* can't even spell her) sequence. I admire them, and wish to goodness I had your art.

[1] 'Tired of the Boat', 'Sigh No More' and 'Ah, Muriel!', *English Review*, vi (October 1910), 377–9.

[2] vague] prosy

[3] No records of Croydon's branch of the English Association have survived.

'This is deep Hell to be expressionless.'[1]

I have to devote myself to prose. Please, if you are bold enough, persuade somebody to buy my novel *The White Peacock* which Heinemann will publish directly. – (a bit of advertisement.)

But to come to the point. I have only got *Fiammetta* (esoteric creature): if I can't borrow *Rose and Vine* I'll buy it (this is poverty, believe me); but isn't there another, earlier volume? Shall I need it? – would you lend it to me?

Those old ladies would love me to describe you to them,[2] but I won't. I will keep you vaguely in upper air, as a poetess should be.[3]

You said you would ask me to come and see you. Why did you not? – But do not answer that pertinent question. I always shrink more from receiving explanations than from making them.

I have not been into any literary society:– indeed, not in London at all, for months and months. I am not a success, and to be a failure wearies me.

Do you dislike my informalities (euphemism!)?

Yours Sincerely D. H. Lawrence

Do you remember meeting me at Mrs Rhys'?

'Where are the knights that rode away – –'[4]

181. To Rachel Annand Taylor, 3 October 1910

Text: MS UCLA; Ewing [6].

12 Colworth Rd – Addiscombe, Croydon
3 Oct 1910

Dear Mrs Taylor,

I have just got your letter. I was feeling as miserable as the devil, and you just give me the extra twinge which makes a dull smart exquisite. I sympathise with you acutely: I have only to look at your funny little handwriting to wince with sympathy. When one does the 'La Milo' with one's soul, posing to exhibit one's nude beauty of suffering at one-and-sixpence a time,[5] it makes you sick, shivering raw with sensitiveness.

[1] Lord Alfred Douglas, 'Silence', l. 1, *Sonnets* (1909), p. 22.

[2] them] you

[3] In his paper DHL presented Rachel Annand Taylor as: 'purely Rossettian: slim, svelte, big beautiful bushes of reddish hair hanging over her eyes which peer from the warm shadow; delicate colouring, scarlet, small, shut mouth;...long, white, languorous hands of the correct, subtle radiance. All that a poetess should be' (Lawrence–Gelder 234).

[4] Not identified.

[5] Perhaps alluding to the 'Venus de Milo' statue now in the Louvre. Or DHL may have been remembering an extract from Georg Ebers about the Olympic Games, published by Richard Garnett in the *International Library of Famous Literature*, ii. 505–14, in which

I hope you've daubed yourself thick by now with your rancid ointment of cynicism. Your 'Agony of Art'[1] is two-fold – first travail, then shame.

I can't come on Saturday. My mother – and [I've?] never had but one parent – is very ill with a cancer. I must go again up to the midlands to see her. That's a raw place – let's leave it.

It is good of you to want me to come, though. Tell me I may come next week, or in a fortnight. It will be so grateful to vibrate to somebody of delicate susceptibility. (Am I incoherent – I'm afraid I'm on[e][2] degree from sober?). But when one lies exposed and quiveringly vulnerable in print, or at the brutal publishers, it is nice to feel the warm hands of understanding quietening one.

Do not be too kind, giving me your first book.[3] One could laugh at the world better if it didn't mix tender kindliness with its brutality.

Now I'll stop. If one writes towards midnight, with an empty glass at one's elbow, one deserves being stuck in the stocks of public derision.

But tell me I may come and see you soon.

Yours Sincerely D. H. Lawrence

182. To Louie Burrows, [6 October 1910]

Text: MS UN; PC v. The Coronation Stone, Kingston-on-Thames; Postmark, Croydon OC 6 10; Boulton 55.

[12 Colworth Road, Addiscombe, Croydon]
[6 October 1910]

Your news is very interesting. Do come on Saturday. I go home tonight.[4]

Shall expect to see you then.[5] DHL

'Milo of Croton' is challenged by Lysander to a wrestling match: 'The youth and the man stood opposite each other in their nude beauty...' (510).

1 'The Epilogue of the Dreaming Women', *The Hours of Fiammetta*, p. 75: 'To urge you through the agony of Art'.

2 MS reads 'on'.

3 Mrs Taylor did give him a copy of her first volume, *Poems* (1904): he described it (and the 'dried lily of the valley' it contained) in his lecture (Lawrence–Gelder 236).

4 DHL had permission from the Education Office to be absent on 7 October 1910 (School Log).

5 Attached to this MS (UN LaB 75) is a note by Louie Burrows: 'I went – and we walked home by the canal and then to his train at Ilkeston. Our first knowledge of our love came on that evening – but it was unexpressed though both knew – it was communicated – as it were electrically by a handshake.'

183. To Rachel Annand Taylor, 12 October 1910

Text: MS UCLA; Ewing [7].

12 Colworth Rd, Addiscombe, Croydon
12 Oct. 1910

Dear Mrs Taylor,

You are very kind. I will come on Saturday at 7.0. I hope your stay at Hampstead will revive you. I shall go up there for the Saturday night.

It is true I'm as miserable as the devil, and I find agony no subtle silk, nor cruelty no cold clear diamond:[1] but a rope that saws one red, very rough and ugly. I think life is very unartistically cruel, and I wish it would let me go a bit.

But I promise not to be lugubrious on Saturday. It behoves me to be gay, I am so sick inside.

You shall moan me out some of your poetry, and I will laugh to myself in lieu of crying. Addio D. H. Lawrence

184. To Grace Crawford, 12 October 1910

Text: MS UT; Fraser 148–9.

12 Colworth Rd, Addiscombe, Croydon
12 Oct 1910.

Dear Miss Crawford,

I was glad to hear from you again. As you are going away so soon, I will reply immediately.[2]

I am very glad you had such a good time in Norway, and glad that things are jolly for you. It must be delightful to go about freely as you do.

About the coming of the first novel I have no news. I corrected and returned the proofs three weeks ago. Since then, Pawling, Heinemann's director, has not written me, save very curtly to say that I owed it him on promise to have sent him the MSS of the second novel by the end of August. But Mr Hueffer had the MSS in Germany when last I heard of it, a week or two back. I have written him, appealing him to send the thing to

[1] Cf. Rachel Annand Taylor:
Since from subtle silk of agony
Our veils of lamentable flesh are spun
('Perils', *The Hours of Fiammetta*, p. 14);
Though cold clear cruelties like diamond
Burthen this silken text of dim surmise
('Reservations', *The Hours of Fiammetta*, p. 71).

[2] Grace Crawford had written to DHL telling him of her plans to go with her mother to Rome from early December till Spring 1911 (Fraser 148).

Heinemann, but I can get no answer. So the publisher is at outs with me, and will tell me nothing – it is true, I've asked nothing – about the first novel, while the second book is wandering vaguely in the irresponsible hands of Mr Hueffer. Do you know where he is, and how I can get at him? I wish you would tell me if you can. What makes you wish to read that MSS ? – please tell me, for if it is only a vague notion that you would find the stuff pleasing which prompts you, then I shall be chary of giving you the book, for it would not, I am afraid, interest you much. It is rather sloppy. Hueffer abused me for it roundly. But if you really and seriously wish to see the work, then you shall have it immediately I can get it back from Pawling: for I want to revise it after he has seen it. That is the state of my literary affairs – damnable. – I'm glad you liked the verses: it was courteous of you. – As for Synge, his folk are too bodiless, mere spirits, but nevertheless he is a great dramatist and I love his work.

Myself, I am as miserable as the devil. Things at Nottingham are all upset. I went home last week-end to see my mother, who is very ill. It makes me sick to think of, and recall. And then – but you are the last person to whom I should pen my jeremiads.

I am glad you wrote to me. I look forward to seeing you. My regards to your mother.

Yours sincerely D. H. Lawrence

P.S. Can you get me Pounds address? I've heard nothing of him.

185. To Rachel Annand Taylor, 16 October 1910

Text: MS UCLA; Ewing [8].

Hillcrest, Ardwich Rd, Hampstead
16 October 1910

Dear Mrs Taylor,

I forgot to ask you if you would mind lending me *Rose and Vine*. You will think me shamelessly importunate.

I liked coming to see you. Whether you liked my coming is another matter.[1] Your muted, slyly malicious manner makes me obstreperous. If it were Violet Hunt I should be witty (sic), and if it were Elizabeth Martindale – I should be sweet and refined. But your slow, soft burning like almost invisible alcohol, with a yellow tip of cynicism now and again makes me

[1] Nearly forty years later she recorded her impressions of DHL on this visit: 'He was a terrific snob, he was definitely a cad, yet in this early period he was touching, he was so artlessly trying to find his way...he was possibly a genius, with all the flaws that the presence of genius usually creates in a personality' (see R. Aldington, *Portrait of a Genius But*..., (1950), p. 94).

crackle like burning straw. I am afraid I was a nuisance: if so, don't ask me again. But lend me *Rose and Vine*, please.

Excuse this paper. I've used all the fancy printed stuff – the private note-paper – I can lay hands on, and I don't want to disturb the claretty after-dinner doze of my cousins.[1]

Yours Sincerely D. H. Lawrence

186. To Sydney Pawling, 18 October 1910

Text: Huxley 4–5.

12, Colworth Road, Addiscombe, Croydon.
18th October, 1910.

Dear Mr. Pawling,

I am glad, and much relieved, to hear that you have the MSS. of the S[aga] of S[iegmund] in your hands. (By the way, don't you think the title idotic? I am a failure there. How would The Livanters do?) I shall wait with some curiosity to hear your opinion of the work. It contains, I know, some rattling good stuff. But if the whole is not to your taste, I shall not mind, for I am not in the least anxious to publish that book. I am content to let it lie for a few years. Of course, you have only got the rapid work of three months.[2] I should want, I do want, to overhaul the book considerably as soon as you care to return it to me. I am not anxious to publish it, and if you are of like mind, we can let the thing stay, and I will give you – with no intermediary this time – my third novel, Paul Morel,[3] which is plotted out very interestingly (to me), and about one-eighth of which is written. Paul Morel will be a novel – not a florid prose poem, or a decorated idyll running to seed in realism: but a restrained, somewhat impersonal novel. It interests me very much. I wish I were not so agitated just now, and could do more.

When you say 'the plates of *The White Peacock* were sent from New York'[4] – do you mean the plates of the cover design, or what? I am a trifle curious. I *do* want that book to make haste. Not that I care much myself. But I want my mother to see it while still she keeps the live consciousness.

1 DHL was staying with his cousin Ethel (daughter of his maternal aunt Ellen and John Richard Staynes) and her husband, Max Hunger. Hunger, variously described as 'foreign correspondent', 'yarn agent' and (on the printed notepaper used by DHL) 'Manufacturers' Agent and Importer', had rented an apartment from the Staynes in The Park, Nottingham, and married their daughter.

2 Composition and revision of *The Trespasser* occupied DHL March–August 1910.

3 The first mention of the novel which was later to be entitled *Sons and Lovers*.

4 Heinemann imported plates (or moulds) from the American publisher, Duffield & Co., New York, and used them (with some alterations and re-setting) to produce the English edition.

She is really horribly ill. I am going up to the Midlands again this week-end.[1]

But you will think I have a sort of 'Mr. Bunbury'.[2]

I don't want to bother you to write, but let me know about the second novel when you're ready, please.

Yours truly, D. H. Lawrence

187. To Rachel Annand Taylor, 26 October 1910

Text: MS UCLA; Ewing [9].

12 Colworth Rd, Addiscombe, Croydon
26 October 1910

Dear Mrs Taylor,

I have received this morning a copy of *Rose and Vine* from Adrian Berrington.[3] Was it to him you introduced me at your rooms? I am much obliged to him for the loan of the book.

I like *Rose and Vine* – but not so much as *Fiammetta*. The former are very choice and charming and curious and careful. But they are rather like the clothes a woman makes before her first baby is born: they have never been worn; they 'cleave not to the mould'.[4] One longs for touch of harshness. And I don't like your arrangement of vowel sounds: it is not emotional enough – too intellectual. One can get good Swinburnian consonant music by taking thought, but never Shakspearean vowel-loveliness, in which the emotion of the piece flows.

I like the first two pieces best:[5] that I suppose, is commonplace to say. I would never have written 'The Appeal to the Artist' – it is arrogant.

Forgive me if I'm stupid. I like *Fiammetta* better: I like 'The Doubt' – and the 'Epilogue', very much.

But why do you persist in separating soul and body?[6] I can't tell, in myself, or in anybody, one from the other.

[1] Presumably DHL took advantage of his school's being closed on Friday 21 October for the 'annual stocktaking' (School Log).

[2] Imaginary character in Oscar Wilde's *The Importance of Being Earnest* (1899); he serves as an excuse for visits to various places.

[3] Adrian Berrington (1886–1923), recently qualified from the University of Liverpool as an architect. Associated with the First Atelier of Architecture; commissioned in Royal Engineers during 1914–18 War; practised in Paris subsequently; and in 1920 appointed Professor of Architecture and Town-Planning at the University of Toronto (see obituary, *The Builder*, 13 April 1923, p. 593).

[4] *Macbeth* I. iii. 145 ['...their mould'].

[5] 'Music of Resurrection' and 'The Roman Road'.

[6] Cf. 'Soul and Body', *The Hours of Fiammetta*, p. 33:
Not less these Twain, being one, are separate
Like lovers whose love is tangled hard with hate.

I have been a long time answering your other letter. I've been rather tired this week. Next week, I think, I shall go home again.

You are better, are you? The beeches in the country are feathered orange like buff-orpington hens. You should go and see them.

Auf wiedersehen D. H. Lawrence

188. To Grace Crawford, 9 November 1910

Text: MS UT; Fraser 150.

Davidson Rd Boys School, South Norwood SE.
9th[1] Nov. 1910

Dear Miss Crawford,

The time slips by very fast. Are you yet back from France? I have been waiting to hear from Pawling, so that I could send you the MSS you wanted. But he has gone to Germany, and will not tell me what he thinks of the second novel until he returns. The first novel too, is very slow: I have had no news of it for a fortnight, when they said they had received the plates from New York.

My mother gets rapidly weaker. I have been home every other week.[2] This week-end I shall stay in London, however, and I will, if you are at home, call in either on Saturday or Sunday. Perhaps I can bring you another bit of MSS – if you like.

The boys keep bothering me to mix paints – we are painting scenery for a little play.[3] It is rather good sport. A bientôt D. H. Lawrence

189. To Sydney Pawling, 14 November 1910

Text: MS UT; Unpublished.

12 Colworth Rd, Addiscombe, Croydon
14 Novem 1910

Sydney S. Pawling Esq
21 Bedford St. W.C.

Dear Sir,

Your estimation of that second novel of mine is so long in reaching me

[1] 9] 8

[2] DHL had been home for the previous weekend and had obviously taken Monday, 7 November, in addition (School Log).

[3] Perhaps in preparation for the School Concert on 30 November 1910 (School Log). The play was probably Yeats' 'A Pot of Broth' (from *The Hour Glass and other Plays*, 1904): see the reference in Letter 245.

that I wonder if you have temporarily forgotten the matter. I really am very curious to know what you think of that rather curious work. I am also day by day anxious to receive a copy of the *White Peacock* for my mother. Will there not soon be one ready?

Yours Sincerely D. H. Lawrence

190. To Rachel Annand Taylor, [15? November 1910]

Text: MS UCLA; Ewing [10].

Davidson Rd Boys School, South Norwood S.E.
Tuesday[1]

Dear Mrs Taylor,

I hope I have not been too clumsy in expressing myself. As for the clothes simile which I foisted on your verse, surely it is an ancient one enough – 'He garments his whimsical soul in verse fastidious –' – and for myself, I know it is always[2] hard to get my verse cut close to the palpitating form of the experience: and all I meant was that some of the poems in *Rose and Vine* seemed made to fit experiences which you have hidden in yourself and then dreamed different, so that the verses seem fingered by art into a grace the experience does not warrant. But I suppose I only make matters worse by enlarging.

It is true, you disconcert me – and I am hasty always. But surely I admire your verse most sincerely. I think I should put you first among the poets of today: perhaps that is not saying much. To the Croydon folk – who are not all old ladies, really, but mainly educated men – I shall say of you nothing but good. What I said, I meant and mean: but the much more I did not say is the greater part of my meaning.

You see, my mother has only a fortnight longer, the doctor says,[3] and it is true, we have been great lovers. Then my betrothal of six years standing I have just broken, and rather disgracefully:[4] I have muddled my love affairs most ridiculously and most maddeningly. So, my times being very much distorted, I am disagreeable.

I am very sorry you have to go in a nursing home: it is dreary to look

[1] The letter must antedate that of 18 November by which time DHL had given his paper on Rachel Annand Taylor; it postdates that of 26 October with its 'clothes simile'; and if the doctor's forecast that Mrs Lawrence had two weeks to live was at all accurate, 15 November was the most likely Tuesday.

[2] always] often

[3] Probably Dr H. M. Gillespie who subsequently signed the death certificate (see Nehls, iii. 744–5, n. 65).

[4] DHL's unofficial engagement to Jessie Chambers, broken off on 1 August 1910.

forward to. I hope you will come forth vivid with energy – unless you like better the languorous part. Don't sarc. me, and be displeased.

Yours Sincerely D. H. Lawrence

But I like some of *Fiammetta* best.

191. To Grace Crawford, 17 November 1910

Text: MS UT; Fraser 150–1.

12 Colworth Rd, Addiscombe, Croydon
17 Novem. 1910

Dear Miss Crawford,

Here is the MSS.[1] I shudder to think of its intruding like a muddy shaggy animal into your 'den', sacred to the joss-stick and all vaporous elegantly-wreathed imaginations of literature. I like something in which the outline is fairly definitely laid. I like corporeality. You have a weakness for spirits – not bottled, but booked. But I shall be very impatient to know what you think. If this weren't the only bit of MSS I can lay my hands on, except verse, I would *not* send it to you. As it is, I yield myself up, and thank God it is an obscure foggy day, with millions of cubic wall of fog 'twixt me and you.

Give the thing to Miss Hunt, please. Tell her I hope she may consider the work fit for staging, after necessary clipping and tinting. Don't let her laugh at the idea. Give her my address, and then, if you're gone to Rome,[2] she can send me the papers back.

Don't let Mrs Crawford read the thing – it's too common. Mothers like stuff to be decently high-falutin.

'Into thy hands –'[3] Vale D. H. Lawrence

192. To Adrian Berrington, 18 November 1910

Text: MS Temple; F. J. Temple, *D. H. Lawrence, L'œuvre et la Vie* (Paris, 1960), p. 97.

12 Colworth Rd, Addiscombe, Croydon
18 Novem 1910

Adrian Berrington Esq
37 Gt Ormond St WC.

[1] Grace Crawford believed the play in question (which she sent on to Violet Hunt) was *A Collier's Friday Night* (Fraser 150); but Violet Hunt (*The Flurried Years*, p. 151) remembered it as *The Widowing of Mrs. Holroyd* (Kennerley, New York, 1914). The references to Holroyd in Letter 199 confirm the accuracy of Violet Hunt's memory.

[2] Cf. p. 182 n. 2.

[3] Luke xxiii. 46.

Dear Sir,

At last I return your *Rose and Vine*, for the loan of which I thank you heartily. The paper on Mrs Taylor went very well.[1] Croydonians seem to find the poetry highly provocative, if no more. They raved at me for bringing them this fantastic decadent stuff: but they were caught in the spell of it, and I laughed.

I hope I have not kept the book too long. Again I thank you.

Yours Sincerely D. H. Lawrence

193. To Louie Burrows, [29 November 1910]

Text: MS UN; PC; Postmark, Eastwood NO 29 10; Boulton 56.

Eastwood
Tuesday

Les fleurs sont arrivées, fraîches et exquises; ma mère en est charmée. Vous êtes gentille; et nous vous remercions de bon cœur.

Je crois aller à Leicester Mercredi ou Jeudi. DHL

[The flowers have arrived, fresh and exquisite; my mother is delighted with them. You are kind; and we thank you very much.

I am thinking of going to Leicester Wednesday or Thursday. DHL]

194. To Rachel Annand Taylor, 3 December 1910

Text: MS UCLA; Ewing [11–12].

Lynn Croft, Eastwood, Notts.
3 Dec. 1910

Dear Mrs Taylor,

I did not know where you were. I am glad you wrote to me.

I have been at home now ten days. My mother is very near the end. Today I have been to Leicester. I did not get home till half past nine. Then I ran upstairs. Oh she was very bad. The pains had been again.

'Oh my dear' I said, 'is it the pains?'

'Not pain now – Oh the weariness' she moaned, so that I could hardly hear her. I wish she could die tonight.

My sister and I do all the nursing. My sister is only 22. I sit upstairs hours and hours, till I wonder if ever it were true that I was at London. I seem to have died since, and that is an old life, dreamy.

[1] Since the records of the English Association branch are lost, the precise date of DHL's lecture cannot be determined.

I will tell you. My mother was a clever, ironical delicately moulded woman, of good, old burgher descent. She married below her. My father was dark, ruddy, with a fine laugh. He is a coal miner. He was one of the sanguine temperament, warm and hearty, but unstable: he lacked principle, as my mother would have said. He deceived her and lied to her. She despised him – he drank.

Their marriage life has been one carnal, bloody fight. I was born hating my father: as early as ever I can remember, I shivered with horror when he touched me. He was very bad before I was born.

This has been a kind of bond between me and my mother. We have loved each other, almost with a husband and wife love, as well as filial and maternal. We knew each other by instinct. She said to my aunt – about me:

'But it has been different with him. He has seemed to be part of me.' – and that is the real case. We have been like one, so sensitive to each other that we never needed words. It has been rather terrible, and has made me, in some respects, abnormal.

I think this peculiar fusion of soul (don't think me high-falutin) never comes twice in a life-time – it doesn't seem natural. When it comes it seems to distribute one's consciousness far abroad from oneself, and one 'understands'. I think no one has got 'Understanding' except through love. Now my mother is nearly dead, and I don't quite know how I am.

I have been to Leicester today, I have met a girl[1] who has always been warm for me – like a sunny happy day – and I've gone and asked her to marry me: in the train, quite unpremeditated,[2] between Rothley and Quorn – she lives at Quorn. When I think of her I feel happy with a sort of warm radiation – she is big and dark and handsome. There were five other people in the carriage. Then when I think of my mother:– if you've ever put your hand round the bowl of a champagne glass and squeezed it and wondered how near it is to crushing-in and the wine all going through your fingers – that's how my heart feels – like the champagne glass. There is no hostility between the warm happiness and the crush of misery: but one is concentrated in my chest, and one is diffuse – a suffusion, vague.

Muriel is the girl I have broken with. She loves me to madness, and demands the soul of me. I have been cruel to her, and wronged her, but I did not know.

Nobody can have the soul of me. My mother has had it, and nobody can

[1] Louie Burrows.

[2] But see Letter 197, 6 December, where DHL tells Louie Burrows of a conversation between himself and his mother 'a month or six weeks' earlier about the possibility of his marrying Louie.

have it again. Nobody can come into my very self again, and breathe me like an atmosphere. Don't say I am hasty this time – I know. Louie – whom I wish I could marry the day after the funeral – she would never demand to drink me up and have me. She loves me – but it is a fine, warm, healthy, natural love – not like Jane Eyre, who is Muriel, but like – say Rhoda Fleming[1] or a commoner Anna Karénin. She will never plunge her hands through my blood and feel for my soul, and make me set my teeth and shiver and fight away. Ugh – I have done well – and cruelly – tonight.

I look at my father – he is like a cinder. It is very terrible, mis marriage.

They sent me yesterday one copy of the *Peacock* for my mother. She just looked at it. It will not be out till spring.[2]

I will tell you next time about that meeting when I gave a paper on you. It was *most* exciting. I worked my audience up to red heat – and I laughed.

Are you any better? – you don't say so. Tell me you are getting strong, and then you and I will not re-act so alarmingly – at least, you on me.

Goodnight D. H. Lawrence

195. To Jessie Chambers, [5? December 1910]

Text: E.T. 183.

[97 Lynn Croft, Eastwood]
[5? December 1910][3]

I was in the train with X. [Louie Burrows] on Saturday and I suddenly asked her to marry me. I never meant to. But she accepted me and I shall stick to it. I've written to her father...I'll go over the old ground again, if you like, and explain. Do you want me to say little, or nothing, or much? I'll say anything you like, only I can't help it, I'm made this way.[4]

[1] Meredith's character in his novel by that name (New York, 1865).

[2] The novel was not published in England until 20 January 1911 but a copy was specially bound up for DHL to present to his mother.

[3] Jessie Chambers wrongly stated that she received this letter 'a fortnight or so' before DHL's mother's death (on 9 December). It must have been dated between 3 December (when DHL proposed to Louie) and 6 December (when he says that Louie's father had not replied to his letter).

[4] Another version of this letter contains the additional sentence: 'I shiver at the thought of your father and mother' (see Delavenay 705).

196. To Arthur McLeod, 5 December 1910

Text: MS Martin; Moore, *Intelligent Heart* 100–2.

Lynn Croft, Eastwood, Notts
5 Dec. 1910

My dear Mac

I was glad to get your letter, which is very kind and graceful. Myself, I should have written before, but for this frustration of suspense. While you're watching a blow coming, and feeling the top of your head tingle in preparation, then you may have the will, but hardly sufficient detachment, to correspond with your friends.[1]

Mother is very bad indeed. It is a continuous 'We watched her breathing through the night –',[2] ay, and the mornings come, snowy, and stormy, and like this 'chill with early showers',[3] and still she is here, and it is the old slow horror. I think Tom Hood's woman looked sad but beautiful: but my mother is a sight to see and be silent about for ever. She has had a bloody hard life, and has always been bright: but now her face has fallen like a mask of bitter cruel suffering. She was, when well, incredibly bright, with more smile wrinkles than anything: you'd never know that this was the permanent structure on which the other floated. I sit hour after hour in the bedroom, for I am chief nurse, watching her – and sometimes I turn to look out of the window at the bright wet cabbages in the garden, and the horses in the field beyond, and the church-tower small as a black dice on the hill at the back a long way off, and I find myself apostrophising the landscape 'So that's what you mean, is it?' – and under the mobile shadowy change of expression, like smiles, on the countryside, there seems to lie the cast of eternal suffering. Banal!

But that's getting morbid, and I won't go on like it. I hope one day you may long as I do for the peace (no exclamation) and happiness of Davidson Rd. Mother is very bad this morning: she refuses even water. It is half past nine. I think – 'If I were only rushing into Mac's room with a newspaper-cutting, to launch forth into unmitigated condemnation of somebody or other, wouldn't it be lovely.' And I say 'Oh, if I were only taking arithmetic, and abusing Burridge!'[4] The desire of my life, at present, is to have mother buried and to be myself back at Davidson.

[1] According to the School Log DHL had been absent from school since 24 November (and was not to return until 14 December): hence the need to exchange letters with his Davidson Road colleague.

[2] Thomas Hood, 'The Death-Bed', l. 1. (The poem was reprinted in both Palgrave's *Golden Treasury* and the *International Library of Famous Literature*.)

[3] Ibid. l. 14.

[4] Probably the name of one of DHL's pupils.

I'm glad the concert went well[1] – and proud that my awning should so approximate the work of Almighty God as to deceive people into a belief in its reality – unless you're telling me an aimiable fib, for which I forgive you. Philip had better read some of my prose before engaging me as school play-wright: it'll cure him of desiring me. And he is a born author: substitute 'purse' for 'heart' in his couplet, and you have an exhortation equal to the best of Peter the Hermit:

> When shall tight purses be unsealed,
> Each school possess its playing field
> And I my gracious influence wield
>   Unhampered! etc etc.

Oh, there's one thing I'll tell you – if you'll promise not to give me away. I went to Leicester on Saturday. There I met an old girl friend of mine, with whom I've always kept up a connection – she was 'my girl' in Coll, though there have been changes since. Well, we were coming down from Leicester to Quorn, where Louie lives. There were five women with us in a small corridor compartment. We had been talking very sympathetically, and had got to Rothley, next station to Quorn. 'And what do you think you'll do, Bert, – after Christmas?' said Louie. I said I didn't know. 'What would you like to do?' she asked, and suddenly I thought she looked wistful. I said I didn't know – then added 'Why, I should like to get married' – She hung her head. 'Should *you*?' I asked. She was much embarrassed, and said *she* didn't know. 'I should like to marry you' I said suddenly, and I opened my eyes, I can tell you. She flushed scarlet. – 'Should *you*?' I added. She looked out of the window and murmured huskily 'What?'. – 'Like to marry me?' I said. She turned to me quickly, and her face shone like a luminous thing. 'Later', she said. I was very glad. The brakes began to grind. 'We're at Quorn' I said, and my heart sank. She suddenly put her hand on mine and leaned to me. 'I'll go to Loughboro' she said. The five women rose. 'I can come back by the 8.10,' she said. The five women, one by one, issued forth, and we ran out among the floods and the darkness. There are such floods at Loughboro – I saw them going up.

So I have written to my other girls, and I have written to Louie's father. She is a glorious girl: about as tall as I, straight and strong as a caryatid (if that's how you spell them) – and swarthy and ruddy as a pomegranate, and bright and vital as a pitcher of wine. I'm jolly glad I asked her. What made me do it, I cannot tell. Twas an inspiration. But I can't tell mother.

[1] See p. 186 n. 3.

I tell you because I want to tell somebody who is interested – and you will not look shocked and doubtful as would those who know my affairs more fully. But the rest can go to the devil, so I have Louie.

But I told her 'My wealth is £4··4··2½' – for I counted in my pocket – 'and not a penny more.' – which is true. I haven't another boddle.[1]

'And I haven't twice as much' she confessed. – Then we laughed. But I wish I had £100. – I shall try for a country school and get married – as soon as possible.

Now look here – you often tell Philip things I don't want you to tell him. I shall be ever so mad if you tell him this – or anybody. But tell him all the rest, because I don't want to force myself to write to him.

I have got my copy of the *Peacock* – but I don't think Pawling will publish till after the election.[2] It looks a nice book – very nice – from the outside: I haven't looked in – haven't wanted. Mother just glanced at it. 'It's yours, my dear,' my sister said to her. 'Is it?' she murmured, and she closed her eyes. Then a little later, she said, 'What does it say?' – and my sister read her the tiny inscription I had put in.[3] Mother has said no more of it.

I have just turned her over – she cannot move. 'Bert – ' she said, very strange and childish and plaintive – half audible 'It's very windy.' – She had just been able to make out what the noise was. The cellars and chimneys are roaring, and the windows banging. – You have no idea – I hope – how many degrees of death there are. My mother's face – almost all but the cheeks – is grey, as grey as the sky.

What a mixture! – Well – auf wiedersehen. You won't be so glad to see me as I to see you. Yours D. H. Lawrence

Give my regards to Aylwin[4] and Byrne[5] – and Philip – and casually – to Humphreys[6] and Miss Rollston.[7] Miss Mason[8] owes me a letter.

[1] A small copper coin.

[2] Polling was completed on 19 December 1910.

[3] It reads: '2nd Dec 1910. To my Mother, with love, D. H. Lawrence.'

[4] Robert Henry Aylwin (1885–1931), colleague at Davidson Road School; he left with Philip Smith and McLeod in 1913 for Norbury Manor School; commissioned in the Army 1916–19; died in New Zealand. Presented as 'Allport' in *The Trespasser*.

[5] Algernon M. Byrne (1889–1928), teacher at Davidson Road School, 1909–28. DHL used his surname for a self-portrait in *The Trespasser*.

[6] Ernest Arthur Humphreys (b. 1882), teacher at Davidson Road School, 1908–21; war service, 1916–19; later at Tavistock School, Croydon; retired 1945. 'Holiday' in *The Trespasser*.

[7] Miss A. Rollston, a colleague at Davidson Road School; she left in 1911 to become headmistress of a school on Limpsfield Common.

[8] Agnes Louise Eliza Mason (1871 – c. 1950), senior mistress at Davidson Road School and the only colleague who showed DHL hospitality early in his career there (Helen Corke, *DHL Review*, vii (1974), 227). Taught at the school 1907–23; retired c. 1934. 'Louisa' in *The Trespasser* and 'Cecily Morton' in Helen Corke's *Neutral Ground*. Introduced DHL to Helen Corke, whom she taught at the Croydon Pupil-Teachers' Centre (see Helen Corke, *In Our Infancy*, p. 105ff).

197. To Louie Burrows, 6 December 1910
Text: MS UN; Boulton 56–9.

Lynn Croft, Eastwood, Notts
6 Dec. 1910

It is morning again, and she is still here.[1] She has had the 'thrush'[2] rather badly: they say one must have it, either on coming or going. Many have it when they are little babies: and others when they're dying. Mother's is nearly better. But she looks so grievous, pitiful this morning, still and grey and deathly, like a hieroglyph of woe. [. . .] One mustn't be bathetic: but there, one is vitiated by sitting up: Ada and I share the night.

I look at my mother and think 'Oh Heaven – is this what life brings us to?' You see mother has had a devilish married life, for nearly forty years – and this is the conclusion – no relief. What ever I wrote, it could not be so awful as to write a biography of my mother. But after this – which is enough – I am going to write romance – when I have finished Paul Morel, which belongs to this.

This anxiety[3] divides me from you. My heart winces to the echo of my mothers pulse. There is only one drop of life to be squeezed from her, and that hangs trembling, so you'd think it must fall and be gone, but it never will – it will evaporate away, slowly. And while she dies, we seem not to be able to live.

So if I do not seem happy with the thought of you – you will understand. I must feel my mother's hand slip out of mine before I can really take yours. She is my first, great love. She was a wonderful, rare woman – you do not know; as strong, and steadfast, and generous as the sun. She could be as swift as a white whip-lash, and as kind and gentle as warm rain, and as steadfast as the irreducible earth beneath us.

But I think of you a great deal – of how happy we shall be. This surcharge of grief makes me determine to be happy. The more I think of you, the more I am glad that I have discovered the right thing to do. I have been very blind, and a fool. But sorrow opens the eyes. When I think of you, it is like thinking of life. You will be the first woman to make the earth glad for me: mother, J[essie] – all the rest, have been gates to a very sad world. But you are strong and rosy as the gates of Eden. We do not all of us, not many, perhaps, set out from a sunny paradise of childhood. We are born with our parents in the desert, and yearn for a Canaan. You are like Canaan – you are rich and fruitful and glad, and I love you.

[1] Mrs Lawrence died from carcinoma of the stomach three days later (see Nehls, iii. 745 n. 65).
[2] *Candida albicans*, an infection of the mouth and throat.
[3] anxiety] anxiety and grief

I have been translating some of those Fellah songs which are done into German.[1] Here is one, called

Self-Contempt
A laborer speaks

I, the man with the red scarf, I
Will give thee what I have left of my week's wages
So thou wilt take it and be mine: it will buy
Thee a silver ring to prove thyself by.

More I have nothing; yea, I will wear
A cap of sweat day-in, day-out, and thou
Shalt see me come home with steaming hair,
Shalt know then the worth of that money there[2]

Near the Mark

Come hither, cousin, cousin my dear!
I think my cousin cannot hear,
So I'll wave my sleeve for a sign 'Come here!'
Come here, my cousin, cousin my dear,
I am here, and God is near
The gladsome God is very near
I am smiling towards thee for good cheer.
Oh cousin, my cousin, oh very dear
Kiss me, for God is standing near.[3]

They are ingenuous and touching, I think. But I am a bad translator.

I am also copying a picture of Frank Brangwyn's for Ada: it is called the *Orange Market* – an impressionist,[4] decorative thing, rather fine.[5] Ada says I shall have to begin to paint for myself. That seems very strange. I have

[1] DHL's uncle Fritz Krenkow translated some Egyptian folk-songs from Arabic into German; DHL then translated them into English. Cf. Letter 229, 11 February 1911. (It has not proved possible to identify the Arabic originals of these poems.)

[2] l. 3 it...it] them...they; l. 5 More I have] And besides this I have

[3] l. 6 God] god; l. 7 I...thee] Smiling upon me

[4] Cf. *A Collier's Friday Night*, Act III: 'And then we talked about those pictures at the Exhibition – about Frank Brangwyn – about Impressionism – for ever such a long time ...You wouldn't care whether it's Impressionism or pre-Raphaelism.' 'Impressionist' does not connote French Impressionism; it relates to the style of English painting, presents a contrast with Pre-Raphaelitism and suggests a rapid statement which avoids minute details.

[5] DHL's copy of *The Orange Market* by Frank Brangwyn (1867–1956) is reproduced in Lawrence–Gelder plate 9. He used as his source the version of Brangwyn's picture painted in 1901 and reproduced in *English Water-Colour*, ed. Charles Holme, 1902, Pt. 6. He had been given six of the eight parts of this work by the Chambers family for his twenty-first birthday (cf. 'Making Pictures', *Phoenix II*, p. 605).

no acquisitive faculty. To possess property worries me – I give everything away that I can. Ada has got all the books I have bought – dozens – and various people the pictures I have done, and so on. I cannot accumulate things. Possessions all go under the heading 'Impedimenta' – for me. I must mend my ways.

Perhaps you could come here to dinner on Saturday – if you would. It is funny. I said – but you know, my mother has been passionately fond of me, and fiercely jealous. She hated J. – and would have risen from the grave to prevent my marrying her. So I said,[1] carefully, about a month or six weeks ago 'Mother, do you think it would be all right for me to marry Louie – later?'

Immediately she said 'No – I don't' – and then, after half a minute 'Well – if you think you'd be happy with her – yes.'

So you see, I know she approves, and she always liked you.[2]

Your father has not answered my letter. But he won't be exactly anxious to do so. I'm glad they're not hostile, very glad. I like their talking about our being young – what about themselves?[3] I am 25 – you 23: very good ages – in fact, the best, I think.

That new way of doing your hair makes you look like your mothers family. I don't know whether I like it better than the old way or not – I must see it again.

When I think of you, I can always see your mouth, because I should like to kiss you.

I told you you would get £90. Isn't it funny to think of you going to a new school.[4] Oh, I wish I could get some money. There was a money-spider on my hair this morning, dangling in front of my nose. I thought to myself 'Oh, if only that meant £100 – we might be married after Christmas.' Because all you want, if we had money, you could buy.

Don't love me too much. I have a fear of being ticketed too high, and having to be bated down at purchase. I am rather showy – don't price me too high.

You are not showy: you are full-fruited and rash and open as a sunflower. – we shall be shy for all that – because we can't help it. I shall laugh at you – and I shall be most timid. When a man and a woman are together – the man is always the younger. I wonder if you'll come. If only I could twirl

[1] said,] said to her,

[2] Louie Burrows always believed this to be true. In a private family letter, 26 February 1962, she said: 'She [Mrs Lawrence] was very fond of me.'

[3] Alfred and Louisa Burrows were twenty-three and twenty-two respectively when they married.

[4] Louie was to become headmistress of Gaddesby, Leicestershire, on 9 January 1911.

the time round quick, and make it be gone. Well – pomegranate – that's your symbol – I won't for shame begin another page. My love – I must mend the fire. –

Which – being done – having wiped my fingers on my trousers – I must tell you I've got a cold with going to sleep on the floor in the midst of my watch. – And is your cold better? – but I think you hadn't one, had you? Mine is nothing.

I think that's the doctor – now I think it isn't.

The fire is black and red – thou art like a fire, and I sit by thee. It would conclude with 'I kiss you a thousand kisses', if it weren't such a flagrant lie.

I don't see why I should end. What shall I call you, my dear? But your name is enough. Addio – Louie DHL

198. To Louie Burrows, 12 December 1910

Text: MS UN; Boulton 59–60.

Lynn Croft, Eastwood, Notts.
12 Decem. 1910

My dear Louie,

I am so tired. The funeral is over. I have been generalissimo. Now, I feel as if I have scarcely energy to hold the pen. Everybody has gone. Tomorrow I go to Croydon: Ada goes to school on Wednesday. I too begin to hate trains – loathe them.

I have a peculiar wretched feeling of being old. That comes when your energy's gone – it comes again in the morning.

We want to go to Brighton for the first week of the holiday: Ada, Frances Cooper, and I. You come – yes do come. Come to Brighton the first week of the holiday with me.

How should I think you a forward hussy: you make me laugh. I understood you perfectly on Saturday – and that's the best way. I hate clinging to, and sympathy poured out like oil: your way is best. Don't find fault with yourself – there's no need.

Oh yes. Now don't feel like a snail in salt.[1] But why did you cut your 'soupçon de moustache'? – I liked it. – Why did you do it? Don't do it any more.

I wish thou wert here. Somebody to rest with – you perhaps don't know what a deep longing that may be – perhaps you do know. I saw J[essie] on Sunday and tried to make it look right to her. I think she does, a bit more.

[1] i.e. mortified.

I think this is finally the bitter river crossed. It certainly feels like one of the kingdoms of death, where I am. It is true, I have died, a bit of me – but there's plenty left for you.

It is thee in the flesh I want. D. H. Lawrence

199. To Violet Hunt, 13 December 1910

Text: MS NYPL; cited in Violet Hunt, *The Flurried Years* [1926], p. 151.

12 Colworth Rd, Addiscombe, Croydon
13 Dec. 1910

Dear Miss Hunt,

I am very sorry to learn that you have had a break-down:[1] it seems to me horrifying to go in a nursing-home where I imagine everybody in list slippers[2] murmuring vaguely. I sincerely hope you won't be long detained (forgive the word).

I myself have only just got back this evening from home, where I have been this last three weeks, nursing and putting up with suspense. We buried my mother yesterday: and there is gone my love of loves.

Thanks for appreciating the play.[3] Mr Hueffer accuses me of Dostoieffskyism – it is an accusation, for all the dear cranky Russian's stuff is as insane as it can be. But you make me very sad. I was trying to persuade myself that I had really got the tones flat enough for an act-able play: you know what I mean – as in a decorative picture the tones are flat – say in Frank Brangwyn – and the figures are parts of a design rather than individuals – so I thought these Holroyd folk were nicely levelled down. Woe is me!

I don't know what Holroyd suffered. He was my uncle, and his name was Lawrence.[4] I heard my Grandmother[5] say, 18 years ago 'Like a blessed smiling babe he looked – he did that.' But my mother looked beautiful, dead – like a maiden dreaming – yet the past fortnight has been unutterable. So we shall never know.

But what am I to do with these plays? Do tell me. I want some money to get married. If I can't stick my head in some hole – c'est à dire, a woman's bosom – I soon shall be as daft as Dostoieffsky. I'm fed up. There's another play[6] more raggy than *Holroyd*. Shall I send you that, or will it be too rowdy

[1] In a letter to DHL, 3? February 1911 (MS UN LaB 187) Violet Hunt says she was ill 17 August – 1 December 1910. (See also *The Flurried Years*, pp. 149–51.)

[2] i.e. made of strips of woollen selvage.

[3] *The Widowing of Mrs. Holroyd* (see *The Flurried Years*, p. 151).

[4] James Lawrence (1851–1880) had been killed in a mining accident. (He was first husband of Mary Ellen ('Polly') Renshaw and father of Alvina.)

[5] Louisa (b. 1818), wife of John Lawrence.

[6] *A Collier's Friday Night.*

for a nursing home? I began, in the interminable watches of the bedroom, still a third play[1] – which *shall* be playable. It is high comedy. When things get too intolerably tragic one flies to comedy, or at least romance – and is cured, I hope, of heavy heroics and Jeremiahishness.[2]

Wm Heinemann – that is Pawling – is going to publish my first novel in the spring: indefinite season. He sent me one copy of the book a few days back. It looks nice outside. – He won't even take the trouble to have the MSS of the second read: pressure of business is too great – God bless him.

Well, you'll think I have a nice cheek running on to this length: and to a lady muffled in[3] a nursing home.

Excuse this paper – my landlady's – but I wont accuse anybody. I only got here a couple of hours ago.

Give me some tidings of Mr Hueffer will you? He wrote me some time ago from Germany, but I did not answer, the address was undecipherable.

I really am sorry that you should be played all out of tune, like a cruelly handled violin. It's a shame – and I should curse.

I'm afraid I'm incorrigibly ill-bred.

Yours very Sincerely D. H. Lawrence

200. To Louie Burrows, [c. 13 December 1910]

Text: MS UN; V. de S. Pinto and Warren Roberts ed., *Complete Poems of D. H. Lawrence* (1972), 882, 1051–2.

[12 Colworth Road, Addiscombe, Croydon]
[c. 13 December 1910][4]

Elixir

Nay Cousin, Dearest
What sort of love-sorrow has come over you?
Surely, if you saw my breasts
Like pomegranates on my body, like a Jew
You would let yourself die in ignominy
Without turning your face from folks jeering 'Hue!'

If I unveiled myself
And you saw my ear-rings neath my hair

[1] 'The Merry-go-Round'.

[2] i.e. pessimism or lugubriousness (in allusion to the biblical 'Lamentations of Jeremiah').

[3] muffled in] in

[4] On 14 December 1910 DHL remarks, 'No translation today'; this seems to presuppose the existence of translations more recent than in the letter of 6 December. Also his remark on 15 December – 'The translation *was* translation' – appears to support the same conclusion.

Like a fool they might bedizen you
And you would not notice, you would not care.[1]

Ain't it funny how a little love in oneself makes a lot of stuff you'd have called daft, very pertinent and particular.

You'll have to burn all these papers – and I keep no copies. Joke!

Baiser DHL

The Witch II

Thou, strange maiden, I can see nought but the glistening
Pictures of thine eyes – I am blind.
– The strange one put silk trash across her bosom
And round her throat strung pearls did wind
And hid her hair with red and golden ramel[2]
– Nay dear friend, canst thou go and find
Her, mount thee on my swift, high, rustling camel
  Bring her to me here that I may unbind
The precious thing from out her precious trash
  That we may lie together, twined
Like corn together in the night's soft sash.[3]

201. To Louie Burrows, 14 December 1910

Text: MS UN; Boulton 60–1.

Davidson Rd Boys – South Norwood, S.E.
14 Decem 1910

My dear Louie,

Here I am back at school. It is exam., so there's not much to do. For some reason or other – physical, I suppose – I feel most doughily wretched. It is the late afternoon and early evening always that drives me cranky. I've got a devilish little nerve in the middle of my forehead, just under the hair, that clicks away like a ticking spider. I'm not going to write or read till January – not much, at any rate – just paint, which is soothing.

The boys this morning began for exam. a ginger-jar with the straw handles, and 3 reddish oranges: it looks so pretty.[4]

[1] l. 5 let yourself] go and; l. 6 jeering] mock

[2] i.e. rubbish (Midlands dialect).

[3] l. 5 red and golden ramel] ramel of; l. 6 canst] cant; l. 7 my] a

[4] DHL's water-colour of a ginger jar and oranges is inscribed 'Davidson Rd. 15 Dec 1910' (*Young Bert*, pp. 64–5).

Do you think you'll come to Brighton? – I'm going to write to the Inspector[1] here about a country school. If we can do no other, perhaps they'd have me at Gadsby in your stead, with you as assistant – how'd you like that. I feel as if I can't stand a long spell of lodgings.

Your wreath did not come till late. Ada and I took it down on Tuesday. It was very pretty, all maiden hair, and cold chrysanthemums, and a bunch of Neapolitan violets. I wore one or two of the violets, and I kept catching their scent all the way down to London, in the warm carriage.

No translation today, because I am in school.

I'm so miserable about my 'matouchka'.[2] When I am not in good health my mind repeatedly presents me a picture: no matter what my thoughts are, or what I am doing, the image of a memory floats up. This afternoon, it is just the winsome, wavy grey hair at my mother's temple, and her hand under her cheek as she lay. – Sometimes life ceases to carry us forward unknown, like creatures moving in a great river: then we have to struggle like water-beetles stranded and toiling in mud. Ugh – indigos!

Don't take any notice of such effulgence. You are sane and strong and healthy. Praise be to Jehovah. But you are nearly as unattainable as the insouciante moon. I can hardly believe in you, you are so far away. And this twilight is yellow grey, and sterile. There seems a feeling of sterility over the world.

So I've had the gas lighted. I wish I might light myself at your abundant life.

My dear, in short, I ought not to write just now, when, as the Japs say, silence is a poetic and graceful thing, holy and desirable.

But thou art a long way off, and if I say anything, I shall be forced, like the turtle dove[3] of old renown,[4] to make my moan of solitude.

Farewell – Lèle. I wish you'd tell me whether you approve of my translations.

It is 4.0 o'clock: 25 more minutes – and then 'The desert of Sahara'. No – I shall go out to tea. I want you, not to write to you. Oh damn!

DHL

[1] Stewart A. Robertson (1866–1933), a regular visitor to Davidson Road School as the School Log attests. Author of *A Masque of Monarchs* (Stirling, 1902); *Two Voices. Verses in Scots and English* (Glasgow, 1911), etc.

[2] Lettie Beardsall uses this term of her mother in *The White Peacock*, II. iii, and Ernest Lambert of his mother in *A Collier's Friday Night*, Act I.

[3] turtle dove] turtle of dove

[4] Cf. *The Winter's Tale* V. iii. 132–4.

202. To Louie Burrows, 15 December 1910
Text: MS UN; Boulton 62–3.

12 Colworth Rd, Addiscombe, Croydon
15 Dec. 1910.

My Louie,

I will write just six lines, because if I get to seven I shall be Jeremiahish. And now I feel I don't know what to say. I'd better take *Nouvelle Heloïse* down and copy.[1] But I hate love letters – as such.

Oh – tonight I have told Aunt Ada. I don't care in the least how she takes it.

We go to Brighton on the 24th and return on the 31st – I to Leicester, Ada to Eastwood. I wouldn't go to Brighton, but that I shouldn't be any nearer you if I didn't: Aunt Ada is going to Hampstead.[2]

I want you so much I daren't say anything.

I know – I have just got your note – that we are very poor. My poverty at this time is nearly absolute: but for the hope of you. I'm glad you will never understand.

The translation *was* translation. Should I have been so pathetic?

I rather like Mrs Root. Give her my kind regards. I have great hopes of her cake.

I always remember the snowdrops and aconite you sent me,[3] when I think of Mrs Root.

It's taken me half an hour to write this, so I'll stop.

I remind myself of Gissing staring with fierce eyeballs in a pie-shop – and going away more famished.[4]

This is the seventh line.

Goodbye – what a brood of little eternities in Life's belly: Like *Faery Queene* dragonettes.[5] Goodbye love D. H. Lawrence

The Wind, the Rascal

The wind knocked at the door, and I said
'It is my coy love come to me!'
But oh wind, thou knave that thou art
To make merry over my sorrowful heart.[6]

---

[1] Rousseau's epistolary novel (1761) telling of the love of Julie and Saint-Preux.

[2] Probably to see her niece Ethel Hunger.

[3] Cf. Letter 103.

[4] See *The Private Papers of Henry Ryecroft*, Spring, chap. 10.

[5] Cf. Spenser, *The Fairie Queene*, I. xii. 10.

[6] An early version of the poem published in *Poetry*, January 1914 (see *Complete Poems*, ii. 731, 1039). DHL used it as an autograph-book poem: see Harriet Cohen, *A Bundle of Time* (1969), pp. 33–4; Roberts 153.

a pure translation.

and another *The Physician*

I am hurt, I am very much hurt
Oh bring me my physician!
I am hurt in my heart, in my heart!
Sir, fetch my full-bosomed magician

---

and again: Dusk-flower, look hither

Thou dusk, thou voluptuous dusk flower,
look hither
Over the land at me.
Then looked she out from her dusk gold eyes
Shining so wondrously
Like the humming of two dusk-gold bees
– And longing tortures me.
'Have pity, look hither at my miseries!'[1]

203. To George Lawrence, [c. 15 December 1910]

Text: E.T. 188.

[12 Colworth Road, Addiscombe, Croydon]
[c. 15 December 1910][2]

[Lawrence informed his brother of his engagement 'On a blooming postcard.']

204. To Louie Burrows, [17 December 1910]

Text: MS UN; Boulton 63–5.

[17 December 1910]

Having come to a concert[3] all by myself, I am bored to death in the interval, for there is no 'foyer' and no 'bar'. I have been thinking a lot of things. Tonight I called to see our Inspector: he's very sweet with me, and says he thinks I'm wise to want a country school. He will do anything for me he can – and he's very nice. So henceforward I shall study the *Schoolmaster*[4] weekly, and try to get a decent shop. I may succeed – I hope so.

[1] l. 4 dusk] moon; l. 5 so] most

[2] It is assumed that DHL would have announced his engagement to other members of his immediate family at the same time as he told his aunt (see previous letter).

[3] The letter was written over the programme of an orchestral concert given by the String-Players' Club in the Public Hall, Croydon, 17 December 1910.

[4] The weekly magazine and official organ of the National Union of Teachers.

I wondered why you didn't send me a letter this morning. Truth to tell, I was disappointed. When I don't write to you it is because I am afraid I shall be lachrymose and disgusting. I will not write lamentations to you – if I write nothing at all.

It is funny. I have had a tooth filled today – and I hardly thought about it. It is reminding me just now with a sore little aching. But this morning I lay in the chair and let the dentist drill away, hardly minding the pain though it's always pretty bad. That's how sorrow acts as an anaesthetic. I am sure I am half stupid just now. So I can't write nice letters. Just wait a bit.

There – they've begun. I wish I could get a drink. – I love Debussy.[1]

I'll continue in the Café. I think J[essie] is taking it quite nicely – I heard from her yesterday. But don't you write to her yet.

I am wondering how long it will be before I shall have enough money to furnish a house. It seems what grains of happiness we get are to be condensed most painfully from our breath of labour and suffering.

There – I'm beginning. – Have you ever read *Jude the Obscure*?[2]

As for those translations – when I have written a letter I hastily seize the book and rattle them off. They never take me ten minutes: so don't talk about my working at them. At present I am merely painting.

I have wondered whether you want any 'Confessions' from me. I suppose you have a right to claim such. But you are welcome to a brief résumé of my life – if you want it. There's nothing very striking, I think: nothing, to my mind, very bad.

There's a fat old woman drinking sherry who will not stop staring at me. I don't know why I'm interesting. To be sure – I am alone – and am not eating. The waiter in this place seems so familiar to me, as if I'd known him since childhood. I'm sure his name is Fritz.

Oh, I forgot to say that I appreciated the managers' choice of books.[3] What a damn farce! I have begun to buy old books for our library – God help us. I've got *Religio Medici* to begin with.[4] I'll send it you. It is adulterated with *Paul et Virginie*[5] and some early Spanish Ballads[6] – job lot, 1/2.

I daren't ask you if you are coming to Brighton – are you? Are you writing to Ada? Do.

[1] Claude Debussy's *Two Dances for Piano and Strings* was in the programme.

[2] The novel (1895) by Thomas Hardy (1840–1928).

[3] Presumably Louie Burrows had told DHL which books her school managers had agreed to buy for teaching purposes.

[4] Sir Thomas Browne's religious and philosophical reflections (1642).

[5] Romance (1787) by Bernardin de St Pierre (1737–1814).

[6] Most likely *Ancient Spanish Ballads, historical and romantic*, trans. J. G. Lockhart (1823). It was by far the most popular collection and most frequently reprinted.

I am not living, I swear. You will get no translation tonight – and I should think this won't reach you till Monday.

Tonight, my mood is dark red: like a very black night at home, with the blood-red blotch of Benally[1] burning. C'est à dire – une passion. I wonder if you'll be afraid of me – ever. I wonder if love will turn out, to you, not what it seems. I wonder. 'Garçon, un bock!' – that's a very ugly tale of Maupassants.

Louisa, my love, I could kiss the very marble of the table top, so do I ache to kiss you.

I like very much the taste of vermouth.

Oh dear – do say you love me – and don't be so restrained. Some savage in me would like to taste your blood. Oh dear, you'll have to burn this. – No, I never bother to make a copy of the beloved translations.

A week tonight I shall be in Brighton. What do I care where I shall be – I'd as lief be in Hell. But there's you. 'Sole star of my life' etc etc.

Well, I've nearly come to the end of my paper – and it's nearly eleven o'clock – when Fritz will tell me 'It iss eleven, Sir.' Shall I ever have any money to marry you. Ach, Louisa! I wish Fritz would sing me a most melancholy love song – I'm sure, by his phiz,[2] he's quite capable.

It's a muggy, mucky night. Do you love me? There's a silly girl having a slice of cake and smiling at me. I look at her, and say to myself 'What a fool you are! – as if *you* were Louie.'

Oh, you'll have to burn this paper. How I chuckle, seeing you doing it. Hell – or here – or you. Dear dear – if I could put my arms round you. – I'm not tipsy, only writing without bar.

Goodnight – I'm going home. A kiss – good God – not one.

Goodbye DHL

205. To Louie Burrows, 19 December 1910

Text: MS UN; Boulton 66.

12, Colworth Road, Addiscombe, Croydon.
19 Dec 1910

My dear Lou,

It is horrid of me (the ink is thick, and there ain't no more, so I've put a drop of beer in to thin it) – not to write to you. But how long did I miss – two days or one? Now look here about my health: always abuse me if I say I'm sick; I'm never ill unless I want to luxuriate in a little bath of

[1] The reference (with its phonetic spelling) is to Bennerley Iron Works which DHL would pass between Eastwood and Cossall. The vivid glare from the works, especially at times of 'casting-off', was locally famous.

[2] i.e. face (physiognomy).

sympathy. I shall never die unless I fling wide my arms and say, Hamlettian – 'Come death etc'; or unless some stilettoed sickness steal behind me and stick me unaware: which is very unlikely, being well trained as I am in the habits of these bravados. I have a pallid and Cassius aspect,[1] but I'm like a birch tree, tenacious in the extreme. As for thee, thou beech – eh, beware a frost.

I have written to Truro, Cornwall, tonight, for application forms for a small place on the North Coast – salary £115 per annum.[2] Think of us, by the brawling ocean in a land of Cornish foreigners blowing out our lonely candle as the clock quavers ten. – Oh, there's plenty to think about. – But it'll take me months and months to get a school.

I am not coming to stay at your house: I'm too shy. And I get rather reserved, which would never do at your house. I shrink from so much boisterousness. A day or two if you like – but not a full week. – Now you are blushing with small mortification – dont.

I dreamed of you, that I was asleep and you were awake with me. It was lovely.

I am always saying 'Hush' to the next thing I am going to say to you – or else 'Shut up, Fool!'

I have been interrupted to give Pa Jones a lesson in oil painting. He paints like a bird pecking crumbs off the doorstep – it is funny.

Look here, I promise you I will be in electric health when I come north to you. I will not be flaccid: Oh dear no. It is a promise.

I think your mother is very nice.

For my life, I don't know what to say next. What a joke! I always think you have a nice mouth.

I hate ending letters. Vale D. H. Lawrence

I believe you'd like letters 'à la *Nouvelle Heloïse*' – oh dear, how disappointing these must be. I'm sorry – Thine DHL

206. To Croydon Education Committee, [19 December 1910]

Text: TMS Pollinger; Unpublished.

[12 Colworth Road, Addiscombe, Croydon]
[19 December 1910][3]

[Lawrence informs the Committee that he is seeking a post elsewhere and requests a testimonial.]

[1] Cf. *Julius Caesar* I. ii. 194.
[2] All correspondence of this date at County Hall, Truro, has been destroyed.
[3] The date is established by a letter from Croydon Education Committee, 20 December 1910, responding to DHL's 'letter of yesterday's date' in which he requested a testimonial.

207. To Louie Burrows, 20 December 1910

Text: MS UN; Boulton 67.

12, Colworth Road, Addiscombe, Croydon.
20 Dec 1910

My dear –

it is ten minutes to post time – been to the kiddies party at school. Don't let me sadden you – I could not bear to do so.

I told J[essie] she could marry me if she'd ask me. Unawares I had let our affair run on: what could I do! But she wouldn't have me so – thank God. I don't want to marry her – though she is my very dear friend. She has not any very intrinsic part of me, now – no, not at all.

As for the other 3 – you were one, and J another: well, I lied. They only liked me and flattered me. I am a fool. One is a jolly nice girl who is engaged now, and whom I hope you will know.[1] She's a school-mistress in Yorkshire. One is a little bitch, and I hate her: and she plucked me, like Potiphar's wife:[2] and one is nothing. I'll tell you verbatim when you ask me.

I am wild and sudden by nature – but I shall be true and try to make you happy – I am as sure of myself as I can be sure of anything. I have a tiresome character. But don't doubt me – dont. I do love you. When we are together, and quiet, it will be beautiful. I do want you to be peaceful with, to grow with, to slowly and sweetly develope with – it's only now and then passionate. Oh dear – I wonder if you'll ever wish you'd had Court.[3] I wish I were just like ordinary men. I *am* a bit different – and god knows, I regret it.

Nay, my love, don't doubt me. I love you truly. D. H. Lawrence

208. To Louie Burrows, 22 December 1910

Text: MS UN; Boulton 67–70.

Davidson Rd Boys School, South Norwood, SE
22 Dec 1910

My dear Lou,

I did not write you yesterday, because I spent all the evening shopping. You see I've six kiddies to buy for: four nephews and nieces and the Colworth's[4] – besides hosts of grown-ups – so I've got a couple of nights'

[1] Agnes Holt.

[2] Cf. Genesis xxxix. 1–20. (The person to whom DHL was referring cannot be identified.) 'plucked' here carries the sense of 'humiliated'.

[3] Ernest Court, a friend of Louie's in Loughborough.

[4] In addition to the two children of his landlady, DHL refers to the following: Ernest (1898?–1972), Edward Arthur (1900–74) and Flossie (1905–76), children of George Lawrence; and Margaret (b. 1909), daughter of Emily King.

work cut out. You should see me in a great store, being wafted hither and thither by shopwalkers and bewildered young ladies, buying a little umbrella, some little handkerchiefs, a little silver and enamel brooch. Finally I discover myself in the Bedlam of the great Bazaar, spotting out Books, and little tea-parties, as Mary calls them, and boxes of bricks and beads. Finally, I can hardly get into the tram. It's such a joke: but an awful fag. When I get home, it's nearly eleven: and, in respect to my Father Christmassy appearance, my tower of parcels, everybody is very benign and sweet. It would amuse you to see how tenderly the shop-ladies handle me. They seem to be mutely asking themselves: 'Is the poor young fellow[1] a widower? – and at his age! I wonder how many he's got – perhaps they're twins. Poor dear – we must be sweet to him.'

I am now terrified lest I should not have enough cash to see me through the holiday. I shall have to keep my weather eye open, for there's no one I can borrow from: I'd scorn to go to Aunt Ada. And I'm so disappointed: I wanted to buy you a lovely silver and enamel brooch – only 4/6 – that I've had my eye on – and I can't. I'm sure you do not know the multitudes of claims there are on me. I hate to seem paltry. And all I can give you is this volume of Gorki:[2] which I spotted for you on Saturday, and which is a fine volume, but don't let your father read it: put it in your bottom drawer. Poor Gorki: I'm very much of an English equivalent of his. I have not read all the tales, so I'll have a look at them when I'm over. Are you disappointed in me?

I shall come up to Leicester, either on Saturday evening, New Year's Eve, or on Sunday, New Year's morning – because then I could get a trip: though I might manage one on Saturday evening. If you like, I'll come straight to you, and stay with you till Monday. Do you like? I know they run half day excursions to London from Loughboro – perhaps they do from Quorn. You could get me a ticket and send it on – then come and meet me on Saturday evening. That's nine days hence – not long. What do you say? Then I won't go to Leicester till the Monday or Tuesday, if your mother can put up with me for so long.

I shall like to go to Ratcliffe party with you: it will be jolly. As a matter of fact, I'm looking forward to it more than to the Brighton week. I don't want to go there, save for Ada's sake. It will be very fine[3] to be at Quorn. And Auntie is quite nice, really: a bit huffy, perhaps – but she'll come round. When you go to see her, Lou, be colder. She doesn't matter a damn: think

[1] fellow] fellower

[2] Perhaps *Tales from Gorky*, trans. R. Nisbet Bain (1902).

[3] fine] nice

so, and let her see it. It's not good to give Ada Krenkow too long a rope. Don't let her make you feel like a trespasser: be cool.

I shall have to go down to the class.

I am wondering when I shall manage to get a school. You see so many places now are filled up, as are those in Leicestershire, by the local people. There are very few remain open for foreigners. Literature is disgustingly slow. Heinemann won't bring out the *Peacock* till March, I suppose – and even then it wont do much for me. I shall not be any nearer having money – unless, indeed, the notices bring me in a fair amount of magazine work. I wish we could have been married right away – but not in Croydon. I did not fill in the Cornwall forms – since you didn't want it. It is altogether very riling.

We do not break up till tomorrow – Friday morning. I meet Ada on Saturday, 1.25 at Kings Cross. I suppose we shall go straight to Brighton. Although I have done nothing all day, I am despicably tired. At present I have eleven boys – and they've been reading all afternoon – 'not a sound breaks the stillness, as – –' etc etc. It is four oclock. At playtime there was an immense gold sunset pouring on everything in a flamy stream. The boys looked beautiful with red faces shining like lamps as they came up the lobby. (ugly word, lobby!) (If I were an artist I should say 'porch'.)

They've just sent me a slab of Christmas pudding in from St[andar]d I. It represents Std I's Nature Study lessons for the last fortnight. It now takes the form of a lesson on mastication. Happy Std I. I have eaten a scrap – it's not bad, – and given Manser[1] the rest. He's a dwarf with red hair and a Sunny Jim[2] grin: he always sits on the seat with his legs crossed and feet under him, so as to appear Normal size: he's going to be a tailor.

The days go drearily and the nights are very heavy. Fessissimus sum.

Well, Cara mia – I wish three things: to be with you; to be very drunk; to be – I don't know.

No translations, since I'm at school – and since they are shocking. Do you wish I would write in the 'Be Good, sweet maid and let who will be clever'[3] – style? I will try, to please you, one day.

I do not run to endearments – don't feel light hearted enough, to tell the truth. But if there is one thing on earth that I wish, it is to be with you altogether – that we were married securely.

My love – goodbye DHL

[1] Presumably a pupil; not identified.

[2] A famous character in a cereal advertisement.

[3] Charles Kingsley, 'A Farewell' l. 9 ['...let who can...'].

209. To Sallie Hopkin, 23 December 1910
Text: MS NCL; cited in Pollak 26.

12, Colworth Road, Addiscombe, Croydon.
23 Dec 1910

Dear Mrs Hopkin,

Now we've broken up I've got the damned blues. It makes me laugh in spite of myself, I am so lugubrious.

Ada and I are going away to Brighton tomorrow for the week. She will return to Eastwood I to Leicester, to be soothed at the bosom of love. I could adore any maiden just now if she were sufficiently fruitful and reposeful in her being. But God preserve us from the acid sort just now.

Time crawls on like a prostrate beast – damn!

Well – I wish you may have a good warm time – a flare-up. I think flare-ups are precious beyond gold, yea, more than[1] – but I leave it to Mr Hopkin to wax scriptural.

My regards to Enid. Write to me sometime.

Yours D. H. Lawrence

210. To Louie Burrows, 23 December 1910
Text: MS UN; Boulton 70–1.

12 Colworth Rd, Addiscombe, Croydon
23 Dec 1910

Geliebte,

This has been one of the days when I have not known what to do with myself: that's why I have not written earlier. Now the 11.0 p.m. post has gone. I am very sorry.

You do not want to leave Ratcliffe – you shrink from the thought of Gaddesby – you are miserable for an evening – and then you understand why I do not write when I am worried. Very good. Then you understand why I have not written today.

My dear – sometimes I feel as if I shout – crêver. My temper is damnably serious and melancholic. If I had not a few grains of reason I should be a maudlin idiot. But oh, my love, you do not know what these days cost me. I want you to succour me, my darling – for I am used up.

But enough. This is my Christmas letter. And how will you be jolly at this rate. Pa Jones has just come in: he's rather tipsy, but is very clever at hiding it. Ma Jones can't twig it. But I, through long experience, can tell to a shade how far gone in drink is any man I know at all. It is rather amusing – and rather ennuyeux, to watch this comedy.

[1] Psalms xix. 10.

This is my Christmas letter. I like to think of you being jolly all the time. I hate to think of you crying your eyes up. Don't cry.

But Oh, my darling, my darling – Pa Jones has had a bottle of whiskey for a christmas box, and we're just going to have a drop. Forgive me if I'm horrid.

If I but had any hope of being with you, near you – I would dislike whiskey – but what am I to do.

Tomorrow I am going to Brighton. It seems horrid, – but the thought of next week wearies me. I shall have to be nice and bright and strong, and support and comfort Ada, and keep her, or make her, cheerful. And I want comforting myself, like a kid, and cheering, like a tearful girl. But it is rather despicable – and I shall be ever so glad to see Ada. She and I are very near to one another. I would give a very great deal to make her even a bit happy. But I feel nearly bankrupt – no I don't – at least I shan't tomorrow. You, my love, are my capital. You are my funds. I wish I could but draw on you a little. But it is all so mixed with passion and complicated.

This is my Christmas letter: I want it to be Christmas for you. I want you to forget me – for I'm sure I must fret you – and be gay, gay, gai. If you say you're not jolly I shall curse. Dear, my darling, I shall make you a good husband. I am very faithful to my own.

I wait for you. As [I] hope for salvation, I hope for you, and a home with you. But I dream of my mother. You do not know. If I told you all, it would make you old, and I don't want you to be old.

This is my christmas letter. Is it better to play with jests, and say nothing? Nay, my love, I want you to clasp me soul to soul, as much as we can. I feel as if I could not go another stride away from you. But it is bedtime.

This time next week I shall be coming – next week. But the tracts of days between. Never mind. – next week – my love. DHL

211. To Jessie Chambers, [c. 23 December 1910]

Text: E.T. 122–3.

[12 Colworth Road, Addiscombe, Croydon]
[c. 23 December 1910]

['At the Christmas that immediately followed his mother's death he sent me [Jessie] Leon Daudet's *Le partage de l'enfant*,[1] saying it would help me to realize the position of the child in a home where the parents do not get on well together.']

[1] Published Paris, 1905.

212. To Arthur McLeod, [23 December 1910]

Text: Moore, *Intelligent Heart* 105.

[12 Colworth Road, Addiscombe, Croydon]
[23 December 1910]

Nice of you to remember that I wanted those Latin poems: I'd forgotten myself: which makes it all the pleasanter now. [Lawrence sent McLeod the Everyman's *Aucassin and Nicolette*,[1] with the injunction] Be Jolly.

213. To Louie Burrows, 25 December 1910

Text: MS UN; Boulton 71–2.

c/o Mr Richards,[2] Davigdor Rd, Hove, Sussex.
25th Dec 1910

My dear Lou,

I have just finished *Undine* – de la Motte-Fouqué's old romance.[3] Do you know it? – it is often a bit absurd and German, but contains spots of real beauty. It makes me think of you: of love – and some sad things.

It is a beautiful day. We went out about 10.0. The mild fresh wind was blowing more and more blue into the sky, till soon it was clear as a blue bowl, and the sun shone on the sea, and the wind was sparkling. It is a lovely day. Now a few clouds are orangey over the west.

All morning Ada and I have walked up and down the esplanade, talking, and laughing at the people. They are very dressy; the throng is salted strong with Jewesses and their attendants. It is rather amusing to watch folk. You would like it because it's rather swelly (sic) – and a swell has an immense appeal for you. Don't you pray nightly – 'May I live to be a lady, and die in the cream of fashion'? I know you do.

But I'm only laughing at you. I never dare say to you the things I am going to say. Which makes my letters jerky and pattering. You see 'I am daring on paper'. – but I've a few grains of discretion. No, I don't mean anything shocking.

It rather often seems to me as if we were – if not married, then on the brink of marriage. My chest seems lifting in expectation towards you, and I feel as if the banns had been uttered. I wish I were gifted with second sight, and could believe myself.

I tore up that Cornwall application form. Then I saw the same school,

[1] *Aucassin and Nicolette, and other Mediæval Romances and Legends*, trans. Eugene Mason, Everyman's (1910).

[2] Arthur Richards, foreman with a firm of cabinet-makers, who took in paying guests.

[3] Published in 1811.

with another like it, advertised again, and I wrote for two forms – today. That first I tore up because you didn't want to go to Cornwall. But if I should get the school to Cornwall you shall go, or to the Devil.

There – I don't mean it. I'm on paper, you see.

I meant to go and call on the boss: he's at a boarding house here. I thought I'd have tea with him.[1] But it's getting too late. Those clouds have gone heliotrope.

I wish you were here. We are jolly comfortable – lovely – Brighton would suit you down to the ground – big and 'swelly'. You are a 'jeune fille', you know. Well, I like you so.

Court would have called you the darling of his heart: Do you regret him? You don't seem particularly far off from here – why? – I can manage you better in person than through the post. So I await next week to be serious.

DHL

See about that ticket for me, will you – and trains. DHL

214. To Louie Burrows, 27 December 1910

Text: MS UN; Boulton 73–4.

Davigdor Rd, Hove, Sussex
27 Dec 1910

My dear Lou,

I wondered when your letter was going to come. It seemed as if Christmas were specially designed to put a silence between me and everybody. But I received your 'envoi' just now: it is noon, Tuesday, and the letter was not the Croydon one – but the Hove direct letter. The former is not yet arrived.

Do you know, things have rubbed a lot of the elastic capacity for pure happiness out of me: and it is my nature. I am rather 'cured' with the salt and salt-petre of bitterness and sorrow. I have a certain hardness of texture now, the knowledge of which grieves me rather when I think that I have[2] not the beautiful pristine fervour of a young Feverel[3] to meet you with. I am very much afraid indeed of disappointing you and causing you real grief for the first time in your life. It is the second me, the hard, cruel if need be, me that is the writer which troubles the pleasanter me, the human who belongs to you. Try, will you, when I disappoint you and may grieve you, to think that it is the impersonal part of me – which belongs to nobody, not even to myself – the writer in me, which is for the moment ruling. When

[1] DHL's headmaster, Philip F. T. Smith. By his account, DHL and his sister Ada called on him on Christmas Day (Nehls, i. 141).

[2] have] shall

[3] The hero of Meredith's *The Ordeal of Richard Feverel* (1859).

you see it in my eyes, take no notice, chatter as if it were not so. Remember I love you and am your husband: but that a part of me is exempt from these things, from everything: the impersonal, artistic side. Do you understand? – and does it trouble you? But you don't believe me. It is just as well. I love you sincerely, and when I was thinking that now it would be easy for me to fulfil[1] my old desire and go to France, I was amused, France seems to have grown so distasteful. We'll go some time together.

Here I am very gay – all the time gay. I live in my impersonal self. Nothing matters in the least, and most things amuse me, and very little touches me. I dance, at a boarding house where the boss is staying, and am quite a bright spark. But nobody has any personality to me, so you needn't be jealous. It's a rather pleasant shadow-theatre kind of existence: I am really jolly.

At the boss', there is a young Frenchman, Monsieur Didier, who has been in the army four years and has now come here to acquire the language. We go[2] out together every day, and talk French all the time. It's good fun.

At the petite danse last night there were three Asiatics from India. They are extraordinarily interesting to watch – like lithe beasts from the jungle: but one cannot help feeling how alien they are. You talk about 'brother men': but a terrier dog is much nearer kin to us than those men with their wild laughter and rolling eyes. Either I am disagreeable or a bit barbaric myself: but I felt the race instinct of aversion and slight antagonism to those blacks, rather strongly. It is strange.

I shall have plenty of time to chatter chatter at Coteshael, and then you shall hear, along with the rest, all about everything. But these people are rather sanctimonious, and oh, the mental atmosphere is so stale.

I had just as lief you were a Christian: I have my own religion, which is to me the truth: you have what suits you: I will go to Church with you – frequently.

Of course, tell everybody about our engagement: I do. They all know, at home and elsewhere.

I must run to meet my Frenchman. We shall walk to Rottingdean over the downs. It is very sunny, but *so* rough. The girls will rest this afternoon after their morning blow.[3]

Give my regards to your mother and father: say nice things to them on my behalf. When they are bigoted, take no notice. It's no good booing a persistent ox for plodding its bit of a track: it would be no good abroad, at large. Some folk are best fitted with a narrow creed, as are docile horses with a bluff:[4] they're not scared and bewildered, and theyre more useful.

[1] MS reads 'fulful'.
[2] go] stay
[3] His sister Ada and Frances Cooper.
[4] i.e. blinkers.

I'm not sarky – oh no, n'a bit.

Well my dear – I am running away down to Brighton. The day *will* come when I have you – Vale D. H. Lawrence

215. To Louie Burrows, 28 December 1910

Text: MS UN; Boulton 75–6.

Davigdor Rd, Hove, Sussex
28 Dec. 1910

Carissima,

It has been a very sunny morning, with a mist like grey silk veils, and the sun-walk on the sea narrowing and darkening to orange and burnished copper and vanishing ruddily on the horizon into a closed door of fog. 'Varrry prreety', as my Frenchman would say. A morning framed for me and thee, but thou wert out of the picture, and I missed thee from it. Comment by the Frenchman 'What peety!'.

Ada, Frances and I have walked the miles of esplanade looking at curio shops, ladies, riders, the sea, fog, the sun, shops, books, people, pet-dogs of all descriptions: 'and so ad infinitum', as Swift would say.[1]

I am glad you are so happy in anticipation. It pleases me immensely to hear it. Ada is always saying 'Oh I shall be miserable to go back: shan't you?' – But then she's had Eddie for three long years, and the savour of expectation is gone. In three years time – in three years time – what? – That's the best of life, it's such a bran-tub. And though we've only fished out tin trumpets and tear-bottles so far, yet we're quite sure that among the bran there are treasures for us, if we rummage. Philosophy.

I want to come up on Saturday by the 6.20, I think. If you take a day trip, I can come by that train, which is a fine one. You see I must dispatch Ada and Frances safely from Kings Cross on the G[reat] N[orthern] R[ailway] at 5.30, then return to Marylebone.[2]

Why isn't Cornwall wise? I think it is. Do not think me rash: I am rarely that, except in trifles. But let us appreciate promptitude in action. I detest vacillation and waiting.

I've been to have a 'Sticky-Back' taken this morning. They are tiny photos with gummed backs, 3d. a dozen if you've got a coupon. I had a coupon. Ada went first and paid her three 'd to a woman at the shop counter. A little man waved her into a box. Before a minute was over she emerged, saying 'Well!'. Immediately I found myself in the box. The little man murmured,

[1] Swift, 'On Poetry: a Rhapsody', l. 340.

[2] DHL would use Marylebone Station for Quorn.

The Lawrence family, c. 1893:
Emily, George, Ernest;
Ada, Mrs Lawrence, David Herbert, Mr Lawrence

Emily King, c. 1905

Ada Lawrence
(Mrs W. E. Clarke), c. 1917

Jessie Chambers, 1909

The Chambers family, 1906:
May, Alan, Jessie, Hubert, Bernard;
Molly, Father, David, Mother

Rev. Robert Reid, c. 1913

William Hopkin, c. 1910

Alice Dax and her children, 1913

Blanche Jennings, 1909

Louie Burrows, c. 1910

Thomas Smith, 1914

Fritz Krenkow, 1949

John William and Marie Jones, c. 1906

Hilda Mary Jones, 1914

Philip Smith, c. 1906

Arthur McLeod, 1946
from a portrait by Drummond

Agnes Holt, 1933

Helen Corke, c. 1912

Ford Madox Hueffer, c. 1909

Violet Hunt, c. 1911,
from the drawing by
Kathleen Shackleton

Grace Crawford, c. 1912

Rachel Annand Taylor, c. 1916

Florence Wood, c. 1903

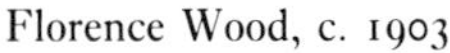

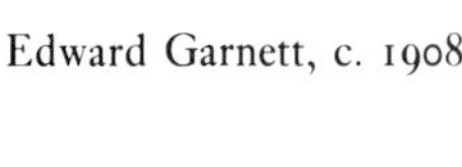

Edward Garnett, c. 1908

William Heinemann, c. 1913

Sydney Pawling, 19

Below left,
Martin Secker, 1912,
from a Photograph
by E. O. Hoppé

Below right,
Walter de la Mare,
1923

Ernest and Frieda Weekley, 1911

D. H. Lawrence, 1912

David Garnett, 1918,
from a portrait by Carrington

Antonia Almgren, c. 1906

Ernest Collings, 1912,
from a portrait by
Austin O. Spare

Tuesday

Now I can't stand it any longer, I cant. For two hours ~~I~~ I have'nt moved a muscle – just sat and thought. ~~and suffered~~ I have written a letter to Ernst. You need'nt, of course, send it. But you must say to him all I have said. No more dishonour, no more lies. Let them do their – silliest – but no more subterfuge, lying, dirt, fear. I feel as if it would strangle me. What is it all but procrastination? No, I can't bear it, because it's bad. I love you. Let us face anything, do anything, put up with anything. But this crawling under the mud I cannot bear.

I'm afraid I've got a fit of heroics. I've tried so hard to work – but I cant. This situation is round my chest like a cord. It mustn't continue. I will go right away, if you like. I will stop in Metz till you get Ernst's answer to the truth. But no, I won't utter or act or willingly let you utter or act, another single lie in the business.

I'm not going to joke, I'm not going to laugh, I'm not going to make light of things for you. The situation tortures me too much. It's the situation, the situation I can't stand – no, and I won't. I love you too much.

Don't show this letter to either of your sisters – no. Let us be good. You are clean, but you dirty your feet. I'll sign myself as you call me. – Mr Lawrence

Dont be miserable – if I didnt love you I wouldnt mind when you lied. But I love you, and Lord, I pray for it.

Lawrence's letter to Frieda Weekley, 7 May 1912 (see pp. 392–3)

like a worn out gramophone 'Take a chair, please.' I sat on a pew. He gave me a card, and suddenly turned on a bright light. 'Lord', I said to myself 'I'd better look amused.' At the same instant he was mechanically murmuring 'keep still a moment.' I rushed, (mentally), to find a suitable expression, when the light vanished, and the little man murmured like the last utterings of a phonograph 'Any time tomorrow after six' – then I found myself in the shop exclaiming 'Well!' – while Frances hovered in fear near the opening. If it's a good caricature – the stickyback – I'll give you one for your amusement.

This will reach you on Thursday (-Friday-Saturday). If I were but Lovelace[1] – which I nearly was, – if the potter hadn't bungled and made a beer-pot of my fine china, should have been – I would say 'How can this fair earth please me, or the seductive ocean allure me, when I consider thee'. I wish you'd tell me which of my epistolary styles you prefer: the gay, the mocking, the ironic, the sad, the despairing, the elevated, the high romantic, the didactic, the emphatic, the bullying, the passionate, the disgraceful or the naïve, so that I can be consistent.

Didier is so serious – he nearly makes me burst with laughter. He is *always* serious. He's a poor little devotee of Corneille: has lent me four vols.: and I've got to begin with *Cinna*:[2] then he's going to expound to me the passages 'plus nobles, plus élevés'. Oh Lordy! The noble and the lofty – how tedious! The farcical, the comic, the ironical – they're amusing.

If I miss writing to you tomorrow it'll be because we're out all day. It depends upon the weather.

Well golubchick (pretty word!) – little pigeon – oh black swan.

Farewell.

I wish to goodness you were here – I've captured an afternoon for myself. I shall think of you.

D. H. Lawrence

216. To Louie Burrows, [29 December 1910]

Text: MS UN; Boulton 76–8.

Davigdor Rd, Hove – Sussex
Thursday 3.0 p.m.

Dear Little Ousel,

I have received today your book, two letters, the ticket and the bill: all of which is very sweet. And I laugh at you again: do you not see that I can return by any train after 6.20: and do you not know that, unless it be altered,

[1] In Richardson's *Clarissa Harlowe* (1748).
[2] Corneille's tragedy (Paris, 1640).

there is a slow old crawler which leaves M[ary] le Bone at 6.25, and gets in Quorn about 10.0 p.m. (look it up): and of course that is the train I shall come by: and we'll go to the watchnight[1] if you like, and I'm in in time: and all shall be respectable and comme-il-faut: and they shall not laugh at you: Ooray.

Let me see – what do you say? Oh – church – all right, I am plastic in your hands – but treat me gently. Cornwall! I haven't yet received the application forms. When I do, I shall fill them in: and if I get the job, 'to Cornwall we will go great boys, to Cornwall we will go – we'll catch a little –'.[2] And if you won't follow me, you'll have to: a little later, peut-être. It is £115 a year. Also I'll go and help you find digs in ridiculous Gaddesby. You always go to places with daft names. – What else? Oh, whiskey. I've just had a glass of Irish: Mrs Richards[3] was so good: but I prefer Scotch. That is true. But I'm always squibbing you, and you're always jumping, because every red spark you see you imagine to be a fearsome cracker that will explode and do God-knows-not-what damage. You won't begin your reforming by insisting on my signing the total abstinence pledge, I hope. Good Lord, what a mill I've got to go through. Sometimes when I have horrors – the ashy sort – I drink a little – to mend the fire of my faith and hope, you see: I can't stand cold ashes of horrors. But, Good Lord, I don't drink. Think of the paternal example. The Good God made whiskey, as I have rather lately discovered. And, as we all know, too much of any divine thing is destruction. Even then, too much whiskey is better than too much melancholies: and a drinking bout better than a bout of ferocious blues. Remember, I am not an imbecile, and I don't know that I want to turn my brains into beery mud. Don't be alarmed, I have no vicious habits, and no vicious tendencies, I believe: save an inclination to blundering forwardness.

We have had a lovely morning. At 10.0 we met the Smiths' – my boss, his young second wife, and his daughter of 15;[4] we walked over the cliffs and downs to Rottingdean. A warm, dimmish day, sunny, with the waves low down and small washing back and forward at the foot of the white cliffs, gulls flashing and daws gleaming, a great wide wake of sunlight slightly dimmed, oxidised with mist: a little wind. Rottingdean is a delicious village in a fold of the downs, gold with lichens. We walked back over the downs. I did wish very heartily that you were there – except that I've got into that

[1] The service held at or near midnight on 31 December, the day of DHL's arrival.

[2] Apparently a free adaptation of words and rhythm associated with the children's game, 'A Hunting we will go'.

[3] The proprietress of the boarding-house where DHL was staying.

[4] Philip Smith married Alice Cox (1883–1961) after the death of his first wife, Edith (1874–1904). His daughter, Doris, was thirteen in 1910.

rather comfortable and grown-up habit of not wishing keenly for what I can*not* have.

Next week! This is like driving slowly towards a destination, to a place where I have never been: as I might be driving to Cornwall, wondering what it is like. For I can't *imagine* next week. That's a trick my imagination plays me. I can imagine everything else: but next week eludes me.

Don't be alarmed, I shall be as good as gold: that is, I intend to be: and I am fairly amenable.

I'm going out to see the sunset. I do wish you could come. I take care not to allow any blank spaces in these days. Tonight we are going to a Tchaïkowsky concert in the Dome.[1] If I have a blank space, I begin to shut my teeth and want you there and then – or whiskey – or – Gott in Himmel! The nights are rather bad. But I am very jolly, you know.

Well, dark dove – little pigeon of my breast – I wish I'd got Renan's 'Canticle' (Song of Solomon) to send you.[2]

I'll go and see the sunset and feel sentimental. In 56 hours or so. I wish we could turn into storks or swans, like Fairy tale folk.

Good evening D. H. Lawrence

217. To Jessie Chambers, [1911?]

Text: E.T. 185.

[12 Colworth Road, Addiscombe, Croydon]

[1911?][3]

Write to me whenever you feel like it. Don't wait for it to be your turn, but write whenever you feel you have something to say.

218. To Reverend Robert Reid, 13 January 1911

Text: MS UN; Postmark, Croydon JA 13 11; Unpublished.

12, Colworth Road, Addiscombe, Croydon.

13 Jan. 1911

Dear Mr Reid,

I am very sorry to hear from Ada that trouble has begun between her and father. Last week he earned 28/6, and of this kept 6/8. She was angry.

[1] A Tchaikowsky concert was given on 29 December 1910 by the Brighton Municipal Orchestra as one of a series of special Christmas concerts (*Brighton Gazette*, 31 December 1910).

[2] *The Song of Songs. Translated from the Hebrew by Ernest Renan...Done into English by W. R. Thomson* (1895).

[3] Jessie Chambers associates this letter with the year after Mrs Lawrence's death.

Several times in the week he got drunk or tipsy, and there was much bad blood. This week he has[1] done only $2\frac{1}{2}$ days' work, so will have very little money. It is not likely that she should spend all her little earnings to keep on the house for a man who is disgusting, irritating, and selfish as a maggot.

Yet I am sorry for him: he's old, and stupid, and very helpless and futile. I have written to him tonight. Also I have written Ada to tell her to try and bear with him, equably, dispassionately, without letting herself forget the issues in bursts of irritability, until Easter, and then we will finally decide. But father must understand that now he must either keep within the mark of consideration for Ada, or be separated from her, and go into lodging. If any woman would have him, and he'd marry, we should be thankful. But the old home cannot be kept on with drunkenness and ill-feeling in it.

I can't come down till Easter[2] – and I've no money. Will you try and see things square at Lynn Croft? It's a shame to trouble you with such a job – but I know you are good.

After all, we only seem to learn from Life that Life doesn't matter so much as it seemed to do – it's not so burningly important, after all, what happens. We crawl, like blinking sea-creatures, out of the Ocean onto a spur of rock, we creep over the promontory bewildered and dazzled and hurting ourselves, then we drop in the ocean on the other side: and the little transit doesn't matter so much.

But if it hadn't been all so cruel for my mother, I could accept it better. But whatever happens, I compare it with my mother's face, during the last few days, and when she was dead – and what is it.

My regards to Mrs Reid. Yours D. H. Lawrence

219. To Frederick Atkinson, 20 January 1911

Text: MS UT; Unpublished.

12, Colworth Road, Addiscombe, Croydon.
20 Jan 1911

Dear Mr Atkinson,

I received half a dozen copies of the *Peacock* this morning,[3] and beg to thank you therefor. Do you remember that I am thus one to the good? – Excuse the slang.

Will you let me know what the reviews say, in your good time? – and the reviewers? of course – Yours Sincerely D. H. Lawrence

[1] has] had

[2] Easter] Christmas

[3] The copies arrived on the very day *The White Peacock* was published in England (it appeared in America on 19 January).

220. To Jessie Chambers, [c. 20 January 1911]
Text: E.T. 189.

[12 Colworth Road, Addiscombe, Croydon]
[c. 20 January 1911]

[On the publication of *The White Peacock* Lawrence wrote] I its creator, you its nurse.

221. To Frederick Atkinson, 25 January 1911
Text: MS UT; Unpublished.

12, Colworth Road, Addiscombe, Croydon.
25 Jan 1911[1]

Dear Mr Atkinson,

Will you please let somebody send me three copies of the *Peacock*, with the bill therefor? Three rapacious relatives are turtling[2] with indignation at my neglect; if they were not ten times better able to spare the cash than I, I might tell them to buy their own books and go to the devil; as it is, I am constrained to play the poor but obliging (save the '*but*') cousin.

One of my aunts gave me the *Dop Doctor*.[3] I think you called it a fine book. Dear me, I seem to have met a great deal of it before at a penny a time. The *Peacock*, on the other hand, is – – –! (If you'll tell me how you fill in my blank blanks, I'll give you my candid rendering of yours.)

Will you let me have the books quick.

Yours Sincerely D. H. Lawrence

222. To Jessie Chambers, [c. 25 January 1911]
Text: E.T. 185.

[12 Colworth Road, Addiscombe, Croydon]
[c. 25 January 1911][4]

I am not strong like you. You can fight your battle and have done with it, but I *have* to run away, or I couldn't bear things. I have to fight a bit, and then run away, and then fight a bit more. So I really do go on fighting, only it has to be at intervals...At times I am afflicted by a perversity amounting to minor insanity. But the best man in me belongs to you. One me is yours,

1 1911] 1910
2 i.e. stretching the neck forward like a turtle.
3 By 'Richard Dehan' (Clotilde Inez Mary Graves) (Heinemann 1910): '...a bewildering book of which it is difficult to render a faithful account' (*TLS*, 28 April 1910).
4 Jessie Chambers dates this letter 'early in the year'. Possibly it was her reply to this that caused a slight tiff between DHL and Louie Burrows (see Letter 225, 30 January 1911).

a fine, strong me...I have great faith still that things will come right in the end.

223. To Frederick Atkinson, 27 January 1911

Text: MS UT; Unpublished.

12, Colworth Road, Addiscombe, Croydon.
27 Jan 1911

Dear Mr Atkinson,

It was good of you to have the books forwarded so promptly. But there is no bill enclosed, and I do not know how much I am charged, so I cannot send the money. Let some one make me a bill, please.

You do not really think the *Dop Doctor* is great literature, do you? I know it has sold wonderfully, which is not surprising. And perhaps it is true, in this life, that fine figures make fine books. God forbid that I should sneer at fine figures.

There have been as yet no [r]eviews of the *Peacock*? – is it early? I know that unless the book has been puffed a bit behind scenes there is scarcely any chance of it's being really well noticed; like the *Corn of Wheat*, with which, as far as I saw, no reviewer seemed to get any further than just to chew the title and spit it out.[1] Poor *Corn of Wheat* ! – What was it like, by the way?

Is there, do you think, any chance of the *Peacock*'s being well noticed? I do not expect a great deal from it in the financial way. I feel that I have forfeited such expectations, and I do not mind, seeing that I could not help myself. But I had hoped, and I think justifiably, that the book would break me an entrance into the jungle of literature; that it would give me a small but individual name by which I should be known; and that it might bring me a bit of monthly work to eke out my lamentable state. It would not be fair to it or to me, I think, that the book should fall dead:– and I know its faults pretty well.

And I do find life a damned hard drag – as do most folk, I suppose. Spare me the 'good for a man that he bear this yoke in his youth' quotation;[2] [ ][3]

You must find me an awful bore. Don't answer this if it wearies you.

Yours Sincerely D. H. Lawrence

[1] By Emily Hilda Young (Heinemann, 1910).
[2] Lamentations iii. 27 ['...bear the yoke...'].
[3] MS torn; two words are illegible.

224. To Louie Burrows, 27 January 1911

Text: MS UN; Boulton 78–9.

12, Colworth Road, Addiscombe, Croydon.
27 Jan. 1911

My dear Lou,

So you did not get my letter in the evening after all. I am sorry. You would see it was posted before school in the morning: but of course, you have no night delivery. I knew you would worry: how naughty of you.

My cold is getting better quite rapidly. I shall soon be able to sing like a lark, and shall have forgotten the croaking crow of this week.

You will be disappointed not to have seen any reviews. I am myself a wee bit disappointed. But I know it's not often a novel gets critted before a fortnight or so, therefore next week is the time. You must not think, my dear, that a work walks up to a man, a public man, and, nipping him by the nose, says 'Behold and proclaim my merit'. It's this way: The publisher sends a copy of the book to the office of the newspaper or magazine, together with a slip saying when the book is to be issued. If the publisher has puffed the book behind scenes, at his club, where he meets the big newspaper men – or if the writer has friends among the literary circles and clubs – or influence – then the book has been talked about, so the editor pounces upon it and writes it up in reviews. If the book has no friends, and the publisher, knowing there is no chance of *Scarlet Pimpernel* sales,[1] does not trouble much, then the best book in the world might fall dead. It gets handed to the hack-man for a twelve line review. We must take things as they come. I shall be very sorry if I get no success – that is to say, not even a little individual name in the literary world – from the *White Peacock*: chiefly, because it will leave me miles further off from marrying you; also, because I want a measure of success, and the book deserves it. But no amount of lamentation will stop tomorrow's rain from falling, so it's best to take the weather as it comes, without caring much. One has to have the essential life indoors, quite inside oneself, independent of whatsoever may happen outside. Voilà.

I have not got the least tiny scrap of news, and at night one does not want to chatter. I wish you were here, to be still with. What else is there to say?

Look, Louie: I – we both have agreed that we cannot marry unless I have £100 in cash and £120 a year income. Father is working very little – will soon have done. I shall have to continue to help, as you will. I cannot save £5 a year without descending to petty carefulness. When shall we marry then? We trust to luck and literature. I have worked hard enough at that damned

[1] Baroness Orczy's novel which went into its twenty-fourth impression within two years of publication in January 1905.

mill to obtain a reward so insignificant in cash. We hope much, but expect very little. Isn't that so, my dear? I am very much afraid of disappointing you. It's such a beastly mill to go through, disappointment. Well – we can have infinite patience if need be – eh?

Goodnight, my dear D. H. Lawrence

225. To Louie Burrows, 30 January 1911

Text: MS UN; Boulton 80–2.

12, Colworth Road, Addiscombe, Croydon.
30 Jan. 1911

My dear Lou,

So you are smitten? Now don't have influenza, don't. Tomorrow is your third day: I shall be ever so mad if you continue to be knocked up. I shall be telling 'whatever Gods there be'[1] that they are a parcel of fools: which would never do.

Did I call somebody's coat old? – Dear me! With a great struggle I have recalled a coat – an astrachan coat – a caracul coat, that is it – a double-breasted caracul coat that used to make my dear aunt[2] look like a bison with a skirt on. She sent it to Emily – the caracul coat – along with a suit of clothes – and I wrote to Mrs Smithard[3] – 'received the jacket suit today, together with the old coat my Aunt has sent'. The *old* coat! Did I say old? – Well, I believe it *is* just a trifle passé. That caracul coat seems like a bit of history to me. I connect it with the callow days when, poor reverent youth, I would close my eyes against its loathsome treatment of my aunt. For I believed in her slimness and her grace as dearly as in my own. 'Would you, you brute', I'd address the caracul coat 'would you make my Aunt Ada look like my Aunt Lettie (in a tightish skirt) who's been fifteen stone this last ten years? – *Would* you, you blasphemous obscenity!' I have shaken that caracul coat in my teeth like any waxy little dog with a rabbit skin. And now, it visits its wrath upon me!

'Raro antecedentem scelestum
  Deseruit pede poena claudo'[4]
'Rarely does lame foot retribution
  relinquish the trail of the offender.'

[1] Swinburne, 'The Garden of Proserpine', l. 84 ['...may be']; or W. E. Henley, 'Invictus', l. 3.

[2] Lettice Berry.

[3] Not identified.

[4] Horace *Odes* III. ii. 31–2 ['Seldom has Vengeance abandoned a wicked man though she is lame of foot and he has got a start on her'].

But if every garment, incensed by that calumnious 'old', is going to rise upon its skirt or basque or waist band to pursue us, waving malignant sleeves – I, for one, will have no friend unless she go naked.

To put a stop to this nonsense, I have just received from *The Times* this very damnatory review.[1] I am cut down like a poppy that gives only one red squint out of the pod before the mowing machine trips him up. It is '*The Times*' – and I am low, very low. It is, perhaps, cruel to send you the slip, but here it is.

The other cutting Mac found for me. It is not a severe cutting. It came from the *Observer*, a paper of some standing, I believe.[2]

I am glad the posts have finished for tonight. They've brought letters – oh dear! – one from a friend of mine, a not very close friend, tis true – in Plymouth – asking me to lend him £5 so that his wife can have an operation to replace the womb.[3] He was married last midsummer, and it appears his wife had been strained in some way before that. – I haven't got five pounds in the world, and am just considering not paying my dentist's bill, borrowing the addition, and sending him the fiver. What do you say?

Don't bother about Aunt Ada. She is vexed with me because I wont answer her last dithyrambs – I mean didactics (what's becoming of my head) – and because Ada wrote her very coolly over a little matter, and we are altogther a thankless lot, ill in grace, and rude to our maternal aunties. I hear a faint resonance

'Dies irae
Dies illa.'[4]

Don't go to Leicester – just send postal order and be sufficiently nice – then leave the dear lady alone.

I'm glad you liked Aunt Let.

I have meant to tell you that one of the three snowdrops you sent spread perfectly, and is still blithely flying. It will last tonight out, anyway – so that'll make a week. It's a long time for a snowdrop.

How strange of you to be angry with J[essie] for writing. I believe it was

[1] *The White Peacock* was briefly reviewed in *TLS*, 26 January 1911 (see Draper 33). It was praised for its natural descriptions but censured for its lack of 'a well-knit plot', its 'aimlessness', and the banality of much of the conversation.

[2] McLeod had sent the *Observer*'s review, 29 January 1911; it remarked that *The White Peacock* was 'a confusing, strange, disturbing book; but that it had the elements of greatness few will deny'.

[3] The request was made by Arthur Stanley Corke on behalf of his wife Annie, née Southgate (d. 1973). The £5 was subscribed jointly by DHL and Helen Corke.

[4] From the hymn of Thomas of Celano, translated as 'Day of wrath, O day of mourning'.

in answer to some question of mine, and it certainly wasnt an amatory epistle. Don't be jealous, will you? On the whole, it is not a nice feeling.

Then – I had forgotten for a moment that I was enumerating tonight's post – there came a letter from America asking me to give an order to the 'Press Cuttings Company' – allowing them to send me the American notices of the book – in return for five dollars. Their letter and pamphlets are just flaming under the grate.

Then I had a letter from Grace Crawford in Rome. She complains of having written before: her mother also wrote me very kindly: so I have answered her at once, being in a quaint humour for a wonder.[1]

The translations don't go well at all – nothing does (Whoa!!)

Don't be mad about *The Times* diatribe. They are anti-progressive, you see. But I wonder why so vindictive.

Now I am going to close – like a daisy afraid of the night.

Goodbye, my dear DHL

226. To Violet Hunt, 2 February 1911

Text: MS NYPL; Unpublished.

12, Colworth Road, Addiscombe, Croydon.
2nd Feb. 1911

Dear Miss Hunt,

I have not heard whether or not you are recovered from your illness, and released from the nursing home. I sincerely hope you are.

Will you be so good as to give me Mr Hueffer's address. He is still in Germany, I think; and I owe him a letter: and I wish to write to him.

With all good wishes for your returning health,

I am Yours Sincerely D. H. Lawrence

227. To Violet Hunt, 9 February 1911

Text: MS NYPL; cited in Violet Hunt, *The Flurried Years* [1926], pp. 158, 164.

12, Colworth Road, Addiscombe, Croydon.
9th Feb. 1911

Dear Miss Hunt,

Many thanks for the letter,[2] and for your generous appreciation of the

[1] The letter has not survived.

[2] The letter reads as follows (MS UN LaB 187):

Feb 3

Dear Mr Lawrence

I was meaning to write to you and tell you what I ventured to think of your book – when your letter came.

book. I had a long letter from Mr Hueffer the other day, full of sage advice and ironical cynicism. Mr Hueffer is really such a lot better fellow tha[n][1] he thinks he ought to be, to belong to this shabby frame of things.[2] So he daubs his dove-grey kindliness with a villainous selfish tar, and hops forth a very rook among rooks: but his eyes, after all, remain, like the Shulamites, doves eyes.[3] He makes me jolly mad. I think the ironic attitude, consistently adopted, is about as tiresome as the infant's bib which he says I wear for my mewling and puking[4] – in other words, he says it, mind. Some things are jolly bad, and while we're afflicted, the best thing to do is to howl to the ever-attentive heavens – if we feel like it. – The grin-and-bear-it attitude is very riling: it's so much grin foisted off on folk, and no one will thank you for a grin.

My head's in an awful buzz, because Ive just been playing with the kids: Mary is three, and Winnie seven; both healthy, bonny, and both tartars. I get so hot and so tired. They're in their nightgowns, so they have the advantage. Mary makes a praying stool of me. She kneels on my knee and says 'Ph-Peh-Ph Ph' – then suddenly, very loudly 'Amen', whereupon she opens like the sun looking over the end of a cloud, laughs, and the racket begins. Her prayer pleases me immensely. She's begun at the right end.

Thanks, I ll come to the Club on the 24th, if you'll promise that it's not swelly. I'm as shabby as a married curate, and you know I'm not well-mannered. So be good to me and warn me if need be.

I keep looking at the *Chronicle*[5] to see myself swelling out like Alice when

It was sent me by the *Chronicle* to review and I have said most truly what I thought there: and in a covering letter to the Editor I urged him to have the credit of being one of the first to welcome you as a great man.

George Saxton is a beautiful character – of a piece with the natural objects and the aspects of nature you reveal so well – You almost bewilder me with your wealth of knowledge and illustration but then the country does have that effect on me. Talk of crowds! The country at certain seasons, when it wakes and when it lies down (not in Aug, or Winter) is bewilderingly full and insistent.

Ive been ill – fr 17 Aug to 1 Dec: 1910 – now I'm better than I ever was.

Come to this – if you are in town.

Mr Hueffer address is 29 Nordanlage, *Giessen*, Germany.

Yours very truly Violet Hunt

[1] MS reads 'that'.

[2] Cf. *Macbeth* III. ii. 16.

[3] Song of Solomon i. 15. (DHL is assuming that, in this work, Solomon is addressing a Shulamite woman of great beauty.)

[4] *As You Like It* II. vii. 144.

[5] Violet Hunt's enthusiastic review of *The White Peacock* (as a 'political document developed along the lines of passionate romance') appeared in the *Daily Chronicle*, 10 February 1911 (see Draper 38–9).

she nibbled the mushroom.[1] There's a very amusing, very favorable review in today's *Morning Post* – funny.[2] Mr Hueffer says he's reviewed me. If that was he in the *Standard* – and it was in his 'Jove-abdicated-in-disgust' tone – I'll never forgive him.[3]

You are still ill, I'm afraid. I'm very sorry. I have the struggle of my life to keep off the sick list – but I manage it. You are not offended by my lack of reserve, are you? Yours very Sincerely D. H. Lawrence

228. To Ada Lawrence, 9 February 1911

Text: MS Clarke; cited in Lawrence–Gelder 78–9.

12, Colworth Road, Addiscombe, Croydon.
9 Feb. 1911

My dear Ada,

What sad news to send: Joe King dead in Chili[4] and Miss Holmes mother[5] gone so suddenly. I'm very sorry. Emily has not written me. Tell me about Joe King, will you. Mother would not have been able to suppress a little exult, would she.

I'm sending two bob for father's birthday.[6] Give him it on the right day, with my love. And will you tell me when Margaret's birthday comes off[7] – don't let me miss it. I shan't send much, but I'll not let it go by if I can help it.

I haven't got any news. Violet Hunt wrote me very nicely the other day, and asked me to go to the authors' club.[8] She's going to hail me in the *Chronicle* as a great man – God help us. I had a great long letter from Hueffer too: he's very friendly. Still[9] in Germany, you know.

[1] Lewis Carroll, *Alice's Adventures in Wonderland* (1865), chap. 5.

[2] See p. 229 n. 1. The review concluded: '*The White Peacock* is a book not only worth reading but worth reckoning with, for we are inclined to believe that its author has come to stay' (Draper 37). (The reviewer's identity cannot be established: no records of the *Morning Post* survived.)

[3] The tone of the *Standard*'s review, 3 February 1911 is suggested by the opening paragraph: 'There is nothing whatever about novel writing as an art that Mr Lawrence has not still to learn. At the same time there are an infinite number of things in this book that no rules or advice or lecture could ever teach him; it is a book of quite extraordinary promise and of no performance whatever.' (It is not possible to identify the reviewer: the *Daily Express* group have no pre-1914 files or marked cuttings.)

[4] Joseph King (1883–1911), brother-in-law to DHL's sister, Emily King. He was based at Valparaiso, working on the Chilean railway; he died a few days before he was due to return home.

[5] Not identified.

[6] On 18 June.

[7] Emily's daughter, Margaret, was two years old on 9 February.

[8] This would not be the 'Authors' Club': women could not be members of it.

[9] Still] There

There's a long and good review in todays *Morning Post*, which is a conservative, very aristocratic paper. They amuse me highly by wondering if I'm a woman.[1]

Tell me when you're going to Louie's. Is your cold quite better. I think I'm about sound now. George is better. He wrote me that the *Guardian* is stirred up on my behalf[2] – so that Nottingham will perhaps shortly have me on its tongue: that is, if whoever it is that reviews appreciates. I shan't want to come home at Easter – folk will stare at me.

Tell me all the news about everybody – I'm ever so interested. Here things are quiet.

Well – goodbye. Are you going to get a week-end down here? – Let me get a scrap of cash, and then I'll only be too glad to see you.

Your loving brother D. H. Lawrence

When *do* you move.[3] I shan't come home to Lynn Croft. I don't much want to come to Eastwood at all. Let us go away again, shall we? I *dont* want to come to Eastwood. DHL

229. To Frederick Atkinson, 11 February 1911

Text: MS UT; Unpublished.

12, Colworth Road, Addiscombe, Croydon.
11 Feb. 1911

Dear Mr Atkinson,

I have been thinking about the 'Siegmund' book, which has been sunk in my consciousness for some time. You are going to tell me some nasty things about it. I guess I have told them, most of them, to myself – amid acute inner blushes. The book is execrable bad art: it has no idea of progressive action, but arranges gorgeous tableaux-vivants which have not any connection one with the other: it is 'chargé' as a Prince Rupert's drop (if you know that curiosity):[4] its purple patches glisten sicklily: it is, finally, pornographic. And for this last reason, I would wish to suppress the book, and beg you to return the MSS to me, with any additional comments. I shall not publish it ever

1 *The White Peacock* 'is a book that piques one's curiosity in many ways. To begin with, what is the sex of "D. H. Lawrence"? The clever analysis of the wayward Lettie, surely a woman's woman, and the particular way in which physical charm is praised almost convince us that it is the work of a woman...' (Draper 36).

2 The evidence does not bear out George's remark.

3 The move took place on 9 March 1911. 'The Eastwood home was broken up and Ada looked after her father' (Lawrence–Gelder 79–80).

4 i.e. a drop of molten glass which has fallen into cold water and become shaped like a tadpole; it disintegrates with a loud bang if its tail is broken.

in its present state; and in any state, not for some years. This is not a whim, but a resolve, and I have no doubt you will commend me.

The third novel 'Paul Morel', sticks where I left it four or five months ago, at the hundredth page. I've no heart to tackle a serious work just now. I amuse myself translating – or rather writing up Arabic Stories and Verses which my Uncle, who is a German and a fairly well-known orientalist, does into German for me. When I can get some money I shall marry and settle down to steady work.

The *Peacock* is getting noticed, a bit, I see. I've had the *Standard*, *Daily Mail*,[1] *Morning Post*, and the *Daily Chronicle*. Violet Hunt is very ingenious in her effort to advertise me. – I have seen also the *Observer* and the *Times* supplement. Will you tell me if there's anything else appeared – and if the Americans have got anything to say – and if the book is 'going' at all.

I am Yours Sincerely D. H. Lawrence

P.S. I wish I'd remembered before to ask for the MSS back, and thus saved you the bother of it. I know you hate handwriting. DHL

230. To Ada Lawrence, 17 February 1911

Text: MS Clarke; Postmark, Croydon FE 17 11; cited in Moore, *Intelligent Heart* 107.

12, Colworth Road, Addiscombe, Croydon.
17 Feb 1911

My dear Ada,

I am very sorry father is proving such a nuisance to you. Never mind: he will be much humbler when he's not got his own house to be boss in. Let him then eat a bit of the bread of humility. It is astonishing how hard and bitter I feel towards him.

It was a cruel thing, Joe King's death: and how cruel little Billy Limb's state![2] Think how everything has turned out! – How jolly we used to play in their house! I often dream of Mabel Limb – oh, so often. I am tired of Life being so ugly and cruel. Now, I long for it to turn pleasant. It makes my soul heave with distaste to see it so harsh and brutal.

I'm glad you like Louie. When she is a bit older, she'll be more understanding. Remember she's seen nothing whatever of the horror of life, and we've been bred up in its presence: with father. It makes a great difference. I have noticed myself the attitude of insolent criticism at their

[1] In the *Daily Mail*, 3 February 1911, DHL was complimented on having written 'a story of great power and beauty', even if the power 'at times grips all too tightly' and the beauty is melancholic.

[2] Probably the brother of Mabel (who had died in 1909).

house. I used to mock them. When I went out, I used to call the people horribly for all the things they *weren't*, just in Ethel's[1] best manner. You should have seen them all cockle.[2]

I've been painting lately. Don't send your pictures to be framed till you see if you like these I've done for Nellie Allam better[3] – then you can have your pick.[4] I've not written much: I find I can't.

The publisher has not written to me lately. He owes me a letter. I believe the *Peacock* is going pretty well. Did you see that rageous review in the *Daily News*.[5] It amused me. I'd upset *that* man, whoever he was, hadn't I. But he acknowledged my power very sincerely.

People here are very nice – at school and everywhere. I shall stop on at Croydon, I think, yet awhile.

Emily has been very short with me lately: postcards in reply to letters – and very scant thanks either for the *Peacock* or the p[ostal] o[rder] for Margaret.

It was Louie's birthday on Monday, and I didn't know. I've bought her rather a pretty brooch of paste brilliants. Don't be jealous of her. She hasn't any share[6] in *your* part of me. You and I – there are some things which we shall share, we alone, all our lives: you know, also, that there is more *real* strength in my regard for you than there is for Louie. You are my one, *real* relative in the world: only you. I am yours: is it not so?

I don't care much about the *Peacock* – really, I don't. And I'm going to suppress the Siegmund book. It is better so.

I've not written Aunt Ada since Christmas and I'm not going to. She's a poor shoddy object, of limited vision. I have no respect for her. – She is mad with me – ah poor fool, that she is.

You know my sympathy is with you –

Your brother D. H. Lawrence

My regards to Minnie[7] and everybody. DHL

[1] Louie Burrows's sister.

[2] i.e. crow like a cock or cackle like a hen (dialect).

[3] Mary Ellen ('Nellie') Allam (b. 1886), daughter of his aunt 'Polly' and her second husband, James Allam. m. John Edward Watson, 1 June 1911: DHL's pictures were to be a wedding present (see Letter 232).

[4] One of those she probably chose was 'Two Apples', a water-colour signed DHL and dated 10 November 1910 (Levy, *Paintings*, monochrome no. 6).

[5] *Daily News*, 14 February 1911. The reviewer remarked that *The White Peacock* is 'able to force a mood on the reader whether he resist or not. The writer has a power of arresting attention for a moment, of casting a spell, but it is painful attention, and a blighting spell' (Draper 40).

[6] share] part

[7] Unidentified.

231. To William Hopkin, 20 February 1911

Text: MS NCL; Postmark, Croydon FE 20 11; Huxley 5–6.

Davidson Rd Boys School, South Norwood, S.E.
20 Feb. 1911

Dear Mr. Hopkin,

I had a letter from Ada this morning telling me that Hall's are kicking up a bit of a dust over the representation of Alice.[1] In my thinking, she ought to be flattered. She's shown as highly moral and salted with wit enough to save even the insipid Sodom of Eastwood – 'sauf votre respect', – that is.

However, if they really feel that their noble chapel-going dignity is impaired, I wish you would assure them that I will contrive to have, in the next impression, the name changed to Margaret Undine Widmerpuddle, or any such fantasy they shall choose, far away from the sound of Hall or Gall.[2] – I suppose it's Holditch, snuffing idiot. I'll have a whack at him, one day – so let him beware.

The book's going moderately, but the shekels are not deluging me yet. Alas, no!

I'm afraid my sister is having a rough time with father. I wish he were in – no, I won't say it aloud. Is one never to have five minutes peace?

Apologise to Mrs. Hopkin on my behalf, please, because I have not answered her letter. I will do so. Congratulate Miss Potter for me, and tell her I shall want her to speak up for me on the Judgment Day.[3] – And, I exhort you, try to keep Enid away from this deadly contamination of pen and ink. – 'Est et silentio tuta merces'[4] – I don't know whether the quotation's correct, but it means that the 'reward is for faithful silence.' I wish I merited it.

Try and soothe off the virtuous indignation of the Halls, I beg you. I don't want the publishers to be annoyed: it is they who are responsible, you see. I can get the name changed without much trouble, myself. Really, if many more perverse things happen, I shall betake myself to Job's muck-heap,[5] putting a potsherd in my pocket, and advising one or two or my prosperous friends in Uz and such-like places, of my intention. In short, I'm fed up.

[1] Alice Beatrice Hall (b. 1880?), a companion of DHL's youth, teacher at British School, Eastwood, and now married to White Holdich (d. 1930). Holdich had threatened DHL with a law-suit over his presentation of Alice as Alice Gall in *The White Peacock*. William Hopkin was instrumental in frustrating the threat (see Harry T. Moore, *Priest of Love*, p. 129; Delavenay 675–6).

[2] The character's name remained unchanged.

[3] Louie Potter, cousin of Mrs Hopkin (née Sallie Potter); lived with the Hopkins and assisted in the Post Office.

[4] See p. 47 n. 2.

[5] Job ii. 8.

My regards to Mrs Hopkin. Thanks for puffing me in the Rag.[1]

Yours, D. H. Lawrence

I was very young when I wrote the *Peacock* – I began it at twenty. Let that be my apology.

232. To Ada Lawrence, 1 March 1911

Text: MS Clarke; Postmark, Croydon MR 2 11; cited in Lawrence–Gelder 80–1.

12, Colworth Road, Addiscombe, Croydon.
1st March 1911

My dear Ada,

I was wondering when you were going to write to me. You did not tell me how father is working and behaving. You should do, for I want to know, and if you do not tell me, I only wonder and wonder. So pray tell me plainly, will you, all that concerns the home.

No, there is nothing I want – saving the woman, and, if you like, the black vases, which will always remind me of home: not, God knows, that one wants too much to be reminded thereof.

Yes, I will come home at Easter. It would cost a lot for us to go away, and I want to see folk. But I hate Eastwood abominably, and I should be glad if it were puffed off the face of the Earth. – I am glad you are moving:[2] yet how strange it will be to come to mill fields: stranger, far, than going to Ramsgate or some unknown place. What a lot of things one has to do that one doesn't in the least want to do.

I promised Nellie Allam three pictures: two I will have framed and give her for a wedding present, one I will give her unframed. I have now done five – two I believe Aunt Ada wants – or one – et nous voilà. But you shall choose among them.

I have not heard for quite a long time from the publisher about the *Peacock*. I guess he has no news, and will write me when he has. I believe the book is doing moderately well. It will not make me much money, and Heaven alone knows, at that rate, when I shall be able to settle down. But no matter: what one can do for two months, one can do 'ad infinitum'.

[1] Under the pseudonym, 'Anglo-Saxon', Hopkin wrote a weekly miscellaneous column in the *Eastwood and Kimberley Advertiser*. On 10 February 1911 he reviewed *The White Peacock* very favourably: 'it is extremely well worth reading, for it is a good book well written...let me strongly advise my readers to buy a copy'. He drew special attention to the portrait of 'Alice Gall', 'a rollicking, larky sort of a lass...Unfortunately, she married a man with a halo, and they are always a nuisance to human folk like Alice, and to most others for the matter of that.'

[2] To Bromley House, Queens Square, in Eastwood.

Sometimes I have a fit of horrors which is very hard to put up with. It is often a case of living by sheer effort. We pay very heavily for this boon of living.

I often think of Flossie.[1] If I don't write to her – well – she will understand. But I know what she's had to go through, and has: and I think of her very often, with sympathy.[2]

In about six weeks tomorrow I shall be coming home. I used to say that to mother. – It rather gets worse than better – *that* – doesn't it.

My love to you DHL

Tell me you get the p[ostal] o[rder] all right.

233. To Louie Burrows, 3 March 1911

Text: MS UN; Boulton 82–3.

12, Colworth Road, Addiscombe, Croydon.
3 March 1911[3]

My dear Lou,

I wish you could have come – I do wish you could. Never mind: one learns patience in the long run. It is a hard lesson for me. I am a long time indifferent: I don't bother with much useless vain desire: but once a thing is visible and I want it, and it is feasible, I would go mad to have it immediately. I could wait for ever for a far-off thing: but for the slow coming of the sun out of a cloud I could go mad.

I have promised to go to Hampstead tomorrow: I had promised.[4] So think of me in London.

Tonight, for four hours, I have been drawing the *Idyll* – you know, Maurice Greiffenhagen's thing.[5] It is to be a big picture – as big as ever my board will hold. It is for you. It has taken me four hours, and I have not

[1] Florence Cullen (1879–1924), daughter of George Henry Cullen (James Houghton of *The Lost Girl*, Secker, 1920); m. George Hodgkinson, (1872–1965), a local miner's son. A trained nurse, she nursed Mrs Lawrence in her final illness; DHL acknowledged her kindness by inscribing a complimentary copy of *The White Peacock*: 'Addiscombe 21st Jan. 1911 To Flossie Cullen in gratitude to her, for her rare kindness to my mother.' She would be in DHL's thoughts when he was writing 'Paul Morel': Miriam in the novel is transplanted to the Cullen household Flossie Cullen was the basis for Alvina in *The Lost Girl*.

[2] sympathy] deep sympathy

[3] 1911] 1910

[4] To visit the Hungers (see p. 184 n. 1).

[5] See p. 103, n. 3. DHL eventually completed four copies of the *Idyll*: one for Louie; a second (smaller) for his sister Ada (Letter 242); a third as a wedding present for Agnes Holt (Letter 281); and a fourth for McLeod (Letter 357). It is impossible to establish which reproduction DHL was copying; among the possibilities are the following: *Examples of Great Artists*, Pt. 17, 3 July 1902; *The Nation's Pictures*, Pt. 1, 1901, folio 3; or *The Nation's Pictures*, 2nd series, 27 March 1907. (The picture is discussed in *The White Peacock*, I.3.)

finished drawing. It will take me to finish 12 or 14 hours in all. Then I will give it you, and voilà, a day of my life. –

I have learned such patience as almost surprises me: patience in executing a work. By nature I am rapid and facile. But by teaching, and horrid discipline of life, I get very much schooled to accuracy.

Perhaps you will come next week. In five weeks we shall be coming home – no, in six. Six weeks today I shall be with you (DV). I wish it weren't at Eastwood. If it weren't that they insist, I'd rather stop in school than go there: I'd rather have no holiday.

But I want very much to see you. I dream, and dream, and dream, very sweetly, often, about us. But it is inclined to make one bitter after. The reality is so absurdly different, and so unnecessarily insufficient.

I still do not hear from the Publisher – I am not sorry: he will only bother me. Oh, if only I were just a private individual, with not any bartering with the public, how glad I should be. I wish all this toil of writing were put away, and we were perfectly untroubled and unanxious, in a quiet country school.[1] – But who can alter fate, and useless it is to rail against it. When I get sore, I always fly to the Greek tragedies: they make one feel sufficiently fatalistic. Im doing *Oedipus Tyrannus* just now – Sophocles. I wish[2] with all my heart I read Greek. These Greek tragedies make one quiet and indifferent. They are very grand, even in translation.

Well, if you were coming tomorrow, how nice it would be – I shall do another hour's work, and then go to bed – work is a fine substitute for a wife. I work work – you will marry a very ant. How horrid for you.

But if you were here, I shouldn't need to work. But you are not here, for God knows how long. So it is 'laisser aller'.

I kiss you – – I paint love pictures to you. Ah – I kiss you closely next week. Addio DHL

234. To Jessie Chambers, [c. 7 March 1911]

Text: E.T. 154.

[12 Colworth Road, Addiscombe, Croydon]
[c. 7 March 1911][3]

['Lawrence wrote to me [Jessie] that X. [Louie Burrows] was to spend a week-end in Croydon, staying as a guest of the family with whom he lodged, as his sister, and myself, and other friends had done.']

[1] MS has 'schools'.

[2] wish] will

[3] Louie Burrows spent the weekend, 11–12 March, in Croydon; this is foreshadowed in Letter 233 and confirmed in Letter 236. DHL would receive her letter accepting his invitation on about 6 March; he was then able to pass the news to Jessie Chambers.

235. To Ada Lawrence, 8 March 1911

Text: MS Clarke; Postmark, Croydon MR 8 11; cited in Lawrence–Gelder 81–3.

12, Colworth Road, Addiscombe, Croydon.
8 March 1911

My dear Ada,

You will be reviling me again for not writing. But I loathe the idea of letters to be written. Let me go once a fortnight, will you? I have to fairly kick myself towards a sheet of notepaper.

You are moving tomorrow. Oh, I do hope it will all be a success. If not, you'll have to split again, and send father into digs. It is very wearying and bothersome.

I am sorry you are still so troubled. Oh dear – there's nothing to do but to grin and bear it. And don't meddle with religion: I would leave all that alone, if I were you, and try to occupy myself full in the present, the present. I find the only antidote is work. Heavens – how I do but slog. It gets the days over, at any rate. – I wish we were nearer, to be company. I find that folks aren't company for me: I am as much alone with the friends here as if I were solitary. But how used one gets to a lonely life. I'm sure I've now no intimate friends here – and I don't want any. I am sufficient unto myself, and prefer to be left alone.

I am sorry Mr Reid is leaving[1] – it will desolate you. But he'll be happier, poor man. I must write to him, and subscribe to his testimonial.

I went to Hampstead on Saturday. They are very nice with me indeed. They say Louie can go there for the night next Sat – not this, as she had arranged. I don't know whether or not I shall take her, though. I shall see. She had arranged to come this Saturday, and if it's fine, I think she'd better. She could stay at Miss Reynolds'.[2] We have got a little old cousin of Mrs Jones from South Africa.[3] She's an amiable little body – but I don't know how long she's going to stop.

I have mortally offended Aunt Ada, by writing her a bit of a stinging letter. I'm glad – insolent, mean cat that she is.

The publisher has not written to me. I told you I had said to him I would not have the Siegmund book published. That has offended him, I suppose. I don't care a snap. He can go to the devil.

I'm glad, though, Alice Halls business blew over. Silly little fool – and

[1] Rev. Robert Reid left Eastwood for Pendleton, Lancs., where he remained till 1919.

[2] Lilian Reynolds (1877–1954), teacher in Croydon; friend of Helen Corke and Agnes Mason; became headmistress of school at Redhill, September 1911. DHL was a frequent visitor to her house, 'Kenella', in Croydon (cf. Letter 290); Louie Burrows stayed there 11–12 March.

[3] Mrs Wilkinson (see Letter 250).

the ass Holditch! I had a letter from Willie Hopkin. It was good of him to stick up for me.

Now I'll close. If I had any money I should wish you'd come and see me. But I must wait for you, – till Easter. With my heart's love DHL

236. To Louie Burrows, 13 March 1911

Text: MS UN; Boulton 83–4.

12 Colworth Rd, Addiscombe, Croydon.
13 March 1911

My dear Lou,

Are you feeling sad now the week-end has gone? – I am. We could be so happy if we could be together, and alone it is so difficult. However, it is useless to moan.

I have begun Paul Morel again. I am afraid it will be a terrible novel. But, if I can keep it to my idea and feeling, it will be a great one.

I am wondering what you will be saying to me tonight. Are you being serious and telling me your trouble? – I wonder. We cannot marry yet awhile for a long time. That, I can see, is your most serious and settled conviction: and to anything you seriously decree, I bow my obedience. But sometimes life pushes very hard, and we have to be careful.

I want you to speak before I say anything. Between life and death and honor, it is a rum pass.

Oh dear, I am a cursed nuisance. I must pluck the very concentrated heart out of each of my mysteries and desires. I go straight, like a bullet, towards my aim. I cannot loiter by the way. I cannot slowly gather flowers as I saunter. I wish to heaven I could. I cut straight through like a knife to what I want. I cannot, cannot slowly enjoy watching the rose open: I can't help it, Louie, I can't. I am really dangerous in my fixed mad aim. I love my rose, and no other: and when I can have her I shall want no other. But when I have her not, I have nothing. Your pleasure, which you enjoy, in the thought of me, is nothing to me. What I want I want and quarter measures are nothing to me. I am a nuisance and a trouble to everybody. Always I am cursing myself, but it doesn't alter me what I am.

I will borrow a translation of *Trésor des Humbles*[1] for you, because I want

[1] By Maurice Maeterlinck (1862–1949), Belgian poet and dramatist. Published in 1896 it was translated by Alfred Sutro as *The Treasure of the Humble* (1897). Louie might well have found Maeterlinck's 'morale mystique' somewhat baffling: 'it can increase reverence where it does not touch understanding' (Edward Thomas, *Maeterlinck*, 1911, p. 155). Yet she would recognise his insistence on women's greater spirituality and intuitive power, on the transforming and vitalising power of love, and on love as the way to mystical truth.

you to understand it thoroughly. It will help you to understand yourself and me.

Life is a strange, inflexible, dreadful thing which turns us slowly in its lathe. The thing is not to resist too strenuously this graving tool.

Oh Lou, how horrid it all sounds. I wish before heaven I was like you. Never mind, things will turn out all right for us, and you shall be happy.

My dear, I feel such a wretch and a nuisance. Gott in Himmel.

But what am I going on about – Smoke.

I kiss you, my dear. Court is less worthy of you even than I am – else I'd say have him. But he's got no understanding. But a man who causes sorrow by his deeds and yet has understanding is better than a righteous stiffnecked fool who gives disgust.

Which is vanity on my part.

And after all, I'm not doing anything wrong, so what am I talking about.

You will never let me make you unhappy, will you?

Goodnight, my love D. H. Lawrence

237. To Jessie Chambers, [post 13 March 1911]

Text: E.T. 154.

[12 Colworth Road, Addiscombe, Croydon]
[post 13 March 1911]

[Louie Burrows] was here for the week-end, but it's no good. Somehow as soon as I am alone with her I want to run away.

238. To Helen Corke, [14 March 1911]

Text: MS UT; cited in Huxley 7.

12 Colworth Rd
Tuesday

Sometimes it strikes me one way – sometimes another. Sometimes I think it is the beastliest of selfishness – sometimes I think it is poltroonery – sometimes it seems to me perfectly natural – my way.

After all, Helene – what difference is there between your arrangement and mine? You say – let us be together, because it stimulates you. – You know you would take my arm when we were alone: you know, when I was a bit tormented, you would put your arms round my neck. Now if you can tell me any difference between this and the ultimate, I shall thank you. I tell you this, because you are moved to irony against me. Might I not also turn round to you in irony, when you proffer your request.

If I became necessary to you, would it be because of the physical intimacy? Would there be no necessity developed from companionship as soul-intimate as ours is sure to be? We are always so intimate, vitally – that the other seems to me merely natural, like a phrase[1] in the conversation. If it is not natural and good, God is an idiot. Between my proposal and yours, Helene, in the eyes of the Seer, what difference is there? – You ask me for my intimate company – I say, all right, so long as I need not keep a clutch on a discord. Finally – to your heart of hearts I speak – and be truthful: *Could* we marry without making a horrible smash? – 'We[2] have broken down the bounds of the individual' – it is true – that's why it is perfectly honorable for you to take me: but with the bounds of the individual broken down, there is too deadly concentrated an intercourse not to be destructive. (bad English – can you understand?)

You have this on your side: that I[3] look on my life as moving on phase by phase, you on yours, unhappily, as being all one-coloured web. Then, if I went, you might be at a loss to find life. But, my dear – Siegmund went, and inevitably, loving as you love – your lover must go – unless you love differently, lighter, more reservedly. You are passionate, ay, as much as I. But your passion smoulders, and consumes your energy that way. I tend to blow your passion into flame – and [...] even then I cannot – it is a heavy, sullen smoulder – and mine is top-heavy with flame.

Do you remember Beatrice in *Tono Bungay*? do you, do you? – *There* – that is your way.

Look here, Helene – I genuinely believe I was *not* wrong in what I asked you.

And if you had not asked me for what I consider is all – you see, it is, for the time, all, for me – and your reservation is as much as mine; only yours is in the past, mine the future – I should not have asked the moiety extra. Don't you see, Helene – we could not go on as friends – we have known each too well: you know what the end would be: then I should feel a coward.

You think of me what you like – and be as ironical as you like – I do not mind.

There, Helene – let's have done. It is sickening, this cats-pawing. I have begun 'Paul Morel' again – glory, you should see it. The British public will stone me if ever it catches sight.

The publisher remains obstinately silent – offended by my cool cheek in asking for the Saga back. You shall have the MSS if you like – when I get

[1] a phrase] fine phrase
[2] smash? – 'We] smash? – you have [...] – 'We
[3] I] for

it. Though, you remember – you say it's not – not – anything of yours except in name, I suppose you mean. Vale Helene DHL

The common everyday – rather superficial man of me really loves Louie. Do you believe that? But do you not think the open-eyed, sad critical, deep seeing man of me has not had to humble itself pretty sorely to accept the imposition of the masculine, stupid decree. There is a decree for each of us[1] – thou shalt live alone – and we have to put up with it. We may keep real company once in our lives – after that we touch [...], now and again, upon someone else – but do not repose.

A few of those vague things, which I used to hesitate over, I feel pretty certain of now. It doesn't much matter. The laws of life, even of Nature, are made for the unseeing, unintelligent mass, and we have to submit also, nous autres. But, entre nous, and entre nous alone – we can make our own laws. Step out of the common pale, and the old laws [...] drop obsolete – you know that – and new[2] laws suddenly reign. But you judge me by the old laws. – The light has gone out – suddenly fallen.

Tenébres DHL

239. To Frederick Atkinson, 15 March 1911

Text: MS UT; Unpublished.

12, Colworth Road, Addiscombe, Croydon.
15 March 1911

Dear Mr Atkinson,

I had a letter from Mr Austin Harrison of the *English Review*, asking why a copy of the *White Peacock* had not been sent to him to review. Would you mind letting one be forwarded to him; please – 11 Henrietta St W.C? – Don't you think *English Review* criticisms worth much? – they are very good fun, to my reckoning. But – Noblesse Oblige – will you send a copy?[3]

Why haven't you answered my last letter? – of how many weeks standing? Haven't you yet waded through the Siegmund MSS? But you will send it back, to me, will you not? I really don't want it to go out. There's no need to read it if it's not going to be published. – I've begun again 'Paul Morel'. I swear it'll be a fine novel: no balderdash. But that *Daily News* reviewer – wa[sn]'t that funny? – will lie on his back and kick like a black-beetle under Keatings,[4] if he happens to read it.

[1] of us] man [2] new] the

[3] One was sent. In a letter, 6 April 1911 (see p. 254 n. 3), Harrison remarked: 'Let me congratulate you on your book – Excellent.' Henry Savage reviewed the novel ('as a work of artistic and literary excellence') in *English Review*, viii (May 1911), 356–7.

[4] i.e. Keating's powder, a famous brand of household insecticide.

I wish you'd tell me what the Americans say of the *White Peacock*. I had a letter from one of their snipping firms, and it said: 'We have now collected 10 reviews from the journals, and shall be pleased to forward them to you on receipt of a dollar.' That was very tantalising.

With all good wishes for your health.

Yours Sincerely D. H. Lawrence

240. To Henry Savage, [post 18 March 1911]

Text: Nehls, i. 210.

[12 Colworth Road, Addiscombe, Croydon]
[post 18 March 1911]

[Lawrence wrote to Henry Savage[1] to thank him for the review of *The White Peacock* he had published in the *Academy* on 18 March 1911.]

241. To Louie Burrows, 27 March 1911

Text: MS UN; Boulton 85–6.

12 Colworth Rd, Addiscombe, Croydon
27 March 1911

My dear Lou,

You may put in my room (imaginary) a scarlet cactus plant in blossom – no more. Now let's quarrel about it, just to enliven this deadly dull day.

The almond blossom is out, full out, mixing in grey miserable rain, poor little devils. There's a lot of almond blossom in Addiscombe, and I like it. The hedges are in rosettes. Hawthorn leaves, opened no further than half blown rosettes, on a wet evening, are the vividest green things I know.

It is a very cold day, after yesterday also cold. I ought to go out to see Humphreys: he's not been to school – more work for us. But it's too cold to visit the ruddy sick.

I've been reading Swinburnes 'Tristram of Lyonesse'. Some parts of it are very fine, parts again are barren to excess, stretches of noisy desert. You mustn't try to put too much thought into verse, as I often try, and – presumptuous contiguity – Meredith does. But to let your metronome go on

[1] Henry Savage (b. 1881?), free-lance journalist and essayist, was on the staff of *Vanity Fair* then under the editorship of Frank Harris. First met DHL on 16 July 1913 at Kingsgate, Kent. Joint editor of *Academy*, 1915; later assistant editor, *Bookman's Journal* and London editor of *Book Notes*. Author of *Richard Middleton* (1922), etc. (See autobiography, *The Receding Shore: Leaves from the somewhat unconventional life of Henry Savage*, 1933.)

ticking when the music and meaning is gone is tiresome. Swinburne is shallow. Do you know Merediths poetry – 'Love in a Valley' – and 'Woods of Westermain' and 'Modern Love': very fine indeed. 'Love in a Valley' is a bag of jewels, rare, precious as can be, and beautiful – but they want a bit of setting.

[ ][1] [re]ad them together some day [ ] you like poetry – I know I've enough long neck and soulful aspect for two – but I'll shorten my gizzard and you can share the soulfulness, – make you look 'intéressante' – then we'll have sweet and ring-dovey times.[2]

I send you a little volume of French kids songs.[3] Learn them and we'll sing them at Easter, for fun. Learn them, and astonish and delight the private parties of Gaddesby: if you don't show 'em the book. It is the dodge of an artist – and most folks are artists where their own ends are concerned. Sneak a thing from a simple obscure source, and then make the catch to shine as a light through a chink, indicating a houseful of bright knowledge – so we attain greatness and distinction. You can make Gaddesby believe that you are intimately acquainted with the French young heart.

Oh dear, what a lot of rot. You know Lou, you make me ashamed of passion – I've finished the *Idyll*, by the way – and ashamed of lamenting, and ashamed of complaining, and ashamed even of dreaming – I know I'm given to disgraceful extravaganza – so remains only to be trivial and ironic. I beg your pardon. I am, and always shall be, a bad writer of love letters.

I hope Miss Cox is better – give her my love.[4] I wish it were Easter – will it be a beautiful yellow morning on Good Friday, with all the primroses out in Berkshire – as it has been other years – or will it rain. It is only 17 days after you get this. There is time to forget all separation and fallings short. We'll have a good week. Till then, we rest patient.

With love Yours DHL

242. To Ada Lawrence, 27 March 1911

Text: MS Clarke; Postmark, Croydon MR 27 11; cited in Lawrence–Gelder 83–4.

12 Colworth Rd, Addiscombe, Croydon
27 March 1911

[1] MS torn.

[2] Cf. *As You Like It* v. iii. 17–19. (DHL was currently teaching this play at school.)

[3] Perhaps *French Song and Verse for Children*, ed. Helen Terry (1908).

[4] Sarah Elizabeth Cox (1859–1946). Louie Burrows lodged with her at Wesley Cottage, Gaddesby.

My dear Ada,

I have owed you a letter a long time. Never mind – perhaps you read Emily's. How are you going on? – do you keep well? – and how does the new house suit? You should have quite a budget of news to tell me.

How is Flossie? What is she doing? Has she forgiven me for not writing her letters? I simply cannot screw up my courage, or my energy, or something, to correspondence. It's not that I think any the less of them – more, perhaps. But I can't get letters written. How are the Coopers? – do they come to see you? I'm going to write to Mr Reid tonight. Will he be gone away by Easter? I'm sorry he's leaving: at the bottom, I like him: and I always respect him.

Isn't it awful weather. I have a damned cold which hangs on abominably. I'll really have a go at shifting it this week.

It's not long to Easter. I'm glad, for the sake of the holiday and of seeing some of my own people. But I don't want to come to Eastwood. You'll not get me in the town much, I can tell you.

I think I shall come home on the Friday morning – there'll be a trip – and Lou could join the train at Loughboro; if that would suit you – would it? If you'd rather she came after me, tell me, and I'll arrange.

I've painted you a little *Idyll* – about 14″ × 7″. Do you remember I began to draw it the night mother died? – and I said I should never finish it. Now I've done a big one for Louie, and a little one for you. It looks nice.

When one is a bit off in health, how it all comes back, worse than ever. No one understands but you. Lou doesn't understand a bit – and I never say anything. I'm afraid she's one I shan't tell things to – it only seems to bother her. But it's just as well. In the things that matter, one has to be alone, in this life – or nearly alone. I never say anything to anybody – but sometimes I can hardly swallow the meals. And there is no refuge from one's own thoughts – day after day.

It's no good writing in this strain, however. Bear a thing, as if it weren't there – that's the only way. Folk hate you to be miserable, and to make them a bit miserable.

Tell me all the news – how baby is[1] – and Father. School goes quietly – I often go to the boss' for an evening. – J[essie] doesn't write to me – except a postcard now and then. It was funny of her to send that joint Christmas card. But there's no need to laugh at her now, is there?

Aunt Ada has not written to me for ages. She's decidedly 'got the needle'[2] as they say down here. Let her have it.

1 Margaret King, then aged 2.

2 i.e. is irritated.

My regards to Eddie – and Flossie – and everybody. Love to the kindchen and Emily and Sam,[1] and you, my dear.

Your brother D. H. Lawrence

243. To Reverend Robert Reid, 27 March 1911

Text: MS UN; Postmark, Croydon MR 27 11; Unpublished.

12, Colworth Road, Addiscombe, Croydon.
27 March 1911

Dear Mr Reid,

I am very sorry to hear from Ada that you are going away from Eastwood. That will be a loss to her and to Emily, a loss to many people in the place.

I would like, if I may, to say that I am very grateful to you for your goodness to my people. My mother held you very high, and the debts of gratitude the dead leave we can never discharge. If I have ever been unmannerly or inimical towards you, I beg you to forgive me. I have a sense that your generosity has exceeded mine by a great way. In the fret of differing opinions we mark and disfigure a real heart-esteem – which I have done. For me, flesh and blood are the Scriptures; and turning back two or three years, and reading again, I am very sorry for having done an injustice to a fine page. I often turn, in the same way, back into the Bible, and am ashamed of my old insolence. – If only we were allowed to look at Scripture in the light of our own experience, instead of having to see it displayed in a kind of theatre, false-real, and never developing, we should save such a lot of mistakes. It's the narrowness of folk's barb-wire restrictions we get our raw wounds from – and then blame the world.

Give my regards to Mrs Reid. I wish you may have a happy life in the new church. Will you leave Robert[2] behind?

Yours very Sincerely D. H. Lawrence

I thank you again for your kindness to me.

[1] Samuel Taylor King; m. DHL's sister Emily on 5 November 1904. Driver of steam-engine truck; on demobilisation in 1918 took a grocer's shop in Nottingham (see also p. 416 n. 1).

[2] Reid's son (d. 1955).

244. To Helen Corke, [c. 27 March 1911]

Text: Huxley 7.

[12 Colworth Road, Addiscombe, Croydon]
[c. 27 March 1911][1]

...I have received your letter, and fail to find its exceeding frankness or brutality – you are quaint. Certainly you shall treat me with humour and asperity: and I will laugh. No – but I will be better....Really, I have got a bit indifferent. Life seemed so paltry, so short of generosity. It would give its half measures with much benignity – very Christian-like. Really, the one beautiful and generous adventure left seemed to be death.

And this is not because I am inactive altogether. My soul has strenuous work in intimacies to do. But then I scorn the intimacy, when it's formed; it is always a lot short...

245. To Louie Burrows, 29 March 1911

Text: MS UN; Boulton 86–8.

Davidson Rd Boys School, South Norwood, S.E.
29 March 1911

My dear Lou,

I think I will write you from school. Here, before night falls, and I'm at Colworth, I'm more good humoured. Forgive me for being disagreeable. I'll mend – how many times do I say that – but I'll mend, surely.

We have just finished *As You Like It*. It's very jolly, and the boys enjoy it: only they do want to caper round in a dance while Rosalind delivers the epilogue, and there's not enough room. Poor Orlando forgot to take the duster off, so he was married with his arm in a sling. We act as if the front of the class were a stage: good fun. And they spy so anxiously to see if I laugh: as a rule it's up my sleeve I'm grinning, but they're satisfied.

To tell the truth my cold has not quite gone, and has left me rather low. But I shall be all right in a fortnight. – Humphreys is back at school, thank Goodness.

I'm going to Lil Reynolds to tea this evening. I'll give her your love. Your *Idyll* looks ever so nice. I began a new sketch, but have spoiled it through not being in the painting humour. Strange, when I can write I can't paint, and vice versa. I'm just amusing myself with a short story.

Austin Harrison – *English Review* – wants to see some stories. I've got a dozen in rough but none done up. So I'll do one or two. Tomorrow I'm

[1] It is assumed that Helen Corke replied to DHL's letter of 14 March, and that this is his response to her.

going to call in the evening to see him about the story he's got, which I think he wants altering a bit.[1] – I'll tell you what he's like – though I may not be home in time to write tomorrow evening.

As to the black furniture – do as you like. I've got a bit of verse to you somewhere – a teasing bit, merely – nothing serious

'I will give you all my keys
  You shall be my châtelaine
You shall enter as you please
  As you please shall go again

———

When I hear you jingle through
  All the chambers of my heart
I shall sit and smile at you
  Playing your housekeeper's part.'[2]

etc etc – but this is all of the 'jingle' I can remember.

I must must get some composition marked: oh the stack that awaits me. The boys are very funny. I gave them 'a newspaper account of any event.' – One boy took the school concert, and I found this jewel, '"A Pot of Broth" an Irish play, was perfectly performed under the direction of Mr MacLeod, before gorgeous scenery, exquisitely painted by Mr Lawrence.[3] The Head master, Mr Smith, was very busy in control, running hither and thither, whilst Mr Aylwin and Mr Byrne attended to the stage carpentry.'

There's nothing so aimiable and decent as boys – big boys, when they know you. I'm having VII again next year. Really, while I am at school, I never wish myself elsewhere. I look at the register. Two more weeks to fill in – what a little way! I look back at the term's twelve – I look back at last terms sixteen or seventeen – Heavens – I stick my face hard to the future, I don't want ever to look back. The future will be fine, must be. Oh yes, this day of ours – chronologically, our lives are about at 11.0 o'clock, aren't they – will brighten up. I know I shall have 'a gorgeous afternoon, exquisitely painted towards evening by x x x.'

Au revoir, my dear, I have thousands and thousands of kisses for you, ready to burst onto wing.

[1] 'Odour of Chrysanthemums' was 'the story' in question. In July 1910 DHL had been asked to cut five pages from it (see Letter 168); he probably re-wrote it during the summer of 1910. He was informed in September (see Letter 179) that there was then no room in the *English Review* for prose; presumably he left it with Harrison and had recently been told again that it required some further revision.

[2] An early version of the much longer poem published as 'Teasing', in *Poetry and Drama*, December 1914 and as 'Tease' in *Amores* (Duckworth, 1916).

[3] See p. 186, Letter 188 and n. 3.

I can smell a pink hyacinth in the window, as I write. The boys in the hall are singing a German spring song.

I've wasted (no) all this spare lesson I have for marking composition. No matter. In school, you are nearer than anywhere, being also in school. I feel as if I would like to turn tramp, and wander north to Leicestershire, and wander till I forget the weedy creek of life I've been bred in. I want to get into a nice running fresh current of life, that has no tang and no taint.

Goodbye, my dear. I wish things happened like *As You Like It*. I reckon you're a lot like Rosalind. I always think of you.

Baisers – baisers. DHL

246. To Louie Burrows, 1 April 1911

Text: MS UN; Boulton 88–90.

12 Colworth Rd, Addiscombe, Croydon
1st April 1911

My dear Lou,

It is unusual for you to miss both Friday and Saturday. Are you scolding me?

I went to *Cavalleria Rusticana* and *Pagliacci* at Croydon last night – one shilling in the pit. It's an Italian company from Drury Lane – Italians of the common class – opera in Italian.[1] But I loved the little folk. You never saw anything in your life more natural, naïve, inartistic, and refreshing. It was just like our old charades.[2]

I love Italian opera – it's so reckless. Damn Wagner, and his bellowings at Fate and death. Damn Debussy, and his averted face. I like the Italians who run all on impulse, and don't care about their immortal souls, and don't worry about the ultimate. My immortal soul can look after itself – what do I care about it. I don't know the creature, even. It's a relative I only know by hear say.

Comment, that, on Italian opera!

But if you were here tonight we'd go to *Carmen*, and hear those delicious little Italians love and weep. I am just as emotional and impulsive as they, by nature. It's the damned climate and upbringing and so on that make me cold-headed as mathematics.

[1] Cavaliere Castellano's Italian Grand Opera Company presented Mascagni's *Cavalleria Rusticana* and Leoncavallo's *Il Pagliacci* on 31 March, and Bizet's *Carmen* on 1 April, at the Grand Theatre, Croydon.

[2] On DHL's delight in charades see J. D. Chambers, 'Memories of D. H. Lawrence', *Renaissance and Modern Studies*, xvi (1972), 11–12.

I've done the transcript of the Legend tale. It's jolly good. If Austin Harrison wants it, you can have the proofs.[1] – And soon, in a day or two, I'll send you the 'Chrysanthemums' to copy – shall I.[2]

Ada seems very miserable. She's dipped into disbelief. Tragedy is like strong acid – it dissolves away all but the very gold of truth. Poor Ada – I'm very sorry. I would not, for worlds, have her go through this, bloody bludgeonings[3] of unbelief, and the struggle for a new faith. But I suppose it's fate. What life has set in progress, life can't arrest: There is nothing to do but to leave her with her own sorrows, to lose, to smash up the old Idea which is nothing but an Idol, and to find in the emptiness a new presence. – Rhetoric! – but it'll suit you better than harshness.

Will you, I wonder, get through life without ever seeing through it. I will never, if I can help it, try to disturb any of your faiths. You will secure yourself by praying for my conversion, eh? – There the balance.

Am I ironical again? – It's Ada has upset me. I'd rather a thousand things than that she were in the mill of truth, being milled.

I've got a blue bowl full of daffodils, with green expanded buds of lilac twigs, and two or three small boughs of beautiful almond blossom. I wish you could see it – it's very pretty. I will take a walk into the country and see how the primroses are. Your violets are just dead – still they smell faintly: 'Odours when the violets sicken'.[4]

I haven't got any verses; those lately are sad ones. The Egyptians[5] have lost interest for me: you will say 'Fie!' I am sorry. When I am – but I can't write to order – I'm sorry. Very soon I shall be meeting you at Loughboro, and we shan't need ink.

Now I'll dust. I got up so late, and larked with the kiddies in my bedroom till after 10.0. So, having made Mrs Jones late, I dust to make up for it. Thank Heavens there's no ornaments.

The weeks will be gone immediately. Mother's constant motto to me 'Blessed is he that expecteth little, for he shall not be disappointed' – makes me laugh now. She lived up to it very well, in latter years: and I begin just to understand it a bit. And as you are not inclined to bolt through the hedge

[1] Harrison published it as 'A Fragment of Stained Glass', *English Review*, ix (September 1911), 242–51.

[2] DHL had presumably made alterations following his meeting with Harrison (see the previous Letter), thus necessitating a fresh copy.

[3] Cf. W. E. Henley, 'Invictus', ll. 7–8:

> Under the bludgeonings of chance
> My head is bloody but unbowed.

[4] Shelley, 'To Music', l. 3 ['...when sweet violets...'].

[5] i.e. the Fellah songs (cf. Letter 197).

of circumstance – why, circumstance, like a hedged lane, will have to lead us where it will. I suppose in the end, since we are each determined to take each turning usward, our separate lanes will debouch to an aimiable, grassy camping ground, like a couple of gipsy caravans met. Meanwhile, I can't see over my hedges, nor you yours – so the lanes have it all their own way. They'll come out when they will. 'Ambulo' – I amble.

Goodbye, my dear. I feel like doing a little prance, with the shadow of my own wilfulness for partner.

And – one-two-three-four
Off we go
To peep behind the shut door
And see the show.

I believe I'm a wicked tease – as Mrs Jones says I am.

Addio – addio DHL

I've had a letter from Agnes Holt. I think she's going to marry in August, and live in Ramsey. – We'll then go and see her. I like her very much – and you will like her too. I want you to know her. Somehow, I always feel sorry for her – she's not strong in health. Poor A!

247. To Louie Burrows, 2 April 1911

Text: MS UN; Boulton 90–1.

12 Colworth Rd. Addiscombe, Croydon
2 April 1911

My dear Lou,

Here are the MSS – it's a really good story.[1] The desideratum is to shorten sufficiently the first part. Of course that part has to reveal the situation. I hope you'll manage to make out all the alterations:[2] it's not particularly plain. Send it me when you've done, will you. You need not hurry. Write small enough, will you – and don't be flourishy, my dear. If I haven't sent enough paper use any sort – exercise or any sort.

It has been a most horrid day; yellow as a guinea. I have not been out. I must go somewhere tonight – the kids are so obstreperous. We've still got 'Mignonette' – the African lady. But she's cleared off to the Plymouth Rock[3] meeting. You should hear the Jones carry on about her immediately her back is turned. It wearies me very much.

[1] 'Odour of Chrysanthemums', the first, heavily corrected proofs of which DHL sent to Louie Burrows. See James T. Boulton, *Renaissance and Modern Studies*, xiii (1969), 5–48.

[2] alterations] parts

[3] Nickname for a member of the religious sect, the Plymouth Brethren.

Sunday evening is a damnable time – the fag end of everything, the wretched hesitation between two weeks. I hate it. I'll go and see Aylwin I think – or to a concert: too far to Wallington[1] – I'll decide when I'm shaved.

I wish we were a bit more accessible one to another. Tonight I'd give anything to be able to spend a quiet evening with you. It is this spinning on a loose end which is so risky. I'm always trying to avoid doing things you'd reproach me for. I don't always succeed to my thorough satisfaction: but then, who would.

A fortnight today is Easter Sunday. I hope it's not like today in weather.

It has taken me such a long long time to write those last two[2] pages of the story.[3] You have no idea how much delving it requires to get that deep into cause and effect.

I am reading Meredith's *Tragic Comedians*, which is wonderfully clever: not a work of art, too turgid.

I went into the country yesterday and found the first primroses. It's very pretty here, between Addington and Farley. I love that part of the country – some time I'll take you.

It's an evening gloomy as hell, outside. How's Miss Cox? My regards to her. Oh for you, a little warmth and cosiness!

Addio – je vous embrasse de tout mon coeur[4] – I really want you very badly indeed.

DHL

248. To Louie Burrows, 4 April 1911

Text: MS UN; Boulton 91–3.

12 Colworth Rd, Addiscombe, Croydon
4 April Tuesday 1911

My dear Lou,

Your letter did not come till noon: I wonder why. And then, being new note-paper, and your handwriting so altered, I could hardly recognise it. Did you feel in a wild mood towards the close? Sometimes I get in such an extravagant paddy with things I wish I could pull fortunes or fates toppling on my head like the stones of the Temple on Samson.[5] So long as one says nowt, moods don't much matter.

I wish I could go violetting with you: it sounds so jolly, and so goodly. I wish with all my heart I could be – I was going to say Gaddesby railway

[1] The home of Philip F. T. Smith.
[2] last two] two last
[3] They were entirely rewritten (see Boulton, art. cit, 46–8).
[4] 'with much love'.
[5] Cf. Judges xvi. 30.

porter, but there isn't such a thing. Lord, how we beat ourselves bloody against the face of circumstance.

No matter. I'm sorry I was disagreeable. I know you'd help things only too speedily if you could. Some day the ravel will untwine. Your father is not better then? If I get some money, if we marry, part of the income is yours, and with that part you do as you like. If I had anything, you should have it to do just as you liked with. Then that way you could help your father: I should be glad. But it's easy talking when I've got nowt, and no prospect. I swear I'll be a good husband: it's now, as exile, or separé, that I wouldn't vouch for myself, as an impeccable person. No matter!

Don't sark me[1] by telling me I said I didn't expect much of you. I expect everything – life almost: but not – and I never know whether to say unfortunately or happily – a companion in my philosophy: – happily, for it's a philosophy that, shared, would be aggravated to abstruseness and uselessness.[2] Forgive me when I'm priggish and superior. One part of me is insolent and overbearing to a degree. But you very brutally put your foot through the paper thereof when we're together: to my great ultimate joy.

The wind is in the north again hang it. There are touches of snow now and again, among the almond blossom. The wind is like the edge of a hatchet. Thus spring comes in.

I have just been to the library and got *Rouge et Noir.*[3] I shall enjoy it. The worst of being a novelist, and having dreams and fancies, is that you know all this is fiction. You know the inanimate dumminess of them – and demand life direct like a blow.[4]

A week or so and we are at home. I am annoyed that I can scarcely look forward, anticipate – even a day. I am peculiarly hour-bound – as regards the future – I can't project myself even into tomorrow: and everything not immediate seems a tale.

Oh Lou – I feel like a river out of its banks: a straying[5] Hoang-ho.[6]

And I love you – whatever. Goodbye, my love DHL

You are quite right – in your way – and I never want you to alter. My way is a form of abnormality. – damn it. DHL

1 i.e. be sarcastic towards me.
2 abstruseness and uselessness] abnormality
3 Stendhal's novel (Paris, 1831).
4 blow] knucle
5 straying] strayed
6 i.e. Hwang Ho (Yellow River).

249. To Louie Burrows, 6 April 1911

Text: MS UN; Boulton 93–4.

Davidson Rd Boys School, South Norwood, SE.
6 April 1911

My dear Lou,

On Thursday afternoon I have the last lesson off to get my marking done. Behold me, in the boss' room, with a stack of composition books at my elbow untouched.

Isn't it cold. I look down and see the field and everywhere dried pale drab with cold, the sky leaden grey, and only a handful of steam flying from a train, sheer white and vivid.

My cold is about better, thanks. I've forgotten all about it by now. But I hate cold weather: I swear I'll flee to the tropics first opportunity. You would look well in a scarlet bandanna.

Do you know, I've had your yesterdays and Tuesday's letters both this morning: how funny! The letter posted on the 4th got here not till noon: the one posted yesterday, at 8.0 this morning. The officials of the post office are cracked, I think.

I'm glad you like the story. Mind you leave out all I have crossed away. All the playing part – most of the kiddies share – goes out, I think. I intend it to.[1] The story must work quicker to a climax. The other story wont want copying, I think. I think it'll stand just as it is. You shall see it in a day or so.[2]

By the way, will you send me – no, bring it to Eastwood – the book of pictures J[essie] gave you. Tear off the cover and the inscription – which is an impertinence – and I may get a copy or two out. I've painted nothing since the *Idyll*: am busy with these silly short stories. Don't worry about my fame: it'll certainly not trouble you too deeply during my life-time, I think.

Men and women are very different in some respects. Man's the animal baby 'who won't be happy till he gets it – whatever he wants'[3] – woman is the queer reluctant thing, who, I verily believe, enjoys much more the dream and anticipation, than the realisation, with its pangs.

This seems a very little letter – but it's nearly 4.20. I think of going to

[1] The proofs of 'Odour of Chrysanthemums' show frequent excisions of childish chatter and action in the early part; thus the original prominence of the children is greatly reduced.

[2] 'A Fragment of Stained Glass'. (The MS of this story is among the Burrows papers with an earlier title, 'The Hole in the Window', crossed out.)

[3] From an advertisement for Pears' Soap (cf. 'The Merry-go-Round' III. ii: 'like the Pears' Soapy baby – "He won't be happy till he gets it".').

Purley to tea, for a bit of music. Laura MaCartney[1] – remember she's 35 or 36 – plays Chopin's nocturnes very well indeed. I do love somebody to play the piano well to me. I wish – that's the one thing I wish you could do – play really well. You are such a scandalous splasher, aren't you. You'll splash away at me, just the same: which makes me chuckle to contemplate.

Don't talk about 'my heights' – they aren't heights. I winna be sarked.

There are three rooks strutting like mad old maids in black, down below in the field. Three for a letter.[2]

A week today, at this minute, we shall be broken up. Oh yes, Time limps along famously. We shall be fifty before we know where we are. Imagine *you* fifty – what a joke.

There's a patter of a myriad feet, I close. Goodbye – this room's as cold as the grave. I guess you're nice and warm, O mon nid! – I hum a bar of the Tear and the sigh![3] – Addio – I can hear Sammarco in *Traviata* 'Addi-i-i-i-o'.[4] It gives my heart a twinge.

Addio – if I were but near you, then – – Hélas! Addio. DHL

250. To Louie Burrows, 7 April 1911

Text: MS UN; Boulton 95–6.

12 Colworth Rd, Addiscombe, Croydon
7 April 1911

My dear Lou,

It's just striking nine, and here I've been all this time larking with the kiddies. It's their bath night. I really think Mary is the prettiest youngster in England. And she's such a rascal. When she's bathed, her hair comes out in full blossom like a double flower, and her face is like apple blossom buds. She insists on sitting on my head, and kicking her heels against my neck. Then she sneaks off and drinks my beer. You should see her with her mouth in the froth, her eyes glancing askance at me, before I rush for her. She likes beer, wicked little sinner that she is.

Pa is out tonight, and that crumpled petal, Mrs Wilkinson, has betaken herself to a 'Rock' meeting – so Mrs Jones and I are 'en famille'. I believe

[1] Sister to H. B. MacCartney ('Siegmund'); Helen Corke introduced DHL to her. He went to musical evenings at her house in Purley; one occasion – with a melodramatic ending – is recorded in his story 'The Witch à la Mode' (first called 'Intimacy').

[2] Cf. *The White Peacock*, I.7 where Lettie, seeing a crow, recites the jingle: 'One for sorrow, two for joy,/Three for a letter...'.

[3] Probably alluding to the final duet of Violetta and Alfredo in Verdi's *La Traviata*.

[4] Mario Sammarco (1873–1930), famous Italian baritone; he performed regularly at Covent Garden, 1904–14.

she enjoys the house best, and I'm sure I do, when we are thus on our own. Pa is really a bit gênant. There are rather rotten rows occasionally. But there, it's not my business to talk.

I meant to write a story – but I'm a bit out of the humour. I feel free and easy. If only you were here, I should be so likeable for you tonight. You wouldn't find any fault with me – because the artist is sunk, and I'm aimiable.

Today, we've had an American chap to lecture us, after school, on handwriting[1] – He was very funny. I will be telling you this time next week. Then this afternoon I've been overhauling and checking the library – 162 volumes. I shall be having it changed soon. This is the second year I've been librarian, and it's rather a fag. I'll chuck it up after August.

Where shall we go for Midsummer? Let's go abroad. Let's go to France – Normandy, Brittany, Paris. It wouldn't cost much. We'll persuade Ada to go with us. She is my nearest relative[2] now: do you know, it feels to me as if she were my only relative.

Eh dear – how cold it is. Austin Harrison says he's putting in the *English* two bits of verse I don't want publishing.[3] Never mind – it'll be a scrap of money, and in the state we are, that's the essential.

We'll go into the country at Easter if only it'll be fine. We shall have a good time. Ah, if only[4] we were married and Mary were my own and thine, I think I should be a fine man for you. As it is, a vapourer, unstable.

Vogue la galère.

Give my regards to everybody at Coteshael. I cant, can't screw up my courage to write – to anybody. I can't bring myself to write to Ada – it's such an effort. But next week I come home – next week. And I am in such a perfect

[1] The School Log records no such lecture. Perhaps the same person visited Dering Place School: see Helen Corke, *In Our Infancy*, p. 217.

[2] relative] real

[3] DHL is referring to a letter of 6 April 1911 (MS UN LaB 188):

Dear Mr. Lawrence,

I am keeping 'Sorrow' and 'A Husband Dead', which, though I cannot say I like personally, I feel I *ought to* publish. The other one I am returning.

I am looking forward to see 'Chrysanthemums' with all its old atmosphere and the old ending, and less of the early talk. Also the other stories you mentioned.

Yours sincerely Austin Harrison

P.S. Let me congratulate you on your book – Excellent.

In fact Harrison published neither of the two poems. 'Sorrow' (*Complete Poems*, i. 106–7) first appeared as 'Weariness' in *Poetry*, December 1914; 'A Husband Dead' was published as 'A Woman and her Dead Husband' in *Poetry*, January 1914. (Later it was renamed 'A Man who Died', *Complete Poems* i. 55–7; ii. 993 n.)

[4] only] I

open humour – and I've nothing to do but read *Rouge et Noir* – which – I don't want to, now. Wo bist du?

My dear, goodnight. To be your husband is my supremest wish. And so, goodnight. DHL

251. To Louie Burrows, [9 April 1911]

Text: MS UN; PC; Postmark, Croydon AP 10 11; Boulton 96.

[12 Colworth Road, Addiscombe, Croydon]
Dimanche – minuit

Merci de ton petit billet – je l'ai reçu ce matin.

Le train part de Marylebone à 11.30, Vendredi. Ce doit donc arriver à Loughboro vers deux heures. Oui, il y arrêtera pour te prendre. N'aie pas de peur – je ne me laisserai pas passer de toi.

Je me porte bien et j'attends le Vendredi. Demain je t'écrirai.

Vale. DHL

De quelle espèce est le nouveau chapeau? – grande? – bleue? DHL

[Sunday – midnight

Thanks for your short note – I received it this morning.

The train leaves Marylebone at 11.30 on Friday. It should arrive at Loughboro about two o'clock. Yes, it will stop to pick you up. Don't worry – I will not go on without you.

I am well and long for Friday. I'll write to you tomorrow.

Goodbye DHL

What's your new hat like? – big? – blue? DHL]

252. To Ada Lawrence, 9 April 1911

Text: MS Clarke; cited in Lawrence–Gelder 85–7.

12, Colworth Road, Addiscombe, Croydon.
9 April 1911

My dear Ada,

I'm going to write you just a little little letter, because it's late at night. It reminds me of how often I used to sit down towards midnight to write mothers' weekly script. And one is inclined to regret, were regret not so useless now.

I am sorry more than I can tell to find you going through all the torment of religious unbelief: it is so hard to bear, especially now. However, it seems to me like this: Jehovah is the Jew's idea of God – not ours. Christ was infinitely good, but mortal as we. There still remains a God, but not a personal God: a vast, shimmering impulse which wavers onwards towards some end, I don't know what – taking no regard of the little individual, but taking regard for humanity. When we die, like rain-drops falling back again into the sea, we fall back into the big, shimmering sea of unorganised life which we call God.[1] We are lost as individuals, yet we count in the whole.

It requires a lot of pain and courage to come to discover one's own creed, and quite as much to continue in lonely faith. Would you like a book or two of philosophy? – or will you merely battle out your own ideas? I would still go to Chapel, if it did me any good. I shall go myself, when I am married. Whatever name one gives Him, in worship we all strive towards the same God, so we be generous hearted: – christians, Buddhists, Mrs Dax, me – we all stretch our hands in the same direction. What does it matter, the name we cry.

It is a fine thing to establish one's own religion in one's heart, not to be dependent on tradition and second hand ideals. Life will seem to you, later, not a lesser, but a greater thing. This which is a great torment now, will be a noble thing to you later on. Let us talk, if you feel like it, when I come home.

I shall come on Friday – London 11.30 – Nottingham about 2.15 or 2.30 I suppose. The trains will be Sunday trains[2] – we shall not be home till teatime, I am afraid. You won't come to Nottingham to meet us? I shall pick Louie up at Loughborough.

You grumble because I don't tell you anything about myself. There is nothing to tell. I work, I think about things – and, for the rest, I don't care many jots. Things don't bother me: they can happen or not, it makes no difference. I will tell you plenty when I come home. My cold is better now, and I am all right. And there is nothing, really, for you to scold me for. – I shall see you on Friday.

Mrs Mann's stories ought not to upset you.[3] But a very small spark will

[1] As Richard Aldington observed (*Portrait of a Genius But*..., p. 76), the imagery here is strongly reminiscent of Edwin Arnold's Buddhist poem, *The Light of Asia*. See for example, viii. 112–30: the waters of 'Being's ceaseless tide' flow

> Into the seas. These, steaming to the Sun,
> Give the lost wavelets back in cloudy fleece
> To trickle down the hills, and glide again;
> Having no pause or peace.

DHL's earlier quotation from the poem (Letter 45) contains an analogous image. (Richard Garnett included two extracts from Arnold's poem in his *International Library*.)

[2] Sunday services would operate on Good Friday.

[3] Mary E. Mann (d. 1929), a prolific and moralising writer, author of *One Another's Burdens* (1890), *The Sheep and the Goats* (1907), *Astray in Arcady* (1910), etc.

light hot straw. Never mind – we'll settle things at Easter. If you weren't at Eastwood I wouldn't come – no, never.

Ah well – in a very short time I shall be seeing you. Give my love to Emily, and the baby, and Sam, and Father.

I'll drop Pem[1] a card during the week.

I am not very anxious for the holiday, are you? But don't tell Lou.

There – Goodnight.

With my best love (I mean it). Your brother D. H. Lawrence

253. To Louie Burrows, 10 April 1911

Text: MS UN; Boulton 96–7.

12 Colworth Rd, Addiscombe, Croydon
10 April 1911

My dear Lou,

Having been larking with the kiddies in the garden I am in a breathless and careless mood. Winnie is behind my chair getting undressed, peeping over my shoulder, and when I turn round to look at her she croodles[2] down to hide her dishabilly state. She always looks so funny in her combins: like, I say, a puffin or a penguin or a deacon in his shorts. She's very tubby. Mary is anxiously awaiting the finish of this to fly down to post with me. She loves to go out and see the dark and the stars and the moon.

'What are they?', she asks of the stars.

'Little girls going to bed with their candles,' I tell her.

'Where do they go to?'

As I can't answer that – 'Look!' I say 'the wind's blowing 'em out.' She clings close round my neck, and puts her cheek on mine, looking up in wonder –

None of which'll interest you.

Now I've got a bracelet of red wool and tape to wear. There's no peace in this life.

I shall look out at Loughboro for you on Friday. That makes me feel quite excited. It's not far off: about 2.0 on Friday afternoon. We'll be very jolly.

There's not an item of news. Oh, do send me the story if it's ready. I want to get them off before the holidays.[3]

Another break – Mary removes my bracelet, wipes my nose, and kisses me thrice. That's one better than your two. Never mind – kisses galore next week – eh?

[1] Family nickname for Emily King.

[2] i.e. crouches (the dialect verb strictly means to huddle together for warmth or protection).

[3] The specific story was 'Odour of Chrysanthemums'; for the others see p. 258 n. 3.

I'm going to write to Aunt Ada tonight. She's been very poorly, she says. Writes to me quite mildly, half apologetically.

Is your Dad all right? I do wish Eth. had got a dozen distinctions. I *must* send her a card. Four evenings from now – je t' embrasse – je te serre contre le sein: je me colle la bouche sur la tienne – quatre jours!

À bientôt – bientôt[1] DHL

Do you want Zola's *Debâcle* or *L'Assommoir*. I've got 'em both to give away.

254. To Louie Burrows, 12 April 1911

Text: MS UN; Boulton 97–9.

Davidson Rd Boys School, South Norwood, SE.
12 April 1911

My dear Lou,

What a beautiful day. It makes Friday imminent. I suppose you don't break up till Thursday morning, so I'll send this to Gaddesby.

It's so quiet. We've just finished reading Stanley Weyman's *Under the Red Robe*.[2] It's not much as literature but it's a good tale – the boys like it. I am afraid I am becoming a down-right romanticist. Of course you'd find me realistic because of subject, but the manner is shockingly romantic.

I've got a pack of books to mark – but I'll write this letter first. I've finished the fourth story – it's the 'White Stocking' written up. Mac says it's fantastic. Really, it's not up to a great deal. But I intended to do four, and four are done.[3] I'll send them as soon as I get the 'Chrysanthemums' from you. Then Austin Harrison can see how he likes 'em. Though – unless I get 'Chryanthemums' in the morning, it'll not be much good sending till after the holiday. I don't care. – I have just done one folio, a dozen MSS pages, of Paul Morel. That great, terrible but unwritten novel, I am afraid it will die a mere conception.

It is such a sunny day, and I feel so easy and indolent. Nothing more strenuous than making love would suit me just now, and that I could do deliciously.

At this time, in two days, we shall be in Nottingham, you and I. I fully expect it to be a beautiful day, as it was last year.

How tiresomely and rebelliously the blood beats in spring. I wish we were

[1] 'I shall be kissing you – pressing you to my breast: I shall cover your mouth with mine – four days! See you soon – soon.'

[2] An historical novel (1894; 1908).

[3] The four stories were: 'The White Stocking', 'Odour of Chrysanthemums', 'A Fragment of Stained Glass' and perhaps 'Intimacy'.

only fauns and nymphs. This black suit of convention is most gênant. I feel a very wicked and riotous person got up to look and behave like a curate. And my temper is so sudden and impetuous, I am astonished. Not irritability – inflammability. I should like to suggest all the – you would say wicked – plans in the world. I say, only that is wicked which is a violation of one's feeling and instinct.

The poetry you are curious over is not love poetry – saddish. You shall have out of me what you like if you'll ask for it – in two days time. But remember, I am not a very ready talker, about my own work especially.

Where shall we go on Easter Monday. Let's go to Bakewell or somewhere there. I am very shabby, and have only one suit: I shall be too shabby to go out anywhere on Sunday.

Let's talk about France, and let's determine to go. Anywhere – I'd give anything to be able to do something rightdown rash.

Goodbye – je te cherche, bouche et gorge, pour t'embrasser.[1]

DHL

255. To Arthur McLeod, [17 April 1911]

Text: MS UT; PC v. The Plague House, Eyam; Postmark, Matlock-Bath AP 17 11; Unpublished.

[17 April 1911]

Hope the number is right – or are you 18 – ? Quandary![2]

Hope you'll like this highly interesting card, and that you'll be instructed by the explanation.[3]

Hope you're enjoying yourself as much as I. Hope you'll sometimes sit with your girl (– what a derogatory word for your 'choice') and watch the green Derwent wriggling past in green Spring time

The only pretty ring time etc. etc.[4]

But Matlock's too trippery for anything: no privacy.

Addio DHL

[1] 'I long for you, mouth and throat, to kiss you.'

[2] DHL correctly addressed the postcard to 17 (having deleted 22) Hunter Road, Thornton Heath, London S.E.

[3] The card carried details of the courage of the Rector of Eyam and his wife during the Plague of 1665–6.

[4] Cf. p. 242 n. 2.

256. To Louie Burrows, 24 April 1911

Text: MS UN; Boulton 99.

12 Colworth Rd, Addiscombe – Croydon
24 April 1911

My dear Lou,

Here we are then, back again, and settled as if we have never been away.[1] But all day I have belonged to the yesterdays of last week, so that school has been like a tale one reads without taking in. I swear I've never really seen the boys today. It is lonely, and meaningless, this life. With the meaning gone out of it, it is a dull, sleep-heavy sort of business. And it has been such a sunny sweet day, and I have smelled hyacinths keen in the sunshine several times. It makes me shiver for to have you. It is true, this shallow dim remnant of life which is left when we're apart, is not worth having.

I've been and had my hair cut. The barber is a Frenchman and we talked a bit of Fr [ ][2] in, a dark and rudd[ ] Never two mortals more alien than at that moment; I indifferent to almost everything, he to nothing; I as quiet as a pebble, he noisier than a paroquet. I wonder what he thought. I still am faintly surprised at the foreignness between us. His bold eyes, like bright brown glass, seem curious to me still.

Coming home, near East Croydon, I saw a pear-tree in full blossom overcast by the lamps behind me to a cream gold in the low twilight; then, right back, the sky was green as verdigris, with a fine evening star.

I am going to write a bit of Paul Morel, if I have any luck with myself.

I have not any news, except[3] the little unpleasantnesses deriving from the cockle-shell cousin.[4]

I think, my dear, it will be best for me to write only twice or three times a week. I have to push myself into correspondance. All that I have to tell you is not for words, and much less pen and ink. It's no good talking about [ ]

257. To Sallie Hopkin, 26 April 1911

Text: MS NCL; Huxley 7–8.

12 Colworth Rd, Addiscombe, Croydon
26 April 1911

Dear Mrs Hopkin,

I am sending you the dramas as I promised. No doubt it will surprise you to find me so scrupulous. *Riders to the Sea* is about the genuinest bit of

[1] The term began on 24 April after the Easter holiday (School Log).
[2] MS torn.
[3] except] of except
[4] Perhaps Ellen Inwood.

dramatic tragedy, English, since Shakspere, I should say: and you can read it in half an hour. Don't, I beg you, tell me you have no time to read these books. The *Trojan Women* is the finest study of women from ancient times. Ah but how women are always the same! – but men vary – do they? I don't know. – *Oedipus* is the finest drama of *all* times. It is terrible in its accumulation – like a great big wave coming up – and then crash! *Bacchae* I like exceedingly for its flashing poetry – These are very great things.[1]

When you have read them, will you give them to Ada to read? And will you tell me what you think? – and will you also tell me your thoughts about Louie: if I am not impertinent. And will you tell me where I am wrong – since you put your head on one side and close your eyes so shrewdly, declaring me at fault.

My regards to Mr Hopkin and Enid.

Yours Sincerely D. H. Lawrence

258. To Ada Lawrence, 26 April 1911

Text: MS Clarke; Postmark, Croydon AP 27 11; Lawrence–Gelder 87–9.

12 Colworth Rd, Addiscombe, Croydon
26 April 1911

My dear Ada,

I had a good journey down on Sunday; and arrived in Croydon in time for tea. Here I found everything much the same: but the Afric[2] has gone to Eastbourne today for the week, thank God.

My dear, I don't know what to say to you. There is nothing to do with life but to let it run: and it's a very bitter thing, but it's also wonderful. You never known what'll happen next. Life is full of wonder and surprise and mostly pain. But never mind, the tragic is the most holding, the most vital thing in life. – And, as I say, the lesson is to learn to live alone. Do that – but don't be too hard on Eddie. He doesn't understand, and it's not fair to him – it hurts him too much. I think he really loves you: and the thing you have to do, in the midst of pain, is to remember him also and say 'Ah well – if he doesn't understand, he doesn't –.' I never want Lou to understand how relentlessly tragic life is – not that. But I want her not to jar on me by gawkiness, and that she must learn. She may give me up –

[1] DHL probably read all three plays, which he received from McLeod (see Letter 258), – Euripides' *Trojan Women* and *Bacchae*, and Sophocles' *Oedipus* – in verse translations by Gilbert Murray. In 1913 (see Letter 554) he asked McLeod to send 'the Gilbert Murray translations...They have a fearful fascination for me still.'

[2] See p. 236, Letter 235 and n. 3.

I shall not her. I should be very sorry if she did. But she can take her own way in it. Try, when you are feeling very irritable and bitter with folk, to remember 'Ah well – they don't understand – if they did, this cruelty for them also.' It is well for the balance of the world that it be mostly blind to the tragic issue. It is best so for Emily, and perhaps Eddie. But I know what horrible pain it is for you: and unfortunately, it's a thing we can't bear vicariously: I wish we could. I never pass long without thinking of you. Don't judge me by exterior. It is all rattle, like dead leaves blown along the road.

I have sent Mrs Hopkin some of MacLeods books, which I want you particularly to read – then you can return them to me. They are tragedies – but all great works are. Tragedy is beautiful also. This is my creed. But sometimes also it leaves me full of misery. Never mind, my dear.

I kiss you – your brother D. H. Lawrence

259. To Louie Burrows, 28 April 1911

Text: MS UN; Boulton 100.

12 Colworth Rd, Addiscombe, Croydon
28 April 1911

[ ][1]

You are really overcast, and by what? No matter, one must know all kinds of weather.

I have just read past the trial and condemnation of Julien in *Le Rouge et le Noir*. It is a terrible book which almost makes me laugh. Life seems such an escapade. And I feel so much like Julien Sorel – except that, of course, I am English and sentimentalist, – poet to please you – that I marvel at Stendhal's wonderful cleverness – marvellous to me. Yet he misses out the religion, the philosophy, if you like, of life. He is not a bit metaphysical. He doesn't satisfy my sentimentality.

A week has gone by like a mist evaporating. Do you know I simply cannot work. I have done only about five pages of MSS, 'Paul Morel'; and that only from sheer pressure of duty. I don't want to work: and I don't care a damn about it. But what William Heinemann Esquire, Great Cham of [ ] publishers, will say when I fail to p[ ] a book within the required time, I don't [ ] care. Vogue la galère.

I have not any newses. Unlike you, [ ] have exciting times at school. Everything flows smoothly.

With having read *Rouge et Noir* for about $4\frac{1}{2}$ hours, I naturally think in French, and have to hold my pen down to English.

[1] MS torn.

Life has a rum fatality about it, and it will go which way it chooses, whatever we say or worry. No matter. The interest is in watching it go. It's like watching a big beetle wander across the table, waiting for the exciting moment when it will go – flop! – over the edge. All of which is Stendhal's influence.

I feel myself a 'Black and Red' myself – black coal bubbling red into fire. Hélas, que vous êtes loin d'ici, que votre corps loin du mien.[1]

Vale DHL

260. To Louie Burrows, 29 April 1911

Text: MS UN; Boulton 101.

12 Colworth Rd, Addiscombe, Croydon
29 April 1911

My dear Lou,

So you've been a bit off colour: we'll say it's the weather, which couldn't be more beautiful.

This time next week we shall be going to Eastwood: it will be downright jolly, and I look forward to it very much.

The evenings are so perfect – O my dear God.

I've begun a painting for Aunt Ada tonight – she needs another. It's the first thing I've done since Easter. – It is the most exquisite jewel twilight you ever saw: jacinth, and topaz and amethyst. It's nine oclock. I'm going to do a bit of Paul. I send you this mass. I'm afraid it's heterogeneous; since I have never read it through, very blemishy. Correct it and collect it will you, and tell me what you think. This is a quarter of the book.

Mr Jones has shaved off his moustache, and I dont like him. He's got a small, thin mouth, like a slit in a tight skin. It's quite strange. It shows up a part of his character that I detest: the mean and prudent and nervous. I feel that I really don't like him, and I rather liked him before.

Write to me as often as it doesn't weary you. You don't bore me – why say so. I like to see your letter when I get down in the morning. You know I do.

I'll do a scrap of Paul. What will you think of it, I wonder. I want to take it to Ada at Whitsun.

By Jove – what an empty life! Au revoir D. H. Lawrence

[1] 'Alas, how far you are from me, how far your body from mine.'

261. To Louie Burrows, 1 May 1911
Text: MS UN; Boulton 101–2.

12 Colworth Rd, Addiscombe, Croydon
1st May 1911

My dear Lou,

I suppose you will be writing to me tonight, so that our letters will again cross. I see the new moon is out, with a small star in attendance. I caught sight of it for the first time as I came down the steps of the library this evening. 'Bless you, you little devil of a weapon', I said. 'You're supposed to be lucky, but you snip the top of one's hopes off, reminding one.' Such a blue bright night over such ripe still yellow lamps: and at the end of it, pen and ink only. I curse these circumstances in their being and their results – let them be cursed.

At your behest I wrote yesterday fourteen pages of Paul Morel, and I sit with the paper before me to continue when this is done. I should like to be able to execute a will such as this – 'I, D.H.L. do hereby bequeath to the devils, daemons, or Gods, all such power or fantasy as makes me a writer. I do divest me of all my extraordinary powers. I do bequeath my body and my life unto Louisa, daughter of – – .' Don't you wish I could do it. I would sell birthrights and deathrights for an embrace of thee, Louisa: toss 'em out of the window, poetic powers, perceptivity, intellect – pouf: for a few kisses and a tight clasp. God help us, what a state.

Well – you see how my letters run riot. Sorry – forgive me.

Thine David Herbert Lawrence

262. To Louie Burrows, 4 May 1911
Text: MS UN; Boulton 102–3.

Davidson Rd Boys School, South Norwood, SE.
4 May 1911

My dear Lou,

How the year slips on: I have only just realised that it is May. Time seems to me to be straying, lost, somewhere near February. I have never known the seasons, the weather, the opening leaves to go round so unnoticed as they do this year: one seems to have lost sight of them.

I am glad you are resolving to practise patience. It is a thing that wears out patience quickest, I reckon. The best way is to drug oneself with work and unhopefulness, then the time drifts like the clouds overhead, without sound of footsteps, no echoes, no impatience.

What the devil am I so high-falutin about this morning. It is a beautiful bright day, with handfuls of white cloud pitched across a very blue sky, and veritable choruses of dandelions shining broad-yellow everywhere.

You asked me if I smoke. I have had, have consumed, nine cigarettes since the return. Will you allow me so many? Do not be afraid, I am not a child to damage myself for a very little longing.

I have written 90 pages of Paul Morel. I think about 7 of these pages may be called amusing, and 20 perhaps pleasant. The rest are 'navrant'. I wonder how Paul will work out.

I am going to Purley to tea today, that's why I write in school. I'm glad your scare is settled in Gaddesby. That about the holiday is the devil. But you may be at Quorn. At any rate, you won't be booked for all August, will you? At any rate, I will come and stay a bit in Gaddesby, unless it were too shocking. We will see.

Till then, I work. 'Laborare est orare.' Never blame me for irreligiousness at that rate. I admire the Jesuits.

Goodbye – Un baiser à la bouche. D. H. Lawrence

Am just writing to Hilda Shaw.[1] DHL

263. To Louie Burrows, 7 May 1911

Text: MS UN; Boulton 103–4.

12 Colworth Road, Addiscombe, Croydon
7 May 1911

My dear Lou,

I have managed my ten pages of Paul: I'm now on with the 112th. I wonder what it'll be like; at present it seems to me very rummy. It is four oclock. I have promised to go to Philip Smith's, but[2] I won't go to tea because Ive no clothes to go in. The only black suit I've got is the one I wear in school. I can't afford to buy another, for God knows when. I am too shabby to go through the town, where folk know me, in daylight, on Sunday. I daren't go out of black yet awhile. So I'm not going to Philip's till this evening. Then he'll be mad. But I don't care in the least whether he is.

I went yesterday a very beautiful walk into the country, over Westerham way, about twelve miles out, in Kent. At Limpsfield the hills are covered with primroses, and the bluebells are just coming out. I got heaps of flowers. I was alone all day long – got home about nine o'clock.

[1] Doubtless Louie Burrows had told DHL that Hilda Shaw feared the onset of tuberculosis; in fact she was in the Ransom Sanatorium, Mansfield, by this date (UN MSS LaB 195–6, 16 April 1911).

[2] Smith's, but] Smith's, to tea but

Will you send me the Corot,[1] by the way?

The beech-trees are very beautiful, as if afire with the vividest green.

I don't think the last chapter of Paul has action enough, moves sufficiently. It is the bane of my life, to get the action of a novel hurried along.

What about your coming down before Whitsun? It's a month today. Are we going to Eastwood for the first? I don't like to impose too much upon Emily. Then to yours for a day or two? Then Auntie wants me a bit at Leicester. It will need arranging. I must begin to think about it.

What about your coming down for the week-end? It would be nice. Can you afford it. I suppose I can squeeze that out all right. It is very beautiful weather.

I must be getting shaven. I think I am stupid this afternoon, and fear this is a stupid letter. Never mind. I wish you could come down here for good. We will talk about midsummer at Whitsun. Oh, work!

Addio – it will be a fine evening, if only you were here.

Addio D. H. Lawrence

264. To Louie Burrows, 9 May 1911

Text: MS UN; Boulton 104–5.

12 Colworth Rd, Addiscombe, Croydon
9 May 1911

My dear Lou,

Sorry I worried you about this cursed suit. It troubles me at no time except just when I want to change and get into something decent. I wrote immediately before getting ready to go to Wallington. Today I don't care a damn.

Will you really only come[2] for the day on Saturday? It is such a rush! But half a loaf's better than no bread. We can hardly go into the country: we can go to the Zoo,[3] where I never have been; and I'll take you to the Tate – though there is no 'New Tate' – only a new room.[4] There is a pretty little garden by the Houses of Parliament where we can sit and look at the River and talk. Let me know what time you get in, and what time you go again. Then I can think what we shall do.

The 112 pages of Paul are pages such as this on which I write. Am I a newspaper printing machine to turn out a hundred sheets in half an hour?

[1] Unidentified.

[2] come] stay

[3] In Regents Park.

[4] Probably a reference to the 'Turner wing' of the Tate Gallery opened in 1910 to accommodate the bulk of the Turner paintings and drawings transferred from the National Gallery.

This weather is wonderfully fine – one can scarcely think of work.

Oh – as for Whitsun – we shall have to give them a few days at home – say till Wednesday: then till Friday at Quorn – then just Saturday at Leicester. You know I don't in the least mind Billy and Nora's racket:[1] but one has to hold oneself to an attitude, I don't quite know how, when one is with one's opposites. I think you understand.

I had a letter from Hilda Shaw this morning. I think she will get well again. She writes me very nicely – her letters are worth reading. I must answer her soon.

Well – I must close. Saturday is very near. These evenings are so beautiful, it is cruel to waste them writing. I wish you were here, so we could walk together. It is the knowledge that the holiday is so brief which makes it pass so strangely when we are together.

I kiss you bon soir – D. H. Lawrence

265. To Louie Burrows, 11 May 1911

Text: MS UN; Boulton 105.

12 Colworth Rd, Addiscombe, Croydon
11 May 1911

My dear Lou,

Having got a vilainous headache owing to the thunder, I'm only going to write half a line. You get in at 10.40, don't you? That's the time I shall be at Mary le Bone unless you contradict. And I'm sure, with a day ticket, you can go back by a later, an express train. I am sure, because Auntie does. Bring a bill.[2] I look forward to Sat – or I should if I weren't squint-blind just now. A day, no more. Did you write to Ada? Will you send or bring Corot. Un jour seul. Addio – je t'aime D. H. Lawrence

266. To Jessie Chambers, [c. 11 May 1911]

Text: E.T. 186.

[12 Colworth Road, Addiscombe, Croydon]
[c. 11 May 1911][3]

I have read your story[4] but I don't think you'll get anyone to publish it with

[1] Louie's youngest brother and sister, aged six and four respectively.

[2] i.e. a handbill giving details of excursion trains.

[3] Jessie Chambers dates this letter 'some time in the spring of 1911'. DHL's complaint about his intense headache appears to echo that in the previous letter.

[4] Based on the occasion when DHL had told her that he could not love her 'as a husband should love his wife' (E.T. 66, 186).

alacrity; it's too subtle...You say you died a death of me, but the death you died of me I must have died also, or you wouldn't have gone on caring about me...They[1] tore me from you, the love of my life...It was the slaughter of the foetus in the womb...I've got a grinning skull-and-crossbones headache. The amount of energy required to live is – how many volts a second?[2]

267. To Gertrude Cooper, [13 May 1911]

Text: MS Clarke; PC v. Buckingham Palace, London. The Blue Drawing Room; Postmark, London May 13 11; Unpublished.

[13 May 1911]

My dear Grit,

Well, how's the world by now? Do you wish you were with me in London – I wish I were out of the city, somewhere a bit cooler. So let's swap. Are things going just as giddily as ever at Lynn Croft? You want to get frisk[y][3] and dance round a bit.

Addio DHL

268. To Louie Burrows, 14 May 1911

Text: MS UN; Boulton 106.

12 Colworth Rd, Addiscombe, Croydon
14 May 1911

My dear Lou,

We were bound to forget something – here is your scarf.

Doesn't yesterday seem as if it belonged to another existence? I have been in bed all day, that's the reason. I'm afraid I wasn't as jolly yesterday as I should have been: but I was feeling queer, having been rocky since Wednesday. I don't know what it is – nothing – the weather, I suppose. I've been in bed today, following your sage advice: and as soon as the bed's made, I'm going back. One must occasionally sing soft. I wouldn't be ill in digs, not for any money. I shall be all right for school in the morning.

You look also a bit queer. It's love and the weather, like me, eh? But we're neither of us die-ers, and there's no need to worry. I intend to have a good time somewhere in the future – I don't hanker for Orcus.[4] We won't let the filching rascally Fates pick the future from our pockets, will we.

[1] Jessie's narrative (E.T. 64–6) points to Mrs Lawrence and Emily as those principally responsible.

[2] Another version of this letter (Delavenay 706) omits the second sentence and substitutes 'day' for the final word of the text.

[3] MS damaged.

[4] i.e. the nether world.

Sursum corda and vogue la galère which is, translated 'Lift up your hearts, however the dam boat cockles.' – if only it didn't make one sea sick.

And now 'To bed, to bed, to bed.'[1]

Embrasse D. H. Lawrence

Sympathetic to Miss Cox – fellow feeling.

269. To Louie Burrows, 16 May 1911

Text: MS UN; Boulton 106–7.

Davidson Rd Boys School, South Norwood, S.E.
16 May 1911

My dear Lou,

How strange! – it makes me laugh. You imagine I imagine you are mean – how mean of me! I could never mean that you are mean or even slightly mercenary, for I know, – need I tell you so, that you're generous more than ordinary. How could you think that I should sink to such a depth of base suggestion? – it makes me blush and crimson flush to be the object of such a question.

The idea is, my dear, just mad enough to send me dotty: – whoa!

But what ever made you think such things? I never for a moment doubt your splendid generosity – nor doubt you in any way except to wonder whether I shall ever get you: which is, of course, only the doubt of the baby in the Pear's Soap bath.[2] You are very fantastical, my dear, in your imaginings: they really amuse me, like *Alice in Wonderland*.

'Twas brillig, and the slithy toves
Did gyre and gimble in the wabe'[3]

No, but I am so Hamletty – I am so confoundedly and absurdly Hamletty, it's enough to make you sick. When I begin to rant in the 'To be or not to be' style, you should say 'Hello, he's off again', and wait for the rhyme which rings conclusion if not reason. Sithee? And if I say about seeing me with J[essie], why I only mean for half an hour: and doubtless, soon or late, you will see me with J for half an hour: and doubtless you won't mind a scrap.

Do lay this to your gentle feminine soul: that, in the opinion of the lady in the Chapter House, I am surely mad.[4] Say to yourself, on lots of occasions

[1] *Macbeth* v. i. 75.
[2] Cf. p. 252 n. 3
[3] 'Jabberwocky' ll. 1–2, in Lewis Carroll, *Through the Looking-Glass* (1872).
[4] Probably a reference to some incident in Westminster Abbey during their day together on 13 May.

that will arrive: 'Well, the lady in the Chapter House says he's mad......' You can fill in the dots.

If you can cook you will be perfect: two cakes! I shall keep henceforth a list to appraise and condemn you by. 'My wife can cook thirty seven puddings and fifteen different cakes: all plain roasts, all haricot stews, curries etc etc etc –.' Kindly keep me informed, so that I can compare you with other men's wives, to my renown.

I, for my part, am going to struggle like the devil to establish my health. A thin blade stands best, goes deepest, and cuts nearest: but if you get too thin in the blade you double up. I proceed to substantiate. Either I shall become a 'garçon solide', or else a mere blessed wraith.

I didn't write any Paul last night – went to bed quite good and early.

It's a very close day today.

I don't feel like undertaking Ordeals, do you?

I'm supposed to be teaching Composition at this minute. I'll now recite the 'Ode to Duty',[1] to get my muscle up, and then I'll fall to.

Addio – I wish it were holidays.

Addio, carissima D. H. Lawrence

270. To Louie Burrows, 23 May 1911

Text: MS UN; Boulton 108–9.

12 Colworth Rd, Addiscombe, Croydon.
23 May 1911

My dear Lou,

Have you yet recovered from your indisposition? Dont let it trouble you long.

About Whitsun – they are raising such an outcry at home, because I say I will come late to Eastwood. Ada seems quite upset at the thought. I must not stay at Quorn long: not longer, probably, than the Monday evening. Shall we go home to Eastwood on Monday evening? Your people wouldn't mind, would they? Ada will be very disappointed even then that we are so late in coming: I would not delay further. Shall I write to your mother to thank her for the invitation and to say the time of my departure? – our departure, I mean, of course. I hope to goodness you haven't let me spoil your Grandpa's[2] visit: I wouldn't have that for anything.

And will you, this week-end, make enquiry if there is the Saturday half day trip to London on Whit-Saturday? I'm afraid lest it should be knocked

[1] Wordsworth's famous poem: 'Stern Daughter of the Voice of God!/O Duty!'

[2] William Ralph Burrows.

off. If it's not I'll come by the return half. The ordinary fare would beggar me to pay. What a damnation to be so penurious! Never mind, we might be much worse.

It is only a very short time to Whit now.

Everybody here seems a bit off colour and cranky. It's tiresome to live with people who jangle.

I can only work a very little, which annoys me.

Why do you dream such unfinished dreams? – You never did ride, you see. It makes me think of Browning's 'Last Ride Together' not coming-off.

You'll get Quorn I suppose.[1] When shall you go, in that event? Before August? – No.

We'll discuss Coronation at Whit.[2]

Your folk are getting quite tolerant of you.

Have you ever read Hewlett's *Spanish Jade*?[3] I'll give it Ada at Whit, unless you'd care for it. I don't value it myself, much.

I hope you'll be sound and well at Whit. Addio. D. H. Lawrence

271. To Louie Burrows, 26 May 1911
Text: MS UN; Boulton 109–10.

12 Colworth Rd, Addiscombe, Croydon
26 May[4] 1911

My dear Lou,

You see I was writing 26 April – I am wool-witted. Today has been sultry, full of black vapour, with brownish fiery lightning, and thunder like enormous cats bounding on a sound-board ceiling. – Very fine that!

I remark that you have broken up, and felicitate you on the point. It will be very nice to lie low awhile. I wish we had broken up. The fever has not been your enemy. Was it scarlet, or typhoid, or typhus, or malaria, or which, by the way? I imagine a lurid, malignant disease rampant in your little school room, but know not how to name the brute.

I am quite sure that your father and I will get on heavenlily before long, being, as we are both, 'bons garçons, bons enfants'. Forgive me if I'm impertinent. The weather gets in my head.

1 Against her better judgement Louie was persuaded by the school managers and her father to apply for the post (which she obtained) of headmistress at the Quorn Church of England Junior School. Her appointment at Gaddesby ceased on 31 July; that at Quorn began on 1 September. DHL considered that the move would rob Louie of her independence and he resented it.

2 The Whitsuntide break, 5–9 June, was shortly to be followed by a week's holiday to celebrate George V's coronation on 22 June 1911 (School Log).

3 Maurice Hewlett's novel (1908).

4 May] Ap

Again, I have not answered the question concerning the verses. If you will allow me, I will not give them to you. They are all very well dancing up and down the pages of my little note book, shut safely in the cupboard – but wandering, even as speech from me to you, as yet, 'no', permit me to say. – My style is certainly 'fetching'. – But at Whit I will show you the first two hundred pages of 'Paul', that book of books.

My health is so-so: I do not grumble. In truth, or rather in act, I am as good as an angel. I am sure I do nothing to the detriment of my physical well-being: I go to bed pretty early, I eschew pleasures of all kinds, I keep a cheerful frame of mind; I do nothing in excess, nor work, nor read, nor think, nor drink, nor eat, nor smoke. Docile, I am, and good as an angel. I offer myself to your commendation: and I never even fib to you. I *am* very tolerably well, I thank you. I *will be* better.

Dreams! I could cap you there. My sleep, in the morning, is a passionate second-life of dreams. This mornings was you: yesterday mother's: so that my dreams seem by far the realest part of my life at present. The day is only a drift, a sort of sleep walk – oh quite aimiable.

I dare scarcely tell you this mornings dream. I dreamed we were bien mariés, et que tu étais accouchée de notre premier enfant. Tu souffrais beaucoup; tu gémissais de douleur, et moi, en entendant, je sentis les entrailles me fondent. Et puis, je[1] m'éloignais un peu, et tout était sombre. Revenant ensuite, tu te guérissait, tu sourissait, et on m'a montré l'enfant: garçon très joli et doux, avec les yeux bleu foncés. Quand je l'avais vu, c'étais moi qui devait disparaître de la scène, et il y avait une ombre noire à ma place. – Je puis encore ressentir les entrailles se fondre[2] dans mon corps au son de les gémissements, et je puis encore ressentir le coeur me bondir de joie et de grâce en voyant l'enfant.

– Et après, c'était ma soeur Emilie, et ce n'était pas toi: tout était confus!

Mon rêve sans doute te fait rougir – j'en demande pardon.[3]

In a week I shall be coming north – I wish it were tomorrow.

[1] je] tu

[2] fondre] fondant

[3] 'I dreamed we were really married, and that you were giving birth to our first child. You were suffering greatly; you were groaning with pain, and, listening to you, I felt my insides melt away. And then, I moved a little way off, and everything was dark. When I came back, you were recovering, you were smiling, and they showed me the child: a boy, very pretty and placid, with deep blue eyes. As soon as I had seen him, I was the one who had to disappear from the scene, and there was a dark shadow in my place. – I can still feel my insides melting away in my body at the sound of your moaning, and I can still feel my heart leap with joy and thankfulness on seeing the child.

– And afterwards, it was my sister Emily, and not you: everything was confused!

My dream is doubtless making you blush – do forgive me.'

I salute you. My regards to all of your family.

Yours D. H. Lawrence

They say it's a very bad dream in our family to dream of a new-born baby.

272. To Louie Burrows, [30 May 1911]

Text: MS UN; PC; Postmark, Croydon MY 30 11; Boulton 110–11.

Croydon –
Tuesday.

J'ai été tellement occupé ce soir, ayant commencé un autre tableau pour ma tante: la femme d'un pêcheur, tenant son enfant, et regardant loin sur la mêr.[1] En souvenez vous? Je crois qu'il viendra bien, mon tableau, et je veux qu'il était pour vous. Chaque fois que j'arrive à une bonne effet, je me dis 'Cela devrait être pour Louie'.

Avez vous reçu Paul? – et a-t-on vous fait payer une surcharge sur le paquet. Je n'avais que trois timbres-postes, et il fallait quatre. M'en pardonnerez vous?

Et, si vous aller à Leicester cette semaine, vous me ferez un bonté si vous m'apportez le tableau que j'ai donné à ma tante aux Pâques, et auquel il faut faire une réparation; il y a un morceau de papier à colle s'attaché au visage de la femme, et on veut que je le peigne de nouveau, ce morceau. Je peux le faire à Quorn, car je ne veux pas aller à Leicester.

Il ne reste que quatre jours. Dieu, comme je m'impatiente! Je vous embrasse, amante.

Beaucoup de choses de ma part à votre famille.

D. H. Lawrence

[I have been so busy this evening, having begun another picture for my aunt: a fisherman's wife, holding her child, and looking far out over the sea. Do you remember it? I think my picture will turn out well, and I wish it were for you. Every time I manage a happy effect, I say to myself 'That ought to be for Louie'.

Have you received Paul? – and did you have to pay excess postage on the parcel. I only had three stamps, and needed four. Will you forgive me?

And, if you go to Leicester this week, you would do me a favour if you brought me the picture I gave to my aunt at Easter, and which needs repairing; there is a piece of gummed paper stuck to the face of the woman,

[1] DHL was copying *A Fisherman's Treasure* (1887) by George Wetherbee (1851–1920). It was reproduced in a special number of *The Studio*, Spring 1906, 'The Royal Institute of Painters in Water-Colours', ed. Charles Holme.

and they want me to paint that bit again. I can do it at Quorn, because I don't want to go to Leicester.

Only four days to go. God, how impatient I am! I kiss you, my love.

Kind regards from me to your family. D. H. Lawrence]

273. To Louie Burrows, 1 June 1911

Text: MS UN; Boulton 111–12.

12 Colworth Rd, Addiscombe, Croydon
1st June 1911

My dear Lou,

Thanks for fetching the picture from Leicester. I have got on pretty well with the other – I shall finish it tomorrow. It doesn't look bad, so far. I get quite a dab hand at manipulating water color. If I had time I would do original stuff – but it is impossible.

Re – the holidays: I'm very glad you will be restored to us for August; and I guess that, in the end, we shall go to the Lakes: I am always a devil for complaisance. It is true, I was rather keen on France: and it would cost no more than England. Lodging is *so* dear in this country, that folk after folk say to me: 'I can't take a holiday in England, it's so dear. I go on the Continent.' However – heaven is on the side of the big battallion[1] – which word I can't spell – tell me, when you write, how to.

I'm glad you like Paul, but doubt whether you tell me 'the truth, the whole truth, and nothing but the truth – so help me God.'

I've painted till nightfall – and talked to the neighbours over the fence till dark – and written to Kit Holderness – it's *such* a long time since I heard from her – and now I write to you. It is quarter to ten: shall I do a few pages of Paul? – or is it too late. Too late, I think. I will vegetate, as Kit says.

Yesterday we had such a storm: the lightning beat about in the sky like a frightened bird (is that over poetic for you? – Sorry!) – And I had a 'Nuit blanche'. And this morning I would have given anything to be near you, near enough to rest. And tonight I bristle with activity and irony. I shall never rest in this life – not long. I think I shall go out now for a while – from 10.0 till 11.0. There is a young moon.

Auntie was quite concerned on a postcard this morning, about my health. How funny things are!

Why weren't you going boating with Tom Smith – he's no lady-killer, for sure – and lonely, poor devil.

[1] Voltaire, Letter to M. le Riche, 6 February 1770, in *Œuvres Complètes*, xiv (Paris, 1882), 551.

Oh, will you write and tell Ada what time we shall get in Newthorpe on Monday night. Do please.

I shall come to Quorn by the 6.25 from M[ary] le Bone.

I shan't do any Paul tonight – I'll go out awhile.

You are too far away – it is abominable. Tonight is tonight – and where is Sunday? I kiss you! D. H. Lawrence

274. To Martin Secker, 12 June 1911

Text: MS UInd; Huxley 8.

12 Colworth Road, Addiscombe, Croydon
12 June 1911

Martin Secker Esq[1]
5 John St, Adelphi.

Dear Sir,

I am very much flattered by your offer to publish a volume of my short stories: to tell the truth, I sit in doubt and wonder because of it.[2]

There have appeared in print, in the *English Review*, two and two only of my tales.[3] Because nobody wanted the things, I have not troubled to write any. So that, at present, I have two good stories published, three very decent ones lying in the hands of the Editor of the *English Review*,[4] another good one at home,[5] and several slight things sketched out and neglected.[6] If these would be any good towards an autumn volume, I should be at the top of happiness. If they are not enough – I am in the midst of a novel, and bejungled in work, alas.

[1] Martin Secker (1882–1978), publisher. Entered publishing, 1908, in the office of Eveleigh Nash. Started on his own account in the Adelphi, 1910. Published DHL's *New Poems*, 1918; continued as his publisher till 1930.

[2] DHL was responding to Secker's letter, 2 June 1911:

> Dear Sir,
>
> I was extremely interested in your novel, and the excellent story in this month's *English Review* which I have just read prompts me to ask if you would care to offer me a volume of short stories, when you have sufficient material. I should like to have published *The White Peacock* and I am looking forward to reading your second book when it appears.
>
> Yours truly

([Martin Secker], *Letters from a Publisher: Martin Secker to D. H. Lawrence and others, 1911–1929*, 1970, p. 1.)

[3] 'Goose Fair' (February 1910); 'Odour of Chrysanthemums' (June 1911).

[4] 'A Fragment of Stained Glass'; 'The White Stocking'; and perhaps 'Intimacy'.

[5] Most probably 'A Modern Lover', earlier entitled 'The Virtuous'.

[6] Perhaps 'Lessford's Rabbits' and 'A Lesson on a Tortoise'.

My second novel is promised to Wm Heinemann. It is written, but I will not publish it, because it is erotic: in spite of which Mr Heinemann would take it. But I am afraid for my tender reputation. Therefore I stick at my third book like a broody hen at her eggs, lest my chickens hatch in a winter of public forgetfulness.

Of course I am sensible to the honour you do me – only wish I could make more satisfactory return.

Yours Sincerely D. H. Lawrence

275. To Louie Burrows, 14 June 1911

Text: MS UN; Boulton 112–13.

12 Colworth Rd, Addiscombe, Croydon
14 June 1911

My dear Lou,

Let me write in pencil again.

Isn't it damnably cold? I hope the weather'll warm up for next week.

This week has got the lid on – I merely exist in a box of days, until Saturday. So I'm not going to write much of a letter.

I've heard from Secker and from Hueffer – both very nice.[1] The book of short stories is practically promised for the Spring: agreeable all round.

I've worked quite hard: begun a picture, long promised, for Mac., and written a short story, 32 pages long, in two nights.[2] Smart work, eh?

Don't worry, I shall be lively enough next week.[3] But the nights are cold as the icy tomb.

[1] In answer to the previous letter DHL had heard again from Secker:

June 13 1911

Dear Sir,

I am much obliged for your letter, and am very glad that you are inclined to view favourably the idea of publishing a volume of short stories. The material for such a book should run to at least 60 or 70 thousand words, and I hope that in the course of time you will allow me to make you an offer for the publication of a book about this length. In any case, I shall not be publishing any fiction until next spring, so that in these circumstances it may be possible that you might have the material for a volume ready by that time.

I can understand how busy you are getting your third book ready for publication while the public still remembers the success of *The White Peacock*, and perhaps from this point of view the volume of stories next spring might be of advantage. But at any rate I hope you will be good enough to let me know as soon as you have a collection of stories which you would like to see in volume form.

Yours very truly

(*Letters from a Publisher*, p. 2.)

[2] Perhaps 'The Old Adam' (though the extant MS of this story is 27 pages).

[3] The holiday to celebrate George V's coronation.

I don't believe there's an item of news. Oh, by the way, would you like to come down to the Suffragette procession on Saturday?[1] I enclose bills. It will, I think, be very nice – and we could return 6.25, or 7.30, or midnight as you please. Puccini's new opera is on in the evening:[2] but alas – my debts are very deep already – oh dear!

Please yourself about coming – but tell me.

I don't want to work – I don't want a bit to work – Oh damn.

Gut Nacht, meine lieben Schatz. (Brahms)[3] D. H. Lawrence

By the way, I've got a 'Swan' number of the *Studio*.[4] Shall I bring it? Rather a nice tiger.

276. To Arthur McLeod, [23 June 1911]

Text: MS UT; PC v. [House with woman and child]; Postmark, Eastwood JU 23 11; Unpublished.

Queens Sq – Eastwood
[23 June 1911]

Don't be so blessed Christian – sending in a claim for an Aureole and a front seat so early. You *are* good – I've no doubt the angels are tooling you a nimbus – but, in the name of modesty, *do* pretend to be unconscious.

And thanks very much for the *Blue Boy*.[5] My sister says, 'Is Mr MacLeod ikey?'[6]

'Indeed no,' I reply. 'He's verily one of the great aristocrats of the perfect Highland "Mac" strain of aristocracy.'

My sister accepts it that your blood is as blue as a cornflower.

I've just had to sign an *English Review* protest against the *Spectator* – more advertisement – but Galsworthy, Thomas Hardy and Yeats are before[7] me, so I sign, though grudgingly.[8] But – 'faiblesse oblige' – or 'pauvreté'.

Thine D. H. Lawrence

[1] The suffragist demonstration on 17 June proved to be larger than any before: *The Times* reported a five-mile procession of 40,000 people.

[2] *La Fanciulla del West* was performed at Covent Garden on 17 June.

[3] Op. 14, no. 7 ['...liebester...': 'Good Night, my dearest Sweetheart'].

[4] *The Studio*, June 1910, p. 2, reproduced a study of a tiger's head by the animal painter John Macallan Swan (1847–1910). DHL later copied it in charcoal (see Lawrence–Gelder, plate 5). McLeod recalled DHL's interest in 'a whole series of Swan's animal studies' (Nehls, i. 90; see *The Studio*, xxii (1901), 74–86, 150–61).

[5] Presumably McLeod had sent DHL a postcard reproduction of Gainsborough's painting (1805).

[6] For explanation see Letter 390, p. 365.

[7] are before] are all before

[8] The *Spectator*'s article, 'The Great Adult Review', 10 June 1911, pp. 875–6, declared that notices about or advertisements from the *English Review* would no longer be printed. The *Spectator* condemned 'the tone and tendency of the *English Review* on moral questions'; it refused to condone 'garbage being dumped on the nation's doorstep'. Austin Harrison

The view is my sister's (married) – house – with her ma-in-law.[1]

I'm bringing you *Howards End* – it is exceedingly good and very discussable – Hope I shan't forget it.[2]

Was in Nottingham yesterday for the fireworks – very pretty.[3] In Leicester Wednesday – very gay. Addio.

277. To Louie Burrows, 23 June 1911

Text: MS UN; Boulton 113–14.

11 Queens Sq, Eastwood, Notts
23 June 1911

My dear Lou,

I had a very exciting time yesterday. George had been waiting at the station for me, and then missed me. There was no news of Ada. We went to the Castle 'en famille' – and by the way, the local artists are very good indeed – Tom Gillott has got the Second prize of the year.[4] When we were coming down Friar Lane, there was Sam bolting by for dear life. And then Ada, Frances, Gertie Floss Eddie, Emily and Baby discovered feeding at Lyons:[5] ices all round, and up to Forest. Such a crowd you never saw: Nottm teemed and spewed with people. The fireworks very pretty – reminded me of Cowes, with mother, two years back.[6]

Sam had driven the party in a wagonette – behold us sailing home towards midnight, singing, and roaring to everybody we passed – most common, but extremely jolly. I sat in front, arm round Floss, because she found it rummy to be so perched. I wished indeed you were there. The subcurrent of passion, oh Lord, makes you shudder.

Perhaps you'll come to Croydon soon. Gott!

Bring me *Howard's End* on Sunday, if you can.

Love to all Baiser D. H. Lawrence

replied in *English Review*, viii (July 1911), 666–70; his reply was prefaced by the names of 96 contributors to the *Review*. Hardy, Shaw, Conrad, James, Yeats, Galsworthy, Tolstoy, Gorky, etc. head the list; there are 90 names before DHL's.

[1] Mrs Ann King (1852–1940).

[2] The novel by E. M. Forster (1879–1970), published October 1910.

[3] To mark George V's coronation.

[4] Thomas Ignatius Joseph Gillott (b. 1886) entered two works in the annual Local Artists' Exhibition held in the Castle Art Gallery; one of them, *A Country Fair* – probably the prizewinner referred to – was acquired for the Gallery. Gillott was born in Eastwood and DHL obviously knew him.

[5] The Nottingham branch of the national chain of restaurants.

[6] On 6 August 1909 during the family holiday on the Isle of Wight (see Letter 118).

278. To Louie Burrows, 27 June 1911
Text: MS UN; Boulton 114–15.

Purley, Surrey
27 June 1911

My dear Lou,

I'm having to scribble a quick note here, because I've not had a glimpse of time at home. Ma Jones and the family went out for the[1] day, so I had Mac to dine with me, and had to be host, hostess and maid in one. But it was jolly.

Then I got a card from Miss Macartney asking me to tea and a musical evening. So far I've been mowing the grass – such a stretch – with old Macartney, who is grumbling because his gardening man hasn't turned up this week. It's a nice garden – big walnut tree in the centre, and long regiments of great delphiniums blue as strips of heaven – and pink roses, heavy and full.

I thank you for your belated advice – won't work too hard, I promise. Damn Paul. Why mustn't I write Old Adams? – and New Eves are much wickeder I assure you.[2]

I think the holiday has been very good for me – too short – damn it. As for midsummer, I'm sure it'll all turn out A1. – only let it be quick. I was rather looking forward to your coming to Croydon soon. But we'll take what comes, for the best.

Now for a Beethoven Sonata.[3] Love DHL

279. To Louie Burrows, 30 June 1911
Text: MS UN; Boulton 115–16.

Davidson Rd Boys School, South Norwood – SE.
30 June 1911

My dear Lou,

You write also very hastily: I suppose there is no news: except the important point about Gaddesby. This time next week, and you will be spending your last session with the Gaddesby kiddies. You will find a big change at Quorn – no more 'en famille' at school: no more the patriarchal – or matriarchal system. You won't like the other so well, but it will be a

[1] the] a

[2] The reference is to DHL's story 'The Old Adam'. 'New Eves' is likely to have been a slightly risqué play on 'Old Adams' rather than a reference to DHL's story 'New Eve and Old Adam' which is of later vintage.

[3] Presumably played by Laura MacCartney (at whose house DHL was writing this letter).

change for you, and you'll soon get used to it: and, heaven knows, it will be easy enough, even at Quorn. You'll like it all right.

I'm very glad that you will go to Wales with me. France seems off, because of money chiefly. I have written to Auntie for the addresses of the cottages at Pwllelli – or Pwllelhi, however they spell it – and will try and arrange for the first three weeks of August, if not for the month. Do you know, the Hall's want to go with us, as of yore. So that would mean Coopers. I should like it all right, if you would. You see, it would mean that Ada would have more pals – and it is very jolly. Then, if we kept the cottage for the month – if we could – we might have Emily or Ethel[1] or even Tom Smith – if he'd come – for a week or so. We must see. Don't say anything about it yet, except just that we propose to go to Wales.

I had a letter from Ethel[2] this morning: they are moving today to St Margaret's on Thames, wherever that may be: somewhere near London. 'Oak Lodge' – sounds rather nice. I am going for the week-end in a fortnight.

And in a month today we shall have broken up – thank the Lord. I feel less and less like work. Certainly I shall have to turn gentleman, and do nowt. I wish we could be married: it is such an effort to carry all things on, sans aide ni appui. Well – in a month we shall have a month to ourselves – which is more than everybody can look forward to.

I[t] is rather cold and dreary here today: I wish I were at Coteshael: I think that[3] is more like home to me than Queens Square. Don't tell Ada I said that – but it's true. Regards to everybody.

With love to you. DHL

280. To Louie Burrows, 4 July 1911

Text: MS UN; Boulton 116–7.

12 Colworth Rd, Addiscombe, Croydon
4 July 1911

My dear Lou,

So your managers are being fussy? – damn them.[4] Say now – are you *sure* you won't go back on the eighth? Of course, in the safety of July you ll protest your will, but when August creeps on us – what then. O damn the fools, why can't they be sensible.

[1] i.e. Etheldreda Burrows.
[2] i.e. Ethel Hunger.
[3] that] it
[4] A letter to Louie Burrows (UN MS LaB 198, 1 June 1911), possibly from the chairman of the Gaddesby school managers, assures her that no obstacles would be presented to her leaving – 'if we can find another to take your place'. Presumably it was proving difficult to replace her.

The Hall's, also, fatheads, want to go to Barmouth. I've partly arranged the Pwllheli digs – sounds ever so nice. We might have a sweet bungalow cottage for £2··10 a week. I have sent the letter to Eastwood for them to consider and decide. They'll let us know. But do try to wring from the necks of your managers some words of certitude.

Don't talk about honey-moons – the atmosphere's too inflammable. It's only 3 weeks to breaking up.

Do you know I went to the Opera on Sat. and heard *Bohème*. Melba took leading part: very good, but a bit tense, strenuous as a singer.[1] Twas nice – wished you were there.

Was there anything I had to answer you? – I forget. Yes, I'm very well – and you? I've done a fair amount of Paul – theres no more news.

We break up in three weeks – how I harp on it. It won't be long going. I wish something nice would happen.

You will be enjoying yourself tea-ing with so many folk. I'm glad you're going out a bit. Don't get thin – I like you to be fat – dont get any thinner. I am a Turk – like my houri plump. Sounds bestial – it's only brevity.

The *English* hasn't paid me yet:[2] Devils!

I've insured father for £9··12: he wasn't insured.

Here's my mouth. D. H. Lawrence

281. To Louie Burrows, 7 July 1911
Text: MS UN; Boulton 117–18.

12 Colworth Rd, Addiscombe, Croydon
7 July 1911

My dear Lou,

I hardly know how your calendar goes from now. Have you done at Gaddesby? – unless you are constrained to start again in August? Do you put in your first day at Quorn on Monday?[3] I suppose you will be very excited and turmoilsome this week-end: and then the heat. For the Lord's sake, don't go and knock yourself up. I often wonder, as I walk along in the still, intense heat, going to school, whether you are flagging like a broken holly hock. It doesn't ill-suit me, this weather.

Ada has applied for the bungalow – for the first two weeks of August, I

[1] Puccini's opera *La Bohème* (1896) was performed at Covent Garden on 1 July with (Dame) Nellie Melba (1861?–1931) in the leading rôle.

[2] For 'Odour of Chrysanthemums' published in June.

[3] Her new appointment officially began on 1 September, but she appears to have taken up the post in July.

believe. If we get it, how jolly! I sincerely hope that the Halls[1] won't go, then we shall be a jolly little party. I believe its a very nice place – I dreamed of it the other day. At any rate we shall see the sun set over the west sea.

Nothing happens here – the days go slowly by, like barges. I began a nice big Corot, half did it, spoiled it, and tore it in thirty pieces. Shame! Now I've begun a little *Idyll* for Agnes Holt. She marries in early August, and has asked me for this picture. I must race and get her a couple done.[2]

I think we are going to live in Clyde Rd. near here in September. The house is a nicer one than this, pleasantly situated. They are negotiating terms. I had thought that when the lease of this house expired I should be far away – but things turn out differently. I may be here a long time. Even we make between us little arrangements for the school year that follows next – that goes on into 1913. Shall I be here then – and still with the Joneses? Gott in Himmel!!

We break up on Thursday 26th.[3] I shall come up on that day – to Quorn for the night at least, eh? – for the two days, eh? I hope holidays turn up trumps.

I wish you were here. This sultry weather makes one burn like a fire that wants feeding. I wish you were nearer. It's no good saying I kiss you, because I can't. Ah well – in three weeks.

Love. D. H. Lawrence

282. To Ada Lawrence, 11 July 1911

Text: MS Clarke; Postmark, Croydon JY 11 11; cited in Lawrence–Gelder 92.

12, Colworth Rd, Addiscombe, Croydon
11 July 1911

My dear Ada,

Don't revile the *English* – they have at last sent me twice the amount I expected.[4] I enclose a birthday sovereign: use it as you like.[5] 'Boots' will

[1] Halls] Coop[ers]

[2] For her wedding on 5 August 1911 DHL painted two pictures (both now owned by the University of Nottingham): *Idyll* (see Letters 92 and 233) and *Wind on the Wold*. The *Idyll*, $10\frac{3}{4}'' \times 5\frac{1}{2}''$, is reproduced in *Paintings*, ed. Levy, monochrome plate 9. *Wind on the Wold*, water-colour, $21\frac{1}{4}'' \times 11''$, is a copy of a painting (1858) by George H. Mason (1818–72) with the same title, now in the Tate; it is reproduced in *Paintings*, monochrome plate 7. For this picture DHL's probable source was a reproduction of Mason's picture in *The Nation's Pictures*, 1st series, pt. 39, 1 April 1903, and again in pt. 8, 2 January 1907.

[3] Thursday was 27th (DHL corrects himself in Letter 283).

[4] The *English Review* paid DHL £10 for 'Odour of Chrysanthemums'.

[5] Ada's twenty-fourth birthday fell on 16 June 1911.

match the brush (joke!).[1] I forget how much that cost – either 16/6 or 17/6.

I also enclose Georgie's letter, and hope you can tell me where the 'scrotum' is. Poor creature, his is a sad case. Tell Floss to let him go to the devil.[2]

I think it'll be nice at Nevin. Don't worry about expenses: I send you ten bob towards them, and if you're short, you will consider my money is yours. I'm not married yet.

I have been wondering whether to send Aunt Ada the £3 which she paid to Dr Eddy for mother.[3] Shall I, or shall I not? It might hurt her feelings – but I feel very much inclined to do it. Shall I?

You see, we break up on the Thursday, and so I can get the half day up. Probably I shall go to Quorn till the Friday or Saturday. At any rate, if I went from London to Pwllheli by trip, I should have to *return* to London – so it's as broad as it is long.

I will go to Kit's. We will go for three days. We will go for the Monday, Tuesday and Wednesday of the first week we are back from Wales, shall we? I will write to her also.

Then I have promised Tom Smith I will go to Lincoln for a short time.[4] I will give him also three days. Him I will write now, and arrange. Also I will answer Georgie, very coolly.

The heat has not treated me badly: you know I like it. I suppose it has upset Lou. You know she soon flags. That is why she hasn't written you, I suppose.[5]

I am glad Grit is going with us to Wales. It will be a rather feminine party, but that I don't mind.[6] It is definitely decided that we go on Sat 29th July, is it not? I hope we get the girl for the work. There will be eight of us, including Lou. Get me a bed out – I shan't sleep with Mr Hall:[7] I'll pay.

It is strange that in about a fortnight holidays will be here. It is mother's birthday a week on Thursday. – I don't feel very keen for the midsummer, do you?

Well – we will have a good time, nevertheless –

love D. H. Lawrence

1 A punning reference to Boots, the pharmaceutical chemists (whose shops would also sell toilet requisites).

2 The two persons concerned were George Neville and Flossie Cullen.

3 See p. 176 n. 3.

4 Smith's home was in Lincoln (where his father, Alfred Smith, was a railway engine-driver).

5 Ada had written to Louie on 29 June (MS UN LaB 199).

6 don't mind] don't care about

7 Alice Hall's father; he had accompanied the young people on their Shanklin holiday in 1909.

Don't tell Emily I've sent you 30/- – and don't tell Louie. DHL

We've got a days holiday tomorrow[1] – I am glad.

I enclose also 2/6 for pocket-money for father. –

Send those excursion books for Miss Reynolds, will you? Mid[land] and G[reat] C[entral].[2]

283. To Louie Burrows, 11 July 1911

Text: MS UN; Boulton 118–19.

12 Colworth Rd, Addiscombe, Croydon.
11 July 1911

My dear Lou,

I hear from Ada today that the bungalow in Nevin is taken – that they're getting a girl at ten bob a week to do the work – and I think everything will go like a coon song,[3] now you are safe and sure. Halls are going, worse luck: and Frances and Gertie – not Neville, because he's not breaking up till the 4th.

Ada complains you haven't written her. Georgie, by the way, is playing the goat: hasn't answered Floss' letter for three weeks. I've done with him – he's a fool.

Now for holidays, which will be here in a fortnight. We break up Thursday 27th, as I told you. Shall I try and get off by the morning trip – I will. If I can't manage it, I'll come by return half. I really ought to go to Eastwood, because of dragging all my luggage to Wales. What shall I do? – Shall I stay with you and we'll join the party together in Nottm on the Sat. morning, or shall I go on to Eastwood on Friday? We must decide.

Oh, and I'll tell you now so you won't revile me when I come: We've[4] promised a few days to Kit Holderness from the 3rd week, Ada and I – and I'm booked to Lincoln a few days for the 4th week. Now *don't* say I haven't told you.

The *English* have paid me at last, and more than I expected, so that I shall be able to pay off all my encumbrances, get some boots and shirts and a suit, and have just a bit left. I want, when I come up, to bring Mrs Burrows something really nice. Will you tell me what. If you don't tell me something worth getting, I'll spend a quid on table-cloths for her – for *her*, not for you, mind you.

[1] 'On occasion of Annual Sports' (School Log).

[2] Lilian Reynolds required information about excursion trains on the Midland and Great Central Lines which served the Nottingham region from London.

[3] i.e. as smooth as a Negro song.

[4] We've] I've

And if still there remains anything – I have such elastic ideas of £10 – then[1] you and I we will not pinch a bit in the holiday, eh? – I've had to send a tidy bit to Eastwood, to settle matters there.

Tomorrow we've got a holiday for the sports. I am glad, for I am as tired as a dog. I think I shall go to St Margarets – which is just over Richmond Bridge – and see how Max and Ethel have settled down.[2] It will be a relief, this hot weather, to get into Richmond Park.

How are you: you sounded very sweaty and enervated in your last. But the Welsh sea will pull you together, I am sure.

I shall miss your wretched Quorn post, which goes so early. Tell me how you have gone on: I've been wondering every morning and afternoon. Tell me how you are. Your letters are scroddier[3] even than mine.

Give the girls a kiss round from me (I shall ask them if you did it). I look forward to getting to Quorn again.

And by the briny in a three week's time, we will be veritable Tristan and Isolde. What!

Now I'll rush to post. I kiss you, you flagging hollyhock.

Tell the Time to shuffle along.

Goodbye – goodnight – au revoir –

x Baisers x x x D. H. Lawrence

284. To Helen Corke, [12 July 1911]

Text: MS UT; Unpublished.

12 Colworth
Wednesday midnight

I was not surprised to find your letter when I got back from Dover. Do not be hurt – I am only hasty in wording. Surely, surely it is *my* tenet, that an emotion is genuine even though next day an antagonistic feeling supplants it. What we are to each other, we are. Some of you I should always love. Then again, I must break free. And I *cannot* marry save where I am not held. Even set me down that disgraceful thing, abnormality, so long as you believe me. I love Louie in a certain way that doesn't encroach on my liberty, and I can marry her, and still be alone. I must be so, if I marry – alone in soul, mostly.

What is between you and me is sex. I was good on Saturday so long as I remained just sufficiently dimmed by alcohol. But in the end comes the

1 then] that
2 He went to Dover instead.
3 i.e. scrappier.

irony that you know is stultified passion. And on Sunday, when I hadn't been able to get a drink because like a fool I had come without money, then I was a nuisance. It is wearying.

On Sunday night, after I left you, I threw away, over St James' railway bridge, the two little articles Jones gave me months back, and which were my articles of temptation. It is no use saying that was another little death I died. I am sick of talking.

But I will never ask for sex relationship again, never, unless I can give the dirty coin of marriage: unless it be a prostitute, whom I can love because I'm sorry for her. I cannot stand the sex strain between us – that's all my judgment – And I'll never ask you again, nor anybody. It is a weakness of mine – I can't stand the sex strain. Of course, with a girl like Gussy,[1] it doesn't act – it merely runs by titillation into harmless flirting. But there has been more between you and me.

I have been extraordinarily happy by myself at Dover. There has been nothing to push back, nothing to get ironic over. The moon rose close against my breast. I think I can manage to live alone body and soul as long as must be. Never, never, – and I *can* keep my soul's vows – never never will I ask a woman for anything again: I will pay her market price.

Note that I write at twenty to one, after an excursion: and so discount a great deal of this as sentimentality. Yours – D. H. Lawrence

285. To Louie Burrows, 13 July 1911

Text: MS UN; Boulton 120.

12 Colworth Rd, Addiscombe, Croydon
13 July 1911

My dear Lou,

I am afraid you are falling out with me for not attempting to save. And does 10 quid seem much to you. Pah – it is nothing. Shall I make you out a bill of how I spend it? Shall I say how much goes to Eastwood, what I give Agnes Holt for a wedding present, et cetera. No, my dear – we won't quibble about the money for 'Chrysanthemums'. Remember, my shirts are patched, my boots are – well, not presentable. Hueffer asks me to the Reform Club – I can't go because I've not got a decent suit. Well well – and what is left out of ten mere quid. You haven't told me what to get for your mother, so I am left to my own devices. – I don't chuck money about – ten quid doesn't seem to me a lot of money – but a scroddy bit. – I went to Dover

[1] Unidentified.

yesterday alone – trainfare 2/6 – tea 1/- – oddments, 1/-. I suppose it *was* extravagant. No matter, it's done.

But listen; – if I don't make money in a fairly large sum, I can never save: I have too many calls. So beware – chuck me if you're going to be sick of my failures: but they may be successes.

I can see you're offended.

I'll come up Thursday – today fortnight. We'll meet 'tothers at Nottm. I have promised Kit the Monday Tuesday Wed of our return. They *wont* let me leave Eastwood the moment I get back. I can't help it – I am not able to do first simply what I prefer. There are many ties, many influences.

When I feel you are a bit offended, I'm no good at a letter.

Shall I send you Olive Schreiner's *Woman and Labour*?[1] – the library copy. Say yes at once if you'd care for it, so that you can send it back before the holiday.

It is only a fortnight: such beautiful hot weather – such heavy thick blood! A fortnight seems a lifetime. But it'll come –

Addio D. H. Lawrence

286. To Louie Burrows, [15 July 1911]

Text: MS UN; Boulton 121.

12 Colworth Rd.
Saturday

My dear Lou,

How horrid of me! – I'm awfully sorry. And the tone of your letter in answer was really beautiful, and I love you for it. My dear, it was the answer of a gentlewoman, I fairly rejoice over it. The artist in me rejoices in sympathy with the man. I love you profoundly at this minute. – The profundity of love is a thing that varies, eh?

Oh, I've been writing all day long, 38 pages of a long short story.[2] I've written all day long and all night. And now its ten o clock, I'm going out. I wish you were here – there's nowhere to go.

Nevin is off – can't arrange about the house. Halls are not going. I want to go to France. Write to Ada; let's go abroad. We shall go somewhere, at any rate. I'm glad Halls aren't going. I wish it were here, the holiday. Don't have headaches. I kiss you most sweetly, my dear.

Your lover DHL

[1] This very popular sociological work had been published in February 1911.
[2] See Letter following and n. 1.

287. To Louie Burrows, [16 July 1911]

Text: MS UN; Boulton 121–2.

12 Colworth Rd, Addiscombe, Croydon
Sunday evening

My dear Lou

Well, I've finished the short story – called 'Two Marriages'[1] – and you can see it as soon as you come to Croydon: it's not worth sending by post.

I send you *Woman and Labor*. Parasitism is not bad – nor Woman and War.[2] Myself I skip the rhetoric. But read the book, will you. I think it's worth it. You'll see, it's short.

I wonder what we shall do about the holidays. What fun if we really go abroad after all. What ever we do we'll make a good time out of it. Only a fortnight now – it seems very near, thank goodness.

Excuse me if this is a tiny note – it's late. I hope your headaches are better, and that you've forgiven me my nastiness of the last letter but one: I repent me still: which is a long time for me.

We shall know each other better
When the mists have rolled
away
When the mii-i-ists etc![3]

Lord, that hymn. No, Ive not been to church. Write to Ada, do. Love to everybody.

With my love to you. DHL

288. To Louie Burrows, 17 July 1911

Text: MS UN; Boulton 122–3.

12 Colworth Rd, Addiscombe, Croydon
17 July 1911

My dear Lou,

I am a failure at everything tonight – writing, verse, painting, reading, everything. It is one of the times when one feels as if one were in a 'cachot' or in an 'oubliette'. There's nothing to do but sit and pant – but it's near enough to bed-time. I don't know what's the matter with me this week-end

[1] Later entitled 'Daughters of the Vicar'. On the various stages of this story see Brian Finney, *Studies in Bibliography*, xxviii (Charlottesville, 1975), 329–31.

[2] 'Parasitism' and 'Woman and War' are titles of chapters in Schreiner's book.

[3] By Annie Herbert from Moody and Sankey's famous *Gospel Hymns*.

– I am quite well. But I feel as if I'd got a bandage over my eyes and mouth ugh! I've tried to do a lot of things, and in the end I can only sit still and wait to go to sleep. If you were here! This is one of the times when you are indispensable: this, now, is much less aimiable than death, I swear.

No, I've not done any Paul lately. I've only done a short story.

You got a letter from me this morning, surely. You don't say that you did. And I've sent the book. They will shortly be teasing you with your number of epistles received.

This evening, and last evening it's been ghastly. – But what's the use of talking.

I think it will turn out that we go to France 'en quatre'. You, me, Ada, Neville. – and the second week: that is, sail August 3rd. Will you like it? It is not far off, by calendar.

I am going to bed. You shouldn't make me tell you how dreadful today is, and yesterday.

If I had my way, of course I should have come long ago: or rather, you would be here living with me. But I have no way, at present – and there is no way, at present. But August is very near. It is foolish of me to get like this.

I hope Ethel will have a suave and romantic time.

Goodnight, my love D. H. Lawrence

289. To Louie Burrows, [19 July 1911]
Text: MS UN; Boulton 123–4.

Le Train 5.15.
[19 July 1911]

Ma chère Lou,

Me voici en train pour Londres. C'est aujourd'hui le jour de naissance de ma mère, et je veux l'oublier.

J'ai été un peu frappé de votre lettre. Cependant, je ne suis nullement mis en courroux. Ada s'est decidé d'aller à Prestatyn, en N. Wales, pour le premier quinze jours. Il y aura Ada, moi, et vous. Cela, est il assez pour votre vertu, ou doit on avoir une vielle tigre de femme de plus. N'importe quoi qu'on dit, nous irons, moi, et vous, et Ada, à Prestatyn, le 29 de ce mois. Qu'est ce qu'on veut, donc? Dis nettement à ta[1] mère notre dessein, et ne permets pas de question. Mon dieu – sommes nous des enfants. Il est possible que Neville vienne à Prestatyn pour la seconde semaine. Il a été blessé par un bal de criquet: en ai-je vous parlé? La blessure a été telle qu'on

[1] ta] votre

ne la peut pas nommer. Cependant, il se guérit, et probablement il viendra chez nous en villégiature. Si cela va compliquer la question, en tais toi. Que de sottises! Je n'ai pas compris très exactement ta lettre (Je le trouve difficile à te tutoyer). Est ce que vous voulez dire que votre famille ne croit guère dans mon amour pour vous? Mais pourquoi? – Peut être je me trompe: votre style n'est pas précis.

Nous passons tout près du Crystal Palais. Ce pays ne cesse pas d'être étranger.

En huit jours je vais venir chez vous. Il me parait impossible. Et en dix jours, nous voilà en route pour Wales. Assurément on trouvera Ada assez de chaperon. Ah, quelle sottise!

Comment allez vous – mieux? Je l'espère. Je ne peux pas travailler cette semaine. J'erre par ici, par là, comme un papillon de nuit. Tu devrais aimer un autre que moi, garçon plus solide, plus stupide, plus convenable. Je ne te donnerai que des chagrins.

Il fait très chaud. Nous sommes à New Cross.

Adieu. D. H. Lawrence

[The Train 5.15.

My dear Lou,

Here I am on the train to London. It's my mother's birthday, and I want to forget it.

I was rather perplexed by your letter. But I am not at all angry. Ada has decided to go to Prestatyn, in N. Wales, for the first fortnight. There will be Ada, me, and you. Is that enough to protect your virtue, or must we have an old dragon of a woman as well. Whatever anyone says, we shall be going, I, and you, and Ada, to Prestatyn, on the 29th of this month. Whatever do they want? Tell your mother plainly about our plans, and don't tolerate any questions. My God – are we children. Neville may possibly come to Prestatyn for the second week. He was injured by a cricket ball: did I tell you about it? The injury was such as to be unmentionable. However, he's recovering, and will probably come to stay with us for a holiday. If that's going to complicate things, keep quiet about it. What a lot of nonsense! I didn't fully grasp your letter (I find it difficult to address you as 'tu'). Do you mean that your family scarcely believes in my love for you? But why? – I may be mistaken: your style is not clear.

We are passing very near Crystal Palace. This district always seems to be foreign.

In a week I shall be coming to see you. It seems impossible. And in ten days, we shall be on our way to Wales. Surely Ada will be enough of a chaperone. What a lot of nonsense!

How are you – better? I hope so. I can't work this week. I flit hither and thither like a moth. You should love some fellow other than me, someone more reliable, more dull-witted, more respectable. I'll bring you nothing but sorrow.

It's very hot. We are at New Cross. Goodbye. D. H. Lawrence]

290. To Louie Burrows, 21 July 1911

Text: MS UN; Boulton 124–5.

12 Colworth Rd, Addiscombe, Croydon.
21 July 1911

My dear Lou,

So things do not go so well with you at Coteshael.[1] It is there, if anywhere, that the rub of the change will be felt. But that is not for me to say.

I find I should really have to leave too early to come by the morning excursion on Thursday, so if you will be good enough to send me the excursion ticket I will come in the evening as I have done before. You will not forget the ticket, will you?

I have been thinking that it would be better for me to buy your mother her table cloths in Leicester, while you are there. That would save my carting them from London: and I shall have a month's luggage, – though I'm not bringing many clothes – and also it would prevent my buying the wrong size. So that this day week we will have a days shopping in Leicester: or at least, half an hour's shopping. On Saturday morning we shall be en route for Wales. That will leave us assez peu de temps à Coteshael: qui est ce que nous voulons. I think I would tell them exactly how we are going to Wales: they are sure to ask me, and I shall not trouble to equivocate. But please yourself, only tell me if there is anything I must reserve. Il est tout très stupide.[2]

You will be pleased to hear that Miss Reynolds has got a school in Redhill – about eight miles south of Croydon, in the Reigate district: the average attendance is 150 – salary £110: which is for her a fall of £10, but that is not serious. She commences duties on Sept 4th I think: at any rate, finishes here on Sept 2nd. So you will never stay at Kenella again, I am afraid. Never mind: Mrs Humphreys would always put you up.[3]

[1] Louie Burrows wrote much later: 'I had already been told to choose between home and DHL; while I was at Gaddesby it was easy to be independent' (family letter, 8 February 1962).

[2] 'That will leave us little enough time at Coteshael: which is what we want. . . . It's all very silly.'

[3] Wife of DHL's colleague, Ernest Humphreys.

I send you the MSS of the story that is to appear in the September *English.*[1] I have corrected and returned the proofs. Hope you will like the tale.

It is exceedingly hot here. Coteshael will not be a particularly restful place this weather. I commiserate. Are you flagging again? – is it your 'malaise' which makes votre monde a little bit displeased with you: or have you been venting advanced opinions? You really shouldn't.

Ah well – in a week's time today we shall have done our shopping in Leicester. It seems impossible. We'll laugh at everything in seven days' time – will we not? Good night – love D. H. Lawrence

291. To Louie Burrows, [23 July 1911]

Text: MS UN; PC v. The Thames, Richmond; Postmark, Twi[ckenham] JY 23 11; Boulton 125.

St Margarets on Thames.
[23 July 1911]

Am down here for the week end. Max has got a delightful house, just a meadow down from Richmond. We have been on Eel Pie Island, – open air restaurant, river crowded with boats, and just beginning to twinkle with lights – everybody at the tables and on the terraces, dressed in white – très gai, très charmant. I wish you had been there – but we'll go one day.

DHL

292. To Louie Burrows, 24 July 1911

Text: MS UN; Boulton 126–7.

12 Colworth Rd, Addiscombe, Croydon
24 July 1911

My dear Lou,

That's all right then, if things square themselves out pleasantly for you at Coteshael. I was afraid there was a certain – increasing – amount of incompatibility between you and the rest. I am glad if it is not so. As for your flinging yourself at me – I like you for this frankness – I only wish you flung yourself a bit farther. I wish we were married, could be married. God alone knows when it will be possible. Honestly, my dear, when I think how I may keep you dragging on, I am in a temper, and feel like telling you to give me up. I have not any great hopes of material success:– Which doesn't mean that I'm wallowing in melancholy: simply, I cannot see success on the

[1] 'A Fragment of Stained Glass', in *English Review*, ix (September 1911), 242–51.

horizon, gaze as I may. By success I mean an assured income of £150, and a hundred quid to marry on: oh, that ancient problem, how to arrive at this much! However, tonight I care less than usual whether it's success or just Mean Street which leads down into my future: and by success I mean merely enough to marry on. I *do* want to get married. But damn it all, what's the good of worrying. If you can't eat, why, curse it, starve and have done with it. That's what Neville heroically writes me.

Which ends my tirade for tonight.

Ada wants to know about the railway tickets. I shall write and say to her she is to book us both from Kimberley along with her own ticket, and that we will go to Eastwood on Friday. Do you hear – it will be much more convenient for us to go to Eastwood on Friday afternoon. I shall write and tell Ada we will come then. Do you decide on the train, and inform her of that.

You *do* misuse the English language. How can you write to me '*Won't* you come by the early train.' I *will*. I will come tonight, now, I will hurry off to East Croydon. But I *may* not. We break up on Thursday morning at 12.0. The excursion leaves London at 12.15, Midland. I could not get to St Pancras till 1.15. We are a teacher short:[1] I *cannot* ask for time off. I cannot, cannot come by the early train. Please send me my ticket, and expect me by the 6.25.

Thank you for your eulogium on the 'Stained Glass' story. It is a bit of tour de force, which I don't care for. – the tale I mean.

I had a pleasant time at St Margarets during the week end. The new house I find very charming. We must go there some time.

I shall be quite willing to discuss Olive Schreiner with you. Do not worry, pray, about Parasitism in your own case. If you married me I'm afraid you'd find plenty to do. You'd have to be

'O I am the cook an' the captain bold[2]
And mate of the 'Nancy' Brig.
An' bosun' tight, and the midship-mite
And the crew of the captain's gig'[3]

No – I'd be the 'captain bold' – and you could be all the rest. I fancy you reciting, in rhetoric vein

'O Captain, my Captain, our fearful trip is done.'[4]

But it ain't begun yet.

[1] Miss Rollston had left on 27 May and had not been replaced. [2] bold] too
[3] Sir W. S. Gilbert (1836–1911), 'The Yarn of the Nancy Bell' in *The Bab Ballads* (1869).
[4] Walt Whitman, 'O Captain, My Captain' in *Drumtaps* (1865).

It's actually raining, and the very rain smells musty. If I were capable of an effort, I could write well tonight. But I loathe the thought of effort – I shall read a bit then go to bed.

I wish we were at Prestatyn. Ah well – we groan so often, I wonder 'Time' doesn't refuse to budge. I often remind myself of a half drunk ill-tempered driver bullying the meagre beasts of my own little applecart: but they jog on unheeding, and at last I hear myself, and laugh. Gott – Gott –

Addio, my dear. Ton amant D. H. Lawrence

Ethel[1] sent her love to you – much good may it do you.

293. To Arthur McLeod, [31 July 1911]

Text: MS UT; PC v. Meliden near Prestatyn; Postmark, Prestatyn 31 JY 11; Huxley 9.

'Rosewood' – Victoria Avenue – Prestatyn, N. Wales

[31 July 1911]

We are installed very happily[2] – very pretty place – face N.W. – Gt Ormes a faint smudge crouching down, W., Snowdon, S.W., a big faint smudge standing up between two sons,[3] at the back of two galloping ranges: 3 tone study: extremely geographic: reminds me of your plasticine relief map. The hills jump up a mile from the sea – coast plain flat – shore sandy, blue with sea holly. The tide goes out far off, leaves streaks of water – I've been out bathing both mornings – alone – 'on a wide wide shore'[4] – amid a disagreeable peevish pack of seagulls – felt quite primeval and near to Nature: and swallowed a most ghastly mouthful of deadly brine: the sea is very choppy.

This is quite as good as a Charles Garvice novel[5] – hope you appreciate it. What are you doing?

Vale. D. H. Lawrence

The 'love', à la Garvice, shall come later.

[1] Ethel Hunger.

[2] Louie, Ada and DHL had 'very nice rooms – quiet and good with relatives of a Methodist parson' (Louie to her mother, n.d., MS LaB 223). On 21 August 1911 (MS LaB 200), the landlady, Annie J. Mellor, wrote to Louie suggesting that she and DHL should spend their honeymoon at 'Rosewood' at 'the time of Stoke Wakes'. (Stoke-on-Trent's next Wakes would be 3–10 August 1912; their significance in this context is obscure.) Annie Mellor also mentions a postcard she had received from DHL; it has not been traced.

[3] DHL's description is topographically accurate: from Prestatyn he would see Snowdon between the two smaller peaks of Carnedd Llewelyn and Carnedd Moel-siaeod.

[4] Coleridge, 'The Ancient Mariner', l. 233 ['...wide wide sea'].

[5] Charles Garvice (1851–1920), popular and prolific 'romantic' novelist. Author of *Just a Girl* (1898), *Her Heart's Desire* (1900), *The Heart of a Maid* (1910), etc.

294. To Arthur McLeod, [3 August 1911]

Text: MS UT; PC v. Llandrillo Church, Colwyn Bay; Postmark, [Col]wyn Bay AU 3 11; Unpublished.

[3 August 1911]

We're doing Colwyn and Llandudno today. It's really very pretty and not too hot: rather cloudy, with just a tiny dash of rain very occasionally – ever so nice. You go away tomorrow? Why haven't you sent me a card? – I gave you my address. Have a gay time. Yrs D. H. Lawrence

295. To Louie Burrows, [14 August 1911]

Text: MS UN; PC v. Southwell, The Palace Ruins; Postmark, Eakring 14 AUG 11; Boulton 127–8.

[14 August 1911]

Arrived here about two after a sweltering ride and a flood of cider. It's such a quaint place, Eakring – a bit Ratcliffey, but pretty: red houses among trees like apples in foliage. The school house is attached to the school, which is about twice as big as yours at Ratcliffe.[1] I drink a brew of fermented honey and eat apples. I m changing my name to Corydon or Damon[2] and think of adopting a leopard skin. Southwell is just the same.

Love to all D. H. Lawrence

296. To Louie Burrows, [17 August 1911]

Text: MS UN; PC; Postmark, Eastwood AU 18 11; Boulton 128.

Eastwood –
Thursday night.

I have written to T.A.S[mith] to ask him to let me off from my visit to Lincoln – if he will, I will come to Quorn on Tuesday at the latest: and not before Monday, for Shirebrook[3] is a clinched thing. I'll let you know as soon as Tom writes: I don't want to go to Lincoln now – I don't. Ada is at Leicester – Auntie is not seriously ill. I would liefest of all come to Quorn on Monday. I hope I may. Love DHL

[1] Louie Burrows had returned to Quorn (on 12 August) at the end of their two-week holiday; DHL was now staying at the home of George Holderness, headmaster of Eakring Elementary School, and his daughter Edith.

[2] Rustic figures in pastoral verse.

[3] The home of Alice and Henry Dax.

297. To Louie Burrows, [19 August 1911]

Text: MS UN; PC v. Old School House and Rock Cottages, Shirebrook; Postmark, Shirebrook AU 20 11; Boulton 128.

[19 August 1911][1]

Biked here – a Hell of a place – Mr and Mrs Dax very well. I got your card – you are in a high feather of adventure. Don't get damaged in the riots.[2] I shall get to Quorn on Tuesday if I can.

Love D. H. Lawrence

298. To Louie Burrows, [22 August 1911]

Text: MS UN; PC; Postmark, Eastwood AU 22 11; Boulton 129.

Eastwood –
Tuesday

T.A.S[mith] is rather cross, and won't let me off since this strike is settled.[3] I am sorry, but shall have to go to Lincoln: I had promised so definitely, you see. I will leave on Thursday though. Perhaps I may have to run straight into Leicester from Lincoln – but I'll let you know that later. Do not be cross, I beg you: I can't help it. Go and see Ada – Auntie is rather seriously ill. What a business altogether!

Love to everybody D. H. Lawrence

299. To Louie Burrows, [23 August 1911]

Text: MS UN; PC v. Lincoln Cathedral, Galilee Porch; Postmark, Lincoln AU 23 11; Boulton 129.

3 Colegrave St – Lincoln.
[23 August 1911]

I will come tomorrow by the first train after 6.15 from Arkwright St. I get in the Midland at Nottm at 6.15 p.m.[4] I can't see what train is forward to Quorn. They are fearfully cross with me here for departing so soon – I am in hot water in every direction. T.A.S[mith] is going to slay you when he sees you, and I tell him you are going to slay him: funerals!

My love to everybody – Your renegade D. H. Lawrence

[1] Since the postcard was postmarked 9 a.m. 20 August, it was most probably written on 19th. DHL is unlikely to have cycled to Shirebrook on 20th, written the card and posted it before 9 a.m.

[2] A national railway strike caused rioting in many places including Derby where Louie was staying with her uncle, George Campbell Burrows.

[3] The majority of railwaymen resumed work on 21 August 1911 (*Times* report, 22 August). There were exceptions, however, in the North-Eastern and Midland systems.

[4] DHL would arrive at the Midland Station from Lincoln and leave for Quorn from Arkwright Street Station.

300. To Arthur McLeod, [24 August 1911]

Text: MS UT; PC v. Lincoln, Jew's House; Postmark, Lincoln AU 24 11; Unpublished.

[3 Colegrave Street, Lincoln]
[24 August 1911]

Last day in Lincoln – seen a fire and a riot – such fun.[1] I *dont* want to come back to Croydon.

What misery! Addio D. H. Lawrence

301. To May Holbrook, [24 August 1911]

Text: MS UN; PC v. Lincoln Cathedral, South Porch; Postmark, Lincoln AU 24 11; Nehls, iii. 620.

[3 Colegrave Street, Lincoln]
[24 August 1911]

Last day in Lincoln – seen riot and a fire – great fun. But I'm dreading the return to school. I went to Shirebrook – wonder when I shall see you again.

Addio D. H. Lawrence

302. To Edward Garnett, [25 August 1911]

Text: MS NYPL; Postmark, Leicester AUG 25 11; Huxley 9–10.

'Coteshael', Cheveney Lane, Quorn, Leicestershire
[25 August 1911]

Edward Garnett Esq.[2]

Dear Sir,

Many thanks for your letter, which I have not received until today, as I have been moving about.

I have several short stories[3] which I shall be very pleased to send to you

[1] Lincoln suffered serious public disturbances consequent on the railway strike: the Midland Railway Co. offices were set on fire; shops were looted; troops were called out.

[2] Edward Garnett (1868–1937), critic, essayist and dramatist. Son of Dr Richard Garnett, Keeper of Books at the British Museum. Literary adviser to several publishing firms: to Fisher Unwin, Heinemann, Cape and, at the time of meeting DHL, Duckworth. Encouraged and helped to publicise Conrad and Galsworthy (who thought him 'one of the greatest of English critics') as well as DHL. Author of *An Imaged World* (poems – 1894), *Hogarth* (1911), *Turgenev* (1917), *Friday Nights* (essays – 1922), *The Trial of Jeanne D'Arc and other Plays* (1931), etc. Lived at the Cearne, near Edenbridge, Kent, and in London at 19 Grove Place, Hampstead. (See *Times* obituary 22 February 1937; Carolyn G. Heilbrun, *The Garnett Family*, 1961.)

[3] Stories known to have been written by this date were:
'A Fragment of Stained Glass' (formerly 'Legend');
'The White Stocking';
'A Prelude';
'The Vicar's Garden' (later 'The Shadow in the Rose Garden');
'Lessford's Rabbits';
'A Lesson on a Tortoise';

for your approval on behalf of the Century Co,[1] in a week or so, when I shall be back in Croydon. I have promised to give the publisher a book of short stories for next Spring. If the Century Co should honour me by accepting any of my work, they would allow me to use their stories for the book?

When I get back to Croydon, I will make haste to send you some stuff,

Yours truly D. H. Lawrence

303. To Louie Burrows, 29 August 1911

Text: MS UN; Boulton 130–1.

12 Colworth Rd, Addiscombe, Croydon
29 Aug 1911

My dear Lou,

Two days of school over – and I must say they have been pretty rotten. My new kids – well, they are not my old ones: and I have 50 – and, at the bottom, I don't like teaching – it wearies me to death. Amen.

How have you gone on with your fleas, all slippers and tongues, is it?

I find Colworth queer after a month of absence. Mr and Mrs Jones are very quiet – not on the very best of terms. Mary is the wildest and rampagest kid on the face of the earth. I have just sported with her for an hour: she's a real brick. I popped her in the back yard at tea-time, and she howled till Addiscombe re-echoed. But all the neighbourhood knows Marys howl by now: if not, it ought. I've been reading William Morris' 'Defence of Guinevere etc'. Do you know, I am rather fond of Morris. That should please you. And then Mrs Jones has been telling me things – very un-Morris-like: marital and faintly horrifying.

I had back the play that Hueffer had sent to Granville Barker[2] – with a 'read it with much interest but afraid I don't want it' note. Hueffer has gone again to Germany. I hope you haven't expected the Lincoln bit

'Goose Fair' (published February 1910);
'Odour of Chrysathemums' (published June 1911);
'A Modern Lover' (formerly 'The Virtuous');
'The Fly in the Ointment' (formerly 'A Blot');
'Second Best';
'Intimacy' (later 'The Witch à la Mode');
'The Old Adam';
'Two Marriages' (later 'Daughters of the Vicar').

[1] A New York publishing house.

[2] The play sent to the dramatist and critic Harley Granville-Barker (1877–1946) was probably an early version of *The Widowing of Mrs. Holroyd*, itself an expansion of DHL's story 'Odour of Chrysanthemums'.

in the *Daily News*:[1] it won't come now: that, however, I dont mind, myself.

I am just going to do another story for Austin Harrison. I did one last night – I will send him a couple. Then some for Edward Garnett.

I feel very unsettled. I should like to lift up my feet and depart again from here – to Hades or elsewhere, I don't mind. Really, I think I shall have to turn that proverbial tramp.

It is not that it seems a long time since Sunday, but that everything further than an hour back seems fictional – all a mere drift of a tale. I really must begin to suck permanency out of something. I suppose it'll have to be work: so I'll begin. Prosper with your wood carving – be busy, it'll keep you happy.[2]

Goodbye – love D. H. Lawrence

304. To Louie Burrows, 1 September 1911

Text: MS UN; Boulton 131–2.

12 Colworth Rd, Addiscombe, Croydon
1st September 1911

My dear Lou,

I'm glad your school is going to turn out another Gaddesby – let me write in pencil, will you, I want to write on my knee. – My kids aren't horrid – only different and rather stupid, and I hate being back in school because of the confinement – nothing else. And it's not so bad at all these later days.

I am interested to hear of the wood-carving. I know how those gouges do score out lumps. Sometimes when the boys are doing wood carving in the workroom I have a go myself, if the kid's a raw one. But it's a thing, so it seems to me, in which one can acquire a fine nicety of touch. I will paint you a Fisherwoman when I get a bit of time.[3] I did not mean I had written a new story on Monday, but I've done one up. I sent two, yesterday evening, to Austin Harrison. I was advised to send something to Edward Garnett for his approval for the *Century*, an American mag. Tonight and tomorrow I am going to spend doing up a couple for him.[4] I will let you know if anything comes of it. I am glad you feel sure of soon prosperity: my prophetic instinct isn't working just at present. I am using my vol of Morris in school just now – Mac[Leod] gave it me – but I will send it you later on. You will like it, I think.

1 Presumably DHL offered to the *Daily News* an account of his experiences in Lincoln.

2 This was an interest inherited from Louie's father who was a skilled wood-carver (see Boulton x).

3 Cf. p. 273, Letter 272 and n. 1.

4 One was 'Intimacy' (cf. Letter 312). None of DHL's works appeared in the *Century*.

It is most exquisite weather here – most beautiful. It would be rich if you were here. But then we should only be falling into a conflict of unaccomplished passion, so perhaps it's as well. I'm wondering about your coming down to London this term. I must get somebody here to take you in – Mrs Humphreys or somebody. I'm not keen for you to come to Colworth, and I don't like fragments of days ripped off. However, it's full early to bother – we're only a week back.

If you happen to be in Leicester and to pass that bookshop, will you look if there still remains that volume of verse by Jean Moréas,[1] which I hesitated over and didn't buy – to my eternal regret. A volume of verse has the value of several days' life: and this is only 6d.

I've got to work when I don't want. I'm simply topsy turvy with lovingness – every woman I meet I think looks sweet and kissable – not that I want to kiss her – but – and here I am – nothing but ink.

Jones is playing Miserere Domine, and singing it falsetto. He'll borrow a dollar from me in half an hour.

Goodnight – je t'embrasse. D. H. Lawrence

305. To Louie Burrows, 7 September 1911

Text: MS UN; Boulton 132–3.

Davidson Rd Boys School, South Norwood, SE
7 Sept 1911

My dear Lou,

I have just finished marking my science books. Oh Lord, what a fag! These close afternoons, it is enough to keep oneself alive, without bothering correcting books and kids. But the class is in quite comfortable order again – settling down. Oh, we're all serene.

Today I've got 14 boys away. The Cherry Blossom Boot Polish people are giving a free day at the Palace,[2] so half Croydon has trooped off. You can get in with a tin lid, or something like that. Mrs Jones has gone with the kids, so I shall have a quiet night of work. I have had two off nights – one at a party of one of the teachers – Tuesday – and I was out to tea down Kenley last night. I really must get a bit of writing done, though I don't feel much like it. I feel like wandering and dodging about.

On Saturday Laura Macartney is giving one of her famous music parties.

[1] Jean (Papadiamantopoulos) Moréas (1856–1910), French poet. Author of *Les Syrtes* (1884), *Cantilènes* (1886), *Les Stances* (1899), etc. (See *English Review*, v (May 1910), 377–84 for obituary and appreciation.)

[2] i.e. Crystal Palace.

It will be jolly, but I'd rather go as I did last week right down into the country and pick blackberries. It was really fine down at Leith Hill.

I haven't got a bit of literary news – I've not written anything: Hueffer has gone to Germany: Harrison has gone to Paris, but will be back sometime next week. I have not had a letter for two days, which is a miracle for me.

How funny that the folk in Hilda's sanatorium should be so poor. I thought surely she would be among the swells there. I am sorry she's got no pals. Yes, I will certainly write her. It makes me sorry I dropped my N[ational] U[nion] [of] T[eachers] subscription – I did it all unknowing when I was at Eastwood last fall – when I hear how good they have been to her.[1] I am glad to hear of it. What's Nell Slater like – just the same?[2] Is there no news of the Coll folk to be told?

It is very hot down here. I think of you and wonder if Quorn is the same. Everybody flags, even I, in the afternoon. It is a weariness of the flesh[3] to teach and make efforts in the heat. – What a joke you have got a sudden desire for dress. Well – I can make myself fairly smart just now, to keep you company. Addio – je vous embrasse. D. H. Lawrence

306. To Edward Garnett, 10 September 1911

Text: MS NYPL; Huxley 10.

12 Colworth Rd, Addiscombe, Croydon
10 Sept 1911

Edward Garnett Esq.
Dear Sir,

I beg to send you the accompanying two stories for your approval on behalf of the Century Co. I am afraid they may not be of the requisite length: as for the kind of thing, would you mind telling me if these are suitable. If not, I must do up something else. I have not very much time for writing.

I shall be very glad if you can dispose of a little of me in the *Century*. Certainly, my work is not in demand. And if, anytime, you would give me a word of criticism on my MSS, I should go with surer feet.

I thank you for giving me your consideration.

Yours Sincerely D. H. Lawrence

[1] Hilda Shaw would benefit from the National Union of Teachers' Benevolent Fund.
[2] Mary Ellen Slater qualified as a teacher along with DHL, Louie Burrows and Hilda Shaw.
[3] Ecclesiastes xii. 12.

307. To Louie Burrows, 11 September 1911

Text: MS UN; Boulton 133–4.

12 Colworth Rd, Addiscombe, Croydon
11[1] Sept 1911

My dear Lou,

How funny, I bungled at the date![2] I got your parcel at breakfast this morning. The clock made me laugh. Why a clock, O impulsive! But it is very pretty: it will adorn your bedroom sweetly. I should always call the rooms yours. It seems to me inconceivable that I should own property: a house. It will have to be yours. The serviette ring is just as I like it – nice and severe in cut. It will accompany me through the ages, I hope: and you will be so used to setting it by my plate. How strange it all seems, stranger than the stories I write, by far. And the strangeness is fascinating too. I wonder, when will it be that you will take my serviette out of our sideboard, and lay it beside my place[3] for dinner. I cannot believe it – but I wish it were here. I wish we had a home in the country, away from school. The boys are all right, only issued from God a good deal below sterling intelligence: but they are nice enough. Only school trammels me and makes me feel as if I can't breathe.

Emily sent me some handkerchiefs, and Mrs Jones gave me some. Ada is going to send me a dressing gown. She insists.

I sent last night two stories to Edward Garnett. I wonder, will he accept. The *Century* would pay well. But the stories are not of the length he wished. That I cannot help. I am going to write another short story tonight, or part of one.

I hope Loughboro fair won't come too near to Goose Fair. You know my brother George is coming down here then. You must find out, and tell me, and we will have a wild time.

Do not think Laura Macartneys music is wonderful: it is not. She only plays well. We had a jolly time at the party.[4] This week, no parties. I think I shall manage to work a good bit.

Mrs Jones' mother has come.[5] She is old, over seventy. It is a great age to be coming sight seeing. And this week, I think, while she is here, we are going to move to No. 16 Colworth.

There, the light is nearly gone. I wish, in some little country house of our own, you were lighting the lamp for me. Mein Gott!

I kiss you. D. H. Lawrence

[1] 11] 21
[2] DHL's birthday.
[3] place] plate
[4] This may be the occasion described by Helen Corke, *In Our Infancy*, p. 210.
[5] Mrs Mary Blaylock (who lived in Liverpool).

308. To Helen Corke, [12 September 1911]

Text: MS Corke; Unpublished.

[12 Colworth Road, Addiscombe, Croydon]
[12 September 1911]

As for Louie's claim on me it is I who discount it, not you.[1]

309. To Louie Burrows, 15 September 1911

Text: MS UN; Boulton 134–5.

Davidson Rd Boys School, South Norwood, SE.
15 Sept 1911

My dear Lou,

You will not mind if I write to you from school. Somehow, I feel more like writing you from Davidson than from Colworth.

We have had a fine old rousing week: four inspectors in for two days.[2] Of course they're all all right: in fact they are rather flattering – and very considerate indeed. But it mucks up the work so. As a matter of fact, I am rather tired of school. There are so many things I want to do, and can't. I can't settle down of an evening nowadays. This week I haven't written a scrap. Should you be cross if I were to – and I don't say I shall – try to get hold of enough literary work, journalism or what not, to keep me going without school. Of course, it's a bit risky, but for myself I don't mind risk – like it. And then, if I get on with literature, I can increase my income, which is a process so slow at [ ][3] to be discreditable. I may try: I'll tell you when [I] do: I am really rather, – very – sick of teaching when I want to do something else.

But don't think of this seriously. It is only a small idea.

I was pleased to get Ethel's card. Neither of you tells me when Loughboro wakes comes.[4] I think it's the Goose Fair in a three week (is it?). I haven't written to George. I must do so.

After all we shall not get the removal over this week, owing, I think, to

[1] This extract was supplied by Helen Corke before the MS was destroyed.

[2] The School Log records a visit by W. K. Spencer and colleagues on 13 and 14 September 1911. A congratulatory report on the Inspectors' visit was received from G. A. Turner, H.M. Inspector, on 11 October 1911. No individual teacher was mentioned by name but DHL's work was referred to in the remark: 'The Drawing reaches a high standard. The brush drawing of the Upper Class shows unusually bold and vigorous treatment.' (The headmaster, Philip F. T. Smith, testified that DHL 'particularly directed the art training of the upper divisions' and that the Inspectors' report highly commended the results. Lawrence–Gelder 95–6.)

[3] MS torn.

[4] A three-day local festivity beginning on the Thursday nearest to 11 November.

the plumbers. It is very stupid. The new house is painted, and looks very nice. It is almost exactly the same as No. 12. We shall go in some time next week.

Last night I was at Humphreys to tea. They have staying with them a young French girl of about 15, who would serve me in good stead for practice of my French, but she is very stupid and wordless. We went to the Picture Palace in the evening, and I was nearly killed with laughing. Really, they are very daft, these pictures. But as they get more melodrama and intensity into the gestures, they get the humanity out. It is a pity. Now, it is often rather like pictures of wonderful marionettes – the individuality is gone. – It is a day, sunny and cloudy and fresh, rather like March. When *is* Loughboro wakes?

Je vous embrasse.

310. To Louie Burrows, 21 September 1911

Text: MS UN; Boulton 135–6.

12 Colworth Rd, Addiscombe, Croydon
21 Sept 1911

My dear Lou,

I shall have to snatch this dinner hour for a letter or else goodness knows when you'll hear from me. We're in the last anguish of removal. I sit in a stark room, bare floor, bare walls, and[1] the poor little isolation of a dinner table with its chairs creeping under it, all forlorn. I've just got ten minutes to write you. Tonight Mrs Humphreys is giving a little party, and I've promised to go. I was out Tuesday and last night. I feel quite a gad-about. Tonight the last goods are going to No 16, all but the beds. Tomorrow night I shall work at house arrangements like the deuce. I shall have all pictures to hang and books to arrange and so on and so on. By Jove, what a life.

Edward Garnett sent me back the *Century* Stories because they aren't suitable to the stupid American taste. I am to write something more objective, more ordinary. I shall when I do – when I have time.

Last night I dined with Austin Harrison at the Pall Mall Restaurant – quite swelly. After dinner we went to the Haymarket. Harrison had got seats. *Bunty Pulls the Strings* is the play, a delightful comedy[2] on Scotch manners of 1845 (circa).[3] The play amused me very much. Harrison is very friendly.

[1] and] with

[2] comedy] Scot

[3] The very popular play by Graham Moffat (1866–1951). (First performed on 4 July 1911, it was reviewed as one of the 'Plays of the Month' in *English Review*, ix (October 1911), 525–6.)

He suggests that I do a bit of reviewing for the *English*. I think I shall. He bids me select from the forthcoming books one I should like to review. What shall it be?

Garnett – who is a very well known littérateur, editor of big things like the World's Famous Literature,[1] wants me to go and see him and take lunch with him some Wednesday or Tuesday. Unfortunately the day is wrong for me. I will try to go some time or other.

I think this is all the news – except Harrison says he'll make me an appointment to meet Frank Harris at dinner next week.[2] But I'm not keen a bit on being a swell – I'd rather not bother to go.

I'm sorry the bookbinding has gone pop. But there 'the best laid schemes' etc etc.[3] Mine all go up the flue. I shall be jolly glad when we're settled in peace again. George hasn't written me yet to say he'll come at the Fair. He's very dilatory. I hope I s'll have some money for Loughboro Wakes – I must mind my p's and q's. What a penniless set we are. Oh, that house in the country! Where on the map of Fate is it?

I *must* answer Eth's card – my love to her.

I'm sorry to scramble the letter so –

Love D. H. Lawrence

I'll send you this month's *English* when we get settled.[4]

311. To Louie Burrows, 25 September 1911

Text: MS UN; Boulton 137–8.

Davidson Rd Boys School, South Norwood, SE
25 Sept 1911

My dear Lou,

You sound désesperé – what's up? Is it the remoteness of Loughboro fair. We'll stalk it, and wing it yet.

We're safe in 16 – it'll be comfy by and by. Why should Garnett see us flitting, by the way? – and he's not great, and I should certainly tell him myself that he'd have to invite me other days than Tuesdays or Wednesdays, if I were mad on seeing him. But I'll contrive to get an hour off some Wednesday – and I'll try to send him something American (God help me) – what have I got to say to Harrison? – at any rate I'll say it. I am sure I listen to you – but what do you want me specially to heed.

[1] The editor of *The International Library of Famous Literature* was Edward's father, Richard Garnett. Cf. p. 50 n. 2.

[2] Frank Harris (1856–1931), editor, journalist and author.

[3] Burns, 'To a Mouse', l. 39.

[4] The September issue contained 'A Fragment of Stained Glass'.

I've got a cold like hell – that's flitting – feel as if my long pipe[1] were a stove chimney got red hot. Dear o me, what a state! And now you'll have more injunctions to give me. But the cold'll be better by your next letter.

I'm not going to frivol this week. If Harrison doesn't want me to dinner on Tuesday, I'm going to hear Moody-Manners folk murder *Samson and Dalila* in Croydon.[2] That's all I m going out – unless I go to Scott's to hear him brilliantly render Grieg on the piano. He's only a young chap of 18, swotting BA – a good, individual pianist, though.[3] Perhaps he'll make a mark. I'm not keen on Grieg, though.

I dont know whether George is coming at Goose Fair – he won't answer yes or no. But he'll come. After that, perhaps you'll come, if you have any cash. I shall have some when I m paid for the next story. I think Ada intends a visit this autumn. She sent me her photo – the Leicester one. It is jolly good, but she looks older.[4] Will you have your photo taken, a decent sized one, not midget.

It is rather a bother to get translation work. The only thing for Miss Rutter[5] to do would be to translate part of some work she admires – or a short story – and send it to a publisher, with stamps for return, as a specimen of her cleverness in rendering French style into English. If she wants to do fiction, she d better try Wm Heinemann or Methuen – or if it's anything racy, John Long; if it's essays, Duckworth or Martin Secker or Dent; if its Drama – well, drama's a bit risky; if its philosophy – a complete Montaigne, for instance – then 'The Open Court'[6] – or Macmillan. You see, there's the French copyright to arrange, then the English publisher, then the translator's fee. It's a bit of a toil, but with patience, and an admirable specimen, she might do all right. But literature is a toil and a snare, a curse that bites deep, and Miss Rutter is wise to avoid it.

Having a bit of a cold, and being a bit tired, makes one a bad, distant letter writer. But count your damson stones – this year, next year, sometime, never – mine usually come this year. You like tokens. I would be glad if this fulfilled itself – I would be glad enough for the house in the country – God knows. Be happy – I kiss you with all my heart. I will get some work done – that is the only way.

Love D. H. Lawrence

[1] pipe] pipes
[2] A performance of the opera by Camille Saint-Saëns (1835–1921) was given by the Moody-Manners company at the Grand Theatre, Croydon, on 26 September 1911.
[3] Not identified.
[4] older] very
[5] The daugher of a tailor at Loughborough.
[6] The British subsidiary, recently established at 149 Strand, of a Chicago publishing house.

312. To Edward Garnett, 25 September 1911

Text: MS NYPL; Huxley 10–11.

16 Colworth Rd, Addiscombe, Croydon
25 Sept 1911

Edward Garnett Esq.
Dear Sir,

I received your letter with the stories the other day. Thanks for the advice concerning 'Intimacy'. I myself had felt the drag of the tale, and its slowness in accumulating.

I send you this, which, I think, would easily split up into three.[1] It is only the first writing, rough, and not sufficiently selective. Bear with me if the first part is tedious – there are, I think, good bits later on. I tried to do something sufficiently emotional, and moral, and – oh, American! I'm not a great success. If you think this is really any good for the *Century*, I will revise it, and have it typed. But if it's not fairly hopeful, I won't have it typed out. I am badly off.

I also should like to – to be seen, if you will have it so. But I teach in school, in Croydon. I will try to get an hour off, and will call on you at Messrs Duckworth's next week – 3rd or 4th of October – if you wish. I hardly like foisting this lump of MSS on anybody.

Yours Sincerely D. H. Lawrence

313. To Edward Garnett, 2 October 1911

Text: MS NYPL; Postmark, Croydon OC 2 11; Huxley 11.

16 Colworth Rd, Addiscombe, Croydon
2nd October 1911

Dear Mr Garnett,

Thanks for the return of 'Two Marriages' with such good hopes. I am doing it up, will split it in three, and will keep it between 12 and 15 thousand words.

I will come to Messrs Duckworths on Wednesday, if it is your pleasure. My train will be in Charing Cross 12.58, so I shall not be very late at Henrietta Street – if you will allow me a minute or two. I shall have to depart again from Charing Cross at 2.6 – am sorry I must stick so strictly within the bounds of an hour.

Yours Sincerely D. H. Lawrence

[1] The story in question was 'Two Marriages' (cf. p. 288, Letter 287 and n. 1).

314. To Louie Burrows, 2 October 1911

Text: MS UN; Boulton 138–9.

16 Colworth Rd, Addiscombe, Croydon
2 Oct 1911

My dear Lou,

I was glad to hear you restored to exuberance again in your last letter. Certainly it is good luck to have got the school: if it's not too much work. I think night schools are a frightful fag. But you are taking it very nicely – I congratulate you. I hope it will again be like a family – or friendly – gathering. I will send you some drawings later on – when you've started. But my things as you know are very rough and, I am afraid, hardly good models to set before meticulous village girls. However, you'll have your way.

I've been bowing my head and been quite subservient – sent Garnett a long – 3 part story which he thinks the *Century* may accept when I've had it typed out, and I've promised to go and lunch with him on Wednesday. Now do not be excited, nothing tremendous will happen. He is merely curious to see what sort of animal I am – and I'm willing to be seen. Nothing more. But he's very nice.

Yesterday I had a ripping time – went to Peckham to tea and for the evening to Miss Herbert's – German lady, 45 (circa), quite ordinary. She lives with her brother-in-law Franklin – an elderly but brisk German, a bit of a bounder, speaks 7 languages, travelled God knows where.[1] There was there a Portuguese lady from Brazil – with her husband. She spoke hardly any English, so we chattered in French. She is the most exquisite woman pianist I have ever heard. She played me Chopin's 'Nocturnes' – which I love exceedingly 'Quelque chose de triste et un peu ironique pour vous',[2] as she said, smiling. She was very good looking, and 'vive' – about 26. She is giving a recital in the Bechstein Hall on Thursday.[3] I shall go if I can. But probably George is coming – I think he will. He is a model of indecision. If I don't have to meet him at the wrong hour, I shall go to the Bechstein, to hear[4] Mrs Miller.

It is very wintry, and cold now. You will be glad. Do you keep pretty well? – you have not told me. I am all right – there's no news.

I should like you to hear Antonietta Miller play Debussy's *Jardin sous la*

[1] Emma Herbert and her brother-in-law Edgar James Franklin (b. 1841 in Berlin) lived at 122 Peckham Park Road. Franklin (naturalised 1 January 1887) was a free-lance export-import agent and possibly a business associate of Fritz Krenkow or Max Hunger.

[2] 'Something sad and slightly ironic for you.'

[3] Antonietta Rudge-Miller (from San Paulo, Brazil) performed at the Bechstein on 5 October.

[4] hear] see

Pluie. I am so busy revising 'Two Marriages' for the type-writer.[1] What a rush this life is.

Goodbye – je t'embrasse, ma chère. D. H. Lawrence

315. To Edward Garnett, 6 October 1911

Text: MS NYPL; Huxley 11–12.

16 Colworth Rd, Addiscombe, Croydon
6 Oct. 1911

Dear Mr Garnett,

I send you this, the one play I have at home.[2] I have written to Mr Hueffer for the other two.[3] This is the least literary – and the least unified of the three. I tried to write for the stage – I tried to make it end up stagily. – If I send it you at once, you can read it at your leisure. The first scenes are good.

The MSS of the story is with the type writer. As soon as it comes back I will send it on – and I can tell you of the time I shall arrive at the 'Cearne' – this time next week. I look forward to it.

Yours Sincerely D. H. Lawrence

316. To Louie Burrows, 10 October 1911

Text: MS UN; Postmark, Croydon OC 10 11; Boulton 139–41.

16 Colworth Rd, Addiscombe, Croydon
10 Oct 1911

My dear Lou,

You've waited a long while for my letter. George's visit fagged me frightfully – chasing round.

I saw Garnett on Wednesday. He's quite sweet. I am going to stay with him this week-end at Edenbridge, Kent. He's going to try and get me published a vol of verse, for Spring[4] – and would also get the three plays placed, for publishing – only two of them are missing. I sent them to Hueffer, as you know, before the holiday. And last night I had a letter from Hueffer to say he'd never had them and that he didn't know anything about them – and he's married Violet Hunt.[5] However, no doubt the plays will turn up.

[1] The typist referred to here and in subsequent letters was Arthur Stanley Corke (see p. 168 n. 4).

[2] *The Widowing of Mrs. Holroyd.*

[3] *A Collier's Friday Night* and 'The Merry-go-Round'. (The MS of the second bears Ford Madox Hueffer's name in pencil; see Tedlock, *Lawrence MSS* 117.)

[4] DHL's first volume of verse, *Love Poems and Others*, was published by Duckworth, but not until 1913.

[5] Hueffer secured a 'divorce' in Germany and 'married' Violet Hunt, but subsequently both proved invalid.

While Garnett and I were having lunch who should come in the place but Atkinson, Heinemanns man. Garnett doesn't like Heinemann's people, so he was beastly sarky with him. I hate Atkinson – I don't go to Heinemanns because I don't like the sneering, affected little fellow. But he made me promise to call there. I did last Thursday. It appears my contract with Heinemann was for yearly payment – so the *Peacock* money is not justly due till February.[1] They owe me £40 – and Atkinson said they'd send me on a cheque. It's not come yet. I shall put it all away, if I can. I shall probably lend it Auntie, to make up her partnership share.[2] I am afraid I have offended Heinemann's people mortally. I haven't done a stroke of Paul for months – don't want to touch it. They are mad, and they are sneery. I don't like them.

George and I had a very hustling time if nothing else. We went to *Sumurun*, the wordless play at the Savoy, on Saturday evening. I liked it very much.[3] On Sunday we were at St Paul's for part of the afternoon service; at the City Temple, hearing R J Campbell in the evening.[4] I liked him all right, but I could preach as well myself. But it was as good a sermon as you'd hear in England – on the positivity of death. George didn't care for it.

I am very busy now getting verse ready to take to Garnett on Friday. Life is such a rush with me. I haven't time to think of anything but the things that are pressing close around.

I should think that this Spring will give me a bit of a reputation. I hope the dramas will turn up. I should be angry were they lost. It is just like Hueffer.

For half an hour, I've got the house to myself. I am fagged after the weariness of George's visit. I must get some of that stuff done. I am in quite good health – how is your cold? – better, I hope. Don't talk about cossetting. I feel as if I should never know a bit of quiet, neglectful cossetty life again. I am swallowed up in worrying through my affairs – not worrying *about* them, I don't do that.

When is Loughboro wakes? I am in debt. I hope the *English* or Heinemann will send me a cheque soon.

[1] DHL's contract with Heinemann allowed for royalties to be paid 'on or before Midsummer Day in each year'.

[2] This was likely to be in a hosiery company. Fritz Krenkow was cashier for Messrs Herbert L. Driver Ltd, Hosiery Manufacturers, Leicester.

[3] 'Since the Bacchanale of Pávlova and Mordkin, London has seen no such beautiful and artistic a thing as the Persian fantasia on *The Arabian Nights*, called *Sumurūn*, now played by Max Reinhardt's company from the Deutsches Theater at the Coliseum' (*English Review*, vii (March 1911), 745).

[4] See p. 37 and n. 2.

You shall see the Christmas shops – bien! These pressures of one thing and another make me feel very affairé. I cannot imagine myself looking at Christmas shops.

But that'll come like everything else. Ah well – goodbye – It is goodness knows how far to Quorn. Addio D. H. Lawrence

317. To Edward Garnett, 11 October 1911

Text: MS NYPL; Postmark, Croydon OC 11 11; Unpublished.

16 Colworth Rd, Addiscombe, Croydon
11 Oct 1911

Dear Mr Garnett,

I will come to the 'Cearne' on Friday evening by the train which arrives in Oxted at 6.32. Do not trouble to meet me at all – I shall like the walk.

The verses I will bring with me – or at least some of them. The other two plays, I hear from Mr Hueffer, are gone astray. He doesn't know where they are. But they'll turn up. The wretched type writer hasn't returned the story yet.

I look forward to Friday. Yours Sincerely D. H. Lawrence

318. To May Holbrook, 11 October 1911

Text: MS UN; Nehls, iii. 620–1.

16 Colworth Rd, Addiscombe, Croydon
11 Oct 1911

My dear May,

It was nice of you to send me the eggs – they are scarce as gold here. They are bonny ones, too. But ye should sell 'em, my dear, not waste 'em on the likes o' me.

I have had the most wearisome week end, rushing round with George. Rush, rush its one big struggle, nowadays, to get things done. It's eleven now, at night. I've been working since 7.0, at verse, getting it ready to take to Edward Garnett on Friday. Oh my dear Lord, I am so tired. I tell you what I should like, now. You know we're living here in the kitchen, small and bare and ugly, because the electric isn't connected up – all too poor to have it done – truth. I should like a small house of my own – small as yours[1] – one warm, sweet room – a woman who loved me to rest me. God! And night after night one stumbles up, half blind with work or with wastefulness – ah bosh.

[1] According to Jessie Chambers (E.T. 205) DHL particularly liked her sister May's cottage.

Jones is just jawing me how to make my fortune in literature. I listen patiently, then resume my pencil. I have worked all night at verse – you don't know what that means. Life is a bit disproportionate, don't you think – either all struggle and bludgeoning and battle by oneself, or dependence, and ease, with overmuch softness of rest. This week, I am very tired. But I shall work it off.

I am wondering if I shall see you at Christmas. I may not be near Eastwood – What a long time.

I had a letter tonight, from an admirer of the *White Peacock* – saying Mrs Thurston, the lady novelist who died a while back, read my book a short time before her death, and thought it so beautiful, and was so much moved by it.[1] She is dead – and she read the *Peacock* – and mother never read it. How funny everything is.

I will go to bed – Goodbye D. H. Lawrence

319. To Maud Villiers-Stuart, 12 October 1911

Text: AMSC NWU; Huxley 12.

12 Colworth Road, Addiscombe, Croydon
12 Oct 1911

Dear Madam,[2]

I read your letter with considerable feeling.[3] I remember very well the death of Mrs Thurston: I was sorry. *John Chilcote* is the only one of her books that I have read, but that I admire sincerely. It seems very strange that a discriminating soul like Mrs Thurston's has read *The White Peacock*, and

[1] Katherine Cecil Thurston (1875–1911), author of *The Circle* (1903), *John Chilcote, M.P.* (1904), *The Gambler* (1905), etc.

[2] Maud Villiers-Stuart, née Hutcheson (1867–1943), from Columbus, Ohio; m. Gerald Villiers-Stuart, author and playwright. They lived at Richmond House, Co. Waterford, Ireland. Both were closely connected with the Irish and London literary scenes. (The text of this letter follows that of a copy of DHL's MS made by Mrs Villiers-Stuart.)

[3] Richmond-Cappoquin
County Waterford – Ireland.

October 1911

Dear Mr Lawrence

I cannot resist writing a few lines to you though I am a complete stranger. I thought perhaps it would give you pleasure to know that Mrs Thurston (the novelist) spoke of your book to me as 'wonderful'. She offered to lend it to me and said 'You must read it at once'. As I was going to Venice I told her I would read it when I came back. I never saw her again – as you know she died quite recently and tragically. I have just finished the book which I read with peculiar interest. I understand *her* feeling for *The White Peacock*.

Yours Sincerely Maud Villiers-Stuart.

now is gone away into Death. It makes me wonder at life. I am glad you told me. The publishing of the book has brought me very little but bitterness. A good many folk have been hostile – practically all America:[1] and my Mother died a few days before it was published. My health, and time, haven't allowed me to get on very well with the second novel. But in Spring there will be a book of short stories, and I trust, a volume of verse – my dearest treasure. I hope these may give you a little pleasure.

I thank you for your appreciation.

Yours Sincerely D. H. Lawrence

320. To Ada Lawrence, 12 October 1911

Text: MS Clarke; cited in Lawrence–Gelder 91–2.

Davidson Rd Boys School, South Norwood, SE.
12 Oct 1911

My dear Ada,

You'll be grumbling at me again. But I seem to have so small time for letters.

I have just remembered I owe you the insurance.[2] If I send this quid it will go on a few weeks more – and, if you have paid the tanners, you will have been saving money. They gave me £10 for the story.[3] I am going to pay for some MS. typing, then I shall save the rest against Christmas, and against my visit to Quorn. I am running down there in a week or two's time, for the week end.

What shall we do at Christmas, by the way? I should like to go somewhere seasidey, yet somewhere whose folk we know, so that we could share their christmas. I can only think of Agnes Holt. How would you like to go to Ramsey?[4] – for Christmas? Let us begin and arrange – this is the seventh week back at school. Can you think of anything. I don't know whether Louie would come – I suppose she wouldn't.

You know I'm going to Garnetts this week end. It'll be nice, I think. I heard from Hueffer in Germany the other day. He's married Violet Hunt over there. She writes me very sweetly. I shall visit her in London.

[1] An exaggeration: the *New York Times*, 9 June 1911, for example, considered the novel, though too long, 'one of remarkable power'. The reviewer felt like that 'Watcher of the skies,/When a new planet swims into his ken.'

[2] Cf. Letter 280.

[3] Presumably for 'A Fragment of Stained Glass', published in *English Review*, September 1911. £10 was the same fee as the *Review* paid for 'Odour of Chrysanthemums' (see p. 282 n. 4).

[4] Agnes Holt had married Walter E. Blanchard, headmaster of Ramsey Grammar School, Isle of Man.

I think George had a good time – we went nearly everywhere. It fagged me a good bit. Ethel and Max were so nice and cordial. Won't *you* come down this Autumn and go there? But we'll have a good Christmas together, at any rate. Say where we shall go – don't ask Frank.[1] – There's the bell – love to all. Your brother D. H. Lawrence

P.S. Do write me a newsey letter.

P.S. I had such a nice letter last night, from Ireland, from an admirer of the *Peacock*. The lady said that Mrs Thurston, the lady novelist who died suddenly in Ireland, had spoken to her so warmly and deeply of the book, said it was such a beautiful book, and had moved her so much. It made me feel a bit queer. DHL

321. To Louie Burrows, 16 October 1911

Text: MS UN; Postmark, Croydon OC 16 11; Boulton 141–3.

16 Colworth Rd, Addiscombe, Croydon.
16 Oct. 1911

My dear Lou,

At last I can sit down to this letter which I want to write to you. I have been to tea to Ansell's – at the Actors' Home.[2] It is rather nice. They have two great houses in Morland Road, which they have turned into a home. Mr Ansell takes beautiful photographs; he is a genuine artist. There are goodness knows how many daughters of the house, such rum girls. It is very funny to go there. They keep great dogs, danes, enormous creatures, which bound about you.

I had a fine time at Edward Garnetts. He has got one of these new, ancient cottages; called the Cearne.[3] It is a house thirteen years old, but exactly, exactly like the 15th century: brick floored hall, bare wood staircase, deep ingle nook with a great log fire, and two tiny windows one on either side of the chimney: and beautiful old furniture – all in perfect taste. You would be moved to artistic rhapsodies, I think. The house stands on the last drop of the north downs, sheer overlooking the Weald of Kent. The wood in which the cottage is lost ends with the scarp slope. It was very fine. Garnett was alone – He is about 42. He and his wife consent to live together or apart as it pleases them. At present Mrs Garnett[4] with their

[1] Perhaps Frances ('Frankie') Cooper.

[2] Walter Ansell, warden of the Actors' Orphanage, 32–4 Morland Road (cf. p. 97 n. 1).

[3] For another description see David Garnett, *The Golden Echo*, pp. 16–21.

[4] Constance Garnett, née Black (1861–1946) took a First in Cambridge Classical Tripos, 1883; m. Edward Garnett 1889. She visited Russia 1892 and 1904. The celebrated translator of Turgenev, Dostoevsky, Tolstoy, Gogol, etc. – seventy volumes in all. (See Heilbrun, *The Garnett Family*; David Garnett, *The Golden Echo*, pp. 4–16 *et passim*.)

son[1] is living in their Hampstead flat. She comes down to the Cearne for week ends sometimes. Garnett generally stays one, or perhaps two days in the week, in London. But he prefers to live alone at the Cearne. But he is very fond of his wife also – only they are content to be a good deal apart.

We discussed books most furiously, sitting drinking wine in the ingle nook, cosy and snug in the big, long room. We had a fine time, only he and I. He thinks my work is quite extra. So do I, of course. But Garnett rather flatters me. He praises me for my sensuous feeling in my writing.

The country looks very charming on the north downs – all the trees are quite fluffy and thick with yellow, like fires among them.

We have got a new little dog called Fritz – that the Ansells gave me. He is such a jolly little chap, black, with white paws, and very frisky. I like him very much. He is weeping on the hall-mat because Mrs Jones has gone out.

Did I tell you Ford Madox Hueffer had married Violet Hunt. I think it is scarcely legal in England, as the divorce – so Garnett says – was never really accomplished.[2] They were married in Germany. I heard again from Violet Hunt from Brussels. She is coming home on Saturday. I shall go and see her in South Lodge in a little while.[3] She wants me to.

Garnett is going to introduce me to quite a lot of people. I am not keen on it, but he says my business is to get known.

Heinemann and I have been squaring up our accounts. Really, my agreement is a yearly one. i.e., I should be paid for the *Peacock* next February. I have asked him to leave it like that, then I can draw the whole cheque at once, since this is the legal arrangement. I have promised to go to Lunch with Wm Heinemann on Friday. He wants to make some or other terms with me. Damn him – but I shall have to go.

I am very busy indeed with one thing and another – so busy, that I have only time to think about work and the things I've got to do tomorrow. I have no leisure for thinking or worrying. It is very funny to live so. Things I've got to do, things I've got to do – there seems nothing else in the world but that.

When is it I come to Quorn? – is it a fortnight on Friday? I want to arrange

[1] David Garnett (1892–), trained as botanist, Royal College of Science; later, novelist (*Lady into Fox* awarded Hawthornden and Tait-Black prizes, 1923); editor (*Letters of T. E. Lawrence*, 1938; novels of Peacock, 1948 etc.); and autobiographer (*The Golden Echo*, 1953; *The Flowers of the Forest*, 1955; *The Familiar Faces*, 1962).

[2] It was a continuing embarrassment: in 1913 and 1925 Violet Hunt was prosecuted for representing herself as 'Mrs Hueffer'. In *The Flurried Years* (1926) she admitted: 'I never did become his legal wife' (p. 187).

[3] Violet Hunt's home at 80 Campden Hill Road, Kensington (a famous literary centre associated with Hueffer, Pound, Wyndham Lewis, etc; see Goldring, *South Lodge*, pp. 12–13, 46, *et passim*).

my week ends. I have promised Miss Reynolds a week end, and I must fix the date. I will come on Friday evening.

It is queer to think of Quorn just now. It seems out of the atmosphere of all this. It would be nice if there were not so many folk. It will be, after all, only a change from one form of rush to another. But after all, I suppose that is what suits me.

Now I must get to work – my dear, I canna write a love letter – there are too many things in my head. When I come you shall have the love. I put it aside nowadays, and work instead. I kiss you (what a farce to write it).

Goodbye – I dreamed of you last night – you looked sad.

Goodbye D. H. Lawrence

322. To Ada Lawrence, [16 October 1911]

Text: MS Clarke; Postmark, Croydon OC 16 11; Lawrence–Gelder 92–3.

16 Colworth
Monday

My dear Ada,

I didn't post the letter before because I wanted to cash the cheque and then to get the p[ostal] o[rder].[1] I hope you're not impatient with me.

I had such a ripping time at Garnetts. The Cearne is a big cottage, built in the 15th Century style, and you'd think it was a fine old farm house – everything old, thick blue earthenware, stone jugs for the beer – a great wood fire on the open hearth in the ingle-nook – fine – and all buried in the middle of a wood, hard to find. I like Garnett ever so much. I shall go and stay with him again soon.

Hueffer has married Violet Hunt in Germany. They'll be home soon, living in her house. I shall go and see them next week, I think.

Garnett is going to get my verses published, and perhaps a vol of plays, in Spring. I am terribly busy.

I've got to go and lunch with Wm Heinemann on Friday. My agreement is a yearly one – i.e. I should draw my cheque next February. I could have it now, but I think I shall wait. I wonder what the little bear wants with me now.

I'm glad father's got a lighter job. Give him my love. Does he want for anything. Write me a letter soon.

With much love Your brother D. H. Lawrence

Love to Emily and baby x x

I hope Margaret is better. DHL

[1] See Letter 320: cheque for £10, postal order for £1.

323. To Edward Garnett, 20 October 1911

Text: MS NYPL; Postmark, Croydon OC 20 11; Huxley 12–13.

16 Colworth Rd, Addiscombe, Croydon
20 Oct 1911

Dear Mr Garnett,

I have been up to Wm Heinemann's today, at that gentleman's request. He, and his satraps, are very much sweeter. It is very remarkable. Last week they were sneering and detestable: today they are of the honeycomb. Heinemann wants to publish the verses. That will be all right, it will save[1] you the bother. He will publish them in Spring.[2] Will you send me the batch, at your convenience? Do you want to see the others before Heinemann has them? – I know you are not keen on verse. Then he wants me definitely to promise the next novel – the one that is half done[3] – for March, and to withhold the short stories from Martin Secker until autumn. That, I suppose, is a fairly good arrangement. I forgot to ask him about the 'erotic' MSS[4] – and Miss Hunt (Mrs Hueffer) will see to the plays tomorrow.[5]

I enjoyed *The Breaking Point* very much.[6] What I like is its clean bareness – it is Greek[7] in that. That is so much better than my ravels of detail. It is a fine, clean moulded tragedy, *The Breaking Point*. I have always got such a lot of non-essential stuff in my work. The Norse play is very interesting[8] – coloured. But it hasn't the bare force of the other.

I hope you received the copy of the *White Peacock* – I am glad you wanted it. The Chart country will be much less beautiful this week, today, than last week.

Yours Sincerely D. H. Lawrence

324. To Jessie Chambers, [c. 20 October 1911]

Text: E.T. 190.

[16 Colworth Road, Addiscombe, Croydon]
[c. 20 October 1911][9]

[Lawrence 'sent the entire manuscript [of Paul Morel] to me [Jessie], and asked me to tell him what I thought of it.']

[1] save] send
[2] Cf. p. 309 n. 4.
[3] *Sons and Lovers.*
[4] *The Trespasser.*
[5] Cf. p. 309 n. 3.
[6] Garnett's play, *A Censured Play. The Breaking Point* (1907).
[7] is Greek] is almost Greek.
[8] Garnett's *The Feud* (1909).
[9] After the prompting from Heinemann (alluded to in the previous letter), DHL presumably sent off his MS to Jessie Chambers; she had returned it with her comments and he had begun the final draft by 3 November (see Letter 331). (The MS of Jessie's reply is at the Humanities Research Center, Austin, Texas.)

325. To Edward Garnett, [22 October 1911]

Text: MS NYPL; PC; Postmark, Croydon OC 22 11; Unpublished.

16 Colworth Rd
Sunday

My dear Garnett,

Glad you like the verses – keep them as *long* as you *like*. – I'll send some more tomorrow.

D. H. Lawrence

326. To Edward Garnett, 23 October 1911

Text: MS NYPL; Unpublished.

Davidson Rd Boys School, South Norwood, S.E.
23 Oct 1911

My dear Garnett,

Excuse me if I write from school on any scrap of paper: I'm squeezed dry of time. And tonight I've promised to go out for tea and all evening with one of my friends – one of the fellows here: his wife is awfully flirty, so he won't have me as a rule: but he wants me to help to entertain visitors – a French man and his sister.[1] The Frenchman[2] speaks such glutinous French I have to struggle like grim death to make a grain of meaning out – and he doesn't know a word of English – and my friend's wife doesn't know a word of French – it is awful: and Humphreys is fearfully jealous, and Mrs Humphreys lays her hand on your arm when she talks to you, and Laisné blushes purple – he's swarthy – and Mademoiselle is wildly caustic in French – Oh Lord! I feel a bit tired, so I funk it rather.

Here's the rest of the verses. Keep them while you want them – and tell me what you think of them – and tell me any you don't approve of, please. These are more recent than those you have read – more anti-*Daily News*, I am afraid.[3]

Oh – don't invite me up to Lunch on weekdays, please. I don't like to take the time from school. Never mind if I can't meet Scott-James: he'll be just as well content, no doubt.[4]

[1] Albert and Cecile Laisné from Rouen (information from DHL's address-book).

[2] Frenchman] man

[3] Obscure. Perhaps an allusion to the *Daily News* review of *The White Peacock* in which DHL was censured for 'cloying descriptiveness' and 'brutality'. Some of the poems (e.g. 'Cruelty and Love') might have been defiantly inviting similar reactions.

[4] Rolfe Arnold Scott-James (1878–1959), journalist, editor, critic. With the *Daily News* from 1902; literary editor 1905, and subsequently leader-writer. 1934 editor of the *London Mercury*. Author of *The Making of Literature* (1928), etc. Influential in literary circles which included Bennett, Galsworthy, Wells, Yeats, etc.

I'm supposed to be marking Composition – such a stack of blue exercise books at my elbow. How's that for MS? – it is awful: it'll be the death of me one of these days.

Damn – there's the bell. Vale D. H. Lawrence

327. To Louie Burrows, 23 October 1911

Text: MS UN; Postmark, Croydon OC 23 11; Boulton 143–4.

Davidson
23 Oct 1911

My dear Lou,

Scuse me if it's a scrap I write. Shall I come to Quorn this week end – I think I will. I've got a central timetable and I cant get an excursion on Friday night – I want a week-end – I can come first thing Sat. morning. I will, however, try Midland to Quorn, and let you know. Ada wants to see me in Nottm. on the Sat. I come up – and Gert Cooper is in hospital again – not very serious – so I must go and see her.

Heinemann was very sweet – no news to speak of. He's mad with me for promising the stories and verses. [...] I've had to withdraw the offer of the verse from Duckworth, and give Heinemann the promise of the things.[1] I shall send in the MS in a week or so, and they'll be out in Jan. or February. Then I've promised to withhold the stories from Secker, and to let Heinemann have the MS of a novel – probably Paul Morel – in March. You can see I am going to be kept most damnably up to the neck.

I was down the Chipstead Valley – down in Surrey – on Sat. The country is very beautiful – very much like John Linnell.[2] Tonight I'm promised to tea with Humphreys – they've got a Frenchman I'm to entertain – but he speaks most awful glutinous French – it is such a struggle. I wish I hadn't promised. I *must* get these damned verses shipshape.

I hope I shall be able to come on Friday night – I'll let you know directly. Do you write and tell me at once whether you want me to come. I hope your cold is better, and that Mrs Adams has subsided for good.[3] I laugh to think of you being so sweet, over and above your wrath.

Friday or Saturday then – here is Philip – I fly – tis 12.30.

Goodbye – love D. H. Lawrence

[1] At a luncheon, 20 October 1911 (see Letter 323), Heinemann had persuaded DHL to withdraw verses from Duckworth and short stories from Secker.

[2] See p. 88 n. 4.

[3] Possibly the mother of Ethel Adams (b. 1883), a teacher at Quorn from 1902, and herself a teacher.

328. To Louie Burrows, 26 October 1911

Text: MS UN; Postmark, Croydon OC 26 11; Boulton 144–5.

16 Colworth Rd, Addiscombe, Croydon
26 Oct 1911

My dear Lou,

I will come tomorrow – Friday – evening, by the 6.20 out of Marylebone, which gets in Leicester at 8.14. There I shall have to change and come on by the 8.34, or something like that. At any rate, you'll know the train.

There was no excursion, so I shall have to come up ordinary. But for the return I have got a half day excursion from Nottingham, so that I can go back with the return half, by the train leaving Victoria at 7.30 on Sunday night, getting in Kings Cross 10.40. That was the only excursion available.

In that case, you see, I think it will be much better for us to stay Saturday night in Eastwood. Therefore, when we meet Ada in Nottingham on Saturday morning, we will have a jig round the town, and then return to my home. It will be best, all ways round, for they were rather cross with me the other way.

It will not be long at Quorn, will it – but, as I say, it's the best I can do. I wish I had a holiday tomorrow.

I am very glad I am coming. I think of it in school, and when the rain comes sweeping, I wonder how it will look over the midlands. You will be better, you say? That is right. I myself am very well.

If you are in Leicester tomorrow, stay for me. In 24 hours I shall be 'en train'.

Goodnight then – tomorrow I will say it in person.

Je t'embrasse D. H. Lawrence

329. To Louie Burrows, 30 October 1911

Text: MS UN; Postmark, Croydon OC 30 11; Boulton 145–6.

16 Colworth Rd, Addiscombe, Croydon.
30 Oct 1911

My dear Lou,

I got home by midnight, quite sober, and quite sound. I have not got a cold, my insurance policy has not increased in value by one denarius. Voilà.

But it is very damnable. Today it has rained like Hell. 'It rains outside, and it rains in my heart' as I've read somewhere or other (very toshy).[1] But

[1] Verlaine, *Romances sans Paroles:*
Il pleure dans mon cœur
Comme il pleut sur la ville.

the long slow drag of hours is very trying. I've now got to digest a great lot of dissatisfied love in my veins. It is very damnable, to have slowly to drink back again into oneself all the lava and fire of a passionate eruption. I have to say to myself all day – 'Don't natter the kids – it's your own fault – don't growl – it's your own fault – don't scowl – why inflict it on anybody else – go on, make another effort' – and so one goads oneself through a livelong day. It is just the same with you I guess – perhaps worse: but it can't be worse, or you wouldn't keep your presence of mind.

How did you find Ilkeston, and your Aunt Nell?[1] Very well, I hope.

But oh damn, I can't get through the platitudes.

I wish the next four or five days would get over. I feel as if I'd got lead in my veins – it's quite a business to drag about. Damn it. It's the digesting of one's spleen with a vengeance.

'What is love?' said jesting Pilate.[2]

The most of the things, that just heave red hot to be said, I shove back. And that leaves nothing to be said. All this, you see, is very indelicate and immodest and all that...and I always want to subscribe to your code of manners, towards you – I know I fail sadly.

Goodbye – just imagine all the things I don't say – they're there.

Goodbye D. H. Lawrence

330. To Louie Burrows, 3 November 1911

Text: MS UN; Postmark, Croydon NO 3 11; Boulton 146–7.

16 Colworth Rd, Addiscombe, Croydon
3 Nov 1911

My dear Lou,

I am very sorry about that train – it must, you see, have been the fault of the time-table, which was 3 months old: I think I looked out the right thing.

I think I have finished the verses. I must send them off at once. You see Heinemann will be waiting for them. When they come back from him, I will send you the proofs. Patience, ma chère. I wish the typewriter would send me back 'Two Marriages' for the *Century*. Damn him, he is devilish dilatory.

Tonight I am going to begin Paul Morel again, for the third and last time. I shall need all your prayers if I'm to get it done. It is a book the thought of which weighs heavily upon me. Say a Misericordia.

[1] Helen Burrows, a teacher in Ilkeston.
[2] Bacon, 'Of Truth' ['...is truth?...'].

Tomorrow I am going to Miss Reynolds. I have been buying a couple of dishes for Mrs Reynolds. I wonder when I shall buy things for ourselves. One of the bowls was so pretty – a French theme in violets and grey leaves, on pure china. It is a nice shop for pots – Birds, in Croydon – one of the nicest I've ever seen. And Mrs Bird, I like her.

I have been to a Promenade Concert in our Public Hall this week.[1] They did Schubert's 'Unfinished' Symphony, which I like very much. Alice Esty was singing. She sang the Miserere scene from *Trovatore*, which made me laugh very much. She's not bad, – just a trifle meaty and common.

I read Leroys letter with – I must confess – only rather faint interest.[2] I could show you a hundred times more interesting page in Baedeker. Leroy is too impersonal to be interesting.

I really dread setting the pen to paper, to write the first word of Paul – which I'm going to do when I've written the last word of this.

I should be thankful for a cottage with one room up and one down. This eternal cultivation of the habit of going without what one wants – needs – is very damnable.

I kiss you goodnight. D. H. Lawrence

331. To Jessie Chambers, [c. 3 November 1911]

Text: Delavenay 670.

[16 Colworth Road, Addiscombe, Croydon]
[c. 3 November 1911][3]

[Lawrence 'asked me [Jessie] to write what I could remember of our early days together, just as a help to him, because he didn't remember those days so well as I did.']

332. To Edward Garnett, 7 November 1911

Text: MS NYPL; Huxley 13–14.

16 Colworth Rd, Addiscombe, Croydon
7 Nov. 1911

1 The first promenade concert given by the Croydon Symphony Orchestra, 1 November 1911. Alice Esty – a prima donna from Covent Garden Opera House – sang 'the Great Miserere Scene from *Il Trovatore*', with the tenor, Aubrey Standing (*Croydon Advertiser*, 28 October 1911).

2 See p. 75 n. 3.

3 Jessie Chambers places this letter close to the time when DHL 'entirely recast his novel'; she had scarcely begun to respond to his request 'when DHL fell ill with pneumonia' on 19 November (Delavenay 670).

Dear Garnett,

I received your letter, much to my joy, about an hour ago. I wondered whether you had gone away.

The *Nation* was very nice to take the poems:[1] I am afraid you must have bullyragged them into it. If ever you show Scott-James any of the things, show him such as are quite respectable, and black and white, will you.

When are you going to the 'Cearne' – you do not say? I will send this to Duckworths.

I have been thinking – shall I ask William Heinemann to allow me an income of £100 a year for one, or two years. He will owe me £50 in February. He shall have another novel before June – not to mention the verses. Shall I ask him. This last fortnight I have felt really rotten – it is the dry heat of the pipes in school, and the strain – and a cold. I must leave school, really.

Hueffer seems actually to have lost the other two plays. It's a nuisance.

I've got another rather ripping long short story – shall I show it you?[2] Don't let me be a bore.

I'm sending the last, best verses, the latest, and most substantial, to the Cearne tomorrow. You will be back?

Yours D. H. Lawrence

333. To Edward Garnett, 7 November 1911

Text: MS NYPL; Moore 84.

16 Colworth Rd, Addiscombe, Croydon
7 Novem. 1911

Dear Garnett,

Just got your letter – I am very glad with the *Nation* – thanks very much.

I send you the best, the latest, and, I am sure, the best of my verses. I hope sincerely that I dont try your patience.

When you've done with the others, perhaps you will let me have them – I'll send the things to William Heinemann in batches. You got the *second* bundle of verses a fortnight ago, didn't you – the one with 'Nils Lykke' and 'Transformations' and 'Another Ophelia'.[3]

The plays seem quite lost with Hueffer – I am sorry.

I can't get the story back from the soldier, either.[4] Just like a soldier.

[1] The *Nation* printed 'Lightning' and 'Violets' on 4 November 1911.

[2] Probably 'Love among the Haystacks'.

[3] 'Nils Lykke Dead' (another early draft of 'A Man who Died'), 'Transformations' and 'Another Ophelia' (later 'Ballad of Another Ophelia') are all poems in the Clarke Notebook (see *Renaissance and Modern Studies*, xiv (1970), 21–3).

[4] Arthur Stanley Corke.

I shall be delighted to meet Scott-James and the other 'nice' man – who is he?

Yours D. H. Lawrence

You see the address was right.[1] DHL

334. To Ada Lawrence, 8 November 1911

Text: MS Clarke; cited in Lawrence–Gelder 93–4.

Davidson Rd Boys School, South Norwood, SE.
8 Novem. 1911

My dear Ada,

Am I a long time in writing? But then, why not you have first go, and begin by writing to me!

I don't know whether you'll want this music – it's part of a batch belonging to a girl who is going to Australia at Christmas.[2] I hope you'll like the stuff. Do play the 9th Sonata – I like it very much. You'll find all the pieces rather good, I think – and you haven't any Bach, nor Gade, nor Henselt nor Moszkowski[3] – pronounce Gā -da, Moss – kov – ski.

And these verses – Garnett put them in last week's *Nation* all unknown to me. I am pleased to get a footing in the *Nation*. It is a sixpenny weekly, of very good standing. I am afraid you will not care much for the verses. The 'Violets' is printed all wrong[4] – you see I had no proofs or anything. Let Mrs Hopkin see them some time at your convenience.

Things are going on very slowly down here: I don't get on very well with my writing: shall have to buck up. I expect a week on Sat. I shall be going to Garnett's again, and Scott-James, the editor of the *Daily News*, will be there.[5] He may do me some good. I want to leave school now as soon as I can. There is a review by me in the *English* of this month.[6]

[1] The previous letter was sent to Duckworth's, this to Garnett's flat at 19 Grove Place, Hampstead.

[2] Perhaps Elsie Stanley Hall the Australian pianist (cf. p. 155 n. 3).

[3] Niels W. Gade (1817–90); Adolf von Henselt (1814–89); Moritz Moszkowski (1854–1925).

[4] This appears to be an exaggeration: at least, a collation between the texts of the (dialect) poem in *Nation*, 4 November 1911, and *Love Poems and Others* reveals only two substantive variants.

[5] Perhaps the weekend described by Scott-James in 'Edward Garnett', *The Spectator*, 26 February 1937: 'We sat by the fire at night feasting on the genial eloquence of our host as he warmed to the theme of Lawrence's genius. "Lawrence's genuis, you see," he would begin, and go on to explain just how, with that background, it lent itself to that fearless exposure of body and soul which was the reality of creative art. And Lawrence, at first shyly, but with growing confidence, began to see himself through Garnett's eyes and to relish the *rôle* of the distinctive "genius" allotted to him.'

[6] Review of *Contemporary German Poetry*, ed. Jethro Bithell. (See Carl E. Baron, 'Two hitherto unknown pieces by D. H. Lawrence', *Encounter*, August 1969, 3–5.)

Ask Emily to get me that mixed pickles recipe – and to tell me when is Aunt Ada's birthday.[1] I shall have to send something.

The boys have nearly finished singing, when I shall be on duty again – and I want to pack the things. How is your concert going? How are you? Do write and tell me all the news.

My love to Emily and Margaret – and to Father and Sam.

Regards to Floss – any news of Georgie?[2] – I have none.

Goodbye – best love. Your brother D. H. Lawrence

335. To Louie Burrows, 10 November 1911

Text: MS UN; Boulton 147–8.

16 Colworth Rd, Addiscombe, Croydon
10 Nov 1911

My dear Lou,

Your bundle of news makes me feel impoverished: I have nothing to send you in that line.

You know, by the way, that I must be at home for Christmas itself. I think I told you – I know I told Mrs Burrows. I shall have to spend at least the first week in Eastwood – otherwise the whole world of mine would be set by the ears. You will have to come over after the party, since you are bound. And when *is* Maggie's wedding, by the way?[3] I will contrive to give you half a quid to her wedding present. Really, you know, I have a lot of claims. To a good many people, I am well off, and they are poor – et voilà.

The verses aren't at Heinemanns yet – they have gone via Garnett – who has[4] done me a good turn in putting me in the *Nation*. Then, when that supreme publisher has gone through them, and selected[5] them, I shall still have a bit more revising – so I don't expect the proofs 'll be here till directly after Christmas. I'm in no hurry – but I'm sorry if you are disappointed. Perhaps you'll like the plays Garnett gave me.[6] *Don't* show them to your people: it will be enough for them that *The Breaking Point* is censored, to make them look at me very much askance. And I really hesitate to send the *Belgian Poetry*[7] into Coteshael – although none of your family are great poetasters.

[1] On 19 November.

[2] Either George Neville, or George Hodgkinson who married Florence Cullen.

[3] Louie Burrows's favourite cousin, Marguerite, (daughter of Campbell Burrows) married Percy Burgess, 26 December 1911.

[4] has] had

[5] selected] revised

[6] Plays referred to in Letter 323.

[7] *Contemporary Belgian Poetry*, ed. Jethro Bithell (May 1911) which DHL mentions in the opening sentence of his review of Bithell's *Contemporary German Poetry* (see previous Letter).

Next week I am probably going again to Garnetts for the week-end – to meet Scott-James, editor of the *Daily News.* I rather want to get him on my side.

I am really very tired of school – I can*not* get on with Paul. I am afraid I shall have to leave – and I am afraid you will be cross with me – and I loathe to plead my cause.

I am glad your father is better: I have most terrible visions of Mrs Burrows as a widow.

It is so – I am on the brink of a complaint – I'll right about –

When I come down Everton Road,[1] and see the man and the woman laughing in the firelight, which picks out the silver of the tea-table in red. (oh Lord, how long winded!) – I do, my dear good God I do wish we also had a hearth. It is very dreary here. I am ashamed, however, to wish for a home, because I seem to get no nearer. Think – it is a year.

The alternative is – don't think.

I don't care for Garnetts plays – they are not alive. A *Little Dream* is rather good – a bit mechanical.[2] But you'll like it. Mac gave it me on my birthday. I kiss you – I mean I wish I could –

Goodbye D. H. Lawrence

336. To Edward Garnett, 11 November 1911

Text: TMS NYPL; Moore 85–6.

16 Colworth Road, Addiscombe, Croydon
11 November 1911

Dear Garnett,

Thanks for the verse which I received last night. I send it today to the Great Cham of publishers.[3] I am afraid I bore you frightfully with the stuff.

I shall be delighted to come to the Cearne next Saturday. I am very curious to know who is the specially nice man.

This morning I hear from a mate of the soldier that the latter rascal went on drink when he got my p[ostal] o[rder] of payment. He never used to be like that. If marriage has driven him to it already, it is a sad look-out. However the pal will get the thing done directly. I am sorry you have been put to inconvenience. Truly I have worried him almost to death about the thing.[4]

[1] On his way to Colworth Road from school.

[2] John Galsworthy, *The Little Dream: an allegory in six scenes* (July 1911).

[3] William Heinemann.

[4] 'Two Marriages' (cf. p. 309 n. 1 and Letter 339).

As for Hueffer, he is in Germany, and I don't know his address. But I will write to Mrs Hueffer.[1]

I will do as you say about asking Heinemann for anything.

I wish I could think of better titles for my stories. Dare I ask Harrison, of the *English Review*, to publish this thing as a little serial?[2]

I look forward to next Saturday,

Yours Sincerely, D. H. Lawrence

P.S. What do you think of my first go at type-writing?

337. To Edward Garnett, [15 November 1911]

Text: MS NYPL; PC; Postmark, Croydon NO 15 11; Unpublished.

Addiscombe
Wednesday

Will you tell me what time to come to the Cearne on Saturday – afternoon or evening? If I'm to come alone, it had better be before dark.

Yours Sincerely D. H. Lawrence

338. To Louie Burrows, 15 November 1911

Text: TMS UN; Boulton 149–50.

16 Colworth Road, Addiscombe, Croydon
15 Nov. 1911

My dear Lou,

It is very swanky to write you in type. Mr Jones brought home an office typewriter the other day, and already I am quite proficient. I shall soon take to writing novels on a machine.

I am frightfully busy this week. On Monday I was up at Covent Garden to hear *Siegfried* – Wagner – one of the *Ring* cycle that I had not heard.[3] It was good, but it did not make any terrific impression on me. And now George has asked me to take a friend of his – a Nottingham chap – to the theatre tomorrow evening – in London. The man is quite a stranger in London. Then on Friday I have promised the boss I will go to a glee-singing party Mrs Smith is giving. And on Saturday I am going again to Edenbridge to stay the weekend with Edward Garnett, who has asked Scott-James – editor of the *Daily News* to be there. So you see I am rushed. Poor Paul, I don't know when he will be done.

[1] i.e. Violet Hunt.

[2] 'Love among the Haystacks'.

[3] On 13 November 1911 *Siegfried* was performed in German with the Covent Garden orchestra under Franz Schalk.

You always tell me such a lot of news, I forget it. What shall we do about Christmas? Will you come to Eastwood on the Thursday, and I will return with you to Quorn on the following Monday or so. Let us not this time muddle – always either your mother does not know what we're doing, or Ada doesn't, or somebody. Let us be pretty definite. Of course I know it depends also on Maggie's wedding.

It is only five weeks to Christmas – how time flies. And I have done so little work this term. I dont know when I shall have time to get finished. It is Aunt Ada's birthday on Sunday, and I dont know what on earth to get her. I shall have to cudgel my brains.

I will let you know what sort of folk I meet at Garnett's. Meantime I feel so squashed with work, I can't write a letter fit to read. It will not be long to Christmas – it will not be long till 1961 – tempus fugit.

Now I will to Paul. I need not say to you cheer up, because by this time you will be quite gay and frisky. These black and starry evenings, I should like to go a walk. I echo you, 'why cant we live our own lives'. Ah well.

Good-bye, I wish you were here. My mouth seems to be lifted blindly for something, and waiting, puzzled. It is shocking how I curse within myself.

Good-bye D. H. Lawrence

339. To Edward Garnett, 21 November 1911

Text: MS NYPL; Unpublished.

16 Colworth Rd, Addiscombe, Croydon
Nov. 21 – 1911

Dear Garnett

Here is the MSS of 'Two Marriages' at last – The soldier writes long and mournfully but does not reach my heart. Thanks for delightful week end.

Yours D. H. Lawrence[1]

340. To Jessie Chambers, [December ? 1911]

Text: E.T. 193.

[16 Colworth Road, Addiscombe, Croydon]
[December? 1911][2]

Did I frighten you all? I'm sorry. Never mind, I'm soon going to be all right.

[1] Though doubtless written at DHL's dictation, this letter is in the hand of Mrs Jones, his landlady. DHL became ill as the result of a chill caught at the Cearne. He developed pneumonia on Sunday 19 November; it is confirmed in a letter to Garnett from Ada Lawrence (MS NYPL 26 November 1911) who came on 25 November to nurse her brother. DHL never taught again: the School Log records his absence from 20 November onwards.

[2] DHL was critically ill in late November. Ada Lawrence wrote to Louie Burrows on 28 November: 'tomorrow or next day is the crisis and please God all may be well' (MS UN

341. To Louie Burrows, 2 December 1911

Text: MS UN; Boulton 150.

16 Colworth Rd, Addiscombe, Croydon.
2 Dec 1911

My dear Lou,

The roses are very sweet smelling, and the yellow jasmine I am fond of. I look forward to seeing you next week.

Love D. H. Lawrence

342. To Louie Burrows, [4? December 1911]

Text: MS UN; Boulton 150–1.

[16 Colworth Road, Addiscombe, Croydon]
[4? December 1911]

[Ada Lawrence begins]

Dear Louie,

Bert reads his own letters now. When you come you can sleep with me. I shall be so glad to see you – let me know when you will arrive.

I'm hoping by Saturday Bert may be able to sit up in bed, but of course we mustnt be too venturesome seeing he has not yet moved off his back. On Wednesday Mr Garnett is coming to see him.[1] For his dinner today he's going to have an egg and toast – doesn't that sound alright?

Love Ada.

He's always talking about you coming.

[Lawrence begins]

My dear Lou

I am going on still very well. I wish I could sit up. It is very wearisome, always on one's back.

The roses are still living, and I can smell them in the room.

I look forward to seeing you on Saturday.

It is very nice of Billy and Alf.[2] Love D. H. Lawrence

LaB 203). It is inconceivable, therefore, that he could write to Jessie Chambers before December. She claims: 'When he was convalescent the first thing he wrote was a tiny pencilled message to me' (E.T. 193).

1 Ada Lawrence had written to Edward Garnett, 2 December 1911: 'My brother wishes me to tell you he would very much like you to come and see him, as he is now improving so nicely' (MS NYPL). Garnett was due on 6 December: hence the conjectural dating of this letter.

2 William Ralph (b. 1905) and Alfred (1900–76), Louie's brothers.

343. To Edward Garnett, 4 December 1911

Text: MS NYPL; Moore 86.

16 Colworth Rd. Addiscombe, Croydon
4.12.11

Dear Garnett,

I have sent to the Cearne, the MSS of the erotic novel[1] which I have at last extorted from William Heineman. I didn't undo the package because if there is any note inside, it is sure to be quite trivial.

I shall like to hear your opinion of the work. Hueffer called it 'a rotten work of genuis',[2] but he was prejudiced against the inconsequential style; said that erotic literature must be in the form of high art.

This Saga, on the contrary, is based on brief notes made from actuality. Nevertheless I swear it has true form.

I shall be glad to see you on Wednesday about six.

Take the Addiscombe car at East Croydon and come to the terminus, then you are here.

Yrs Sincerely D. H. Lawrence[3]

344. To May Holbrook, 6 December 1911

Text: TMSC UT; Nehls, iii. 621–2.

[16 Colworth Road, Addiscombe, Croydon]
Wednesday 6 Dec 1911

My dear May

The eggs have come – they are very pretty – one only cracked: that is to be made into a custard pudding. It is very good of you to take so much trouble.

I am much stronger – but still on my back – 17th day. Neither to right nor to left can I lie, nor may I be propped up half an inch. But soon the doctor[4] will let me be reared up.

I am pretty happy – except at evening when I always feel rotten. I can sleep fairly well. When I wake there is Nurse crocheting in the shade-light.[5] She crochets so slowly and clumsily, I laugh at her. Sometimes she is asleep. But usually she is at me with milk or medicine, much to my disgust. At six oclock I don't pretend to sleep any more. Then Nurse draws the blind up and we talk while it grows day. When it rains, the day won't come. I'm always

[1] *The Trespasser.* [2] Cf. Letter 178.

[3] Except for the signature, this MS is in Ada Lawrence's hand.

[4] Dr William Fielding Addey (1872–1947), the Jones family doctor.

[5] Despite a Croydon address for 'Nurse' in DHL's address-book, her identity cannot be traced.

glad when its eight oclock. Now Nurse brings me coffee and toast for breakfast.

I am allowed to read. I have got to review a book of German poetry and a book of Minnesinger translations. I like the German poetry, but not the translations.[1]

It is sunny today. I envy the sparrows and the starlings. This is the most I've written since I've been ill.

My regards to Will. I will write to you again.

Love D. H. Lawrence

345. To Louie Burrows, 7 December 1911

Text: MS UN; Boulton 151.

[16 Colworth Road, Addiscombe, Croydon]
7 Dec 1911

My dear Lou

Were you very much disappointed when you got Ada's letter?[2] I am very sorry – but the doctor is emphatic. When will you come? Will you come at Christmas, when I am up. When I am in bed, I am no good to visit.

I think the doctor will let me go to Bournemouth, or somewhere, for the New Year. Will you come too for the week? What shall we do?

I mayn't sit up in bed yet. That is very wearisome. But one must be patient.

Your little clock still gains an hour in the night, silly little thing. I can't read very much today – only a very short time. Then I have to give up, and be still. And I mustn't have anybody to see me. It is very stupid to be ill.

In a fortnight it is Christmas. You must come then and stay with me.

You are a great one for a romance. I hope Ethel's will flourish.

I won't write any more – Goodbye.

I give you my love D. H. Lawrence

[1] The *English Review*, x (January 1912), 373–6 carried DHL's reviews of *The Oxford Book of German Verse*, ed. H. G. Fiedler (1911) and *The Minnesingers*, vol. 1, by Jethro Bithell (1909). To the first his general reaction was: 'no book, for a long time, has given us the pleasure that this has given'. Of the second he wrote: 'The book is very interesting in spite of its faults.'

[2] It has not survived among the Burrows papers.

346. To Louie Burrows, 9 December 1911

Text: MS UN; Boulton 152.

16 Colworth Rd, Addiscombe, Croydon
9 Dec 1911

My dear Lou,

I am propped up in bed – it is the doctor's order. He wants to get me up and get me away. It makes me feel a bit queer, and soon tires me.

It is great news, is it not, that we may go straight to Bournemouth in a fortnight. I am glad. I want to leave Colworth now. I want to leave Mrs Jones, and Mr Jones, and the children. It is queer, how I have turned, since I have been ill. But I do not want to be here for Christmas. What will you do – find an excursion and go straight to Bournemouth on the Friday, if we can go then – or the Saturday, as best suits? Will the journey scare you?

Do not tell me so often to be patient. Do I complain so much? I think I do not. I accept the inevitable, and say nothing. And I take very little nursing – Ada crochets and reads for hours, without paying me any attention, except to give me my medicine, or milk. Do you imagine I fret and chafe? – I know too well it's no good. I am progressing very well – I have [ ][1] passive. But I must read. My mind is so active, [ ] it some stuff to work on, it would grind itself away. Rem[ember we?] are different natures: I am intense and concentrative, you [ ] a muser. I cannot muse – do not prescribe it me.

[The] jasmine you sent is very charming. [ ] me of primroses, and of spring. It is delightf[ul when?] it opens and opens afresh. I like it better than flowers which cost more.

It will be delightful, a fortnight hence. It will make up for everything, to be in a warm place at the seaside. And it will soon be here. I make wonderful progress, the doctor says. Let that be a proof to you that I handle myself wisely.

Nurse says a knitted waistcoat would be a fine thing for me. But, my dear, it would take you ages to get it done. You choose the color, so long as it is nothing startling, it will suit me.

We will let the next week-end go, then, and you will come straight to Bournemouth with us. That will be fine. There are pine trees at Bournemouth, pine woods, and a warm sea. And it is only a fortnight.

I must lie down now – Goodbye, my dear – I kiss you.

D. H. Lawrence

[1] MS torn.

347. To Louie Burrows, 11 December 1911
Text: MS UN; Boulton 153.

16 Colworth Rd, Addiscombe, Croydon
11 Dec 1911

My dear Lou,

I am glad you went to see Auntie, and that you cheered each other up. Tell her I am sorry she has been poorly again.

The doctor is not so sure, now, when we can go away. He says the Wednesday after Christmas. But I do not want to be here for Christmas, if it can be helped. We must see.

I can sit up in bed quite a long time now – propped up with the pillows, of course. And I have done such a feat today – I have shaved off my red beard. Nurse clipped it short, and lathered me, then she held the glass while I shaved. It was a good, clean shave too, I can tell you. My nerves are wonderfully steady. It is a thing I rather pride myself on, my control.

Nurse bids me say, I am very patient and cheerful, I bear everything with becoming fortitude, I swallow everything that is given me, I leave nothing to be desired as a patient. – This I have written at her dictation – 'tis none of my own saying. She laughs so much when I tell her you are counselling me once more to be patient. She is very jolly.

A fortnight today is Christmas day: a week today, the doctor says, I *may* go downstairs. It seems to come quite suddenly, this change. Perhaps he will let me get out of bed on Thursday. Somehow, I am not very anxious, now, to get up.

Eddie has sent two fowls today. I do hope you get this in time to reprieve your wicked young cockerel, to spare his life for a week or so. I will pray the sentence may not have been executed before morning, that his neck be not yet wrung.

There, I am tired, I have had a big morning, what with shaving and writing letters to Emily and you and Agnes Holt. She wants me to go to Ramsey. I say, later.

Christmas will soon be here – and I shall be getting up. The yellow jasmine is so bonny.

I kiss you with love D. H. Lawrence

348. To Edward Garnett, 13 December 1911

Text: MS NYPL; Moore 87.

16 Colworth Rd, Addiscombe, Croydon
13 Dec. 1911

Dear Garnett,

I ought to have thanked you before for the books. I will send them back directly, with *Torrents of Spring*.[1] What a curious man James Prior is![2] I did not know him, and he so near home. I was very much interested. But what curious, highly flavoured stuff! *Nature in Downland* is very delightful.[3]

I still get on well. There was talk of my getting up a little today, but my temperature is up. I do not care. I am not anxious, somehow, to be perched in a chair feeling sick.

The doctor will send me to Bournemouth on the 27th I think – at least, very soon after Christmas. So after all I shall be here for Christmas. But I do not care.

There is no news. My sister wishes me to commend her to you.

Yours Sincerely D. H. Lawrence

349. To Grace Crawford, 13 December 1911

Text: MS UT; Fraser 151–2.

16 Colworth Rd, Addiscombe, Croydon
13 Dec 1911

Dear Miss Crawford,

I was so surprised to get your letter this morning. As soon as nurse gave me the envelope, I knew from whom it came. When we meet, we shall certainly have to quarrel over these letters. I vow and declare that I wrote last to you, to Rome. Those other letters of yours, where are they?

I have been laid up in bed for the past month, with pneumonia. It is very stupid of me, I know. It *is* stupid to be ill – almost unpardonable. But I am quite convalescent. The doctor did say I might sit up a little today, for the first time. Now he hums and haws about the temperature and the pulse. I don't care much. I'm not at all keen on being huddled into a dressing gown and perched in a chair, to feel sick.

[1] By Turgenev, trans. Constance Garnett (1897).

[2] James Prior Kirk (1851–1922), b. Nottingham; lived in the county all his life. Unsuccessful as solicitor's clerk, teacher, shopkeeper and farmer; acquired a reputation as Nottinghamshire's regional novelist. Author of *Forest Folk* (Heinemann, 1901), *Hyssop* (Heinemann, 1904), etc.

[3] By W. H. Hudson (1900).

Nurse has pounced on me with the thermometer and her watch. She scores over the pulse, I over the temperature. I am down to 98° – a triumph for me. She says I mustn't write, because of the pulse. I tell her not to bully, it excites me. She says she wants to wash me. I tell her she must crochet awhile, to calm herself, she is much too heated to handle an invalid. I score this go: she retreats. It is almost my first victory over her. I am a very biddable patient, and she's jolly nice.

I have not been in good trim this year. I have let things slide and haven't bothered to do much writing. I have not cared much about it, and I have scarcely been in London at all. You would find two or three stories of mine in the *English*[1] – and I have done a bit of review work[2] – and there have been verses in the *Nation*.[3] But I have not troubled much about getting published. Wm Heinemann is supposed to be bringing out a volume of my verse about February. But he is notoriously dilatory. I have promised him a novel for June, and I have promised Martin Secker a vol. of short stories for next[4] year. I ought to be very busy. I suppose I shall have to be, when I get up.

Directly after Christmas, the doctor is bundling me off to Bournemouth. My sister is here with me – we shall go to the seaside together. The doctor is tyrannous – he wouldn't let me come to London before I go to Bournemouth. But when I come back, towards the end of January, then, if I may, I shall be delighted to come and see you. I shall not stay in the South. For at least six months, I shall be away from London, staying with my sister and other friends in the north.

Have you seen Ezra Pound?[5] I heard from Scott-James that he was in London, and considerably down at the mouth. I should like to have seen him, but it is scarcely possible.

I am sorry I cannot go to the lecture: I hope you will allow me to return the tickets. I should like to hear you sing 'O Cessate' now your voice is stronger.[6] You must be very happy.

Commend me humbly to Mrs Crawford – My respects to Mr Crawford.

Yours Sincerely D. H. Lawrence

[1] 'Odour of Chrysanthemums' (June 1911) and 'A Fragment of Stained Glass' (September 1911).

[2] Cf. p. 331 n. 1.

[3] Cf. p. 323 n. 1.

[4] next] this

[5] The close friendship between Grace Crawford and Pound had 'quietly dwindled until [her] departure for Rome in December [1910] brought it entirely to an end' (Fraser 144).

[6] Cf. p. 171 n. 3.

350. To Louie Burrows, 13 December 1911

Text: MS UN; Boulton 154.

16 Colworth Rd, Addiscombe, Croydon
13 Dec. 1911

My dear Lou,

Why do you regret my red beard? I hated it. Oh, no more of it for me. I shaved again today. Nurse lathers me like a barber's assistant. She laughs so much when the soap goes in my mouth. I row her like fury for doing me wrong, but she doesn't mind.

I was to sit up a bit today, but my pulse and temperature haven't been behaving quite as they should, so it's a bit doubtful. I am not anxious to get up. The thought of sitting bundled in a dressing gown in a chair makes me feel queer.

Ada is sending the waistcoat. It is one I shall want to wear, so let me have it back as soon as you can. Ada will write another time, she says.

I have done the reviews and sent them off. They were only trifles.

The waistcoat is very exciting. Don't go pedgilling[1] at it and wearying yourself out. I had rather not have it than that.

It is probable Eddie will be down here for Christmas. I am trying to arrange little outings for us. We do not want always to be in number 16.

Hueffer wants to come and see me, but I am not anxious that he should.

It really seems now as if I should soon be going into the world again. It is so queer – and strangely enough, I am half reluctant to get up and start again. But next week I shall be keen enough.

Already this week has nearly gone. Before we know where we are, you will be here. Things seem to whirl round so strangely of their own accord, one ceases to wonder or to bother.

I am sorry about that bird – truly. What a nuisance your mother must think us. Give my love to all at Coteshael.

I kiss you goodbye. D. H. Lawrence

351. To Louie Burrows, [15 December 1911]

Text: MS UN; PC; Postmark, Croydon DE 16 11; Boulton 155.

Addiscombe
Friday

My dear Lou,

I have sat up for half an hour today. It is a weird experience. Tomorrow I shall sit up longer. Emily is coming.

[1] i. e. struggling hard.

We shall get away on the 27th almost for sure. Ada is going to write for rooms. I do not know what they will be – not much, be easy.

I am very well. This time next week we shall be thinking of your coming. That is very jolly. We wondered not to have heard from you at all today. I hope you have not knocked yourself up – it is what I expect. Do not be queer for next week. Addio – Love to all D. H. Lawrence

352. To Edward Garnett, 17 December 1911

Text: MS NYPL; Huxley 14–15.

16 Colworth Rd, Addiscombe, Croydon
17 Dec. 1911

Dear Garnett,

I got the cheque yesterday, and accept it gladly from you.[1] But a little later, when I have some money, you must let me pay it back to you, because that seems to me honester.

I am very well. Yesterday I sat up to tea for an hour. It is a weird, not delightful experience, which makes me feel like the seated statues of kings in Egypt. My chest gets rapidly well, but my brain is too active. To keep myself at all in order, I ought to be up and doing. By nature I am ceaselessly active. Now I sleep badly, because I don't do enough – and I mustn't work, because then away goes my strength. But I feel my life burn like a free flame floating on oil – wavering and leaping and snapping. I shall be glad to get it confined and conducted again.

The doctor says I mustn't go to school again or I shall be consumptive.[2] But he doesn't know. I shan't send in my notice, but shall ask for long leave of absence. Then I can go back if I get broke. The head-master grieves loudly over my prolonged absence. He knows he would scarcely get another man to do for him as I have done.

I shall look for you on Wednesday. Don't bring back that novel MSS.[3] unless you have read all you want to read. I don't want it a bit. It is a work too chargé, too emotional. It's a sponge dipped too full of vinegar,[4] or wine, or whatever – it wants squeezing out. I shrink from it rather. I wonder whether Jefferies used to wince away from the *Story of my Heart*.[5]

This is too long a letter to send to a busy man: excuse me.

Yours Sincerely D. H. Lawrence

[1] Probably a loan of 7 guineas. Cf. Letter 388.

[2] Ada Lawrence in a letter to Garnett, 17 December 1911 (MS NYPL), confirms this remark: 'Of course my brother will be very liable to consumption and as the doctors say will always need great care. He has to give up school, too.'

[3] *The Trespasser.*

[4] Cf. Matthew xxvii. 48.

[5] By Richard Jefferies (1883).

353. To Louie Burrows, 17 December 1911

Text: MS UN; Boulton 155–6.

16 Colworth Rd, Addiscombe, Croydon
17 Dec 1911

My dear Lou,

Am I becoming again a bad correspondent? I have off days.

Emily came yesterday. Ada went up to meet her, and they did the London shops. They enjoyed it very much. Wouldn't you like to do the same next week? It will be your only opportunity, and I think you'd enjoy it. You'll see enough of me afterwards. Miss Mason stayed with me till[1] three oclock, while Ada was away. She is very nice. Shall you mind sleeping at her house.

I sat up for about an hour at tea yesterday. It did not tire me so very much. But I can't stand on my legs for my life. That disgusts me very much. When shall I be able to get downstairs – heaven knows. I doubt whether we shall get to Bournemouth on the 27th – the 29th perhaps. Ada does not very much want to go, because of the expense. Already she has had to pay out some £15, and it scares her: for not half the bills are paid, she says. That of course is not true. Most of the bills are paid. Nurse has gone today. I shall miss her very much – Ada is glad, because of the expense. But do not think we are short of money – we are not.

I think Ada would rather like to go home at the New Year, and send us to Richmond for the week,[2] and then I[3] should go alone to Bournemouth. I do not know what we shall do, and don't care much. It depends on when I can walk.

I am tired of being invalid, and I won't be so much longer.

Do not imagine you will get much *rest* in this house. You forget the family. At least I cannot rest here – not much.[4]

In a very short time Saturday will be here. I shall very likely be able to go out on Sunday. We must get on.

I wait for next week.

A bientôt D. H. Lawrence

Of course I will come to Quorn later – when the flowers begin to come – I shall love it.

[1] till] from

[2] i.e. to stay with Max and Ethel Hunger.

[3] I] she

[4] not much] not too much

354. To Edward Garnett, 18 December 1911

Text: MS NYPL; Postmark, Croydon DE 19 11; Huxley 15–16.

16 Colworth Rd, Addiscombe, Croydon
18 Dec 1911

Dear Garnett,

Your letter concerning the Siegmund book is very exciting. I will tell you just what Hueffer said, then you will see the attitude his kind will take up.

'The book' he said 'is a rotten work of genius. It has no construction or form – it is execrably bad art, being all variations on a theme. Also it is erotic – not that I, personally, mind that, but an erotic work *must* be good art, which this is not.'

I sent it to 'our friend with the monocle'.[1] He wrote to me, after three months: 'I have read part of the book. I don't care for it, but we will publish it.'

I wrote back to him 'No, I won't have the book published. Return it to me.'[2]

That is about fifteen months ago. I wrote to Hueffer saying: 'The novel called "The Saga of Siegmund" I have determined not to publish.'[3] He replied to me 'You are quite right not to publish that book – it would damage your reputation, perhaps permanently.'

When I was last up at Heinemanns, two months ago, I asked Atkinson to send me the MS. He promised to do so, and said 'I have never finished it. It's your handwriting, you know.' – a sweet smile 'Perfectly legible, but so *tedious*' – a sweet smile.

That's all the criticism he ever ventured.

Is Hueffer's opinion worth anything, do you think? Is the book *so* erotic? I don't want to be talked about in an *Anne Veronica* fashion.[4]

If you offer the thing to Duckworth, do not, I beg you, ask for an advance on royalties. Do not present me as a beggar. Do not tell him I am poor. Heinemann owes me £50 in February – I have enough money to tide me over till he pays – and that fifty will, at home, last me six months. I do not want an advance – let me be presented to Duckworth as a respectable person.

[1] F. M. Atkinson, Heinemann's general editor.

[2] See Letter 229.

[3] Letter missing.

[4] e.g. John O'London in *TP's Weekly*, 22 October 1909, wrote: '*Ann Veronica* seems to me to be a dangerous novel'; John St Loe Strachey in *Spectator*, 20 November 1909, thought *Ann Veronica* 'capable of poisoning the minds of those who read it...a piece of dangerous and demoralising sophistry' (see *H. G. Wells, The Critical Heritage*, ed. Patrick Parrender, 1972, pp. 162, 169, 172).

Atkinson has not yet said anything about the poems. I told him I preferred only to publish about 25 of the best, impersonal pieces. He has not answered at all. I shall be glad when I have no more dealings with that firm.

You would get my yesterday's letter before you left the Cearne today – ?

We will, then, discuss the book on Wednesday. I shall change the title. Shall I call it 'The Livanters' – is that a correct noun from the verb 'To Livant'. To me, it doesn't look an ugly word, nor a disreputable one.

Yours Sincerely D. H. Lawrence

355. To Louie Burrows [18 December 1911]

Text: MS UN; PC; Postmark, Croydon DE 18 11; Boulton 156–7.

Addiscombe
Monday

My dear Lou,

How wonderfully you have got on with mon gilet. I shall henceforward believe you capable of anything.

I am very well. If the temperature is high Ada doesn't register it. We wait awhile, then I drink cold water, then lo, it is normal – a huge joke – the doctor gets so jumpy if I'm high. But I am very well, really; distressed only by my legs, which *won't* hold me up. I feel like the poor man sick of the palsy.[1]

Emily came Saturday – it was jolly to have her, but her stay was so short. What a blessing yours won't be a week-end. Eddie comes Saturday midnight – St Pancras at 3.25 in the morning. Heaven knows when he'll be down here.

Bring the bird on Saturday, and we'll have him for dinner on Sunday – the four of us. Won't it be jolly. I can eat anything now – in reason, and in small quantities. I am to be fed, the doctor repeats eternally.

You make me laugh, talking about rest. I shan't be able to walk half a mile, so I cant rush you about much.

My love to all at Coteshael. Yrs D. H. Lawrence

356. To Louie Burrows, 20 December 1911

Text: MS UN; Boulton 157–8.

16 Colworth Rd, Addiscombe, Croydon.
20[2] Dec 1911

[1] Matthew ix. 2.
[2] 20] 19

My dear Lou,

Don't, don't, don't alarm yourself. I can drink as much cold water as I like (doctor's permission), and I only take it to make my mouth cold to reduce the thermometer. I drink cold water at all hours of the day and night. The doctor has just been in and has the impudence to say I shall do well if I am down by Christmas day. He is a fibber – I shall go down on Sunday. This morning I strolled into the bathroom, prancing like the horses of the Walküre, on nimble air. I am enlarging my *Voyage autour de ma Chambre.*[1]

You will not get to Bournemouth – your visions of the racing Channel go pop. I should be mad if – if things really bothered me. I am awfully wild when I find a chocolate liqueur – a Kirsch – in bed with me. But it scarcely bothers me at all, what the Fates and Furies may roll out of their laps.

You will be very late coming on Sunday. Even Eddie will be here to Sunday breakfast. Tot is looking forward to meeting you – do not deprive her of the pleasure.[2]

I am waxy about going downstairs – I *hate* entertaining in the bedroom. Garnett is coming today, and Lil Reynolds will be here to tea tomorrow. I have had several folk to tea, and it is great excitement, I can tell you, in this little bedroom.

My damned pulse is the bother – fancy having a heart that ticks like a lady's watch! There's no room for endearments – à dimanche.

con amore D. H. Lawrence

So sorry Mr Burrows is ill. Condole with him from me. DHL

357. To Arthur McLeod, [22 December 1911]

Text: MS UT; PC; Postmark, [Cro]ydon DE 22 11; Unpublished.

Addiscombe
Friday

My dear Mac,

Jolly nice of you to send me *Toil of Men*[3] – I've hankered after it. This year I receive and give not[4] – it's an unholy condition. I sketched the *Idyll* for you in the week – I wanted to do the painting for you – but the lumbering drawing-board was too much for me, damn it. I will try if I can get the thing done before I go away.

[1] A pun on the title of the novel by François Xavier de Maistre (Paris, 1794).

[2] Ada Lawrence told Louie by letter, 20 December 1911 (MS UN LaB 205) that Agnes ('Tot') Mason would meet her (presumably at the station).

[3] By Israel Querido (1874–1932), trans. F. S. Arnold (1909).

[4] Cf. Acts xx. 35.

I can go downstairs on Christmas Day. And today I have struggled into my trousers, and walked into the bathroom. Now I lie like a warrior taking his rest, with my martial shawl around me.

Do come and see me. Oh how I execrated Ernie – how I suffered at his hands. You *might* have kicked him downstairs. Come any time and see me, I shall perforce be at home – and come soon.

[...] I'd put a Christmas verse if there were room.

Addio D. H. Lawrence

358. To Louie Burrows, [22 December 1911]

Text: MS UN; PC; Postmark, Croydon DE 22 11; Boulton 158.

Addiscombe
Friday

My dear Lou,

We shall expect you then on Sunday at about 4.45. You'll just be in time for tea.

The doctors says I shall be lucky if I am downstairs on Christmas day. But I shall be down to take tea with you on Sunday.

Miss Mason will meet you, and you'll be all serene. I hope you will be feeling more fit.

My love and Christmas greetings to everybody at Coteshael.

A bientôt D. H. Lawrence

P.S. Mrs Barker, the char-woman, has given us the sack – great indignation on Ada's part. DHL

359. To Edward Garnett, 30 December 1911

Text: MS NYPL; Huxley 16–17.

16 Colworth Rd, Addiscombe, Croydon
30 Dec 1911

Dear Garnett,

Have I kept the *Downland* too long?[1] – I am sorry. For a day or two I have intended writing, and returning it, but one is so dilatory convalescent.

I am getting on very well. Yesterday I went out for the first time, a little way down the road. I could walk like a grenadier guard, but for my left leg, which slumbers on, when all the rest of me is awake. The doctor says it is neuritis. However, it gets much better.

[1] See Letter 348.

Christmas was all right. My sister had her boy[1] down. He follows her round like a dog. They had tea tête-à-tête – I was lying on the couch with my back to them. When I scanned round, he sat holding a mince-pie minus one large round bite, and leaning forward to her so pathetically. She gave him a quick kiss, he bowed his head and humbly bit his mince pie. All the time they kept up their trivial conversation, and I should never have known – if I hadn't glegged.[2]

I'm not a bit like that – much more brûlant. My girl is here. She's big, and swarthy, and passionate as a gipsy – but good, awfully good, churchy. She rubs her cheek against me, just like a cat, and says 'Are you happy?' It makes me laugh. But I am not particularly happy, being only half here, yet awhile. She never understands that – so I have to pitch all my wits against her. It's very weird.

The Americans are just as stupid as we expected. Their reason, however, is really comical. It amused me – that's something unexpected.[3] – Keep the MS. as long as you like.[4]

I am to go to Bournemouth – Lord, how sick I am of this ordering and countermanding – I loathe to be an invalid – It is nearly unendurable to have to wait for one's strength to come back – like Penelope. I hate my legs, miserable defaulters – I detest them. I hate to be waited on, and to be treated gently. If ever I'm ill again I shall die of mortification. – I am to go to Bournemouth some time next week – probably Friday.

I think I'll send you this story.[5] My sense of beauty and of interest comes back very strong. I wrote this story last week, in bed – before I could sit up much. You'll find it, perhaps, thin – maladif. I can't judge it at all – one reason why I send it.

There's no news. My sister sends her greetings.

Yours Sincerely D. H. Lawrence

P.S. For a title to that MS. called at present The Saga, will 'Trespassers in Cythera' or The Trespasser or something like that, do? Or for 'Cythera' what can one put – what are the Isles of the Happy – ? Evin, Evna?[6] – Help me out.

I shall begin re-writing the first part today. DHL

[1] W. E. Clarke.

[2] i.e. taken a sly look, peeped.

[3] that's something unexpected] so that's something gained

[4] Of 'Two Marriages' (cf. Letter 339) rejected by the *Century*.

[5] 'The Soiled Rose', later entitled 'The Shades of Spring'. For confirmation see Letter 579.

[6] DHL's reference is obscure.

360. To Edward Garnett, 3 January 1912

Text: MS NYPL; Huxley 18.

16 Colworth Rd, Addiscombe, Croydon
3 Jan 1912[1]

Dear Garnett,

I hope you got *Nature in Downland* all right – it was posted on Saturday. I return you the rest – for which many thanks. The whole household, from Mrs Jones downwards, has devoured James Prior. *Why* is he a failure – Wm Heinemann said he was:

'We had a fellow from your way – a James Prior – did some Sherwood Forest novels. Very good, I thought – but went quite dead, quite dead.'

I saw myself also 'quite dead, quite dead' in William's hands – ghastly spectacle!

I am actually going to Bournemouth on Saturday – to 'Compton House, St Peters Rd. Bournemouth' a boarding house. God help us.

I have begun the Saga again – done the first chapter – heaps, heaps better. There was room for improvement, by Jove! – I was so young – almost pathetically young – two years ago. What do *you* say of me today – I guess you laugh.

A long fare well D. H. Lawrence

P.S. I don't care for *Torrents of Spring* – though perhaps because I read it too soon – too ill. DHL

361. To Edward Garnett, [7 January 1912]

Text: MS NYPL; Huxley 18–20.

Compton House, St Peters Rd, Bournemouth
7 Jan 1911

Dear Garnett,

Many thanks for the play.[2] I like it best of all yours; I think it's ripping: I wish I could say it were satirical or cynical. It looks such a damn mess between the men and the women altogether. – Henderson, the Philistine, I think you're a bit hard on: just a bit. Harding, the artist, is most appallingly true: it's a case of 'behold thyself' – with this difference – I don't think I should go about swearing undying love. It is a much more delicate thing to make love and to win love, than to declare love. But in plays you have to

[1] 1912] 1911

[2] *Lords and Masters* published under Garnett's pseudonym 'James Byrne' (1911); first produced by B. Iden Payne, Gaiety Theatre, Manchester, 22–7 May 1911 (see Rex Pogson, *Miss Horniman and the Gaiety Theatre, Manchester*, 1952, p. 202); reviewed in *Manchester Guardian*, 23 May 1911.

be bald. Mrs Henderson – I mean the young one – I could shoot her. She is typical of all that is exasperating in women. She is most abominably true. But Harding must have managed her very badly. – It is a disturbing, damnable little play – I should never have guessed you for the author. – The women in it are best aren't they? I wish I had been in Manchester to see the acting.

As for the *Century* man, I'm certain I haven't a story he'd take. The three he might have had, the *English* has published. For the rest, you've seen most of the Secker volume. There's the one you've got – the two you've got – and the 'Haystacks' one – and the two I sent you first – and a couple that Austin Harrison has – and a couple or so more.[1] That's enough for a volume I believe – and nothing, absolutely, for the *Century*'s holy eyes. What shall I say to Secker? – he is 5 John St, Adelphi, is he not?

I was away at Red Hill[2] for a couple of days, when your letter came, so I couldn't root out any more stories for you – and I came straight from Red Hill here.

I don't like it very much – It's a sort of go-as-you-please boarding house, where I shall be far more alone than if I had gone into apartments, as I wanted to do.[3] I think I get a bit impatient of people. But there, one is always churlish after an illness. When I'm better tempered I shall like the old maids and the philistine men and the very proper and proprietous maidens right enough. It is always raining – so stupid of it.

When I come back to Croydon, in a month's time, I shall be very glad to come and see you at the Cearne. Then I shall go home to the midlands.

I will try and get the *Trespasser* done in a month or so. I should[4] like him published this spring. Must I tell Wm Heinemann about him? I have heard nothing of the poems.

The world – there are some 50 people in the house – is going to church, so I can write in peace.

If you've anything really nice to read – send it me, will you.

Yrs D. H. Lawrence

[1] DHL here points to his output of short stories to date. *English Review* had published 'Goose Fair', 'Odour of Chrysanthemums', and 'A Fragment of Stained Glass'. The two Garnett had were 'Two Marriages' and 'The Soiled Rose', together with 'Love Among the Haystacks'. Of the two sent him 'first', one was 'Intimacy'; the second and the 'couple or so more' were from the following: 'A Prelude', 'The Vicar's Garden', 'Lessford's Rabbits', 'A Lesson on a Tortoise', 'A Modern Lover', 'The Fly in the Ointment', 'The Old Adam'. The 'couple that Austin Harrison has' were 'Second Best' and 'The White Stocking'.

[2] Staying with Lilian Reynolds and her mother.

[3] Compton House is described in *Kelly's Directory* 1911, as a 'Boarding House'; the name of T. B. Robb is attached to the entry.

[4] should] must

362. To Arthur McLeod, [7 January 1912]

Text: MS UT; PC v. Compton House, St. Peter's Road, Bournemouth; Postmark, Bournemouth JA 7 12; Unpublished.

[Compton House, St. Peter's Road, Bournemouth]
[7 January 1912]

Here I am alone in a crowd – Lord! Write me, for the love of heaven.
DHL

363. To May Holbrook, 7 January 1912

Text: TMSC UT; Envelope MS UN; Postmark, Bourne[mouth] JA 7 12; Nehls, iii. 622–3.

Compton House, St. Peter's Road, Bournemouth.
7 Jan 1912

My dear May,

Isn't it scandalous that I haven't written you before. But now I'm convalescent, I am more reluctant to do my duty than ever.

I came down here yesterday. It is a big house – 45 folk in now – there were 80 last week. I am still a forlorn lost lamb – but am getting used to things. I write in the billiard room, and a fellow is giving physical demonstrations, very weird, to a little Finnish chap.[1] The latter I have chattered to. It is wonderful what chances for being interesting some people miss. He looks like a Mongol – the Finns are Mongolian – and he speaks like no one else on Earth. But he talks commonplace. It's a shame.

The place is pretty – a big town set among trees – and such heaps of pine trees, very dark. The cliffs are golden – sand-stone, quite soft. They look very nice with the sun on them: and the sea, like a great churning of milk with golden patches far off, coming in long rollers and smashing high up, the loveliest of smashed waves, white and leaping, and slewing all over the promenade. It is very pretty. Now it is moon-light – after dinner. The bay is very long, and double, like this

[rough sketch]

so we look along the surf at the moon. The white light glitters like fire on the front of each wave, just as it rears to fall. Then, in the flat wash, the foam is shadow like dark lace, and then skerts off the water like silver grey silk – lovely. I wish you were down here to see it all.

Your cheese was so nice, by the way. I wondered however in winter you had managed to make it. It was awfully good of you.

The Finn is waiting for me to go out. The sea has been like milk, and

[1] Mr Scheinen (b. 1891).

like white steel, all day. I will write you a nice letter later – this is a scrawl. Write to me here – I am so forlorn.

Regards to Will. I shall be home in 5 or 6 weeks – Hurray!

Love D. H. Lawrence

364. To Louie Burrows, 8 January 1912

Text: MS UN; Postmark, Bournemouth JA 8 12; Boulton 158–9.

Compton House, St. Peter's Road, Bournemouth.
8 Jan 1912

My dear Lou,

It is the end of the second day – we've just finished coffee, after dinner. It's a jolly place – you would like it. I wish always you had come. There are 45 people in, all sorts. One gets up at 8.30, and breakfasts at nine – very prolific breakfasts – bacon and kidney and ham and eggs – what you like. I chatter in the smoke room till about 10.30 – then work in my room where I have had a fire made – until 1.30, when we have lunch – which is a bigger meal, or as big as our usual dinners. In the afternoon I go out, or if its wet, like today, I just stop in the recreation room and we play cards and games. After tea I went out with a man for a stroll, then a gin and bitters, then dinner. When I've done this letter I'm going up to the rec. again for games. It is really rather jolly. You must come some time.

I get such a lot better – the air suits me. The weather is wet, but it's not cold.

The town is very pretty. When you look back at it, it's quite dark green with trees. There is a great bay, and long, smashing waves, always close to the prom., because there are four tides a day. At night, with the full moon along the surf, and the foam smashing up, it is lovely. Then I go out alone, and I wish, I can tell you, that you were here. We would have some lovely times now I am getting well and shall be able to walk nice long ways.

I do not flirt with the girls – there are some very pretty – only with the old, old maids.

I am going out to tea tomorrow at Mrs Steel's.[1] She is a friend of Miss MacNairs,[2] and has a house in Lansdowne Rd.

I do about 2 hrs work a day, and get on. When it is finer I shall go out more. I will be very good, and get very fat, and come home 'like a giant refreshed',[3] to use your language.

[1] Mrs Eliza Steel (d. 1921?) who lived at 66 Lansdowne Road.
[2] Unidentified.
[3] Psalm lxxviii. 66 (Book of Common Prayer).

I hope school has gone down well, and that Mrs A[dams] is inclined to be sweeter.

They make such a row here, in the billiard room, this is sure to be a scrappy letter.

It would be so fine if you were here. But I shall soon come home. Give my love to all at Coteshael. I shall expect your letter tomorrow.

Addio – love D. H. Lawrence

365. To Alice Smith, [9 January 1912]

Text: MS UT; PC v. Compton House, St. Peter's Road, Bournemouth; Postmark, Bournemouth JA 9 12; cited in Moore, *Intelligent Heart* 108.

[Compton House, St. Peter's Road, Bournemouth]
[9 January 1912]

You didn't come and see me in the holiday – for which, 'je vous en veux' (French!!)[1] Bournemouth is all right. This house is jolly. – 45 folk in – a fair leaven of old permanent ladies, but nevertheless, some solid young folk, quite gay.

I am becoming a 'garçon fort solide' – it's actually sunny this morning.

Vale! D. H. Lawrence

366. To Edward Garnett, 10 January 1912

Text: MS NYPL; Unpublished.

Compton House, St Peters Rd, Bournemouth
10 Jan 1912

Dear Garnett,

Harrison sent me back this story yesterday, and he's publishing one I don't like a bit – a poor one.[2] Isn't it a nuisance. I suppose he wont have the 'Haystacks' one – too long – he doesn't say. This is a wicked story, perhaps, but it's clever. – I will send you all I can.

Thanks for the letter of this morning. I'll tell Heinemann. Do you mean Walter de la Mare?[3] – if so, how ripping! I hope Atkinson *has* gone. But what of my verses?

[1] According to her husband, Mrs Alice Smith, like DHL, 'was interested in French literature. They read French verse and we sang French songs' (Nehls, i. 89).

[2] Harrison returned 'The White Stocking'; he published 'Second Best', *English Review*, x (February 1912), 461–9.

[3] Walter de la Mare (1873–1956), poet, writer of prose fiction, essayist; he succeeded Atkinson as Heinemann's resident reader in January 1912. He had already published *Songs of Childhood* (pseudonym 'Walter Ramal', 1902); a novel, *The Return* (1910), etc.

I get on very slowly with the 'Saga'.

The books haven't come – am I a great nuisance?

In haste D. H. Lawrence

P.S. The books have just come. I love books of Short stories. Andreyev is not burningly interesting, is he?[1]

Shall I write to Secker and what shall I say? DHL

367. To Louie Burrows, [10 January 1912]

Text: MS UN; PC v. Norman Tower, Christchurch; Postmark, Bournemouth JA 11 12; Boulton 160.

[Compton House, St. Peter's Road, Bournemouth]
[10 January 1912][2]

I have been here today by car – it is a wonderfully fine church, and a queer situation, between two rivers, now in flood.[3]

I am very well – can walk $1\frac{1}{2}$ miles like a bird. The weather has been fine today and yesterday – and so warm. I am glad to miss the snow up in the midlands.

One has scarcely a minute here – all full up. Love to all –

Love D. H. Lawrence

368. To Louie Burrows, 12 January 1912

Text: MS UN; Postmark, Bournemouth JA 12 12; Boulton 160–1.

Compton House, St. Peter's Road, Bournemouth.
12 Jan 1912

My dear Lou,

Did you get my Christchurch card on Thursday? I believe I posted it in the house, after the box was cleared. I am sorry.

Today there is a big fog. When I was on the West Cliff yesterday afternoon, I saw it coming in from over the sea. It is a peculiar colour, this sea – either milk white, or a very pale, pure stone colour, or a dove grey: so pale and ghostly, with opalescent tints. I admire it very much.

We have real good times. I have a fire in my room and write when I may. If it's fine we go out in the morning. Always, we have games in the recreation

[1] Leonidas Andreyev. Garnett may have sent his *Silence, and Other Stories*, trans. W. H. Lowe (September 1910).

[2] The opening paragraph of the next letter makes clear that this card was posted on 10 January 1912 but too late for collection the same day; it was thus postmarked on 11 January.

[3] Christchurch, Hants., at the junction of the rivers Stour and Avon; noted for the priory church of Holy Trinity.

room. It is a big, cosy room, with a turkey carpet and deep chairs. There are some ripping chairs here, and some delightful folk, men and women. The Miss Brintons have just had their billiard lesson from the little Finnish fellow.[1] He makes such a row: you would die to hear him. There is a little Russian girl named Stein who has him on an awful string.

I went to see Trubeen's[2] friend, Mrs Steel, on Wednesday – was there for tea. It is a nice house, and they are exceedingly pleasant. But they don't love Trubeen, notwithstanding they send their 'best love'.

We usually tea out. It is the fashion here. The house tea is a bit dreary, and there are some lovely restaurants. Tea should be a cosy meal.

We seem to feed so much. There is always such heaps of butter and toast and biscuits about – then four meals a day – and three of them *big* meals. I tell you, I am coming on fast. I eat as much as I can, decently. Already my legs are about as big as before I was ill.

Have you heard from Auntie that Hannah Krenkow[3] wants me to go to Germany, to Waldbröl near Cologne, in Spring. And I want to go in April or May. Won't it be just all right. If I get a living knowledge of German and French, then any time, if necessary, I can go into Secondary teaching.

I always wish you could be down here, it is so nice. But in Summer the house is crowded – 70 to 80 folk. That is too much.

I don't think I have any more news. Keep well, and be happy.

My love to everybody at Coteshael. Love D. H. Lawrence

369. To Louie Burrows, 17 January 1912

Text: MS UN; Postmark, Bournemouth JA 17 12; Boulton 161–2.

Compton House, St. Peter's Road, Bournemouth.
17 Jan 1912

My dear Lou,

It's raining here like the devil – it rained ditto yesterday, clearing up for an hour or two about noon But it was a beautiful rough sea. I have moved downstairs on to the first floor, where I have a bigger room – a large armchair, a broad fire place with a quite impressive mantel of white marble. I have a fire and am cosy as can be, when I want to retire from the madding crowd. But they won't leave me much alone.

[1] Though the Misses Brinton are listed in DHL's address-book as at 14 Fortune Green Road, Hampstead, they have not been traced.

[2] Possibly a reference to Miss MacNair (Letter 364).

[3] DHL referred to her later as his 'cousin'; their relationship was by marriage only. Hannah (b. 1881?) married Fritz Krenkow's relative, Karl. She appears as Johanna in 'German Impressions: II. Hail in the Rhineland' (*Saturday Westminster Gazette*, 10 August 1912).

My rash is better – I am very well – by the time I come home I shall be quite solid. I've had a cold but I think it's better. I drink hot milk morning and night, like a good un. We have some real fun. Now, I have got quite fond of the semi public sort of life: always plenty of folk, plenty to do, no chance to be dull, and yet, if you like, real privacy, such as domestic life never gives. It is not bad. I believe, do you know, you'd like it. You'd be rid of the nuisance of house-keeping. If one were well enough off, would you like to live in an hôtel, do you think.

This is the MS of a story that is to appear in next month's *English*.[1] I don't care much for it.

I think, like you, I have no news. I am glad you are scoring off Mrs A[dams] so well.

Damn the dirty morning – I wanted to go out, and I s'll have to play games instead.

Goodbye – keep well – give my love to everybody – snowdrops are out here – spring's near, all right.

Vale, my dear D. H. Lawrence

P.S. Don't fret, I dont work much.

370. To Edward Garnett, 19 January 1912

Text: MS NYPL; Huxley 20.

Compton House, St. Peter's Road, Bournemouth.
19 Jan 1912

My dear Garnett,

What do you think of the enclosed?[2] Is it merely soft sawder? I really don't think the Saga was ever read at Wm Heinemann's – not by anyone. But they make me feel so uncertain and down about the wretched thing. I am always ready to believe the worst that is said about my work, and reluctant of the best. Father was like that with us children.

I have done the first 135 pages of the *Trespasser* – rewritten them. Shall I send them on? At the bottom of my heart I don't like the work, though I'm sure it has points, and I don't think it retrograde from the *White Peacock*. It surprises me by its steady progressiveness – I hate it for its fluid, luscious quality.

Harrison is putting in Next month's *English* a story I do *not* care for. Altogether, I am out of sorts in my literary self just now.

[1] See p. 348 n. 2.

[2] A (missing) letter from Heinemann; it tried to persuade DHL not to give *The Trespasser* to Duckworth (see Letter 375).

I've had a vicious cold, but it's nearly better – and it is a fine morning at last. We have had torrents of rain, but no snow. Are you quite well – I have been wondering.

Tell me, shall I send that so much of the *Trespasser* – and will you be severe on it when you have time to go through it.

I hope to get away from here in another fortnight. I have promised to visit friends in Germany in April or May.

Oh – it seems to me evident Heinemann doesn't want the verses very badly. Isn't he a nuisance. It's because of their rotten form, I suppose. Still, he could find a *few* good ones – and he might let me know what he does want. I wish he'd give them me back.

Shame to bore you with all this.

Yours Sincerely D. H. Lawrence

371. To Arthur McLeod, [19 January 1912]

Text: MS UT; PC v. Compton House, St. Peter's Road, Bournemouth; Postmark, Bournemouth JA 19 12; Unpublished.

[Compton House, St. Peter's Road, Bournemouth]
[19 January 1912]

Your letter was so brief and scanty, it doesn't deserve a reply. But are you better from your cold. Oh the damnable weather!

Harrison is putting me a story in next month – but such a rotten one. I am on tenterhooks of literary shame.

– I'm pretty well – had a damned cold. Lets hear from you.

D. H. Lawrence

372. To Louie Burrows, [20 January 1912]

Text: MS UN; PC v. Christchurch; Postmark, Bournemouth JA 20 12; Boulton 162.

[Compton House, St. Peter's Road, Bournemouth]
[20 January 1912]

Another view of Christchurch – you must go there sometime. Yesterday I was out at Poole Harbour – drove there with the Jenkinsons[1] – it was delightful, such a sweet day, and all so pretty. I am really very well – be at your ease.

Yours Sincerely D. H. Lawrence

[1] Walter (1876–1917?) and Elizabeth Anne Jenkinson of 2 Studley Road, Harrogate.

373. To Edward Garnett, 21 January 1912
Text: MS NYPL; Huxley 21–2.

Compton House, St. Peter's Road, Bournemouth.
21 Jan 1912

My dear Garnett,

I received your letter yesterday, and the books this morning. It is very good of you, and it makes me wonder how you, who are as busy and as public a man as most literary fellows, can find the time and the energy. Hueffer impressed it on me, it couldn't be done: by the time a man was forty, the triviality of minor interests could only command a rare slight attention: and I had begun to believe it. But you are so prompt and consistently attentive, where you gain nothing, that I begin to reconsider myself.

I will send you herewith the 180 or 190 pages of the *Trespasser* which I have done. It won't take me much longer, will it? I hope the thing is knitted firm – I hate those pieces where the stitch is slack and loose. The 'Stranger' piece is probably still too literary – I don't feel at all satisfied.[1]

But this is a work one can't regard easily – I mean, at one's ease. It is so much oneself, one's naked self. I give myself away so much, and write what is my most palpitant, sensitive self, that I loathe the book, because it will betray me to a parcel of fools. Which is what any deeply personal or lyrical writer feels, I guess. I often think Stendhal must have writhed in torture every time he remembered *Le Rouge et le noir* was public property: and Jefferies at *The Story of my Heart*. I don't like the *Story of my Heart*.

I wish the *Trespasser* were to be issued privately, to a few folk who had understanding. But I suppose, by all the rules of life, it must take open chance, if it's good enough.

I like the first two stories of Gertrude Bone immensely[2] – she is wonderfully perceptive there. She's got a lot of poetic feeling, a lot of perceptivity, but she seems scarcely able to concentrate it on her people she is studying: at least, not always. Something in Andreyev makes him rather uninteresting to me, and *House of Cobwebs* is, as Seccombe suggests, chiefly of interest as

[1] Helen Corke commented (in a private letter): '"The Stranger piece" is the chapter XIII, in which the "outside" character Hampson is introduced. It was DHL's way of indicating his own place in the story. He brought it to me when first written and asked if I had any objection to its inclusion – I had not.' On a fragment of *The Trespasser* MS in its unrevised state is a critical note probably by Edward Garnett: 'Something is wanted to carry off this passage with the Stranger, i.e., – you must intersect his talk with little realistic touches to make him very *actual*. He must not spring quite out of the blue & disappear into it again. He's too much a deus ex machina, for your purpose. Make him seem in talk more ordinary & natural & slip in the pregnant things at moments' (Tedlock, *Lawrence MSS* 8, 11).

[2] The reference is probably to her *Provincial Tales* (Duckworth, 1904); if so 'the first two stories' are 'Poverty' and 'The Right Eye'.

footnotes on Gissing.[1] Gissing hasn't enough energy, enough sanguinity, to capture me. But I esteem him a good deal.

I am pretty well – have had a damnable cold, which lingers. The weather here is soft and inclined to fog. I would rather be braced a little, now.

I shall leave here on Feb. 3rd and will come straight to the Cearne, if that is convenient. I have promised to go home to Nottingham on Feb 8th. Can you keep me at the Cearne about four days?

Here I get mixed up in people's lives so – it's very interesting, sometimes a bit painful, often jolly. But I run to such close intimacy with folk, it is complicating. But I love to have myself in a bit of a tangle.

Thanks very much for the things.

Yours D. H. Lawrence

374. To Louie Burrows, 23 January 1912

Text: MS UN; Boulton 163.

Compton House, St. Peter's Road, Bournemouth.
23 Jan 1912

My dear Lou,

Your pippiness in the last letter is very quaint and unusual for you. It accords with the 'disgusting dreary desert' state I often suffer from. It is no use talking about Ethel – what she will do, she will do, and will only be thought the better of, in the end. Folk who have their own way in spite of everybody's wishes, seem, miraculously, to win the esteem and affection of the same everybody.

I am very well again, after my cold. It is poor sort of weather. Saturday was lovely: we were up on the hills in the pine woods, and had dough cakes and milk in a very charming cottage. Sunday was blank fog – I never stirred out. Yesterday was dullish, but fine: sea an 'eau de Nile' colour. I am beginning to suffer from 'wanderlust' again. I want to go over sea. When the Jenkinson's went up to London yesterday, I would have given anything to go too. Yet, here is as nice as any place could be. But I would willingly move.

I have promised to go to Garnetts on Feb. 3rd. The Haleys[2] want me to stay on till the 5th, when they are going up to London. I may do so. If the weather is decent I shall probably come up to Eastwood on Feb. 9th. It is Margarets birthday then, and Emily wants to give a party in honor thereof, and of my homecoming. We'll see how it comes off.

[1] In Thomas Seccombe's 'The Work of George Gissing: an Introductory Survey' prefixed to Gissing's *House of Cobwebs* (1906), pp. xlviii–xlix.

[2] Unidentified fellow guests.

Today is a bit misty but quite decent. I should rather like to go to Poole – I must see.

Tomorrow it is the 21st birthday of Mr Scheinen – the little fellow from Finland. The girls are getting up a sort of bun fight down in the recreation room, to celebrate the event. Scheinen has promised to drive us out in the big motor car belonging to the establishment. We'll see how that also comes off.

There are rather fewer people in the house, but as my table party remains – save the Jenkinsons, who went yesterday, to my sorrow – I am not very much affected.

When is your birthday, by the way?[1] I have forgotten again. Dont let me neglect it – you know what I am.

By this time you will have bucked up and will be quite gay again, I hope.

This, with my love D. H. Lawrence

375. To Arthur McLeod, 24 January 1912

Text: MS UT; Postmark, Bournemouth JA 24 12; cited in Moore, *Intelligent Heart* 109.

Compton House, St. Peter's Road, Bournemouth.
24 Jan 1912

My dear Mac,

I was very glad to hear from you – but is it *such* a fag to write. Whom has Aylwin assaulted, how bad is it – and what is to be the result. Where is Humphreys now? Why won't your cold get better? Do be careful. Don't go my way, and get chesty. It is the very devil in the end.

Implore Miss Mason to put in her letter the school *news*: to tell me how Philip is behaving, and how Bennetto[2] has come to Hades etc. She at least has some length about her: you and the rest are stumpy correspondents.

I am getting very well, I think. I've had a fierce and fiendish cold which lingers – but notwithstanding all, I get fatter – 'fatter' is the term, I think – in preference to 'more corpulent'.

How can I, in a far-off land, tell you interesting things – unless I become geographical. Of me, there is nothing to say. But you are the Davidson chronicler, and a jolly bad one.

Atkinson has left Heinemann, and it was rumoured Walter de la Mare was to take his place. With Atkinson my verses are left also – I wrote

[1] 13 February.

[2] R. M. Bennetto (d. 1912) joined the staff of Davidson Road School, 30 August 1911; he became ill on 2 February 1912. The School Log laconically reports: '20 Feb. 1912 R. M. Bennetto left service of [Education] committee. (Died 20th Feb 1912).'

Heinemann – William is away – they were indefinite concerning the poems – and tried to soft-sawder me into not giving the second, love-novel which they practically refused, to Duckworth. But to Duckworth it shall go, if I can revise it to my taste. It is to be called *The Trespasser*, so we'll know how to speak of it. I do very little work – just the revising of this novel – no creative work.

I'm writing in the billiard room where a little Finn, whose 21st is today, is playing billiards with an old gent from South Africa. I live in constant dread of a cue in my ear and a ball in my eye. Also Scriven and I were celebrating our acquaintance – with scotch – in his room – till the small hours – so I'm as dull as cold tea.

The old ladies continue to mother me – the young ones – shall we say, to sister me. The men are very aimiable, but nearly teetotallers, now. There was one chap[1] here last week, with whom I[2] had fine sport. He was mad with his wife on Friday, so he went out with me to Poole Harbour. There he went on the razzle. I had a fiendish time. He kept it up when we got back here: walked away with a baby in a pram in Christchurch Rd – tried to board and drive off with a private motor car – nearly had a fight in the Central Hôtel, and got us turned out. We were four, arm in arm, swaying up the main street here. . people dodging out of the way like hares. It was hot. In the end, I had to throw all the drinks they kept forcing on me, onto the floor, lest I got as drunk as they.

Then, when at last, after superhuman struggles, I got him home – he was a big, well-built Yorkshire man of 35 – plenty of cash – had been in the army – *I* – *I* had to stand the racket from Mrs Jenkinson, whom I like, who is young and pretty and has travelled a good bit – and who sits at my table. I wished most heartily on Friday evening that I was over Lethe's soothing stream.

But now I am forgiven. It is raining today – the weather is so-so – it has never been cold. I can scarcely say when I shall be back in Croydon – if ever. But I'll tell you later: I don't think I want to return to Davidson – but we'll let that dog lie, also.

I wish I could see you. I suppose you don't feel like taking a trip down here on Sunday? – only five bob – I should love it.

My fond affection to thee – regards to all the world.

D. H. Lawrence

How's that business of the house, and the law-suit, by the way?

DHL

[1] Walter Jenkinson.

[2] I] we

I had, from Barrie Robinson,[1] a warm eulogy on the *Peacock*. He says he's a hero-worshipper – hero, myself! How's that to counterbalance the shrivelled Marshall?[2] 'out of the mouths of babes and sucklings'.[3]

DHL

376. To Helen Corke, [26 January 1912]

Text: MS UT; PC v. The Needles. I.O.W.; Postmark, Poole 26 JA 12; Unpublished.

[26 January 1912]

Poole is awfully pretty – we've come here by car – on the way to Wimbourne where I'm going to read the bible – the ancient chained one.

Yrs D. H. Lawrence

377. To Louie Burrows, [28 January 1912]

Text: MS UN; Postmark, Bournemouth JA 28 12; Boulton 164.

Compton House, St. Peter's Road, Bournemouth.
Sunday

My dear Lou,

I don't in the least know when I last wrote you, but I suppose it's my turn.

Your questions trouble me considerably.

I do *not* want to go with a bushel of maidens to the castle. I shall be delighted to accompany you to Bingham, but don't fix the date yet. What else? Oh, I will remember the 13th – what an unlucky date.

Was that all I had to answer? My memory's really gone to pot since I've been crocky.

It's such a ripping day. We've been along the sands to Branksome Chine – 2 or 3 miles – where we had hot milk and chocs. It is very beautiful here when the weather's decent. Now, and yesterday and Friday have been sunny as you like. On Friday we went to Poole, and then to Wimburne – some 10 or 11 miles. Poole is very pretty – a round harbour, with islands

[sketch-map][4]

and swans and gulls mixed. Wimburne has an old minster – Saxon and

[1] D. Bartlett ('Barry') Robinson (1886–1945), a teacher at Woodside and at Portland Schools, Croydon (both neighbouring schools to Davidson Road); 1929 headmaster of Ecclesbourne Boys School, and, 1936–45, of Winterbourne Junior Boys School.

[2] Possibly Miss I. Marshall, a member of Croydon Education Committee, 1904–19, whose name (as a visitor) appears in the School Log.

[3] Psalms viii. 2 ['...mouth...'].

[4] Showing Poole in relation to 'the Haven' (and, wrongly, to the east of Bournemouth).

Norman – very fine: ancient oak, old tombs of the Somersets, a chained library, and the lord knows what. It's really very interesting. We had lunch in the Kings Head and then walked back to Poole – six miles – *now* am I not a garçon solide. But sometimes I lapse. However I shall not shortly.

Well really – I am invited to Scrivens room to coffee. He often collects the decent folk on Sunday afternoon – and if Im not off I shall find the lot of the beverage swallowed by – goodness knows whom.

We tea'd yesterday at the Haven – on the verandah. Red sunset in S.W. – very rough sea coming over the bar on the left[1] – still harbour right – very nice – refer to map.

The folk here admire my writing so much.

I nearly won the whist drive prize on Friday – a bottle of scotch. I hope Scriven's got some in.

I shall be seeing you directly.

Love and Kisses D. H. Lawrence

378. To Edward Garnett, 29 January 1912

Text: MS NYPL; Huxley 22–3.

Compton House, St. Peter's Road, Bournemouth.
29 Jan 1912

My dear Garnett,

My time here is running out. They want me sadly to stay till today week – the 5th – but I think I'd rather come on the Saturday. I shall leave here by the 2.0 p.m. train, which arrives in London – Waterloo – at 4.0. It is a non-stop. Would you mind to send me a train from Victoria or anywhere down to Edenbridge? You choose the time, and I will abide by it. Do not bother with a trap – I can walk quite well. I can do six miles by now.

The Trespasser goes quite fast. In the dirty weather of the last week I have got on with it. I am past the 300th page now. It really isn't bad, is it – but too florid, too 'chargé'. But it can't be anything else – it is itself. I must let it stand. At any rate, not many folk could have done it, however they may find fault. – I shall finish by the time I come to Edenbridge – or at any rate before I leave you. So, when you can find time to go over the thing, we can decide about the publishing. If it is to come, I should like April or May for the month, as you suggested.

We have had three beautiful days – most lovely. I am very sensitive to the exquisite atmospheres of down here – I have delightful passages. In health, too, I am sure I make good strides. But at the bottom I am rather

[1] left] right

miserable. I can never decide whether my dreams are the result of my thoughts, or my thoughts the result of my dreams. It is very queer. But my dreams make conclusions for me. They decide things finally. I dream a decision. Sleep seems to hammer out for me the logical conclusions of my vague days, and offer me them as dreams. It is a horrid feeling, not to be able to escape from one's own – what? – self – daemon – fate, or something. I hate to have my own judgments clinched inside me involuntarily. But it is so.

What tosh to write. I don't know what ails me.

Just tell me about the train. I will bring the rest of the *Trespasser*.

Yours D. H. Lawrence

379. To Helen Corke, 1 February 1912

Text: MS SIU; Moore 97–8.

Compton House, St. Peter's Road, Bournemouth.
1st. Feb 1912

Why are you so sarky? I tell you again I am not altering the substance of the Saga, so that, in spite of my present tone, you will not find it perverted from what of original truth it had. I re-cast the paragraphs, and attend to the style. As soon as I can, I will send you the MS., that you may satisfy yourself.

But, as you remember saying yourself, the Saga is a work[1] of fiction on a frame of actual experience. It is my presentation, and therefore necessarily false sometimes to your view. The necessity is not that our two views should coincide, but that the work should be a work of art. Why should I want to falsify it? I am not flippant with the Saga. But you shall see for yourself.

Send the books to Eastwood just at your convenience, will you? Have you got Hueffer's *High Germany* poems?[2] You see he gave that to me. And the *Hibberts*, – I think either you or J[essie] had it – would you mind giving it to Mrs Dax some time. I want her to read it.[3]

Why should things that were real to me become false? I don't understand you perfectly. Surely it has always been one of my tenets, that a truth, or a vital experience, is eternal, in so far as it is incorporated into one's being, and so is oneself. How am I one thing today, and another tomorrow? It is an absurdity. Yet you urge it against me very often: it is almost my chief

[1] work] framework

[2] *High Germany. Eleven sets of verse* (1911).

[3] DHL was referring to the *Hibbert Journal*, x (October 1911), 1–23, which contained A. J. Balfour's article, 'Creative Evolution and Philosophic Doubt'. (Information from Helen Corke.)

characteristic, in your eyes. You never believe that I have any real unity of character.

An illness changes me a good deal – like winter on the face of the earth: but that does not mean I am shook about like a kaleidoscope. It would be to deny identity. One may seem very different from one's past, but one is nevertheless the new child of one's yesterdays.[1]

You will smile, and say I am again taking up the prisoner at the bar position. But it is only by answering charges that I can substantiate my bit of a life philosophy.

I wonder how barren all this is to you!

Valete D. H. Lawrence

380. To May Holbrook, [2 February 1912]

Text: MS UN; PC v. Compton House, St. Peter's Road, Bournemouth; Postmark, Bournemouth FE 2 12; Nehls, iii. 623.

[Compton House, St. Peter's Road, Bournemouth.]
[2 February 1912]

Are you wondering what has become of me? I am scandalously lax in my correspondence.

Tomorrow I leave here – and for some things am very sorry. I go for a week to Garnetts, down in Kent – then, on the 9th or 10th I shall come to Eastwood. I look forward so much to seeing you and having a bit of a razzle.

Yrs D. H. Lawrence

Regards to Will.

381. To Jessie Chambers, [ante 3 February 1912]

Text: E.T. 194.

[Compton House, St. Peter's Road, Bournemouth]
[ante 3 February 1912]

I advise you never to come here for a holiday. The place exists for the sick. They hide the fact as far as possible, but it's like a huge hospital. At every turn you come across invalids being pushed or pulled along. Quite a nice place of course, everything arranged for the comfort of the invalid, sunny sheltered corners and the like, but pah – I shall be glad when I get away.

[1] yesterdays] past

382. To Stewart Robertson, [ante 3 February 1912]
Text: Glasgow Herald, 8 March 1930.

[Compton House, St. Peter's Road, Bournemouth]
[ante 3 February 1912]

[Lawrence wrote from Bournemouth and 'recalled that Robert Louis Stevenson had also gone thither as an invalid'.][1]

383. To Louie Burrows, 4 February 1912
Text: MS UN; Postmark, Edenbridge FE 4 12; Boulton 165.

The Cearne, Nr. Edenbridge.
4th Feb. 1912

My dear Lou,

You will be wondering why I am so long in writing. I have been thinking what the doctor at Croydon and the doctor at Bournemouth both urged on me: that I ought not to marry, at least for a long time, if ever. And I feel myself my health is so precarious, I wouldn't undertake the responsibility. Then, seeing I mustn't teach, I shall have a struggle to keep myself. I will not drag on an engagement – so I ask you to dismiss me. I am afraid we are not well suited.

My illness has changed me a good deal, has broken a good many of the old bonds that held me. I can't help it. It is no good to go on. I asked Ada, and she thought it would be better if the engagement were broken off; because it is not fair to you.[2]

It's a miserable business, and the fault is all mine.

D. H. Lawrence

[1] He was there 1884–7.

[2] Ada Lawrence wrote to Louie Burrows, [16 February 1912] (MS UN LaB 206):

> ...We are all quite upset about this affair, but speaking for my self, knowing what I know of Bert, I think its kinder to you to break off now than to drag on an engagement which would I'm certain end in nothing.
>
> Its surprising how very much changed Bert is since his illness, and changed for the worse too, I think.
>
> I've had a serious talk with him about it too – his flippant and really artificial manner gets on my nerves dreadfully. Perhaps he may get alright by and by but he's very strange now, I can tell you....
>
> You really deserve someone better than Bert Louie, I wouldn't marry a man like him, no, not if he were the only one on the earth.

384. To Helen Corke, 5 February 1912

Text: MS Roberts F. W.; Postmark, The Chart FE 6 12; cited in Corke, *In our Infancy* 215.

The Cearne, Nr. Edenbridge. Kent
5 Feb. 1912

It is so quiet here, and so lonely after Bournemouth, with such a far off spreading of snow in the plain, and such uncanny black and white mingling of snow among the trees on the hill, with withered beech as red as blood, sprinkling[1] its spray of leaves, that I don't know whatever's the matter with me. There are just the books I want to read, and there is just the opportunity to write, yet I moon about like a moulting bird, and do nothing.

Garnett and I are alone in the house – the housekeeper leaves at sundown now, to help with a sick neighbour. It is a dull night tonight, with the earth brighter, paler than the sky. Yet I wish you were here to walk with through the woods.

Should you like a walk one evening, before I go? On Friday I leave here. Should you like to meet me outside Miss Rollstons School on Limpsfield Common, as early as you can one evening. Then we could walk down here, and you could see the Cearne. Perhaps even you might stay the night, if you would consent.[2] You would not mind Garnett. He is most beautifully free of the world's conventions.

There is no sound except the fluttering of the logs on the open hearth. I am uneasy tonight.

Yours D. H. Lawrence

385. To Arthur McLeod, [6 February 1912]

Text: MS UT; PC; Postmark, The Chart FE 6 12; Unpublished.

The Cearne, Nr Edenbridge
Tuesday.

My dear Mac,

I don't know when I shall get off that letter I owe you – I am unutterably lazy. I wish you were here to revel with me among these books – they are ripping. There's everything the heart could desire. By the way Lascelles Abercrombie's *Emblems of Love* are rather fine[3] – magnificent phraseology, but a bit over toppling. Tell Miss Mason its time I had a letter from

[1] blood, sprinkling] blood, that sprinkling

[2] For Helen Corke's response to this invitation, see *In Our Infancy*, p. 215. She believed DHL wrote his poem 'Passing Visit to Helen' (earlier called 'Intime') at this time (see *Complete Poems*, i. 150–2).

[3] *Emblems of Love, designed in several discourses* (1912) by Abercrombie (1881–1938).

her. I leave here on Friday, for Eastwood. Soon I'll write you at length.
Yrs D. H. Lawrence

What did you think of that damn story of mine?[1]

DHL

386. To Louie Burrows, 7 February 1912

Text: MS UN; Postmark, The Chart FE 7 12; Boulton 165.

The Cearne, Nr. Edenbridge.
7 Feb 1912

My dear Lou,

I'm sorry I could not wire back as you wished.[2] But I do really feel it would be better to break the engagement. I dont think now I have the proper love to marry on. Have you not felt it so?

But I will see you next week – I will think out a time and a place.

Yours D. H. Lawrence

387. To Jessie Chambers, [c. 9 February 1912]

Text: E.T. 195; PC.

[13 Queen's Square, Eastwood]
[c. 9 February 1912][3]

I hear you're in digs at the moment. If you are still in digs next week, I'd like to come and see you, if I may.

388. To Edward Garnett, 10 February 1912

Text: MS NYPL; Postmark, Eastwood FE 10 12; Huxley 23–5.

13 Queens Square, Eastwood, Notts
10 Feb 1912

Dear Garnett,

I found Hueffer getting very fat – 'be not puffed up' came into my mind.[4] But he's rather nicer than he was. He seems to have had a crisis, when, dear Lord, he fizzed and bubbled all over the place. Now, don't you know, he seems quite considerate, even thoughtful for other folk. But he *is* fat.

[1] 'Second Best'. See p. 348 n. 2.

[2] Presumably, on receiving Letter 383, Louie had pleaded for a decision on their engagement to be deferred, and had asked for a reply by telegram.

[3] DHL was in Eastwood 9 February – 2 March; it is likely that he contacted Jessie Chambers early in his stay.

[4] I Corinthians iv. 6 and xiii. 4.

It's Violet's good influence. Do you know, I rather like her – she's such a neat assassin. I evoked the memory of various friends that were her friends twelve months ago. Behold, she nicely[1] showed me the effigies of these folk in her heart, each of their blemishes marked with a red asterisk like a dagger hole. I saluted her, she did the business so artistically: there was no loathsome gore spilt over the murdered friends.

She looked old, yet she was gay – she was gay, she laughed, she bent and fluttered in the wind of joy. She coquetted and played beautifully with Hueffer: she loves him distractedly – she was charming, and I loved her. But my God, she looked old.

Perhaps because she wore – she was going to some afternoon affair of swell suffragettes – a gaudy witch-cap stitched with beads of scarlet and a delicate ravel of green and blue. It was a[2] cap like a flat, square bag: the two points she pulled over her ears – and she peeped coquettishly under the brim – but she looked damned old. It rather hurt me. Something like this.[3]

I think Fordy liked[4] it – but was rather scared. He feels, poor fish, the hooks are through his gills this time – and they *are*. Yet he's lucky to be so well caught – she'll handle him with marvellous skill.

They sport a carriage now – have one on contract, I[5] believe. Hueffer drove me in great state to the Court Theatre, where we heard some Morality Players – Yeats and Rev Something Adderley.[6] It wasn't any *very* great shakes – but rather nice. Hueffer is really rather decent:– he likes to sark (verb to be sarcastic unto) me because I am 'a serious person at grips with life'.

I met Jane[7] and kissed her farewell at Marylebone – my heart was awfully heavy.

Here they take my critical case with Louie very seriously. I feel rather frit.[8]

Heinemann has settled my account £49··15··10.[9] You will have to wait still further for your seven guineas,[10] because I've got to pay the doctor

[1] nicely] neat

[2] was a] was like a

[3] DHL provided two sketches emphasising Violet Hunt's hat.

[4] liked] rather liked

[5] contract, I] contract now, I

[6] On DHL's way from the Cearne to Eastwood, 9 February, he was taken by Hueffer to a matinée performance at the Royal Court Theatre. The Morality Play Society presented the first performance of *Epiphany* (1912) by the Hon. and Rev. J. G. Adderley (1861–1942); *The Hour Glass* (1903) by W. B. Yeats; and *The Travelling Man* (1909) by Lady Gregory (1859–1932).

[7] Not identified. She was certainly not (as has been suggested) another lodger in the Jones household.

[8] i.e. alarmed (Nottinghamshire dialect).

[9] Royalties on *The White Peacock*.

[10] Cf. Letter 352.

and my sister and so on. But I'll square up as soon as I can. – Not a word, by the way, from the divine William, cock of Bedford St, concerning my invaluable poems.

Austin Harrison – in two lines – wants to meet me on Monday afternoon, and to know what books I want to review. I'm glad I shan't have to go to him, to have the fount of my eloquence corked up. But what books *do* I want to review? For the lords sake, tell me.

Tell Miss Wale[1] that the wickedness is all on top – like the scarlet sweets we used to suck, and get bloody mouths. The inside is pure white sugar. My love to Miss Wale.

D. H. Lawrence

389. To Louie Burrows, 10 February 1912

Text: MS UN; Postmark, Eastwood FE 10 12; Boulton 166.

Queens Square, Eastwood, Notts
10 Feb. 1912

My dear Lou,

I came on here yesterday, and am very well. Shall I meet you in Nottingham on Tuesday? By a cursed irony, that is your birthday. Mrs Dax has asked me to be in town to meet her on Wednesday.

Shall I see you on Tuesday at 2.30 at the Victoria Station? All send regards.

D. H. Lawrence

390. To Edward Garnett, [14 February 1912]

Text: MS NYPL; Huxley 25–6.

Queens Sq, Eastwood, Notts
12 Feb 1912[2]

Dear Garnett,

I saw Louie yesterday – she was rather ikey (adj. – to be cocky, to put on airs, to be agressively superior). She had decided beforehand that she had made herself too cheap to me, therefore she thought she would become all at once expensive and desirable. Consequently she offended me at every verse end – thank God. If she'd been wistful, tender and passionate, I should have been a goner. I took her to the castle, where was an exhibition from the Art

[1] Elizabeth ('Li') Whale, formerly of Scearn Bank Farm, lived at the Cearne as housekeeper until about 1913. (See David Garnett, *The Golden Echo*, pp. 58–9.)

[2] Though dated by DHL '12 Feb' it appears (from Letters 389 and 393) that his meeting with Louie Burrows was on 13 February and that therefore this Letter was written on the 14th.

School – wonderfully good stuff.[1] She stared at the naked men till I had to go into another room[2] – she gave me a disquisition on texture in modelling: why clay lives or does not live; – sarked me for saying a certain old fellow I met was a bore: could not remember, oh no, had[3] not the ghost of a notion when we had last visited the Castle together, though she knew perfectly: thought me a fool for saying the shadow of the town seen faintly coloured through a fog was startling – and so on. I took her to a café, and over tea and toast, told her for the fourth time. When she began to giggle, I asked her coolly for the joke: when she began to cry, I wanted a cup of tea. It's awfully funny. I had a sort of cloud over my mind – a real sensation of darkness which lifted and trembled slightly. I seemed to be a sort of impersonal creature, without heart or liver, staring out of a black cloud. It's an awfully funny phenomenon. – I saw her off by the 5.8 train, perfectly calm. She was more angry and disgusted than anything, thank God.

The sequel – which startled *me* – I will tell you personally some time. It shall not be committed to paper.

I have another rendez-vous today – and one Ive had to put off. But I can't tell you those things via the post.

I send you these sketches. I think they're not bad. Would the *Saturday* or the *Nation* look at them. I'm awfully sorry to trouble you so – really. The colliery one[4] à propos the Strike, might go down.[5]

The weather here is livid – I loathe it. In May I go to Germany. God speed the day.

Don't smite the trembling edifice of my character in Miss Whale's eyes – and give her my regards.

D. H. Lawrence

[1] The biennial exhibition mounted in the Castle Museum by the Nottingham School of Art, opened on 4 February 1912.

[2] It is impossible precisely to identify the exhibits; no catalogue was produced. One picture at which Louie Burrows may have 'stared' is Thomas Gillott's *Life Class*, painted in 1911 under the direction of life master, Wilson Foster (see *Young Bert*, pp. 58–9).

[3] had] could

[4] 'The Miner at Home' (although the miner's notice of resignation in the story is submitted on 14 February 1912).

[5] The miners had threatened strike action from early February; on 2 February their Federation proposed a new schedule of wages; negotiations continued throughout the month; the Prime Minister's intervention on 20 February failed and the strike began on the 26th. It lasted till 6 April.

391. To Louie Burrows, 15 February 1912

Text: MS UN; Postmark, Eastwood FE 15 12; Boulton 166.

Queens Sq, Eastwood, Notts
15 Feb 1912

My dear Lou,

I was glad to get your letter, and to know you would rather be friends. That is as I wish it. By all means keep the brooch: it's little enough I've ever given you – and it seems so vulgar, sending back the small things that were given in such good spirit. So, I don't think I shall send you the ring or the waistcoat – it's not nice. Keep what of my books you will.

I wanted to get you something for this birthday, then I dared not, under the circumstances.

I hope Ethel and the rest are better.

Vale D. H. Lawrence

392. To Arthur McLeod, 23 February 1912

Text: MS UT; Postmark, [East]wood FE 23 12; cited in *News Chronicle* 14 September 1957.

Queens Sq, Eastwood, Notts
23 Feb 1912

My dear Mac,

I don't believe I've any news to tell you, because you hear all of me from Miss Mason. Nothing happens in the literary world: I await Duckworth's decision on *The Trespasser*. Secker asked again for Short Stories, but I have had to put him off.[1] 'Paul Morel' is going pretty well, now I have once more tackled it.

As for myself, I am very decent in health: just the little twists and turns of ordinary convalescence. I think I get fatter – I think I look better than I did six months ago. I feel about all right – have odd bad days, when – I suppose it's when my liver asserts itself – don't know, I'm sure. But I shan't teach again – no, I'll be a tramp rather. As I live longer – i.e. six weeks longer – I loathe the idea of school more and more. To think of the amount of blood and spirit I sold the Croydon Education Committee for £100 a year makes me wild. They were very mean devils – they stopped my pay – did

[1] Secker wrote to DHL on 2 February 1912 to follow up his enquiries of 2 and 13 June 1911 (see p. 275 n. 2 and p. 276 n. 1): 'You were good enough to say last summer that when you had sufficient material for a volume of stories you would consider their publication in book form. If you have such a collection ready, I should be pleased to make you an offer for the book-rights, for publication this summer on a royalty basis' (*Letters from a Publisher*, p. 3). DHL's reply is missing.

not even give me December's money clear[1] – and not a word have I had from them, except a loving letter from Robertson, damn him. I hate the whole Croydon crew violently – and, as time goes on, I seem to detest Philip. I can't write to him. Isn't it funny how one's feeling goes, sets, fixes, all independently of one's consciousness. I shall send in my resignation next month, because they owe me, don't they, a bit of my wages they have kept for insurance or some such scheme.

Tell Philip I think of sending in my resignation: tell him about the salary also: but tell him it is for health's sake I don't return. If there *should* arise a suggestion of a farewell token to me from Davidson, I beg you to squash it at once. I hate to think of Philip's or Humphrey's or Bennetto's or Byrne's putting his hand in his pocket for me, even to the extent of sixpence.

I have agreed to go to Germany in early May. I should like to stay abroad some time – perhaps a year or two. I suppose you wouldn't care to come up here for a week-end? I should be glad if you would – any week-end, almost. You see Easter is such a crowded time, when everybody has a holiday, and so everybody is in demand of everybody. Though it would be nice for a gang of us to meet at Matlock or Bakewell, wouldn't it? One is chary of asking you to anything.

I really must get on and do a bit of work. Everybody in Eastwood is so jolly – I am always out – have scarcely a moment's time for anything. I've got a dozen or two engagements to fulfil – when I can get them in.

Give my regards to Aylwin – tell him I *will* write to him. Meanwhile give him what news of me would interest him, I beg you.

I'm glad your cough is better – write to me more than I write to you.

Yours D. H. Lawrence

393. To Edward Garnett, 24 February 1912

Text: MS NYPL; Huxley 26–7.

Queens Sq, Eastwood, Notts
24 Feb 1912

Dear Garnett,

I enclose another 'billet-doux' from our mutual friend.[2] He doesn't want to publish the poems. I think he's pretty just, isn't he. Shall I write and say to him 'all right'!

[1] On 23 January 1912 the Croydon Elementary Education Sub-Committee confirmed that twelve teachers, including DHL, should suffer a deduction of salary 'for absence occasioned by personal illness...more than the number of times allowed by the Standing Orders'. For DHL the deduction was £1·5·11 (Committee Minute No. 19).

[2] Heinemann.

Has Duckworth said anything about *The Trespasser*? I'm afraid he also will not want to publish me. The only thing to do is to get on with this third novel.[1] It goes pretty well. I think I shall finish it by May.

My sister and I were at a bit of a dance last night at Jacksdale – mining village four miles out. It was most howling good fun. My sister found me kissing one of her friends goodbye – such a ripping little girl – and we were kissing like nuts – enter my sister – great shocks all round, and much indignation. But – life is awfully fast down here.

I am very well. Dont bother to answer me if you're busy. My regards to Miss Whale. Yours D. H. Lawrence

P.S. Louie writes, repenting of her horrid behaviour on that Tuesday – beseeching me to take an excursion with her down into the country next Saturday – just to show I forgive her. I daren't accept – and shan't.

DHL

394. To Croydon Education Committee, [28 February 1912]

Text: TMS Pollinger; Unpublished.

[Queen's Square, Eastwood]
[28 February 1912][2]

[Lawrence resigns his teaching post at Davidson Road School.[3]]

395. To Louie Burrows, 28 February 1912

Text: MS UN; Boulton 167.

Queens Sq, Eastwood, Notts
28 Feb 1912

My dear Lou,

I am very glad things are looking up at your house: it is unusual for Coteshael to be afflicted with maladies.

I am keeping awfully well, really, and not working much. Don't you believe TAS[mith]. I went to see him in Coll. last Thursday, and he told me he had met you.

This Saturday I have promised to go to Shirebrook[4] – and am going on thence to Eakring.[5] The weather is so nice I may as well move about a bit. But we'll have a jig when I come back.

[1] *Sons and Lovers.*
[2] The date is established by reference to the next letter.
[3] DHL's resignation was reported in the Minutes of the Elementary Education Sub-Committee, 5 March 1912.
[4] See p. 295 n. 3.
[5] See p. 295 n. 1.

Today I have sent in my resignation to Croydon. I don't want that to be dragging on any longer.

The men are out today[1] – and I believe, most of 'em highly rejoiced. I hope they'll soon go back, that I do.

Keep well Yours D. H. Lawrence

396. To Walter de la Mare, 1 March 1912

Text: MS UN; Unpublished.

Queens Square, Eastwood, Notts.
1st March 1912

Dear Sir,

I was surprised to receive your letter this morning. I am sorry I shan't be in London again, maybe not for a long time: because I should have liked so much to meet you. I delighted in that first little book of poems, by Walter Ramal, and *The Return* is one of the books that lives with me.[2] But I am too badly off to make excursions to London.

I have given up teaching altogether, and shortly intend going to Germany. Having been knocked up since October, I have not been able to finish another novel. But now it is going well. I shall have it done by May – and it is a good novel.

So shall we not bother about the poems? I don't think Mr Heinemann is very keen on publishing them, and I am not particularly keen on having them in print, so may they not as well wait?, and later on I will work at them. You will find them very amateurish, I know.

Will you let this letter be private? – and if you think I had really better come down, I will do so.

Yours Sincerely D. H. Lawrence

397. To Walter de la Mare, 4 March 1912

Text: MS UN; Unpublished.

Station Rd Pharmacy, Shirebrook, Near Mansfield
4 March 1912

Dear Mr de la Mare,

Your letter has come on here to me. Certainly do as you will about the poems. I quite understand that you did not want to talk to me about my pleasure in writing, but that you wanted to suggest improvements in the

[1] See p. 366 n. 5.

[2] See p. 348 n. 3.

volume of verse. But I had thought, from the tone of Mr Heinemanns two previous letters, that he was scarcely anxious to put the verses into print, and that they might as well lie by until such occasion as might see them better worth publishing.

I am very busy with the novel – at which I am working hard, and in which I don't want to be seriously interrupted just now, as I wish to finish it before I go to Germany, which I hope to do this spring. And poetry takes me a long time to re-cast. And I know the stuff is full of blemishes.

However, please act entirely as you think best.

Yours Sincerely D. H. Lawrence

P.S. I have not much verse beyond that you have – but you shall have it. DHL

PPS. I stay here till Friday – 8th. – then to Eastwood again.

DHL

398. To May Holbrook, [5 March 1912]

Text: MS UN; PC v. Clumber Terrace Steps; Postmark, Worksop MR 5 12; Nehls, iii. 623.

Worksop –
Tuesday

– Rather rum old place – snied with[1] colliers – just been in a pub and found it crowded out – Going to the Priory[2] – Shirebrook's too slow for anything. Hows Bill – DHL

399. To Edward Garnett, 6 March 1912

Text: MS NYPL; Postmark, Shirebrook MR 7 12; Huxley 27–8.

Station Rd Pharmacy, Shirebrook, Near Mansfield
6 March 1912

My dear Garnett,

They forwarded me your letter on here. It is awfully good of you to write me so promptly. I had a letter from de la Mare about the poems. As Heinemann hadn't seemed keen on publishing the things, and as I am very busy indeed at the colliery novel, which I wish to finish before I go to Germany, I said to de la Mare, shall we not trouble with the poems[3] at the present! Then he took me to task rather sharply for my unbusinesslike reply – whereupon I said he could do just what he liked with the verses, and I

[1] i.e. full of (Lincs. dialect). (The *Worksop Guardian*, 8 March 1912, reported the town crowded with strikers.)

[2] Priory Church.

[3] the poems] them

would alter them when I had time. You see I can't work at novel and verses at once just now, because the former takes all my attention. However, I suppose they will do as they choose.

Don't you bother so much about the sketches: it's not fair. By the way, would you care to see the MS of the colliery novel, when it is finished, before it goes to Wm H? I have done two thirds or more.

Duckworth is jolly nice. Of course he can have the novel after this I am now doing. But what will William of Bedford Street[1] say? I have written putting off Martin Secker.

I am here only till Friday. This last fortnight I have not been so well, but it's nothing. I'm not going to tell you any stories, because at breakfast you are a sort of Father Anthony;[2] and I am afraid of you.

Here, in this ugly hell, the men are *most* happy. They sing, they drink, they rejoice in the land. There were more 'drunks' run-in from the Crown and the Drum here last week-end, than ever since Shirebrook was Shirebrook. Yesterday I was in Worksop. It is simply snyed with pubs. Every blessed place was full of men, in the larkiest of spirits. I went in the Golden Crown and a couple of other places. They were betting like steam on skittles – the 'seconds' had[3] capfuls of money. There is some life up here this week, I can tell you. Everywhere you go, crowds and crowds of men, not unhappy, as they usually are.

Will you tell me when there is anything I ought to do, and will you remember me kindly to Miss Whale. Yours D. H. Lawrence

400. To Edward Garnett, 8 March 1912

Text: MS NYPL; Huxley 28–9.

13 Queens Square, Eastwood, Notts
8th March 1912

My dear Garnett,

It is good news from the *Forum*.[4] I have altered the story much to my satisfaction. What do you think? I enclose also the duplicate. Will the title do? Shall you send the duplicate to the *English* and ask Harrison to publish it simultaneously with the *Forum*? You know better than I.

I enclose a story I wrote three years back, and had forgotten.[5] It is on

[1] Heinemann.

[2] i.e. stern and ascetic.

[3] had] have

[4] Presumably the editor of the American magazine, *Forum*, had accepted DHL's 'The Soiled Rose'. The story appeared in March 1913 (it was not published in the *English Review*).

[5] Probably 'A Modern Lover' which DHL had shown to Jessie Chambers in December 1909 (see Delavenay, ii. 694). (It was not published until 1933.)

the same theme, and I thought it might interest you – it is really curious. But before it was ever submitted to a publisher, I would like thoroughly to revise it.

I had a letter from Duckworth, which I shall answer now 'yes'. But he says the title *Trespasser*, is not particularly strong, and will I find another. I have cudgelled my brains into smithereens, and can find nothing. God help us.

What do you mean by Miss Corke's MS, by the way?[1] Has she sent you something.

I had two shocks this morning, by the post. One of the men who taught in the school at Croydon with me, has died suddenly of pneumonia.[2] And Neville – my very old[3] friend, the Don Juanish fellow I told you of – went and got married three months back, without telling a soul – and now boasts a son: 'Jimmy, a very fine lad.'[4] – He writes me eight pages, closely packed,[5] this morning. The girl is living at home, with 'Jimmy' in Stourbridge. The managers asked George – Neville – to resign his post, because of the blot on the scutcheon. He said 'he'd see them frizzled first.' In the end, he was removed to a little headship on the Stafford–Derby border[6] – has been there six weeks – alone – doing fearfully hard work. Don Juan in hell, what ho![7]

[1] Helen Corke wrote to Edward Garnett, 3 March 1912 (MS NYPL):

192 Whitehorse Rd,
Croydon
March 3rd.

Dear Mr Garnett,

I think I would like you to see this of mine. It is a sequel to the writing from which the Saga was drawn. There is nothing in it but actual experience expressed as directly as expression came. To me there is a kind of unity about it, a kind of definite progression that gives it a value for me – but I do not know at all whether it has any impersonal value. That is partly why I send it to you. Miss Chambers has read the whole, Mr Lawrence some of it – but they are too near me to see it well.

....You will understand when you have read it, that I have no desire for its publication. But if for you it is true in tone – if there is anything of music in it – I shall be glad that it was written.

Helen Corke.

The MS referred to was entitled 'The Cornwall Writing 1912' (see Helen Corke, *In Our Infancy*, p. 203); it consists of five folio gatherings. When Garnett returned the MS it was laid aside until 1918; then Helen Corke incorporated it into her novel, *Neutral Ground*, pp. 235–58. (Information from Helen Corke.)

[2] R. M. Bennetto (cf. p. 355 n. 2). [3] old] of

[4] George Neville married Ethel Gertrude Piper (b. 1888) at Amblecote, Stourbridge, on 4 November 1911. Their child was born in January 1912 (baptized 18 February).

[5] packed] written

[6] Neville left his teaching post in Amblecote for the headship of the school at Bradnop, near Leek, Staffordshire.

[7] G. B. Shaw's *Man and Superman* (1903), Act III includes a dream scene of Don Juan in Hell; it was presented as a one-act play – *Don Juan in Hell* – at the Royal Court Theatre in June 1907.

He implores me to go and stay a week with him. I suppose I s'll have to. This has upset me – One never knows what'll happen. You know Georgie has already got one illegitimate child.[1] It's a lovely story, the end of it: the beginning was damnable. She was only nineteen, and he only twenty. Her father, great Christian, turned her out. Georgie wouldn't acknowledge the kid, but had to pay, whether or not. That's five years back. Last October, I am told, the girl got married. Before the wedding – two days or so – she went to Neville's home with the child, and showe[d] it to Georgie's father and mother.[2]

'I've come, Mr Neville, for you to own this child. Who's the father of that – ?' pushing forward the small girl.

'Eh bless her, it's just like him,' cried old Mrs Neville, and she kissed the kid with tears.

'Well Lizzie,' said Neville to the girl, 'if our George-Henry says that isn't his'n, he's a liar. It's the spit and image of him.'

Whereupon Lizzie went away satisfied, got married to a collier, and lives in Cordy Lane.[3] She, with one or two others, will rejoice over George's final nabbing. Isn't it awful!

All this, by the way, is quite verbal truth.

Vale! D. H. Lawrence

401. To Ernest Weekley, [9? March 1912]

Text: Delavenay 706–7.

[Queen's Square, Eastwood]
[9? March 1912][4]

[Lawrence wrote to Ernest Weekley[5] refusing his invitation to lunch.]

[1] Born c. 1905, a girl who died at the age of 12.

[2] James Neville (d. 1939?) and Sarah Ellen Neville (d. 1918).

[3] Near the pit at Underwood.

[4] The date assumes the following chronology: DHL returned to Eastwood from Shirebrook, 8 March 1912; he received a letter from Ernest Weekley on 9 March; he met Jessie Chambers 'on a certain Sunday in late February or early March' [10 March] and told her that he had refused Weekley's invitation (Delavenay 706). Within 'a few days' (Delavenay 707) he met Jessie Chambers again; by now he had already accepted the lunch invitation, this time from Frieda Weekley. DHL and Jessie Chambers agreed to meet, yet again, on the same day as he was to lunch with the Weekleys; this day was certainly a Sunday (compare Jessie Chambers's account in Delavenay 707 and E.T. 199); and 17 March seems most likely. He was in Nottingham on that day (see Letter 405).

[5] Ernest Weekley (1865–1954), University Professor. Educated privately, then at the Universities of Berne, Cambridge, Paris and Freiburg. 1898–1938 Professor of French, University College, Nottingham. m. Frieda von Richthofen, 1899. Well-known etymologist. Wrote *Romance of Words* (1912), *Romance of Names* (1914), *Etymological Dictionary of Modern English* (1921), etc. (For obituary see *The Times*, 8 May 1954.)

402. To Walter de la Mare, 13 March 1912

Text: MS UN; Unpublished.

Queens Sq, Eastwood, Notts
13 March 1912

Dear Mr de la Mare,

It's awfully good of you to show my verses to the *Westminster* man.[1] Mr Harrison of the *English* promised to publish something – 'Snapdragon', I believe this month – but he evidently forgot.[2] Do just as you will with the poems. I should like them to appear in mags, then I should hate their faults worse.

And this novel – it won't be a *great* success, – wrong sort – should be finished in a month, and then I'll come to London to hear your advice concerning the improvement of the poems.

I hope somebody will have the things if only for the £ s d they'd bring.

Yours Sincerely D. H. Lawrence

403. To Edward Garnett, 14 March 1912

Text: MS NYPL; Unpublished.

Queens Sq, Eastwood, Notts
14 March 1912

My dear Garnett,

I'm afraid you won't find this sketch very enlivening.[3] But it happened to run into my mind, and unfortunately it is true in detail and fact. I got the *Nation* proofs this morning.[4]

I am doing another sketch, which I will send you tomorrow. But I must not bother you too much.

I suppose you got the story back.[5] Tell me later what you'll do with the duplicate. I heard from de la Mare. He will send selections of my verses to the *Westminster* and the *English*. Good of him, is it not?

I hope this sketch 'll do. But if not, it's not a great loss.

Yours D. H. Lawrence

[1] Probably John Alfred Spender (1862–1942), editor of the *Saturday Westminster Gazette*, 1896–1922. Cf. p. 424 n. 1.

[2] 'Snap-Dragon' appeared in *English Review*, xi (June 1912), 345–8.

[3] In this and the two letters following DHL refers to three 'sketches'. They are: 'The Collier's Wife Scores' (later entitled 'Strike-Pay I, Her Turn' and finally 'Her Turn'); 'Strike Pay' (first published as 'Strike-Pay II, Ephraim's Half Sovereign'); and 'A Sick Collier'. (The second and third both allude to an actual football match played on 13 March 1912.) It is not possible to determine which story DHL was referring to in a particular letter.

[4] Proofs of 'The Miner at Home', published in *Nation*, 16 March 1912.

[5] 'The Soiled Rose' (cf. p. 372 and n. 4).

404. To Edward Garnett, 16 March 1912

Text: MS NYPL; Unpublished.

Queens Sq, Eastwood, Notts
16 March 1912

My dear Garnett,

Here's the second sketch. I'll do one more tomorrow, then I'll take breath.

I'll send you back the Bush Stories also.[1] A woman borrowed them, or I'd have returned them before.

I had a letter from Hueffer this morning saying the plays had turned up after all.[2] Do you want to see them? – are you awfully busy? – The things were at the Authors' club all the while.[3]

Yours D. H. Lawrence

405. To Edward Garnett, 17 March 1912

Text: MS NYPL; Unpublished.

[43, Laurel Street, Nottingham][4]
17 March 1912

My dear Garnett,

Here's the last of these damned articles. I'm sick of 'em. They're as journalistic as I can make 'em, but why in the name of all that's fortunate do I kill my own pig before I've driven it to market. There's stuff in all the damned articles that nobody will want to print. But I can't make a silk purse out of a sow's ear.

Console me. Yours D. H. Lawrence

406. To Frieda Weekley, [c. 20 March 1912]

Text: Frieda Lawrence 22.

[Queen's Square, Eastwood]
[c. 20 March 1912][5]

You are the most wonderful woman in all England.[6]

[1] Probably *Children of the Bush* (1902) by the Australian writer Henry Hertzberg Lawson (1867–1922). (Information from David Garnett.)

[2] See p. 309 n. 3.

[3] Hueffer was a member of the club from 1908 (Douglas Goldring, *The Last Pre-Raphaelite*, 1948, p. 131).

[4] The letter is written on notepaper headed: 'Hunger Hill Road Baptist Sunday School, Nottingham'. Among the officers' names printed is: 'Secretary, Geo. A. Lawrence, 43, Laurel Street'. It is assumed that DHL wrote from his brother's house.

[5] DHL wrote this soon after their first meeting (Frieda Lawrence 22) which is thought to have been on 17 March 1912 (see p. 374 n. 4).

[6] Emma Maria Frieda Johanna Weekley, née von Richthofen (1879–1956), b. Metz; m. Ernest Weekley, 29 August 1899, in Freiburg; lived in Nottingham; bore three children. Eloped with DHL, 3 May 1912; they married on 13 July 1914. (See her *Not I, But the Wind*... Santa Fe, New Mexico, 1934.)

407. To May Holbrook, 27 March 1912
Text: MS UN; Nehls, iii. 623–4.

c/o Mrs Plumb, Bradnop, Leek, Staffs
27 March 1912

My dear Jonty,[1]

I am here since Monday – shall be home again – D.V. on Saturday evening. It's a truly rural sort of place. Diddler[2] and I dodge about at evening. His school has 51 kids – a girl for the infants. It's pretty – Derbyshireish – grey stone – fields dark green. I gave the little clods a lesson on color yesterday afternoon – they gorped like frogs. Afterwards the vicar[3] and I had a heart-rending discussion for an hour and a half, on the church. In the evening Diddler took me a tat-tah, and of course got lost. We wriggled over a river on a rail. It's very Switzerlandish, just over the Long Shaw. Later we called at a farm, where the old woman reigns supreme in a fur shoulder-cape, and the old man, deaf as a post, blorts like a bullock occasionally, nearly making you jump out of your skin.[4] Mrs Titterton is the masterful sort. She gives me to understand she would mother me: manage me, that means. She mothers her own three great sons to such an extent that they will never marry. She keeps them in order, but they're very happy: live good and healthy animals. Jack runs the rig in Leek occasionally.[5] A woman throned is really – !

I'll bring you *Man and Superman* on Sunday. I suppose J[essie] will be at the cottage.[6] The play was very good. I said nothing to Mrs Weekley about coming over. Will discuss it further with you.

Messages to Bill. Love D. H. Lawrence

408. To Austin Harrison, 28 March 1912
Text: MS Harrison; Moore 104–5.

'Mount Pleasant', Bradnop, Leek, Staffordshire
28 March 1912

Dear Mr Harrison,

I received your letter this morning. Certainly Mr Garnett is no literary agent, and I should be very sorry to think I had lost your favour. I merely

[1] A nickname for May Holbrook, derived from the name of her grandfather Jonathan Chambers (see Nehls, iii. 746 n. 88).
[2] George Neville (with whom DHL was staying).
[3] Rev. Arthur Peters, Vicar of Onecote with Bradnop, 1905–17.
[4] George Titterton (d. 1928) and his wife (d. 1931) lived at Apesford Farm.
[5] John Titterton (d. 1959).
[6] Jessie Chambers describes DHL's visit to the Holbrooks' cottage on 31 March (E.T. 205–8); she was present.

asked Mr Garnett if he would entreat some Review or other to print me.[1] He sent 'The Soiled Rose' to the *Forum*: they said they would print 'this most unusual story', and would the author arrange for its simultaneous publishing in England. Then Mr Garnett[2] forwarded the story to you: I did not even know he had done so. Of course you must consider the interests of *The English Review* primarily. I don't suppose any other Review would publish 'The Soiled Rose'. As to 'Love Among the Haystacks' – I am sorry it is so long. I suppose it would not split.

Do you remember you promised to publish some of my verse. Mr Heinemann is holding over the volume till my next novel has appeared, so as to give the verses more chance. Mr de la Mare, who was arranging the verses for Mr Heinemann, said he would send you a selection for your approval for the *English*.

Do not write to my 'Croydon' address any more, please. I have given up teaching, and left London altogether. My address is 'Queens Square – Eastwood – Notts.' Publish me something when you can, will you. It is a nuisance I should have to come to depend on literature.

Mr Duckworth is publishing a novel directly[3] – he has the MS in hand, and has accepted it; and Mr Heinemann will publish me another novel in the autumn.[4] But give me a little shove until these things come off, will you?

I am going to Germany in early May, chiefly for my health. It is one of your countries, I understand. Yours Sincerely D. H. Lawrence

409. To Edward Garnett, 1 April 1912

Text: MS NYPL; Huxley 29–30.

Queens Sq, Eastwood, Notts
1 April 1912

My dear Garnett,

I was away in Staffs when your letter came. I can't think of another title. Would:

A Game of Forfeits
or The Forfeit
or The Man and the Dreaming Woman[5]

[1] See Letter 400. [2] Mr. Garnett] he

[3] *The Trespasser* appeared on 23 May 1912.

[4] The reference is to *Sons and Lovers*; in the event Duckworth, not Heinemann, published it.

[5] The concept of 'the dreaming woman' may derive from Rachel Annand Taylor. It reappeared in the final lines of DHL's poem 'Repulsed' (printed in *Love Poems*, 1913): 'How we hate each other tonight,... As a man hates the dreaming woman he loves, but who will not reply.' (See M. C. Sharpe, *Essays in Criticism*, xi (January 1961), 38.)

or anything like that do? I try to get something that would catch. Even *The Trespasser* has been used before, I believe by Gilbert Parker.[1] I haven't received any proofs from Duckworth. The *Daily News* sent me back the article – 'The Colliers Wife Scores'.[2] Would *The Eyewitness*[3] have it, I wonder.

Father has just come in with his strike ballot. He's balloted for – here, I'll send you the paper.[4]

My two sisters are raving because the meeting was rowdy, and many of the men ballotted 'against': every evil that could be urged against a working man is urged by his woman-folk. They are all aristocrats, these women, to the back-bone. They would murder any man at any minute if he refused to be a good servant to the family. They make me curse.

Hueffer wrote and asked for my address so that he could send the plays. I sent the address, but the plays haven't come.

It's cold here – I hope you are well. D. H. Lawrence

410. To Louie Burrows, 2 April 1912
Text: MS UN; Boulton 167–8.

Queens Sq, Eastwood, Notts.
2 April 1912

My dear Lou,

I am sorry I have neglected to write to you. But I have been away a good deal. Last week I was in North Staffordshire with Neville. He is married – did you know? – last November, on the q – t. His baby was born in January. He had to leave Amblecoate. They gave him a tiny temporary place in the country near Leek, where I stayed with him. His wife is with her parents in Stourbridge, some 50 miles away. He lives 'en bachelier'. Which is quite a story!

I have got a bit of a cold, with the harsh winds, but otherwise am all right. Occasionally I hear of you from Tom Smith.

They are all pretty well here – we shall be glad when the strikers go in. Father, of course, enjoys it.

[1] Sir Gilbert Parker (1862–1932), journalist and popular novelist. His *Trespasser* appeared in 1893.

[2] See p. 375 n. 3.

[3] Founded by Hilaire Belloc (1870–1953) as a radical journal; it ran 22 June 1911 – 27 December 1913.

[4] Strikers were asked: 'Are you in favour of resuming work pending a settlement of the *minimum* rates of wages in the various grades by the district boards to be appointed under the Mines (Minimum Wage) Act?' (*The Times*, 1 April 1912). Nottinghamshire miners marginally rejected the proposal; nationally the miners rejected it; but the union Executive Committee considered the margin too slender for a continuation of the strike.

Ada says she will write to you directly. The holiday will do you good, no doubt.

Yours D. H. Lawrence

411. To Edward Garnett, 3 April 1912

Text: MS NYPL; Postmark, Eastwood AP 3 12; Huxley 30–1.

Queens Square, Eastwood, Notts
3rd April 1912

Dear Garnett,

Austin Harrison writes me concerning the *Forum* story: is not exactly keen on publishing it, because he doesn't love the *Forum*.

He wants to put one of my poems in in June;[1] so, he says, shall he return me 'Love among the Haystacks', and fix a date – either July, August, or Sept., for the publication of 'The Soiled Rose' – the *Forum* story; Or shall he return me 'The Soiled Rose', and publish the 'Haystacks' story in July.[2] Which shall I say? He wants a definite answer directly.

He also says, if I want books to review, will I write at once, naming the works. But I don't know what is out. Can you tell me of anything? I beg you, do.

I like your Dostoievsky review in the *Daily News* today.[3] They won't have you much oftener, I'm afraid, altho. you've tried to put a sort of 'liberal' complexion on it. Isn't the *D.N.* enough to break one's heart nowadays. Did you read its notice of the *English Review*, and its emphasis of Sickert's dislike of the nude?[4]

I was round with a friend delivering Relief tickets yesterday. It's not that the actual suffering is so great – though it's bad enough – but the men seem such big, helpless, hopeless children, and the women are impersonal – little atlases under a load that they know will crush them out at last, but it doesn't matter. They aren't conscious, any more than their hearts are conscious of their endless business of beating. They have no conscious life, no windows. It makes me ill.

Don't tell Harrison I wrote for your advice – he likes to think he's a personal benefactor.

[1] Cf. p. 375 n. 2.

[2] 'Love among the Haystacks' appeared posthumously as the title story to a volume (Nonesuch, 1930).

[3] *Daily News*, 3 April 1912 carried Garnett's favourable review of J. A. T. Lloyd, *A Great Russian Realist: Feodor Dostoieffsky* (Paul, March 1912).

[4] In 'The Futurist "Devil-among-the-Tailors"', *English Review*, xi (April 1912), 147–54, Sickert wrote briefly on (among other things) 'the incessant and dispiriting study of the nude'. The *Daily News*, 3 April 1912, reviewing the April issue of *English Review*, selected from Sickert's article only his remarks about the nude in painting.

I shall finish my Colliery novel this week – the first draft. It'll want a bit of revising. It's by far the best thing I've done.

Yours D. H. Lawrence

P.S. Had a p.c. from Violet Hunt today to say, was Queens Sq my right address. I expect the plays in a week or two. DHL

412. To Edward Garnett, 5 April 1912

Text: MS NYPL; Huxley 31–2.

Queens Square, Eastwood, Notts.
5 April 1912

Dear Garnett,

Thanks for your letter. I wrote Harrison and asked him to publish the 'Haystacks' story. But you didn't suggest any books for me to review.

Mrs Hueffer sent me the plays today. It appears 'my poor Ford' has had a breakdown, and mustn't even dictate a letter 'if he can help it'. They are at Sandgate.[1] Mrs Hueffer is 'so sorry the plays were delayed. They might have taken quite well, while collieries are in the air.[2] But perhaps it is not too late. You must get them published, with the aid of Mr Garnett.'[3] So you see the fat's in the fire there. The plays are very interesting, but again, formless. Form will never be my strong point, she says, but I needn't be quite so bad. 'But never mind, Ford and I always call you a genius.' I have thanked her for the sarcasm.

The first batch of proofs of the *Trespasser* arrived last night. I will wage war on my adjectives. Culpa mea! I think I have no occasion to write to Duckworth. But I'll send Belloc the sketch.[4] Those others, shall I send him them also? I suppose you have them. I mean the other two Strike articles.

I have just found the list of books on your letter – thanks awfully. I'll write to Harrison. He seems inclined to deflate.[5] On Tuesday he wrote me a cocky

1 After a 'honeymoon', Hueffer and Violet Hunt 'returned to England as a married couple. Violet's friend, Lady Houston, lent them her house at Sandgate which was conveniently near Ford's friends, Conrad and Marwood.' Ford then suffered 'a fresh attack of neurasthenia that lasted three whole years' (Goldring, *South Lodge*, p. 99).

2 A national conference of miners' delegates was due to be held the next day, 6 April, to decide on a resumption of work or a continuation of the strike. (Work was resumed the following week.)

3 DHL probably sent the MS of *A Collier's Friday Night* with this letter. On the MS he wrote in pencil: 'This was written when I was twenty-one – almost before I'd done anything. It's most horribly green. DHL.' Edward Garnett published this note in his edition of the play (1934, p.v), adding that he received the MS in April 1912.

4 'The Collier's Wife Scores' (cf. Letter 409).

5 deflate] crow

letter, yesterday, a sweet and friendly one. Publishing people are more sickly than lepers. I am thankful to be safe out of London.

Yours D. H. Lawrence

413. To Philip Smith, [9 April 1912]

Text: MS UT; PC v. On the Trent: Boat leaving for Colwick Park, Nottingham; Postmark, Nottingham APL 9 12; Moore, *Intelligent Heart* 111–12.

[9 April 1912]

Here's Miss Mason on the scene[1] – thinner – you're working her to the bone, I know.

The books are so nice – I'm on the point of tears like anything – It's really too ridiculous in a restaurant. I should love to come back to Davidson, if there were no kids – or only half a dozen or so.

My regards to Mrs Smith and Doris – I will answer your letter (peccavi) just now.

Your obedient servt D. H. Lawrence

414. To Arthur McLeod, [9 April 1912]

Text: MS UT; PC v. Nottingham Castle; Postmark, Nottingham APL 9 12; Unpublished.

[9 April 1912]

Here's Miss Mason – and the books – and here am I in tears (of love) for all of you. I wish you'd come up too – damn you. I do want to see you again before I go abroad – I really must weep.

Goodbye D. H. Lawrence

Miss Mason sends love and – – DHL

415. To Walter de la Mare, 11 April 1912

Text: MS UN; Unpublished.

Queens Square, Eastwood, Notts.
11 April 1912

Dear Mr de la Mare,

How awfully glad I am to see these verses in proof. It is very good of you. For a title, will 'Heart of a School-Teacher' do?[2] I haven't made much

[1] DHL's colleagues at Davidson Road School had jointly bought some books to mark his resignation; Agnes Mason delivered them to him.

[2] De la Mare had facilitated the publication of the series of poems generally entitled 'The Schoolmaster' in *Saturday Westminster Gazette*, 11 May – 1 June 1912. Cf. Letter 402.

alteration, because I am correcting just now the proofs of the Duckworth novel, and my mind is full of prose.

By the way, is there any news of any of my articles?[1]

I have finished in its first form the colliery novel. Now I want to leave it for a month, when I shall go over it again. There are parts I want[2] to change. Shall I send it to you for your opinion now at once, before I do any revising, or shall I pull it close together before you see it? As you will.

Don't leave the title 'The School Master', will you? I dont like it. And to call me C. E. Lawrence is – well! –

Yours Sincerely D. H. Lawrence

416. To Walter de la Mare, 16 April 1912

Text: MS UN; Unpublished.

Queens Square, Eastwood, Notts
16 April 1912

Dear Mr de la Mare,

I shall most probably be in London next week, from Thursday till Sunday. Will you see me then, to jaw me about those poems? I think you said Thursday was one of your free days. I will hold myself at your disposal that afternoon – the 25th, that will be.

You got the proofs of the school verses, which I returned to you, did you not?

Yours Sincerely D. H. Lawrence

417. To Edward Garnett, 17 April 1912

Text: MS NYPL; Postmark, Eastwood AP 17 12; Huxley 32–3.

Queens Square, Eastwood, Notts
17 April 1912

Dear Garnett,

Did I answer your last letter? – I can't for my life remember. Why do you take so much trouble for me? – if I am not eternally grateful, I am a swine.

[1] The 'sketches' earlier sent to Garnett (see p. 375 n. 3); two ('Strike-Pay' I and II) were later published in *Saturday Westminster Gazette*, 6 and 13 September 1913; and De la Mare may have placed them for DHL.

[2] I want] I very want

It is huge to think of Iden Payne acting me on the stage:[1] you are like a genius of Arabian Nights, to get me through. Of course I will alter and improve whatever I can, and Mr Payne has fullest liberty to do entirely as he pleases with the play[2] – you know that. And of course I don't expect to get money by it. But it's ripping to think of my being acted.

I shall be in London next week, I think – from Thursday to Sunday – then I can see Walter de la Mare, and Harrison, who want to jaw me – and you who don't want to jaw me. Mrs Weekley will be in town also. She is ripping – she's the finest woman I've ever met – you must above all things meet her. Wife of one of my College professors – Weekley has just published some book or other on words, through John Murray, and the *Athenæum* held him sky-high a week ago[3] – she is the daughter of Baron von Richthofen,[4] of the ancient and famous house of Richthofen – but she's splendid, she is really. How damnably I mix things up. Mrs Weekley is perfectly unconventional, but really good – in the best sense. I'll bet you've never met anybody like her, by a long chalk. You *must* see her next week. I wonder if she'd come to the Cearne, if you asked us. Oh but she is the woman of a lifetime.

I shall love to see you again. Don't be grumpy.

Yours D. H. Lawrence

418. To Walter de la Mare, 19 April 1912

Text: MS UN; Unpublished.

Queens Sq, Eastwood, Notts
19 April 1912

Dear Mr de la Mare,

I've scrambled through the proofs again. Certainly leave the title 'The Schoolmaster', if it is preferred. I like you to suggest what displeases you. Now for the alterations. Will:

[1] Ben Iden Payne (1881–1976), actor and producer. Acted with F. R. Benson's company; directed for Miss A. E. F. Horniman at the Gaiety Theatre, Manchester, 1908–11; toured with his own repertory company; went to the Fine Arts Theatre, Chicago, 1913; returned 1935–42 to direct at Stratford-on-Avon; finally became Professor of Drama, University of Texas, at Austin. m. Mona Limerick (Mary Gadney), 1906.

[2] Probably *A Collier's Friday Night*.

[3] Weekley's *Romance of Words* was very favourably reviewed in the *Athenæum*, 6 April 1912: '...Professor Weekley is both learned and careful...we wish many to share the enjoyment which the book has given us.'

[4] Baron Friedrich von Richthofen (1845–1915), regular soldier. Entered Prussian army, 1862; wounded in Franco-Prussian war and removed from active duty. Garrison administrative officer in Metz at this time.

'The snow descends as if the dull sky shook
In flakes of shadow down –' –[1]

do for the two lines in V.

And:

'Into rollicking suns, and their lost gold rots compressed'[2]

for the one line in III.

If you don't like these suggestions, and if you can think of anything better, *do* put it in. There's no need to consult me.

Yours Sincerely D. H. Lawrence

419. To Philip Smith, 22 April 1912

Text: Huxley 33–4.

Queen's Square, Eastwood, Notts.
22 April, 1912.

Dear Mr. Smith,

It was awfully nice of you and the other chaps and Miss Mason to get me those two books. The plays are exceedingly interesting. I hope you read them. Tchekhov is a new thing in drama.[3]

What changes and variations at Davidson nowadays. When I think back, it seems to me we were pretty peaceful those last two years of mine. But school is hard work, anywhere.

I am probably going to Germany on the 4th May. It is just possible that I may be detained by business, but I think to depart on Saturday week. I am going first to Metz – for only a short time; then to Waldbröl, near Bonn, and near the Rhein: I shall stay a month or two in Waldbröl, after which I have an invitation to Munich. So you see about where I shall be fixed. Do you think of going to Germany again this summer? – to the Black Forest at all? – then I could see you and Mrs. Smith. It would be very jolly.

I am pretty well in health, as Miss Mason will have told you. It is such beautiful weather, and so pretty with blossom in the country. Sometimes I think of playtime at Davidson: 'Please, Mr. Lawrence, Mr. Smith says, will you blow the whistle.' It's a nice playground at Davidson, such a space of

[1] This version was printed in 'A Snowy Day in School', *Saturday Westminster Gazette*, 1 June 1912.

[2] This line appeared in 'Evening', *Saturday Westminster Gazette*, 25 May 1912.

[3] The only volume of Chekhov's plays listed in the *English Catalogue of Books* as currently in print was *Two Plays: The Seagull; The Cherry Orchard*, trans. George Calderon (February 1912).

view, and a lot of sky. Sometimes I think I should like to come and take my Nature lessons; cool, and jolly, with the boys happy. But I'm glad, when I hear them in the school at Beauvale here, that I'm not a prisoner.[1] Liberty to work, oh, such a lot.

By the way, you may find very shortly in the *Saturday Westminster Gazette*, a string of verses of mine about school, that might interest you.

If Mr. Robertson comes in, remember me to him, will you. Tell everybody at Davidson I'm awfully fond of them. My regards to Mrs. Smith and Doris.

Yours sincerely, D. H. Lawrence

420. To Edward Garnett, 23 April 1912

Text: MS NYPL; Postmark, Leicester APR 23 12; Huxley 34.

20 Dulverton Rd, Leicester
23 April 1912

Dear Garnett,

I had a letter from Iden Payne appointing me a meeting at the Managers Club[2] on Thursday, to which I have written agreeing. I shall come back here to Leicester on Thursday evening, by the excursion.

I want to come to the Cearne on Saturday with Mrs Weekley. I am most awfully fond of her. Things are getting difficult. Are you *quite* sure you would like her and me to come to your house? If so, will you fix a train for Saturday evening? We should go away again on Sunday. But don't mind to say 'No', if you feel the least hesitating.

Mrs Weekley is going to Germany on the 4th of May. I want to go then, because we could have at least one week together. I should think it wouldn't matter, would it, if I weren't in London when the little play was performed? And I wanted to see it, but as things are, I want to go to Germany more. The world is so full of mean, rather brutal people. It makes me tired.

You will write me here, c/o Mrs Krenkow.

Yours D. H. Lawrence

P.S. I have written a comedy – middling good.[3] Should I send it you?
DHL

[1] DHL himself attended Beauvale Board School.
[2] At 5 Wardour Street, London.
[3] 'The Married Man' (based on Neville's amatory adventures).

421. To Walter de la Mare, 24 April 1912

Text: MS UN; Unpublished.

20 Dulverton Rd, Leicester
24 April 1912

Dear Mr de la Mare,

I am sorry if I put the wrong dates in my letter of last week. But did I not say I should be in London this week from *Thursday* – 25th – till Sunday?

I only got your letter this morning. I hope my wire will find you at Heinemanns.

Tomorrow – Thursday – I have an engagement at 4.0 in the afternoon, but could give you from 3.0 to 3.45 – also I could meet you any time on Friday, or after lunch on Saturday. I shall be found at

Oak Lodge, St Georges Rd, St Margarets on Thames
c/o Mrs Hunger

on Friday and Saturday. If I hear from you there on either of those days, I am at your disposal.

Yours Sincerely D. H. Lawrence

422. To William Holbrook, [26 April 1912]

Text: TMSC UT; PC v. Temple of the Sun, Kew Gardens; Postmark, Brentford AP 26 12; Nehls, iii. 624.

[26 April 1912]

Oh Bill – it's ripping down here – slightly different from the cottage – Heaven on a lower plane, shall we say? By the end of this razzle, I shall sigh for peace under a pear-tree.

Love D. H. Lawrence

423. To Louie Burrows, [26 April 1912]

Text: MS UN; PC v. The Queen's Cottage, Kew; Postmark, Brentford AP 26 12; Boulton 168.

[26 April 1912]

Am in London on business till Monday – then going home. I was in Leicester only one clear day. It is lovely to be down here again.

DHL

424. To Edward Garnett, 29 April 1912

Text: MS NYPL; Postmark, Leicester APR 29 12; Huxley 35.

20 Dulverton Rd, Leicester
29 April 1912

Dear Garnett,

I believe Mrs Weekley after all left those first chapters of my Heinemann novel 'Paul Morel' in your book-room: I am sure they are there. And I left my scrubby gloves. Send me them on to Eastwood, will you. I am going home today. Probably I shall go to Germany on Friday. I am so anxious to know what Weekley will say. She is going to tell him today. He is a middle class, gentlemanly man, in whom the brute can leap up. He is forty six, and has been handsome, is usually ironic, pessimistic and cynical, nice, I like him. He will hate me, but really he likes me at the bottom. He is forty six, and has had a bad illness a year or two back. He is getting elderly, and a bit tired. He doesn't want a wife like Frieda, not to monopolise her. But he loves her, and in a jealous monogamistic fashion. I wonder what he'll say.

Tell me what you think of Mrs Weekley. I am afraid of your suddenly donning a cassock of a monk, and speaking out of the hood. Don't sound wise, and old, and– 'When you've lived as long as I have' sort of thing. It's insulting.

Tell me when Duckworth will publish the novel.[1]

Today isn't like yesterday. I hate this house – full of old books, gloomy as hell, and silent with books. I hate the glum silence of ranks of shut books. I imagine your appleblossom. It seems so sociable and lovable in comparison.

Vale! D. H. Lawrence

425. To Frieda Weekley, [30 April 1912]

Text: MS UT; Frieda Lawrence 27.

Eastwood –
Tuesday.

I feel so horrid and helpless. I know how it all sickens you, and you are almost at the end of the tether. And what was decent yesterday will perhaps be frightfully indecent today. But it's like being ill: there's nothing to do but shut one's teeth and look at the wall and wait.

You say you're going to Gladys[2] tomorrow. But even that is uncertain.

[1] See p. 378 n. 3.

[2] Gladys Bradley, daughter of Frederick James Bradley, J.P. She and her sister Madge were close Nottingham friends of Ernest and Frieda Weekley; they actively promoted the relationship between DHL and Frieda.

And I *must* know about the trains. What time are you going to Germany, what day, what hour, which railway, which class?[1] Do tell me as soon as you can, or else what can I do? I will come any time you tell me – but let me know.

You must be in an insane whirl in your mind. I feel helpless and rudderless, a stupid scattered fool. For goodness sake tell me something, and something definite. I would do anything on earth for you, and I can do nothing. Yesterday I knew would be decent, but I don't like my feeling today – presentiment. I am afraid of something low, like an eel which bites out of the mud, and hangs on with its teeth. I feel as if I can't breathe while we're in England. I wish I could come and see you, or else you me.

D. H. Lawrence

426. To Edward Garnett, 1 May 1912

Textg: MS NYPL; Postmark, Eastwood MY 1 12; Unpublished.

Queens Square, Eastwood – Notts
1 May 1912

Dear Garnett,

Here is the thing you want.[2] Isn't it hateful, this sort of business! If I haven't done it right, you alter it, will you? In these matters I feel so awkward.

Thanks so much for the MS. of the novel.[3] I was a wee bit worried over it.

Have just got the drama from Payne. He rather amuses me – He was going to show me what he wanted altering, but now says I know what wants doing without his troubling. So I do.

Tell me when Duckworth will publish the novel, when you write next. I go to Germany on Friday. Then I will write you my news.

Yours D. H. Lawrence

427. To Frieda Weekley, 2 May 1912

Text: MS UT; Frieda Lawrence 28.

Queens Sq. Eastwood – Notts
2 May 1912

I shall get in King's Cross tomorrow at 1.25. Will that do? You see I couldn't come today, because I was waiting for the laundry and for some stuff from

[1] Frieda's notes for what probably was a reply to these questions are found on the verso of this MS: 'Charing X 2 o'clock Outside 1st Class Ladies Room'. That they met at and left from Charing Cross is certain (see Frieda Lawrence 25).

[2] Perhaps some publicity material for *The Trespasser*.

[3] See Letter 424.

the tailors. I had prepared for Friday, but Thursday was impossible. I am sorry if it makes things tiresome.

Will you meet me, or let somebody meet me, at King's Cross? Or else wire me *very* early, what to do. It is harassing to be as we are.

I have worried endlessly over you. Is that an insult? But I shan't get an easy breath till I see you. This time tomorrow, exactly, I shall be in London.

I hope you've got some money for yourself. I can muster only £11. A chap owes me twenty five quid, but is in such a fix himself, I daren't bother him.[1] At any rate, eleven pounds will take us to Metz, then I must rack my poor brains.

Oh Lord, I must say 'making history', as Garnett puts it, isn't the most comfortable thing on earth. If I knew how things stood with you, I wouldn't care a damn. As it is, I eat my blessed heart out.

Till tomorrow, till tomorrow, till tomorrow (I nearly put à demain)

D. H. Lawrence

P.S. I haven't told anything to anybody. Lord, but I wonder how you are. DHL

428. To May Holbrook, [4 May 1912]

Text: TMSC UT; PC v. Metz. – Totenbrüche, Pont des Morts; Postmark, Metz 4 5 12; Nehls, iii. 624.

[Hotel Deutscher Hof, Metz]
[4 May 1912]

Here I am at last – it's a wild long journey. Everything went quite smooth however. I'm already drinking my third pint of German beer. Heaven knows what a size I shall be by the time I get back. Lord, these German mugs.

Love D. H. Lawrence

429. To Frieda Weekley, [6 May 1912]

Text: MS UT; Frieda Lawrence 29–30.

[Hotel Deutscher Hof, Metz]
[6 May 1912]

Damn the rain! I suppose you won't go out while it continues heavily. I'll venture forth in a minute – 9.15 already. I don't know where you live exactly – so if I can't find you I shall put this in Number 4.[2] That's the nearest I can get; is it right.

[1] Perhaps Arthur Stanley Corke.

[2] Because of confusion at Frieda's parents' home, both she and DHL were occupying separate rooms in the same hotel.

If I don't meet you, I suppose I shan't see you today; since this is the festive day.[1] I don't mind. At least, I do, but I understand it can't be helped.

I shall go into the country if it'll keep a bit fine – shall be home here about 2.30 I suppose. I can work as soon as I like.

Let us go away from Metz. Tell Else I'm not cross.[2] How should I be? You are the soul of good intention – how can one then be cross with you. But I wish I had the management of our affairs.

Dont love me for things I'm not – but also don't tell me I'm mean. I wondered what had become of you this morning. Were you being wise and good and saving my health. You needn't. I'm not keen on coming to your place to lunch tomorrow – but I am in your hands – 'into thine hand, O Lord, I commend etc.'[3] I want you to do as you like, over little things such as my coming to your father's house. In oddments, your will is my will.

I love you – but I always have to bite my tongue before I can say it. It's only my Englishness.

Commend me to your sister.[4] I lodge an appeal with her. I shall say to her – it's no good saying it to you – 'Ayez pitié de moi.'

No, I'm only teasing. It doesn't matter at all what happens – or what *doesn't* happen, that's more to the point – these few days. But if you put up your fingers, and count your days in Germany, and compare them with the days to follow in Nottingham, then you will see, you – I don't mean it – are selling sovereigns at[5] a penny each. No, *you* are not doing it – but it's being done.

Don't be hurt, or I shall – let me see – go into a monastery – this hôtel is precious much like one already.

This is the last day I let you off – so make the most of it, and be jolly.

[1] To celebrate the fiftieth anniversary of Baron von Richthofen's entering the army.

[2] Else Jaffe, née von Richthofen (1874–1973), older sister to Frieda. m. Edgar Jaffe (1866–1921) in 1902. Pupil of Max Weber (1864–1920) at Heidelberg University. Professor of Social Economics; German translator of DHL's *The Boy in the Bush* and *The Fox*; *The Rainbow* (Methuen, 1915) dedicated to her. (See M. Green, *The Von Richthofen Sisters*, 1974.)

[3] Psalms xxxi. 4 or Luke 46.

[4] Johanna ('Nusch') von Schreibershofen, née von Richthofen (1882–1971) Frieda's younger sister and (from 1900) wife to Max von Schreibershofen (b. 1864), an officer on the German General Staff. After divorce in 1923, m. Emil von Krug (1870–1944).

[5] at] for

430. To Ernest Weekley, [7 May 1912]

Text: Nottinghamshire Guardian, 20 October 1913; cited in *News of the World*, 19 October 1913.

[Hotel Deutscher Hof, Metz]
[7 May 1912][1]

You will know by now the extent of the trouble. Don't curse my impudence in writing to you. In this hour we are only simple men, and Mrs. Weekley will have told you everything, but you do not suffer alone. It is really torture to me in this position. There are three of us, though I do not compare my sufferings with what yours must be, and I am here as a distant friend, and you can imagine the thousand baffling lies it all entails. Mrs. Weekley hates it, but it has had to be. I love your wife and she loves me. I am not frivolous or impertinent. Mrs. Weekley is afraid of being stunted and not allowed to grow, and so she must live her own life. All women in their natures are like giantesses. They will break through everything and go on with their own lives. The position is one of torture for us all. Do not think I am a student of your class – a young cripple. In this matter are we not simple men? However you think of me, the situation still remains. I almost burst my heart in trying to think what will be best. At any rate we ought to be fair to ourselves. Mrs. Weekley must live largely and abundantly. It is her nature. To me it means the future. I feel as if my effort of life was all for her. Cannot we all forgive something? It is not too much to ask. Certainly if there is any real wrong being done I am doing it, but I think there is not.

D. H. Lawrence[2]

431. To Frieda Weekley, [7 May 1912]

Text: MS UT; Frieda Lawrence 31.

[Hotel Deutscher Hof, Metz]
Tuesday

Now I can't stand it any longer, I cant. For two hours I haven't moved a muscle – just sat and thought.[3] I have written a letter to Ernst.[4] You needn't, of course, send it. But you must say to him all I have said. No more

[1] This letter, printed in the account of Ernest Weekley's divorce proceedings October 1913, is dated 'May 8th' by the *Nottinghamshire Guardian*. If in the next letter DHL refers to the writing of this, then that date is slightly inaccurate; but this letter to Weekley may have been *posted* on 8 May. (Ernest, writing to Frieda Weekley, 10 May 1912, says: 'I had a letter from Lawrence this morning', Tedlock 180.) The MS seems to have disappeared.

[2] The newspaper's account gave the signatory's name as 'W. H. Lawrence'.

[3] thought.] thought – and suffered

[4] DHL enclosed the previous letter with this and gave Frieda the responsibility of deciding to send it or to incorporate its message in a letter of her own to Weekley.

dishonour, no more lies. Let them do their – silliest – but no more subterfuge, lying, dirt, fear. I feel as if it would strangle me. What is it all but procrastination? No, I can't bear it, because it's bad. I love you. Let us face anything, do anything, put up with anything. But this crawling under the mud I cannot bear.

I'm afraid I've got a fit of heroics. I've tried so hard to work – but I cant. This situation is round my chest like a cord. It *mustn't* continue. I will go right away, if you like. I will stop in Metz till you get Ernst's answer to the truth. But no, I won't utter or act or willingly let you utter or act, another single lie in the business.

I'm not going to joke, I'm not going to laugh, I'm not going to make light of things for you. The situation tortures me too much. It's the situation, the situation I can't stand – no, and I won't. I love you too much.

Don't show this letter to either of your sisters – no. Let us be good. You are clean, but you dirty your feet. I'll sign myself as you call me

– Mr Lawrence

Don't be miserable – if I didn't love you I wouldn't mind when you lied. But I love you, and Lord, I pay for it.

432. To Frieda Weekley, 8 May 1912

Text: MS UT; Frieda Lawrence 32–3.

Hôtel Rheinischer Hof, Trier
8 May 1912

I am here – I have dined – it seems rather nice. The hôtel is little – the man[1] is proprietor, waiter, bureau, and everything else, apparently – speaks English and French and German quite sweetly – has evidently been in swell restaurants abroad – has an instinct for doing things decently, with just a touch of swank – is cheap – his wife (they're a youngish couple) draws the beer – it's awfully nice. The bedroom is 2 Marks 50 per day, including breakfast – per person. That's no more than my room at the Deutscher Hof, and this is much nicer. It's on the second floor – two beds – rather decent. Now, you ought to be here, you ought to be here. Remember, you are to be my wife – see that they don't send you any letters, or only under cover to me. But you aren't here yet. I shall love Trier – it isn't a ghastly medley like Metz – new town, old town, barracks, barracks, cathedral, Montigny.[2] This is nice, old, with trees down the town. I wish you were here. The valley all along coming is full of apple trees in blossom, pink puffs like the smoke

[1] DHL's headed notepaper named the proprietor as M. Hermesdorf.

[2] The adjoining town and home of Frieda's parents.

of an explosion, and then bristling vine sticks, so that the hills are angry hedgehogs.[1]

I love you so much. No doubt there'll be another dish of tragedy in the morning, and we've only enough money to run us a fortnight, and we don't know where the next will come from, but still I'm happy, I am happy. But I wish you were here. But you'll come, and it isn't Metz. Curse Metz.

They are all men in this hôtel – business men. They are the conoisseurs of comfort and moderate price. Be sure men will get the best for the money. I think it'll be nice for you. You don't mind a masculine atmosphere, I know.

I begin to feel quite a man of the world. I ought, I suppose, with this wickedness of waiting for another man's wife in my heart. Never mind, in heaven there is no marriage nor giving in marriage.[2]

I must hurry to post – it's getting late. Come early on Saturday morning. Ask the Black Hussy at Deutscher Hof if there are any letters for me. I love you – and Else – I do more than thank her.

Love D. H. Lawrence

433. To Edward Garnett, 9 May 1912

Text: MS NYPL; Huxley 35–6.

Hôtel Rheinischer Hof, Trier
9 May 1912

Dear Garnett,

I've not had any letters since I've been here – since Friday, that is – so I don't know what is taking place. Write to me, I beg you – I am staying in Trier till next Monday or Tuesday – then, for a week or two, my address will be

c/o Frau Karl Krenkow, Waldbröl, Reinprovinz.

Of course I've been in Metz with Mrs Weekleys people. There's such a hell of a stir up. Nothing is settled yet. Weekley knows everything. Oh Lord, what a mess to be in – and this after eight weeks of acquaintance! But I don't care a damn what it all costs. I'll tell you how things work out. At present all is vague.

I had to quit Metz because the damn fools wanted to arrest me as a spy. Mrs Weekley and I were lying on the grass near some water – talking – and I was moving round an old emerald ring on her finger, when we heard a faint murmur in the rear – a German policeman. There was such a to-do.

[1] Cf. 'The whole hillside bristles with sticks, like an angry hedgehog', 'German Impressions: I. French Sons of Germany', *Phoenix* 73.

[2] Matthew xxii. 30.

It needed all the fiery little Baron von Richthofen's influence – and he is rather influential in Metz – to rescue me. They vow I am an English officer – *I* – *I*!! The damn fools. So behold me, fleeing eighty miles away, to Trier. Mrs Weekley is coming on Saturday. Oh Lord, it's easier to write history than to make it, even in such a mild way as mine.

But don't you think she is very fine? But you don't know her. You should see the Richthofens at home – three sisters – one, the eldest, a professor of psychology and economics – left her husband, gone with two other men (in succession)[1] – yet *really* good – good, the sort of woman one reverences. Then there's Frieda. Then the youngest sister, very beautiful, married to a brute of a swanky officer in Berlin – and, in a large, splendid way – cocotte. Lord, what a family. I've never seen anything like it.

Tell me if my literary affairs are shifting at all. Regards to Miss Whale.

Yours D. H. Lawrence

Isn't it all funny!

434. To Arthur McLeod, [9? May 1912]

Text: MS UT; PC v. Ehrenbreitstein bei Koblenz a/Rh; Postmark [ ]; Huxley 36.

[Hôtel Rheinischer Hof, Trier]
[9? May 1912]

I suppose you wonder what on earth has become of me. Oh, fearful and wonderful things are happening. I have to leave Metz quick, because they're going to arrest me as a spy – I come on to Trier – but no, I won't tell you what happens at Trier.

I am going up the Rhine on Monday. Write to me c/o Frau Karl Krenkow – Waldbröl – Reinprovinz, there's a dear. How is everything going? I sit among the blossoming apple-trees, above the vineyards of the Mosel, above the ancient town of Trier, hearkening to the cuckoo sing; and thinking of Davidson and of thee. I would not be in Davidson – no, not for anything. Escape my dear, escape.

My love to everybody. D. H. Lawrence

Psalm MCI[2]

[1] Else had affairs with Otto Gross (by whom she had a son in 1907) and with Max Weber. By 1910 she lived apart from Edgar Jaffe; her 'lover' (see Letters 457 and 458) now was Alfred Weber (1868–1958).

[2] Possibly an error for XCI, a psalm which assures the faithful of divine protection.

435. To Frieda Weekley, [9 May 1912]

Text: MS UT; Frieda Lawrence 34–5.

Hôtel Rheinischer Hof, Trier –
Thursday

Another day nearly gone – it is just sunset. Trier is a nice town. This is a nice Hôtel. The man is a cocky little fellow, but good. He's lived in every country, and swanks about his languages. He really speaks English nicely. He's about 35, I should think. When I came in just now – it is sunset – he said 'You are tired?' It goes without saying I laughed. 'A little bit,' he added, quite gently. That amuses me. He would do what my men friends always want to do, look after me a bit in the trifling, physical matters.

I have written a newspaper article that nobody on earth will print, because it's too plain and straight.[1] However, I don't care. And I've been a ripping walk – up a great steep hill nearly like a cliff, beyond the river. I will take you on Saturday – so nice: apple-blossom everywhere, and the cuckoo, and brilliant beech trees. Beech-leaves seem to *rush* out in spring, with éclat. You can have coffee at a nice place, and look at the town, like a handful of cinders and rubbish thrown beside the river down below. Then there are the birds always. And I went past a madonna stuck with flowers, beyond the hill top, among all the folds and jumble of hills: pretty as heaven. And I smoked a pensive cigarette, and philosophised about love and life and battle, and you and me. And I thought of a theme for my next novel. And I forgot the German for matches, so I had to beg a light from a young priest, in French, and he held me the red end of his cigar. There are not so many soldiers here. I should never hate Trier. There are more priests than soldiers. Of the sort I've seen – not a bit Jesuitical – I prefer them. The Cathedral is crazy: a grotto, not a cathedral, inside – baroque, baroque. The town is always pleasant, and the people.

One more day, and you'll be here. Suddenly I see your chin. I love your chin. At this moment, I seem to love you, because you've got such a nice chin.[2] Doesn't it seem ridiculous?

I must go down to supper. I *am* tired. It was a long walk. And then the strain of these days. I dreamed Ernst was frantically furiously wild with me – I won't tell you the details – and then he calmed down, and I had to comfort him. I am a devil at dreaming. It's because I get up so late. One always dreams after 7.0 a.m. (German Vorm.)

The day is gone. I'll talk a bit to my waiter fellow, and post this. You

[1] 'German Impressions: I. French Sons of Germany', *Saturday Westminster Gazette*, 3 August 1912.

[2] you've got...chin.] I love your chin.

will come on Saturday? By Jove, if you don't! We shall always have to battle with *life*, so we'll never fight with each other, always help.

Bis Samtag – ich liebe dich schwer.[1] D. H. Lawrence

436. To May Holbrook, [9 May 1912]

Text: MS UN; PC v. Berncastel-Cues, Burg Landshut; Postmark, Trier -9 5 12; Nehls, iii. 624–5.

Hotel Rheinischer Hof – Trier
[9 May 1912]

This is a most delicious place – Trier.[2] There's a wild old cathedral, *most* catholic, great black stone gateways – oh it's a sweet town. It lies right down in the valley – like Matlock Town[3] – like this picture. I am sitting on a steep hill, looking between the trees at the town below, and the river. The foot of the hills is covered with vineyards. How you would love it! But Moorgreen seems sweet to me. There's my address till Monday.

Love and to Will D. H. Lawrence

I had to leave Metz, because they were going to arrest me for staring at their idiotic fortifications. DHL

437. To Louie Burrows, [9 May 1912]

Text: MS UN; PC v. Burg Cochem; Postmark, Trier -9 5 12; Boulton 168.

Hotel Rheinischer Hof – Trier
[9 May 1912]

I have come on here from Metz. Trier is a delicious place – a crazy old cathedral, fearfully Roman Catholic – sleepy town, river, hills like Matlock with vineyards and woods – the Lord knows what. I don't love the Germans, but this country is awfully pretty. I think on Monday I go on to Waldbröl – about 200 miles up the Rhine. You'll soon be having Whitsuntide.

Yrs D. H. Lawrence

438. To Frieda Weekley, [11 May 1912]

Text: MS UCB; PC v. Trier Porta nigra; Postmark, [Fra]nkfurt -11. 5. 12; Frieda Lawrence 36.

[11 May 1912]

Here is your Porta Nigra, that you have missed three times. I think I am quite clever. It is a weird and circuitous journey to Waldbröl – 7 hours. Now

[1] 'Until Saturday – I love you dearly.'

[2] May's sister, Jessie Chambers, also received a postcard: 'a beautiful view of Trier Cathedral' (E.T. 216).

[3] In the Derwent Valley, Derbyshire.

I am at Niederlahnstein, – Rechtreinisch[1] – having just come over from Coblenz. I go on to Troisdorf – ever heard of such places! – then to Hennef – and at last Waldbröl – 4 changes – umsteigen[2] – 7 hours journey. But isn't the Mosel valley pretty? The Rhein is most awfully German. It makes me laugh. It looks fearfully fit for the theatre. Address me

c/o Frau Karl Krenkow, Waldbröl Reinprovinz.

Anything new and nasty happened? This is *my Sentimental Journey*.[3]

Love D. H. Lawrence

439. To Florence Cullen, [11 May 1912]

Text: MS Clarke; PC v. Trier – Mariensäule; Postmark, Troisdorf 11. 5. 12; Unpublished.

[11 May 1912]

Ada says you are cross with me – no, don't be so – pray forgive me. I am just going from Trier – it's a lovely old town – 200[4] miles up the Rhine to Waldbröl. By this time I am tired of travelling. Two hundred miles this afternoon, by railway – and it's as hot as H[ell]. Tell Ada my address is

c/o Frau Karl Krenkow, Waldbröl – Reinprovinz.

Love D. H. Lawrence

440. To Frieda Weekley, [11 May 1912]

Text: MS UCB; PC v. Trier Basilica; Postmark, Henn[ef] 11 [...]; Frieda Lawrence 36.

[11 May 1912]

Now I am in Hennef – my last changing place. It is 8.30 – and still an hour to wait. So I am sitting like a sad swain beside a nice, twittering little river, waiting for the twilight to drop,[5] and my last last train to come. I shan't get to Waldbröl till after 11.0 – nine hours on the way – and that is the quickest it can be done. But it's a nice place, Hennef, nearly like England. It's getting dark. Now, for the first time during today, my detachment leaves me, and I know I only love you. The rest is nothing at all. And the promise of life with you is all richness. Now I know.

D. H. Lawrence

[1] The right bank of the Rhine. [2] Change of train.

[3] DHL alludes to *A Sentimental Journey through France and Italy* (1768) by Laurence Sterne (1713–68), described by the author as 'a quiet journey of the heart in pursuit of Nature, and those affections which arise out of her'.

[4] 200] to

[5] DHL's poem 'Bei Hennef' (written on this occasion) opens: 'The little river twittering in the twilight...'

441. To Frieda Weekley, [13 May 1912]

Text: MS UT; Frieda Lawrence 37–8.

adr. Frau Karl Krenkow, Waldbröl – Reinprovinz
[13 May 1912]

It's really very nice here – Hannah is very bright and so decent with me. Her husband is 'very good man' – uninteresting. She never loved him – Married him because she was thirty and time was going by. Already she's quite fond of me – but do not mind, she is perfectly *honorable* – the last word of respectability – Then there is 'Opar O'pa' – how do you spell it? – Stülchen – He is 73 – a lovely old man – really a sweet disposition, and no fool. Now he is really lovable. It was Kermesse[1] at one of the villages yesterday – Sunday – and we went to look. It was jolly. Onkel Stülchen bought us a Herz – a great heart of cake, covered with sugar, and sugar grapes, and sugar roses, and a bird, a dove – and three pieces of poetry. It's rather quaint. Strange, how deep symbolism is in our soil. Herr Stülchen brought up Hannah, since she was five years old. He[r] father was killed – or died awhile after – the Franco Prussian. Now I am fond of him.

Here, I am so respectable, and so good – it is quite a rest. We are not dull – Hannah is really intelligent. We amuse ourselves a good deal with my German. In three months here I should know quite a lot.

It's a quiet – dead little village – miles from everywhere – rather pretty in a tame sort of way – a bit Englishy. Once they let me begin, I shall knock off quite a lot of work. There is that novel on my conscience.[2]

I write in the morning, when one is wonderfully sane. Waldbröl is good for my health – it is cooler, more invigorating. Trier was like a perpetual Turkish bath. I like this air.

If you must go to England – must you? – go before I leave Waldbröl. Don't leave me stranded in some unearthly German town. How are you? I am not going to sound worried over you, because I am so a bit. You might write to me and tell me a few significant details. The tragedy will begin to slacken off from now, I think.

I wrote to you yesterday, but it wasn't a nice letter, so I didn't send it. Things are better, surely, and growing – better – Oh yes!

Nun muss ich aus gehen mit Onkel Stülchen, ein Halbes zu trinken. Der Morgen ist kühl und rein, nach dem gestern-Abends Gewitter. Es war viele Blitzen in unsern Himmel, abert nicht nahe vorbei. Sie sollten wohl lachen an meinem Deutsch.

[1] A fair.

[2] *Sons and Lovers.*

Habe ein gutes Hertz, meine Geliebte, bitte sei nicht traurig. Ade nun. Bleib stark.[1]

Ade D. H. Lawrence

442. To Edward Garnett, [13? May 1912]

Text: MS NYPL; Tedlock 182.

[Frieda Weekley begins]

c/ Herrn Baron von Richthofen, Montigny bei *Metz*
[13? May 1912][2]

Dear Mr Garnett,

I think of you often and your friendly cottage and the appleblossoms and your own wonderfully hospitable self, you have a *genius* for hospitality. It has helped Lawrence and me through a lot of horrors that we had to go through. I love him with a 1000 different loves, I want everybody to love him he deserves it. There is no fight between us, we want the same thing and our fighting will be against other people *never* with each other. I see you laugh, and I am serious, but I am not taken in, I think you are awfully good. Have you written what you were going to write? May I come to you again some time? Dont laugh at me!

Yours gratefully Frieda Weekley

[Lawrence begins]

Of course you must laugh at us. I am terrified of you when you are serious – you're rather like other people then.

D. H. Lawrence

443. To Frieda Weekley, 14 May 1912

Text: MS UT; Frieda Lawrence 42–4.

pr Adr Herrn Karl Krenkow, Waldbröl – Rheinprovinz
14 May 1912

Yes, I got your letter later in the day – and your letter and Ernsts and yours to Garnett, this morning. In Ernst's, as in mine to Ernst, see the men combining in their free masonry against you. It is very strange.

[1] 'I must go out now with Uncle Stülchen, for a beer. The morning is cool and clear, after the storm yesterday evening. There was a lot of lightning in our sky, but not nearby. You will probably laugh at my German.

Be of good heart, my love, please do not be sad. Farewell now. Stay strong. Farewell.'

[2] In the next letter, 14 May 1912, DHL says he received Frieda's 'to Garnett' that day; she would probably write it on 13th; presumably DHL forwarded it, with his own postscript, on 14th.

I will send your letter to Garnett. I enclose one of his to me. It will make you laugh.

With correcting proofs,[1] and reading Ernst's letter, I feel rather detached. Things are coming straight. When you got in London, and had to face that judge, it would make you ill. We are not callous enough to stand against the public, the whole mass of the world's disapprobation, in a sort of criminal dock. It destroys us, though we deny it. We are all off the balance. We are like spring scales that have been knocked about. We had better be still awhile, let ourselves come to rest.

Things are working out to their final state now. I did not do wrong in writing to Ernst. Do not write to my sister yet.[2] When all is a 'fait accompli' then we will tell her, because then it will be useless for her to do other than to accept.

I am very well, but, like you, I feel shaky. Shall we not leave our meeting till we are better? Here, in [a] little while, I shall be solid again. And if you must go to England, will you go to Munich first – so far? No. I don't want to be left alone in Munich. Let us have firm ground where we next go. Quakiness and uncertainty are the death of us. See, tell me exactly what you are going to do. *Is* the divorce coming off? – *Are*[3] you going to England at all? Are we going finally to pitch our camp in Munich? Are we going to have enough money to get along with? Have you settled anything definite with Ernst? – One *must* be detached, impersonal, cold, and logical, when one is arranging *affairs*. We do not want another fleet of horrors attacking us when we are on a rather flimsy raft – lodging in a borrowed flat on borrowed money.

Look, my dear, now the suspense is going over, we can wait even a bit religiously for one another. My next coming to you is solemn, intrinsically – I am solemn over it – not sad, oh no – but it is my marriage, after all, and a great thing – not a thing to be snatched and clumsily handled. I will not come to you unless it is safely, and firmly. When I have come, things shall not put us apart again. So we must wait and watch for the hour. Henceforth, dignity in our movements and our arrangements – no shuffling and underhandedness. And we must settle the money business. I will write to the publishers, if necessary, for a sub. I have got about thirty pounds due in August – £24[4] due – and £25 more I am owed. Can we wait, or not, for that?

Now I shall do as I like, because you are not certain. Even if I stay in Waldbröl a month, I won't come till our[5] affair is welded firm. I can wait

[1] Of 'Snap-Dragon'. Cf. p. 375 n. 2.
[2] Ada Lawrence.
[3] *Are*] When *are*
[4] £24] 29
[5] our] then

a month – a year almost – for a sure thing. But an unsure thing is a horror to me.

I love you – and I am in earnest about it – and we are going to make a great – or at least, a good life together. I'm not going to risk fret and harassment, which would spoil our intimacy, because of hasty forcing of affairs.

Don't think I love you less, in being like this. You will think so, but it isn't true. The best man in me loves you. And I dread anything dragging our love down.

Be definite, my dear; be detailed, be business-like. In our marriage, let us be business-like. The love is there – then let the common-sense match it.
Auf wiedersehen D. H. Lawrence

This poetry will come in next month's *English*. I'm afraid you won't like it.
DHL

And I love you, and I am sorry it is so hard. But it is only a little while – then we will have a *dead cert*.

444. To Frieda Weekley, [15 May 1912]

Text: MS UT; Frieda Lawrence 39–41.

Waldbröl – Mitwoch
[15 May 1912]

I have had all your three letters quite safely. We are coming on quickly now. Do tell me if you can what is Ernst's final decision. He will get the divorce, I think, because of his thinking you ought to marry me. That is the result of *my* letter to him. I will crow my little crow, in opposition to you. And then, after six months, we will be married – will you? Soon we will go to Munich. But give us a little time. Let us get solid before we set up together. Waldbröl restores me to my decent sanity. Is Metz still bad for you. No? It will be better for me to stay here – shall I say till the end of next week? We must decide what we are going to do, very definitely. If I am to come to Munich next week, what are we going to live on? Can we scramble enough together to last us till my payments come in? I am not going to tell my people anything till you have the divorce. If we can go decently over the first three or four months – financially – I[1] think I shall be able to keep us going for the rest. Never mind about the infant. If it should come, we will be glad, and stir ourselves to provide for it – and if it should not come, ever – I shall be sorry. I do not believe, when people love each other, in interfering there.

[1] I] we

It is wicked, according to my feeling. I want you to have children to me – I don't care how soon. I never thought I should have that definite desire. But you see, we must have a more or less stable foundation if we are going to run the risk of the responsibility of children – not the risk of children, but the risk of the responsibility.

I think, after a little while, I shall write to Ernst again. Perhaps he would correspond better with me.

Can't you feel how certainly I love you and how certainly we shall be married. Only let us wait just a short time, to get strong again. Two shaken, rather sick people together would be a bad start. A little waiting, let us have, because I love you. Or does the waiting make you worse? – no, not when it is only a time of preparation. Do you know, like the old knights, I seem to want a certain time to prepare myself – a sort of vigil with myself. Because it is a great thing for me to marry you, not a quick, passionate coming together. I know in my heart 'here's my marriage'. It feels rather terrible – because it is a great thing in my life – it is *my life* – I am a bit awe-inspired – I want to get used to it. If you think it is fear and indecision, you wrong me. It is *you* who would hurry who are undecided. It's the very strength and inevitability of the oncoming thing that makes me wait, to get in harmony with it. Dear God, I am marrying you, now, don't you see. It's a far greater thing than ever I knew. Give me till next week-end, at least. If you love me, you will understand.

If I seem merely frightened and reluctant to you, – you must forgive me.

I try, I will always try, when I write to you, to write the truth as near the mark as I can get it. It frets me, for fear you are disappointed in me, and for fear you are too much hurt. But you are strong when necessary.

You have got all myself – I don't even flirt – it would bore me very much – unless I got tipsy. It's a funny thing, to feel one's passion – sex desire – no longer a sort of wandering thing, but steady, and calm. I think, when one loves, one's very sex passion becomes calm, a steady sort of force, instead of a storm. Passion, that nearly drives one mad, is far away from real love. I am realising things I never thought to realise. – Look at that poem I sent you – I would never write that to you.[1] I shall love you all my life. That also is a new idea to me. But I believe it.

Auf wiedersehen D. H. Lawrence

[1] The subject of the poem 'Snap-Dragon' was the frustrated sexual desire DHL had experienced over Louie Burrows.

445. To Frieda Weekley, [16 May 1912]

Text: MS UT; Frieda Lawrence 45–6.

Waldbröl –
Thursday

I have worked quite hard at my novel today. This morning we went to see the Ascension Day procession, and it rained like Hell on the poor devils. Yesterday, when we were driving home, luckily in a closed carriage, the hail came on in immense stones, as big as walnuts, the largest. The place seemed covered with lumps of sugar.[1]

You are far more ill than I am, now. Can't you begin to get well. It makes me miserable to think of you so badly off the hooks. No, I am well here. I am always well. But last week made me feel queer – in my soul mostly – and I want to get that well before I start the new enterprise of living with you. Does it seem strange to you? Give me till tomorrow or Saturday week, will you? I think it is better for us both. Till the 24th or the 25th give me. Does it seem unloving and unnatural to you? No? See, when the air man fell, I was only a weak spot in your soul. Round the thought of *me* – all your fear. Don't let it be so. Believe in me enough.

Perhaps it is a bit of the monk in me. No, it is not. It is simply a desire to start with you, having a strong, healthy soul. The letters seem a long time getting from me to you. Tell me you understand, and you think it is – at least *perhaps*, best. A good deal depends on the start. You never got over your bad beginning with Ernst.

If you want Henning, or anybody, have him.[2] But I don't want anybody, till I see you. But all natures aren't alike. But I don't believe even *you* are your best, when you are using Henning as a dose of morphia – he's not much else to you. But sometimes one needs a dose of morphia. I've had many a one. So you known best. Only, my dear, because I love you, don't be sick, do will to be well and sane.

This is also a long wait. I also am a carcase without you. But having a rather sick soul, I'll let it get up and be stronger before I ask it to run and live with you again.

Because, I'm not coming to you *now* for rest, but to start living. It's a marriage, not a meeting. What an inevitable thing it seems. Only inevitable things – things that feel inevitable – are right. I am still a trifle afraid, but I know we are right. One is afraid to be born, I'm sure.

[1] Cf. 'The ditches looked as if stones and stones weight of loaf sugar had been emptied into them', 'German Impressions: II. Hail in the Rhineland', *Phoenix*, p. 79.

[2] Udo von Henning who was killed at Charleroi, 7 September 1914 (letter to Edward Garnett, 13 October 1914).

I have written and written and written. I shall be glad to know you understand. I wonder if you'll be ill. Don't, if you can help it. But if you *need* me – Frieda!

Vale! D. H. Lawrence

446. To Walter de la Mare, [16 May 1912]

Text: MS UN; Unpublished.

pr. Adr. Herrn Karl Krenkow, *Waldbröl*, Rheinprovinz, Germany

15 May 1912[1]

Dear de la Mare,

I wonder if any of this stuff – not the poetry, of course – would be any good to the *Westminster*, or if anybody else would have it. I don't know the papers a bit. If you think it would be any use, would you mind offering the articles to somebody you think probable.[2] I am about reduced to my last shilling again – it's a sort of three-monthly fever of poverty – so I must work[3] my untrustworthy soul, somehow or other, to see if I can coin it into gold. Alas, it's all grit and mud.

But today is Ascension Day, and the bells are ringing, and I've nodded to about sixty Madonnas and Jesuses in the shrines at the cottage doors, and I've walked humbly along the procession way, down the strewn track of leaves and grass and lilac and buttercups and gillives,[4] so I ought to have some luck.

With the patience of a saint, I'm revising the Heinemann novel.[5] I'll send it within[6] a fortnight (D.V. and if I can buy the stamps). Germany is rather jolly – while it lasts.

Commend me to Edward Thomas,[7] and to the 50 – or 25 *Chinese Poems* man,[8] if you happen to see either of them.

It's raining like Hell, and the poor procession is 'en route' from Buschbach. The Lutherans will be gloating – devils!

If you don't want to bother with the articles, merely leave them.

Farewell D. H. Lawrence

[1] DHL wrote on Ascension Day which was 16 May 1912.

[2] 'German Impressions: I. French Sons of Germany' and 'II. Hail in the Rhineland' appeared in *Saturday Westminster Gazette*, 3 and 10 August 1912.

[3] work] stir

[4] i.e. gillyflowers.

[5] *Sons and Lovers* (cf. p. 378 n. 4).

[6] within] in

[7] Edward Thomas (1878–1917), whom DHL may have met through their both having published in the *English Review*. By 1912 Thomas's books included: *The Heart of England* (1906); editor, *The Pocket Book of Poems and Songs for the Open Air* (1907); *Richard Jefferies* (1909). De la Mare later wrote the introduction for Thomas's *Collected Poems* (1920).

[8] Clifford Bax (1886–1962), published *Twenty Chinese Poems, Paraphrased* (1910); 2nd edn (1916) entitled *Twenty-five Chinese Poems*.

P.S. Do you hate this formless poetry? It seems to me so truthful. I suppose you despise it. DHL

447. To Frieda Weekley, [17 May 1912]

Text: MS UT; Frieda Lawrence 47–8.

Waldbröl –
Friday.

That was the letter I expected – and I hated it. Never mind. I suppose I deserve it all. I shall register it up, the number of times I leave you in the lurch: that is a historical phrase also. This is the first time. 'Rats' is a bit hard, as a collective name for all your men – And you're the ship? Poor Henning, poor devil! Vous le croquez bien entre les dents.[1] I don't wonder Ernst hates your letters – they would drive any man on earth, mad. I have not the faintest intention of dying: I hope you haven't any longer. I am not a tyrant. If I am, you will always have your own way, so my domain of tyranny isn't wide. – I am trying to think of some other mildly sarcastic things to say. – Oh – the voice of Hannah, my dear, is the voice of a woman who laughs at her newly-married husband when he's a bit tipsy and a big fool. You fling Henning in my teeth. I shall say Hannah is getting fonder and fonder of me. She gives *me* the best in the house. So there!

I think I've exhausted my shell and shrapnel. – You are getting better, thank the Lord. I am better quite. We have both, I think, marvellous recuperative powers.

You really and seriously and honestly think I could come to Munich next Saturday, and stay two months, till August? You think we could manage it all right, as far as the business side goes? I begin to feel like rising once more on the wing. Ich komm – je viens – I come – advenio.

We are going to be married, respectable people, later on. If you were my property, I should have to look after you, which God forbid.

I like the way you stick to your guns. It's rather splendid. We won't fight, because you'd win, from sheer lack of sense of danger.

I think you're rather horrid to Henning. You make him more babified – baby-fied. Or shall you leave him more manly?

You make me think of Maupassants story.[2] An Italian workman, a young man, was crossing in the train to France, and had no money, and had eaten nothing for a long time. There came a woman with breasts full of milk – she was going into France as a wet nurse. Her breasts full of milk hurt her

[1] 'You will crunch him easily between your teeth.'

[2] 'Idylle' in *Miss Harriet* (*Œuvres Complètes*, Paris, 1908).

– the young man was in a bad way with hunger. They relieved each other and went their several ways. Only where is Henning to get his next feed? – Am I horrid?

Write to me quick from Munich, and I will tell them here. – I can return here in August.

Be well, and happy, I charge you (tyranny). D. H. Lawrence

Eine Wahn

Du muss mich heiraten, nicht mehr Frau Friede Wekley zu sein.[1]

448. To Ada Lawrence, [19 May 1912]

Text: MS Clarke; PC v. Ruine Drachenfels; Postmark, [Königs]winter [...] 2; Lawrence-Gelder 110.

[19 May 1912][2]

We are going down the Rhine on a steamer from Bonn to the Drachenfels. It's awfully pretty – and a lovely day. You would *adore* seeing these Germans – they are delicious. Bonn is a beautiful town. I will write you a letter quite soon.

Love DHL

449. To Arthur McLeod, [19 May 1912]

Text: MS UT; PC v. Der Rhein. Ruine Drachenfels; Postmark, Drachenfels 19 5 12; Huxley 37.

[19 May 1912]

I got your card – you sound down in the mouth. I'm so sorry. I write on top of the Drachenfels, in the café under the trees. One can see miles and miles of Rhine – it twists and seems to climb upwards, till some of it swims in the sky. Has Philip been here? Damn him and his missis and their bicycles. We came here down the river from Bonn – that is a delicious town – masses of horse chestnut trees in blossom. Germany is delightful. If I have to beg my bread, I'll never teach again. Get away if you can – try. Look for a poem in next months *English*.[3] When did the *Westminster* publish me? There was a whole series of poems to come.[4] Write to me, do. I love to have a letter from you. Dont be cross if I only send cards in reply. Ask Miss Mason to be good to me and write me to Waldbröl.

My love to Aylwin and the rest D. H. Lawrence

[1] 'A fancy You must marry me, no longer to be Mrs Frieda Weekley.'

[2] Dated from the two postcards following.

[3] See p. 375 Letter 402 and n. 2.

[4] McLeod had presumably seen the first of 'The Schoolmaster' poems. See p. 382 n. 2.

450. To May Holbrook, [19 May 1912]

Text; MS UN; PC v. Rolandseck, Nonnenwert und Siebengebirge; Postmark, Drachenfels 19 5 12; Nehls, iii. 625.

Sunday.

I write on the top of Drachenfels – high above the Rhine. The river winds and twists till it seems climbing the sky, far off. There are steep mountains – or hills – covered entirely with wood. There is an island right below – with tiny steamers going by – and near at hand, on the air, two red butterflies making love. If they can spin and kiss at this height, there in mid-air – then why should I bother about myself. – There is a faint mist over all the Rhineland – really magical. I hope you'll come one day. We have come down on the steamer from Bonn.

Love – and to Will D. H. Lawrence

451. To Jessie Chambers, [19? May 1912]

Text: E.T. 216.

[19? May 1912][1]

I am going through Paul Morel. I'm sorry it turned out as it has. You'll have to go on forgiving me.

452. To Edward Garnett, 21 May 1912

Text: MS NYPL; Postmark, Waldbröl 21 5 12; Huxley 37–9.

bei Herrn Karl Krenkow, Waldbröl, Rheinprovinz
21 May 1912

Dear Garnett,

I suppose I shall have to keep on amusing you, though I myself am anything but amused. I tell you, making history is no joke.[2] But I won't die in the attempt, if I can help it.

Now that title – the readers at Duckworth's ought to have altered it, for *I* did not know that 'A Game of Forfeits' was finally settled upon.[3] As for 'Author of the *White Peacock*'[4] – now would you expect me to think of it? I wonder you can be so heartless. I've not signed any agreement with Messrs Duckworth – I suppose it doesn't matter. And supposing I actually haven't a penny in the world – at present I've about four quid – would your chief

[1] Jessie Chambers said (E.T. 216) this letter was written a 'week or so' after she received a card from Trier (see p. 397 n. 2). She also recalled that the letter was written from the banks of the Rhine (Delavenay 708). The two facts point to this conjectural date.

[2] See Letters 427 and 433.

[3] Cf. Letter 409.

[4] These words are stamped on the front cover of *The Trespasser*.

give me a sub – £10. But for the Lords sake, don't ask him yet – I'd rather anything. Always, somewhere, I shall find *some* woman who'll give me bed and board. Thank god for the women.

F – that is Mrs Weekley – her name is Frieda – 'The Peaceful' – let me call her F. – she has gone to Munich – hundreds of miles away – and I am eating my heart out, and revising my immortal Heinemann novel 'Paul Morel', in this tiny village stuck up in the Rhineland. If you wouldn't make it a laughing matter – I'd open my poor heart to you – a rare museum. But you are too 'narquois'. I left F. in Trier – 200 miles from here – a week ago. Oh there has been *such* a to-do. Weekley was suspicious. He wrote[1] to her, saying he thought she had deceived him recently. When we came back from the Cearne, F. told him about two *other*, *earlier* men,[2] but not about me. He however suspected. He said 'if it is true, wire to me "Ganz recent" (quite recent).' I saw the letter – we were sitting under the lilacs in the garden at Trier. Oh Lord – tragedy! I took F. straight to the post-office, and she wired 'ganz recent'. Came back a wire 'kein moeglichkeit' – (no possibility – i.e. all is over). Since then, wires and letters, something awful. Of course we want a divorce – though F. vows she shall never marry again. Ernst (Weekley) went to the consul to arrange for one – now he backs out – can't face the publicity. And he loves his wife. Poor devil, I feel as if I could bang my head against the wall, life is so knotty. I wrote to him – he wrote to me again. He is really very decent over it. To live, one must hurt people so. One has to make up one's mind, it must be so. Of course my people at home wonder what I'm up to – I shall tell them all later, but nothing now – and they too are hurt. And F. is making herself ill. Now she's gone to München, to her sister.[3] The Richthofens are an astonishing family – three girls – women – the eldest a Doctor of Social Economics – a Professor too – then Frieda – then the youngest – 28 – very beautiful, rather splendid in her deliberate worldliness. They are a rare family – father a fierce old aristocrat – mother utterly non-moral, very kind.[4] You should know them.

I am going to Munich directly – perhaps Saturday. The soles of my feet burn as I wait. Here, the slow oxen go down the main street, drawing the wagons, under my window – the country is all still, and oxen plough and harrow. In the Gasthaus, the Lutheran choir practises in one room, we drink in the next. My cousin Hannah is newly married – and wishes she weren't. She's getting in love with me. Why is it women *will* fall in love with me.

[1] wrote] said

[2] Will Dowson (in Nottingham) and Otto Gross (in Munich). (See R. Lucas, *Frieda Lawrence*, 1973, 33–8.)

[3] Else Jaffe.

[4] Baroness Anna von Richthofen (1851–1930), née Marquier.

And I haven't an eye for a girl, damn it. I just remain in a state of suspense, till I can go to Munich.

Frieda sort of clings to the idea of you, as the only man in England who would be a refuge. She wanted to write to you – so I send you her letter. Don't be wise and cryptic. After all, Frieda isn't in any book, and I'm not, and life hurts – and sometimes rejoices one. But – you see – in life one's own flesh and blood goes through the mill – and F's eyes are tired now. I hope I can go to Munich on Saturday – it is 15 hours journey from this God-forsaken little hole. But people are wonderfully good to me. The Rhineland is nice – we were at Bonn and on the Drachenfels on Sunday – so magical. But it will always be to me a land of exile – and slow, slow cattle drawing the wagons. Those slow, buff oxen, with their immense heads that seem always asleep, nearly drive me mad as they step tinkling down the street. After them, I could hug the dog in the milk-cart, that lifts his paw quickly and daintily over the shaft, and sits down panting.

Is it Tuesday – I never know how the days go. Miss Whale is quite right when she says I'm good – I *am* good. Give her my love. Only the women have eyes for goodness – and *they* wear green moral spectacles, most of 'em.

Vale! D. H. Lawrence

[Frieda Weekley begins][1]

Dear Mr Garnett,

We thought it would be so nice for us and so good for you if you left the 'homes of England' for a little while and came to us here, we would love to have you! We cant put you up but at a little place quite near and I would give you meals. (Does that frighten you?) I am happy, that is the first and the last, quite simple and commonplace – Your letter to me was good, but you should see less of a woman in me and more a human being. Lawrence is a joy in *all* moods and it's fearfully exciting when he writes and I watch while it comes and it is a thrill. Do come, I *know* you would like it. I shall be rather frightened of all the clever things you will say and I shant quite understand, but I will try my best and thank you for your good letter.

Yours Frieda *sans nom*

[1] Frieda's letter is published in Heilbrun 146–7.

453. To Ada Lawrence, [23 May 1912]

Text: MS Clarke; PC v. Trier Römische Bäder; Postmark, Waldbröl 23. 5. 12; Lawrence-Gelder 109.

Waldbröl –
Thursday.

I am going to München tomorrow, to stay perhaps a month or so. My address will be bei Frau Dr. Jaffe-Richthofen, Wolfratshausen, bei München. From there I will write to you on Saturday. Thank Emily for her letter – tell her the first part of Paul Morel is the first writing – I did it again, and have the whole here - finished all but 10 pages. I got the poetry and everything all right – many thanks. You must have almost ruined yourself in postage. I shall come back to Waldbrol later – it's very jolly here.

Love to all D. H. Lawrence

München of course is Munich – very far – 14 hours journey.

454. To Helen Corke, 28 May 1912

Text: MS UT; Huxley 39.

Gasthaus zur Post, Beuerberg, bei München
28 May 1912.

Ada has sent me a copy of *The Trespasser*, and says there are two more at home, so I thought you might like one from me.[1] Some day I will inscribe it, if you wish.

I am here in Bavarian Tyrol, near the mountains. They stand up streaked with snow, so blue, across the valley. The Isar is a quick stream, all muddy with glacier water now. If ever you come to Germany, come down the Isar-Thal. The flowers are in masses, masses, enough to satisfy any heart alive, and so beautiful. And the clear, clean atmosphere, and the peasants barefooted, and the white cows with their cow-bells, it is all so delightful. Yesterday we were at a peasant play – you know this is the Ober Ammergau Country. It was an old Miracle play, with the Devil and Death, and Christ, and Maria – quaint and rather touching. You would like it very much. Some time, come to Bavaria. It is the Minnesinger Country.[2] I have been in the Rhine land, and the Mosel land, but I like Bavaria best.

Your last letter to me wasn't very nice, I thought.[3] But there, I don't wonder. We leave here on Friday.

Regards to Mr and Mrs Corke.[4] D. H. Lawrence

[1] Cf. p. 378 n. 3.
[2] Medieval German love poets. Cf. p. 331 n. 1.
[3] Helen Corke's reply to Letter 379.
[4] Alfred Corke (1851–1929) and Louisa (1849–1930).

455. To May Holbrook, [29 May 1912]

Text: MS UN; PC v. Oktober 1741 Pfingsten 1912: Beyrberg unter dem Schutze der Rosenkranzkönigin; Postmark, Beuerberg 29 5 12; Nehls, iii. 625.

[29 May 1912]

I am now down in the Isar Valley – 30 miles from Munich. It's a lovely place – wild valley, great blue mountains – snow capped – and masses of the loveliest flowers. You would simply adore it. We are in the midst of this play – it's a sort of OberAmmergau Passion business – ripping. Shall be moving in a day or two.

Love and to Will DHL

456. To Jessie Chambers, [June 1912]

Text: Delavenay 708.

[Icking, bei München, Isarthal]
[June 1912][1]

[Enclosed with a letter for the Chambers family was an envelope] pour vous seule [containing 'his almost hysterical message' about his attachment to Frieda Weekley.] I daren't think of Weekley... I only know I love Frieda... I can think of nothing but of Anna Karenina. Don't tell May, nor Nell Corke, don't tell anyone. Nobody knows, only Ada.

457. To Sallie Hopkin, 2 June 1912

Text: MS NCL; Huxley 39–41.

bei Professor Alf. Weber, Icking, bei München
2 June 1912

Dear Mrs Hopkin,

Although I haven't heard from you, I'll get a letter off to you, because to people I like, I always want to tell my good news. When I came to Germany I came with Mrs Weekley – went to Metz with her. Her husband knows all about it – but I don't think he will give her a divorce – only a separation. I wish he'd divorce her, so we could be married. But that's as it is.

I came down from the Rhine land to Munich last Friday week. Frieda[2] met me there in Munich. She had been living with her sister in a village down the Isar valley, next village to this. We stayed in Munich a night, then

[1] A shorter text of this letter is in E.T. 216. Jessie Chambers dated it 'a few weeks' later than Letter 451.

[2] Frieda] We

went down to Beuerberg for eight days. Beuerberg is about 40 kilometres from Munich, up the Isar, near the Alps. This is the Bavarian Tyrol. We stayed in the Gasthaus zur Post. In the morning we used to have breakfast under the thick horse-chestnut trees, and the red and white flowers fell on us. The garden was on a ledge, high over the river, above the weir, where the timber rafts floated down. The Loisach – that's the river – is pale jade green, because it comes from glaciers. It is fearfully cold and swift. The people were all such queer Bavarians. Across from the inn, across a square full of horsechestnut trees, was the church and the convent, so peaceful, all whitewashed, except for the minaret of the church, which has a black hat. Everyday, we went out for a long, long time. There are flowers so many they would make you cry for joy – alpine flowers. – By the river, great hosts of globe flowers, that we call bachelor's buttons – pale gold great bubbles – then primulas, like mauve cowslips, somewhat – and queer marsh violets, and orchids, and lots of bell-flowers, like large, tangled, dark-purple harebells, and stuff like larkspur, very rich, and lucerne, so pink, and in the woods, lilies of the valley – oh, flowers, great wild mad profusion of them, everywhere. One day we went to a queer old play done by the peasants – this is the Ober Ammergau country. One day we went into the mountains, and sat, putting Friedas rings on our toes, holding our feet under[1] the pale green water of a lake, to see how they looked. Then we go to Wolfratshausen where Frieda's sister has a house – like a châlet – on the hill above the white village. Else – Dr Jaffé-Richthofen – is rather beautiful, but different from Frieda – you see, she's aesthetic – rather lovely. She's married – but has a lover – a professor Weber of Heidelberg, such a jolly fellow.[2] Her husband, also a professor, but at Munich, doesn't mind. He lives mostly in their Munich flat.

Now Frieda and I are living alone in Professor Weber's flat. It is the top story of this villa – quite small – four rooms beside kitchen. But there's a balcony, where we sit out, and have meals, and I write. Down below, is the road where the bullock wagons go slowly. Across the road the peasant women work in the wheat. Then the pale, milk-green river runs between the woods and the plain – then beyond, the mountains, range beyond range, and their tops glittering with snow.

I've just had to run into the kitchen – a jolly little place – wondering what Frieda was up to. She'd only banged her head on the cupboard. So we stood and looked out. Over the hills was a great lid of black cloud, and the

[1] under] in a

[2] Alfred Weber, brother of Max. Professor of Sociology and Political Science. Educated at Bonn, Tübingen and Berlin; taught at Prague and (from 1907), Heidelberg.

mountains nearest went up and down in a solid blue-black. Through, was a wonderful gold space, with a tangle of pale, wonderful mountains, peaks pale gold with snow and farther and farther away – such a silent, glowing confusion brilliant with snow. Now the thunder is going at it, and the rain is here.

I love Frieda so much I don't like to talk about it. I never knew what love was before. She wanted me to write to you. I want you and her[1] to be friends always. Some time perhaps she – perhaps we – shall need you. Then you'll be good to us, won't you?

The world is wonderful and beautiful and good beyond one's wildest imagination. Never, never, never could one conceive what love is, beforehand, never. Life *can* be great – quite god-like. It *can* be so. God be thanked I have proved it.

You might write to us here. Our week of honeymoon is over. Lord, it was lovely. But this – do I like this better? – I like it so much. Don't tell anybody. This is only for the good to know. Write to us.

D. H. Lawrence

458. To Edward Garnett, 2 June 1912

Text: MS NYPL; Huxley 41–3.

bei Herrn Professor Alf. Weber. Icking, bei München
2 Juni 1912

Dear Garnett,

You'll never guess where I am now. And your letter was so down we were beastly sorry. It's that damned play.[2] Why, why should we be plagued with literature and such like tomfoolery? Why can't we live decent honorable lives, without the critics in the Little Theatre fretting us? When I was coming down to München, last Friday week, I happened to see a man going by on Niederlahnstein platform, with a *Morning Post*. It contained your play's announcement, and then I knew you were going to have a flaming hard struggle to get through.[3] They didn't seem to care for the plot, nor the character, the *feel* of the play. Fools – they're all fools.

But listen to me. I've had my week's honeymoon. We went down to Beuerberg Saturday[4] week ago. This is down the Isar Valley, in the Bavarian

[1] her] she

[2] Iden Payne and Mona Limerick appeared at the Little Theatre, London, 22 May 1912, in *The Spanish Lovers* adapted by Edward Garnett from *La Celestina* (1492–1502) by Fernando de Rojas (1465?–1541).

[3] *Morning Post*, 24 May 1912.

[4] Beuerberg Saturday] Beuerberg on Saturday

Tyrol, near the Alps. We stayed at a Gasthaus, and used to have breakfast out under the horse-chestnut trees, steep above the river weir, where the timber rafts come down. The river is green glacier water. Bavarian villages are white and gay, the churches are baroque, with minarets, white with black caps. Every day it was perfect. Frieda and I went long ways. There are masses and masses of Alpine flowers, globe flowers, primulas, lilies, orchids – make you dance. The river was in flood. Once we had to wade such a long way. Of course that just delighted Freidas heart. The lovely brooks we have paddled in, the lovely things we've done!

Now, Weber, Professor at Heidelberg University ([. . .] Political economics) – lover of Frieda's sister, who has a house in the next village,[1] has given us his flat whilst he is back in Heidelberg. It is quite tiny. This is our first morning. We have the upper story of the cottage, and a balcony. I on the balcony in a dressing gown am respectable, but Freida in her nightgown isn't, I say. There's a little white village below, then the river, and a plain of dark woods – all in shadow. Then there's the great blue wall of mountains, only their tops, all snowy, glittering in far-off sunshine against a pale blue sky. Frieda is awfully good-looking. You should see her sometimes. She is getting the breakfast. We are both a bit solemn this morning. It is our first morning at home. You needn't say things about her – or me. She is a million times better than ever you imagine – you *don't* know her, from literature, no, how can you. *I* don't. She is fond of you. I say she'd alarm you. She's got a figure like a fine Rubens woman, but her face is almost Greek. If you say a word about her, I hate you. I am *awfully* well – you should see me. I wish Weekley would divorce her, but he won't. I shall live abroad I think for ever. We shall scramble along. I don't want any money from Duckworth. I'm sending the colliery novel to Heinemann – it's rather great. Can you send me the notices, sometime, on *The Trespasser*?[2]

D. H. Lawrence

F, in a scarlet pinafore, leaning out on the balcony, against a background of blue and snowy mountains, says 'I'm so happy I don't even want to kiss you.' So there, you see, Love is a much bigger thing than passion, and a woman *much* more than sex.

DHL

[1] Wolfratshausen. DHL on several occasions used that as a forwarding address even when he was not writing from it.

[2] By 2 June one review had appeared: unsigned in the *Athenæum*, 1 June 1912 (Draper 44–5).

459. To May Holbrook, [8 June 1912]

Text: MS UN; PC v. A. D. Goltz pinx. Die Quelle. La source; Postmark, München 8 JUN 12; Nehls, iii. 625–6.

Icking, bei München, Isarthal.
[8 June 1912]

Your card followed me down here. What a long way off you seem! Bavaria is lovelier than a dream, thick with flowers that even our garden would hardly grow. We have breakfast on the balcony. Below, the peasants work in the wheat – one stroke of the hoe in five minutes. Beyond, in the pine woods, the pale green glacier river, icy to look at. Beyond, a great lot of mountains, all day long changing. In the evening, their snow is like flame on the dusk. I wish you could see it all. Today we are shopping in München.

Love and to Will D. H. Lawrence

460. To Emily King, [8 June 1912]

Text: MS Clarke; PC v. Rob. Schiff: Bei der Prozession; Postmark, München 8 JUN 12; Unpublished.

[8 June 1912]

We are in Munich for the day – it's a lovely town, all artists, pictures galore. This is rather a pretty card – they had the Corpus Christi procession in Wolfrats-hausen Thursday, almost exactly the same.

I was awfully sorry to hear Sam has nothing to do at present[1] – but I know he won't be long out – and this time let him find something he can *really* put his heart into. Ada says Peggy is well – I am glad.

We have lovely weather here, but hot, and among the mountains, thunderstorms. I am fearfully wel[l] getting so brown.

Love – xxx DHL

461. To Walter de la Mare, 10 June 1912

Text: MS UN; Unpublished.

Haus Vogelnest, *Wolfratshausen*, bei München, Isarthal.
10 June 1912

Dear De la Mare,

I sent that novel 'Paul Morel' off to William Heinemann yesterday. Now I know it's a good thing, even a bit great. It's different from your stuff –

[1] Samuel King, after temporary unemployment, went to Glasgow on 10 June 1912 as a driver for the Scottish Farmers' Association (letter from Ada Lawrence to Louie Burrows, 10 June 1912, MS UN LaB 207); he remained in Glasgow as a dairyman till mobilised for the army.

by the way, I'm fearfully interested to hear of some new poems you have out.[1] It's not so strongly concentric as the fashionable folk under French influence – you see I suffered badly from Hueffer re Flaubert and perfection – want it. It may seem loose – and I may cut the childhood part – if you think better so – and perhaps you'll want me to spoil some of the good stuff. But it is rather great. Some Germans who really know a good thing when they see it speak in high praise.

Sounds as if I had to cry my wares in the market-place, doesn't it? But be as nice as you can about the thing, when you speak to William Heinemann, will you. That novel may get me onto my feet.

I haven't had to sell my boots yet – though the postage for the damned parcel was 2/9. The fool of a post-master swindled me. Still, the gods are merciful. Folk down here are awfully nice. Do you know München and the Isarthal? I can recommend it to you any day for a treat – it knocks the Rhineland into a cocked hat.

I haven't seen an English newspaper nor an English body, for a month. Do you know, it's rather nice. Not that I don't love my country and my countrymen – I do. But this is rest, sweet rest.

Did you see *The Trespasser* – the Duckworth novel? Tell me what you think of it, will you. Garnett seems fearfully down at the mouth about his play. Oh literature, oh the glorious Art, how it preys upon the marrow in our bones. It scoops the stuffing out of us, and chucks us aside. Alas!

Take my part with W. H, and I'll say a prayer for you at every shrine I pass in Bavaria – which is saying a great deal; – and also, of course, if you want my petitions to be lifted on your behalf, not otherwise.

Adieu. Do you want any more poetry? Haven't you got enough for that volume of verse of mine, which lies in the womb of Time?[2]

Adieu, D. H. Lawrence

462. To Arthur McLeod, [15 June 1912]

Text: MS Whiteson; Unpublished.

Prof. Dr. Edgar Jaffé, Herausgeber des Archivs für Sozialwissenschaft und Sozialpolitik, München N.O.2.

15 June 191[2]

My dear Mac,

Your letter made me miserable for you. I got it at Beuerberg. I shall never forget Beuerberg. It is near the mountains, in the wonderful meadows at the

[1] *The Listeners, and Other Poems* (February 1912).

[2] Cf. *Othello* I. iii. 377.

head of the Loisach – a white, tiny village, with a great church, white-washed outside, with a white minaret and a black small bulb – half renaissance, half moorish – brought back from the Turkish wars, a reminiscence – but inside, baroque, gilded, pictures, gaudy, wild, savagely religious. We stayed at an old inn, a great forsaken place. The peasants dined in the long table in the hall, looking out of the open door at the chestnut trees and the cloister. There I read your letter. I was on my honeymoon. I am not legally married. Perhaps some day the great scandal will come out. But I don't care. I have been fearfully happy. I long to go back to Frieda on Monday. I am in love – and, my God, it's the greatest thing that can happen to a man. I tell you, find a woman you can fall in love with. *Do* it. *Let* yourself fall in love, if you haven't done so already. You[1] are wasting your life. How miserable your last letter! Nowadays, men haven't the courage and the strength to love. You must *know* that you're committing slow suicide. Do for the lord's sake find some woman you can respect and love, and love her, and let her love you. Decide to do it. As you go on, you die. Now decide to live. After all, what is golf to Aylwin? – nothing in the end. He wants life – he wants love. But he is afraid to risk himself. I tried several women – I did it honestly – and now, thank God, I have got a woman I love. You have no idea what it means.

I won't tell you details – don't mention this to Miss Mason or anybody – it is what the world calls a scandal. But we'll straighten out the tangles. Lord, it's a great thing to have met a woman like Frieda. I could stand on my head for joy, to think I have found her. We've been together for three weeks. And I love her more every morning, and every night. Where it'll end, I don't know. She's got a great, generous soul – and a splendid woman to look at.

But I'm afraid I sound a fool. You know I'm not frivolous. All this I say to you, is really earnest.

Do you know, I don't think you were fond enough of me. I was very fond of you. But you don't trust yourself, or you don't trust other people. You won't let yourself be really fond, even of a man friend, for fear he find[2] out your weaknesses. As if your good qualities wouldn't outweigh, a dozen times, your failings! But you mistrust folk – even decent folk. It is a blemish in you, a lack of courage, a want of faith and of higher generosity.

All this because you perplex and distress me so. Don't say it was only a mood, your last letter – it was not. It is a permanent thing, this sadness of yours, because you feel your life, as a life, is going to waste. Don't let it. Buck up and do something with it. Look at Aylwin too!

[1] You] I

[2] find] found

Don't be angry with me, will you. Write and tell me how you liked *The Trespasser*. I sent Paul Morel to Heinemann on Thursday. I *hate* Davidson – I *hate* Philip.

It is Walpurgis Night festival tonight[1] – I should have gone – but it rains.

Do you want me to buy you some Geographical picture-postcards, or anything, down here? Tell me if you do.

Address me

bei Herrn Professor Alf. Weber, *Icking*,
bei München, Isarthal. Vale! D. H. Lawrence

463. To Edward Garnett, 29 June 1912

Text: MS NYPL; Huxley 43–4.

Icking, bei München, Isarthal.
29 June 1912

Dear Garnett,

Thanks for the cutting from the *Westminster*[2] – quite good, wasn't it? – who was it? I had a letter from England yesterday, telling me the *Daily News* says I must 'cultivate an intenser vision'.[3] Which makes F[rieda] shriek with laughter.

You needn't think we spend all our time billing and cooing, and nibbling grapes and white sugar. Oh no – the great war is waged in this little flat on the Isarthal, just as much as anywhere else. In fact, I don't think the *real* tragedy is in dying, or in the perversity of affairs, like the woman one loves being the wife of another man – like the last act of *Tristan*. I think the real tragedy is in the inner war which is waged between people who love each other, a war out of which comes knowledge and –

But Lord! – I'm off on the preach again. All I want to say – we have fearfully good times together, but are in no danger of being killed with kindness or surfeited with sweet.[4]

I had a fearfully affected letter from Saga woman[5] the other day, fishing for me back. She thanks me for *The Trespasser* – and winds up, 'We are such stuff as dreams are made on[6] – but aye we make fair dreams, what matter!'

[1] St Walpurgis, protectress against magic arts; commemorated at various times, principally on 1 May.

[2] An unsigned review of *The Trespasser* on 8 June 1912.

[3] The *Daily News* reviewer, 21 June 1912, remarked: 'We look forward to the day when Mr Lawrence will burn with an intenser vision than anything he communicates here. If only he can get below surfaces, he has in him the makings of an artist in literature.'

[4] *The Taming of the Shrew* IV. i. 211; *A Midsummer Night's Dream* II. ii. 137.

[5] Helen Corke.

[6] *The Tempest* IV. i. 156–7.

F. tore up the letter in great disgust, and pitches 'aye we make fair dreams' at me at every verse end.

The papers have been decent to the *Trespasser*, haven't they? I've only had the one cutting. I wonder if anybody would have a short story now. While here, I've written three.[1] But, under the influence of Frieda, I am afraid their moral tone would not agree with my countrymen.

Things are a bit unsettled with England. Prof. Weekley is not definite about a divorce. Folk down here are very nice, and the country is lovely. F. raves over glow-worms, I over fire-flies, and we nearly murder each other.

I haven't seen an English newspaper for six weeks. What's the Parliamentary Reform Bill?[2]

Love rather suits me. I am getting fat, and look awfully well. You don't know how surprised I am, considering the rate we go at. One man's meat is another man's poison, I suppose.

F. reads my letter before I send it, so I must be careful. Is there any news about anybody? Have you got over that play yet? It was a beastly swindle. It's so fearfully nice to get away from the British public, altogether.

Don't be miserable, and cynical. – Oh, and by the way, you can now say all the horrid things you like – we shall enjoy them. Sometime I'll write you a letter when F.'s gone out.

Yours D. H. Lawrence

464. To Edward Garnett, 3 July 1912

Text: MS NYPL; cited in Huxley 45.

Icking, bei[3] München, Isarthal.
3 July 1912

Dear Garnett,

Your news of the *Trespasser* is rather cheering.[4] Everything else is pretty bad. Weekley it seems, is going half crazed. He is *fearfully* in love with F[rieda]. There are storms of letters from England, imploring her to renounce for ever all her ideas of love, to go back and give her life to her

[1] 'New Eve and Old Adam', 'Once' and, probably, 'Delilah and Mr Bircumshaw'.

[2] On 17 June 1912 the Franchise and Registration Bill had been introduced into the House of Commons. Its aim was to simplify electoral law and to abolish plural voting along with university franchise.

[3] Icking, bei] 'Haus Vogelnest', Wolfratshausen, bei

[4] News of largely favourable reviews e.g. unsigned in *Athenæum*, 1 June 1912 (Draper 44–5); Basil de Selincourt in *Manchester Guardian*, 5 June 1912 (Draper 46–7); unsigned in *Saturday Westminster Gazette*, 8 June 1912; unsigned in *Morning Post*, 17 June 1912 (Draper 48–9); unsigned in *Standard*, 21 June 1912; unsigned in *Saturday Review*, 22 June 1912.

husband and her children.[1] Weekley would have her back, on those conditions. The children are miserable, missing her so much. She lies on the floor in misery – and then is fearfully angry with me because I won't say 'stay for my sake'. I say 'decide what you want most, to live with me and share my rotten chances, or go back to security, and your children – decide for *yourself* – Choose for yourself.' And then she almost hates me, because I won't say 'I love you – stay with me whatever happens.' I *do* love her. If she left me, I do not think I should be alive six months hence. And she won't leave me, I think. God, how I love her – and the agony of it. She is a woman who also makes a man suffer, by being blind to him when her anger or resentment is roused. She is staying in Wolfratshausen with her sister's[2] children for the four nights[3] – her sister is away, and the nurse has just left. The letters today have nearly sent us both crazy. I didn't know life was so hard. But really, for me, it's been a devilish time ever since I was born. But for the fact that when one's got a job on, one ought to go through with it, I'd prefer to be dead any minute. I can't bear it when F. is away. I could bang my head against the wall, for relief. It's a bit too much.

And William Heinemann – may his name be used as a curse and an eternal infamy – kindly sends me this letter in the thick of it all.[4]

I had a rather nice letter from somebody – 'Hugh Walpole'.[5] Is he

[1] Charles Montague (b. 1900), Elsa Agnes Frieda (b. 1902) and Barbara Joy (b. 1904).

[2] her sister's] her

[3] Else Jaffe's children were: Friedel (b. 1903), Marianne (b. 1905), Peter (1907–15), and Hans (b. 1909).

[4] Heinemann wrote as follows, 1 July 1912 (TMS UT):

Dear Mr Lawrence

I have read PAUL MOREL with a good deal of interest and, frankly, with a good deal of disappointment, especially after what you wrote to me with regard to your feeling about the book and the view you took that it was your best work.

I feel that the book is unsatisfactory from several points of view; not only because it lacks unity, without which the reader's interest cannot be held, but more so because its want of reticence makes it unfit, I fear, altogether for publication in England as things are. The tyranny of the Libraries is such that a book far less out-spoken would certainly be damned (and there is practically no market for fiction outside of them).

In declining this manuscript, with many regrets, I would like to say that I am a great admirer of your writing, that certain parts in PAUL MOREL strike me as good as anything I have ever read of yours; but as a whole it seems to me painfully mistaken, if for no other reason than that one has no sympathy for any character in the book. A writer must create interest in his characters. Even, after a while, one's interest in Paul flags, – while, in the early part, the degradation of his mother, supposed to be of gentler birth, is almost inconceivable.

I need hardly say that I shall at all times be glad to read anything of yours, and it is a real disappointment to me to have to decline this book. The manuscript goes back to you in a separate parcel, registered.

Yours sincerely

[5] (Sir) Hugh Seymour Walpole (1884–1941), author of *The Wooden Horse* (1909), *Mr Perrin and Mr Traill* (1911), *Rogue Herries* (1930), etc.

anybody? Could I wring three ha'porth of help out of his bloody neck. Curse the blasted, jelly-boned swines, the slimy, the belly-wriggling invertebrates, the miserable sodding rotters, the flaming sods, the snivelling, dribbling, dithering palsied pulse-less lot that make up England today. They've got white of egg in their veins, and their spunk is that watery its a marvel they can breed. They *can* nothing but frog-spawn – the gibberers! God, how I hate them! God curse them, funkers. God blast them, wish-wash. Exterminate them, slime.

I could curse for hours and hours – God help me.

It doesn't matter a bit what Miss Whale tells any inquiring lady. The trouble is, that Weekley *won't* get a divorce. I want Frieda free.

Why, why, why was I born an Englishman! – my cursed, rotten-boned, pappy hearted countrymen,[1] *why* was I sent to *them*. Christ on the cross must have hated his countrymen. 'Crucify me, you swine,' he must have said through his teeth. It's not so hard to love thieves[2] also on the cross. But the high priests down there – 'crucify me, you swine.' – 'Put in your nails and spear, you bloody nasal sour-blooded swine, I laugh last.' God, how I hate them – I nauseate – they stink in sourness.

They deserve it that every great man should drown himself. But not I (I am a bit great).

My dear Garnett, at this eleventh hour I love you and understand you a bit. Don't sympathise with me, don't.

Yours Sincerely D. H. Lawrence

P.S. And Heinemann, I can see, is quite right, as a business man.

465. To Walter de la Mare, 3 July 1912

Text: MS UN; Unpublished.

Icking, bei München, Isarthal.
3 Juli 1912

Dear Mr De la Mare,

Thanks for your letter and the proofs of the article.[3] After all, it is a bit rough on you, to put you to all this trouble. I hope you'll forgive me. I don't mind when the *W*[*estminster*] *G*[*azette*] publishes the verse[4] and the articles, so long as it brings them out at all. As for the payment: they sent me a cheque for £4..13 the other day, and I can wait till they are ready, for the next.

[1] MS reads 'countryman'.
[2] MS reads 'theives'.
[3] One of the two articles entitled 'German Impressions'.
[4] None of DHL's poems appeared in *Saturday Westminster Gazette* after this date (the 'Schoolmaster' series having been completed on 1 June 1912).

Thanks also for your remarks on the Paul Morel novel. I shall have to go over it again, and I shall remember what you said.[1] I suppose you know Wm Heinemann has refused it – not over pleasantly. But there, a publisher holds the right to dispense with decency. And from a business point of view, I can sympathise with his rejecting the thing. But in spite of all and everything, I maintain it is rather a great work. However, I'm not out to make converts.

I am rather ashamed of the amount of trouble I have been to you. What about the poems? He doesn't mention them. I don't mind if he sends me them back also: Someone else would have them, I guess.

Yours Sincerely D. H. Lawrence

PS. God helping me, my next novel shall be of the 'sweet' order. I must live.

466. To Edward Garnett, [4 July 1912]

Text: MS NYPL; PC; Postmark, München 4. 7. 12.; Unpublished.

Wolfratshausen
Thursday

Dear Garnett,

I have posted to you today the MS. of the Paul Morel novel. Anything that wants altering I will do. Your letter cheered me immensely.

F[rieda] sends love – because she says you'll stick to me.

Excuse the card. D. H. Lawrence

467. To Edward Garnett, [8 July 1912]

Text: MS NYPL; cited in Huxley 43.

Icking, bei München, Isarthal.
Monday

My dear Garnett,

I sent you the novel to the Cearne, before I heard from you asking for it to go to Duckworth's. I hope you won't mind. You are still down at Lewes? I will make what alterations you think advisable. It would be rather nice if you made a few notes again.[2] I will squash the first part together – it is too long. I am really very much interested to know what you'll say.

[1] The letter to DHL is lost, but De la Mare's view of *Sons and Lovers* when it was submitted to Heinemann is clear in his letter to Edward Garnett, 27 May 1913 (TMS UT): 'I read it in MS., and thought – apart from the fineness of individual passages – that it was badly put together and a bit too violent here and there.' See also p. 424 n. 1.

[2] As he had done on *The Trespasser*.

The other day I heard from de la Mare. He is a bit funky, as you said – sort of half apologetic. What's *Loves Pilgrimage* – by whom – that he says the libraries have banned.[1] He sent me proofs of some articles that the *Westminster Gazette* had accepted – which is something. He said he was taking my poems to W[illiam] H[einemann] today. I hope the rotten little Jew won't have them. De la Mare says he'll recommend them strongly. Fancy De la Mare recommending anything strongly. Oh generation of tender feet.

We are still at Icking for a time; F[rieda] and I – have been through alleys and avenues of tragedy. W[eekley] got more and more desperate – F. wrote definitely she could never come back – he said, then she must forego the children. There was a cyclone of letters. I wrote also. Now things are beginning to calm down. W. is really *awfully* good: what the English *can* be if they are hauled by the neck into it, is something rather great. I should like to bludgeon them into realising their own[2] selves. Curse you, my countrymen, you have put the halters round your necks, and pull tighter and tighter, from day to day. You are strangling yourselves, you blasted fools. Oh my countrymen!

There will be no divorce (damn it!) – W. will settle things well, I know. He's rather fine – never, for one moment, denies his love for F, and never says anything against her herself, only against the previous lover, a German, who put these 'ideas' into her head.[3] He says I am 'ehrlich' and have a great future – I should think I *am* honest: good God, I reckon I'm an angel!

In a week or ten days we are going walking through the Tyrol. I have got about £12 and F. about as much – which is all we have in the world for the present. But it'll do. I don't want anything from Duckworth. I think we shall walk over Innsbruck to Verona.

I don't want to come back to England. For the winter I shall get something to do in Germany, I think. F. wants to clear out of Europe, and get to

[1] Perhaps in a letter to DHL, certainly in one (c. 1 July 1912) to Edward Garnett, De la Mare mentioned Upton Sinclair's book published by Heinemann, May 1912. To Garnett he wrote (MS UT):

Dear Garnett

This is the last address I had from Lawrence. The MS. of 'Paul Morel' has gone back to him there.

W[illiam] H[einemann] thinks the Libraries would ban the book as it stands; and judging from the fact that Smith's refused *Love's Pilgrimage* I should imagine he is right. But apart from this altogether, I don't feel that the book as a whole comes up to Lawrence's real mark. It seems to me to need pulling together: it is not of a piece. But the real theme of the story is not arrived at till half way through. This of course is only my own personal opinion: and I should like to hear what you think. The best in it is of course extraordinarily good.

L. sent me some excellent German sketches which I sent on to Spender. They will appear in the *W*[*estminster*] *G*[*azette*] after the series of his poems is finished....

[2] own] real

[3] See p. 409 n. 2.

somewhere uncivilised. It is astonishing how barbaric one gets with love: one finds oneself in the Hinterland der Seele,[1] and – it's a rum place. I never knew I was like this. What Blasted Fools the English are, fencing off the big wild scope of their natures. Since I am in Germany, all my little pathetic sadness and softness goes, and I am often frightened at the thing[2] I find myself.

Now F. and I are going swimming in the Isar. She swims finely, and looks fearfully voluptuous, rolling in the pale green water. It's all lonely and wild, so we can bathe naked, which one should. You really ought to try life down here.

Nothing pleases me like the 'Reprehensible Jaunt' of the *Nottingham Guardian*.[3] My beautiful *Trespasser* called a Reprehensible Jaunt. It is the joy of F.'s soul.

I hope things will continue to go a bit decently. F. brazenly sends her love. It's a sunny day, for bathing.

Yours D. H. Lawrence

468. To May Holbrook, [13 July 1912]

Text: MS UN; PC v. Wolfratshausen, Isartalbahn; Postmark, RB Bahnpost 13 JUL 12; Nehls, iii. 626.

[Icking, bei München, Isarthal]
[13 July 1912]

What an exciting letter that was! The emigration idea is, I should say, a fine one. Australia is a new country, new morals: it is *not* a split from England, but a new nation. But which of the States? – you don't say – N. S. Wales or Queensland? I shan't come back to England for a long time, if I can help it. Now, I want to wander. Your notes were *good* – rather fascinating – do go on, I should love the rest.

I think, at the end of next week I am going on a walking tour, over Innsbrück and the Austrian Tyrol to Verona. I am not sure yet. But I will let you have addresses later on. 'Haus Vogelnest' – Wolfratshausen will always find me. – But move, tell Will he must move. I will write to him. – It is so hot here now, I want to get up to the snow.

Love D. H. Lawrence

[1] i.e. unknown reaches of the soul. [2] thing] savage

[3] A review of *The Trespasser* appeared in the *Nottinghamshire Guardian*, 2 July 1912, under this heading. The reviewer's hostility led him to write as follows: 'Reading his pages is like walking through the Wierz Museum, for sometimes we are astonished at his cleverness in putting all sorts of strange emotions into words and discriminating the slightest shades of sensation, but there are passages which convey no meaning to us, and we cannot believe the author is much better off...The philosophy is neither paganism nor sensualism, but what we call animalism, which is human animalism.'

469. To Louie Burrows, [13 July 1912]

Text: MS UN; PC v. Wolfratshausen a. d. Loisach. Isartalbahn; Postmark, [...] 13 JUL 12; Boulton 169.

[Icking, bei München, Isarthal]
[13 July 1912]

Thanks for your letter – what a great shame about your cast! You don't say how long you are staying in Castle Donington. I have been down here in the Isar valley for some time now – near Munich – 20 miles south. It is very lovely, near the Alps. But next week I think I am going on a walking tour through the Austrian Tyrol, probably down into Verona, over Innsbrück, so I can't give you an address just now. I will when I get somewhere. I am awfully well. It is warm here, and lovely. I hope you'll have a good time on the holiday. I can't say when I return to England.

Yrs D. H. Lawrence

470. To Sallie Hopkin, [c. 13 July 1912]

Text: Photocopy NCL; PC; Postmark, [...] JUL 12; Unpublished.

[Icking, bei München, Isarthal]
[c. 13 July 1912][1]

We never answered your letter and it made us so happy! But things have been fast and *hard* like anything, *yet* they seem to have been worth it for all the horror! We send our love and your generous warmth did us good.

F. Weekley
D. H. Lawrence[2]

471. To Edward Garnett, 18 July 1912

Text: MS NYPL; Postmark, RB Bahnpost 19 JUL 12; Unpublished.

Icking, bei München, Isarthal
18 July 1912

Dear Garnett,

Thanks very much for the notes on P[aul] M[orel]. I agree with all you say, and will do all I can. I'll do my best. Send the MS here.

F[rieda] and I are going on a tramp through the Tyrol to Italy – start on the 28th or 29th I think. We should *love* to see David.[3] Tell us his address. Send him to see us here – quick, because of our going away. He comes here from the Isarthal Bahnhof. I can introduce him to Professor Jaffé, at the

[1] The conjectural date relates to a second postmark: Nottingham JY 15 12.
[2] Frieda wrote the card; both signed it.
[3] See p. 315, n. 1.

University – a nice man. It would be lovely if we could do just a little for him – all we can.

Frieda sends love. D. H. Lawrence

P.S. I am amusing myself writing a comedy.[1]

472. To Edward Garnett, [22 July 1912]

Text: MS NYPL; Postmark, RB Bahnpost 23 JUL 12; Huxley 45–6.

Icking, bei München
Monday

Dear Garnett,

Our letters bow to each other in passing in the post, every time. I suppose you do in the end get my notes – yours ramble in to me.

I got Paul Morel this morning, and the list of notes from Duckworth. The latter are awfully nice and detailed. What a Trojan of energy and conscientiousness you are! I'm going to slave like a Turk at the novel – see if I won't do you credit. I begin in earnest tomorrow – having spent the day in thought (?)

We shall be awfully glad to hear of your son David.

There is talk of getting me some lecturing in München for the winter. I dread it a bit. Here, in this tiny savage little place, F[rieda] and I have got awfully wild. I loathe the idea of England, and its enervation and misty miserable modernness. I *don't* want to go back to town and civilisation. I want to rough it and scramble through, free, free. I don't want to be tied down. And I can live on a tiny bit. I shan't let F leave me, if I can help it. I feel I've got a mate and I'll fight tooth and claw to keep her. She says I'm reverting, but I'm not – I'm only coming out wholesome and myself. Say I'm right, and I ought to be always common. I *loathe* Paul Morel.

F sends love. D. H. Lawrence

I'll do you credit with that novel, if I can.

473. To David Garnett, [23 July 1912]

Text: MS NYPL; Postmark, RB Bahnpost 23 JUL 12; cited in David Garnett, *The Golden Echo* (1953), p. 241.

Icking, bei München
Tuesday.

Dear Mr Garnett,

I was waiting to hear from you – Edward Garnett had told me you were coming to München.

[1] Probably sketching out 'The Fight for Barbara'; it was to be finally written in October (see Letter 510).

It will be awfully jolly to see you. Could you come down here by the 1.35 train tomorrow, from the Isarthal Bahnhof. You take tram number 10 or 20 from the Marien Platz or the Sendlingerthor Platz. I don't know where the Zwieblandstrasse is – but you'll easily find the Isarthal station. You get in at Icking 2.24, and I shall be at the station to meet you.

I must explain to you first that I am living with a lady who is not my wife, but who goes as my wife down here in Bavaria.

Yours Sincerely D. H. Lawrence

I look fearfully English, and so I guess do you, so there is no need for either of us to carry the Union Jack for recognition.[1]

DHL

474. To David Garnett, [26 July 1912]

Text: MS NYPL; Postmark, [...] 2[...] JUL 12; Unpublished.

Icking, bei München
Friday

Dear Garnett,

After all we are not going to München this week-end, as it is no longer necessary, and Frieda infinitely prefers the country.

Perhaps you would come out on Sunday, by the 10.15 in the morning, will you? If I'm not at the station, you know the way.

Frieda and I enjoyed your coming immensely, as you could see.

Yours Sincerely D. H. Lawrence

If you come on Sunday, you'll stay the night, will you, but dont bother to bring anything to wear.

If you could, would you just buy us a penny tube of sticky stuff in town, to mend Frieda's mirror.

475. To David Garnett, [30 July 1912]

Text: MS NYPL; PC; Postmark, Ebenhausen 30 JUL 12; Unpublished.

Icking
Tuesday

Do you care to come Thursday for the midday meal, stay the night as you will. Be prepared to amuse us, you are so rare and delicious.

Love – and from F[rieda].

D. H. Lawrence

[1] See David Garnett, *The Golden Echo*, pp. 240–2, for his description of the meeting to which this letter gave rise.

476. To Edward Garnett, 4 August 1912
Text: MS NYPL; Huxley 46–8.

Icking, bei München
Sunday 4 Aug 1912

Dear Garnett,

What can have become of you, that we have not heard from you for so long? And we ask Bunny (so he will have it) – but[1] he knows nothing of you. He's awfully like you, in a thousand ways – his walk, his touch of mischief and wickedness, and nice things besides. But he hasn't got your appetite for tragedy with the bleeding brow: perhaps he'll get it later: some female or other will create the want for it in him. (F[rieda] reads my letters).

We are awfully fond of him. I reckon he's a lucky dog. But I'd rather have a dog lucky and adorable, like him, than unlucky and lugubrious, like myself. You should see him swim in the Isar, that is effervescent and pale green, where the current is fearfully strong. He simply smashes his way through the water, while F. sits on the bank bursting with admiration, and I am green with envy. By Jove, I reckon his parents have done joyously well for that young man. Oh but you should see him dance Mordkin[2] passion dances, with great orange and yellow and red and dark green scarves of F's, and his legs and arms bare; while I sit on the sofa and do the music, and burst with laughter, and F. stands out on the balcony in the dark, scared. Such a prancing whirl of legs and arms and raving colours you never saw: And F. shrieks when he brandishes the murderous knife in my music-making face; and somebody calls in German from below: 'Go and trample somewhere else,' and at last he falls panting. Oh the delightful Bunny! – it is incredible that he is also so much like you. He should have come and stayed with us last night, but didn't turn up. I suppose he's on the razzle in München.

We are going away from here tomorrow. Oh, I must tell you how the Baroness von Richthofen 'schimpfed'[3] me on Friday night. She suddenly whirled in here on her way from The Tyrol to Constance, stayed an hour, and spent that hour abusing me like a washerwoman – in German, of course. I sat and gasped. 'Who was I, did I think, that a Baronesse should clean my boots and empty my slops: she, the daughter of a high-born and highly-cultured gentleman' – at the highly-cultured, I wanted to say 'I don't think!' – 'No decent man, no man with common sense of decency, could expect to have a woman, the wife of a clever professor, living with him like

[1] but] and
[2] Mikhail Mordkin (1882–1944), famous Russian ballet dancer and partner of Anna Pavlova (1885–1931).
[3] 'cursed'.

a barmaid, and he not even able to keep her in shoes.' – So she went on. – Then in München, to Else, her eldest daughter, says I am a lovable and trustworthy person. – You see I saw her off gracefully from the station.

We are going away tomorrow morning, early. – F. is just holding forth – reciting, I call it – that everybody in the world is a rotter, except herself. Why I'm a rotter at the present moment, it will be interesting to hear later. – I have at last nailed F.'s nose to my wagon. At last, I think, she can't leave me – at least for the present: despite the loss of her children. I am sick to death of the bother, – Weekley whining bullying threatening, the Richthofen lot funking and trying to boss and being really rather nice – bother and worry and sentiments and harrowings from week end to week-end. The only bit of real peace we get is when we are both asleep, touching each other. Of all this, nothing has been really worth it, but the nights in the little bed where we sleep together. It's the rotten outsiders who plant nettles in paradise. But, thank God, we are going away: walking to Mayrhofen, about 10 miles from Innsbrück – stopping there for a week or two – perhaps Bunny will come – then going on down into Italian Switzerland, where we shall spend the winter, probably on Lake Garda, or Maggiore.[1] We've got £23 between us, at present. We shall have to live cheap as mice, but I think we shall manage. I hope Weekley will at last get the divorce. He funks so – won't be definite any way. Oh Lord, I am so tired of them all. I think we shall get a bit of peace in Austria.

I had a letter from Austin Harrison re a story. His is a wishy-washy noodle, God help me. My stories are too 'steaming' for him. I sent him 3 more,[2] and asked him to forward to you at the Cearne all the MS. of mine he doesn't want. Heinemann is hesitating over the poetry – swine. He – or rather Dela mare, wants to know, do I think of publishing a book of German sketches such as those of which the *Westminster* has accepted three[3] – and would I let W.H. have the rejection thereof. I s'll say yes (a lie). Won't somebody in America have my stories now the *Trespasser* is out there?[4] I am going to write six short stories. I must try and make running money. I am going to

[1] Lake Garda had long been favoured by German tourists, partly on account of Goethe's association with it.

[2] Cf. p. 420 n. 1.

[3] The history of these 'sketches' is complicated. According to DHL here, three had been accepted; on 4 August (Letter 478) he says five were written; but only two ever appeared, on 3 and 10 August 1912. By 22 August 1912 (Letter 487) the *Saturday Westminster Gazette* had decided that two of the remaining sketches were too anti-German and rejected them. These two rejected MSS disappeared; DHL made efforts to locate them (in Letters on 7, 13 and 24 August 1913); apparently without success. Of the five, then, two were published; two were rejected and were lost; and one remains a mystery.

[4] Published by Mitchell Kennerley, May 1912.

write Paul Morel over again – it'll take me 3 months. But Duckworth won't bring it out till Jan., will he? Write me to 'Haus Vogelnest', Wolfratshausen, bei München, if you don't get an address from me. I hope you are well, and all that – I've thought of a new novel - purely of the common people - fearfully interesting.[1]

Vale! D. H. Lawrence

477. To David Garnett, [4 August 1912]

Text: MS NYPL; PC; Postmark, RB Bahnpost 5 AUG 12; Unpublished.

Icking –
Sunday

Dear Bunny,

What's the meaning of this! – why have we heard and seen nothing of you? – we're *cross*. In the morning we rise with the lark – 5.30 a.m and set off on our pilgrimage – to Mayrhofen, bei Innsbrück. Let us hear from you. Prof. Jaffé's address is Irschenhausen bei Ebenhausen – and the Wolfratshausen is 'Haus Vogelnest'. Frieda only says she is cross with you, unless the girl was *very* delightful, then she'll forgive you.

Yours D. H. Lawrence

478. To Walter de la Mare, 4 August 1912

Text: MS UN; Unpublished.

'Haus Vogelnest', *Wolfratshausen*, bei München, Isarthal.
Sunday 4th Aug 1912

Dear de la Mare,

I was glad to hear from you again concerning the verses. At present, I have written five German sketches in all. No doubt I shall keep on. Then, certainly, if it pleased W[illiam] H[einemann] to publish them, I should be most grateful to him.

Duckworth has accepted 'Paul Morel'. I think I shall write a good deal of it again – as, of course, I would have done for Mr. Heinemann. I shall keep your opinion in mind – it will help.

I am going away tomorrow to some place in the Tirol beyond Innsbrück – I don't know the address at all – but if you write me at Wolfratshausen, as above, it will always find me.

Shall I continue to send sketches to the *W*[*estminster*] *G*[*azette*] – or have

[1] Probably the novel later called 'Scargill Street' (see Letter 510) which DHL never completed.

they enough? I suppose Mr Heinemann doesn't want a book of short stories. I had half promised Secker[1] – but I am in no hurry to bother about them, the stories: they pay nobody, in a volume, I am told.

Yours Sincerely D. H. Lawrence

479. To Arthur McLeod, [8 August 1912]

Text: MS UT; PC v. Glashütte – Stuben; Postmark, Kufstein –8. VIII. 12; Unpublished.

[8 August 1912]

I have been on the point of writing to you 20 times – I'm a lazy devil. Your letter was fearfully nice. I'm walking over to Mayrhofen – 20 miles S. of Innsbrück. It's raining for ever, damn it, among these thundering mountains. Last night I got hopelessly lost, and slept in a hay hut. This card I write in the cottage of a hunter, beloved of the Kronprinz.[2] Life seems to spin on in an amazing fashion. How are you.

Yrs. D. H. Lawrence

480. To Gertie Cooper, [8 August 1912]

Text: MS Clarke; PC v. Glashü[tte...] Café Hubertus; Postmark, Kufstein – 8. VIII. 12; Unpublished.

[8 August 1912]

I'm always sending a thought your way, but can't scrape you a card, can I? I'm walking over into the Tyrol – this is the last place in Germany – I cross the Austrian border in half an hour. Last night I got lost in the mountains, and had to sleep in a hay-hut. Now it's raining like — and I write in a hunter's cottage. It's jolly, altogether. What are you doing? Write me a p.c., do, to *Mayrhofen*, Zillertal, Tirol (Postlager). The last word is (Postlagernd[3]). Love – and to F[rances].

Yrs. D. H. Lawrence

1. See Letters 274 and 392.
2. Archduke Franz Ferdinand (later murdered at Sarajevo, 28 June 1914). The scene in the forester's cottage at Glashütte is described and the Crown Prince is mentioned in the original ending – later deleted – to DHL's 'A Hay Hut Among the Mountains' (see *Phoenix II* 43).
3. The department of a post office ('Hauptpostlagernd', a main post office) where letters are kept till called for.

481. To Edward Garnett, [11 August 1912]

Text: MS NYPL; PC; Postmark, Mayrhofen 11. VIII. 12; Unpublished.

bei Fräulein Schneeberger, *Mayrhofen* 138. Zillertal, Tirol – Austria
[11 August 1912]

We got here last night after various adventures. There are no letters postlagernds,[1] so either your letter is not written or it is at Wolfratshausen. Nor do I know where Bunny is.

It is fearfully lovely here. – snow mountains on top of one's head, a 'raging torrent' going by under the bedroom window, so that I keep waking up and imagining a locomotive is blowing off steam, a ghastly Austrian dialect spoken, that I can't understand, no shops, nothing but mountains draped in white chiffon clouds, and determined looking people going by with Alpenstocks. F[rieda] is gorging bilberries and cranberries. Do let us hear about London.

Regards to Miss Whale. D. H. Lawrence

482. To Ada Lawrence, [11? August 1912]

Text: MS Clarke; PC v. Mayrhofen (Zillertal); Postmark, [ ]; Lawrence–Gelder 108–9.

bei Fräulein Schneeberger, *Mayrhofen* 138, Zillertal, Tirol – Austria
[11? August 1912]

Have walked through the mountains to this adorable place, where I shall stay 2 or 3 weeks. There is no letter from you in the Postlagernd – perhaps it is at Wolfratshausen. I am staying in a farmhouse at the foot of the mountains, just by a lovely stream, that tears along, and is as bright as glass. On Wednesday night there was quite a heavy fall of snow, only a little way up the mountains. Do let me hear how you are going on. Underline *Mayrhofen*. Love to all D. H. Lawrence

483. To Edward Garnett, 13 August 1912

Text: MS NYPL; Moore 138.

bei Fräulein Schneeberger, *Mayrhofen 138*, in Zillertal, Tirol – Austria
13 Aug 1912

Dear Garnett,

Hueffer sends me this.[2] What shall I say? Would it be much use to me

[1] letters postlagernds] letters in the postlagernd

[2] Hueffer wrote as follows, 31 July 1912 (MS NYPL):

Dear Lawrence,

Seckers tell me that they are anxious to make you an offer for a novel and indeed to run you rigorously for the rest of time. I think it would be well worth your while to pay attention if Secker ran me for the rest of time? It might be, eh? Does Duckworth really want the 'Paul Morel' novel? Shall I offer Secker that? You see I must get some money from somewhere, shortly. And how I hate to worry you. The *W[estminster] Gazette* is publishing me some sketches. Do you know of anybody else who might. And should I send you some bits of poetry for the *Nation* or somebody. I ll do you one.

I wonder if anything is the matter. It is ages and ages since I heard from you. I'll copy you just one piece of verse.[1] It is rather long, but good, I think.

If ever you know anybody who is tempted to run away with another man's wife, warn him to be very sure of himself. There come such ghastly times, such ghastly letters from England. But I don't regret one jot or tittle. Only it's hard that the other folk are so much hurt.

I *must* hear from you or of you. Yours D. H. Lawrence

Just had a jolly letter from Bunny – he is coming here.

F[rieda] sends her love – wants me to copy more poetry to send you – shall I? I'm too tired tonight.

The Young Soldier with Bloody Spurs.[2]

by D. H. Lawrence

A Servant Girl Speaks.[3]

The sergeant says that eight and twenty wagons
Are coming behind, and we must put out all
The water we can at the gate, for the horses. – He gallops
To the next farm, pulls up where the elderflowers fall.

The wheat on both sides of the road stands green,
And hundreds of soldiers on horseback have filed between
It, gone by our farm to the mountains that stand back blue
This morning.

I think perhaps the man that came
To Wolfratshausen last winter's end, comes through
This place today. These soldiers wear the same

to this and to drop them a line. I don't known where you are myself so I am sending this to Croydon.

I deduce from the public prints that you have published the 'Saga' novel under another title. Well, well, –

Anyhow, drop Secker a line his address is 5 John St, Adelphi. Yours FMH

[1] The poem below, first published in Huxley 51–5.

[2] The Young soldier with Bloody Spurs] Bloody Spurs.

[3] A Servant Girl Speaks.] A Young Servant Woman Speaks.

Helmets as his he lost in the wood that night,
And their uniforms are the same of white and blue – –

It was cold, and he put his cloak right round me
As we walked; dark, so he held his arm close round me.
In the stillness, he took off his helmet to kiss me –
It snowed, and his helmet was lost, he forgot me, he did not miss me.

The Isar whispers again in the valley; the children
Are ducking their heads in the water tubs at the gate
As they go from school; some of the officers rally
At the door of the gasthaus down the road: great
Threads of blue wind far and down the road
I wait for the eight and twenty wagons to come.

At last I hear a rattle, and there away
Crawls the first load into sight – and now there are some
Drawing near, they cover the München road.

Nay,
I dread him coming; I wonder how he will take it.
I can see his raging black eyes blaze at me
And feel him gripping my wrist as if he would break it.

Here comes the first of the wagons, a grey, a dreary
Shut-up coffin of a thing, with a soldier weary
In the box, and four hot horses going drearily,
And a soldier in the saddle of the left-hand draught-horse, sitting
wearily.

One by one they go by – At last
There he sits in the saddle of this the five
And twentieth wagon. – And he will not drive past,
He pulls up for our water; would he drive
On if he knew that *I* was at this farm – ?

And he swings his heavy thigh
Out of the saddle, and staggering
With stiffness comes for the water that I
Have poured for the horses – a dark-blue, staggering

Strong young man. – He leans sighing
With heat against the shaft, and takes
His helmet off, and wipes his hair, trying
To ease himself in his clothes. It makes
Me want to cry, to see him so strong and easy,
Swarthy and strong with his damp thick hair
Pushed up on end – and the breath sighing
Between his thick lips. – I wonder where
He thinks I am – if ever he thinks at all.
But his handkerchief is white with a broad blue border,
A nice one, I like it. – He'll think it's a tall order
When I say he ought to marry me. – And small
I feel to have to tell him.
                                        But why, before
He waters the horses does he wash his heel?
Jesus! – his spurs are red with shining blood!
He splashes water from the pail upon them,
And rubs the silver clean with his thick brown fingers,
Bending backwards awkwardly,
And anxiously, like a boy afraid to be found out.
And he goes and washes the belly of his horse,
A poor roan thing: it's hind leg twitches
Forwards as he rubs the wound,
And bloody water falls upon the road
Soiling the clean white dust. – He rubs the belly
Carefully again, and again, to stop the bleeding.
Jesus! – his fingers are red!
And again, rolling in his heavy high boots,
He comes to the side of the road and washes his hand,
And looks round again at his heel, the bright spur,
And bends again and looks at the belly of the horse,
And kicks dust over the red stain in the road.

And all the time his handsome, swarthy red face
With savage black eyes is sulky: and all the time
He frowns as if he were worried, as if the place
On the horse's belly hurt him, for he was rather gentle
To the thing, and rather fretted. And his thick black hair
Was wet with sweat, and his movements strong and heavy.
– I wonder, will he care!

Now I take the big stone jug of water
Down to the gate, and stand and wait
For a word. He is coming towards the gate –
His eyes meet mine as he takes the jug of water,
He knows me, but does not speak: instead
He drinks and drinks, then turns away his head.

'Do you remember me?'
– 'Yes!'
'Who then?'
– 'Maria, of the Gasthaus Green Hat, Wolfratshausen.'
'I am with child by you – '

He looked at me, and his heavy brows came over
His eyes and he sulked. – He had another lover.

'It is true,' I said.
– 'And what do you want?'
'What do you think?' I said.

He looked away down the road.

Suddenly his horses [. . .] began to start.
He shouted, ran heavily after them,
And jerked back their bridles, pushing their heads apart.

I waited, but he would not come back to me,
He stayed with the horses, sulkily
Till the whistle went. – Then swiftly he

Swung strong and heavy to saddle again
And called to his horses, and his strong blue body
Had its back to me;
And away went the last of the wagons.[1]

[1] l. 48 cry] die

484. To David Garnett, [13? August 1912]

Text: MS NYPL; PC; Postmark, Mayrhofen [...]; Unpublished.

Mayrhofen 138
[13? August 1912]

Dear Bunny,

Your delicious and delightful letter has just arrived. *Don't* be so beastly deprecating.

F[rieda] would just love somebody to be sentimental with – says I'm like a smoked sausage. Do come and unbosom yourself – only let me be there to enjoy the fun. We are bogged in tragedy from England. Come before the 20th. It's lovely here. You can take auto. from Bad[1] Kreuth. It rains and bes fine by turns. F. adores you, so I s'll have to put up with you. Do come as soon as you can – it's quite cheap.

Yrs D. H. Lawrence

We shall be walking on over the Brenner soon after the 20th – you'll be coming too?

[Frieda Weekley begins]

Are you feeling sorry for yourself? I do sympathise though of course cannot approve, people should feel olympic. But I am feeling myself so small to-day, like a small cat I want to crawl under the bed and miow. Try it, perhaps it is a consolation.

485. To Edward Garnett, [13 August 1912]

Text: MS NYPL; Tedlock 182–4.

[*Mayrhofen* 138, in Zillertal, Tirol – Austria]
[13 August 1912][2]

[Frieda Weekley begins]

Dear friend and patron,

I feel how really you take part in our riggle, it is a riggle to keep going at all, sometimes. – Your boy is so nice, quite a treat, I feel him so much a kin to me, he seems to have the same sort of whole hoggerish generosity (if I may swank), where it will land him God only knows, I hope not in quite such tight places as myself. My husband is a perfect agony, the loads of crucifixes here seem joyful round-about-horses [Lawrence interjects: She

[1] i.e. Wildbad.

[2] This date is consistent with: the reference to Secker in Letter 483; the established friendship with David Garnett and his visit shortly afterwards (see Letter 487); and DHL's having already written to Edward Garnett on the same day. (Tedlock supplies the wrong address; none appears on the MS.)

means merry-go-rounds] compared to him; I wanted love, now I have more than I can bear. Perhaps I will go to England soon and see Ernst, you would see me then, would'nt you, it would be a great help, it will be so hard to see him suffer so. Yet I cant be only sorry. Lawrence is great in his way, that seems so little sometimes,[1] but always human, always alive. He has taught me the feel and the understanding of things and people, that is morality, I think. Sometimes our car gets badly stuck and the spokes in the wheels are clogged, but it all comes right in the end, I wont give in – neither will he. Even the money does not seem a worry, we have jolly little, but I think we shall soon have a tiny[2] place somewhere, because L. wants to work. Dont worry about us, even if things went wrong and they *wont*, we have had an honest try. I wish you would come out, you will soon, please, will you? Good-bye and thank you so much, that you are there, somewhere with a friendly feeling, I dont believe I have anybody really, who can put up with me. This sounds quite whiny. – You must get out of London, there is too much ink spilt all in one spot. – Dont think me anything out of the way, please, I don't even prance theories or anything else of the sort any longer. L says, he did it for me, I call him a liar, but there is some truth in it, I am afraid.

Yours (I will *not* say gratefully, if you put me in a 'sark' nothing but a miserere will do).

Frieda

[Lawrence begins]

Your letter has just come. Don't bother about my stuff – it's a fearful shame to worry you. – And you always sound so miserable. F. says – 'Does he hate women?' – I say: 'I think so.' Then she says 'So will that boy of his; before long. But he wouldn't if *I* had him.' – She's naturally vain, I'm sorry to say – As a matter of fact, we are fearfully fond of one another, all the more, perhaps, when it doesn't show. We want remarkably the same thing in life – sort of freedom, nakedness of intimacy, free breathing-space between us. You don't know how fine it is between us – whatever either of us says.

We want now – we are going now – to take some little cottage in Italy, by Lake Garda, furnish it with a few things – we really need very little – and live the winter there. We shall manage to have enough money to live on, I think.

You don't think the quality of my work is going down, do you? – It isn't. I want soon to be settling down, to have a go at it – Paul Morel. But we have lived so hard lately. Don't be cross with me about Secker. I know you

[1] MS reads 'some, times'

[2] MS reads 'tinty'.

don't care much for the Paul Morel novel, that's why I thought you'd perhaps be glad to be rid of it.

Bunny is coming here on Sunday. He won't swim, it is too cold. We *do* try to keep him out of danger. I wish you sounded jollier. – I sent you another letter – perhaps you'll get this first. – Still the tragedy simmers. This is a bellyfull. But I pay without regretting.

D. H. Lawrence

486. To Sallie Hopkin, 19 August 1912

Text: MS NCL; Huxley 48–50.

Mayrhofen 138, in Zillertal, Tirol – Austria.
19 Aug 1912

You know that it is not forgetfulness, makes us not write to you. You know you are one of the very, very few who will take us into your heart, together. So, if the months go by without your hearing, I know you will understand – I know you[1] will be sticking by us, and we shall be depending on you. I wanted my sister to come and talk with you, but she wouldn't; you see, it is harder for her, she is young, and doesn't understand quite. And she is going to marry Eddie Clark in the spring,[2] is going to become a hard, respectable married woman – I think the thought of me is very bitter to her – and she won't speak of me to anybody. Only she, of all my people, knows. And I told Jessie, to leave her a chance of ridding herself of my influence: nobody else. Mrs Dax writes me – I told her I was with another woman – but no details. I am sorry for her, she is so ill.

Things have been hard, and worth it. There has been some sickening misery. Prof. W[eekley] wanted F[rieda] back, and thought she would come. Also he was furious, and raved. He is breaking up the Nottingham home, taking the three children to live with himself and his old parents in Chiswick.[3] F. is to see the children, and stay with them, next Easter. It has been rather ghastly, that part of the affair. If only one didn't hurt so many people.

For ourselves, Frieda and I have struggled through some bad times into a wonderful naked intimacy, all kindled with warmth, that I know at last is love. I think I ought not to blame women, as I have done, but myself, for taking my love to the wrong women, before now. Let every man find, keep on trying till he finds, the woman who can take him and whose love he can take, then who will grumble about men or about women. But the thing

[1] you] the
[2] Ada and Edwin Clarke were married on 4 August 1913.
[3] Charles Weekley (1834–1918) and Agnes (1840–1926).

must be two-sided. At any rate, and whatever happens, I do love, and I am loved – I have given and I have taken – and that is eternal. Oh, if only people could marry properly, I believe in marriage.

Perhaps Frieda will have to come to London to see her husband, in the autumn. Then she might want you to help her. Would you go to London, if she needed you?

We think of spending the winter in Italy, somewhere on Lake Garda. We shall be awfully poor, but don't mind so long as we can manage. It is Prof. W. and the children that are the trouble. You see he loves Frieda madly, and can't let go.

We walked from the Isarthal down here – or at least, quite a long way – F. and I. – with our German shoulder-bags on our backs. We made tea and our meals by the rivers. Crossing the mountains, we got stranded one night. I found a lovely little wooden chapel, quite forsaken, and lit the candles, and looked at the hundreds of Ex Voto pictures[1] – so strange. Then I found F. had gone. But she came back to the shrine, saying we[2] were at the top of the pass and there was a hay-hut in the Alpine meadow.[3] There we slept that night. In the dawn, the peaks were round us, and we were, as it seemed, in a pot, with a green high meadow for a bottom.

Here we are lodging awhile in a farmhouse. A mountain stream rushes by just outside. It is icy and clear. We go out all day with our Rucksacks – make fires, boil eggs, and eat the lovely fresh gruyère cheese that they make here. We are almost pure vegetarians. We go quite long ways up the valleys. The peaks of the mountains are covered with eternal snow. Water comes falling from a fearful height, and the cows, in the summer meadows, tinkle their bells. Sometimes F. undresses and lies in the sun – sometimes we bathe together – and we *can* be happy, nobody knows how happy.

There are millions of different bells: tiny harebells, big, black-purple mountain harebells, pale blue, hairy strange creatures, blue and white Canterbury bells – then there's a great blue gentian, and flowers like monkey-musk. The Alpine roses are just over – and I believe we could find the Edelweiss if we tried. Sometimes we drink with the mountain peasants in the Gasthaus, and dance a little. – And how we love each other – God only knows.

We shall be moving on soon, walking south, by the Brenner, to Italy. If you write, address us at 'Haus Vogelnest' – *Wolfratshausen* – bei München. F, with me, sends love. Yours D. H. Lawrence

[1] Presented in recognition that prayers had been answered.

[2] we] she

[3] See 'A Chapel Among the Mountains' and 'A Hay Hut Among the Mountains' (in *Love Among the Haystacks and Other Pieces*, Nonesuch, 1930).

P.S. Do you mind giving my younger sister the proofs of *The Trespasser*. She says they are hers. DHL

My sister is going to live with Nellie Allam – Mrs J. E. Watson – in Percy Street. I can't imagine why I have not heard from her for so long.

I think only the *Westminster Gazette* is publishing my articles at present – nothing else. – Regards to Enid and to Mr Hopkin.

487. To Edward Garnett, 22 August 1912

Text: MS NYPL; Postmark, Mayrhofen 22 [...] 12; Huxley 50–1.

Mayrhofen 138, in Zillertal, Tirol – Austria
22 Aug 1912

Dear Garnett,

Right you are about H[ueffer] and Secker.[1] I'll not bother with the latter man. But don't let H. know I said anything to you, will you, or he'll think me a double-dealing swine.

Heinemann sent me back my poems, without a word except 'Your manuscript is herewith returned' – and that after keeping them for six months. De la Mare says he strongly recommended them to Wm H. – and that Atkinson had done so. But I suppose the verses also shocked the modesty of his Jew-ship. Will Duckworth have them? – I should love to have a volume of my verses out – in hard, rough covers, on white, rough paper. I should just love it. De la Mare and Atkinson were both very warm about the poetry. I'm sure it's pretty good. De la Mare made the selection which is held in the clip.[2] I think he has selected and arranged rather prettily – and with some care, I am sure. But perhaps you would like some of the others – which he marked 'doubtful' – included. I should put in 'Lightning' – and the two *Westminster Gazette* school poems that are out of print.[3] – Bunny is here. He suggests Asphodels as a title. F[rieda] says Cabbage[4] Roses. I say 'Asphodels among the Cabbages' – or 'Asphodels in the Kitchen Garden'. F. is drawing a lovely picture – fat purple and green cabbages sitting close to earth, and rising among them, the tall and slender elegant lines of her imaginary asphodels.

Bunny is here – we are fearfully happy together. I swear he'll be all right in F's and my care. We are just going out for the day.

[1] Cf. Letter 483. (Secker had written to DHL on 20 August 1912 expressing interest in his next novel; but the letter, addressed to Wolfratshausen, is unlikely to have arrived by 22 August. See [Secker], *Letters from a Publisher*, p. 4.)

[2] See Tedlock, *Lawrence MSS* 82–5.

[3] Duckworth published *Love Poems and Others* in February 1913; 'Lightning' and three 'school poems' were included.

[4] says Cabbage] says A Cabbage

F. is half contemplating going to England to see W[eekley]. God knows what'll come of it – if she's not careful, a mess.

I want soon to be settling down to work.

F. send love. Yours D. H. Lawrence

We are here for about a week longer, I guess.

I send the verses to Duckworth's.

De la Mare says there are two articles which the *W. G.* decided not to print, because they are too anti- German.[1] He wants to know where I would like them sent – to what paper. Could you suggest anything?

DHL

488. To Ada Lawrence, [29 August 1912]

Text: MS Clarke; PC v. Dominicushütte, (1684 m) mit Schlegeistal, Zillertal; Postmark, Neu B[...] 29[...]; Lawrence–Gelder 105–6.

[29 August 1912]

We have walked two days, and now have spent the night in this place,[2] where one gets guides to climb the glaciers. It is quite snowy everywhere. The guides keep coming in, with edelweiss in their hats, with ice-axes and ropes. It is the most beautiful view you can imagine. We have now got 8 hours to go, over the mountains, to Sterzing. But don't write me till you hear from me, I don't know what address I shall have. Garnett (junior) is here, and a ripping fellow who is spending this time with us on his way from Moscow.[3] My regards to Mrs Limb and Emmie. I'll write as soon as I've stopped moving. Love DHL

489. To Edward Garnett, 30 August 1912

Text: MS NYPL; Unpublished.

Sterzing am Brenner
30 Aug. 1912

Dear Garnett,

Your letter re – the poems has followed me here. I am glad you got the MS. all right. It will be fearfully nice if Duckworth brings them out directly.

[1] Cf. p. 430 n. 3.

[2] i.e. Dominicushütte. (For an account of the occasion see David Garnett, *The Golden Echo*, p. 247.)

[3] Harold Hobson (1891–1974), close friend of David Garnett (see *Golden Echo*, pp. 240, 246). Consulting engineer with Hubert Wailes, 1912–14; with Merz and McLellan, 1914–25; 1925–8 manager of County of London Electricity Supply Co. Finally Chairman of Central Electricity Board. m. (1) Coralie Jeyes von Werner, 1914 (2) Margaret Hand, 1948.

And you will get my letter at the Cearne, telling you about de la Mare's selection – which I think isn't a bad selection, but which ought to include the two *Nation* poems, and the other 'Schoolmaster' things – and perhaps something you would like to add.

This is a charming place. But we have missed David fearfully. I have found five new flowers, and it grieves me bitterly I can't give them to him, he would rejoice over them.[1] He is fearfully lovable, I think. And he will have told you about our walk.

I think, if you write within the next week, the address had better be *Bozen* – in Tirol – Haupt-postlagernd. But leave the money from Duckworth till we are settled, will you please?

This is a scrap of a hasty note. Frieda says she awaits your letter – and sends love. Don't bother with my things while you are so squashed with affairs. Yours Sincerely D. H. Lawrence

490. To Ada Lawrence, [31 August 1912]

Text: MS Clarke; PC v. Sterzing. Burg Sprechenstein; Postmark [ ][2]; Lawrence–Gelder 106–7.

[31 August 1912]

I am staying here only till tomorrow – Sunday – then going on to Meran and then to Bozen. You might write me a letter to *Bozen* – in Tirol – (Hauptpostlagernd). Garnett and Hobson and I had a fine time crossing the mountains here. It was quite snowy. Sterzing is a charming place – already quite Italian in feeling. I shall be in Bozen in about a week, and shall wait for letters – but write at once, and tell me how father is, and everything. My love to Nellie – regards to Edward. How has school gone down?[3] How are you? Love D. H. Lawrence

491. To William Holbrook, [c. 31 August 1912]

Text: MS UN; PC v. Blick von der Rosskopfhütte (2191m) auf Wildekreuzspitze; Postmark, [ ];[4] Nehls, iii. 626.

[c. 31 August 1912]

I'm still on the go – came over the mountains with a couple of fellows – on Wednesday, through the snow. Glory, but it *was* cold. Now it's hotter,

[1] David Garnett trained as a botanist (see *The Golden Echo*, pp. 228–34, 247).

[2] Stamp and frank removed.

[3] Ada Lawrence was teaching at the Eastwood Elementary School; the Autumn term had just begun.

[4] Stamp and frank removed.

and getting Italian in feel. I am fearfully interested about the emigration business. Tell me about[1] your business and things. You might let me have a line to *Bozen* – in Tirol – (Haupt-postlagernd). It is some 70 miles on, so I shall be there next Friday or so. But write me at once and tell me. I must write as soon as I get settled. How is Jont? Love D. H. Lawrence

492. To David Garnett, [2 September 1912]

Text: MS NYPL; PC v. Die neue Jaufenstrasse. Serpentinen an der Passeier Seite; Postmark, Sterzing 2 [. . .]; Unpublished.

[2 September 1912]

We have had the most terrific scramble here, worse by far than the Pfitscher Joch.[2] Frieda lost her patience utterly. We are on our way to Meran.

We have missed you fearfully – oh the flowers I see that I want you to have. By the way, *don't* bother about the Geld[3] – it doesn't matter in the least. What is your Hampstead address? Send us a card to Bozen. Love from both. D. H. Lawrence

493. To Arthur McLeod, 2 September 1912

Text: MS UT; Huxley 55–6.

Sterzing am Brenner
2 Sept 1912

My dear Mac,

You'll wonder what the deuce has come over me, that I never write to you. But I am footling[4] about from place to place, and there are so many folk to write to – don't be disgusted with me.

I have walked here from Mayrhofen – quite an exciting scramble. And last night again we slept in a hut 2000-some odd hundred metres high. It was damnably cold. The water was simply freezing. And I nearly got lost. Don't be surprised if I do vanish some day in some oubliette or other among these mountains.

There isn't much news. I am giving a last look at the Paul Morel novel as soon as I can get ten minutes peace. It is to come out with Duckworth in January. The same gentleman is publishing some poetry, during this or the next months. Walter De la Mare made a rather pretty selection, after

[1] about] if

[2] A col over 6,000 feet in the proximity of Dominicushütte.

[3] i.e. money. 'When we...said good-bye, [DHL] said something about not needing me to repay the money I had borrowed for my fare home' (David Garnett, *The Golden Echo*, p. 248).

[4] i.e. acting in a feeble, ineffectual manner.

his own heart, that I think Garnett will more or less stick to. It will include the *W[estminster] Gazette* poems, of which, however, 3 and 4 are missing. Would it be a great bore to you to get one of the lads to copy them out for me. And those two *Nation* ones – 'Violets' and 'Lightning' – careless swine that I am, I've lost 'em again.[1] Have you got a copy.

When I woke up this morning – in a funny wooden bed-room with walls 4 feet thick, and only a little window level with my feet, and I looked out, seeing the snow on the tops of the mountains, I wondered what day it was. It took me ages to recollect it was Monday, then bang-slap went my heart – ½ past eight on Monday morning – school! You've no idea what a nightmare it is to me, now I have escaped. Sometimes, when it's 3.0 oclock and sunny, I think of play-time, and sweet-williams in Miss Mason's garden, and walking talking books with you, and I should like it again. But when you blew the whistle I should want to disappear. I'm not keen on England. This is so much freer.

From Mayrhofen I walked with Garnett's son and Harold Hobson – son of the social economics writer.[2] We had an awfully good time. We take Rucksacks – shoulder sacks – with food and methylated, cook our meals by some stream – and twice we have slept in hay-huts. Every day F[rieda] and I are on foot, travelling the same.

This, of course, is the highroad from Germany to Italy, and one sees all sorts of queer cuts, from Lords of England to Italian tramps – It is quite interesting. We are going to settle down somewhere not too far south, for the winter – somewhere on L. Garda or just north. I wonder how it will be. I must soon begin to write again, for I've done absolutely nothing lately. I want to get a few articles done for the *W.G.*[3]

Don't give this letter to anybody. F. is the wife of an English professor, and is a German. I should like you to know her. But nobody knows I am with her, except, of course, *her* folk, and my sister. So you will keep the confidence. Do write me to *Bozen*: Tirol: Austria – Poste restante.[4] Tell me all the news you possibly can – I have heard nothing for ages. Dont be cross with me for being such a bad correspondent. I wonder if there's any particular Tauchnitz you'd like, and I could send you.[5]

1 Nos. III ('Evening') and IV ('The Punisher') of 'The Schoolmaster' series were omitted from *Love Poems and Others*. 'Violets' and 'Lightning' were included.

2 John Atkinson Hobson (1858–1940), author of *The Evolution of Modern Capitalism* (1894), *Imperialism* (1902), etc.

3 One was published: 'Christs in the Tirol', *Saturday Westminster Gazette*, 22 March 1913.

4 Poste restante] hauptpostlagernd

5 From 1841 Tauchnitz published a 'Collection of British and American Authors' for sale in Europe, followed by English translations of German authors.

I shan't be long in Bozen – but letters will be forwarded.

Je vous serre la main D. H. Lawrence

494. To Walter de la Mare, 5 September 1912

Text: MS UN; Unpublished.

Villa Leonardi, Viale Giovanni-Prati No 8, *Riva*, Lago di Garda, Austria.

5 Sept. 1912

Dear De la Mare,

I have been walking for the last month or so, and my letters have run after me like a little dog that couldn't catch me up. But I got yours and the poems from W[illiam] H[einemann] when I was in Mayrhofen. I think Duckworth will publish the verses. I liked that little selection you had made. I thought, what a pretty book it would be, if it were published. I know you did what you could for me and for my poems.

Now I have forgotten whether the *Westminster Gazette* is in Salisbury Square or not,[1] so I am sending you these three articles. Should you mind handing them in for me – or just re-addressing them. I am sorry to trouble you. And I suppose, for those things that are printed in the *W. G.*, I ought to get copies of the paper, for they did not return me the MS., nor did they send duplicate proofs, so I have no copy whatsoever. And what the *Westminster* doesn't want, perhaps you would give to Edward Garnett – The Cearne, Nr Edenbridge.

I wonder if I could do anything for you, in return for this trouble. I should be glad. But now I shall probably be at Riva some months, and so I can write direct to the *W. G.* or the publishers.

Thanks for arranging those verses: I should have botched it horribly.

Yours D. H. Lawrence

495. To Edward Garnett, 7 September 1912

Text: MS NYPL; Huxley 56–7.

Villa Leonardi, viale Giovanni-Prati 8, *Riva*, Lago di Garda, Austria

7 Sept. 1912

Dear Garnett,

Now we are going to settle somewhere near here in Riva. It is quite beautiful, and perfectly Italian – about 5 miles from the frontier. The water of the lake is of the most beautiful dark blue colour you can imagine – purple

[1] 12 Salisbury Square, Fleet Street.

in the shade, and emerald green where it washes over the white rocks. F[rieda] and I have got a beautiful room, but it is too dear: 3 Korona – 2/6 for the day – for the two of us. There are roses and oleanders and grapes in the garden. Everywhere the grapes are ripe – vineyards with great weight of black bunches hanging in şhadow. It is wonderful, and I love it.

But you know all about those things. I want you, if you will, to send me the Duckworth money here.[1] Would it be possible for it to come in notes, because cashing a cheque would be rather a bother. It is good of Duckworth to pay me up so soon. That money will have to carry me a long way. However, with God's blessing, we shall manage. I think F. and I will be quite happy to sit here a winter and see nobody: only we should be much happier still if you would come and see us. The winter here is warm and lovely. If you say to yourself, it is possible, – then perhaps it will come off.

I am glad to be settling down, to get at that novel.[2] I am rather keen on it. I shall re-cast the first part altogether. You are back at the Cearne? It seems queer, that while I am straying about here, you are working like a fiend, and hampered with my stuff as well. It worries me because it is unjust – unlevel.

I wish you would come to Italy, because I should love to talk to you – for hours and hours. I feel as if you were father and brother and all my relations to me – except wife. I want to marry F, and feel rather disagreeable with W[eekley], that he won't divorce her. He began by footling about with detectives and God knows what, and then the whole thing fizzles out. Folks are such damned waverers. They flap about like the flame of a spirit-lamp, and their pot never comes to the boil. But W. hangs on to the belief that F. will come back to him. He has cleared out the Nottingham house, taken a biggish place at Chiswick, and gone to live there with his people and the children. He writes to la mère Baronne that I am honest, but no gentleman, and when F. quarrels with me, she will find her mistake – that I am selfish etc etc – yards and yards and yards of letters, all of which come on here – a bit wearisome.

They are ringing the sunset bell. The fear of money frets me a bit, that's all. Tell David I'll send his books directly. Frieda is reading Benvenuto.[3] She sends her greetings to David,[4] and so do I. I wish he were here – the

[1] Messrs. Duckworth's files for this period no longer exist. Nevertheless, on 16 September 1912, DHL announces the arrival of £50 from Duckworth (Letter 498); this may well represent royalties on *The Trespasser*, and be the sum referred to later on 1 February 1913 (Letter 544).

[2] *Sons and Lovers*.

[3] Presumably *The Memoirs of Benvenuto Cellini* (which DHL had read by 1907 – see E.T. 112).

[4] David] him

lake is wonderful to swim in, and fruit is a dream of cheapness and niceness. Do I weary you? Yours D. H. Lawrence

I haven't heard from you lately. DHL

[Frieda Weekley begins]

Dear Mr Garnett,

Do come, you will be in Britanny, it will be *so* cheap and we would love and adore to have you! Though I am frightened of yours and L[awrence]'s male talks, he *will* give me away so! But I suppose that's being a blooming artist! When I detest him, he *always* makes that his excuse – You have written me such a letter I am quite proud of it, swelled on the strength of it and cant come down – It is a good thing there are men like you (I tell L) who *do* appreciate women! Yes, he is many things, but his great points are for a woman, the absolute freshness of things, nothing is ever stale or old and in spite of his lots of unrealities he is simple and real underneath. Life *is* good with him, je ne demande pas mieux, yes and it is *love*, but thank the Lord *passion* as well – It has *really* been a success, in spite of the misery left behind, in spite of the always missing the children, in spite of the no money, and I could say: 'Lord, let thy servant depart in peace'[1] though I dont want him to do it just yet. Your boy is a dear, he walks just like you he has a lot of you in his composition, it will be so interesting to watch him and he *is* original – *Do* come, your boy said you were'nt well of, but there would only be the journey and it *is* such a place –

I hope 'auf Wiedersehen'. Yours 'Frieda'

I have quite forgotten that I am *not* married to L.

I think L. quite missed the point in 'Paul Morel'. He really loved his mother more than any body, even with his other women, real love, sort of Oedipus, his mother must have been adorable – he is writing P.M. again, reads bits to me and we fight like blazes over it, he is so often beside the point 'but "I'll learn him to be a toad" as the boy said as he stamped on the toad.' He has written heaps nicer poems than those 'baby ones' some about his mother and lots since we have been together. My sister,[2] who is elegant has just sent me 4 baldachino hats – L. is trying them on in an undescribable get-up and the most beautiful Asphodel pose! [Lawrence interjects: – by 'get-up', she means 'sans anything'. She always was a brazen bitch.]

[1] Luke ii. 29 (A.V.) ['Lord now lettest thy...'].

[2] Johanna (see Frieda Lawrence 72).

496. To David Garnett, 11 September 1912

Text: MS NYPL; Postmark, Riva 11 IX 12; Huxley 58–9.

Villa Leonardi, viale Giovanni-Prati No 8, *Riva*, Lago di Garda, Austria
11 Sept 1912

Dear Bunny,

Your welcome letter came yesterday, and I sent you the Heine. *Don't* send the other Benvenuto, *don't* send the Swinburne – we can get him here. But, Frieda says, she will be undyingly grateful if you'd get for her a copy of *The Golden Age* – by – who is it by? – Graham something or other.[1] And will you post it to Miss Elsa Weekley – 40 Well Walk, Hampstead. It is Elsa's birthday on the 13th – so you'll be too late for the day. But you won't mind, will you, getting the book. I'll send you the other Benvenuto when Frieda has read it.

We had weird times after you'd gone – quarrelled like nuts. Then we set off to walk to Meran, and got stranded in a wild place, worse than Pfitscher Joch, Frieda dead with weariness, I furious for having come the wrong way, the night rolling up filthy and black from out of a Hell of a gulf below us, a wind like a razor, cold as ice. Then, feeling too Excelsior-like[2] for anything, having decided that the next Hütte would be Peter's porters lodge, where we should knock late but find admittance, we reconciled ourselves one to the other, and, after having given up the ghost, caught it by the tail and pulled it back again, and scrambled over the ridge into the Jaufen house,[3] w[h]ere we found [ ][4] beds and two Englishmen, Algernon Sweet and Herbert Dance of London.[5] We got to Bozen, beautiful but beastly, and slept in a room over a pig sty. Then we moved on to Trient. It's a pure Italian ancient decrepit town, where F had blues enough [. . .] to re-pave the floor of heaven. Now we're at Riva, house-hunting. We know about 10 Italian words. 'Casa' is a house 'd'affitare' is 'to let' – now we'll see where *that* lands us. I write under the olive trees in view of the dark blue lake. I should like some jam and jelly and apples. I would [. . .] forfeit my heritage – like Esau – for a mess of sweet pottage.[6] But for Gods sake, man, *do* stop eating. F. says 'I don't think a man can *love* much if he eats much.' It reminds me of my landlord.[7] 'Such a pretty tart in the "Crown", Mr Lawrence – really warm and fruity.'

'Oh,' I say, 'and didn't you cotton.'[8]

[1] Kenneth Grahame (1859–1932); published 1895.
[2] A possible allusion to Longfellow's poem 'Excelsior'.
[3] Jaufen Wirts-Haus, on the col at the head of the Jaufen and Passeier valleys.
[4] MS torn.
[5] Unidentified.
[6] The chapter heading to Genesis xxv in the *Geneva Bible*.
[7] J. W. Jones.
[8] i.e. make progress.

'No – I'd rather have a good dinner any day.'

That's a common saying among my lower class. 'She's not bad – but – I'd rather have a good dinner.' I think I ought to teach it you, you can say it with much aptness.

How's Iris, that fleeting rainbow dream.[1] – I can feel Noel Olivier is an asphodel – I know she is.[2] – Well, you're a good fat cabbage to match.[3]

[Sketch][4]

For heavens sake forget that money.

I am working like Hell at my novel, and F. hates me for it, because it divides my attention.

Have you heard anything of Harold?

How are the plants going. How much swank have you pulled off yet. Frieda's got a soft blue dress on, instead of that peasant sack. We're in such a grand room – and we have such horrors, sliding the Maggi[5] and the sausage under the couch, when the maid comes in. She's Italian, so she can't say nothing, but looks the more.

My love to you D. H. Lawrence

[Frieda Weekley begins]

I call [?this a] disagreeable letter. I would [ ] a nicer one

[Lawrence continues]

[ ] you should hear what she *says* about you. DHL

[Frieda Weekley continues]

He is telling lies and slanders about me, too bad, but you are used to our ways; I will write you a nice letter soon, your father's quite blew me up like the frog near bursting point – I want to know about your doings. F.

[1] Iris Duddington. Her father, Rev. J. N. Duddington, Rector of Ayot St Lawrence, Hertfordshire, 1905–12, married Natasha Ertel, Constance Garnett's friend and amanuensis.

[2] Hon. Noel Olivier (1892–1969), David Garnett's earliest friend (see *Golden Echo*, pp. 30 ff; photograph p. 69). Daughter of 1st Lord Olivier; educated at Bedales School and University of London; m. W. A. Richards, 1920; became a paediatrician. (DHL's term 'asphodel' – defined in Letter 530 – was quite inappropriate.)

[3] cabbage to match] cabbage, aren't you

[4] Of rainbow, asphodel and cabbage (cf. Letter 487).

[5] A proprietary brand of meat extract.

497. To Louie Burrows, [15 September 1912]

Text: MS UN; Boulton 169–70.

Villa Leonardi, *Riva*, viale Giovanni-Prati N° 8, Lago di Garda – Austria

Sunday.

My dear Lou,

Thanks for your letter and birthday greetings. After all, it was too late to get me at Bozen,[1] so it came along to me here. I heard from Agnes Mason, and she said she had had a jolly letter from you. You had a good time in Whitby.

I have been walking through the Tirol down here. It was very nice – and sounds swanky, but isn't. Riva is fearfully nice – at the head of Lake Garda. It is quite Italian – so is Trient, for that matter – only the Austrians have collared them and stocked them with Chocolate Soldiers.[2] The folk are Italian, speak only Italian, even use a lot of Italian money. But the border is only about 3 miles down the lake. At night, the search lights amuse me tripping and dodging about to catch the poor bits of smugglers. The lake is dark blue, a beautiful colour, and so sunny. Here we have had only one shower in a fortnight. It is beautiful weather, and warm. Figs are just ripe – 2d a lb – and grapes – miles and miles of vineyards – and peaches. They are also just getting the maize. It's fearfully nice.

I think I shall spend the winter in Gargnano – about 20 miles down the lake, in Italy. I don't know any Italian, but it doesn't matter. Gargnano is a funny place, rather decayed, like Italy – fearfully pretty, backed with olive woods and lemon gardens and vineyards. I think I shall be happy there, and do some good work.

Ada, as you know, intends to be married in May or June, and insists on my being in England then. I wonder if I shall be. Out here seems so much freer than England.

Did you know Jessie had got her Frenchman over[3] – he is staying in Tim's house. What'll happen there? – I haven't heard from her for months.

Thanks for all your news. You'll have a lively winter, in that evening dress.

Yours D. H. Lawrence

[1] Louie Burrows had obtained DHL's Bozen address from Ada Lawrence (MS UN LaB 208, [5 September 1912]).

[2] An allusion to the extremely popular comic opera, *The Chocolate Soldier*, music by Oscar Straus and based on Shaw's *Arms and the Man*, which opened at the Lyric Theatre, London, on 12 September 1910; before it closed on 13 November 1911 it had exceeded 400 performances.

[3] Marc Boutrit (from St. Genis de Saintonge), 'a village schoolmaster of peasant family from the Bordeaux district' (Helen Corke, *In Our Infancy*, p. 206). Described by Jessie Chambers to Louie Burrows as 'a very melancholy youth' and 'sluggish-livered' (MS UN LaB 190, 28 June 1908).

498. To Edward Garnett, [16 September 1912]
Text: MS NYPL; Huxley 62–3.

Villa Leonardi, Riva, Süd-Tirol – Austria
Monday.

Dear Garnett,

Your letter came yesterday – of course we got yours and David's from Bozen. And this morning Duckworth sent me £50 in notes – the angel![1] We are both bursting with joy and puffed up with importance. Also we've got a place to live in.

Frieda hates me because I daren't broach these Italians about flats and rooms. We know about 10 words of Italian. She hankered after a red place at Torbole. We hesitated for hours. Then she attacked a man, with three words.

'Prego – er – er – quartiere – d'affitare.'[2]

And he insists on our taking the 3.30 omnibus to Riva, so that at last we run in terror, seeing ourselves in that bus.

But we're going to Gargnano. The hôtel lady sent us to Pietro di Paoli. We found him, a grey old Italian with grand manners and a jaw like a dog and a lovely wife of forty. Frieda adores Pietro and I the wife. They have to let, furnished, the bottom flat of the Villa Igéa – dining room, kitchen, 2 bedrooms, furnished – big pretty rooms looking over the road on to the lake – a nice garden with peaches and bamboos – not big – for 80 lire a month: about 66/- shillings a month – everything supplied, everything nice, nothing common – 3 windows in the dining room – clean as a flower. And so, we are moving in on Wednesday, and you must come to see us quick, it's so nice.

Gargnano is a rather tumble-downish place on the lake. You can only get there by steamer, because of the steep rocky mountainy hills at the back – no railway. You would come via. Brescia I should think. There are vineyards and olive woods and lemon gardens on the hill at the back. There is a lovely little square, where the Italians gossip and the fishermen pull up their boats, just near. Everything is too nice for words – not a bit touristy – quite simply Italian common village – Riva is 20 or 25 kilometres, and Gardone 15. Come quick while the sun shines as it shines now, and the figs and peaches are ripe, and when the grape harvest begins. You can have the other bedroom. There will only be the three of us in the flat. You can go to Venice if you feel swanky. It won't cost you anything at the Villa Igéa, so there's only train fare. F. and I are hugging each other with joy at the

[1] See p. 448 n. 1.
[2] 'Please – flat – to rent.'

idea of a ménage, and gorgeous copper pans in the kitchen, and steps down from the dining room to the garden, and a view of lake, which is only 50 yards away. And you sound so jolly yourself. And if you want to send anybody for a holiday, they can come to us.

Love from both D. H. Lawrence

address Villa Igéa, *Villa di Gargnano*, Lago di Garda, Italy.

Pietro di Paoli writes and talks the most lovely French – quaintest thing on earth. I am hugely pleased about the *Love Poems and Others* – and I shall correct the proofs in Gargnano. What bliss. Only F. thinks they are trivial poems. She wants those concerning herself to blossom forth. DHL

499. To Ada Lawrence, [16 September 1912]

Text: MS Clarke; PC v. Riva. Lago di Garda; Postmark, [ ]; Lawrence–Gelder 110–11.

[16 September 1912]

I got your letter the other day – and a cap from Auntie, with a nice letter,[1] and a sponge and bag from Emily, also with a nice letter. You wrote me in a scuffle and a hurry, and sounded rather as if you were ordering the washerwoman than saying nice things to me. But the idea of a smoking jacket is quite gorgeous – only let it be of some delightful colour – purple or crimson or cornflower blue – nothing dull and uninteresting. I mean it, of course. And if you have not already sent it, address it to 'Villa Igéa, *Villa di Gargnano*, Lago di Garda, Italy.' I am going there on Wednesday and shall probably stay there the winter. *Do* underline the name of the place – Gargnano. I'll write you a beautiful letter directly the coat comes. I've just eaten two pounds of figs, and oh Lord! Duckworth sent me fifty quid today.

Love and to Nellie D. H. Lawrence

500. To Arthur McLeod, [17 September 1912]

Text: MS UT; Huxley 60–2.

Villa Leonardi, *Riva*, Süd tirol – Austria
Tuesday the ?

My dear Mac,

Your letter, rather belated, caught me up here. Why do you write such delightful letters, when you're really rather a grumpy person, and not a literary gent. It ain't fair nor in keeping.

[1] Ada Krenkow had written for DHL's birthday, 11 September.

My exalted head goes about in an old straw hat, shapeless and puffed up, which I bought for 3/6 in München, and which has stuck to me – often literally – through all my wanderings. I'm going to write an article to it. But don't think I intend[1] to singe my hair on the stars – much too 'umble.

Damn the Jones ménage. Now, and only now, do I know how I hated it all. I still dream I must teach – and that's the worst dream I ever have. How I loathed and raged with hate against it, and never knew!

Philip should have answered my last letter – at least by post-card. He didn't – not a word. So – !

I'm sending you back the two *W*[*estminster*] *G*[*azette*] poems.[2] They were too late. The others were in print. But Garnett may have got these two and included them. I dont know. – It won't be a big book – rather a smallish one – a bit exquisite, the collection – à la De la Mare – to convince the critics I was well brought up, so to speak. Damn Robertson and his tufts of hair![3] You were an angel rooting those poems out. Garnett found them. But I thank you very nicely.

Oh Davidson, Davidson! I don't[4] know whether I oughtn't to curse you, but I can never quite get there. I think you weren't so bad, as things go, but why have things such a beastly habit of going hatefully! No – I don't want to see it again yet.

Paul Morel is *better* than the *White Peacock* or *The Trespasser*. I'm inwardly very proud of it, though I haven't yet licked it into form – am still at that labour of love. Heinemann refused it because he was cross with me for going to Duckworth – refused it on grounds of its indecency, if you please. The poems are coming out in about 3 or 4 weeks. *Love Poems and Others* they are called. Sounds sad, eh?

Duckworth sent me £50 the other day. Cheer up the rest of the world with that.

I'm on the Lago di Garda. Riva is still Austria, but as Italian as an ice-cream man. Now I speak in signs. Of course the soldiers are Austrian. Austria is funny – So easy going. The officials are all Chocolate Soldiers. They let you walk through the Customs with a Good day. At Trient there was a great crowd at the ticket office – then the train came. So a man – a higher station official – sauntered up and told them to buck up. It made no difference. You know the free and easy manners of men in a pub – the Austrians have always got 'em – their jolly public-house manners.

[1] I intend] I'm going
[2] 'Evening' and 'The Punisher'. Cf. p. 446 n. 1.
[3] Presumably the school inspector, Stewart Robertson.
[4] don't] never

'Rovereto – Riva – Ala!'

yelled the official suddenly. I, amidst a herd of soldiers and black sombrero'd Italians caught his eye. He put up his finger to me. Then he led me, and two others, into the booking-clerks office. The clerk was leaning leisurely at the 'Schalter'. I could see the mob through. Then my official said to the booking clerk 'Ein Rovereto – zwei Riva – ein Mori.' So the clerk turned aimiably round, left the raging mob, and leisurely booked these tickets. Meanwhile the Italy train sat peacefully in the station, and waited for us. That's Austria I say, it waited for *me*, the train into Italy.

I only talk about my poverty so as not to seem to swank. I can always afford what I want. Indeed, the Villa Leonardi is quite gorgeous and palatial. The figs they send up, fresh gathered out of the garden, are a dream of bliss. Grapes and peaches are ripe – there are miles of vineyards and olive woods. The lake is dark blue, purple, and clear as a jewel, with swarms of fishes. And the boats have lemon-coloured sails. It's an adorable lake.

I'm going tomorrow to the

'Villa Igéa, *Villa di Gargnano*, Lago di Garda, Italy.'

There I shall probably stay all the winter. It is fearfully nice. Gargnano is a tumble down Italian place straggling along the lake. It is only accessible by steamer, because of the rocky mountains at the back. The Villa Igéa is just across the road from the lake, and looks on the water. There, in the sunshine – it is *always* sunny here – I shall finish Paul Morel and do another novel – God helping me. If you feel queer, tell the doctor to order you abroad, and come and spend a holiday with us. Do – I mean it.

And, if you love me, send me something to read. I've not read a thing in English for 5 months, except *Under Western Eyes*, which bored me.[1] Send me something 4½d or 7d, something light and cheap – but do send me something. The postage isn't so much, 'printed matter'. I've not read *New Machiavelli*, nor *Clayhanger* nor any of those.[2] I know nothing about the last six – or nine months of English publishing. I can't get Tauchnitz any longer – nothing but German and Italian, neither of which I can read. And I shall be at the Villa Igéa.

My love to everybody, and to you D. H. Lawrence

What I *could* get you, if you are still making yourself a geographical pot, is some pictures of the lake and such. Want 'em? DHL

[1] Conrad's novel, first published in *English Review*, December 1910 – October 1911.

[2] By H. G. Wells (New York, 1910) and Arnold Bennett (1910) respectively.

501. To Alice Dax, [c. 17 September 1912]

Text: MS Hale; PC v. Lago di Garda – Punta S. Vigilio; Postmark, [ ]; Unpublished.

Villa Leonardi, viale Giovanni-Prati No 8, *Riva*, Lago di Garda, Austria.
[c. 17 September 1912]

I was glad to hear you were going on decently. I am here on the border of Italy, where I think I shall spend the winter. It is a beautiful place. Figs and peaches and grapes are just ripe. Grapes are hanging everywhere, tons of them, very beautiful. The lake is dark blue, really dark blue, and clear as crystal. It is very beautiful indeed. One can go in steamer from one end to the other, in about 6 hours – it is 55 kilometres long. Ask Harry to write me how you are, if you cannot. How dreadful, these last weeks!

love D. H. Lawrence

502. To Ada Lawrence, [23 September 1912]

Text: MS Clarke; PC v. Villa Jgèa. – Villa di Gargnano; Postmark, Bogliaco 23 9 12; Lawrence–Gelder 111–12.

Villa Igéa – Villa di Gargnano, Lago di Garda – Italy
[23 September 1912]

I got your letter and the enclosure from the *W*[*estminster*] *G*[*azette*] here. This card isn't a scrap like the Villa Igéa – the reality is a million times better – fearfully nice. You must make haste and get married and come for your honeymoon. – I am quite well – have just been watching them tread the wine.

Love D. H. Lawrence

503. To Edward Garnett, 3 [–5] October 1912

Text: MS NYPL; Moore 149–50.

Villa Igéa, *Villa di Gargnano*, Lago di Garda[1] – *Italy*
3rd Oct.[2] 1912

Dear Garnett,

It is ages and ages since we heard from you. And when Bunny wrote he never mentioned you, nor said if he'd sent the book to Frieda's little girl.[3] And the proofs of the poems haven't come yet from Duckworth. And altogether we begin to feel afraid that letters can't get here: except the bowel-twisting ones from W[eekley] – they turn up.

We're settled in a lovely flat, looking at the lake, quite grand, with a little garden and oranges and 'ceccia' – 'persimmons' I think we call them – and

[1] MS reads 'Gardo'.

[2] Oct.] Sep

[3] See Letter 496.

roses. It is so lovely. And in the kitchen there's a great open fireplace, then two little things called fornelli – charcoal braziers – and we've got lots of lovely copper pans, so bright. Then I light the fornello and we cook. It's an unending joy. Bunny *must* come and cook over a fornello. There's nothing on earth so charming. And – in Rome etc[1] – we eat spaghetti and risotto and so on, all of our own making. And the flat – furnished – 2 bedrooms, dining room and kitchen – big nice rooms – 80 lire a month – 64/-. Everything outside is Italian and weird and tumble-down, and seems to belong to the past. And the men sing – and the soldiers are always going by – they are so good looking and animal – and some of the women are adorable – they have such fascinating straight shapely backs – and when are you coming? The place smells rather of wine. They [are] treading it in the street, and in the courtyard. And our Padrone: Signor Pietro di Paoli[2] – sends us baskets of figs and grapes and weird fruit, and queer fomenting grape juice – wine in its first stage. And you can go in a wine place – and there's the family[3] at supper by the fireplace, and you drink at another table. The father is a shortish, thick set, strong man – these Italians are *so* muscular – and the wife is straight and I like her – he *clicks-clicks* to the bambino in her arms, across the table. And the white grandfather scolds a little girl, and the old grandmother sits by the fire. And I drink a $\frac{1}{4}$ litre of red wine for 15 centesimi – about 1$\frac{1}{4}$d – and I love them all.

So now you see now nice it is, you come.

It is wonderful how one can keep going further in love – F. and I.

I do my novel well, I'm sure. It's half done.

I got these letters and never answered them – ought I?[4] Do write. F. sends love.

D. H. Lawrence

[1] i.e. when in Rome do as Rome does.

[2] Cf. 'Italian Studies II – The Lemon Gardens of the Signor di P', *English Review*, xv. 210–20.

[3] family] father

[4] The two letters were from the publishers, Hutchinson and Co. and T. Fisher Unwin (MSS NYPL). Hutchinson enquired, on 17 September 1912, as follows:

> We are writing to say that we have read with great interest your books *The White Peacock* and *The Trespasser*.
>
> We believe in your work and we should have pleasure in including you in our list of leading authors and in running your name.
>
> ...we must ask you to be good enough to give us an answer by return.

Unwin wrote on 19 September 1912:

> In conversation with my friend, Mr Austin Harrison, he told me about your work and so I think I may mention his name. Let me say at once that it would give me great pleasure to correspond with you, or to meet you, and discuss the publishing question. I am open for a good strong novel and I should very much like to have one ready to print and publish early in the New Year, sometime even in January. Perhaps you would let me hear from you and come and see me when you are in London and we can talk the matter over.

Saturday

Some proofs of poems have just come – but not all, are they? Did you include 'Violets', and any school poems.[1] The verses look so nice in print. A man called E Marsh has written me from the Admiralty, and wants to put 'Snapdragon' into a vol. of verse of new men he is getting up.[2] I said yes.[3] Must I ask the *Nation* and *English* and *W*[*estminster*] *Gazette*'s permission to have the poems they printed?

DHL

504. To Arthur McLeod, [4 October 1912]

Text: MS UT; Postmark, Gargnano 6 10 12; Huxley 64–6

Villa Igéa, *Villa di Gargnano*, Lago di Garda. Italy
Friday. Oct 1912

Dear Mac,

Your books came today, your letter long ago. Now I am afraid I put you to a lot of trouble and expense, and feel quite guilty. But thanks a thousand times. And F[rieda] thanks you too.

I have read *Anna of the Five Towns*[4] today, because it is stormy weather. For five months I have scarcely seen a word of English print, and to read it makes me feel fearfully queer. I don't know where I am. I am so used to the people going by outside, talking or singing some foreign language, always Italian now: but today, to be in Hanley, and to read almost my own dialect, makes me feel quite ill. I hate England and its hopelessness. I hate Bennett's resignation. Tragedy ought really to be a great kick at misery. But *Anna of the Five Towns* seems like an acceptance – so does all the modern stuff since Flaubert. I hate it. I want to wash again quick, wash off England, the oldness and grubbiness and despair.

Today it is so stormy. The lake is dark, and with white lambs all over it. The steamer rocks as she goes by. There are no sails stealing past. The

[1] See p. 446 n. 1.

[2] (Sir) Edward Howard Marsh (1872–1953), writer and civil servant. Editor of *Georgian Poetry*, 1912–22; private secretary to (Sir) Winston Churchill, 1905, 1917–22, 1924–9; KCVO, 1937. Author of *Memoir of Rupert Brooke* (1915), *A Number of People* (1939), etc. (See Christopher Hassall, *Edward Marsh*, 1959.)

[3] Marsh included DHL's poem in *Georgian Poetry 1911–1912* (1912). The volume was intended to justify the editor's belief that 'English poetry is now again putting on a new strength and beauty' (Preface). Marsh asked De la Mare to address and post his letter to DHL, telling him: 'I very much want D. H. Lawrence's poem in the June *English Review*, "Snapdragon", for my book. I don't know what you think of it. It's far from perfect, but like his two novels it seems to me to have elements of great and rather strange power and beauty. ...if you could spare the time to put in a line saying I'm a respectable person it might be a help – but don't bother' (Hassall, *Edward Marsh*, pp. 193–4).

[4] By Arnold Bennett (1902).

vines are yellow and red, and fig trees are in flame on the mountains. I can't bear to be in England when I am in Italy. It makes me feel so soiled. Yesterday F and I went down along the lake towards Maderno. We climbed down from a little olive wood, and swam. It was evening, so weird, and a great black cloud trailing over the lake. And tiny little lights of villages came out, so low down, right across the water. Then great lightnings spilt out. – No, I don't believe England need be so grubby. What does it matter if one is poor, and risks ones livelihood, and reputation. One *can* have the necessary things, life, and love, and clean warmth. Why is England so shabby.

The Italians here sing. They are very poor, they buy two pennorth of butter and a pennorth of cheese. But they are healthy and they lounge about in the little square where the boats come up and nets are mended, like kings. And they go by the window proudly, and they don't hurry or fret. And the women walk straight and look calm. And the men adore children[1] – they are glad of their children even if they're poor. I think they haven't many ideas, but they look well, and they have strong blood.

I go in a little place to drink wine near Bogliaco. It is the living room of the house. The father, sturdy as these Italians are, gets up from table and bows to me. The family is having supper. He brings me red wine to another table, then sits down again, and the mother ladles him soup from the bowl. He has his shirt sleeves rolled up and his shirt collar open. Then he nods and 'click-clicks' to the small baby, that the mother, young and proud, is feeding with soup from a big spoon. The grandfather, white moustached, sits a bit effaced by the father. A little girl eats soup. The grandmother by the big, open fire sits and quietly scolds another little girl. It reminds me so of home when I was a boy. They are all so warm with life. The father reaches his thick brown hand to play with the baby – the mother looks quickly away, catching my eye. Then he gets up to wait on me, and thinks my bad Italian can't understand that a quarter litre of wine is 15 centesimi ($1\frac{1}{4}$d) – when I give him thirty. He doesn't understand tips. And the huge lot of figs for 20 centesimi.

Why can't you ever come? You could if you wanted to, at Christmas. Why not. We should love to have you, and it costs little. Why do you say I sark you about your letters? – I don't, they *are* delightful. I think I am going to Salò tomorrow and can get you some views of the lake there. I haven't got the proofs of my poems yet. It takes so long. Perhaps I will send you the MS of Paul Morel – I shall alter the title – when it's done.

Thanks – je te serre la main. D. H. Lawrence

[1] adore children] adore the children

505. To Edward Marsh, 5 October 1912

Text: MS NYPL; Postmark, Gargnano 5 10 12; Huxley 64.

'Villa Igéa', *Villa di Gargnano*, Lago di Garda – Italy
5 Oct. 1912

Dear Sir,

Your letter comes only today. I shall be very glad if you will print my poem 'Snapdragon' in your book, which sounds awfully nice. I am just correcting proofs for a volume of verse which Mr Duckworth will publish immediately, but 'Snapdragon' is not included. If there is anything else I could any time give you, some unpublished stuff, I shall be glad. I shall love to see the book. It will be quite profit enough in itself. – My address is as above till spring. Yours faithfully D. H. Lawrence

E Marsh Esq.
Admiralty – Whitehall – London.

506. To Ada Lawrence, [10 October 1912]

Text: MS Clarke; PC v. Gargnano sul lago di Garda; Postmark, Bogliaco 10 [...] 12; Lawrence–Gelder 107.

['Villa Igéa', *Villa di Gargnano*, Lago di Garda (Brescia)]
[10 October 1912]

Glad to get your letter – the coat hasn't come yet. I know I s'll look like a monkey on a barrel, in it. I've just corrected the proofs of a fearfully exciting vol. of verse – for Duckworth. I'll send you the duplicates just now. Heard this morning that Mrs Dax has a daughter[1] – both doing well. Don't send a cap – you might put a coloured tie in – one with big ends – and perhaps my knitted waistcoat – sometimes it's chilly. But don't bother if you've already sent. Love – and to Eddie – and Nellie and Ed.[2]

Stick to the dancing. This house is about the last on the left.

DHL

507. To Edward Garnett, [15 October 1912]

Text: MS NYPL; Huxley 68–70.

'Villa Igéa', *Villa di Gargnano* (Brescia), Lago di Garda – Italy.
Tuesday – Oct – 1912[3]

Dear Garnett,

Very glad we were to hear from you. It was almost like the voice of Orpheus come up from Hell.

[1] Phyllis Maude Dax, b. 6 October 1912.

[2] John Edward Watson (see p. 231 n. 3).

[3] The letter is dated 15 October through DHL's reference to 'a new moon'; this would be visible from 10 October. The stage reached in the re-writing of *Sons and Lovers* also lends confirmation to the date.

All right about the publishers, Hutchinson and so.[1] I'll leave myself all in your hands if you'll let me. You'll see I returned the corrected proofs of the poems to Duckworth before I got your letter. I didn't say 'thanks' in the front. Do say that for me, if it's not too late.[2] And I only made corrections of the most unrespectable lines – I was a bit hurried. I thought the book awfully nice – I loved it. F[rieda] refuses to have sufficient respect for it – but there, she *would*. There are in it too many heroines other than herself. Queer, there is one poem to her 'Bei Hennef' – I wish it had been the last in the book.[3] We are grieved that it must wait till after Christmas – but you know best.

I do want to know your articles of faith, the first of which is the love of women – the second of which – is something cynical, I know – the temporality of that self same love? I shall ask F. to put her fingers to her nose, at you – she can, being an aristocrat.

Did I tell you about Marsh who is putting 'Snapdragon' into a vol. of contemporary poetry that is coming out just now? That'll help perhaps to advertise me.

We are sitting in an olive garden on the lake, and it is sunset of a perfect day. The tops of the mountains across are rose-coloured. In the twilight on the lake below the fishers row standing up. One is drawing in his line, and there are glints of silver. It is so still.

The grapes are gathered, and the vines are all red and gold.

There are wild little cyclamens, rose colour all over the hills, exquisite, smelling of lilies of the valley. When you come, primroses will be out.

I have done $\frac{3}{5}$ of Paul Morel. Can I call it *Sons and Lovers*? – or – this funny hand-writing is F.'s fault.

I wonder if I dare ask you for some books – again, for my lady. She's a cormorant of novels, and it's the only way to keep her good. A friend of mine sent us *The Bracknels* – good.[4] I want to read something romanticky – feel like it. I've got a heap of warmth and blood and tissue into that fuliginous novel of mine – F. says it's her – it would be. She saves me, but can't save herself.[5] That's how all these Messiany people are.

If you hear of us murdered, that also will be F's fault. She empties water out of the bedroom window onto the highroad and a fat old lady who steals along under the wall. I had to keep all doors locked, and we sat in the spare

[1] See p. 458 n. 4.
[2] *Love Poems and Others* contains no acknowledgments.
[3] DHL emphasised the significance of this poem in his Preface to *The Collected Poems* (Secker, 1928): '"Bei Hennef", written in May 1912, by a river in the Rhineland starts the new cycle' of *Look! We Have Come Through!* (Chatto and Windus, 1917). Cf. Letter 440.
[4] Novel (1911) by Forrest Reid (1875–1947), possibly sent by McLeod.
[5] Cf. Mark xv. 31.

bedroom. There are no police. – And the flat is so big, such a long way from everywhere to anywhere, and several rooms locked up – I shall develop an Edgar Allan Poe flavour.

I've had a swollen jaw. F. adores me all the more. – Put *that* in your cynical pipe, and smoke it. – Who'd love *you* with a swollen jaw? Yah!

We've been most god-damnably miserable, the pair of us, over various things from England. My fate's a hard one. But wine is only 7d a litre.

There's a new moon in the pinky evening over the lake. I wonder how much more misery we s'll have been through before it's nibbled away again. F. had carefully studied *Anna Karenin*, in a sort of 'How to be happy though livanted' spirit. She finds Anna very much like herself, only inferior – Vronsky is not much like me – too much my superior.

Oh – for describing me as a woman, a Frenchman, a devil and a conger-eel, F. is your undying enemy. Remember, whatever toe-rag I may be personally, I am the fellow she livanted with. So you be careful.

We found a scorpion in the spittoon – I don't know *why* we have a spittoon – it stands on F's side of the bed, because she smokes. We found a scorpion in the spittoon. F. fled for her life and I tackled the beast with a tooth brush. Instead of calling me St. Lawrence or St George, she said it had come because birds of a feather flock together. As if I could bite with my tail.

Forgive this rubbish – much love from both. D. H. Lawrence

Tell Bunny we don't believe his last scroddy letter was meant for us – it got in the wrong envelope. DHL

508. To Ada Lawrence, [24 October 1912]

Text: MS Clarke; PC v. Gargnano; Postmark, Bogliaco 24 10 12; Lawrence–Gelder 112.

['Villa Igéa', *Villa di Gargnano*, Lago di Garda (Brescia)]

[24 October 1912]

You will have got my letter – your card came today. I *wish* you wouldn't bother about a smoking jacket – let it go, it doesn't matter. Send me a couple of ties instead. I don't really need a cap, so don't bother. But do stop troubling about that jacket. It is an awful hardship on Eddie.

How's the weather? It has at last gone colder here. Your news of Flossie is queer. I wonder how she'll like it. – The trees in front are olives. This is a very true view. Love. DHL

509. To Arthur McLeod, 29 October 1912

Text: MS UT; Postmark, Bogliaco 29 10 12; Unpublished.

'Villa Igéa'. *Villa di Gargnano* (Brescia), Lago di Garda – Italy.
29 Oct 1912

Dear Mac,

Just this minute got your letter, and am in tears of wrath, humiliation and indignation. I am a fool, a fool – why need I put a bit of manuscript in those things – but they have swindled us again. These damned dirty poverty stricken Italians diddle you whenever they get the chance: it's something fearful the way they try to do me. But I'm up to 'em now. I know no Italian – except the numerals and a few names of things – but I know Quanto, which means how much? and troppo – non, molto troppo – which means – no, it's far too much. And the words are always in my mouth. They surcharge me on dozens of things – your books came through – some Garnett sent, and whose postage had been paid *more* than yours, were surcharged. And almost every letter that we get out of Bavaria, there's 2d or 3d to pay – God knows why – and for a parcel – rather a big one and valuable – 13/4. They are *so* poor – all the money is paper and copper – paper from 5/- upwards – filthy rags: It grieves me to change good English money for such trash – fancy 5/- notes. Nobody has ever seen any Italian gold: and half the silver is French or Swiss. They use Austrian, French, Swiss, German and Italian money here – all equally good – But I'm *so so* sorry about that thing, that 5/1, I am in tears. I'll send you some more photos. Would you like little, exquisite ones? Have you read Strindberg? – he's rotten – Garnett sent the *Miss Julia* and *There are Crimes and Crimes.*[1] I hate them. Have you read them? Shall I send them along, and you can forward them to Garnett, if he wants 'em. If he doesn't, you can keep 'em.

Will you come and spend Christmas here? – do, *do* – I should love it so. Fancy seeing an Englishman – fancy having you in the house. The lovely things we could do. F[rieda] may have to go to England, then I should be alone. It would be nicer if she didn't have to go. But come any way. It would only cost your railway fare, and you could get an excursion. Even an excursion to Venice would do – or to Milan – or Verona – or Brescia – or anywhere on the Garda Riviera. We are the Garda Riviera, God help us. Come! You'd get a through train to Brescia, and I'd meet you there. Do come. Tell your mother,[2] and she'll persuade you. Think – why should Philip be so lordly and continental? – Why should you be the only untravelled blighter

[1] '*Miss Julia' and 'The Stronger'* and *There are Crimes and Crimes* by August Strindberg (1849–1912) were both published by Duckworth in September 1912.

[2] Alice McLeod (1850–1929).

in Davidson – you, a geographer. It would be lovely to put you up for a fortnight. We've got a spare room, and you'd have to make your own bed – else I'd do it. How lovely. And if you were bent on travelling, you could go to Venice – 13/- excursion – or up to Bozen and the Dolomiten – about the same – think! Now then – make up your mind and get ready. There's only the cold long journey. You'd come on the Venice route, I suppose – you *might* come by Basel – ask Cooks. I'd meet you on the main line, at any rate. Think of it, how blissful!

Do persuade Ernie he's not vulgar in the grain.[1] Tell him I say I said that for contrast – a sheer bit of fiction altogether. I'm always in a mess, one way or another.

Forgive me that post business – I am so cut up.

How's your new house?[2] Do you like it? Think, it's a year now, almost, since I wrote my name in the time book. Think of it!

It's only eight weeks to Christmas. But I shan't know it *is* Christmas unless somebody comes.

Remember me to Barry Robinson, but tell him my feet are clay, and so's all the rest of me. My hand to Aylwin. Thank the boss from me for his long letter. How can I conciliate Humphreys. Greet Byrne from me – tell Miss Mason I'll leave her out of my will if she doesn't write to me.

Love D. H. Lawrence

510. To Edward Garnett, 30 October [–2 November] 1912

Text: MS NYPL; Postmark, Gargnano 1 11 12; Huxley 66–7, 70.

'Villa Igéa', *Villa di Gargnano* (Brescia), Lago di Garda.

30 Oct 1912

Dear Garnett,

Thanks so much for the books. I hate Strindberg – he seems unnatural, forced, a bit indecent – a bit wooden, like Ibsen, a bit skin-erupty. The Conrad, after months of Europe, makes me furious – and the stories are *so* good.[3] But why this giving in before you start, that pervades all Conrad and such folks – the Writers among the Ruins. I can't forgive Conrad for being so sad and for giving in.

[1] Ernest Humphreys had recognised himself in *The Trespasser*, chap. 30, as Mr Holiday who 'had a disagreeable voice, was vulgar in the grain, but officiously helpful if appeal were made to him.'

[2] McLeod had moved in Thornton Heath from 17 Hunter Road to 5 Carew Road.

[3] In view of the reference to Razumov later, DHL had partly in mind *Under Western Eyes* (cf. Letter 500). The 'stories' may have been *Twixt Land and Sea*, Conrad's latest volume (October 1912).

I've written the Comedy I send you by this post in the last three days, as a sort of interlude to Paul Morel.[1] I've done all but the last hundred or so pages of that great work, and those I funk. But it'll be done easily in a fortnight, then I start 'Scargill Street'.[2] This comedy will amuse you fearfully – much of it is word for word true – it will interest you. I think it's good. Frieda makes me send it you straight away. She says I have gilded myself beyond recognition, and put her in rags. I leave it to the world and to you to judge.

I'll send you the books back in a minute.

We're going to have our first visitor tomorrow – the landlady of the Hôtel Cervo, who is a German. She is *fearfully* honored at the thought of coming to afternoon coffee. I am a howling gentleman and swell here – and those £50 are going to last me till March. – So, because Signora Samuelli is coming tomorrow, I have spent an active afternoon scrubbing the bedroom – why F. insists on having the bedroom scrubbed I don't know – and cleaning the silver – or nameless metal such as we use at table. The 'Wirtin' of the 'Cervo' is a very strict housewife, and calls F. to account sometimes.

In the storey above has come to live a hunchback and his mother and their maid. He is an artist, about 40, a painter. He talks a bit of weird, glutinous French. He's my first acquaintance.

It is *such* a dark night – darker than ever in England. There is a mist on the lake, and the fishing boats with their great sails have seemed to hang in the air, like magic ships, all day long.

Do I bore you? You scare me by being so busy. – I generally get up about 8.0 and make breakfast, but F. stops in bed, and I have[3] to sit and talk to her till dinner time. I am a working man by instinct, and I feel as if the Almighty[4] would punish me for my slacking. Do you think it's wicked? Do I do[5] my fair share of work? – I've got a horror of loafing – and yet – Well, I'll take my punishment later. But I feel guilty. – But we live so hard, F. and I. – And I've written 400 pages of Paul Morel, and this drama. Will *Sons and Lovers* do for a title? I've made the *book heaps* better – a million times.

F. sends her love. Where's Bunny? He's *got* to write us a letter, not a bit of sleep-walking, tell him. – The time goes so fast it takes my breath away.

Yrs D. H. Lawrence

[1] See p. 427 n. 1.

[2] The name proposed for this unfinished novel had close associations with DHL's childhood. Cf. 'Nottingham and the Mining Country' (1930), *Phoenix*, p. 134: 'Down the steep street between the squares, Scargill Street, the Weslyans' chapel was put up, and I was born in the little corner shop just above.'

[3] have] sit

[4] MS reads 'Almight'.

[5] MS reads 'Do I do do'.

I'm in great misery, having broken my spectacles, and have no eyes to write with, so must feel in the dark. DHL

Is your address always Downshire Hill? We haven't heard from you for weeks. DHL

[Frieda Weekley begins][1]

It makes me feel warm to think of you in grey old England; I agree with you, it is not really tame but they have buried a very much alive thing, I do love the English, that's why I shriek so hard about and at them. – It is good to think, that you are there with a kindly feeling for us both, so you only saw me the once, that hospitable once! Your *Jeanne d'Arc* will interest me[2] – I hope you will like the play, it's all of it really lived, Ernst's very words and me, though I dont like myself; L[awrence] makes himself out the strong, silent man, it is'nt fair, authors can have it all their own way; he is'nt half so nice or steady or easy, but I must say he is like the English in the bull-dog quality of hanging on, they say the English never are really roused till they are beaten – I do love that – though I am never *quite* sure whether I love or hate L, I only know I would rather die than[3] do without him and his life along of mine – Ernst offered me a flat in London with the children, I would have loved it a little while ago, but now? I had a photo of my little girls, they look adorable but sad, it seemed to tear pieces of my soul, I shall see them at Xmas, I hope, but I am so scared. This place is so healing, alive and yet restful and beautiful and always different unobtrusive like a tactful lover –

[Lawrence continues]

unlike me then. – I thought we were never going to hear from you. Good of Bunny to write us. Do you think he *could* send us a paper once a week? We never see any news at all, not a line. Frieda's got the blues. It's wonderful what a cheerful person one gets, when the trouble flies thick enough. Today is the feast of all the dead,[4] so we're going to the cemetery to be made bright. It is sunny and warm as June. Yet your Cearne porch and the storm in England sound fascinating. – Of course Conrad should always do the beautiful, magic atmospheres. What on earth turned him to Razumov. I'll bet your play will interest me more than that rotten Strindberg. Is it as good as the James Byrne[5] one that I admired so much? – I suppose you think what a ripping little volume of plays you will leave behind – I believe you're

[1] For some unknown reason the letter was not posted; then one arrived from Edward Garnett and a postscript was added in reply.

[2] Edward Garnett's play, published October 1912.

[3] MS reads 'then'.

[4] All Souls' Day ('il giorno dei Morti'), 2 November.

[5] The pseudonym under which Garnett published *Lords and Masters* (1911).

inwardly conceited like anything – I'm *dying* to know what you think of the 'Fight for Barbara'. You're all vain but me. – Fancy F. being dissatisfied with Barbara!
D. H. Lawrence

511. To Ernest Collings, 7 November 1912

Text: MS UT; Huxley 71.

'Villa Igéa', *Villa di Gargnano* (Brescia), Lago di Garda – Italy.
7 Nov. 1912

Dear Sir,[1]

I was fearfully pleased with your letter and the *Sappho*.[2] That was the nicest thing anybody has ever done to me, in respect of my work, the sending of your goodwill and your book.

The drawings I am so fond of. I like the sort of idea of Sapho as a white spark blown along where everything is flame and smoke. It gives a primeval feeling. I wish there was a bit more flame about in this cold ash of humanity nowadays – we'd put up with the smoke to it, easily.

I feel so fearfully conceited since you say such nice things about those two books of mine. The letter, the last I received before yours, had urged me to repent before it was too late, before I and my books were consumed in the fire of wrath.[3] That made me sad. Even I began to be afraid of my own wickedness. Now my tail is up again, and I snap at the flies.

I don't care for *The Trespasser* so much as the first book. My third will be out in February. Of course I think it's great.

I live in sunshine and happiness, in exile and poverty, here in this pretty hole. If ever you are within reach, will you come and see me? – I should be glad. I shan't be in England again till May or thereabouts.

I like 'Favor thy suppliant's hidden fires' and 'Sweet rose of May' and 'Sad Statue' best among the pictures, I think.[4] You draw Sapho rather hermaphroditic, don't you? But I suppose she was. But no – women are more passionate than men, only the men daren't allow it.

Excuse me if I'm impertinent. And thanks a dozen times.

Yours faithfully D. H. Lawrence

[1] Ernest Henry Roberts Collings (1882–1932), artist and illustrator. Educated King's College, London; exhibited in Chancery Lane, in the Rowley Gallery and the Albert Hall, 1911–13; dedicated his *Outlines: A book of drawings* (1914) to DHL. Joined Artists' Rifles, January 1917; discharged unfit, April 1917. With his wife, Vera Mellor, edited *Hillmn* (1920–1). Published *Modern European Art* (1929).

[2] *Sappho the Queen of Song* (*a collection of translations from the Greek of Sappho*) *arranged by J. R. Tutin. Illustrations from pictures in water-colours by Ernest H. R. Collings* (1910).

[3] DHL's correspondent is unknown.

[4] DHL is quoting the captions to Collings' illustrations (pp. 24, 49, 81).

512. To Edward Garnett, [11? November 1912]

Text: MS NYPL; Postmark, Bogliaco 14 11 12; Edward Garnett, *The Trial of Jeanne D'Arc and Other Plays* (1931), pp. 16–17.

Villa Igéa –
Monday.

Dear Garnett,

I have read the *Jeanne D'Arc*[1] and looked at the Persian atrocity.[2] I wanted to get into a corner and howl over the *Jeanne D'Arc*. Cruelty is a form of perverted sex.[3] I want to dogmatise. Priests in their celibacy get their sex lustful, then perverted, then insane, hence Inquisitions – all sexual in origin. And soldiers, being herded together, men without women, never being *satisfied* by a woman, as a man never is from a street affair, get their surplus sex and their frustration and dissatisfaction into the blood, and *love* cruelty. It is sex lust fermented makes atrocity.

The *Jeanne D'Arc* interests us fearfully – it seems such a living historical document. I can't see it as a play – more as a fact. You've got a fair amount of 'priest' in you, and that's why you do them so well. The people stand off from one another so distinctly. I can't do that. Of course it's a play about the people who judge Joan, rather than about herself. It seems queer to have the keystone figure so small, scarcely seen. That makes the drama more subtle: the play of a lot of these fat flies round the same thing. It still seems to me a human record rather than a play, and I don't know how to criticise it at all. Tell me what the papers say.[4] They treated *Lords and Masters* rather meanly, didn't they?[5] It must have been fearfully hard to get the *blood* into

[1] Cf. p. 467 n. 2.

[2] Garnett had probably sent the pamphlet by the Cambridge Professor of Arabic, Edward Granville Browne (1862–1926), *The Reign of Terror at Tabriz. England's responsibility*, published by Taylor, [Edward] Garnett, Evans & Co., Manchester, October 1912. DHL may well have been familiar with Browne's earlier article, 'The Persian Crisis: Rebirth or Death?', *English Review*, iii (August 1909), 173–81. Browne was well known in the *English Review* circle and to the Garnetts. (David Garnett recalls the indignation among the English radicals and left-wing Liberals at the aggressive behaviour by Russia and England towards Persia.)

[3] Edward Garnett, when printing this 'curiously subjective letter' in 1931, remarked that DHL 'blends his own identity with mine, and generally weaves E.G. into the sex web of DHL's predilections' (*The Trial of Jeanne D'Arc and Other Plays*, p. 16).

[4] Garnett (*Jeanne D'Arc*, p. 16) says the play was 'produced at The Art Theatre, May 1931'; in fact it was first produced in the Ethical Church, 46 Queens Road, Bayswater, on 26 October 1913, by William Poel under the auspices of the Religious Drama Society. DHL's enquiry was, then, directed to newspaper reaction to the play's *publication* in October 1912. Later, on 2 January 1913, the *Daily News* commented: 'Mr Garnett's play...is taken in a slice from the mass of fact...looked at as a whole, its documentary character deadens it. It is a procession of days, all tragic, but moving with something of the clock's exactitude and impassivity.'

[5] Cf. p. 344 n. 2. The *Manchester Guardian*, 23 May 1911, generally favourable, observed: 'You feel all the time as if something were impending' but 'nothing does happen in the play; all the things happened before it began, and we simply see people finding them out.'

a play like *Jeanne*. When the figures are ready made in dry material, I should think it's the devil to breathe life into them. I think the buzzing, sensational atmosphere of *priests* – how I loathe them – is fearfully good. How they relish a sensation, the blow-flies! I think that strictly you ought to have been a mediaeval cleric – of the nice sort, probably. I think I like the English Lords the least – excepting John Grey perhaps. I think you're best at half sexual subtleties. It seems to me queer you prefer to present men chiefly – as if you cared for women not so much for what they were themselves as for what their men saw in them.[1] So that after all in your work women seem not to have an existence, save they are the projections of the men. That is, they seem almost entirely sexual answers to or discords with the men. No, I *don't* think you have a high opinion of women. They have got each an internal *form*, an internal self which remains firm and individual whatever love they may be subject to. It's the *positivity* of women you seem to deny – make them sort of instrumental. There is in women such a big sufficiency unto themselves, more than in men. – You really study the conflict and struggles of men over women: the women themselves are inactive and merely subject. That seems queer. – And I consider the *Jeanne D'Arc* play is an awfully good study of the conflicting feelings of men over the almost passive Maid. – I believe you're a curious monk, a man born to 'gloss' the drama of men and women with queer penetrating notes on the men, rather than to do the drama. That's why I like this play. – Is all this bosh? I am *no* critic at all. But it interests me. – Don't be cross with me if I'm stupid.

[Frieda Weekley begins]

I rather like the elusiveness of Jeanne – of course she is really a fearfully jolly, healthy girl with a bit of the peasant cunning, and then her weird mysticness throws a veil over her and I like it – I am glad she had a St. Michael, and I like the way you treated her, L[awrence] always wants to treat women like the chicken we had the other day, take its guts out and pluck its feathers sitting over a pail – I am just wildly arguing with L and he is so stupid, I think, in *seeing* things, that cannot be seen with eyes, or touched, or smelt or heard – But this is all beside the point just like a woman! I think that there is an individual form as much in a man as in a woman, as a rule; Jeanne I feel as an individual but I say women are not much in the hands of men; We both men and women are frightened of 'It' – call it love or passion – This fear we think is due each to the other! The fear makes brutal

[1] The *Manchester Guardian*, 23 May 1911, remarked on *Lords and Masters*: 'though practically all the interest of the extremely short play is centred in the woman, we are forced to approach her by way of the men, as it were.'

and hopeless and helpless! Poor Jeanne! Whatever you do you rouse one's sympathy for her to such a degree; I would just like to kill a few of the fat, sly, stupid swine! And from *my* point of view your play is a real pleasure, because of its warm sympathy its deep humanity with a twitch of satirical laughter in the corner of its mouth! Poor Jeanne in her simple, broken vitality! Don't you men all love her better because she was sacrificed! Why are *all* heroines really Gretchens? You dont *like* the triumphant female, it's too much for you! I have written some bosh but there! I ask for the kind consideration of the triumphant male being

the poor female! Frieda

513. To Ernest Collings, 14 November 1912

Text: MS UT; Huxley 72–3.

'Villa Igea', *Villa di Gargnano* (Brescia), Lago di Garda, Italy.
14 Nov. 1912.

Dear Mr Collings,[1]

Call me 'Sir'[2] if you will. I assure you I am a man. My name is David Herbert Lawrence. My age is 27 years. I was, but am no more, thank God – a school teacher – I dreamed last night I was teaching again – that's the only bad dream that ever afflicts my sturdy conscience.

How queer to think of 'A Still Afternoon in School'.[3] It's the first thing I ever had published. Ford Madox Hueffer discovered I was a genius – don't be alarmed, Hueffer would discover *anything* if he wanted to – published me some verse and a story or two, sent me to Wm Heinemann with the *White Peacock*, and left me to paddle my own canoe. I *very* nearly wrecked[4] it and did for myself. Edward Garnett, like a good angel, fished me out. Now I am living here on my paltry literary earnings. You should look up, in back *English Reviews* 'Odour of Chrysanthemums' – a story full of my childhood's atmosphere – And the glamorous enough 'Fragment of Stained Glass'. Excuse my cheek.

I can see all the poetry at the *back* of your verse – but there isn't much inside the lines. It's the rhythm and the sound that don't penetrate the blood – only now and then. I don't like the crackly little lines, nor the 'thou wouldest' style, nor 'mighty hills' and garlands and voices of birds and

[1] Mr Collings] Sir

[2] 'Sir'] a lord

[3] 'A Still Afternoon', the title of DHL's first published series of poems (not his first publication), *English Review*, iii (November 1909), 561–5.

[4] wrecked] upset

caskets – none of that. I can remember a few things, that nearly make poems in themselves.

'We met again, and for a short laughing
Did play with words; till suddenly
I knew – didst thou – ?'[1]

And then all the rest is inconsequent, to me.

'The coverings of the doorway
Are flung open:
Superb thou standest, wild-eyed, eager girl,
Letting fall thy gown to feel the little
Winds of the morning soothe thy breasts and shoulders.'[2]

Then you go on 'Walk the Earth in Gladness' – but that girl isn't going to *Walk the earth.*

The first stanza of 'Adventure' is so nice, and I love:

'Now – Go thy way.

Ah through the open door
Is there an almond tree
Aflame with blossom!

A little longer stay –

Why do tears blind me?

Nay, but go thy way.'[3]

That's a little poem, sufficient[4] in itself. Then you go off to the 'Love did

[1] In Collings's MS notebook (the property of Mr Guy Collings) these lines are from 'The Moment' (1911), ll. 1–2, 4.

[2] From 'On "The Gypsy Girl" by Obrovsky', ll. 27–35. (Collings had added: 'Written Spring 1912. Copied 10/7/12. E.C.') His text reads:

...Superb thou standest,
Wide-eyed eager girl,
Letting fall thy gown,
To feel the little winds of morning-tide
About thee playing.
O, walk the Earth in gladness,
For there comes to thee to-day
Before the sun goes down,
A God.

[3] From 'The Return of Love (A Woman Sings)' (1911), ll. 12–17, 22–3.

[4] sufficient] almost

turn to hate' business. And fancy anybody saying 'Boy, wither away?'[1] Then I like:

> 'I think you must have died last night
> For in my[2] dreams you came to me – '[3]

then the rest isn't good. Do them in better form – put them in blank verse or something. Your rhythms aren't a bit good.

Forgive me if I'm nasty. That's what I say to myself, what I say to you.

I think we might get on well together. I'm quite nice really, though nobody will tell you so. If we can't meet in Italy, we may in England. – Fools, to think your Sapho drawings improper.[4] You'd think men were born in trousers that grew on them like skin. Our clothes consume us, like Heracles' garment.[5]

Excuse this horrid bit of paper. And thanks so much for letting me read the poems. I suppose you are between 30 and 40 years of age? Do you mind your papers being squashed into this envelope? –

Yours Sincerely D. H. Lawrence

514. To David Garnett, 19 November 1912

Text: MS NYPL; Huxley 78–80.

'Villa Igéa', *Villa di Gargnano* (Brescia), Lago di Garda
19 Nov. 1912

My dear Bunny,

Your last letter was fearfully welcome. We were just thinking of going to bed – there isn't much else to do here – when it arrived and we ran to great discussions over it. I *love* you as an alarmist.[6] I see myself and Frieda fleeing out of Gargnano, each of us seated upon a fleet ass, scouring for the Austrian border, the Villa Igéa in flames. But everything is so still. The greatest excitement was early Sunday morning, while it was yet dark, when there came great and ferocious howling under the bedroom windows, that hang over the road. Frieda lay in terror – she is a Tedesca (German) so her conscience in

[1] Perhaps an early version of 'Storm' (later printed in *Colour*, i (December 1914), 200, ll. 19–20): '"Boy! Let us go, /The sun is rising."'

[2] my] your

[3] Not from any poem in the MS notebook; the idea is found in Collings's poem 'A Wreath' in *Hillmn*, iv (April 1921), 26.

[4] See Letter 521.

[5] The shirt of Nessus (a story familiar to DHL, see E.T. 181).

[6] David Garnett had transmitted to DHL the views of a Russian revolutionary friend, Boris ('Sokolov') Volkov, that the Balkan War (1912) would lead to a European conflict (see *The Golden Echo*, pp. 249–50).

Italy is bad. But I as Inglese lie with a firm heart, ready to rush to defend the stone staircase should they force the garden gate. But it's only the rejoicings of two wounded sons of 'Villa' returned from Tripoli, and their mates.[1] They have been drinking all night. Frieda says 'If war makes people as sad as that, then – no, it's too bad. That's the saddest noise I've heard.'

'My dear,' I answer, 'it's the wine.' Then I get a curtain lecture, à la Frau Caudle.[2]

Do come here – Italy's so nice to look at, but nothing at all to talk to. I have learned a bit of Italian, but it won't carry me far. I saw a man gathering the olives today. They perch like queer birds on a ladder made so.

[Sketch]

They look queer – but Italians have such good figures and lovely movements. Summoning all my Italian, I say to him 'It's a late harvest.' 'Come?' he says. I repeat – 'A late harvest, Signore', he grins. 'It's very early.' I feel like saying to him: 'Don't be a pig, I've done my best.' But I say instead 'fa bello tempo, oggi.' – 'Oggi!' he repeats, 'Si Signore, oggi.' He's got an offensive grin.

We've had two first visits this week: one from Signorina Feltrelline, who teaches us Italian. It's a screaming farce: she wears black gloves and keeps F. and me in order. I can't help drinking a little wine, to assert my masculine and marital independence, I feel I am put in *so* small a place by Signorina Feltrelline. Like humble children, F. and I lisp our lessons. Of course I'm much quicker than F [Frieda Weekley interjects: a lie] but Signorina Feltrelline – she's 38 and 's got a slight squint – prefers Frieda, and constantly represses me. The lesson goes on in French, German and Italian – I merely swear in English.

Then the Wirtin of the Stag Hôtel – really del Cervo – came to coffee yesterday. Frieda kept me all morning long scrubbing floors like a galley slave – did they scrub floors? But these rooms are big, very big, and the wood of the boards is soft, and there are no carpets. It was no good my pleading my genius, scrub I had to. I felt like Mr Mantelini.[3]

Do send me just one newspaper.[4] I read in Italian about Turkey and Servia, but nothing more interesting.[5] I s'll feel like Orpheus coming up from

[1] Tripoli, occupied by Italy 1911–12, had been ceded by the treaty of Ouchy, October 1912, to the King of Italy.

[2] *Mrs Caudle's Curtain Lectures*, by Douglas Jerrold (1803–57); first reprinted from *Punch* in 1846, and frequently republished. (Mrs Caudle is the nagging wife.)

[3] In Dickens' *Nicholas Nickleby* (1839).

[4] David Garnett is confident that he sent DHL the *Daily News*.

[5] The two governments were in dispute over autonomy for Macedonia.

Hades when I next set foot in England. But come and see us. The place is lovely as a dream.

Your Dad doesn't like the play,[1] and Frieda wants to hit him. But there, you know the war-like tendencies of her family.

Write us some more good letters like the last. Think of Icking and the Isar. Don't fall in love for fear you have to scrub floors and fetch groceries. Remember me to London.

Yours D. H. Lawrence

If these letters coincide[2] – well, you can establish the truth, by comparing them – like the Gospels.

We cook over a charcoal brazier – fornello – we eat macaroni and Maggi and I grate pounds of cheese. I cart a fowl from Brescia (3 hours journey) and we fry it in olive oil. Oh it's great! The weird fish we get – the poor little thrushes and black-caps they bring to the door, on strings – Oh Italy Italy! But I want a cloak – that I can fling over my nose. You should see 'em! But come!

515. To David Garnett, [19 November 1912]

Text: MS NYPL; Tedlock 186–7.

['Villa Igéa', *Villa di Gargnano* (Brescia), Lago di Garda]
[19 November 1912]

[Frieda Weekley begins]

Dear Bunny!

I did enjoy your letter! About Godwin,[3] and London and X;[4] it just was a little bit of life. I thought it was quite a great letter! I am glad you left X, it is the *only* thing if one cant *really* go on, look at the lie and indecency and all, no, if I adored a man till I was black in the face I would rather he went, than stay because he felt he ought. But dont give in, dear Bunny 'le jeu vaut la chandelle' [Lawrence interjects: the game is worth the candle] if I can say it, I am sure any body ought, when I think of all, the children, and Ernst, who says: 'No man can do more than give his life, but I would have gladly been tortured for you and laughed, and now I'll do more, I'll

[1] See Letter 510.

[2] Frieda (Letter 515) and DHL wrote simultaneously and sent their letters together.

[3] Helton Godwin Baynes (1882–1943), house physician at St Bartholomew's Hospital, 1910–11; surgeon in charge of Red Crescent Mission to Turkey in Balkan War, 1911–12. R.A.M.C. 1914–18. m. Rosalind Thornycroft, 1913. Assistant to Jung, 1919–22. Edited and translated Jung's *Psychological Types*, 1921, etc. (For David Garnett's friendship with him, see *The Golden Echo*, p. 166ff.)

[4] Possibly Antonia Almgrem (see p. 520 n. 2).

live.' It makes me quite ill every time. –I was cross with L[awrence] about the play, he makes himself the 'strong, silent man', the *wretch*, he *did* hang on to me, but not quite so unflinchingly and I did *not* wobble [Lawrence adds: (?)] so; he wrote the play when he was in a rage with me! [Lawrence interjects: (No no!!)] So there, but I think it *is* a good play! Do come, cant you at Xmas, it would be a treat! I am *not* going to England before Easter now. Icking and Mayrhofen seem quite a long way back and this place is so beautiful, really a fairy land [Lawrence interjects: (I am Bottom)]. I lie with joy out of a window [Lawrence interjects: She means on the window-sill], that looks on the road and watch the Italians. They are beautiful creatures. The men so loose and soldiers with *such* hats, a foam [Lawrence interjects: (Good god!)] of cockfeathers on them I long for one, a hat not a soldier. I have found 2 women friends, most eminently and superbly respectable, but they bore Lawrence, though the one's rows with her horrid mother-in-law rouse me deeply. They *will* think we are well off, the irony of it! I hope L. does not write the same stuff as I am! How we would love to have you here! Yes, I am proud that most of my people had pluck and made Germany what it is, of course I am an anarchist, and a beastly 'aristo' [Lawrence interjects: a fool!] at the same time, but then these women! – I never look at my scarves[1] without thinking of you and our acting and what a God forsaken idiot [you] looked as Holofernes![2] Good-bye, I must stop,

With much love Frieda

Such maccaroni and good things

516. To Edward Garnett, 19 November 1912

Text: MS NYPL; Huxley 76–8.

'Villa Igea', *Villa di Gargnano* (Brescia), Lago di Garda. Italy
19 Nov. 1912

Dear Garnett,

Your letter has just come. I hasten to tell you I sent the MS. of the Paul Morel novel to Duckworth, registered, yesterday. And I want to defend it, quick. I wrote it again, pruning it and shaping it and filling it in. I tell you it has got form – *form*: haven't I made it patiently, out of sweat as well as blood. It follows this idea: a woman of character and refinement goes into the lower class, and has no satisfaction in her own life. She has had a passion for her husband, so the children are born of passion, and have heaps of

[1] Cf. Letter 476.

[2] 'The last time we met, Frieda asked me: "Do you remember, David, the head of Holofernes?"..."Oh, you looked such a fool!"' (*The Golden Echo*, p. 246).

vitality. But as her sons grow up she selects them as lovers – first the eldest, then the second. These sons are *urged* into life by their reciprocal love of their mother – urged on and on. But when they come to manhood, they can't love, because their mother is the strongest power in their lives, and holds them. – It's rather like Goethe and his mother and Frau von Stein and Christiana –.[1] As soon as the young men come into contact with women, there's a split. William gives his sex to a fribble, and his mother holds his soul. But the split kills him, because he doesn't know where he is. The next son gets a woman who fights for his soul – fights his mother. The son loves the mother – all the sons hate and are jealous of the father. The battle goes on between the mother and the girl, with the son as object. The mother gradually proves stronger, because of the tie of blood. The son decides to leave his soul in his mother's hands, and, like his elder brother, go for passion. He gets passion. Then the split begins to tell again. But, almost unconsciously, the mother realises what is the matter, and begins to die. The son casts off his mistress, attends to his mother dying. He is left in the end naked of everything, with the drift towards death.

It is a great tragedy, and I tell you I've written a great book. It's the tragedy of thousands of young men in England – it may even be Bunny's tragedy. I think it was Ruskin's, and men like him.[2] – Now tell me if I haven't worked out my theme, like life, but always my theme. Read my novel – it's a great novel. If *you* can't see the development – which is slow like growth – I can.

As for the 'Fight for Barbara' – I don't know much about plays. If ever you have time, you might tell me where you find fault with the 'Fight for Barbara'. 'The Merry Go Round' and the other[3] are candidly impromptus. I *know* they want doing again – re-casting. I should like to have them again, now, before I really set to work on my next novel – which I have conceived – and I should like to try recasting and re-forming them. If you have time, send them me.

I should like to dedicate the 'Paul Morel' to you – may I? But not unless you think it's really a good work. 'To Edward Garnett, in Gratitude.'[4] But you can put it better.

1 Respectively Johann Wolfgang von Goethe (1749–1832); Katherine Elizabeth née Textor; Charlotte von Stein who inspired some of Goethe's finest lyrics; and Christiane Vulpius whom he married (1806).

2 Cf. *Fantasia of the Unconscious* (Seltzer, New York, 1922) chap. 10: '...when Mrs Ruskin said that John Ruskin should have married his mother she spoke the truth. He *was* married to his mother.'

3 'The Married Man'.

4 The published dedication reads: 'To Edward Garnett'. (In Garnett's copy of *Sons and Lovers* DHL wrote: 'To my friend and protector in love and literature Edward Garnett from the Author', Heilbrun 149 n. 3.)

You are miserable about your play. Somehow or other your work riles folk. Why does it? But it makes them furious. Nevertheless, I shall see the day when a volume of your plays is in all the libraries.[1] I can't understand why the dreary weeklies haven't read your *Jeanne* and installed it as a 'historical document of great value'. You know they hate you as a creator, all the critics: but why they shouldn't sigh with relief at finding you – in their own conceptions – a wonderfully subtle renderer and commentator of history, I don't know.

Pinker wrote me the other day, wanting to place me a novel with one of the leading publishers.[2] Would he be any good for other stuff? It costs so many stamps, I don't reply to all these people.

Have I made those naked scenes in Paul Morel tame enough. You cut them if you like. Yet they are so clean – and I *have* patiently and laboriously constructed that novel.

It is a marvellous moonlight night. The mountains have shoulder-capes of snow. I have been far away into the hills today, and got great handfuls of wild Christmas-roses. This is one of the most beautiful countries in the world. You must come. The sunshine is marvellous, on the dark blue water, the ruddy mountain feet, and the snow.

F[rieda] and I keep struggling forward. It is not easy, but I won't complain. I suppose, if in the end I can't make enough money by writing, I shall have to go back to teaching. At any rate I can do that, so matters are never hopeless with me.

When you have time, do tell me about the 'Fight for Barbara'. You think it couldn't be any use for the stage? I think the new generation is rather different from the old. I think they will read me more gratefully. But there, one can only go on.

It's funny, there is no *War* here – except 'Tripoli'. Everybody sings Tripoli. The soldiers howl all the night through and bang tambourines when the wounded heroes come home. – And the Italian papers are full of Servia and Turkey – but what has England got to do with it?[3]

It's awfully good of you to send me a paper. But you'll see, one day I can help you, or Bunny. And I will.

You sound so miserable. It's the damned work. I wish you were here for awhile. If you get run down, do come quickly. *Don't* let yourself become

[1] MS reads 'libraryies'.

[2] James Brand Pinker (1863–1922), later (1914–20) to be DHL's literary agent. Agent for James, Conrad, Bennett, Crane and Ford Madox Hueffer. (See James Hepburn, *The Author's Empty Purse*, 1968, pp. 57–65.)

[3] It was important that England as one of the Great Powers should recognise Italy's sovereignty in Tripoli; it also served her interests to make peace between Italy and Turkey.

ill. This is such a beastly dangerous time. You could work here, and live cheap as dirt with us.

Don't mind if I am impertinent. Living here alone one gets so different – sort of ex cathedra.

D. H. Lawrence

[Frieda Weekley begins]

I also feel as if I ought to say something about L.s formlessness. I dont think he has 'no form'; I used to. But now I think anybody must see in Paul Morel the hang of it. The mother is really the thread, the domineering note, I think the honesty, the vividness of a book suffers if you subject to it 'form'. I have heard so much about 'form' with Ernst, why are you English so keen on it, their own form wants smashing in almost any direction, but they cant come out of their snail house. I know it is so much safer. That's what I love Lawrence for, that he is so plucky and honest in his work, he dares to come out in the open and plants his stuff down bald and naked, really he is the only revolutionary worthy of the name, that I know, any new thing must find a new shape, then afterwards one can call it 'art'. I hate art, it seems like grammar, wants to make a language all grammar, language was first and then they abstracted a grammar; I quite firmly believe that L is quite great in spite of his 'gaps'. Look at the vividness of his stuff, it knocks you down I think. It is perhaps too 'intimate' comes too close, but I believe that is youth and he has not done, not by long chalks! Dont think I am impudent to say all this, but I feel quite responsible for 'Paul'. I wrote little female bits and lived it over in my own heart. I am sure he is a real artist, the way things pour out of him, *he* seems only the pen, and isnt that how it ought to be? We *all* go for things, look at them with preconceived notions, things must have a 'precedence'. We have lost the faculty of seeing things unprejudiced, live off our own bat, think off our own free mind. Good gracious, what a tirade! I think you are just *awfully* good to ask me to the 'Cearne' but would'nt my unmarried married condition be awkward for you?

517. To Louie Burrows, 19 November 1912

Text: MS UN; Postmark, Bogliaco 22 11 12; Boulton 170–1.

'Villa Igéa', *Villa di Gargnano* (Brescia), Lago di Garda, Italy
19 Nov. 1912

My dear Louie,

Your letter and the little photo did wander here after me all right. The photo is so like you – it seems queer.

I want to say that it grieves me that I was such a rotter to you. You always treated me really well – and I – well, I only knew towards the end we couldn't make a good thing of it. But the wrong was all on my side. I think of you with respect and gratitude, for you were good to me – and I think of myself in the matter with no pleasure, I can tell you. And now all I can do is just to say this.

I am living here with a lady whom I love, and whom I shall marry when I come to England, if it is possible. We have been together as man and wife for six months, nearly, now, and I hope we shall always remain man and wife.

I feel a beast writing this. But I do it because I think it is only fair to you. I never deceived you, whatever – or did I deceive you – ? I may have done even that. – I have nothing to be proud of. –

I shall only get into a bigger mess if I go on writing. Don't say anything about me and this to anybody, will you?[1] I shall be able to be married and make everything public in the spring, I hope – if the divorce comes off.

I am ever so well in health – poor in pocket – but happy enough. I wish I could make up for what I did to you. But if we go on writing, I feel I am only doing you more wrong, and it would be easier to stop altogether now – wiser perhaps.

The best thing you can do is to hate me.

I loathe signing my name to this. D. H. Lawrence

518. To Louie Burrows, [25 November 1912]

Text: MS UN; PC v. Lago di Garda visto da Nago; Postmark, Bogliaco 25 11 12; Boulton 171–2.

['Villa Igéa', *Villa di Gargnano*, Lago di Garda, (Brescia) Italy]
[25 November 1912]

Votre lettre est venue ce matin. Faites certainement ce que vous voulez des morceaux de vers dont vous parlez. Mais je crains qu'ils ne soient trop rudes pour la musique.

Vous auriez reçue à cette heure mon autre billet. Faîtes-moi en grâce.

Oui, l'Italie est fort belle – je m'y porte bien. Et je suis content de vos nouvelles de Hilda Shaw,[2] et de vos occupations. Il fait un merveilleusement beau temps ici. D. H. Lawrence[3]

[1] A MS note by Louie Burrows on her transcript of this letter makes it clear that she did not know at this time with whom DHL had eloped. She learned Frieda's name through Hilda Shaw.

[2] Presumably that she was recovering from tuberculosis. (In fact she died shortly afterwards.)

[3] This is DHL's last known letter to Louie Burrows. Ada Lawrence gave Louie her brother's address on 7 February 1913 (MS UN LaB 210); if Louie then wrote and received a reply, the latter has not survived.

[Your letter came this morning. By all means do what you like with the bits of verse you mention. But I am afraid they may be too rough for the music.

You should have had my other note by now. Forgive me for it.

Yes, Italy is very beautiful – I'm very well here. And I'm glad of your news about Hilda Shaw, and about your activities. The weather here is wonderfully fine.

D. H. Lawrence]

519. To Arthur McLeod, [28 November 1912]

Text: MS UT; PC; Postmark, Bogliaco 29 11 12; Huxley 80–1.

Gargnano
Thursday

My dear Mac.

The books came today – what a treasureful! You don't know how grateful I am. And F[rieda] thanks you particularly. She's swallowed the *House of Mirth* already[1] – and I'm nearly through Mark Rutherford.[2] How good he is! – so just, so harmonious. I *have* enjoyed him today – it has rained.

I'm sending you a little pretty book a man sent to me – the artist of the illustrations - because he said he admired me.[3] Tomorrow I'm going to Riva, to fetch some of my things – my paints among them. Then, I shall paint you your picture for Christmas. You see all the summer I've had no paints.

Why don't you come and see us – *why*? Your excuses are flimsy. I'll write in a day or so.

Love D. H. Lawrence

520. To Edward Garnett, [1 December 1912]

Text: MS NYPL; PC; Postmark, Bogliaco 1 12 12; Huxley 81.

['Villa Igéa', *Villa di Gargnano*, Lago di Garda (Brescia)]
[1 December 1912]

I sit in sadness and grief after your letter. I daren't say anything. All right, take out what you think necessary[4] – I suppose I shall see what you've done when the proofs come, at any rate. I'm sorry I've let you in for such a job – but don't scold me too hard, it makes me wither up.

[1] A novel by Edith Wharton (1862–1937).

[2] Pseudonym of William Hale White (1831–1913). The book referred to was *The Revolution in Tanner's Lane* (1887) (cf. Letter 521).

[3] See p. 468 n. 2.

[4] Edward Garnett reduced the length of the original *Sons and Lovers* by approximately one tenth.

D[uckworth]'s terms are quite gorgeous –[1]

But I'm so afraid you'll repress me once more, I daren't say anything. Still another man[2] wrote this morning that one of the most enterprising of the younger publishers wants the next novel I can let him have, at very satisfactory terms. – They comfort me after your wigging.

Yrs D. H. Lawrence

Tell me anything considerable you are removing – (sounds like furniture).

Thanks awfully for the newspapers – you don't know what a treat they were!

521. To Arthur McLeod, 2 December 1912

Text: MS UT; Postmark, Gargnano 5 12 12; Huxley 81–3.

'Villa Igéa', *Villa di Gargnano* (Brescia), Lago di Garda
2 Dec 1912

Lieber Mac,

Why am I so sleepy, seeing it's only half past eight! You are the decentest man to me in England. The books are a joy for ever. I've read the *Revolution in Tanner's Lane*, and find myself fearfully fond of Rutherford. I used to think him dull, but now I see he is so just and plucky and sound – and yes, perhaps I like his dullness – when one lives in a whirl of melodrama, as I seem to do just now, one is glad of a glass of good porter like Rutherford. And Frieda is once more to be kept in bounds, since there's a pack of books. A thousand[3] thanks again.

Oh, I've actually painted two pictures. I'm doing several – when they're finished I shall send them and let you have your pick. This is the interlude between novels. The Paul Morel book – to be called, I think *Sons and Lovers* is being got ready for the printer – I'm resting a bit after having delivered it. It's quite a great work. I only hope the English nation won't rend me for having given them anything so good. Not that the English nation is likely to concern itself with me – but 'England, my England'[4] is for me, I suppose, 'Critic, my critic'. Duckworth's going to give me £100 on account. I feel quite like a thief.

What do you think of the *Sappho* book? It has a certain curious interest,

[1] Terms, formally agreed in a contract dated 19 March 1913, gave DHL 15% royalty on the first 2,500 copies, 17½% on all beyond that number, and £100 advance royalties payable 'on day of publication'.

[2] Possibly Curtis Brown (1866–1945), literary agent, to whom DHL wrote on 4 April 1921: 'I wish I'd come to you ten years back: you wrote me just too late.'

[3] MS reads 'thoussand'.

[4] The refrain in W. E. Henley, 'Pro Rege Nostro'.

I think – and purple leather covers. The man who did the drawings said that several London booksellers refused to stock it. He seemed quite proud of the fact. I hope you don't mind my passing on to you a book inscribed to me. But I don't know the man and am not a bibliophile.

You are a duffer not to come at Christmas. Harold Hobson is coming – but I'd rather have had you. I believe you'll be too shy to go through the gates of Heaven – and you'll be hanging round through eternity.

I'm going to bed. This is altogether too stupid. There are lots of big stars. The last steamer has gone. There's one warm little light under the mountains on the opposite side of the lake. And imagine – there's a big jar of Christmas roses and maidenhair fern on the table. They grow wild, such big white beauties, and so many of them. I should love a jaw to you about things. School is gradually sinking over the rim of my horizon. Imagine the bell-turret of Davidson slowly fading over the margin of my eternity – Sounds affecting! I don't think I ever want to see it again. – But this is too hopeless. 'To bed, to bed, to bed!'[1]

Fancy – I had a letter from Dobson today – still in his dignified and sober style.[2]

Tell me some news of people. I daren't think of Ernie[3] – nor of Mrs E[rnie]. But give my love to the rest.

I'm having Italian lessons from the school mistress here. She scolds me and adores me. She is punctual and bores me. Tomorrow I shall offer her a cognac, to make her hair curl. But she's forty, poor thing. And she thinks I'm a howling swell. And I ask her how many kids she's got, and feign such indignation and wonderment at her having 35. I ask her stupid questions about Italian education – which it appears is even stupider than my questions.

I wandered the other day into a lovely little inn in the mountains, where one sits perched high up in the chimney and pokes the sticks under the hanging pot, and eats most ghastly cheese. Then the old lady – the inn is always the family living room – told me her husband was schoolmaster in the village for 40 years, and her three daughters had been to 'Centre'[4] in Toscolano and were now teaching among the mountains.

'Any of 'em married?' I naively asked.

'No Signore!'

The old lady glanced at me half resentful, half ashamed. I had put my foot in it.

[1] *Macbeth* v. i. 75.

[2] Later he was headmaster of Sydenham Road School, Croydon.

[3] See p. 465 n. 1.

[4] A Pupil-Teacher Centre.

'And when are they at home?' I continued.

'All on Friday night.'

I got frightened. The world is too, too much alike.

I was afraid her husband might have been at college with Philip.

Tell me about people – people. – I have painted $2\frac{1}{2}$ pictures – quite decent. I *do* pay my debts – some of 'em. Do you want any of the books back? Next time, would you send me *Tom Jones* ($4\frac{1}{2}$d).

Goodbye – here's my hand

(said Herve Riel)[1]

D. H. Lawrence

522. To Ada Lawrence, [2 December 1912]

Text: MS Clarke; PC v. Strada ponale presso Riva; Postmark, Bogliaco 2 12 12; Lawrence–Gelder 107–8.

['Villa Igéa', *Villa di Gargnano*, Lago di Garda (Brescia)]

[2 December 1912]

Here's a card to wish you a Happy Christmas. Try and have as jolly a time as you can. I will do the same. And give father, from me, five shillings, will you? It's too late to get if off now, but I'll send it you next week. I haven't heard from you. I'm writing father a letter. Give my love and good wishes to Nellie and Edward.

Love from your brother D. H. Lawrence

Thanks for the books you sent.

523. To David Garnett, 5 December 1912

Text: MS NYPL; Moore 166.

'Villa Igéa', *Villa di Gargnano*, Lago di Garda (Brescia).

5 Dec 1912

My dear Bunny,

The enclosed was sent by me for Frieda to her children. Because it was – forgetfully – done under my name, Weekley sent it back, and a letter to Frieda threatening to come and kill us both here in Gargnano, for daring to insult his children with the name of 'that filthy hound' – me. I am keeping a list of the nice names I've acquired this trip. And please watch the newspapers for intelligence concerning us.

[1] Robert Browning (1812–89), 'Hervé Riel', vi:

'Why I've nothing but my life, – here's my head!'
Cries Hervé Riel.

But – for the money! Would you mind going down to Chiswick and cashing it for me. It was sent by D. H. Lawrence, *Villa di Gargnano* – but you know that. It's a shame to bother you. But – you may keep the 1/9 for yourself: it'll enrichen you for Christmas. – I'm only joking. And send me the thirty bob at your leisure – payable at Gargnano, not at Villa. I'm not hard up, so you needn't hurry.

I'm so sick of bloody gushings. Weekley threatens us alternately with murder and with suicide (the latter his own). I always expect a streak of greased lightning to fly out when we open an envelope from him. The Richthofens and W. have made a grand onslaught this week. I believe it is their Waterloo. God knows what sort of a Napoleon I feel, nor where my St Helena is. But Frieda is still in Gargnano. Sympathise with me, Bunny, you lazy devil. I don't feel you half compassionate enough. And send me a *Nation* or something such, will you. And don't curse me for a pest: I'd do as much for you.

Would I had wedded a microscope;[1] I could have kept my eye on it and my heart in my pocket, and been called blessed. And now – ! I will send this letter to Hampstead. I'd love a night at the Cearne: beer, apples, a big fire, and a jaw till midnight.

You're nearly through the long term. How lovely to be young and enthusiastic for work! The night falls – the star of love issues forth in its nakedness – shame on it.

auf wiedersehen D. H. Lawrence

They use sand instead of blotting paper in Italy – benighted lot.

524. To Ford Madox Hueffer, 10 December 1912

Text: MS NYPL; Unpublished.

'Villa Igéa', *Villa di Gargnano* (Brescia), Lago di Garda
10 Dec. 1912

Dear Hueffer,

Thanks for your full opinions on the *Trespasser*. I agree with you heartily. I rather hate the book. It seems a bit messy to me. But whether it injures my reputation or not, it has brought me enough money to carry me – so modestly, as you may guess – through a winter here on the Lake Garda. One must publish to live.

I'm sure I wrote last to you. Did you have a sudden flicker of affection for me that made you write this letter? I'm sure I wish it were so. And no

[1] An allusion to David Garnett's studies towards his Associateship of the Royal College of Science (which he took in 1913).

doubt I am a lax and immoral young man – but ought not that rather to endear me to you than otherwise?

No – I am feathering no nest – I wish I were. I am living on the proceeds of the *Trespasser* and trusting for the future to an advance on the new novel I sent Duckworth a week or so back. – No – you're a better prospector of Tom Tiddlers ground[1] than ever I hope to be.

Yours Sincerely D. H. Lawrence

525. To Else Jaffe, 14 December 1912

Text: MS UT; Moore 167.

'Villa Igéa', *Villa di Gargnano*, Lago di Garda
14 Dec 1912

Dear Else,

I was not cross with your letter. I think you want to do the best for Frieda. I do also. But I think you ask us to throw away a real apple for a gilt one. Nowadays it costs more courage to assert ones desire and need, than it does to renounce.

If Frieda and the children could live happily together, I should say 'Go' – because the happiness of two out of three is sufficient. But if she would only be sacrificing her life, I would not let her go if I could keep her. Because if she brings to the children a sacrifice, that is a curse to them. If I had a prayer, I think it would be 'Lord, let no one ever sacrifice living stuff to me – because I'm burdened enough.' Whatever the children may miss now, they will preserve their inner liberty, and their independent pride will be strong when they come of age. But if Frieda gave up all to go and live with them, that would sap their strength because[2] they would have to support her life as they grew up. They would not be free to live of themselves – they would first have to live *for her*, to pay back. The worst of sacrifice is that we have to pay back. It is like somebody giving a present that was never asked for, and putting the recipient under the obligation of making restitution, often more than he could afford.

So we must go on, and never let go the children, but will, and will, and will to have them and to have what we think good. That's all one can do. You say 'Lawrence kommt mir vor wie ein Held'. I hope he may 'gehen dir aus' similarly.[3] He doesn't feel at all heroic, but only in the devil of a mess.

Don't mind how I write, will you?

Yours Sincerely D. H. Lawrence

[1] i.e. a place where it is easy to pick up a fortune.

[2] because] and

[3] '"Lawrence appears to me like a hero". I hope he may "disappear like one" similarly.'

526. To Ada Lawrence, [ante 16 December 1912][1]

Text: MS UN; Unpublished.

['Villa Igéa', *Villa di Gargnano*, Lago di Garda (Brescia)]
[ante 16 December 1912][1]

[Lawrence tells Ada that 'he has sent "Paul Morel" to Duckworth who is publishing early in the new year.

They are paying him £100 down for it, so that he'll be in clover for a time at any rate.

Harold Hobson, son of Hobson the writer, is going to Gargnano to spend Xmas with him.']

527. To Arthur McLeod, 17 December 1912

Text: MS UT; Postmark, Bogliaco 18 12 12; Moore, *Intelligent Heart* 135–6.

'Villa Igéa', *Villa di Gargnano*, Lago di Garda (Brescia)
17 Dec 1912

Dear Mac,

You are too good to me. Don't send me anything else, will you. The load of obligation is too heavy. The last selection is ripping – I've scarcely read any of them. They will last us a long time now. The *Tom Jones* came on Saturday, before any of the rest. – Don't send me anything else – I feel too guilty. I haven't got any book I could give you – except Garnett's *Joan of Arc*. It is more or less interesting. Don't scorn it.

I am thinking so hard of my new novel, and since I am feeling hard pushed again, am in the right tune for it. It is to be a life of Robert Burns[2] – but I shall make him live near home, as a Derbyshire man – and shall fictionise the circumstances. But I have always loved him, in a way. He seems a good deal like myself – nicer in most ways. I think I can do him almost like an autobiography. Tell Miss Mason the *Life* came all right, and give her my thanks.[3] I am waiting for her letter before I write. – If it would amuse you, just peep round and see if you can spot anything interesting about Burns, in the library, during the holiday. I've only got Lockhart's *Life*. I should like to know more about the Highland Mary episode.[4] Do you think it's interesting?

I haven't done any stories or anything lately. The strain of this business

[1] The contents of DHL's letter were reported to Louie Burrows by letter from Ada Lawrence, 16 December 1912 (MS UN LaB 209).

[2] The surviving fragments of 'A Burns Novel' are printed in Nehls, i. 184–95.

[3] J. G. Lockhart, *Life of Robert Burns* (1828).

[4] Mary Campbell (d. 1786), a Highland servant-girl whose relations with Burns gave rise to a romantic legend.

with Frieda squashes little things out of me. Perhaps after all there will be a divorce. If so, the next time you see me I shall be a married man. I am one now with all the disadvantages of illicity.[1]

Harold Hobson is here – and it's very jolly. But I'd rather you had come. I need one of my own friends rather badly just now. I've done 4 pictures – Harold will bring them to England, and send them to you, and you can pick. But if you can get a copy of the *Idyll*, I'll do you that as well.

Thanks for the Yeats.[2] Why didn't you put my name in? He seems awfully queer stuff to me now – as if he wouldn't bear touching. But Frieda is fond of him.

I'm going to begin again my work. One works in two bursts – Sept. to the beginning of Dec. – and Jan. to March or April. The rest are more or less trivial and barren months. I feel that I am *resisting* too hard to write poetry – *resisting* the strain of Weekley, and the tragedy there is in keeping Frieda. To write poetry one has to let oneself fuse in the current – but I daren't. This state of mind is more like a business man's, where he stands firm and keeps his eye open, than an artist's, who lets go and loses himself. But I daren't let go just now. The strain makes me tired.

I shall give you a copy of the poems and of the *Sons and Lovers* when they come out – so don't think of buying them.

I wish you all jolliness for the Christmas, and own my debt to you.

Yours ever D. H. Lawrence

528. To Edward Garnett, 17 December 1912

Text: MS NYPL; Postmark, Bogliaco 18 12 12; Huxley 84.

'Villa Igéa', *Villa di Gargnano*, Lago di Garda (Brescia)

17 Dec 1912

Dear Garnett,

Thanks for the Stephen Reynolds. *Alongshore* is very interesting indeed.[3] The only thing I find fault with in Reynolds is that he swanks his acquaintance with the longshoremen so hugely. He writes 'de haut en bas' like any old salt talking to a clerk from London – except that he's the clerk himself, carefully got up as the salt. I like his strong intelligence best – better than his imagination – which run to journalese. – I will send all the books back, the Conrad, the Strindberg – he *is* a lurid wooden stalker – and the Reynolds, by Harold Hobson.

[1] illicity] marriage

[2] Perhaps his *Poems* new edition revised, September 1912.

[3] *Alongshore: where man and the sea face one another* (1910) by Stephen Reynolds (1881–1919).

We were awfully surprised to see the latter. He walked in on Wednesday morning while we were at breakfast. His letter had not yet come. I notice you are rather sarcastic about him. I don't think he's so bad. We get on really awfully well, we three together. As for congratulating any of us – I think you might condole with us instead. – No, I can trust H. as my friend now.[1]

W[eekley] writes he will divorce Frieda if she cuts herself off from him and the children. The last sentence – or condition – he'd mitigate, I know. She says a woman can only have one husband – only belong to one man – all tears and trouble. 'Constant dropping will wear away a stone' as my mother used to say. But, by the Lord, I'm dead tired inside – fit to drop. It's just the strain of resisting, of seven months resistance. I feel as if I canna do no more – the rest's got to come.

I've thought of a new novel I'm keen on. It's a sort of life of Robert Burns. But I'm not Scotch. So I shall just transplant him to home – or on the hills of Derbyshire – and do as I like with him as far as circumstances go, but I shall stick to the man. I have always been fond of him, as of a sort of brother. Now, I'll write a novel of him. Tell me if you approve.

I'm glad you don't mind cutting the *Sons and Lovers*. By the way, is the title satisfactory?

It's cold here now, these last two days. I've got a cold, which no doubt accounts for the blues. It seems there's nothing to do but to go on, like a candle guttering and clinging in a draught. I'm sorry for myself just now. It's rather comforting.

I wonder if *Rhythm* would take any of my stories or sketches.[2] I wonder if ever the *Forum* is going to publish that tale[3] – and did the American edition of the *Trespasser* ever come out?[4]

If there is a divorce, we shall stay out here till it is consummated, then come to England married. Frieda says she's not keen on marrying me – but I want some peace. I want to be able to look ahead and see some rest and security somewhere. By the time I am thirty I shall have had my bellyful of hard living, I think, and shall have either to slacken off or go to the devil.

Yours Sincerely D. H. Lawrence

[1] Apparently DHL now knew that on one occasion during the journey from Mayrhofen, Frieda had seduced Hobson (see David Garnett, *The Golden Echo*, pp. 246–7).

[2] None was published in *Rhythm*.

[3] See p. 372 n. 4.

[4] See p. 430, Letter 476 and n. 4.

529. To Sallie Hopkin, 23 December 1912

Text: MS NCL; Huxley 85–6.

'Villa Igéa', *Villa di Gargnano*, Lago di Garda (Brescia)
23 Dec. 1912

Dear Mrs Hopkin,

Your letter has just come. I haven't written only because I've had a venomous cold these last three days. But yesterday and today Frieda and I were talking about you, for quite two hours. I was thinking Ada kept you up in what news I have. And we are the sort who can remain silent for a long time, and still the tie only grows, not weakens.

Frieda and I have been here together for three months now, living alone in this big flat. I wish you could come. Do you think, when primroses and violets are out, you could for this once muster seven or eight pounds and come and see us? You should see the moon rise up behind the snowy mountains across the lake: and you should gather great handfuls of perfect Christmas roses in the clefts of the hills, and in the olive[1] orchards. Yes, you ought to come. We've got two spare bedrooms, and we should be *glad*.

We've had a hard time, Frieda and I. It is not so easy for a woman to leave a man and children like that. And it's not so easy for a man and a woman to live alone together in a foreign country for six months, and dig out a love deeper and deeper. But we've[2] done it so far, and I'm glad. One day I'll tell you all about it.

Weekley talks now of a divorce. Thank God when it comes off and we have some peace. How queer it will be to come with Frieda and stay with you! You are always there, a friend for us to turn to.

My poems are coming out in January, my novel, *Sons and Lovers* – autobiography – in February.[3] They're both good – particularly the second.

Frieda will write you some more. I shall do a novel about Love Triumphant one day. I shall do my work for women, better than the suffrage.

My love to Enid and to Mr Hopkin – and all good wishes for the Christmas. You seem to have done my sister *good* – and again, my thanks. I wish this letter would come on Christmas day, but it is too late.

With love, D. H. Lawrence

530. To Ernest Collings, 24 December 1912

Text: MS UT; Huxley 86–7.

'Villa Igéa', *Villa di Gargnano* (Brescia), Lago di Garda.
24 Dec 1912

[1] olive] wild
[2] We've] I've
[3] Both were later: *Love Poems*, February 1913; *Sons and Lovers*, May 1913.

Dear Collings,

If I had had any decency, and if I had not had a bad cold, I should have got this letter written in time for it to come to England for Christmas. Now it must come late.

I liked your last letter. It struck me as being generous. But I have lost it, and so I can't really reply. I only remember you are having an exhibition of your drawings in the spring.[1] I liked your illustrations to the *Sapho* so much – you might tell me about your art, will you? What do you go in for, on the whole?

You prefer figure to landscape, I suppose. I think I should. I sketch in water-colour myself, as a hopeless amateur. But it is such healing work, I find, to paint a bit, even if it is only to copy, after one has frayed out one's soul with damned emotional drawing. To copy a nice Peter de Wint is the most soothing thing I can do, and to copy a Frank Brangwyn is a joy, so refreshing.[2] Do you mind that attitude to art? I always say, my motto is 'Art for my sake'. If I *want* to write, I write – and if I don't want to, I won't. The difficulty is to find exactly the form one's passion – work is produced by passion with me, like kisses – is it with you? – wants to take.

I'm glad you prefer 'Odour of Chrysanthemums' – I do. But the literary people who have talked to me, so many of them, prefer 'Stained Glass'. But I hate the conventionalised literary person – of the type I call Asphodels. Do you know the Radfords[3] and the Rhys – folk like them? They are so nice, and yet – I suppose it is only I who am too clownish. Do you know J A Hobson – social economics man? We've got his son staying with us, and have a good time. I wonder if our social orbits do touch at any point.

I'm seedy, so I sit in bed chewing Toroni – do you know that adorable sweet? – and writing a bit at a new novel, which seems to me to be so far more clever than good.[4] January sees my poems published, February my novel *Sons and Lovers*. Of course I admire both works immensely. I am a great admirer of my own stuff while it's new, but after a while I'm not so

[1] Collings held a personal exhibition of 15 oil paintings and 20 drawings at the Rowley Gallery, 140 Church Street, Kensington, 30 April – 11 May 1913. (He also exhibited at the Sixth London Salon Exhibition of the Allied Artists' Association at the Royal Albert Hall, July 1913.)

[2] DHL copied Peter de Wint's *A Harvest Scene* in his own water colour (8″ × 11″) *Harvesting*. See *Young Bert* p. 63 and Letter 76, p. 88 n. 4. On Brangwyn see p. 196.

[3] Ernest (1857–1919) and Dollie (1864?–1920) Radford. May have met DHL at Rhys's home in Spring 1910. Loaned Chapel Farm Cottage, Hermitage, to DHL, 1918–19. Ernest published *Translations from Heine and Other Verses* (1882), *A Collection of Poems* (1906), etc; Dollie, *Songs and Other Verses* (1895), *Poems* (1910), etc.

[4] This remark heralds the abandonment, effectively perhaps in December 1912, of the 'Burns Novel'.

gone on it – like the true maternal instinct, that kicks off an offspring as soon as it can go on its own legs.

It all sounds very egoistic, but you don't tell me enough about yourself. It's good of you to be only thirty. These damned old stagers want to train up a child in the way it should grow, whereas if it's destined to have a snub nose, it's sheer waste of time to harass the poor brat into Roman-nosedness. They want me to have form: that means, they want me to have *their* pernicious ossiferous skin-and-grief form, and I won't. – Do tell as many people as you can that I'm a great writer and that my influence is pure and sweet – also that I'm being published just now. I'm so afraid I shall have to take to teaching again.

You won't be coming to Italy? – Best wishes for the New Year – luck to the Artist you.

D. H. Lawrence

I've lost the address and dont know if you'll ever get this.[1]

531. To Sallie Hopkin, [25 December 1912]

Text: MS NCL; Huxley 87–8.

Villa Igéa, *Villa di Gargnano* (Brescia), Lago di Garda.
Christmas Day 1912

Dear Mrs Hopkin,

I did write you a letter, but it's got lost, and I don't like it.[2] I've been seedy, laid up in bed for some days with a cold – damn its eyes. But on the day when your letter came, and the day before, Frieda and I had been talking about you, for two hours. It seemed queer to see your handwriting – like an answer one heard.

We've had such a hard time pegging through this autumn – the children, Weekley, and ourselves. If two people start clean of trouble, without children and other husbands between 'em, it's hard for them to get simple and close to each other – but when it's like this – oh Lord, it takes it out of you. But we've done wonders, really. I am satisfied with what I have done – we have done, I mean – up to now. God help us. Once you've known what love *can* be, there's no disappointment any more, and no despair. If the skies tumble down like a smashed saucer, it couldn't break what's between Frieda and me. I think folk have got sceptic about love – that's because nearly everybody fails. But if they do fail, they needn't doubt *love*. It's their own fault. I'll do my life work, sticking up for the love between man and woman.

[1] Collings noted on the MS: 'Ansrd E C 29/12/12'.

[2] It was not lost; see Letter 529.

Do you think, in the spring, when the snowdrops are going and there are hundreds and thousands of violets and primroses, you could scrape six or seven pounds and come and stay some weeks with us? It would only be the journey. And one *should* take the opportunities that come. It is so lovely here. There have been such perfect clumps of christmas roses, wild, in the olive orchards and by the gullies of streams.

My book of poems comes out next month – my novel in February. They are good. But I shall always be a priest of love, and now a glad one – and I'll preach my heart out, Lor bless you.

Weekley talks about a divorce. Won't it be queer, when Frieda and I are married, and come and stay with you. What a jumpy sea life looks for me – I wonder if I shall make a living. But I don't mind – today.

We've got the son of J A Hobson, the Economist writer, staying with us – we are fond of him.

I wonder if we shall be in England at Easter. If the divorce is coming, we shall probably wait for it.

I am stupid headed – don't mind. Things work out, bit by bit, and we all help one another. Try to come and see us here – it is Italy. My regards to Willie and to Enid.

Yours D. H. Lawrence

Thanks for helping Ada – you did her good.

I love it that one uses sand for blotting paper here – it is such fun.[1]

532. To David Garnett, [29 December 1912]

Text: MS NYPL; cited in Huxley 89.

Villa Igéa, Villa di Gargnano
Sunday 29 Dec

Dear Bunny,

Thanks so much for doing the money business.[2] They gave me 39 lire for the 31/-, and I felt rich again. Your budget of letters was interesting. Of course Harold said *swank*, but Frieda said she liked it, and I'm simply starving to be able to swank myself. Do you think you might persuade one or two quite tender young ladies to lionise me a bit when I get back to England. Frieda pulls all my tail-feathers out, and I feel as if a little gentle adoration would come remarkably soothingly unto me. Not that lions have tail feathers. Put it at a tuft.

[Sketch][3]

[1] Frieda's postscript printed in Moore 173 is not on the MS.

[2] See Letter 523.

[3] Of a maned lion drooping and unsteady on its legs.

This is the kind of lion I feel at present: shall we say a rat-tailed lion?

I've tried hard to make a chivalrous Sir Galahad of Harold. But it's no good. He is a lion indeed – but all bark and bristles. If he and I were rolled into one you'd have a king of beasts. He doesn't bite, really.

Seriously, we've been awfully jolly together, the three of us, and we shall miss him horribly when he goes. If we're here next summer, I see you hopping into that lake: how you'd love it! I think it's possible we might stay here till we can be married: then we should kick our heels if you came.

I envy you your life of toil: it is a sweet vision before my 'amarro far niente'[1] eyes. Think of the rest and peace, the positive sloth and luxury of idleness, that hard work is. I wish the Lord would grant me a little. You see one can only write creative stuff when it comes – otherwise it's [...] not much good. I should love something to swot, or something mechanical, on which to spend my sweat!

Your rag-bag letters are most highly acceptable, one can hear your voice. Don't be long before you write again –

D. H. Lawrence

[Frieda Weekley begins][2]

Dear Bunny!

I am really quite hurt that you think me so tragic! It's all because of L[awrence]'s play,[3] that is *misleading* to put it mildly, some of Harold's language would be more appropriate! Cant you see, what really sad and tragic blokes Harold and Lawrence are? Both of them! Harold's chelp[4] (as L. calls it) is only bluff, that type of creature is *all* tragedy, it's got no outlet for its energies, its strong virility; they are sensitive, miserable consequently, touchy, to the last degree of decency, dont you be humbugged by them, just because you are a male yourself, though fortunately of a different, more restful sort – If you only knew how in Lawrence I discovered abysses of elusive, destructive, spiritual tragedy [Lawrence interjects: balls!], that it took the strength of several St George's to fight the dragon (there's a serpent in the grass, fight it down, fight it, fight it down!). My tragedy is tangible though floods the bed and chews the sheet, it's child's play compared to his – [Lawrence interjects: *Shit*!] They called Harold 'six foot of misery' at the

1 Literally 'bitter do nothing' ('amaro').

2 It is assumed that this letter (printed in Tedlock 188–9) was written concurrently with DHL's and mailed with his.

3 In 'The Fight for Barbara', Frieda is presented as an English woman, Barbara Tressider; she has eloped with James Wesson who is berated by her aristocratic mother and father, and by her professorial husband.

4 i.e. shrill voice or contentious chatter (dialect). Cf. *A Collier's Friday Night*, III. iii.

works!!![1] I had a hell of a time with them, L torturing me, H being that 'umpy, but now we have had some jolly days, peace and goodwill all round [Lawrence interjects: I dont fink], I am really proud of us, it was'nt easy! We saw a red berry that sits on a leaf, is called Butcher's broom[2] and said you ought to have it, there are primroses, huge bunches of Xmas roses in the hedges, I put them on the table and stick them in my hair and get called names for the effort, they *do* abuse me and have no chivalry – We went to see Ibsens *Spettri*[3] in a tiny theatre, we sat in a tiny red box, I fancied myself in a huge, soft velvet hat with huge feathers, black garments Xmas roses and the pretty red of the box. The boxes are tiny and close together, we watched the butcher boy flirting with a pretty damsel, but she was also flirting with a yokel and Harold. It's jolly to know the sailor, who brings the parcels, (Lawrence is jealous of him, I *do* love him, the sailor) [Lawrence interjects: balls-aching rot] the proud Post office lady, the cheesemonger boy in his Sunday best; They all carry-on their conversations, while the conversation on the stage goes on as a secondary pastime – You will hear of Harold's plans! I wonder, if they will come off – How you would love this place, Bunny, and what a restful person, you would be, no tragedy about you now any way; Dont think nasty things about me, Bunny, I have'nt deserved it, I am really quite good and weep no more! [Lawrence interjects: Bitch!] A merry Xmas you had and I wish you a happy year and that we shall see something of you!

Good-bye, Bunny, my love to you, I appreciate your letters, though they dont appreciate me. [Lawrence interjects: Arse-licking.]

Frieda[4]

533. To Edward Garnett, 29 December 1912

Text: MS NYPL; Postmark, Gargnano 31 12 12; cited in Tedlock 189–90.

'Villa Igéa', *Villa di Gargnano*, Lago di Garda – (Brescia)
29 Dec 1912

Dear Garnett,

Frieda wants to thank you for the two novels: she is such a lazy animal that I don't know whether she'll rouse herself to a letter. I don't care

[1] At Hubert Wailes and Co. in Euston Road.

[2] An evergreen shrub of the lily family.

[3] MS reads 'spettri'. According to Letter 533 they saw *Ghosts* on 28 December. The date is confirmed ('the Saturday after Christmas') in 'Italian Studies. By the Lago di Garda: III – The Theatre', *English Review*, xv (September 1913), 221 (later collected in *Twilight in Italy*, Duckworth, 1916).

[4] Next to Frieda's signature DHL drew a hand with two fingers pointing upwards; it is connected by a line to a heavy arrow directed to the words 'come off' eight lines above.

for *Bernadine*, and haven't read the other.[1] But they're amusing enough.

Things are looking up a bit with us. W[eekley] says he won't write any more, and will get a divorce. So no letters are to pass between him and Frieda, or it will be called collusion. I hope to God he'll go through with it this time. There's no surer way of getting to hate anybody, than having them slobber between sentimental pardon and violent righteous wrath. As for the children, heaven knows how their small fates will be settled. They are in abeyance for the time being. We only dread their coming up again, like the ghostly children in *Macbeth*.[2] Sufficient unto the day is the evil thereof.[3]

I'm glad to hear you like the novel better. I don't much mind what you squash out. I hope to goodness it'll do my reputation and my pocket good, the book. I'm glad you'll let it be dedicated to you. I feel always so deep in your debt.

I have been thinking also, when I come back to England, I shall have to find a job of some sort. Either I shall get a teaching place, or if I could I would do some work for a publisher. But I suppose I shall have to leave it till I get back.

We sort of forgot about its being Christmas. It didn't go off with much of a bang here – owing to other Christmases looking so forlornly over the years at us – blast them. So I didn't send you greetings as I might have done if I'd had any decency.

Yesterday we saw Ibsen's *Ghosts* in Italian in the little theatre here. It was awfully well acted, and gave me the creeps.

We've got on awfully well the three of us, while Harold has been here. He will be going I expect next week – Tuesday or New Years day – probably to his people on the Riviera. It'll be horribly quiet again. When are you coming? – don't forget that promise. Primroses are already coming out. Frieda expects to come to England to see the children at Easter. W. promised them[4] to her then some time back. Whether it'll hold good now I don't quite know, but I expect so.

I've stewed my next novel inside me for a week or so, and have begun dishing it up.[5] It's going to have a bit of a plot, and I don't think it'll be

[1] Rosina Filippi, *Bernadine* (Duckworth, November 1912). 'The other' was Lily Schofield, *Elizabeth, Betsy and Bess* (Duckworth, October 1912): see Letter 544.

[2] *Macbeth* IV. i. 77–94.

[3] Matthew vi. 34.

[4] them] that

[5] Perhaps DHL had begun the twenty-page MS (now at Southern Illinois University) which opens, 'My mother made a failure of her life'. This fragment, a reminiscence told in the first person by 'Elsa Culverwell', made use of the material about the Cullen family which DHL had removed from 'Paul Morel'.

unwieldy, because it'll be further off from me and won't come down on my head so often. (A bit mixed in the metaphor.)

We are definitely expecting you in the spring, so keep up to the scratch. I wouldn't mind staying out here till we were married, but F. can hardly come to England alone, and it is so expensive going backwards and forwards. My younger sister gets married in April or May, and she'll take us in if we want. My elder sister and my brother – and of course father – don't know anything. I hope they needn't, for they'd pester.

Frieda is fearfully keen on having a cottage in England, if we go.

I don't bother about those things – work, money, prospects – they must settle themselves gradually. But one must look a bit ahead.

I hope things will go well with you during the New Year: I want nothing to happen to me, but just small easy things. It'll take me a little while to digest this dollop. But it's getting easier – sort of slacking off.

Vale – my dear Authority D. H. Lawrence

[Frieda Weekley begins][1]

Dear Mr Garnett,

Your books were quite a Godsend to me – The tragedy was in its zenith just at Xmas; in spite of heroic efforts and loftiest sentiments one feels more like mincepies and parcels *almost* Xmas cards at that time and of course I was ignored by all my friends, the outcast; even if one says to oneself 'tu l'a voulu, Georges Dandin,'[2] George does'nt feel no better for it – But things are looking up, I like my people-in-law, the children will be happy there, and I must wait, after all they are my flesh and blood and I must trust in the Lord, [Lawrence interjects: Who's he? Some new bloke?] it's really wonderful, how things come right if you only trust enough – I am really rather dense is so many things, but the sort of blind, stupid trust has always brought me through – We are having a good time with Harold, he is good stuff, we say very nasty things to each other, told H. for instance that he would never have the hospitable spirit of the Garnetts. Every day an hour before the postman comes, Harold goes about crying, nobody loves me, nobody loves me, if there is no letter, you should just hear[3] him, perhaps you would rather not – Between them I did have a time, Lawrence *is* wear

[1] The address is repeated at the head of this letter: 'Villa Igéa', Villa di Gargnano. DHL wrote the first three, Frieda the last two words. No date is given. 29 December appears correct: in his letter DHL half-expects Frieda also will write; both thanked Garnett for books; Frieda was clearly writing after Christmas; and since Hobson was still at Gargnano she must have written before 2 January 1913 when he departed.

[2] Molière, *Georges Dandin* (1668). The hero, a tradesman, marries a nobleman's daughter and often comments on his situation: 'Vous l'avez voulu, Georges Dandin.'

[3] MS reads 'here'.

and tear, I am cross with him just at present, he chases my poor emotions, till they drop like panting hares [Lawrence interjects: bleeder!] and if I feel an emotion coming miles away, I'm all of a tremble – But still it's worth it and in the end we shall be a quiet, respectable (Ernst offered to help me to live down my past) couple, quite dull, fancy marrying again, it gives me creeps – [Lawrence interjects: Stinker] Many good wishes for the new year, do remain the good spirit over us – as you have been so far, we are *really* happy; though we fight like blazes, we shall bring it off – Yes, my theories have sadly altered, there are 2 sides to human love, one that wants to be faithful, the other wants to run, my running one was uppermost, but it's going to be faithful now, I used to think I should never have enough love, now I think I have got as much as I can swallow – This letter is all about 'I' I apologise!

With many thanks for the gift and the spirit and goodwill of the sender

Frieda

534. To John William and Marie Jones, [1912?]

Text: Hugh Kingsmill, *D. H. Lawrence* (1938), pp. 38–9.

[1912?]

[After Lawrence's convalescence in Bournemouth 'the Joneses heard from him only once again, some months later, when he wrote mysteriously that something had happened which he was not at liberty to divulge, but which would become known in due course'.]

535. To Arthur McLeod, 2 January 1913

Text: MS UT; PC; Postmark, Gargnano 3 I 13; Unpublished.

Villa di Gargnano
2 Jan 1913

Dear Mac,

Hobson has left today, with the sketches. He will post them all to you, and you are to choose. Put strips of paper round them, in lieu of mounts, before you decide. Then please post them on to Mrs Krenkow, 20 Dulverton Rd, Leicester.

If you can send me a copy of *Idyll* or anything else you *like* – it would give me pleasure to copy it – I will certainly do you a copy. If you want, you may choose two of the sketches. One seems shabby.

Tell Miss Mason I'm not friends with her. That was a ripping selection of books, your last. I've been a bit seedy but am better. My best wishes for the New Year – thank Philip for his card.

My love to Everybody.

Yours D. H. Lawrence

There's no hurry about the pictures.

536. To May Holbrook, 2 January 1913

Text: TMSC Ridgway; Unpublished.

Villa Igea, Villa di Gargnano, (Brescia)[1] Lago di Garda.
2 Jan. 1913

Dear May,

Here goes. I didn't write because I got sick of telling half a lie. I came down here with Mrs. Weekley – we have been living together a long time. I think Prof. Weekley is beginning to get a divorce – then we shall be married. It has been awful – and – well, good enough too. I hope we may be able to be married in some few months' time. We shall probably come to England in April. Don't mention this to anybody. Jessie has known all along. I shrewdly suspect you have heard something. But I *don't* want anybody to know – why should folk wipe their dirty mouths on me. I wanted to tell you before – and couldn't. I know it seems horrid – but it is something else beside. Now be nice with me about it. I shan't say no more.

It seems so plucky of you to go to Australia in the teeth of everything.[2] What is the good of life, after all, but to live. And shifting about breaks down a lot of barriers. But the real living comes from inside – like an engine that goes by the same works wherever it travels to. Still – the stress of my own life would have been a hundred times harder, if it hadn't been for this lake – the sun rises and shines on my face as it comes over the mountain just across the lake, and I look up and see such a lovely glittering road over a milky-white lake, with dark blue mountains and pale blue snow behind. And there have been such lovely bunches of great Christmas roses growing wild by the streams. And primroses are out. It helps one when things get too keen.

I shall have to leave off. The Maestra has come and we are to have our Italian lesson.

[1] TMSC reads 'Brescin'.

[2] The Holbrooks emigrated to Canada not Australia: William went in Spring 1914, May followed in 1915 (Nehls, iii. 637, 747 n. 95 where Holbrook's inaccurate recollection of this letter is quoted).

Now the lesson's over, thank the Lord – I have made molti sbagli.[1] The Maestra is the Schoolmistress – about 45 – old maid – correc[tly?] nice. Already I know quite a decent bit of Italian.

We've had staying with us for the last three weeks a friend of Garnetts whom we met in the Tirol – Harold Hobson. His father is the writer on economics. He was awful. But it made my heart sink when the steamer turned its broad behind on me at Bogliaco and went careering down the lake, this morning. Not that I wanted to go to England – but – I didn't like being left behind. Now he'll be crossing into Switzerland, and tomorrow morning will be in Paris. I'm glad I haven't got the journey, though.

We live in a big flat, half the Villa Igea. The roses are out in the garden, ever so pretty. We are alone, and often wish we had your cottage as well.[2] These big rooms and miles of corridor are a bit disheartening.

You might send me news of everybody – of Arno and all.[3] You will understand I feel I can scarcely write to them.

Christmas was very quiet – it is scarcely a feast here at all – the men just have the day's holiday. Everybody is fearfully easy going. Work knocks off when the twilight bell rings in all the Churches and begins with the Sunrise bell – all the light hours. But the navvies in the road never do more than let a pick[4] fall of its own weight, and they dig out a bit as big as a potato at each shovelful. Lazy devils, they are, but they look so nice one forgives them anything.

I've got one or two more cheap books if you'd like them. Tell Will to get that letter written – a real man's letter of sympathy. It'll give me joy.

All good wishes for the New Year.

Yours D. H. Lawrence

537. To Edward Garnett, 12 January 1913

Text: MS NYPL; Postmark, Gargnano 12 I 13; Huxley 90–1.

'Villa Igéa', *Villa di Gargnano*, Lago di Garda (Brescia)

12 Jan 1913

Dear Garnett,

I am going to send you a new play I have written.[5] It is neither a comedy

[1] 'many mistakes'.

[2] The cottage DHL so much liked, Moorgreen, Newthorpe, Notts. (The Holbrooks left there before 22 February 1913, the date of a letter from Ada Lawrence to Louie Burrows, MS UN LaB 211.)

[3] Arno Vale Farm, Mapperley, Nottingham, where the Chambers family lived after leaving Haggs Farm. (For a description see Corke, *Croydon Years* 24.)

[4] TMSC reads 'lick'.

[5] 'The Daughter-in-Law'.

nor a tragedy – just ordinary. It is quite objective, as far as that term goes, and though no doubt, like most of my stuff, it wants weeding out a bit, yet I think the whole thing is there, laid out properly, planned and progressive. If you don't think so, I am disappointed.

I enjoy so much writing my plays – they come so quick and exciting from the pen – that you mustn't growl at me if you think them waste of time. At any rate, they'll be stuff for shaping later on, when I'm more of a workman. And I look at the future, and it behoves me to keep on trying to earn money somehow. The divorce will come off, I think, for sure. Then Frieda and I must see to ourselves, and I must see to the money part. I *do* think this play might have a chance on the stage. It'll bear cutting, but I don't think it lacks the stuff for the theatre. – I am afraid of being a nuisance. Do you feel, with me, a bit like the old man of the seas? If I weren't so scared of having no money at all, I'd tell you to shovel all my stuff onto Pinker, get rid of the bother of me, and leave me to transact with him. – The thought of you pedgilling away[1] at the novel frets me. Why can't I do those things? – I can't. I could do hack work, to a certain amount. But apply my creative self where it doesn't want to be applied, makes me feel I should bust or go cracked. I *couldn't* have done any more at that novel – at least for six months. I must go on producing, producing, and the stuff must come more and more to shape each year. But trim and garnish my stuff I cannot – it *must* go. The plays I can re-write and re-create: I shall love it, when I want to do it. But I don't want to do it yet.

I'm simmering a new work that I shall not tell you about, because it may not come off.[2] But the thought of it fills me with a curious pleasure – venomous, almost. I want to get it off my chest.

We had a good time with Harold – you may congratulate us all.

It is rainy weather for three days, so that we are amazed and indignant. It has been *so* sunny all the time.

And again, about my getting some work. I shall never go into a big school to teach again. I'll be the proverbial poor poet in the garret first – and I must say I loathe the fellow. I've no sympathy with starvers, Gissings or Chattertons.[3] I might get a little country school. But I don't want to bury Frieda alive. Wherever I go with her, we shall have to fall into the intelligent,

[1] i.e. working at, examining and patching *Sons and Lovers*.

[2] If, on 29 December 1912, DHL was indeed referring to the 'Elsa Culverwell' MS (see p. 496 n. 5), he had now abandoned it and made an enthusiastic start on what was to become 'The Insurrection of Miss Houghton'. By 17 January (Letter 540) eighty pages were written. ('The Insurrection of Miss Houghton', re-written perhaps twice in 1920, was transmuted into *The Lost Girl*, Secker, 1920.)

[3] Thomas Chatterton (1752–70), poet; poverty and despair drove him to suicide.

as it were upper classes. I could get along with anybody, by myself, because, as Frieda says, I am common, and as you say, I am $\frac{1}{5}$ Cockney. I find a servant maid more interesting, as a rule, than a Violet Hunt or a Grace Rhys. After all, I was brought up among them. But Frieda is a lady, and I hate her when she talks to the common people. She is not a bit stuck-up, really more humble than I am, but she makes the *de haut en bas* of class distinction felt – even with my sister. It is as she was bred and fed, and can't be otherwise. So, that really cuts out a country school. I mustn't take her to England to bury her alive. We have had six months without any-body at all. One needs *some* people, to keep healthy and well aired. I ought to live near London. Perhaps I could get some publishers reading to do. We could manage on £200 a year. It ought not to be impossible. You must help me a bit, with advice.

If we come to England at Easter, there is not long here. Frieda wants to see her children then, but I don't know. – I never thanked you for the American copy of *The Trespasser*. It is ugly. – Have a bit of patience with me. You won't come out and see us? – When do the poems appear? – I shall want a dozen copies, I owe so many people a remembrance. But I can pay for them. Frieda sends her regards.

Yrs D. H. Lawrence

538. To Ada Lawrence, [14 January 1913]

Text: MS Clarke; PC v. [Tree-lined road in winter]; Postmark, Gargnano 14 I 13; Lawrence–Gelder 113.

['Villa Igéa', *Villa di Gargnano*, Lago di Garda (Brescia)]
[14 January 1913]

What a shame about your bowl – but never mind, I'll buy you another. I sent you the poem-proofs off. I guess you'll hate the stuff.

Write me a letter – it is overdue.

Love D. H. Lawrence

539. To Ernest Collings, 17 January 1913

Text: MS UT; Huxley 93–5.

'Villa Igéa', *Villa di Gargnano*, Lago di Garda (Brescia)
17 Jan 1913

Dear Collings,

Your letters are as good as a visit from somebody nice. I love people who can write reams and reams about themselves: it seems generous. And the prints are interesting. What a rum chap you are! Are you a celibate?[1] (Don't

[1] Collings was unmarried until 1922.

answer if you don't want to – I'm a married man, or ought to be.) Your work seems too – too – onesided (I've only seen a tiny bit of it, as you know) – as if it were *afraid* of the female element – which makes me think you are more or less a Galahad – which is not, I believe, good for your art. It is hopeless for me to try to do anything without I have a woman at the back of me. And you seem a bit like that – not hopeless – but too uncertain. Böcklin – or somebody like him – daren't sit in a café except with his back to the wall.[1] I daren't sit in the world without a woman behind me. And you give me that feeling a bit: as if you were uneasy of what is behind you. Excuse me if I am wrong. But a woman I love sort of keeps me in direct communication with the unknown, in which otherwise I am a bit lost.

Don't ever mind what I say. I am a great bosher, and full of fancies that interest me. Only these are my speculations over the two drawings.[2] I think I prefer the Sphinx one. And then, when it comes to the actual *head*, in both cases, one is dissatisfied. It is as if the head were not the inevitable consequence, the core and clinching point of the rest of the picture. They seem to me too fretful for the inevitability of the land which bears them. The more or less of wonder in the Sappho I liked better. Why is the body so often, with you, a strange mass of earth, and yet the head is so fretful? I should have thought your conception needed a little more of fate in the faces of your figures,[3] to be expressed: fate solid and inscrutable. But I know nothing about it. Only what have you done with your body, that your head seems so lost and lonely and dissatisfied.

My great religion is a belief in the blood, the flesh, as being wiser than the intellect. We can go wrong in our minds. But what our blood feels and believes and says, is always true. The intellect is only a bit and a bridle.[4] What do I care about knowledge. All I want is to answer to my blood, direct, without fribbling intervention of mind, or moral, or what not. I conceive a man's body as a kind of flame, like a candle flame forever upright and yet flowing: and the intellect is just the light that is shed onto the things around. And I am not so much concerned with the things around;– which is really mind: –but with the mystery of the flame forever flowing, coming God knows how from out of practically nowhere, and being *itself*, whatever there is around it, that it lights up. We have got so ridiculously mindful, that we never know that we ourselves are anything – we think there are only the

[1] Arnold Böcklin (1827–1901), Swiss painter.

[2] The 'Sphinx', which DHL preferred, was probably the drawing later incorporated in Collings's *Outlines. A Book of Drawings* (1914), p. 19. The second drawing was most likely that used as a frontispiece to *Sappho: The Queen of Song*.

[3] MS reads 'figure'.

[4] Psalms xxxii. 9.

objects we shine upon. And there the poor flame goes on burning ignored, to produce this light. And instead of chasing the mystery in the fugitive, half lighted things outside us, we ought to look at ourselves, and say 'My God, I am myself!' That is why I like to live in Italy. The people are so unconscious. They only feel and want: they don't know. We know too much. No, we only *think*[1] we know such a lot. A flame isn't a flame because it lights up two, or twenty objects on a table. It's a flame because it is itself. And we have forgotten ourselves. We are Hamlet without the Prince of Denmark.[2] We cannot *be*. 'To be or not to be' – it is the question with us now, by Jove.[3] And nearly every Englishman says 'Not to be.' So he goes in for Humanitarianism and such like forms of not-being. The real way of living is to answer to one's wants. Not 'I want to light up with my intelligence as many things as possible' – but 'For the living of my full flame – I want that liberty, I want that woman, I want that pound of peaches, I want to go to sleep, I want to go to the pub. and have a good time, I want to look a beastly swell today, I want to kiss that girl, I want to insult that man.' – Instead of that, all these wants, which are there whether-or-not, are utterly ignored, and we talk about some sort of ideas. – I'm like Carlyle, who, they say, wrote 50 vols. on the value of silence.[4] – Send me some drawings, if ever you have any quite to spare. – I liked your photograph, but it wasn't very much of a revelation of you. – I like immensely to hear about your art. Write me when you feel you can write a lot.

Yours D. H. Lawrence

540. To Arthur McLeod, 17 January 1913

Text: MS UT; Postmark, Bogliaco 17 1 13; Huxley 92–3.

'Villa Igéa', *Villa di Gargnano*, Lago di Garda (Brescia)
17 Jan. 1913

Dear Mac,

It's high time I wrote and thanked you for the notes and book. It's a delightful little Burns. And Henley was awfully good, but made me rather wild. Frieda and I have had high times, arguing over Andrew Lang and Henley and Lockhart.[5] As for the book, my novel on the subject, I wonder

[1] No, we only *think*] We want to get our

[2] Sir Walter Scott, *The Talisman* (1825), Introduction.

[3] *Hamlet*, III. i. 56.

[4] John Morley, 'Carlyle', *Critical Miscellanies* (1886), i. 135: 'The golden Gospel of Silence is effectively compressed in thirty fine volumes.'

[5] It is difficult precisely to identify the works referred to other than Lockhart's *Life* (cf. Letter 527). McLeod had possibly made 'notes' on W. E. Henley's biographical essay (*Poetry of Robert Burns*, ed. Henley and Henderson, Edinburgh, 1896, iv. 233–341, and available as

if I shall ever get it done. I have written 80 pages of a new novel: a most curious work, which gives me great joy to write, but which, I am afraid, will give most folk extreme annoyance to read; if it doesn't bore them.

We've got a theatre here, and last night I went to see *Amletto.*[1] Do you recognise our old friend? Now he was, really, the most amazing creature you can imagine: rather short, rather stout, with not much neck, and about forty years old: a bit after the Caruso[2] type of Italian: the Croton type.[3] I almost fell out of my little box trying to suppress my laughter. Because, being one of the chief persons in the audience, and of course the only Englishman, and ranking here as quite a swell – they acted particularly for me. I sat in my box No 8., and felt a bigger farce than the stage. Poor Amletto – when he came forward whispering – 'Essere – o non essere,'[4] I thought my ears would fall off. When the gravedigger holds up a skull and says 'Ecco, signore! Questo cranio è quel – –'[5] – I almost protested. Hamlet addressed as Signore! – No – it was too much. I saw *Ghosts* and gulped it down – it was rather good. I have seen a D'Annunzio play, and rather enjoyed it – fearful melodrama.[6] But they are only peasants, the players, and they play farces: and the queen is always the old servant woman, born for the part; and the King is always the contadino, or the weedy, weedy old father – also born for the part. And Hamlet is usually the villain in some 'amour' – and poor Amletto, if I hadn't known what it was all about, I should have thought he had murdered some madam 'à la Crippen'[7] and it was *her* father's ghost chasing him: whilst he dallied between a bad and murderous conscience, a slinking desire to avoid everybody, and a wicked hankering after 'Ofaylia' – that's what she sounds like. I am muddled.

It is nasty weather – a beastly wind from the Po that has brought the snow right down the mountains, not many yards above us. I object. I came here for sunshine, and insist on having it.

a separately published essay, 1898); and had sent to DHL an edn of Burns's poems edited by Lang (*Selected Poems*, 1905). This would then be the 'delightful little Burns' (274pp. costing 1/6).

[1] For another account see 'Italian Studies III – The Theatre', *English Review*, xv. 227–34; see also 'The Theatre', in *Twilight in Italy*. The local actor-manager playing Hamlet was Enrico Persevalli.

[2] Enrico Caruso (1873–1921), celebrated tenor. Cf. *A Collier's Friday Night*, I: 'Caruso! Caruso! A great fat fellow – !'

[3] Croton, the eponym of Croton in Southern Italy. When using it DHL possibly had in mind the athlete Milo who lived at Croton and was famed for his extraordinary physical strength.

[4] *Hamlet* III. i. 56.

[5] Ibid V. ii. 198–9.

[6] *La Fiaccola sotto il Moggio* (*The Light under the Bushel*). See *English Review*, xv. 224–5.

[7] Hawley H. Crippen (1862–1910), convicted wife-poisoner, hanged on 23 November 1910 after a sensational trial.

I got the blues thinking of the future, so I left off and made some marmalade. It's amazing how it cheers one up to shred oranges or scrub the floor.

I'm wondering what I shall do at Easter. We shall probably be coming to England. Frieda expects to see her children then. You might scan the divorce columns and tell me if ever I appear as Co-respondent. W[eekley] talked of divorce, just before Christmas, but God knows how far he'll get with it. It would wear the heart out of a wheel-barrow trundle, as my father would say, this kind of business. Of course one mostly writes letters just when one is pippy. As a rule I'm very happy. There's always the hyaena of morality at the garden gate, and the real wolf at the end of the street. But simple faith is more than Norman blood, we are told.[1] The question is, how exactly am I going to manage. We shall probably be married this year. I can make, I should reckon £100 a year by novels: I can't live under £200 a year – not as things are. Am I going to try to get publisher's work – reading – in London – am I going to stay abroad and teach – am I going to come to England and get some sort of a teaching job? I leave it to the Lord, but I don't trust him quite implicitly. – But I would never return to a Davidson – never. – How interesting for you to think of moving with Philip.[2] You are so radically shy, that the thought of anything out of the old rut gives you the horrors. But you really should marry – it's worth it.

Did Harold Hobson send you the pictures all right? He's a lazy devil. If they've not come, drop him a p.c. to 3 Gayton Crescent, Hampstead, and ask him if he's posted them to the wrong address. Write me a letter soon: it is nice to feel ones folk in England. Tell F. Turner I'll write him soon.[3]

My love to everybody D. H. Lawrence

Frieda is reading the bible, and suddenly announces 'I rather like Christ'. It seems funny.

[1] Tennyson, 'Lady Clara Vere de Vere', vii.

[2] McLeod left Davidson Road School for Norbury Manor School when Smith also left on 1 April 1913.

[3] Francis W. Turner (1898–1975), a pupil at Davidson Road School (later deputy editor-in-chief of the Press Association News Agency). His twin brother Leonard James Turner (1898–1921) received a postcard (not extant) from DHL and it is likely that he also received one. (Information from the Turner family.)

541. To Edward Garnett, [20 January 1913]

Text: MS NYPL; PC v. Dorothy Boot Homes, Wilford; Postmark, Bogliaco 20 I 13; Huxley 95.

['Villa Igéa', *Villa di Gargnano*, Lago di Garda (Brescia)]
[20 January 1913]

I was fearfully anxious to write a Fore-word to *Sons and Lovers*, and this is what I did.[1] I am a fool – but it will amuse you.

I am glad you think my prospects so good. It is raining here. I wonder how that rheumatism of yours is. I'll write immediately.

Did Harold give you all your books back?[2] DHL

542. To Katherine Mansfield, 26 January 1913

Text: MS NYPL; Moore 181.

'Villa Igéa', *Villa di Gargnano*, Lago di Garda (Brescia)
26 Jan 1913

Dear Miss Mansfield,[3]

I can't send you a story from here, not at once, because I haven't one. But *The Forum* is publishing one either in March or February – I am not sure – called 'The Soiled Rose' – a sickly title, but not a bad story, I think. If it were for March, might you not publish simultaneously? Ask Edward Garnett, will you – he got the *Forum* man to take that story for me. You will find him at Hampstead – 4 Downshire Hill. And if 'The Soiled Rose' is no go, because of the *Forum*'s publishing, ask Mr Garnett to give you another of my stories. And if nothing satisfactory comes to hand, I shall be writing a short tale before many days are out, and I'll send it to you. But ask Edward Garnett for something of mine. I have neither house nor hole, so I left most of my MS. at his place in Limpsfield.

I am as poor as a church mouse, so feel quite grand giving something away. – Oh but I make two conditions – First, that you send me a copy of *Rhythm*, for I've never seen your publication, only somebody said you wrote nasty things about *The Trespasser*;[4] and second, that you

[1] Huxley printed the Foreword with this postcard. It was not, however, sent with this (franked) card and is therefore not printed here.

[2] Cf. Letter 528.

[3] Pseudonym for Kathleen Beauchamp (1888–1923), New Zealand short-story writer. Came to London, 1908. m. George Bowden 1909; divorced 1918. With John Middleton Murry edited *Rhythm*, Summer 1911 – March 1913; they married 1918. Author of *In a German Pension* [1911], *Bliss, and Other Stories* (1920) etc.

[4] DHL's novel was reviewed by 'F.G.' (F. Goodyear) in *Rhythm*, ii (November 1912), 278: '...the story simply doesn't matter; the characters don't even matter. What is important is the curious mood of passion exhibited by Siegmund and Helena on their holiday. ...the

let me have something interesting to review for March[1] – German if you like.

I shall probably be in London at the end of March – immediately after Easter – and then, if your tea-kettle is still hot, I shall be glad to ask you for the cup you offered me.

Yours Sincerely D. H. Lawrence

543. To May Holbrook, [31 January 1913]

Text: MS UN; Postmark, Bogliaco 31 I 13; Nehls, iii. 627.

['Villa Igéa', *Villa di Gargnano*, Lago di Garda (Brescia)]
[31 January 1913]

[. . . . .[2] Now this is positively the last word I am going to say about the whole matter. I swear hereafter to keep out of the pulpit. But I only preach because it] affects me about you.

If you had 24 bob a week, what *would* you do? Oh God, it is a purposeless generation.

I wish you were here. We have a box at the theatre – no it's not like Teddy Rayners[3] – and we see Amleto – who is Hamlet with an Eyetalian hat on – and we nearly die. The men and women are faithful in marriage, on the whole – but they have tribes of children. The butcher said to his wife one night 'You *were* going to have an infant, weren't you?' ['Yes, you dolt', she said. 'I had it this morning. There it is in the cradle.' And she went out to fetch some charcoal in. They are a spunky lot, and no soul or intellect. It's an awful relief to live among them. The theatre is quite grand. On Sunday all the men get blind drunk. I go to a pub in Bogliaco sometimes. It's a rum shop. There's a great open fireplace, about level with your knees, for the guests of honor. So I sit on one with my feet near the fire. And raised up above the company I drink my Vermouth. And now and then the girl comes] to blow up the fire with a great long blow-pipe of iron, the earliest form of

tone is very curious, almost indescribable, and on the whole unsatisfactory. There is something neurotic in the oscillations of the lovers' emotions. ...The book then becomes a study in morbid psychology, and as such is written from an unjustifiable point of view. The sympathy is not that of a rich healthy temperament; it is the compassionate fellow-feeling of kindred weakness.'

[1] 'The Georgian Renaissance', DHL's review of *Georgian Poetry 1911–1912*, appeared in *Rhythm*, March 1913.

[2] Pages 1 and 3 of MS are presumed lost. Passages within the square brackets are taken from Nehls.

[3] Edward Rayner whose travelling (largely family) theatrical troupe dominated the Midland circuit c. 1905–30. 'Rayner's Star Theatre' toured from Belper and Nottingham to Birmingham. (See also Nehls, iii. 746 n. 90.)

bellows. Then I talk to the draper, and learn to play cards with the most awful ugly Neapolitan cards you ever saw – And one man has been in South America, and another talks German, and when they are a bit tipsy their eyes blaze. But they are gentle and awfully nice. They drink new wine – ghastly stuff. One can also get hot punch. I wish you were here – I do, with all my heart. We have an enormous flat to ourselves – and could put up a regiment. I have got wine and brandy, and the stove going, and a great room, and devil a fellow to drink with. It's sad.

I'm not going to settle down. I shall be in England sometime in spring. Then I shall come abroad again for the winter. There's nothing like keeping on the move. I love Italy, and want to go south to Naples. I love these people. They haven't learnt not to be themselves yet. Let me hear what you are going to do. We'd better stick together.

Yours – also to a cinder[1] (it's an oath) D. H. Lawrence

544. To Edward Garnett, 1 February 1913

Text: MS NYPL; Postmark, Bogliaco 1 2 13; Huxley 103–6.

Villa Igéa, Villa di Gargnano, Lago di Garda (Brescia)
1 Febbraio 1913

Dear Garnett,

The three plays – 'Fight for Barbara', 'Married Man', and 'Merry go Round', came this morning. Thanks for them. Frieda is reading them, and will put me through the mill because of them, in a little while.

I believe that, just as an audience was found in Russia for Tchekhov, so an audience might be found in England for some of my stuff, if there were a man to whip 'em in. It's the producer that is lacking, not the audience. I'm sure we are sick of the rather bony, bloodless drama we get nowadays – it is time for a reaction against Shaw and Galsworthy and Barker and Irishy (except Synge) people – the rule and measure mathematical folk. But you are of them and your sympathies are with your own generation, not with mine. I think it is inevitable. You are about the only man who is willing to let a new generation come in. It will seem a bit rough to me, when I am 45, and must see myself and my tradition supplanted. I shall bear it very badly. Damn my impudence, but don't dislike me. But I don't want to write like Galsworthy nor Ibsen, nor Strindberg nor any of them, *not* even if I could. We have to hate our immediate predecessors, to get free from their authority.

[1] i.e. till death.

But Lord, I can't be sententious and keep my dignity.

I don't want neither a Foreword nor a Discriptive notice *publishing* to *Sons and Lovers*. I wanted to *write* a Foreword, not to have one printed.[1] You can easily understand. I am fearfully satisfied with myself as it is, and I would die of shame if that Foreword were printed. [Frieda Weekley interjects: We fought over it.]

You are very comforting about my monetary prospects. But coming of hand-to-mouth poor folk, I never believe in any money that is not in my pocket. Still, I hope one day to be quite, quite rich, and then I shall establish a[2] Little Lord Fauntleroy system, where everything goes so well.[3] That is my dream.

About the book of poems:[4] I want to see it – but I'll enclose a list of addresses. It seems awful cheek to me, but you told me I might.

There are more short stories somewhere – four, for instance, that the *English Review* has published,[5] and still more in MS. I must think them up. Are you cross with me for telling Katherine Mansfield she could have a story for *Rhythm*, for nothing? I wanted to do it. But if you disapprove, then I won't promise any more. You will have heard from her, perhaps.[6] I thought, if the *Forum* were not up to scratch – as I don't suppose they will be – she could have their story 'The Soiled Rose', and publish simultaneously. If not – she might have another – just as you think best – but I should want to revise it, in that case.

About coming to England – Frieda is determined to come at Easter, but we have as yet heard nothing, neither of the divorce, nor of the children, whether she is to have them or not. We shall come to the Cearne. It is the only place in England open to the pair of us. Perhaps you will have us for a week or two, till we can find another place. Don't you think I could get some publisher's reading, or reviewing, to do, when I am in England. I should

[1] See Letter 541.

[2] establish a] establish quite a

[3] In the children's story, *Little Lord Fauntleroy* (1886) by Frances Hodgson Burnett (1849–1924), the hero (Cedric Errol) achieves social and financial eminence with seeming inevitability.

[4] *Love Poems and Others.*

[5] 'Goose Fair', 'Odour of Chrysanthemums', 'A Fragment of Stained Glass', 'Second Best'.

[6] Garnett may have received the undated letter (MS NYPL) from Mansfield:

Dear Sir,

Here it is Im sorry. I explained to Mr Lawrence that we dont pay: I made it quite clear –

Sincerely
K M

(© 1979 Estate of Katherine Mansfield.)

feel then that I *earned* something. The money one gets from novels feels like the manna which falls from the skies.[1] And I'll bet, every morning the Israelites looked out of their tent doors and held their breath, for fear nothing had fallen. I think Frieda and I might get a cottage somewhere. If I had work in London, it would have to be near London. Otherwise, we might take some little furnished cottage at the sea-side for six months. One can get those places fairly easily, I think. I think the divorce is going. Then later we can marry. Perhaps next winter we can come back to Italy. It all depends how the money goes. At any rate, if Duckworth gives me £100 for *Sons and Lovers*,[2] I shall have enough to carry me through September or October. But I don't want him to be creditor to me. I don't want to owe him money. I could get some teaching work if nothing were forthcoming. Will the *Trespasser* bring any more than the £50 I have had, or not?[3] I have got enough money, I think, to bring us to England at Easter – with a little care. Then I must ask Duckworth for some.

I have done 100 pages of a novel.[4] I think you will hate it, but I think, when it is re-written, it might find a good public among the Meredithy public. It is quite different in manner from my other stuff – far less visualised. It is what I *can* write just now, and write with pleasure, so write it I must, however you may grumble. And it is good too. I think, do you know, I have inside me a sort of answer to the *want* of today: to the real, deep want of the English people, not to just what they fancy they want. And gradually, I shall get my hold on them. And this novel is perhaps not such good art, but it is what they want, need, more or less. But I needn't talk about it, when only 106 pages are written.

They call the last three days in January the days of La Merla – the Blackbird – and they are supposed to be the worst three days in the year. They have been. Their Merla sang a true tune this time. But it is sunny again today.

I should think you find me a bit of a burden on your hands. It seems queer, that you do it and get no profit. I should think you've forgotten the Yorkshire proverb 'An' if tha does owt for nowt, do it for thysen.'[5]

Tell Bunny we will write to him. I know he gets all news of us from you – and there is not much to tell.

Yours Sincerely D. H. Lawrence

[1] Exodus xvi. 14–35.
[2] See p. 482 n. 1.
[3] See p. 448 n. 1 and Letter 498.
[4] 'The Insurrection of Miss Houghton.'
[5] i.e. 'and if you do anything for nothing, do it for yourself.'

P.S. I liked *Elizabeth Betty and Bess* quite a lot, but I hated *Bernadine*. Frieda had quite a tender feeling for *Bernadine*, but didn't like *Elizabeth*. I thought[1] Miss Schofield very capable. – We are just quarrelling over *Salve*.[2] Frieda hates George Moore in it. It's a Tauchnitz.

[Frieda Weekley begins]

I am not interested in his fleas and dont see why I should be and *so* superficial, bony Irishmen, I *hate* that Celtic pretence of poetry, it's *sham* not even a *garment*, the sounding brass, own trumpet blowers!

545. To Arthur McLeod, [5 February 1913]

Text: MS UT; PC v. Panorama di Tignale (Lago di Garda); Postmark, Bogliaco 5 2 13; Huxley 103.

['Villa Igéa', *Villa di Gargnano*, Lago di Garda (Brescia)]
[5 February 1913]

Thanks again for the books. It so happens Katherine Mansfield sent me *Rhythm* at the same time. You'll see some of my work in next month's, I believe. The poems are due the first week in March. You know what procrastinators publishers are. I am doing proofs of *Sons and Lovers*; – it is a great novel, but I hope it won't bring the ceiling down on my head. Now again I am not sure when I shall come back. England looks cold and inhospitable towards me. I might be here another year – in Italy, not here. You *should* come. The theatre has gone, alas.[3] Send me now and again a newspaper, will you. This is a good view of the lake villages – all like this, those high up.

Love. DHL

Tell me about Philip's new school, and Rice[4] – what of him. There is lots of news. Send it me quick. How is your health this winter?

Une bonne poignée DHL

[1] MS reads 'though'.

[2] Volume two of George Moore's autobiography (October 1912). On Frieda's reference to 'fleas' in her postscript, see *Salve*, p. 7 for Moore's account of his being bitten by a 'most ferocious flea'.

[3] 'Carnival ends on the 5th of February' ('Italian Studies III – The Theatre', *English Review*, xv. 225).

[4] F. C. Rice, teacher at Winterbourne School, Norbury. Assistant Inspector of Schools, Croydon, from 1903 (and probably known in this capacity to DHL and McLeod); on 1 March 1913 was appointed Inspector of Schools in Cheshire.

546. To Arthur McLeod, [8 February 1913]

Text: MS UT; PC v. Max von Poosch pinx. Bauernliebe: L'amour aux champs; Postmark, Gargnano 8 2 13; Unpublished.

['Villa Igéa', *Villa di Gargnano*, Lago di Garda (Brescia)]
[8 February 1913]

I asked Duckworth to send you a couple of copies of the poems – when they come, will you give one to Miss Mason, with my love, and keep one for yourself, with the same.[1] I am correcting proofs of *Sons and Lovers* – it gives me the blues. I suppose it will be out in a month or so. It is possible I may be in England about Easter – but I don't know, so don't say anything. At any rate, I should see you then. You wouldn't come out here at Easter, if we were staying, would you? It would be ripping.

Yrs D. H. Lawrence

547. To Else Jaffe, 10 February 1913

Text: MS Jeffrey; Frieda Lawrence 81–3.

Villa Igéa, *Villa di Gargnano*, Lago di Garda (Brescia)
10 Feb. 1913

Dear Else,

You don't expect me to stop here, gaping like a fish out of water, while Frieda goes careering and carousing off to München, do you? Je vous en veux.

About the article – Frieda is a nameless duffer at telling anything – the *English Review*, – a shilling monthly, supposed to be advanced and clever – asked me to write an article on modern German poetry – about 3000 words. It is the modern, new stuff they want to hear about – say that which is published in the last ten years – such people as Dehmel, and Liliencron, Stefan George, Ricarda Huch, Elsa Laska Schule.[2] Haven't you got a strong opinion about modern German poetry – pottery, as father calls it–? Well, do write what you think – say Dehmel is ranty and tawdry, if you like, but don't be too classical. If you like, the *English Review* will listen with great respect to dithyrambs on beautiful printing and fine form in book issuing. It will adore tendenz, and influences. And for Heaven's sake, put in plenty of little poems or verses as examples. –It would be rather a cute idea to write about:

[1] In McLeod's copy of *Love Poems* DHL wrote later: 'Remembering the unhappy days and the happy playtimes at Davidson when I solaced myself with his appreciation of some of these miserable poems' (Nehls, i. 90).

[2] Respectively: Richard Dehmel (1863–1920), poet and playwright; Detlev von Lilliencron (1844–1909), poet and novelist; Stefan George (1868–1933), poet; Ricarda Huch (1864–1947), historical novelist and poet; Else Lasker-Schüler (1876–1945), poet and playwright.

'The Woman-Poets of the Germany of Today.'

or 'The Woman-Poets of Germany Today.'

It would fetch the *English Review* readers like pigeons to salt. And surely *Die Frau*[1] has got articles on the subject. I should love doing it myself, if I knew enough about it. [Frieda Weekley interjects: Frechheit, er weiß *nichts*] Nicht wahr[2] – I have reviewed, in England, *two* anthologies of modern German poetry.[3] *Do* write about the women – their aims and ideals – and a bit about them personally, any you know – and how they'd rather paint pictures than nurse children, because any motherly body can do the latter, while it needs a fine and wonderful woman to speak a message. Didn't somebody tell you that? Did she have red hair? Put it all in.

'The Woman-Poets of Germany Today.'

It sounds lovely. Do write it in German – I can read your letters quite easily, because you don't write in gothic hieroglyph.

It is beautiful weather here. We are finding the first violets. There are bunches of primroses everywhere, and Leber Blumen,[4] lovely little blue things, and lilac-coloured crocuses. You must come – you would love it, and we should feel quite grand having you for visitor.

Mrs Kipping[5] has written,[6] forwarding a lawyers letter which was sent to Ernst,[7] and which says 'We should advise Professor Weekley to refer Mrs Weekley to the Court, pending the divorce proceedings. Any request she has to make concerning the children, should be made to the Court.'[8] That of course necessitates the engaging of a solicitor. Frieda says, it is too long to let the children wait another six months without seeing her – they would become too much estranged. Perhaps that is true. Heaven knows how we're going to untangle these knots. At any rate, the divorce is going forward; in England, after the first hearing, the judge pronounces a decree *nisi* – that is, the divorce is granted *unless* something turns up; then at the end of the six months the divorce is made *absolute*, if nothing has turned up. Then Frieda is free again. Till the divorce is absolute, Ernst must have nothing to do with Frieda. So arrangements should be made through lawyers. But the children have holidays only at Easter, and can anything be settled before then. We shall have to see. This is to put you au courant. – Send that 'wonderful' book,

[1] A periodical published in Berlin (1893–1925).

[2] 'What check, he doesn't know *anything*.' 'Not true.'

[3] See p. 324 n. 6 and p. 331 n. 1.

[4] 'Liverwort' ['Leberblümchen'].

[5] Lily Kipping (1867–1949) and her husband Frederic S. Kipping (1863–1949), FRS, Professor of Chemistry, University College, Nottingham, were close friends of the Weekleys.

[6] Mrs Kipping has written] Ernst has written – if Frieda

[7] Ernst] him

[8] See p. 516 n. 7.

do. The 60 francs[1] have come. Frieda is sending a picture that I want to have framed for Prof. Weber at Icking, but she says it is for you.

– And a thousand thanks – D. H. Lawrence

548. To David Garnett, 18 February 1913

Text: MS NYPL; Huxley 106–7.

Villa Igéa, *Villa di Gargnano*, Lago di Garda (Brescia)
18 Feb. 1913.

My dear Bunny,

It's a beastly shame we don't write to you. But you read your father's letters from us, don't you. And I'm sure they're enough, you won't want any more.

I am glad not to be coming to England just yet. It is funny how I dread my native land. But here it is so free. The tightness of England is horrid.

The spring is here – primroses and violets in profusion, and beautiful tufts of heather. F[rieda] and I went to Campione on Sunday – about 10 miles up the lake. It's a queer place – just a flat strip of land at[2] the foot of great cliffs, and then cotton mills, and workmens dwellings – all perfectly isolated, on a little ledge that the lake washes. Well, having got into Campione, we couldn't get out. I wanted to find a road, but Frieda rushed to the first man, and asked him. He turned out to be fearfully drunk, and said he would guide us over the gallery. We went a little way – the gallery is quite a fantastic path that climbs the gorge, under a great spurt of water. Well, I wanted to send him back, because we could go by ourselves, and being so drunk, he was winking at Frieda over my shoulder. She was terrified. He wouldn't think of returning. I had an altercation with him, and he threatened to throw me into the stream – all this on the steps of the gallery, like flies on the side of a wall. We retreated – he was furious. And the dialect they speak is quite unintelligible to me. At last I got some youths to hang on to him whilst we mounted the gallery. There were ropes of ice where the stream leaps over the path. Then one must go through tunnels, on boards laid over the stream, the water running just below ones feet, the rock about neck-high, and beastly dark. It took us an hour and a half, hard going, to climb out of Campione. Then we were among the snow, fearfully wild. And these deserted Italian villages stand so like rubble of rocks between the hills. The old maize stalks shook in an icy wind above a snow-field that gleamed like silver. It is pretty.

In Gardola di Tignale – the next village – the brass band was playing for a major returned from Tripoli, and he was standing in his doorway while

[1] 60 francs] 90 lire

[2] MS reads 'a'.

the band brayed in his honor on his doorstep. – The landlord of the inn[1] was an awfully jolly old sport. The inns are the living room of the family – dogs, babies, boiling pots, villains, and great open chimneys in which one sits. The hearth is raised about 3 ft, so one sits in a high, high chair – a chair on stilts – with ones feet near the ashes, and drinks moscato – Asti Spumanti I think it's called – or muscadine – lovely white fizzy wine – at a lire per litro – quite a lot for fivepence, 3 or 4 tumblerfuls.

If we are here, could you come for the Easter vacation? Fancy, I might be alone. You could come 3rd quite cheaply, I should think. You would adore this country.

How goes work? Have you seen Harold lately. I must write him. But I expected to hear again from him.

How's your heart? – Still fluttering round a microscope?

Send me a book to read, will you – a 4½d that doesn't matter.

It is Easter in a month – good Lord! And so from hour to hour we ripe and ripe.[2] – Write and say something nice to us. 'What rhubarb, senna, or what purgative drug – etc.'[3]

The theatre has gone, much to my sorrow.

But goodbye – viele herzliche Grüssen.[4] D. H. Lawrence

549. To Edward Garnett, [18 February 1913]

Text: MS NYPL; Heilbrun 151–3.

['Villa Igéa', *Villa di Gargnano*, Lago di Garda (Brescia)]
18 Feb.

Dear Garnett,

Do you know a lawyer you co[uld][5] send us to about this matter of Frieda's.[6] Professor W[eekley] says, pending the proceedings, all application from the mother, to see the children, must be made through the court.[7] Of course we don't know what court or anything. Then there is the matter of Frieda's having any legal right to the children after the divorce. Do you know anything about that? She ought, I suppose, to be represented when the case

[1] MS reads 'in'.

[2] *As You Like It* II. vii. 26.

[3] *Macbeth* V. iii. 55.

[4] 'many kind regards.'

[5] MS torn.

[6] Garnett recommended his brother, Robert Singleton Garnett (1866–1932), senior partner of Darley Cumberland and Co.

[7] The court concerned was the High Court, Probate, Divorce and Admiralty Division. There is no record that Frieda applied to see her children pending the divorce proceedings. Ernest Weekley, on 28 July 1913, applied to the President of the Court, Sir Samuel T. Evans, for an order giving him custody of the children and restraining Frieda from attempting to interfere with them. It was granted.

comes on, and the request made for her share in the children.[1] Can you tell me anything about it, and what to do?

We shall not come to England until it is necessary. You see unless Frieda can see the children at the Easter vacation, it will have to be deferred, her meeting them, until the long vacation, in August. Since the divorce comes on immediately after Easter, and since it will take six months, I suppose, we should at any rate be in England in the autumn to get married. I don't see, if I have no work to do in my own, my native land,[2] why I should disgrace it with my presence. I shall continue to live in Italy for a bit, I think.

Thanks so much for offering us the Cearne. What we should do without you God knows: feed the gloomy cypresses instead of your apple trees, as Frieda suggests. But it is devilish hard. And when two people are alone as we are, almost absolutely [ ] in England [ ] Frieda [ ] you, [ ] [?w]as so miserable [ ] that I feel you. [ ] [qui]te eased if you see a cloud [?oth]er than your own. Though ours is a [?sor]t of thunder cloud that burst and leaves off for a while. We gather strength from the Captain Scott.[3] And somehow, translating him from Italian newspapers makes him more poignant.

It always frightens me how life gets reduced down and down to fewer elements the further one goes: Captain Scott had cold, hunger, and death. I've got love – which is Frieda – and the care because of providing for us to live – and nothing more. All the rest has become accessory, after these six months here alone. I don't want to come to England.

I corrected and returned the first batch of *Sons and Lovers*. It goes well, in print, don't you think? Don't you think I get people into my grip? You did the pruning jolly well, and I am grateful. I hope you'll live a long long time, to barber up my novels for me before they're published. I wish I weren't so profuse – or prolix, or whatever it is. But I shall get better.

This new novel is going quite fast.[4] It is awfully exciting, thrilling, to my mind – a bit outspoken, perhaps. I shall write it as long as I like to start with, then write it smaller. I must always write my books twice.

I want my book of poems to come, for a comfort.

[1] At the divorce hearing, 18 October 1913, she was not represented. Ernest Weekley was given custody of the children; Frieda did not apply for (and would probably not have been allowed) access to them.

[2] Sir Walter Scott, *The Lay of the Last Minstrel* (1805), VI. i. 3.

[3] Captain Robert (Falcon) Scott (1868–1912), Antarctic explorer. News of his death on the expedition to the South Pole did not reach Europe until February 1913 (when the search party returned to New Zealand).

[4] 'The Insurrection of Miss Houghton'.

No, I had no agreement for *Sons and Lovers* from Duckworth.[1] As far as that goes I've never had an agreement for the *Trespasser*.

Violets are out here. It is wonderful country. Why won't you come? I shrink rather from imposing so much on you – Frieda and me.

I hope to God I shall be able to make a living – but there, one must.

a rivederla D. H. Lawrence

550. To Ernest Collings, 24 February 1913

Text: MS UT; Huxley 107–9.

Villa Igéa, *Villa di Gargnano*, Lago di Garda (Brescia)
24 Feb. 1913

Dear Collings,

It is quite a long time since I got your letter and the drawings. I do like them immensely. I think my favorite is 'the beauty of the summer morning'.[2] That I think is quite lovely, with its sense of sunshine and atmosphere. I think after all you care more for landscape than for figure, and are much more of a poet than a dramatist. I do think you ought to have come here this spring: it is a perfect place for you, would rejoice you: the cypresses, the olives, the great high rocks and gorgeous contours. And who has ever done the lovely glimmer of olive trees in black, and white – or in colour. You would adore them. And then the lake is blue like nothing else. We may be here still another couple of months – though I am not sure. But if we are, couldn't you squeeze a fortnight here. You should – it would mean a lot to you. We are poor as mice, but have heaps of room, and are glad of a visitor. Carpe diem. I am not sure that I can get used to your straight trunks of pillars – like the one where the bicycle is just disappearing.[3] Somehow or other, when your big figure comes in, – the idol or the satyr or the sphinx – you seem to lose your magic joyful effect. It is as if, in your figures, you become didactic, while in the landscape you are lyrical. There's never the same free grace and joy about your figures, as about your trees. You bother too much about them – are too laborious and effortful with them – you think them too important. – Do tell me if I'm wrong. I think that satyr in the bicycle picture is bossy and stupid. He tries to boss the atmosphere, instead of revealing it in a big glint.

How do you work? Do you start with the idea of the satyr and the bicycle, and moonshine, and develop the rest? But your satyr ought to come out of your moon – your bit of a bicycle does.

[1] Cf. p. 482 n. 1.

[2] Published in *Outlines: A book of drawings*, p. 39, under the title 'Summer'; dated 1910.

[3] Not in *Outlines*; perhaps unpublished.

In the picture that looks like March, where the man is offering fruits, there is rather a delicious feeling of weather, but again the same uneasiness remains, as if you hadn't hit the thing dead certain, not left the picture with the finality one wants.[1] I know how hard it is. One needs something to make one's mood deep and sincere. There are so many little frets that prevent our coming at the real naked essence of our vision. It sounds boshy, doesn't it. I often think one ought to be able to pray, before one works – and then leave it to the Lord. Isn't it hard, hard work to come to real grips with one's imagination – throw everything overboard. I always feel as if I stood naked for the fire of Almighty God to go through me – and it's rather an awful feeling. One has to be so terribly religious, to be an artist. I often think of my dear Saint Lawrence on his gridiron, when he said 'Turn me over, brothers, I am done enough on this side.'

I like 'wide open spaces'[2] – and the Pavlova cover is a treat.[3] Now there I feel you've hit it jolly well. It made me want to design a cover for my next book of poems. By the way, I asked the publishers to send you a copy of my *Love Poems and Others*. Have they done so? If not, I'll send you one from here.

My next book of poems will be a book of Elegies. Sounds bad, doesn't it. If ever I bring it out, will you help me to design a cover?

You should find some of my stuff in March *Rhythm*. It's a daft paper, but the folk seem rather nice.

I am correcting proofs of my novel *Sons and Lovers*. It is by far the best thing I've done. It will be out in about a month.

I am fearfully keen to know what folk will say about my poems. Tell me your opinion when you can. Send me always any drawings you don't want to keep. It is ripping to feel one develops in one's work, don't you think.

Edward Garnett has just written and says the poems were sent off.

Yours D. H. Lawrence

551. To Edward Garnett, [25 February 1913]

Text: MS NYPL; PC; Postmark, Gargnano 26 2 13; Huxley 109–10.

Gargnano –
Tuesday

Dear Garnett,

Thanks again for your letter. Did you not get mine in answer to yours

[1] 'Idol', *Outlines*, p. 35.

[2] 'Open Country', *Outlines*, p. 31.

[3] Collings designed the cover for *Poems to Pavlova* by A. Tulloch Cull (published November 1912, by Herbert Jenkins, Haymarket).

of the 11th? I posted it to Hampstead. The 6 books of poetry came – jolly good of the publisher to send them. I think it looks *awfully* nice, and am in love with it – wonder if it'll do anything.

The last proofs of *Sons and Lovers* come today. I admire my own work a good deal. You did well in the cutting – thanks again. Shall you put in the dedication 'To my friend, Edward Garnett' – or just 'To Edward Garnett' or what?[1]

You are awfully good about the Cearne. But I don't want us to bother you if we can help it. Nothing is certain – except the torment of the present. I shall let you know as soon as there is anything.

I am so anxious to know how the poems will be received. You'll send me some cuttings. – I wonder when I shall see you.

a rivederla D. H. Lawrence

552. To David Garnett, 27 February 1913

Text: MS NYPL & TMSC Garnett D.; Postmark, Bogliaco 28 2 13; Unpublished.

Villa Igéa, Villa di Gargnano, Lago di Garda, Brescia
27 Feb 1913

Dear Bunny,

Frieda and I were discussing your letter when the wire came. If 'Tony' is coming, I hope you'll let me know in time to meet her, at Desenzano, or somewhere.[2]

We think it would be better if she slept at the Hôtel and lived with us, ate with us. The padrona of the 'Cervo' is our friend, awfully nice[3] – and a German – and loves us dearly. It would not cost much, a bed – about 1.50 per night for the two[4] – and we found, to our disgust, we had to pay a lire a night for Harold's single-bedded room, which we took extra – we have no bedding.

We know of rooms in Bogliaco and one or two places, and shall be sure to fix up something decent. We may be here six weeks[5] longer. And then, if she would rather move to München, it's not far.

[1] See p. 477 n. 4.

[2] Antonia Almgrem, née Cyriax (1881–1927), artist. March 1906 m. Per Johan Hugo Almgrem when both were art students in Sweden; separated late 1912. Friend of David Garnett: see *The Golden Echo*, p. 226–7 ('Mrs Anthony' or 'Anthonius' was her pseudonym adopted on separating from Almgrem and in the, perhaps paranoid, belief that he was pursuing her). Under the name Tony Cyriax, she published *Among Italian Peasants* (1919), with her own water-colours of Gargnano and San Gaudenzio.

[3] Cf. Letter 510. (Signora Samuelli, re-named Castelli, appears in *Among Italian Peasants.*)

[4] Antonia Almgrem was accompanied by her daughter Gisela (b. 1909).

[5] six weeks] two months

We shall be awfully pleased to have a friend here too. But I am afraid the place is so lonely, if we leave, and after May, so hot. But all those things we can discuss with Mrs Alengrun – (is that it?). And Italy is not cheap, really. Meat and butter and things are so dear. But that isn't much. If one can get good, cheap, healthy nice housing, and knows the language, one can manage.

We must wait to see exactly how our affairs develop. At any rate, Gargnano is too hot by June – though there are lovely villages just above in the mountains. We must see.

We shall do our best for your friend, you know that.

Love D. H. Lawrence

[Frieda Weekley begins][1]

Dear Bunny,

It will be so nice for us to have Mrs 'Tony' as I only know her. We are always just us two and we live so hard on each other one day like the lions that ate each other, there will be nothing but two tails left. We will do what we can for her, and if we go away from here, I think she might be *too* lonely, then I suggest *München* to her where I am sure my brother-in-law[2] would do what he could for her – and she ought to have people – Poor Harold, yes I hope he and Lola will hit it off.[3] Don't you talk like that about women, one day your turn will come and I bet you will have a decent try, women are not like the tooth-ache, though you would have us so and if women are undecided, what about men? But I shall be interested what you do – I wonder if you read my last wild letter to your father, I do feel like bursting sometimes about the children, Lawrence is in a state of utter misery then and I can't help it much – Rejoicing on the one hand like *anything* that he cares so much on the other the children and the misery of it. I am coming to England anyhow, if I can have the children alone, if Ernst wont let me have them, L and I will both come so that I can see them on the sly – It will be nice to see you! You have only seemed to be fond of L. lately not a bit of me, and I don't think it's nice!

Auf wiedersehen Frieda

[1] The contents of Frieda's letter (which exists only in the form of a typed copy) suggest that it was enclosed with DHL's.

[2] Edgar Jaffe.

[3] Lola Ertel (b. 1890?), daughter of close Russian friends of the Garnetts. Hobson met her, summer 1912, at the Cearne and fell in love; he accompanied the Ertel family when they returned to Russia. (It was on his return from Russia that he joined David Garnett, DHL and Frieda at Mayrhofen.) See David Garnett, *The Golden Echo*, pp. 77–8, 240.

553. To Edward Garnett, 3 March 1913

Text: MS NYPL; Postmark, Gargnano 3 3 13; Huxley 110–11.

Villa Igéa, *Villa di Gargnano*, Lago di Garda (Brescia)
3 March 1913

Dear Garnett,

Frieda thanks you for the address of your brother, and she will write to him.[1] I liked the American reviews – those that weren't screamingly funny understood quite well. It is true, I liked the look of the poetry book immensely – so did the people to whom it was sent. I think it is a good collection.[2] Those who won't be pleased by one thing should find another they like. Whereas De la Mare in his choice only wanted to please the exquisite folk.[3]

I'm glad you got the *Forum* cheque.[4] Send me two five-pound notes. I can't do anything with a cheque. I am coming to the end of my cash. Soon I shall have to ask Duckworth for something. I finished and returned all the proofs of *Sons and Lovers*. I suppose they came all right. It is rather a good novel – but if anything a bit difficult to grasp[5] as a whole, at first. Yet it *is* a unified whole, and I hate the dodge of putting a thick black line round the figures to throw out the composition – Which shows I'm a bit uneasy about it. – I'm very keen to know what the folk will say about the *Poems*.

We met Mrs A[nthony] in Salò. The wire came too late for us to get to Desenzano. She is still just a bit tired, but we shall get along like three bricks. When folks have all had a good few knocks under the jaw, they hang together better.

[1] Cf. p. 516 n. 6.

[2] Cf. David Garnett, *The Flowers of the Forest* (1955), p. 54: 'At Edward's request I had been responsible...for choosing the selection published in *Love Poems and Others*.'

[3] See Letters 487, 489 and 494.

[4] Mitchell Kennerley (1878–1950), American publisher, wrote to Edward Garnett, 15 February 1913 (MS NYPL):

Dear Mr Garnett:

I enclose herewith check for twelve pounds in payment for 'The Soiled Rose' by Mr D H Lawrence, which will appear in the March number of *The Forum*, now printing. I am sorry that it was unavoidably crowded out of the February number.

I enclose herewith duplicate reviews of *The Trespasser* which I think will interest you and Mr Lawrence. I hope soon to hear from you about the manuscript of his new novel. I understood from your last letter that it was completed. The reception of *The Trespasser* has been such that I should like the opportunity of copyrighting the new book.

Did you receive a copy of my edition of *The Trespasser* which I mailed to you some weeks ago.

Yours faithfully

Later, on 30 June 1913 (MS NYPL), Kennerley said that in paying DHL $60 for his story, the *Forum* had 'strained a point' and exceeded the normal maximum of $50.

[5] grasp] grip

I've got a perfectly barren head, so don't mind my letter. There's one thing, Mrs A. can do my share of the housework, thank the Lord. I feel I've cooked cart-loads of food and scrubbed acres of dirty board. Now I'm fed.

The Nottingham people are still haffling and caffling about the children. Probably Frieda will get them before long. Till we know something definite we can say nothing about coming to England. But it's a shame to bother you at the Cearne.

I should think Masefield's masterpieces will do for a sort of heavy hors d'oeuvres – pickled herring, though not so good – to introduce my elegant dishes.[1] He's a horrible sentimentalist – the cheap Byron of the day – his stuff is *Lara* 1913.[2]

Mrs Anthony is just prodding the cauliflower with a fountain pen, to see if it's done. It explains the whole situation.

Do you know anything of Harold? We are quite anxious about him. You Garnetts' are like the spoons in a hell-broth of tragedy – you stir and stir.

Frieda sends love, along o' me. D. H. Lawrence

554. To Arthur McLeod, 5 March 1913

Text: MS UT; Postmark, Gargnano 5 3 1[...]; cited in *News Chronicle* 14 September 1957.

Villa Igéa, Villa di Gargnano, Lago di Garda (Brescia)
5 März 1913

Dear Mac,

I was glad to hear from you, and that you liked the poetry book. Tell me later how you like the new poems.

What times at Davidson! I love to think of Philip getting rid of that Young Man of[3] the Seas, Humphreys.[4] I love to think of Philip disapproving of your methods. You should go to him and say, in honied tones, 'By the way, Mr Smith, I believe you consider my methods underhand.' Do! Do put salt on the snail. He oozes so beautifully. You will owe him an undying dislike now, I know. I am the same myself. It's like when you've had a 'doubtful' egg. I am 'off' Philip for ever. – By the way, your letter made me dream again I had returned to Davidson. You must believe me when I say that is my *only* nightmare.

[1] The reference to John Masefield (1878–1967) is obscure. Possibly Edward Garnett and DHL were agreed in the view – later expressed by Ezra Pound in his review of *Love Poems and Others* in *New Freewoman*, 1 September 1913 (Draper 53) – that 'with the appearance of "Violets" and "Whether or Not" the Masefield boom may be declared officially and potentially over'.

[2] Byron's poem (1814).

[3] Young Man of] Old Man of

[4] Philip Smith, leaving Davidson Road School, with McLeod, Aylwin and Agnes Mason, would leave Humphreys behind.

So you won't have Rice's job.[1] I know it would be a bit of a nuisance – and you would have to face too many folk, for your comfort. I'd have done anything to get out of teaching. What's become of Rice, by the way? And you, and Aylwin, and Miss Mason are to move to the new school with Philip? – not Byrne nor anybody else? No, I don't want to come. Tell Philip I will when I'm starving.

I've sent in the proofs of *Sons and Lovers*. It is quite a great novel. It will be out in about three weeks, I guess.

Yesterday we had the notices of the divorce served on us. A mangy old gentleman insisted on seeing the Signor Lavrenchy, as they pronounce it –. He came in, bowed with a lovely grace and smile, and asked me if I was myself. Then he gave me a long paper, and I saw 'Co-respondent'. Then he made a lovely bow to F[rieda], presented her with a similar paper, saying with gusto 'per la signora'. – 'I am from the English Consul in Verona'[2] he said – I said 'Certainly – there is no need to reply?' He smiled and said 'No, signore – credo no.' I showed him the door. – It says in bald language I have '*habitually* committed adultery.' – What a nasty habit!

Do send me one or two books. Is *New Grub St* cheap?[3] Could you send me a Leonard Merrick?[4] Is *Clarissa Harlowe* done cheap?[5] Send me something fairly stodgy – not Zangwill, though – I hate him.[6] Would you like George Moore's *Salve*? It's not up to much, but I've got it in Tauchnitz if you'd like it. – *The New Machiavelli* isn't done at 7d yet? Oh, send me *White Fang*, for F. Mrs Wharton – *The House of Mirth* woman – is rather good. I've read all the 4½[d] Maxim Gorky's, I believe – I love short stories. But don't spend much, will you? – about two bob. You've got *Georgian Poetry*, or I'd have sent you my copy I had from *Rhythm*.

It is beautiful weather again. Oh, I don't want to come back to school – not even to England. Probably I shall be abroad the whole summer. – The *Forum* publishes a story just now. I haven't bothered much – I am too far away from England.

Write me longer letters – more gossipy – about people – will you? We are just having 'kid' for dinner – it seems so queer. We have got a visitor who

[1] As local Inspector of Schools, cf. p. 512 n. 4.

[2] In 1913 there was no British Consul in Verona. The Milan Consulate (Consul: Joseph H. Towsey) was responsible for Lombardy and Venetia (*Foreign Office List*, 1913).

[3] Gissing's novel (1891), re-issued June 1910 at 6d.

[4] Leonard Merrick (1864–1938), well-known minor novelist: *The House of Lynch* (1907), *The Position of Peggy Harper* (1911), etc.

[5] The only available edn of Richardson's novel was Mrs Humphry Ward's abridgement, 1899, at 2/-.

[6] Israel Zangwill (1864–1926), minor novelist.

has lived in Lapland – very interesting, she is. Tell Miss Mason I'll write to her. If you'd lend me the Gilbert Murray translations – not Aristophanes, the others – I should send them back *carefully*. They have a fearful fascination for me still.[1]

My new novel is a weird thing.[2] I rather love it. It is half written. If ever I can do anything for you, *do* tell me. Don't be so long before you write.

Love D. H. Lawrence

555. To Arthur McLeod, [10 March 1913]

Text: MS UT; PC v. Veduta Generale di Tignale (Lago di Garda); Postmark, Gargnano 10 3 13; Unpublished.

['Villa Igéa', *Villa di Gargnano*, Lago di Garda (Brescia)]
[10 March 1913]

Thanks awfully for the books. Take no notice of my later letter and request. How good Voynich is – awfully good.[3] Mrs Mann disappointed me – and Merrick seemed trivial.

What are you doing for Easter? I suppose there's no getting you out of England. Don't you bother to send me anything else, please. The view isn't a bad one, I reckon.

Love D. H. Lawrence

556. To Edward Garnett, 11 March 1913

Text: MS NYPL; Huxley 111–13.

Villa Igéa, Villa di Gargnano, Lago di Garda (Brescia)
11 March 1913

Dear Garnett,

I received the £10 in notes last night – many thanks.

We are most interested to hear of Miss Chambers MS.,[4] and Frieda is

[1] The famous series of translations, into 'English rhyming verse', of works by Euripides (1902–13); Sophocles, *Oedipus* (1910); and Aristophanes, *The Frogs* (1902). Jessie Chambers dates DHL's interest in Murray's translations from the Croydon period (E.T. 121): doubtless the classicist McLeod was the cause of his interest and continuing 'fascination'.

[2] 'The Insurrection of Miss Houghton.'

[3] Ethel L. Voynich (1864–1960), author of *The Gadfly* (1897; 1912). Cf. Letter 573.

[4] Jessie Chambers had been encouraged by Edward Garnett to continue with her autobiographical novel first called 'The Rathe Primrose' (c. 1910) and revised in early 1911 as 'Eunice Temple' (hence 'E.T.'). She had completed the MS and sent it to him. (A letter from her to Garnett (MS NYPL) shows that he had not acknowledged receipt as late as 24 July 1913.) Jessie told Helen Corke, [16 March 1913]: 'I always intended that [DHL] should see it. I feel it a matter of honour' (MS UN LaM 10).

more anxious to see it than I am. I think I will ask Jessie to send it along. I heard from her the other day in answer to the book of poems – a damned affected letter.[1] But there, it isn't so easy to write naturally to a quondam lover.

I am anxious down to my vitals about the poems. I thought my friends in the field – De la Mare and so on – would review them decently for me. God help us, I've got the pip horribly at present. I don't mind if Duckworth crosses out a hundred shady pages in *Sons and Lovers*. It's got to sell, I've got to live.

I am a damned curse unto myself. I've written rather more than half of a most fascinating (to me) novel. But nobody will ever dare to publish it. I feel I could knock my head against the wall. Yet I love and adore this new book. It's all crude as yet, like one of Tony's clumsy prehistorical beasts – most cumbersome and floundering – but I think it's great – so new, so really a stratum deeper than I think anybody has ever gone, in a novel. But there, you see, it's my latest. It is all analytical – quite unlike *Sons and Lovers*, not a bit visualised. But nobody will publish it. I wish I had never been born. But I'm going to stick at it, get it done, and then write another, shorter, absolutely impeccable – as far as morals go – novel.[2] It is an oath I have vowed – if I have to grind my teeth to stumps, I'll do it – or else what am I going to live on, and keep Frieda on withal. Don't you mind about this tirade.

I think we shall give this place up at the end of this month. Frieda wants to come to England. We might have Mrs Anthony's rooms, down in Ashdown Forest,[3] mightn't we – at least for a time. Then she would have our rent – at least, some of it – and be richer.

She is up at San Gaudenzio, perched on the brim of the mountains over the lake, in a farm-stead of olives and vines, a situation beautiful as a dream. We are going up there this afternoon. I don't think 30 Lire a month much for her room, do you. It's only 24/- a calendar month – and the folk *are* nice.

I have also got some friends who have a small grammar school in the Isle of Man, at Ramsey.[4] I'm sure I could get a bit of teaching there, and I think Ramsey wouldn't be a bad p[lace][5] to live in, for the summer.

We have written to your brother Robert Garnett.

Thank Bunny for his letters. He sounds a bit unhooked – manhood comes

[1] Jessie Chambers recalled: 'I was glad to receive the book, so I asked my sister for his address, and wrote, thanking him for it, and made a few remarks about the poems' (E.T. 219).

[2] This was to be 'The Sisters'.

[3] At Forest Row.

[4] See p. 139 n. 3.

[5] MS defaced.

hard to him, evidently. He's like me, I suppose. I had a devil of a time getting a bit weaned from my mother, at the age of 22. She suffered, and I suffered, and it seemed all for nothing, just waste cruelty. It's funny. I suppose it is the final breaking away to independence.

Forgive me if I am impertinent.

Ask Duckworth to send me £50, will you. That must take me on five months or so, and then if there's any more due, I can draw, and if there isn't, I must wait.

I had rather not come to England this summer. But it is a case of Frieda's children. We wouldn't trouble you at the Cearne for very long – at the most not more than a fortnight. Does it seem an imposition? We can do all our own work, get in food and cook. And we shouldn't come before about the middle of April.

It's very sunny and pretty. Frieda has gone boating on the lake with some Germans. I didn't want to go – have had a damned cold.

I wish somebody would give my poems a lift.

a rivederla D. H. Lawrence

I enclose Bunny an orchid. I find lovely flowers for him, and lose them again.

The novel is *not* about Frieda and me, nor about a Baroness neither.

557. To Jessie Chambers, [c. 13 March 1913]

Text: E.T. 219–20.

['Villa Igéa', *Villa di Gargnano*, Lago di Garda (Brescia)]
[c. 13 March 1913][1]

I think the little poetry book is all right...I'm sending you the proofs of the novel, I think you ought to see it before it's published. I heard from A[da] that you were in digs. again.[2] Send the novel on to her when you've done with it[3]...This last year hasn't been all roses for me. I've had my ups and downs out here with Frieda. But we mean to marry as soon as the divorce is through. We shall settle down quite quietly somewhere, probably in

[1] The letter is dated by reference to one written on a Sunday by Jessie Chambers telling Helen Corke that she was coming 'on Friday' to stay over Easter (MS UN LaM 10). Jessie Chambers' letter therefore originated on Sunday 16 March 1913. In it she remarks: 'Yesterday morning came the proofs of *Sons and Lovers* which makes no pleasant reading for me....' Thus DHL probably wrote to her on 13 March 1913.

[2] Ada had given the same news to Louie Burrows on 22 February 1913 (MS UN LaB 211): 'Jessie is in lodgings again I hear. She doesn't seem to get on at all with her people.' Helen Corke confirms this view of Jessie's unhappiness at home (*Croydon Years*, pp. 24–5).

[3] After glancing 'through some pages' Jessie Chambers at once 'reversed the wrapper and posted the proofs as Lawrence had directed' (E.T. 220–1).

Berkshire. Frieda and I discuss you endlessly. We should like you to come out to us some time, if you would care to. But we are leaving here in about a week, it's getting too hot for us, I mean the weather, not the place. I must leave off now, they're waiting for me.[1]

558. To Arthur McLeod, [15 March 1913]

Text: MS UT; PC; Postmark, Bogliaco 15 3 13; Unpublished.

Gargnano
Saturday

My dear Mac,

More books – but you make me feel ashamed. Don't do so much, please. I've had the *Morning Post* and *D[aily] N[ews]* on my *Poems.*[2] What do you think? The critics will never like me much. There is a story in the *Forum* (March). The novel is not fixed yet. Shall I send you *Salve*? I can get you Wells' *Marriage*[3] – or some poems – look in Miss Mason's Tauchnitz list, and tell me what you'd like. How near Easter is, for you. For me, it is all the same. Write me a nice long letter. Love D. H. Lawrence

559. To Ernest Collings, [22? March 1913]

Text: MS UT; Huxley 113–14.

Villa Igéa, Villa di Gargnano, Lago di Garda (Brescia)
Saturday[4]

My dear Collings,

Thanks very much for your letter and crits. It is awfully interesting to hear what various people say – and on the whole, I agree with you. The book is not going to be received very well, I'm sorry to say.

But I want you to do something for me. Garnett must be mad. In an off-hand sort of fashion he demands that *I* shall design a thing for the wrapper of my new novel *Sons and Lovers.* It seems preposterous. He asks for something suggesting the collieries – headstocks. Fancy doing collieries here in Italy, with no coal within miles and miles, and not an industry worth the mention,

[1] Another version of this letter concludes: '...they're waiting for me at tennis' (Delavenay 709). According to Jessie Chambers (MS UN LaM 10), 'in his note, accompanying the proofs' DHL had also said 'that Garnett had told him of [her] novel and had spoken praise of it, but thought it perhaps too quiet for the public. He wants to see it.'

[2] Both (somewhat ambivalent) reviews appeared on 6 March 1913. The reviewer in the *Daily News* was Max Plowman (1883–1941).

[3] Published September 1912.

[4] Dated by the reference to Collings in the letter following.

and no pictures – oh Lord, it's frightful. One-third or so of the cover is to be picture, the rest a brief notice on the novel. It's a damned nuisance. Would it be a *great* bore to you just to[1] give it a bit of a try. Is it impudence to ask it. Because of course, they don't want to pay *me* for designing a cover, or a bit of a cover. And I am pennilessly poor, always. But we might arrange something that way. At any rate I'll send you the first batch of proofs. If it is too much fag for you, just send the things back and say 'no'. You might get an idea from the proofs – the text, I mean. Oh God, I wish I was a navvy or a policeman.

I enclose a draft of the size of the cover and spacing. They want this thing awfully soon too. If you do it, you might post it to Edward Garnett, at Duckworth and Cos, 3 Henrietta St, W.C.

I am in a mess and a misery all round just now. I believe I am moving to Rome in about ten days – isn't 'Avernus' Hole' somewhere down there – the mouth of Hell?[2] I ought to draw a bit nearer to it.

I'll help *you* when I can, I will really. D. H. Lawrence

[Enclosed is a draft sketch in pencil of headstock, pit-heap and coal-trucks for the cover design]

[Lawrence writes on the verso]

I hate this damned idea altogether – but I have no choice.

The thing is to be black and white. DHL

560. To Edward Garnett, 22 March 1913

Text: MS NYPL; Heilbrun 153–4.

Villa Igéa, Villa di Gargnano, Lago di Garda (Brescia)
22 March 1913

Dear Garnett,

I got the £50 from Duckworth today – and the agreement for *Sons and Lovers.*[3] I have signed, and sent also a receipt.

I have also been trying to draw collieries. It is beastly difficult. One needs the technique of a proper illustrator. I have asked a friend of mine – Ernest Collings, do you know him – if he'd do this thing for me. If he will, he'll send it on to you.

I have also written the brief notice for the wrapper.[4] If it is wrong, tell

[1] just to] to just

[2] Latin mythology placed the entrance to hell close to Lake Avernus in Campania.

[3] See p. 482 n. 1.

[4] DHL was, therefore, probably responsible for the announcement on the dust-jacket of *Sons and Lovers* (Duckworth edn): 'Mr D. H. Lawrence's new novel covers a wide field: life in a colliery, on a farm, in a manufacturing centre. It is concerned with the contrasted outlook

me. Frieda insists on my enclosing her version also. Of course I think it not anywhere near it. I got also the *Times Supplement*.[1] De la Mare was very cautious – I suppose he has to be. I hope Duckworth won't be out of pocket on the book. Katherine Mansfield said everybody was talking about my poetry.

I am still sad and decrepit. I have been seedy these last few days. With doing so little, I feel tired. I began a new, lighter novel and have done 46 pages.[2] It will be quite decent (D.V.). The other one has my love.[3] It will be none the worse for waiting a while. I wish I was a navvy or a policeman. I even wish I was teaching in school again.

Frieda's sister was here for two days, this week.[4] She has told us we should go to Rome. As she is a person who arranges other folk's affairs, I suppose we shall go. That will be in about a week or ten days' time. We shall go first to Florence, then on to Rome. There we shall take rooms and stay for some months. We are neither of us coming to England. It sounded nice, when you talked of that front bedroom at the Cearne. I suppose the Cearne is after all the nearest place to home that I've got. Rough on you that. But Frieda isn't going to see her children yet, at any rate. So we may as well stay abroad. I wish the Cearne were here.

Mrs A[nthony] will probably move to München. She was introduced to Frieda's sister, with that idea, and the thing discussed.

We hear from Harold very regularly. I must congratulate him on his engagement.[5]

It is rainy weather for three days.

I might get some sort of teaching work in Rome.

Bunny will come to see us when we are out there. I began a letter to him and never finished it. Is he aimiable again. 'When is a bunny not a bunny? When he's a bear.' Frieda has made up that lovely conundrum for his benefit.

I feel about as cheerful as Watts' *Hope*.[6]

riverisco D. H. Lawrence

on life of two generations. The title, *Sons and Lovers*, indicates the conflicting claims of a young man's mother and sweetheart for predominance.'

1 *Love Poems* was reviewed on 13 March 1913 in *TLS*.

2 'The Sisters' (which led eventually, after very considerable re-writing, to *The Rainbow*, 1915, and *Women in Love*, 1920).

3 'The Insurrection of Miss Houghton.'

4 Else Jaffe.

5 Hobson became engaged to (and married in 1914) Coralie Jeyes von Werner (1891–1946). She wrote several novels both under her married name and as 'Sarah Salt'.

6 *Hope* (1885–6) by G. F. Watts (1817–1904). Cf. G. K. Chesterton, *G. F. Watts* (1904), p. 98: if a spectator saw *Hope* without knowing its title 'his first thought, of course, would be that the picture was called *Despair*'.

[Frieda Weekley begins]

He *has* got the humpiest hump, O Gawd! I am a heroic person, to stand him day for day, I tell you! I shall not see the children now, I had looked on it as a dead certainty, now it's nothing! [Lawrence interjects: No wonder I have the hump.]

I think I'll put him on a little stool in the garden like his mother, 'now cry there, misery'.

561. To Ada Lawrence, [25 March 1913]

Text: MSS Clarke & NCL; Moore, *Intelligent Heart* 142–3.

Villa Igéa, Villa di Gargnano, Lago di Garda, Brescia.
Tuesday

My dear Sister,

You ought to be enjoying the holiday, you hussy – why aren't you. We've had awful rain for 4 days – but now brilliant sunshine. We are going to Rome. We are tired of being buried alive. Frieda's sister was here last Wednesday. She is in Rome for a month. She will look round for rooms for us. We leave here on Sunday – go to San Gaudenzio – which is a farm about 2 miles up the lake, still Gargnano postal district – stay there 2 or 3 days – then go to Verona – then to Rome, perhaps staying in Florence en route. There will be time for you to write me a card here, before we go. Then I shall send you the address when we get there.

I have received £50 on account of *Sons and Lovers*. I send you £5 on account of all the insurances and things you have paid for me. You will see, when you have read those proofs, why I sent them to J[essie]. These things Frieda will write to you are probably untrue. – I had not heard from J. for 8 months – nor written her. I asked the publishers to send her a copy of the poems. She thanked me. I sent her the proofs and a note. The note came back – I say by mistake. Still, if J. did it on purpose – all the better.[1]

I shant be sorry to move, for some things, but for others, I shall be awfully

[1] It was undoubtedly done 'on purpose': see E.T. 219–22. Jessie Chambers' letter to Helen Corke, 16 March 1913 (MS UN LaM 10), shows how the proofs lacerated her sensibility:

I really can't think why David should have wished me to read the proofs, since nothing now can be altered. He must be extraordinarily inconsiderate. I shouldn't care if it didn't make me so sick, all this turmoil of emotionalism. But it makes me fearfully sick, I can neither eat nor sleep, and I sit in front of the fire and shiver as if I had ague fits...

The Miriam part of the novel is a slander, a fearful treachery. David has selected every point which sets off Miriam at a disadvantage, and he has interpreted her every word and action, and thought in the light of Mrs. Morel's hatred of her.

miserable. This has been my first home – and such a grand one. I doubt I shall never rise to such heights again. In Rome we shall only have two rooms.

I had a cold, which resulted in my usual pippiness and sweetness. It is nearly gone now. Devil of a policeman! Never mind, we have these ups and downs, even the best of us. Pay your ten bob with a grin, my dear.[1]

I wish you could have come out here for Easter – only it poured with rain. The poor folk in the hôtel looked like prisoners staring out of Black Maria, their mournful faces at the window.

I *do* wish you'd tell me about those pictures. Don't you like them? If you dont, then say so. Which are you going to give Dick, and which Alice.[2] You are too bad. If they are ugly, keep them for your back bedrooms.

Yes, I should be most grateful of your support just now against Frieda. She's an awful badgerer. I *do* wish you were here, and that's a fact. But we must to Rome, and you to New Eastwood. We shan't come to England before August.

Keep well. Father gets off best, after all. My love to everybody.

Your afflicted brother D. H. Gummidge[3]

[Frieda Weekley begins][4]

Dear Ada!

I laughed, when you thought of poor me when L[awrence] has the hump! It is a hump, only a monster camel could carry it! I am also looking forward to the time, when we are together! I think we shall laugh and compare notes about L; I sometimes write letters to you but he says, you wont like them and they never go! I am glad to hear, he always had those humps, I thought it was my fault! He told me so! It's been raining for days and days, the people at the Hotels looking with long faces at an astounding pour of rain! But to-day the sun shines gorgeously! Think, Jessie Chambers wrote a novel about L, good, but not quite good enough Garnett says. L asked her for it in a letter, she send the letter back; L.'s letter, I suppose was'nt high falluting enough, but I did think it was nasty of her, I call her only the 'white love, white of egg of my youth'! We are going to Rome, I am looking forward to it,

1 Ada had been fined 10/- for a traffic offence.

2 Respectively Richard Pogmore and Alice Hall.

3 An allusion to Mrs Gummidge in Dickens' *David Copperfield* (1849–50), a character with 'rather a fretful disposition'. Frieda's note which follows makes pertinent Mrs Gummidge's remark: 'I know that I am a lone lorn creetur', and not only that everythink goes contrairy with me, but that I go contrairy with everybody' (chap. 3).

4 The contents of Frieda's note suggest that it was enclosed with DHL's letter; he seized the opportunity to add a postscript concerning practical matters which he had omitted. (From this point to the end the text is from MS NCL.)

now, it has been nice here, but I want to forget how miserable I have been sometimes! My love to you. Frieda

[Lawrence continues]

A letter to Gargnano will always find us – follow us, at any rate.

You might send those MS articles[1] to the

Editor of the *English Review*
17–21 Tavistock St
Covent Garden, W.C.

but there is no hurry.

562. To David Garnett, [25 March 1913]

Text: MS NYPL; Postmark, Bogliaco 25 3 13; Tedlock 192–3.

['Villa Igéa', *Villa di Gargnano*, Lago di Garda (Brescia)]
[25 March 1913]

[Frieda Weekley begins]

Dear Bunny,

Your last letter was *so* nice! But sad I thought, what's the matter? You want to be my Dutch uncle, so let me be something like it to you! Have *you* drunk off some bitter waters of knowing? I think you are quite right, you have too much to give later on, to throw yourself away on mere sensationalism, and that is what those modern damsels want of you; wait, only wait and *she* will come! Yes, I like it, that you are so keen on your work, we think of you at every new flower we come across! Harold and Lola,! she has been flirting and he has felt righteous! I hope for both their sakes, they will make a success of it, but Harold is an 'enfant gâté', and like in the 'Land of Cokayne'[2] he expects the roast pigeons to fly in his mouth! It isnt as easy as that! I like Tony for many things; she is chasing greatness as if it were a rabbit and she wants to put salt on its tail! But I *do* feel sorry for John,[3] he must have taken her seriously and she is cold to give one shivers, even with the child, she is cold and it's cold too! I had a pang of jealousy because of her, but the bubble's pricked, L[awrence] approaches all people (women specially) as if they were Gothic cathedrals, then he finds that they are little houses and hates them for it! But I admire Tony for her independance, she goes her own way! But could'nt anybody tell John, that he is a blithering,

[1] 'Italian Studies: By the Lago di Garda' which appeared in *English Review*, xv (September 1913), 202–34.

[2] i.e. an imaginary land of luxury and contentment.

[3] Per Johan Hugo Almgren (1880–1963?), Swedish sculptor and painter, husband of Antonia ('Tony'). Patronised by Prince Carl of Sweden.

blighted imbecile, duffer and idiot to want her back? She is a sensationalist, loves all this chasing game, would'nt, could'nt do without it now! He *must* leave her, with an effort of will get rid of her inside or he will be quite done for soon! Lord, the messes people are in! I have given Lawrence a hell of a time, that's to say he took it over the children, I was so *very* sure to see them at Easter, it was a fixture in my head, when Ernst would'nt, it was like dangling with my feet in the air! Now we are going to Rome! Cant you come? I am anxious to go! Tony is very likely going to Icking, our flat, she ought to have people and a good time! Your mother seems to have been superhuman to her,[1] I am looking forward to see your mother, she sounds so awfully nice, Harold and Tony seem to love her! Lawrence *has* been having a hump, it's quite killing, when he goes about an incorporated doom, *nothing* is any good and he asks a dozen times a day in all keys, are you miserable, dear? [Lawrence interjects: I never say 'dear' – that's Frieda's marital term for me.] *Most* cheering, when one's got to fight one's own hump off! But still, we are going to bring it off in spite of odds and the shortcomings of this world!

My love to you, Signor Davide, come and see us in Rome, there are trips, cant you manage one?

Auf Wiedersehen Frieda

[Lawrence begins]

Dear David,

I have been seedy as the sickest ass that ever groaned, hence the hump. But Frieda sits on top of the hump, and then it's as big as the 'doom of St Paul's', as my father always says.

You are suffering from 'genitoritis' – the affliction of one's parents. One goes through it like measles. It's hard all round. The only cure is 'love' – à la Harold. We have heard of *your* flight to Moscow – and to love – God bless you.[2] Is Harold in the same frame of mind, only rowing another boat, I wonder, as you when you 'recovered'. – We liked your last letters, and I am awfully sorry not to be seeing you just now. You *must* scramble to Rome later. I'll send you the address when we get to the Eternal City.

Love DHL

1 Antonia had stayed at the Cearne in the late summer of 1911 (see David Garnett, *The Golden Echo*, p. 226).

2 David Garnett had also visited Moscow, Easter 1911, in the cause of love (see *The Golden Echo*, pp. 212–15).

563. To Ernest Collings, [28 March 1913]

Text: MS UT; PC v. Gardola di Tignale (Lago di Garda); Postmark, Gargnano 28 3 13; Unpublished.

['Villa Igéa', *Villa di Gargnano*, Lago di Garda (Brescia)]
[28 March 1913]

You are awfully nice to do that thing – I *do* like the sketch – it's got the poetic quality I wanted. I shall be awfully glad if you will let Garnett have it in a few days, or a week. Don't send back the proofs if you'd care to keep them – and I will send you the rest. They are the revised proofs, and not all have come yet. I want you to like the book. We are here till the 2nd or 3rd April.

Yrs D. H. Lawrence

564. To David Garnett, 5 April 1913

Text: MS NYPL; Postmark, Gargnano 5 4 13; Huxley 114–16.

San Gaudenzio, Muslone, Gargnano
5 April[1] 1913

Dear Bunny,

We were all highly interested in your last letter. You are a varied and boldly-coloured person. It is a little form, a little strength of line that is perhaps lacking. You seem a bit sporadic, and one looks for the 'core of ardour'. If I were you I'd be a plain dull person for a bit.

You'll wonder at my last brief note.[2] It was like the horn of Tristan sounding across the sea – I mean of Isolda. Frieda after all feels she must be near the children – within an hour's train journey of them. So, instead of going to Florence – the luggage was already addressed – we are coming to England. But first Frieda must see her sister in Verona. Else is in Rome now. We meet her, I think, next Friday: that is I believe the 11th. So we should be in England about the 13th. I must let you know. We shall be very thankful to stay at the Cearne for a bit.

At present we are living at San Gaudenzio with Mrs Antony.[3] It is a lovely place. There is a garden over a mile round, with vines and olives. It falls to the cliff-edge above the lake. I sit and write in a deserted lemon-garden which gathers the sun and keeps it. The mountains are covered with snow opposite. – Then the Capelli – the people – are *fearfully* nice. The place is almost like an inn – illegal, there is no licence – so that people are always

[1] April] March

[2] The postscript to Letter 562.

[3] She described San Gaudenzio ('San Lorenzo') in *Among Italian Peasants*, p. 3: 'San Lorenzo was a large farmhouse built on a piece of level ground at the top of a precipice. It was a halfway house between the town on the lake shore below and the little village higher up, but it was much nearer the village...'

coming – handsome young men who are conscripts and just about to flee to America, and so on. One need never be alone. *And* the folk are nice – warm and generous. I reckon Mrs A. is jolly lucky, if you ask me anything, to be in such a lovely spot with such decent folk. We play games at evening. Last Sunday there was a band – cello, mandoline and two weird guitars – playing all evening while we danced.[1] Nay, even there was a wild and handsome one-legged man with a deltoid like a boss of brass, who danced Frieda, and then Tony, like a wooden-legged angel. What can woman want more? We are out nearly all day – up at the charcoal-burners hut on the mountains, or away at the great scree.[2] It is quite wonderful and unspoiled everywhere. There are little grape-hyacinths standing about, and peach blossom is pink among the grey olives, and the cherry blossom shakes in the wind. Oh my sirs, what more do you want.

I register what you say about my 'pottery',[3] and am glad to succeed the salvation army on the throne of your heart. No, I don't think I'm the greatest poet that ever lived – I'm not very conceited. I should not like to say I thought myself as great a poet as Lord Tennyson – perhaps when I've finished, I shall, perhaps I shan't. But let me finish first. You are only twenty yet – I'm only 27.

I wonder where your father is. I hear he is beginning a new book.[4] I drink to it's success, though the wine is miserable stuff. I did 200 pages of a novel[5] – a novel I love – then I put it aside to do a pot-boiler[6] – it was *too* improper. The pot-boiler is at page 110, and has developed into an earnest and painful work – God help it and me.

I'm so sick of the last lot of proofs of *Sons and Lovers*, that I have scarcely patience to correct them. By the way, a friend of mine, an awfully nice fellow Ernest H R Collings – 24 Gorst Rd – Wandsworth Common – did a drawing for the cover of *Sons and Lovers*. Your Dad asked *me* to do it – but Collings is a professional, and has done some good stuff. He sent the thing in to Duckworth's but has had no acknowledgement. Do ask your father to be nice to him about it – he's young and struggling and his stuff is good, if it's not marvellous. But he's an awfully lovable chap – generous. He's older than me – God bless me for my patronising.

I am thinking we may stay at Forest Row for a bit, then get some little crib. I wish I was a lily of the field. I'm sure I don't *want* to sow and spin.[7]

[1] Cf. 'The Dance at the Inn', *Among Italian Peasants*, chap. 2.
[2] Cf. 'Charcoal Burners', ibid, chap. 5.
[3] i.e. poetry (see Letter 547).
[4] *Tolstoy* (1914).
[5] 'The Insurrection of Miss Houghton'.
[6] 'The Sisters'.
[7] Matthew vi. 26–8.

I don't want to bother your father while he is away. When do you go back to College? I suppose we shall be here four or five days longer. With my love and Friedas.

D. H. Lawrence

[Frieda Weekley begins]

I am looking forward to seeing you, I want to read your book,[1] dont be hopeless and dont forget that one's never as hopeless as at 21!

Love F.

[Lawrence continues]

I want to see that book. I'll help you with it if you like. DHL

Mrs Anthony says it's a mean dodge, your trying to extract an unearned letter from a lonely and forlorn lady, who watches the post like Isolda the ships oversea – longing to hear from her [sketch of a rabbit].

565. To Ada Lawrence, 5 April 1913

Text: TMSC NWU; Moore, *Intelligent Heart* 144–5.

San Gaudenzio, Gargnano.
5 April 1913.

My dear Sister,

I'm afraid you'll be grieved to hear that after all we are probably coming to England very shortly. Frieda wants to be within reach of the children. We are staying up here for about a week. Then we are going to Verona to meet Frieda's sister on her return from Rome – then to England. We shall stay a while at the Cearne, then probably in Sussex. Then we should see you at Whitsuntide. But I shall write you again, definitely.

This is a lovely place – a farm high on the mountain side. It has grounds a mile round – vines, olive gardens. I sit in a deserted lemon-garden that gets so warm with the sun. There are little grape hyacinths standing about. They are all over the mountains – and violets. Peach blossom is rosy pink among the grey olives, and cherry blossom and pear are white. We love the people of the farm – such warm folks. At evening we play games in the kitchen. On Sunday there was a band of four – cello, mandolin, 2 guitars, playing in a corner, queer lively Italian music, while we danced. The peasants of the mountains were in. One was a good looking, wild fellow, with a wooden leg. He danced like anything with Frieda and Mrs. Anthony, a friend of ours who is also staying here, and he danced well. So you see we have quite a life of it.

[1] David Garnett informs the editor that the book was untitled and not finished; he adds that DHL rightly considered it no good.

Frieda was awfully pleased with your last letter. She uses it against me as a proof of what a difficult and unpleasant person I am to live with. I say you never meant it in that wise. L. stands for Lorenzo. Mrs. Anthony's kid calls me Lorenzo – the people Signore Lorenze. I shall have collected a list soon.

I haven't any real news – soon I hope I shall see you. I am writing away at a novel rather more cheerful than *Sons and Lovers*.[1] You must tell me what you think of that book – you'll hate it, but it is rather great, I think. A friend of mine has just designed a picture for the wrapper, that looks rather well. I still have not corrected all the proofs. I tell you, I am mightily sick of it.

It seems difficult to think of being in England. I wonder if it will really come off. I am not anxious to be in my native land, but I should love having you with us at Whitsuntide, in Ashdown Forest. Is this two weeks or three, after Easter?

[Frieda Weekley begins]

Yes, so shall I, your letter just came when L. had made me so miserable that I began to think I was the scum of the earth unfit for a human being, *his* misery was all *my* doing, so your letter came as a help to me from the Almighty. L. looks well I think but of course it is hard our life, but now I *hope* the worst is over of misery, the children, illness and all. But of course he is really good and it is hard for him as it is for me! It will be nice to see you, we shall live very quietly till we are married, we might just as well!! (He says I am writing a lot to you, he is already jealous of you, I always tell him, I wish he were as nice as you) So I hope to see you soon.

Good bye, Frieda

[Lawrence continues]

My pen ran dry so I had to come in.

How did the bike go off, the fine?[2] Love, DHL

566. To Gertrude Cooper, [10? April 1913]

Text: MS Clarke; PC v. Lago di Garda – Gargnano; Postmark, Gargnano 11 4 13; Unpublished.

[San Gaudenzio, Muslone, Gargnano]

[10? April 1913][3]

I am just leaving this place – going tomorrow to Verona – from there, God knows where. Perhaps I may soon come to England. How are you? I have

[1] 'The Sisters'.

[2] See p. 532 n. 1.

[3] DHL was due to leave on Friday, 11 April (cf. Letter 564); thus this card was perhaps written on 10 and posted on 11 April. (DHL's reference to 'a couple of days' in Letter 567 is not necessarily precise.)

occasional messages from you, and don't forget you. I suppose Eastwood is still there. My love to Frank[1] and to you – Love D. H. Lawrence

567. To Edward Garnett, 14 April 1913
Text: MS NYPL; Huxley 116–17.

Hôtel Europa E Aquila Nera, Verona
14 April 1913

Dear Garnett,

It is years since I heard from you. We are on the move at last – been here a couple of days. After all we are coming to England, but not direct. We are going tonight to München and shall be there about a week. You might write to me at the

'Haus Vogelnest', *Wolfratshausen*, bei München,

and tell me how you are. Will you have us at the Cearne in about a week's time? Do you know of any little cottage anywhere, that we could rent? – somewhere by the sea if we can. Mrs Anthony says that your brother Arthur Garnett knows those things.[2] We want soon to settle down again. We could furnish a little place for ourselves, if we knew of one.

I sent off all those proofs of *Sons and Lovers*. Did you get the drawing that Collings did? I haven't seen it, but I'll bet it's nice. Do thank him, will you? –

Ernest H R Collings, 24 Gorst Rd, Wandsworth Common.

I shall be so glad to see you, and feel myself in your hands for a day or two.

I may be in Heidelberg on Thursday – but letters to Wolfratshausen will always find me. I want to hear from you. It is so long since I did.

Frieda joins me in love – and to Bunny.

D. H. Lawrence

568. To Ernest Collings, [14 April 1913]
Text: MS UT; PC; Postmark, Verona 14 [...] 13; Unpublished.

Verona –
Monday[3]

My dear Collings,

I did get your letter – thanks awfully for doing the design. Have you heard

[1] i.e. her sister Frances.

[2] Arthur Garnett (1881–1927), youngest son of Richard Garnett, was an old friend of Antonia Almgren. On the staff at Kew Gardens; an horticultural journalist; later he spent some time in Tasmania, returning to England in 1923.

[3] The conjectural date is confirmed by DHL's being in Munich on 15 April (Letter 570).

yet from Garnett? I believe he was abroad. I left the last of the proofs to be sent to you – did they come? I am leaving Italy tonight – going to Munich. But soon I hope to be in England. I shall write you as soon as I have got an address. I want to hear what you think of *Sons and Lovers*. The proofs are supposed to be strictly private, till the book is out. When do you go to Switzerland? A rivederci – D. H. Lawrence

569. To Arthur McLeod, [14 April 1913]

Text: MS UT; PC v. Verona – Interno dell'Arena; Postmark, Verona 14 [. . .] 13; Unpublished.

[Hôtel Europa E Aquila Nera, Verona]
[14 April 1913]

Thanks for the books[1] – I got them at San Gaudenzio. I am leaving Verona tonight for Munich. Before long I shall be in England, then I shall see you. I can't give you any address yet, but I shall see you soon. This is really a wonderful arena.[2]

My love to everybody D. H. Lawrence

570. To Edward Garnett, [15 April 1913]

Text: MS NYPL; PC v. München. Rathaus; Postmark, München 15. 4. 13; Unpublished.

[15 April 1913]

You won't mind if I suddenly turn up in London, will you? I might leave here for England tomorrow. Frieda stays another week.

D. H. Lawrence

571. To Ada Lawrence, 19 April 1913

Text: MS Clarke; Moore, *Intelligent Heart* 145–6.

Villa Jaffe, Irschenhausen, post *Ebenhausen*, bei München, Isartal
Saturday 19 April 1913

My dear Sister,

First of all, the village is Irschenhausen, then the post office is in Ebenhausen, so you draw a line under that, then München, which is Munich, has two dots on it, and then Isartal means Isar-valley, and the Isar is a tributary of the Danube, well known in English poetry as 'Eiser rolling rapidly'

'And dark as winter was the flood
Of Eiser rolling rapidly'[3]

[1] See Letter 573. [2] One of the largest Roman amphitheatres in existence.

[3] Thomas Campbell (1777–1844), 'Hohenlinden', ll. 3–4 ['. . the flow/Of Iser, . . .'].

– it is pronounced 'Eeser', à l'anglaise. Where Hohenlinden is, and when the battle was fought, God knows.[1]

Now you can address a letter to me. I got your letter in München – and your p.c. It was a nice letter. Frieda liked hers.

We are in a lovely little wooden house in a corner of a pine or rather fir forest, looking over to the Alps, which are white with snow – they are some ten miles away. It is quite near Icking, where I was last year. The house belongs to Frieda's brother in law. It is quite new – a lovely little place. Prof. Jaffē lives in Munich, so the house is empty. We make a home here for a week or two – quite alone. Don't you think it is a nice idea? The house stands on a high meadow in an angle of the wood. The meadow has blue patches of gentian and is speckled[2] with Alp primulas and with cowslips. The village is a tiny place. An ox brought up our luggage in dignity from the station. I sit in the little dining room in the lamp-light. It is a room all of wood. There is a warm old stove of green tiles, and queer Bavarian pottery. Directly I am going to bed, because I have a cold. When I woke up at Innsbruck, coming from Italy,[3] I found the whole land under snow. I tell you, it *was* a shock. So the air was fierce after the Garda. But my cold is fleeing with the snow, which is all gone. Now I do not know when I shall be in England – perhaps not before your wedding. I am excited to hear of Emmie Limb being bridesmaid with Hilda Pettit,[4] and having 'delicate sprigged muslin' frocks. Look here, don't you go and be too grand. Don't make Eddie wear a frock coat, for God's sake. I want to wear a jacket. I will wear a white waistcoat and a white buttonhole, if you insist. And I would never give you away.

Parson: 'Who gives this woman away.'

Me: 'I'm sure I don't.'

But father will no doubt be glad of the opportunity. Don't deprive him of his paternal rights.

You keep discreet silence about *Sons and Lovers* – Why?

As for the divorce – it will be a very quiet affair. Don't worry.

It will be nice to stay with you in Ripley. I want to go to Pentrich.[5] And do you remember the pub where we saw Daft?[6] – and the Women's Guild? O Dio Dio!

[1] French forces defeated the Austrians at Hohenlinden (east of Munich) on 2 December 1800.

[2] has blue...speckled] is blue with gentians and

[3] Italy] Germany

[4] Unidentified.

[5] About seven miles north-west of Eastwood; William Hopkin had friends there.

[6] Unidentified.

Give my love to everybody. Frieda is very busy, and sends her love, and she is looking after me. Give my love to Father – has he flitted yet?

Again my love to you

a rivederci D. H. Lawrence

572. To Edward Garnett, [21 April 1913]

Text: MS NYPL; Unpublished.

Villa Jaffē, Irschenhausen, Post *Ebenhausen*, bei München, Isartal
Monday[1]

Dear Garnett,

I have just got your letter. You know you can accept things for me without my knowing, if you think them good. Anyhow I am very glad of Kennerley's offer, and accept gratefully.[2]

Don't be sick of our chopping and changing. I should probably have been in England now – alone. But when I got here, we found Bavaria under snow. That gave me a frightful cold, after the warm Garda. So I dared not move for a while. And now perhaps we stay here a week, even for a month or two. Because Frieda was coming to England, to see the children by hook or crook – chiefly by crook. And I have a horror of her stopping her son as he comes from school, and seeing him so.[3] It is now arranged that Frieda's mother, who lives in Baden Baden, shall ask Prof. W[eekley][4] – with whom she corresponds still amicably – to send the children to Baden Baden, perhaps for Whitsuntide, so that Frieda may see them there. If anything comes of this, we need not come to England. But if W. remains averse, then after a while we must come.

[1] Dated through the similarity of contents to Letter 571.

[2] Kennerley wrote to Edward Garnett, 6 March 1913 (MS NYPL):

> Dear Mr Garnett,
>
> Thank you for your letter of February twenty-fifth. I will certainly take a small edition of Mr Lawrence's book of poems and I look forward to reading the manuscript of the play. I might put this into my Series and print a small edition for Mr Duckworth?
>
> I shall be pleased to receive the advance sheets of the new novel but I do hope that they will come to me well in advance of English publication. We still have about 200 copies left of *The Trespasser* but I will shortly send you a check in settlement of royalties on the entire edition.
>
> Yours faithfully

Kennerley published the first American edition of: *Love Poems* (1913); *Sons and Lovers* (17 September 1913); and *The Widowing of Mrs. Holroyd* (in 'The Modern Drama Series', 1 April 1914).

[3] Montague Weekley attended St Paul's School (see Letter 577).

[4] Prof. W] Ernst

We are in Dr Jaffe's little Holzhaus, here in the country, among the primulas and the gentian, looking away at the Alps. It reminds me a bit of the Cearne, only the Cearne is nicer, and I would rather be there.

After Italy I hate Germany – it feels so narrow and cruel. These moral folk have such a cruel feel about them. I want to go back to Italy – or come to England.

Your letter was rather scant – and you have not written for so long. It has rained a good deal here, but the snow is just gone, and the mountains are very bright in the sun.

Frieda sends her apologies for our indefiniteness.

Yours D. H. Lawrence

P.S. I am sorry about Collings.

573. To Arthur McLeod, [23 April 1913]

Text: MS UT; Postmark, München 24. 4. 13; Huxley 119–20.

Villa Jaffe, Irschenhausen, Post *Ebenhausen*, bei München (Isartal)
Wednesday

Dear Mac,

I'm here instead of in England. It's a jolly little wooden house – oh, don't jump to conclusions, quite luxurious – standing in a corner of a fir-wood, in a hilly meadow all primulas and gentian, and looking away at the snowy Alps. Ecco! F[rieda] and I are quite alone. The place is a little summer house belonging to her brother in law, which he has lent us for a month or two. It is lonely. The deer feed sometimes in the corner among the flowers. But they fly with great bounds when I go out. And when I whistle to a hare among the grass, he dances round in wild bewilderment.

I must thank you again for the books. *Medea* is still very good.[1] But I though[t] her a bit stupid in the end. F. is mightily impressed by her still. I am wading through *New Machiavelli*. It depresses me. I sometimes find it too long. But it is awfully interesting. I like Wells, he is so warm, such a passionate declaimer or reasoner or whatever you like. But ugh – he hurts me. He always seems to be looking at life as a cold and hungry little boy in the street stares at a shop where there is hot pork. I do like him and esteem him, and wish I knew half as much about things. I think the *Gadfly* man[2] has a 'complexe'[3] – some sexual twist – that he likes physical hurt as he does.

[1] Probably one of the Gilbert Murray translations DHL requested earlier of McLeod (see p. 525, Letter 554 and n. 1). Murray published Euripides' *Medea*, 1906 (reprinted at 1/- in 1907).

[2] DHL appears to have forgotten that the author was a woman. See p. 525 n. 3.

[3] Jung's term (1907) had not yet passed into easy colloquial usage.

Those old inquisitors and Sadists and Caligulas of course had perverted sex – which was why they 'savoured' those nasty hurts.[1] The Bergson book was very dull. Bergson bores me. He feels a bit thin.[2]

I don't know when they'll get *Sons and Lovers* out. Duckworths are a damned dilatory lot. Curse them, they'll put forth in their spring – it won't be long, I suppose. – I will give you a copy. – I am doing a novel which I have never grasped.[3] Damn its eyes, there I am at page 145, and I've no notion what it's about. I hate it. F. says it is good. But it's like a novel in a foreign language I don't know very well – I can only just make out what it is about.

I don't know when I shall be in England. But my youngest sister – my only unmarried sister – marries in August, so I shall have to appear about that time. Write to me and tell me lots of news. One can buy such pretty pictures in Munich. Do you want anything particular? Perhaps I shall soon be able to furnish a cottage in England. Then you could come and stay with us. Would you like it? I should.

It broke my heart to leave Italy. I still cannot, cannot believe this landscape is real. I expect it to lift, and clear away, and reveal my bright Garda again. Lord but I am a conservative person.

I make such deep roots wherever I go. Soon I must settle down. I can't bear to tear myself about. And it is so queer to greet the peasants in German. 'Grüss Gott,' they say. In Austria they say 'Servus'. In Italy 'riverisco'. But it hurts me not to say the Italian. One must love Italy, if one has lived there. It is so non-moral. It leaves the soul so free. Over these countries, Germany and England, like the grey skies, lies the gloom of the dark moral judgment and condemnation and reservation of the people. Italy does not judge. I shall want to go back there.

Pray to your Gods for me that *Sons and Lovers* shall succeed. People *should* begin to take me seriously now. And I do so break my heart over England, when I read the *New Machiavelli*. And I am so sure that only through a re-adjustment between men and women, and a making free and healthy of the sex, will she get out of her present atrophy. Oh Lord, and if I don't 'subdue my art to a metaphysic', as somebody very beautifully said of Hardy,[4] I do write because I want folk – English folk – to alter, and have more sense.

[1] Cf. Letter 512.

[2] If McLeod had sent an English translation of a work by Henri Bergson (1859–1941), two were currently available to him: *Laughter* (1911) and *The Philosophy of Change* (1912).

[3] 'The Sisters'.

[4] Probably a half-remembered reconstruction of remarks by Lascelles Abercrombie in *Thomas Hardy* (1912). Abercrombie frequently writes of the relationship between Hardy's art and metaphysic (e.g. pp. 96, 128).

Give my love to everybody. I could send you such heaps of German books, if you could read that floundering language, which is alien to my psychology and my very tissue. I should *never* be able to use German, if I lived here for ever. – But everything is translated into German. Nietzsche said the Germans are the great receptive, female nation.[1]

I must close – auf wiedersehen – Yours D. H. Lawrence

[Frieda Weekley begins]

I also want to thank you for your books, they arrived in such a friendly way at the Villa Igéa; Almost our only connection with outer life! I wish you could see the patches of gentians in the fields, so bluely blue they are! Perhaps I shall see you before long and I shall like seeing you, I know!

Kind regards Frieda

574. To Edward Garnett, [2? May 1913]

Text: MS NYPL; Huxley 117–18.

Villa Jaffe, Irschenhausen, (Post) *Ebenhausen*, bei München

Friday.[2]

Dear Garnett,

Your letter and enclosures came this morning. Will you send the MS of Miss Chambers here, please, at your leisure.[3] We may be here till August – or we may move before that time – but at any rate, not immediately. I see Frieda has written a defence of me against Miriam – or Jessie, whatever she shall be called. It's all very well for Miss Chambers to be spiritual – perhaps she can bring it off – I can't. She bottled me up till I was going to burst. – But as long as the cork sat tight (herself the cork) there was spiritual calm. When the cork was blown out, and Mr Lawrence foamed, Miriam said 'This yeastiness I disown: it was not so in my day.' God bless her, she always looked down on me – spiritually. But it hurt[4] when she sent a letter of mine back: quite an inoffensive letter, I think.[5] And look, she is bitterly ashamed of having had me – as if I had dragged her spiritual plumage in the mud. Call that love! Ah well.

I am sorry the *Poems* only sold 100 – Frieda is very cross. Don't you think Duckworths printers or somebody are very *slow*. If one wants things to go like hot cakes, the cakes should be hot, surely. But the *Poems* hung fire for

[1] A resumé of several of Nietzsche's remarks rather than a precise quotation.

[2] Dated 2? May by the progress DHL had made with writing 'The Sisters': 145 pages on 23 April and 256 pages by 17 May (Letter 576), suggest that 180 pages by 2 May is probable.

[3] See p. 525 n. 4.

[4] it hurt] it did hurt

[5] See p. 531, Letter 561 and n. 1.

months – *Sons and Lovers* does likewise. The interest – what of it there may be – goes lukewarm. It's no good – if *Hamlet* and *Œdipus* were published now, they wouldn't sell more than 100 copies, unless they were pushed: I know that Duckworth will have to wait till my name is made, for his money. I can understand he is a bit diffident about putting me forward. But he needn't be afraid. I *know* I can write bigger stuff than any man in England. And I have to write what I can write. And I write for men like David and Harold – they will read me, soon. My stuff is what they want: when they know what they want. You wait.

Bliss Carmen was very nice.[1] I have half a mind to write to him. Shall I?

We – or rather Frieda – had a letter from Harold this morning.

I am only doing *reviews* for The Blue Monthly, or whatever it is.[2]

Shall I send some poems, and a story, for the *Forum*?[3]

I have written 180 pages of my newest novel 'The Sisters'. It is a queer novel, which seems to have come by itself. I will send it you. You may dislike it – it hasn't got hard outlines – and of course it's only first draft – but it is pretty neat, for me, in composition. Then I've got 200 pages of a novel which I'm saving – which is very lumbering – which I'll call, provisionally 'The Insurrection of Miss[4] Houghton'. That I shan't send you yet, but it is, to me, fearfully exciting. It lies next my heart, for the present. But I am finishing 'The Sisters'. It will only have 300 pages. It was meant to be for the 'jeunes filles', but already it has fallen from grace. I can only write what I feel pretty strongly about: and that, at present, is the relations between men and women. After all, it is *the* problem of today, the establishment of a new relation, or the re-adjustment of the old one, between men and women. – In a month 'The Sisters' will be finished (D.V.).

It is queer, but nobody seems to want, or to love, *two* people together. Heaps of folk love me alone – if I were alone – and of course all the world adores Frieda – when I'm not there. But together we seem to be a pest. I suppose married (sic) people ought to be sufficient to themselves. It's poverty which is so out of place.

I want to go back to Italy. I *have* suffered from the tightness, the

[1] Bliss Carman (1861–1929), Canadian poet and literary journalist. No correspondence between him and DHL has been traced; no review is known by Carman of any work by DHL.

[2] In fact the *Blue Review* (May–July 1913), edited by Middleton Murry and Katherine Mansfield as a successor to *Rhythm*. DHL's review, 'German Books: Thomas Mann', appeared in the *Blue Review*, July 1913.

[3] Perhaps Garnett discouraged him: DHL did not publish again in the *Forum* until 1927.

[4] Miss] Anna

domesticity of Germany. It is our domesticity which leads to our conformity, which chokes us. The very agricultural landscape here, and the distinct paths, stifles me. The very oxen are dull and featureless, and the folk seem like tables of figures. I have longed for Italy again, I can tell you.

I think these letters of ours are typical. Frieda sprawls so large I must squeeze myself small. I am very contractible. – But aren't you writing a book about Dostoievsky?[1] Those things crack my brains. How does it go? – You *are* a pessimist, really. – We have *not* mentioned Mrs G. to anybody, I believe.[2] Tell David to write to me here.

D. H. Lawrence

575. To Ernest Collings, 13 May 1913

Text: MS UT; Huxley 122–4.

Irschenhausen, (Post) *Ebenhausen*, bei München
13 May 1913

Dear Collings,

After straying about all over the shop, and being fearfully unsettled, I am fixed here for a bit. It is a perfect little wooden house – à la mode – standing in a corner of a fir wood looking over at the long line of the Alps. It is very pretty, I assure you. But after Italy I can't bear Germany – even Bavaria – so tidy, so arranged.

I heard from Garnett the other day, that Duckworth sent back your drawing to you, thinking that the idea of a colliery was unsuitable.[3] I don't know how to apologise to you sufficiently. I am so sorry, you don't know. I hate Duckworths – though they are decent to me – but they are dilatory and uncertain and they sort of leave one in the lurch. Garnett *asked* me for a colliery design. And damn it all, when you had been so good. – I don't know now what Duckworth is putting on the cover of the book,[4] and I don't

[1] See p. 536 n. 4. (Garnett never published a book on Dostoievsky.)

[2] Obscure: DHL perhaps intended to write Mrs A[lmgren].

[3] On receiving this letter Collings wrote to Garnett, 16 May 1913 (MS NYPL):

> Dear Mr Garnett,
>
> I hear from Lawrence that Mr Duckworth has decided not to use my sketch for the cover of *Sons and Lovers*; Lawrence says he understands the drawing has been returned to me. As I have not received it and am anxious not to lose it, would you be good enough to look into the matter. Beyond the few words I had with Mr Duckworth on the telephone one day I have not received a line from your firm since I sent in the drawing.
>
> Yours very truly.

[4] On the cover of the book itself, only the title and author's name were stamped. DHL was probably referring to the dust-cover. Except for the paragraph describing the theme and setting of *Sons and Lovers* (see p. 529 n. 4), the entire jacket was devoted to advertising other works published by Duckworth.

care. He half wants to boom the thing, and he is half afraid – and there you are, neither hot nor cold, what is one to do? But don't let it make you offended with me, will you? Curse the publishers. – I wonder if you liked the novel. Will you tell me? It comes out in a fortnight.

Spring is so late here, the apple blossom is only just coming into flower, and a month ago the weather[1] was icy cold. I want to go back to Italy. I feel restless and without a root. But soon I must come to England. And then, if *Sons and Lovers* does not go, I shan't have enough money to return to the South. It's touch and go with me now. – The poems have done pretty miserably – sold 100. The reviewers, some of them my friends, were so faint.[2] They are afraid to write well of me, for fear of the folk coming down on them for immorality. And some of the reviews have been so God-forsakenly stupid, it is enough to break the heart of a granite boulder.

But it is a pretty world – shadows of big clouds coming[3] slowly here across the Isar and up the valley, a shepherd dog scampering round a flock of sheep near the wood, and among the rising[4] corn, great oblong stretches where it is all yellow with dandelions. Then in the sky the hazy mountains, their dim[5] snow looking between the clouds.

By the way, how did you like Switzerland? How was your holiday? Did it make you happy, and is your work going well? Are you giving any drawings to that scoundrel, the *Blue Review*?[6] 'Scoundrel' is half-affectionate, of course.

I am going it strong enough with a new novel, that is two-thirds done.[7] You must say nice things about *Sons and Lovers*, because my spring, like the year's, is very backward and frosty.

Do you know Munich? For some things I love it, and for some things I hate it. I hate it for its puffiness – puffed under the eyes with beer and bohemianism. Then I love it for its indifference. But it should be debonnair in its bohemianism, and it isn't – it is rather unwholesome,[8] and seems conscious of its dirty linen. I hate Munich art.[9] But yet it is free of that beastly, tight, Sunday feeling which is so blighting in England. I like Italy,

1 the weather] it

2 Perhaps alluding (among others) to Edward Thomas's review, *Bookman*, xliv (April 1913), 47 (Draper 51–2).

3 coming] going

4 rising] young

5 dim] white

6 None appeared in it.

7 'The Sisters'.

8 unwholesome] dirty

9 DHL's adverse comments on 'the Secession pictures in Munich', in 'Christs in the Tirol' (*Phoenix* p. 82), suggest that he was aiming at the same target here. Indeed he may have been referring specifically to the pictures shown in 1913 at the Secessionist Exhibition in the Königliche Kunstausstellungsgebäude which opened to the public on 13 March and closed at the end of May.

which takes no thought for the morrow,[1] neither fear nor pride. The English are 'good' because they are afraid, and the Müncheners are 'wicked' because they are afraid, and the Italians forget to be afraid, so they're neither good nor wicked, but just natural. Viva l'Italia!

Well, you'll be sick of my jaw. I shall be glad to know you are all right.

Yours D. H. Lawrence

576. To Edward Garnett, [17 May 1913]

Text: MS NYPL; Postmark, E[benha]us[en] 17 MAI 13; Heilbrun 154–5.

Irschenhausen, (Post) *Ebenhausen*, Oberbayern[2]

[17 May 1913]

[Frieda Weekley begins]

Dear Mr Garnett,

We roared over the 'remarkable females' you just hit them![3] The worst, it's like his impudence, they are *me*, these beastly, superior arrogant females! Lawrence *hated* me just over the children, I daresay *I* was'nt all I might have been, so he wrote this! I know now why Göthe wrote *Iphigenie*[4] [Lawrence interjects: Iphegenie, according to Frieda, is a noble statue to the frosty Frau von Stein; – noble, but done in hate; the cruelest thing a man can do to a woman is to portray her as perfection DHL] so superb she is, but I ll be hanged if any man wants to love her, as well be married to the tablets of the ten commandments, though mind you a man looks for that in a woman too! The book will be all right in the end, you trust me for my own sake, they will have to be women and not superior flounders – I say the book is worthy of his talent, but not of his genius. 'Miss Houghton', whom I am reading now, is a 1000 times 'more', but improper! You will love it (I dont mean for that) sometimes, it's witty too! You wrote me such a nice letter, it warmed my inside and I am grateful, Lawrence was so seedy, and he goes on working and it's simply ghastly, he becomes a writing machine, that works itself out, it made me quite frantic [Lawrence interjects: (a lie – I've written very little)] – Not a word about the children for months now, Monty will be 13 [Lawrence interjects: 14 I think] in June, so I must go on waiting, but we are coming to England, it depends on L's health now [Lawrence interjects: (Not true. It depends on Frieda's will)] – It will be nice to see you and Bunny, we think of him a lot here, where he was with us in the

[1] Matthew vi. 34 (A.V.).

[2] The address-line is in DHL's hand.

[3] Frieda recognised herself in both sisters, Ella and Gudrun, in 'The Sisters' (see Mark Kinkead-Weekes in *Imagined Worlds*, ed. Maynard Mack and Ian Gregor, 1968, p. 371ff).

[4] *Iphigenie auf Tauris* (1779).

Isartal! Miriam's novel is very lovable,[1] I think, and one does feel so sorry for her, but it's a faded photograph of *Sons and Lovers*, she has never understood anything out of herself, no inner activity, but she does make one ache! I only just realised the amazing brutality of *Sons and Lovers*. How that brutality [Lawrence interjects: remains,] in spite of Christianity, of the two thousand years; it's better like that, than the civilised forms it takes! Its only a top plaster [Lawrence interjects: (the civilisation)], and I'm sure brutality ought to develop into something finer, out of *itself*, not be suppressed, denied! Paul says to his mother, when she is dying 'If I'd got to die, I would be quick about it, I would *will* to die.'[2] Does'nt it seem awful! Yet, one *does* feel like that, but not only that after all! There I'm 'Ellaing' again,[3]

[Lawrence begins]

I was glad of your letter about the Sisters. Don't schimpf, I shall make it all right when I re-write it. I shall put it in the third person. All along I knew what ailed the book. But it did me good to theorise myself out, and to depict Friedas God Almightiness in all its glory. That was the first crude fermenting of the book. I'll make it into art now. I've done 256 pages, but still can't see the end very clear. But it's coming. Frieda is so cross, since your letter came, with the book. Before that she was rather fond of her portrait in straight pleats and Athena sort of pose.

Send me the first part back, will you.

Auf Wiedersehen D. H. Lawrence

577. To Edward Garnett, 19 May 1913

Text: MS NYPL; Postmark, [Ebe]nha[usen] 2[. . .] MAY 13; Heilbrun 155–7.

Irschenhausen, (Post) *Ebenhausen*, bei München
19 May 1913

Dear Garnett,

I am relieved when you put me in my place with a quiet hand. One does get all sorts of misdoubting moods. You never take me too seriously, I know, and you never need.

I wonder how you like 'The Sisters'. Not much, I am afraid, or you would tell me. You are the sort of man who is quick with nice news and slow with nasty. Never mind, you can tell me what fault you find, and I can re-write the book.

[1] See p. 525 n. 4.

[2] *Sons and Lovers*, chap. 14: 'Mother if I had to die, I'd die. I'd *will* to die.'

[3] i.e. Frieda was behaving like Ella Templeman (forerunner of Ursula Brangwen) in 'The Sisters'.

Sons and Lovers won't be long then? I hope to God it will sell.

Frieda feels she must make a move about the children. So we shall come to England for quite a short time – perhaps a fortnight. If we land about the 3rd or 4th of June, could you do with us? The idea is that Frieda sees her son Monty at St Pauls School, talks to him, arranges to see the little girls, keeps everything quiet from the father. Then the children shall say to their father 'We want to see our mother in Germany.' – It is a plan I don't like, setting the children between two parents. But there is nothing else for it. Then Frieda wants to see your brother, Robert Garnett, to talk to him. That is our business in England. It should not take longer than a fortnight. We might stop a week at the sea side. One gets to long for a touch of salt in the air. Then we move to Italy again – probably, for a time at least, to San Gaudenzio, near Gargnano. I hope that I shall be able to have enough money for all this. At present I am all right.

You must tell us what you think. – I hope in about a fortnight to have finished 'The Sisters'. It will be quite short. My novel-writing fit usually goes off in June, and I do a bit of poetry, and loafe.

It is not easy to live as close as Frieda and I live, and yet to have this drawn sword of the children between us. I hope it will come all right. We have both of us got some pretty bad – half healed – cuts from it. It sort of makes one tired. When one has come home to find trouble, there is no[1] road leads away from it. But there is no reason why it shouldn't turn out all right.

If we are in Italy for August, will David come out there to us?

Yours D. H. Lawrence

The copy of *Sons and Lovers* has just come – I am fearfully proud of it. I reckon it is quite a great book. I shall not write quite in that style any more. It's the end of my youthful period. Thanks a hundred times.

We got Miss Chambers novel. I should scarcely recognise her – she never used to *say* anything. But it isn't bad, and it made me so miserable I had hardly the energy to walk out of the house for two days. DHL

578. To Arthur McLeod, [21 May 1913]

Text: MS UT; Huxley 121–2.

Irschenhausen, (Post) *Ebenhausen*, Oberbayern
Wednesday[2]

Dear Mac,

Thanks for the books – what a measly thing Shaw's *New Statesman*

[1] there is no] it is no good

[2] Dated with reference to the first issue of the *New Statesman* and the procession presumed to be on the eve of Corpus Christi ('Fronleichnam'), 22 May.

was![1] God help him. – And it is amazing how narrowly Philpotts shaves it, and *just* misses, always.

I sent you a rather miserable Card of Wolfratshausen[2] – thought it might interest you geographically. It looked rather nice on a white mount. *Sons and Lovers* comes out on the 29th. I've had just one copy – it looks nice. If they dont fall on me for morals, it should go. It is my best work, by far.

I have nearly done another remarkable work, called The Sisters. Oh it is a wonder – but it wants dressing down a bit.

I am still sighing for Italy. Bavaria is too humid, too green and lush, and mountains *never* move – they are *always* there. They go all different tones and colours – but still, they are always there.

We are perhaps coming to England end of June – but not to stop. I hope to go back to Italy. Of course a lot depends on *Sons and Lovers*' selling. You talk about the lines falling to me in pleasant places – I reckon a good many of 'em fall in stripes on my back. 'Resigned, I kissed the rod?'[3] Never.

What did you do at Whitsuntide. I live in a green meadow by the budding pines, and look at these damned mountains, and write bloody rot. Oh Gawd, oh Gawd! There's a grand procession today – the folk in Bavaria are the most fervent Roman Catholics on God's earth – Frohn leichnahm – and now it's come on in sheets of thunder-rain. It always does. Damned climate, this. I shall send you some of Arthur Ransome's *Essays* – ought to be entitled 'Je sais tout.'[4] Aren't you well? For the Lords sake don't get ill, or I shall feel as if I heard the props of the earth cracking. I ll have a copy of *Sons and Lovers* sent you. Remember me to Aylwin. Where is he going for his summer holiday? – and you? But I hope to see you before then.

Auf weidersehen D. H. Lawrence

[1] The first issue appeared on 12 May 1913. It was founded by Sidney and Beatrice Webb with money from various sources including £1,000 from George Bernard Shaw. The editor was Clifford Dyce Sharp.

[2] MS missing.

[3] Pope, 'Epistle to Dr Arbuthnot', l. 158 ['...if right, I kissed...'].

[4] The reference is either to Arthur M. Ransome (1884–1967), *Portraits and Speculations* (January 1913), or more likely to one of two collections edited by him: *The Book of Friendship* (November 1909) or *The Book of Love* (November 1910). The sub-title of both collections was: *Essays, Poems, Maxims and Prose Passages*.

579. To Helen Corke, 29 May 1913
Text: MS UT; Huxley 121.

Irschenhausen, (post) *Ebenhausen*, Oberbayern.
29 May 1913

Your letter followed me here. I've left Italy – at least during the hot months. If I can I shall go back in September – if I've got any money.

Perhaps you are a little bit mistaken about the 'Soiled Rose'. I wrote it while I was still in Croydon – still in bed after the last illness.[1] Don't you think it a bit affected? It is a bit stiff, like sick man's work. – So that the philosophy which is in the 'Soiled Rose' didn't hold good for me long after the writing of the story. I had not really seen the best, when I left Croydon. Forgive me if I am a bit stupid after this thundery day and the long walk.

You see, I have been married for this last year. Muriel knew – perhaps she told you.[2] I cannot talk about it, because it involves too much. It has meant a good deal of suffering too, and sometimes I feel old – but then again, very often I feel no age at all. And meine Frau – she has been 'meine Frau' and 'mia Signora', in[3] Italy and Germany, but never 'my wife' – is never very far from me, in any sense of the word. You would be surprised, how I am married – or how married I am. And this is the best I have known, or ever shall know.

I don't know whether we might do any good by keeping up a connection. Muriel wants absolutely to have done with me – neither to hear of me or from me any more. She sent my last letter back – it was in Italy, two months ago. It was a stupid letter – you know how stupid I can be – but it hardly merited being sent back. It upset me. But there, she knew her own affairs best, and it was definite.

It is a pity your people are going to Canada.[4] Wouldn't you like to go with them? I am here in a little house made of wood, standing in a corner of a hilly meadow against a big pinewood, and looking over at the Alps. Sometimes a deer steps out into the wheat, sometimes a hare lobs among the grass. In the bedroom, one can hear the squirrels chattering. We two are alone. We stay here only a little longer. I may come to England for a

[1] i.e. in December 1911.

[2] Jessie Chambers ('Muriel') had told Helen Corke, on 16 March 1913 (MS UN LaM 10): '...I may as well tell you, unless you already know, that ever since he has been abroad he has been living with a married woman. They are accepted as man and wife. Her divorce is to be heard shortly, I understand. I don't suppose you're very surprised. Please, please, digest it quickly and get it over before I come. I am sick, sick to death of David and all that concerns him.'

[3] in] but

[4] Helen Corke's landlord and landlady in Shirley, near Croydon, who were emigrating to join their son and daughter-in-law in Canada.

short time. I don't want to. I want to go back to Italy. I don't want to live in England any more.

Sons and Lovers comes out just now.[1] I remember your telling me, at the beginning, it would be great. I think it is so. I wonder if you will agree.

I seem to have had several lives, when I think back. This is all so different from anything I have known before. And now I feel a different person. It is all queerer than novels. It is enough to make one take life carelessly, it behaves so topsy-turvily. Life unsaddles one so often. But now I don't think it can, not much, any more.

Write to me if you like. Do you read much German? It is a beastly language, one that doesn't fit the cells of my brain.

riverisco D. H. Lawrence

[1] This letter was written on the day of its publication.

INDEX

No distinction is made between a reference in the text or in a footnote.
All titles of writings and paintings by Lawrence are gathered under his name.
For localities, public buildings and institutions etc. in Croydon, Eastwood, London or Nottingham, see the comprehensive entry under the relevant place-name.

58096

PR
6023
.A93
Z53
1979
v.1

Lawrence, David
Herbert, 1885-
1930.

The letters of D.
H. Lawrence

WOODBURY UNIVERSITY LIBRARY
1027 WILSHIRE BOULEVARD
LOS ANGELES, CA 90017

CARD OWNER IS RESPONSIBLE FOR ALL
LIBRARY MATERIAL ISSUED ON HIS CARD

RETURN BOOKS PROMPTLY—A fine is charged
for each day a book is overdue, except Saturdays,
Sundays, and holidays.

REPORT A LOST BOOK AT ONCE—The charge
for a lost book includes the cost of the book plus
fines.